The Origins of Modern African Thought

Africa World Press, Inc.

P.O. Box 1892
Trenton, NJ 08607

P.O. Box 48
Asmara, ERITREA

Copyright © 2004 Robert W. July
First Printing 2004

A Reprint of the Original Edition by Frederick A. Praeger, 1967
A New Foreword by Richard L. Sklar, 2004

All rights reserved. No part of this publication may be reproduced, stored in a retrieval system or transmitted in any form or by any means electronic, mechanical, photocopying, recording or otherwise without the prior written permission of the publisher.

Cover Design: Roger Dormann

Cataloging-in-Publication Data is availabe from the Library of Congress.

ISBN: 1--59221-198-4 (hardcover)
ISBN: 1-59221-199-2 (paperback)

ROBERT W. JULY

THE ORIGINS OF MODERN AFRICAN THOUGHT

Its development in West Africa during the nineteenth and twentieth centuries

Africa World Press, Inc.

P.O. Box 1892
Trenton, NJ 08607

P.O. Box 48
Asmara, ERITREA

To J.H.J.

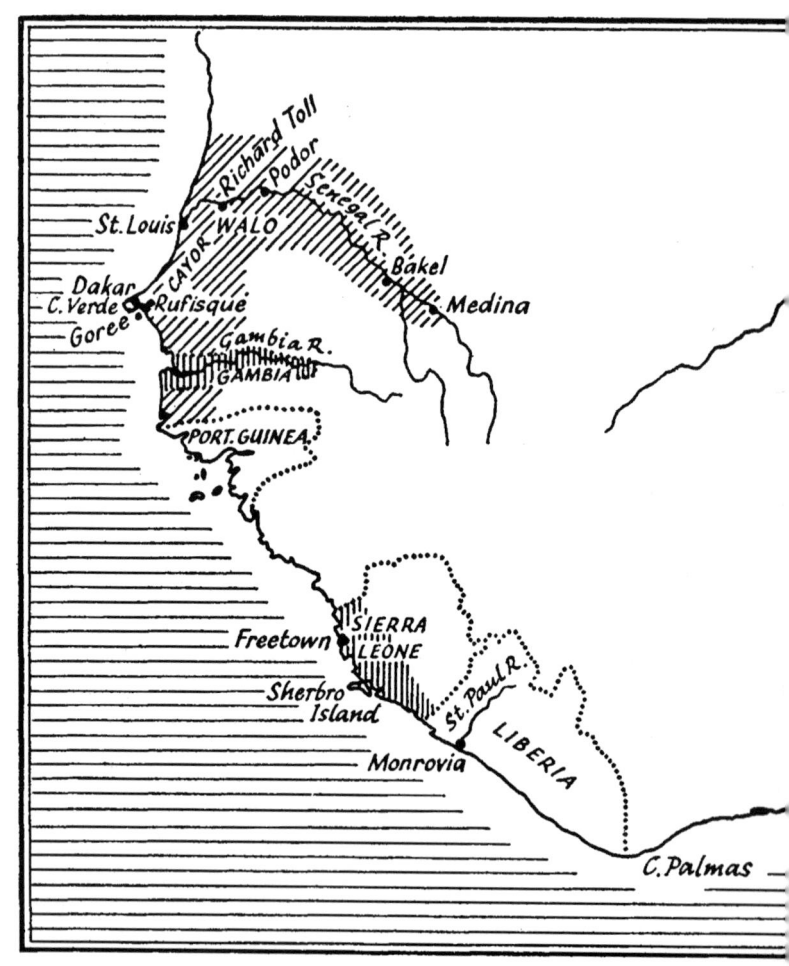

West Africa c. 1880 and Colonial Boundaries in 1914

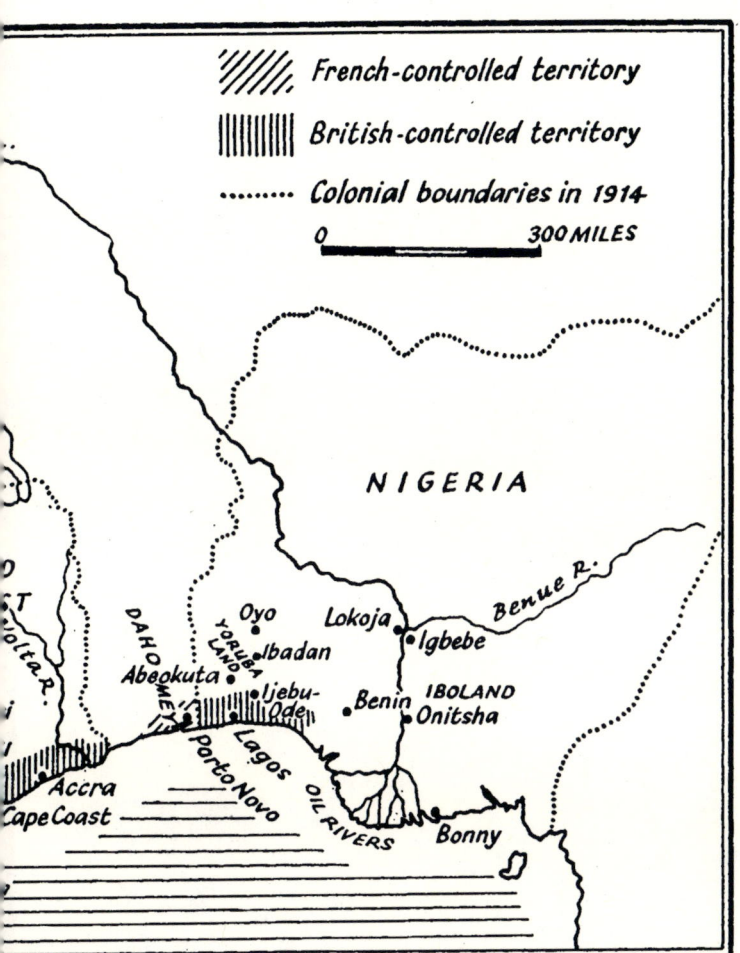

Contents

Foreword by Richard L. Sklar	i-xi
Preface	15
1. Prologue: The European Background	21
2. The Eighteenth-Century Forerunners	33
3. The Founding of the Sierra Leone Colony	48
4. The Establishment of France in Senegal	67
5. The Liberian Experiment	85
6. Africanus Horton and Independence in West Africa	110
7. Mid-Century Freetown: The African Bourgeoisie	130
8. The Évolués	155
9. British Assimilation along the Niger: Bishop Crowther	177
10. Indigenous African Nationalism: Reversible Johnson	196
11. The First African Personality: Edward W. Blyden	208
12. The Politics of Assimilation in Senegal	234
13. The African Historian in West African Thought	254
14. The Dilemma Resolved: Bishop James Johnson	279
15. Sierra Leone: The Twilight of the Creoles	297
16. Nationalism on the Gold Coast	327
17. The Journalist in West African Thought	345
18. The Liberal Nationalists: Herbert Macaulay	374
19. The Assimilation of Blaise Diagne	392
20. The Conservative Nationalists: Henry Carr	415
21. The Metamorphosis of Casely Hayford	433
22. Epilogue: The Emergence of the Modern West African	458
Bibliography	481
Index	494

Illustrations

Map of West Africa — *pages* 6 & 7

PLATES — follow page 160
1. Gustavus Vassa
2. Alexander Crummell
3. Monrovia *c.* 1840
4. Freetown in 1856
5. George Nicol
6. Africanus Horton
7. Bishop Crowther
8. Gaspard Devès
9. St. Louis in 1865
10. Edward W. Blyden
11. James Johnson
12. Lagos Marina *c.* 1885
13. Cape Coast *c.* 1890
14. Samuel Lewis
15. S. R. B. Attoh-Ahuma
16. John Mensah Sarbah
17. C. C. Reindorf
18. J. E. Casely Hayford
19. Henry Carr
20. Lamine Guèye
21. Herbert Macaulay
22. Blaise Diagne

Acknowledgements

The author thanks the following for permission to reproduce photographs and prints: The National Archives, Senegal, for photographs of Blaise Diagne, Lamine Guèye and Gaspard Devès; The Church Missionary Society, London, for photographs of Bishop Crowther, James Johnson and George Nicol; The Africana Collection, University of Ibadan, for photographs of Herbert Macaulay and Henry Carr, also the Nigerian Federal Ministry of Information for the photograph of Carr; Library of Congress, Washington, for the print of Monrovia; British Museum, London, for the print of Freetown, 1856; Professor K. A. B. Jones-Quartey and the University of Ghana for the photograph of J. E. Casely Hayford.

The author also thanks the following publisher and journals: Frederick A. Praeger Inc., New York, for permission to quote from *On African Socialism* by L. S. Senghor: *International Affairs* for permission to quote from 'Some Thoughts on Africa: A Continent in Development' by L. S. Senghor in the issue for April 1962, from 'The Foreign Policy of Mali' by Modibo Keita in the issue for October 1961, and from 'The Republic of Guinea' by Sékou Touré in the issue for April 1960; *Diogenes* for permission to quote from 'African-Negro Aesthetics' by L. S. Senghor in the issue for Winter 1956.

Abbreviations in the Footnotes

C.M.S.   Church Missionary Society Archives, London.
C.O.   Colonial Office Archives, Public Record Office, London.
F.O.   Foreign Office Archives, Public Record Office, London.
N.A.P.O.S. National Archives, Paris, Overseas Section. (Archives Nationales, Section Outre-Mer, Paris.)
N.A.S.   National Archives, Senegal. (Archives Nationales du Sénégal, Dakar.)

Foreword

Richard L. Sklar[1]

For the better part of two centuries, racial domination has been the central concern of African social thought. Other questions, among them national identity, the role of chieftaincy, representation, justice, and constitutional design, have often been defined in relation to preoccupations with racial and colonial forms of domination. During the colonial era, a few African thinkers, notably Edward Wilmot Blyden, Joseph Ephraim Casely Hayford, and Léopold Sédar Senghor, interpreted Africa for intellectuals throughout the world. Many other thinkers of analytical or philosophical merit were scarcely noted by intellectuals outside of their own countries and neighboring lands where they lived and worked. Most of those locally significant thinkers have now disappeared from the recorded history of ideas. So it is that the discovery and elucidation of modern social and political thought in Africa poses a formidable challenge to scholars in the field of intellectual history.

Robert W. July took up that challenge in the early 1960s while he was a scholar in residence at the University of Ibadan in Nigeria. By then, the optimism and euphoria of late colonial times, particularly in British West Africa, had begun to fade into the gathering gloom of postcolonial disillusionment. Meanwhile, on campus, inspirational historians associated with the renowned Ibadan school of African history taught a new generation of scholars to place African, rather than colonial, goals and values at the center of their thought and research.[2] July did not share the methodological preoccupation of the Ibadan school with oral history and its documentation. His own search for the origins of modern African thought was conducted in archives and libraries without recourse to oral evidence. Yet the roster of African thinkers whose works are examined in this book include three historians of the latter nineteenth and early twentieth centuries whose scholarship "anticipated to a remarkable degree those present-day students of Africa's new history" (p. 277). And July's attempt to view "the intrusion of the West as completely as I could through the eyes of those on whom it fell" (p. 17) is genuinely Afrocentric and largely accounts for the enduring influence of this pioneering work.

Reading *The Origins* shortly after its publication, I was reminded of a celebrated study of American social and political thought by Vernon Louis Parrington, published in 1927 and entitled *Main Currents in American Thought*. Many of us who studied the history of political ideas in mid-century America were indebted to Parrington for his illuminating exposition of American thinking over a period of three hundred years, from the early seventeenth century until the early twentieth. Parrington described his three volume work as "a field of American letters which has been pretty largely neglected."[3] In private conversation, July has confirmed the influence of Parrington's achievement on his own plan for a history of African thought. In academe, Parrington was a professor of literature with a partiality for "the claims of aesthetics."[4] July's similar penchant for the study of cultural history reached fruition twenty years after publication of *The Origins* in a work devoted to the contributions of artists, artistic performers, dramatists, educators, musicians, and the literary estate to the movement for independence in Africa.[5] Like Parrington in America, July in postcolonial West Africa contemplated a field of letters that had been "largely neglected" by scholars. To this day, there is no standard history of African thought comparable to *The Origins* in its combination of historical depth and transcolonial breadth within a multi-state region of Africa.[6]

The thinkers considered in this book were either born in sub-Saharan West Africa or resided there as immigrants. The countries concerned extend from Senegal in the west to Cameroon in the east. The predominant colonial powers were Britain and France; Germany was evicted from its colonies (Cameroon and Togo) as a result of its defeat in World War I; Portugal ruled a small Atlantic coastal and island colony, while Spain colonized an island cluster in the Gulf of Guinea. July acknowledges that even within this sub-region of Africa, his study does not encompass African thought comprehensively. He is specifically concerned with Africa's intellectual response to social forces unleashed by the impact of Western imperialism and its accompaniment of Western thought. While his conception of Western thought includes ideas "emanating from America as well as from Europe" (p. 17), he does not examine the influence of ideas introduced by African-Americans in the latter nineteenth and early twentieth centuries, an acknowledged omission that he thought he would address in a subsequent work. Furthermore,

FOREWORD [iii]

his account of modern ideas in West Africa does not include Islamic thought, a subject of crucial importance that intellectual historians have scarcely begun to compare with the body of ideas attributable to Africa's relationship with Europe and America.

In British and French West Africa there were relatively few European settlers by comparison with those countries of northern, eastern, and southern Africa, where many Europeans settled permanently. Moreover, from the latter nineteenth century onward, there was a growing tendency in the British and French West African colonies to extend rights of citizenship to African people. In the aftermath of four centuries during which millions of African slaves were transported to American shores, colonial rule in West Africa was, on the whole, less oppressive than it proved to be in the settler-colonies where Africans were systematically dispossessed of their lands. By the late colonial era, the issue of racial domination in West Africa, despite its great importance, was balanced more evenly by other political and social issues than had been the case in countries where racial despotism defined the system of government until either the onset of independence, as in Kenya, Angola, and Mozambique, or racial emancipation, as in Rhodesia and South Africa. Hence there was a well-established tradition of non-racial political and social thought in West Africa that was unrivalled elsewhere in sub-Saharan Africa. More precisely, in West African thought, racial emancipatory themes have shared their pride of place with anti-colonial motifs; similarly, the rights of persons and citizens have complemented claims by precolonial nations to redress their historic rights. This aspect of West African thought may have weakened the impact of *The Origins* on African studies in the United States of America where nationalist values superceded preoccupations with problems of representative democracy until the final decade of the twentieth century.

There is yet another aspect of African thought that has been underappreciated in the United States; it is the durability of sentiments that sustain special relationships with the former colonial powers. Americans often appear to be oblivious of these profound sentiments and binding ties, manifest in a myriad of functional relationships, e.g., the learned professions, educational norms and methods, parliamentary etiquette, military traditions, commercial practices, religious beliefs, literary and linguistic commonalities, manners, styles, habits and cuisine. Africans rarely explain these matters to their American friends and associates, who frequently lack appreciation for the complexity and cosmopolitan sophistication of African thinking. These qualities of modern African thought are displayed in every chapter of *The Origins*.

The life histories of most of the thinkers whose ideas grace these pages are every bit as remarkable as their intellectual and literary achievements. One marvels at the heroism, fortitude, linguistic competence, literary merit, objectivity, and analytical skill of the eighteenth-century emancipated slaves, Ottobah Cuoango and Olaudah Equiano, portrayed with riveting acuity in this book. Their immediate successors in the world of West African ideas were associated with communities in the Atlantic coastal countries of Senegal, under French rule, Sierra Leone, a British dependency, and Liberia, created by free persons of African descent from the United States. In Sierra Leone, "the Province of Freedom" (p. 49) as it was called by Granville Sharp, its crusading English founder, nurtured successive generations of modernizing intellectuals who, in turn, exerted a powerful transforming influence throughout British West Africa. For Senegalese, the vaunted French "civilizing mission" proclaimed by the French empires, monarchies, and republics of the nineteenth century, implied paternalistic rule facilitated by an intermediary class of mixed African and European descent. As for Liberia, home to several important thinkers who lectured and wrote creatively about racial questions, the settler minority of African descent never came to grips with the problem created by its oligarchic rule of the country. In that respect, among others, the intellectual histories of Liberia and Sierra Leone are similar despite their different statuses until 1962, one an independent republic, the other a British colony.

Among those nineteenth century African thinkers who bequeathed to posterity oeuvres in written form, two individuals achieved towering stature, namely Samuel Ajayi Crowther and Edward Wilmot Blyden. Crowther, a recaptive (one who was freed from captivity by the British navy and returned to Africa) of Nigerian Yoruba descent became an Anglican bishop in charge of missions in the Niger Delta, far inland along the Niger River, and other places in Nigeria, the Gold Coast, Liberia, and The Gambia. He made an extraordinary contribution to the creation of modern, particularly but not only religious, institutions despite the overbearing prejudice against Africans that he encountered within the church hierarchy itself.[7] His humility as a servant of his people as well as the Anglican Church is legendary. As July remarks, he responded to chastisement by prejudiced European associates by offering to undertake the arduous task of founding new mission stations at the age of eighty (p. 194).

Like Crowther, Blyden believed ardently in the modernization of

African societies. But his commitment to the principle of racial self-reliance profoundly influenced the course of African, and African-American, nationalism for generations to come. Born of free and literate African parents in the Danish (now American) island of St. Thomas, Blyden emigrated to newly independent Liberia in 1850, at the age of eighteen. He soon became a Presbyterian minister and a professor of classics at Liberia College, which he later served as president. His governmental service in Liberia included office as Secretary of State, Ambassador to Britain, and Minister Plenipotentiary to Britain and France. He also held official positions relating to the education of Muslims in the British colonies of Sierra Leone and Lagos. Yet his institutional achievements were far less significant than his contribution as a theorist of racial nationalism. He believed that racial sentiments had become the main motivating forces in modern history; that every race has been endowed by the creator with its special potential for achievement; and that the African race was superior to others in matters of spirituality and religion. "Africa," he declared, "may yet prove to be the spiritual conservatory of the world."[8]

As a practical matter, however, Blyden accepted the necessity of cooperation with British and French imperial rule in Africa. He understood that no force on earth could prevent the impending colonial occupation of Africa and he did not regret the tide of history. On the contrary, he viewed political imperialism with favor as a necessary stage of historical development which could, if wisely conducted, have highly beneficial effects for the people of Africa. In that regard, he shared the pro-imperialist sentiments of most progressive and worldly intellectuals of his time, including Marx, Engels, and the younger Lenin. But Blyden was not about to clamber aboard the European bandwagon. The unfailing mark of serious thought is an ability to perceive the divergent implications of related ideas that resemble one another in important respects. Blyden knew and warned that colonial domination would be justified on the despicable ground that African cultural values were inherently inferior to those of Europe. In defense of African values, he constructed a shield of cultural nationalism to repulse the assault of European cultural imperialism. By word and example, he stood for intimate political collaboration with the imperial overlord without ever conceding a cultural strongpoint.[9]

Throughout his life, Blyden was an ardent "black zionist," ever promoting the return of diaspora Africans to the continent of their origin. In his view, a black person in a white country would always be culturally enslaved. He ridiculed the arrogance of Europeans who sought to educate Africans in accordance with Western standards and values; that kind of education, he warned, would only stunt the growth of African genius and thereby diminish Africa's contribution to human civilization. Viewing the colonial era as a relatively brief transitional phase, he particularly favored the British colonial principle of indirect rule because it appeared to minimize the degree of colonial intrusion into African social institutions. Toward the end of his life, Blyden was estranged from many younger nationalists, whom he often criticized for what he took to be premature challenges to European rule. Yet his views and influence were lauded by his many disciples, among them the Gold Coast nationalist, Joseph E. Casely Hayford, whose judgement has been regarded favorably by later thinkers: "The work of Edward W. Blyden is universal, covering the entire race and the entire race problem."[10]

Considering the breadth of Blyden's thought and knowledge, derived from multilingual scholarship (English, Spanish, Greek, Latin, Hebrew, and Arabic), it is tempting to adopt Casely Hayford's perspective and classify twentieth century African thinkers as the heirs of Blyden with respect, for example, to racial exclusivity and self-reliance, black zionism, cultural nationalism, and pragmatic political conservatism. Thus, Nnamdi Azikiwe's rousing call for "mental emancipation," to rescue "mis-educated" Africans was authentically Blydenite.[11] In anticipation of Senghor's concept of negritude, discussed briefly in conjunction with the ideas of other mid-century nationalist thinkers in the final chapter of this book, July captions a section of his chapter on Blyden "Edward W. Blyden and the Philosophy of Negritude" (p. 212); the chapter itself is entitled "The First African Personality" in anticipation of the use of Blyden's phrase, "African Personality" by nationalist leaders of the mid-twentieth century, notably Ghana's Kwame Nkrumah at the First Conference of Independent African States in 1958.

In francophone African thought, attitudes toward colonial authority during the late nineteenth and early twentieth centuries revolved around the rival principles of assimilation and association. The concept of assimilation was predicated on a belief that France had produced a high culture of universal value; assimilationists taught that African people should be incorporated into the world of French civilization, where they would be equal in every respect to the people of France. In opposition to that belief, the concept of association presupposed separate cultural identities for European and African peoples as a natural and permanent condition. France, therefore, should carry out its "civilizing mission" in Africa without the presumptions or goals of racial equality or eventual cultural identity. In Senegal, ardent assimilationists in the African and Creole communities advocated military conscription to promote their vision of one French identity for all. At issue for true believers was not racial differentiation but assimilation of Muslims who comprised an overwhelming majority of the African population.

The African demand for full citizenship, including the right to be conscripted like other French citizens, was asserted by a political movement called the "Young Senegalese" and sponsored in the French National Assembly by the first African, in the racial sense of that term, rather than Creole or European, deputy for Senegal, Blaise Diagne. In 1915 and 1916, with France at war, Diagne achieved the enactment of laws providing for conscription of African inhabitants of incorporated municipalities, and conferring citizenship on them and their descendants in perpetuity. Furthermore, Muslim Africans would henceforth be free to follow the precepts of Islamic law in personal and family matters, including the practice of polygamy. Diagne's African constituents had "secured privileges unique within the French empire" (p. 402). Toward the end of the war Diagne was appointed Commissioner of the Republic with responsibility for military recruitment throughout French West Africa. Through equal valor in combat, he declared, France had become a country of one hundred million people. With deep patriotic conviction, Diagne became the foremost exponent of French colonial policy in public life. Eventually, he even defended the racialist and authoritarian principle of association as a necessary condition for material progress and preparation for the higher ideal of assimilation. July's poignant chronicle of Diagne's decline as a champion of African rights concludes appropriately with an account of his capacity for honest introspection.[12]

In British West Africa, each of four distinct territories included a Crown Colony, which had been acquired before the comprehensive partition of Africa in the 1880's, and an expansive hinterland, known as the protectorate. In the colonies – Bathurst, Freetown and its environs, Lagos, and the Gold Coast – African inhabitants were British subjects with rights of political representation for taxpayers; in the protectorates, however, indirect rule, meaning colonial government through the medium of indigenous authorities, was the main method of choice.[13] Intellectuals clustered in the colonies; there, as elsewhere throughout the ages, renaissance thinkers debated issues that have proven to the timeless. Their intellectual formulations have been recovered repeatedly by successive generations of new thinkers unto the present century. Religious thinkers pondered the compatibility of European theologies with Africa's own cultural heritage. Educational philosophers debated the question of bilingual education in primary schools. Journalists tested the limits of freedom under authoritarian forms of government; they also considered the meaning of journalistic responsibility in their culturally plural societies. Administrative theorists assessed the legacy of indigenous political and legal institutions as well as the role of traditional authority as an instrument of government. Communitarian thinkers grappled with the issues of land ownership, rents, and property taxation. Legalists discoursed on the constitutional prerogatives of legislative councils vis-à-vis colonial administrations. Constitutional theorists compared the forms of government and examined the relationship between ethno-linguistic identities and new nationalities based on the colonial partition of Africa. Pan-African patriots revived Blyden's dream of West African political unity and created an inter-territorial forum of Anglophone intellectuals to pursue that goal. Politicians publicized these and other issues as they mobilized supporters in their quest for office. Thinkers in all of these categories come to life in the latter chapters of this book.

The dramatis personae include two bitter antagonists in colonial Lagos, namely Herbert Samuel Heelas Macaulay, known as the "father of Nigerian nationalism," and Henry Rawlinson Carr, who rose to the rank of Resident (highest administrative official) in the colony. Both of them were repatriates from Sierra Leone and persons of Yoruba ethno-linguistic origin. Macaulay, a crusading journalist, became a tribune of the indigenous people of Lagos, as distinct from that city's substantial immigrant population. His political career was based mainly on his service to the traditional king and chiefs of Lagos. He defended their claims to administer communal land and their asserted rights of recognition in the colony, similar to rights enjoyed by traditional rulers in the Nigerian protectorates. He organized their followers, who comprised a majority of the inhabitants, into a big city political machine that controlled elections to the Lagos Town Council. He was the indispensable link between the traditionalist organization of the masses and their English-speaking elected representatives. As he was a staunch defender of the rights of all Lagosians as British subjects, the chapter on his thought introduces him accurately as the consummate "liberal nationalist" of his time.

By contrast, the chapter devoted mainly to Henry Carr describes the thought of a "conservative nationalist," one who served the colonial government as deputy to the Governor-General of the Colony and Protectorate of Nigeria yet envisioned the timely achievement of self

FOREWORD

government and other nationalist goals. A dedicated modernizer, Carr was repelled by demagogic politics and despised the incumbent traditional ruler as a dismal example of archaic custom. No less than Macaulay, Carr is given his due in this book. Liberals, let us remember, can be more or less conservative, more or less progresssive. On the issues of his day, Carr was no less liberal than Macaulay; on certain issues, including the reform of traditional authority in Lagos, he was surely no less progressive. In his later years, Macaulay outmaneuvered his political opponents in Lagos by leading his traditionalist followers into an alliance with a new generation of militant nationalists. He died while campaigning for Nigerian national independence.

By mid-century, African thinkers had begun to grapple with questions arising from the study of international political economy. The emergence of the Soviet Union as one of two superpowers and the communist revolution in China positioned the twin theories of capitalist imperialism and socialist revolution at the forefront of intellectual discourse in Africa. The debates occasioned by these developments are indicated in July's concluding chapter, where Senegal's Léopold Senghor is shrewdly identified as "the philosopher of twentieth-century Africa" (p. 480) for having followed, independently and in the idiom of francophone philosophy, in the theoretical footsteps of Edward W. Blyden.

During the latter twentieth centurty, socialists in Africa suffered economic, intellectual, moral, and political debacles that were comparable to socialist disasters in other parts of the world. In Africa, as elsewhere, the debacle of twentieth-century socialism was due, in no small part, to an obsession with the methods of socialist revolution at the expense of individual liberty. At the outset of the twenty-first century, new thinkers have begun to revisit the intellectual history of Africa's quest for freedom, liberty, and social progress. For that purpose, they can find reliable guidance in the pages of this masterful work.

Notes

1. Richard L. Sklar is Professor Emeritus of Political Science at the University of California, Los Angeles. During the 1960s he was a member of political science departments at the University of Ibadan and the University of Zambia. His books include *Nigerian Political Parties: Power in an Emergent African Nation* (Princeton, NJ: Princeton University Press, 1963, 1970; New York and Enugu, Nigeria: NOK Publishers International, 1983; Trenton, NJ and Asmara, Eritrea: Africa World Press, 2004); *Corporate Power in an African State: The Political Impact of Multinational Mining Companies in Zambia* (Berkeley and Los Angeles: University of California Press, 1975); *African Politics in Postimperial Times: The Essays of Richard L. Sklar*, ed. Toyin Falola (Trenton, NJ and Asmara, Eritrea: Africa World Press, 2002).
2. J. F. Ade. Ajayi, "The Ibadan School of History," in Toyin Falola, ed., *Tradition and Change in Africa: The Essays of J. F. Ade. Ajayi* (Trenton, NJ and Asmara, Eritrea: Africa World Press, 2000), pp. 377-388.
3. Vernon Louis Parrington, *Main Currents in American Thought* (New York: Harcourt, Brace, 1930), Vol. I, p. i.
4. E. B. Eby, "Vernon Louis Parrington," in Ibid., Vol. III, p. vii.
5. Robert W. July, *An African Voice: The Role of the Humanities in African Independence* (Durham, NC: Duke University Press, 1987).
6. Claude Wauthier's important study, *The Literature and Thought of Modern Africa*, trans. Shirley Kay (London: Pall Mall, 1966), and ibid., 2nd ed., trans. Clive Wake (Washington, D.C.: Three Continents Press, 1979) is organized thematically by contrast with the individual thinker format to which July adheres consistently. In addition to these two comparable books, there are several edited compilations of works by African social and political thinkers, notably J. Ayodele Langely, *Ideologies of Liberation in Black Africa 1856-1970: Documents on Modern African Political Thought from Colonial Times to the Present* (London: Collings, 1979); and Gideon-Cyrus M. Mutiso and S. W. Rohio, *Readings in African Political Thought* (London: Heinemann, 1975).
7. J. F. Ade. Ajayi, "Bishop Crowther: A Patriot to the Core," and "Native Agency in Nineteenth Century West Africa," in Falola, ed., pp. 85-127; Ajayi, *Christian Missions in Nigeria, 1841-91: the Making of a New Elite* (London: Longman, 1965).

8. Edward W. Blyden, *Christianity, Islam and the Negro Race*, 2nd ed., (London: W. B. Whittingham, 1888), p. 143.
9. This paragraph is derived, almost verbatim from Richard L. Sklar, "The Colonial Imprint on African Political Thought," in Gwendolen M. Carter and Patrick O'Meara, eds., *African Independence: The First Twenty-Five Years* (Bloomington: IndianaUniversity Press, 1985.), p. 3.
10. Quoted in Hollis R. Lynch, *Edward Wilmot Blyden: Pan-Negro Patriot, 1832-1912* (London: Oxford University Press, 1967), p. 241.
11. Nnamdi Azikiwe, *Renascent Africa* (Accra: 1937), p. 135.
12. At page 414, July cites a conversation with Diagne reported by his friend, the scholar and former administrator Robert L. Delavignette, in which Diagne's awareness of his ambiguous role in later life is unburdened.
13. Michael Crowder, *West Africa under Colonial Rule* (Evanston: Northwestern University Press, 1968), pp. 199-216.

Preface

Migration, invasion, and conquest—this is one of the great rhythms of history. The continent of Africa, like other continents, has been invaded many times, and like other continents has both suffered devastation and gained fresh techniques and germinal ideas from these invasions. It might be said that the shape of modern Africa has in large measure been determined by the response to two of her most recent invasions—that of Islam beginning in the mid-seventh century after Christ, and that of the scientific-technological revolution introduced from Europe at the beginning of the nineteenth century. Of the two, Islam may yet prove to be the more pervasive for it remains virile and appealing in its message which has slowly spread among the peoples of Africa over thirteen centuries. Nevertheless, the more recent arrival of western scientific-technological thought seems more completely to have influenced the institutions and ideas of the modern states of mid-twentieth-century Africa. In one hundred and fifty years it has already well begun a fundamental transformation of African societies which is potentially, if not actually, the most far-reaching revolution the continent of Africa has yet experienced.

The impact of the scientific revolution on Europe herself is a familiar story—the slow and painful growth of commerce between Europe and the East and within the isolated elements of the European community; the development of inventions, particularly in the field of transportation, designed to facilitate Europe's growing commercial interests; the rise of larger political units needed to police the trade routes and protect newborn commercial enterprise; the gradual secularization of society leading to the substitution of experimental science for metaphysics and magic as a basis for knowledge of natural phenomena; the rediscovery and refurbishing of the vast learning of the ancient world; the rise of a new class in a changing social setting: an urban bourgeoisie devoted to the idea of profit and reinvestment for economic expansion; the replacement of dogmatism with iconoclasm, of faith with scepticism, of resignation with dissatisfaction, of social rigidity with social dynamism.

When, during the Renaissance, Europe began her own metamorphosis towards modernization, she underwent transformations which led inexorably to expansion into other parts of the world. Science yielded the technology both for a developing commerce and industry and for military ascendancy; political change harnessed to economic growth brought a search for markets and raw materials to feed the expanding system. Warfare, slavery, imperial domination, and economic exploitation were visited upon Asia, Africa and the Americas. In Africa the initial confrontation was harsh, its spirit amoral; the interest limited to extracting a profit from trade, first in gold and other goods and then primarily in slaves. Yet the slave trade, for all its inhumanity, had relatively little impact on traditional African societies, certainly far less than the thrust of the later, nineteenth-century penetration which argued, not physical bondage but spiritual freedom; which combined humanitarian objectives with economic goals; which implied man's perfectibility and material progress in the temporal world; and which in essence attempted to introduce into West Africa the ideas and institutions of Europe's own phenomenal revolution of modernization. 'The Renaissance was a conqueror', Léopold Sédar Senghor has said. 'But it exported not only merchants and soldiers; with professors, physicians, engineers, administrators, and missionaries, it also exported ideas and techniques. It not only destroyed, it built; it not only killed, it cured and educated; it gave birth to a new world, an entire world of our brothers, men of other races and continents.'[1]

The response in West Africa to the European penetration beginning in the nineteenth century ranged from uncritical acceptance to vigorous rejection, but the main drift was incontestably towards accommodation and reflected a desire to achieve the full advantages of the scientific-technological revolution as it was already unfolding in the West. The confrontation with the West raised in West African minds a whole range of questions of the most fundamental nature – the shape of the economy, the structure of the state, the adequacy of traditional religion and metaphysics, the role of education and Africa's place in the modern world – in short, the essential functions of society. The African reaction, therefore, was not merely an expression of nationalistic thinking, but a more thoroughgoing examination of man and society in West Africa, with the

[1] L. S. Senghor, *On African Socialism*, 81.

prospect that at last there might be emancipation from those ancient limitations of poverty, ignorance and disease which had fettered West African peoples as far back as memory could recall. When Edward Blyden spoke glowingly of the future of Liberia–'The hills . . . covered with flocks, and the valleys with corn; the increase of the earth . . . fat and plenteous'–he spoke, not only for himself or for one country; he voiced the hopes of all West Africans of his time who had caught a glimpse of the prospect before them.

For an understanding of mid-twentieth-century Africa, both the Islamic and the western intrusions need detailed examination. In the present study, I have attempted to explore the second of these phenomena. In so doing, I have worked within a context of definitions and assumptions which need to be shared with the reader. In the first place, I have thought of the terms, western and European, as being synonymous and have used them interchangeably, primarily so that I might include points of view emanating from America as well as from Europe. Secondly, I have not included within my definition of western influences those ideas which originated with Negroes in America beginning towards the end of the nineteenth century, not because I considered them unimportant or irrelevant but because their importance calls for special treatment which will be the subject of another, later volume. Thirdly, I have tried to treat the impact of western ideas on West Africa, not merely in terms of nationalist thought–although this is an important element–but in the broader context of a fundamental confrontation of two ways of life. Further, I have viewed the intrusion of the West as completely as I could through the eyes of those on whom it fell, who, so to speak, stood on the shore to meet it, who were obliged to deal with its shattering force, and who inherited the fateful task of advising their people how to respond.

Finally, I have undertaken this study with the needs and aspirations of present-day West African nations continually in mind. It seems clear that the new nations of Africa are more than ever concerned with the task of modernization, and are caught up in the problem of how to manage the ideal as well as the material aspects of building a modern nation-state. It is the latest stage in a process which has been unfolding for more than a century and a half, and it can be better understood to the extent that it is illuminated by a fuller knowledge of that process. The Africa of today has grown out of the trials of the past, and the wisdom of Africa's new leadership is rooted in the experience and intellectual discrimination of those earlier leaders who first encountered Europe on West Africa's shores.

Numerous individuals have been most helpful to me in the course of my study. Among those who have devoted valuable time to reading parts of my work and who have assisted with useful suggestions are Dr. E. A. Ayandele, Dr. H. O. Idowu, and Dr. F. I. A. Omu of Nigeria, Dr. Hollis R. Lynch of Trinidad, and Dr. John A. Ballard and Dr. Richard L. Sklar of the United States.

A wide variety of libraries and archives have opened their facilities without stint and greatly assisted, through generous personal attention, the labours of an individual researcher. These institutions include the British Museum in London, the Bibliothèque Nationale in Paris, the Schomburg Collection of the New York Public Library, the Royal Commonwealth Society in London, and the Institut Français d'Afrique Noire at the University of Dakar. In this connection I owe particular thanks to Mrs. Margaret Amosu and her colleagues in the Africana collection of the University of Ibadan library who granted me all the many facilities of their splendid collection. A number of archives have also been of great assistance - the Public Record Office and the Church Missionary Society in London, the overseas section of the National Archives in Paris, the National Archives of Senegal in Dakar, those of Ghana in Accra and the Nigerian Archives in Ibadan.

I am most grateful to my colleagues in the Rockefeller Foundation of New York who arranged a generous sabbatical from my regular duties and who cheerfully took over the burdens of those duties that I might be freed to pursue this study.

I must also express my deep obligation to two others - friends and former teachers - whose long-standing interest and encouragement and whose patient instruction, I hope, have endowed some of my pages with their own rare historical skills and human understanding - Harry J. Carman and Allan Nevins.

Lastly, I owe a great debt to my wife. Not only has she performed unfailingly and well in those more usual wifely roles of captive audience, amanuensis, research assistant and proof-reader, but she has placed at my service both her own splendid historical judgment and an unusually fine editorial talent which have been of enormous assistance in bringing my chapters into final coherence and cohesion.

Nairobi
November 1966

The Origins of Modern African Thought

1 Prologue: The European Background

1 *Ottobah Cugoano Writes a Book*

Towards the end of the eighteenth century, a book was published in London entitled *Thoughts and Sentiments on the Evil and Wicked Traffic of the Slavery and Commerce of the Human Species*. It was written by one who had come to know his subject at close quarters – an African from the Fanti country of the Gold Coast named Ottobah Cugoano. Kidnapped and enslaved while still a child, he had by luck come eventually into the possession of a master who brought him to Britain as a servant. There he became free, perhaps as a result of the James Somerset case in 1772 which put an end to slavery in England. While he was still with his master, he tells us, he learned to read and write, and at some point he was converted to Christianity. Thus it was that he eventually was able to produce his eloquent if rhetorical indictment of slavery and the slave trade. Writing in the baroque style of the England of his day, invoking a Christian God and summoning biblical evidence to support his argument, appealing to the humanitarianism of eighteenth-century Europe, he used his western training and experience to pronounce the equality of all men before God and to assert the right of the African to pursue his own destiny in freedom and with human dignity.

Cugoano's book which was one of the earliest expressions of African thought to reach a European audience, was the result of bringing African experience to Europe where it encountered and mixed with religious and humanitarian ideas then current in England. By coincidence, it was published in 1787, the same year that a group of British philanthropists established a settlement in Sierra Leone for the repatriation of the so-called Black Poor of London. Thus the reciprocity was complete, for this was the first step in the long process whereby European institutions and ideas were to be brought to Africa. There, joining with indigenous forms and shaped by the local environment, they helped to develop the body of ideas, viewpoints, philosophies, ethical codes and systems of moral and religious thought which came ultimately to characterize the modern African mind.

2 The Ideas of the Enlightenment in England and France

The England that Ottobah Cugoano had come to know represented eighteenth-century Europe at the height of her powers. For approximately four centuries the continent had exploded with discoveries and rediscoveries as ancient learning was unearthed and combined with new knowledge in a wide-ranging and effective search to understand man and his universe. The central idea of the Enlightenment—the primacy of rational thought—had brought to light the laws of nature and seemingly given man the means to live in harmony with them. Progress appeared for the first time not only possible but inevitable. Moreover, the idea of progress had no limits; not only enlightened Europe but all mankind was deemed capable of perfection. Hence implicit in Enlightenment thinking was a humanitarian duty to bring the fruits of European civilization to parts of the world still languishing in darkness.

Eighteenth-century Europe already knew a great deal about the non-European world, partly as a result of scientific inquiry, but primarily for the less exalted reason that Europe's commercial needs had already led to territorial expansion on a global scale. During the two and a half centuries after Columbus, vast empires had sprawled across the seas, filling the map of the New World and staking out clusters of enclaves in Asia and Africa. Stimulated by visions of wealth, troubled by economic stagnation or religious persecution at home, the chief maritime powers of Europe had successively established themselves East and West. By 1750 a long series of wars had for all practical purposes reduced the contenders to two—England and France.

Both nations were strong adherents of mercantilism, that economic system which rigorously subordinated the interests of the colonies to those of the mother country. Both believed in economic self-sufficiency which assigned to the overseas possession the function of market for the produce of the metropole, of source for the supply of raw materials, or of convenient station for the reprovisioning of the merchant marine and the basing of the navy. Neither gave more thought than the other to the needs and desires of the colonial populations; yet for all that, there were fundamental distinctions to be drawn between French and English imperial thought and practice.

Primarily, France was a continental power preoccupied with dynastic

THE EUROPEAN BACKGROUND [23]

and religious questions in Europe to the neglect of overseas possessions and commitments. The idea of the glory of France burned bright but it was a glory more of the Bourbon royal house than of the French nation and its fulfilment appeared to rest more in European primacy than in colonial empire. Moreover, merchant groups in France were hampered by the remnants of the medieval guilds, by an archaic system of internal customs duties and tolls and by an autocratic monarchy, and consequently were unable to give effective voice to ideas of commercial development, particularly in relation to a strong and expanding colonial system.

England, on the other hand, insular and isolated, had relied on sea power since the days of the Armada and for the best part of two hundred years had concentrated her energies on the achievement of national economic self-sufficiency through empire. Since Tudor times her commerce and industry had been encouraged and protected and, with the political revolutions of the seventeenth century, the rising merchant class had obtained the parliamentary representation necessary to ensure continued governmental attention to its interests. By 1750 France was headed for bankruptcy and revolution, whereas England was laying the foundations for her subsequent commercial supremacy and already taking her first tentative steps towards industrial development.

The difference in imperial theory between the two nations was most clearly illustrated by the attitude of France at the Peace of Paris in 1763 following the disastrous Seven Years War. The loss of Canada was treated with relative indifference, partly because it was felt that Canada provided neither the agricultural wealth of the sugar islands of Martinique and Guadeloupe nor the trading opportunities of a territory like Senegal. More important, however, the politics of prestige pursued by the French royal house were no longer to be served by colonial empire; it was on the continent that the glory of France would ultimately be secured, and there her energies should be concentrated. England suffered from no such myopia – the acquisition of Canada and the elimination of the French from North America opened a continent to expansion. This was not only prestigious; it was good business as well.

At home diverging political philosophies guided the two countries. In England the idea had become established of a government by the consent of the governed and limited by constitutional guarantees against tyranny in its various forms. Beyond this, the British colonies in America had carried these principles to their logical conclusion. The Declaration of Independence and the war that followed proclaimed the right of all mankind to life, liberty and the pursuit of happiness, and added the vision of a broadly based democracy which was to capture the imagination of future generations, not only in America but eventually the world over.

During the years that England was shifting from a monarchy ruling by divine right to a constitutional government, France remained the prime example of a classical autocracy. Her kings were absolute, the nascent middle class was unable to achieve meaningful power and there was no tradition of legislative government. No such things as constitutional guarantees of personal rights existed, so that arbitrary arrest and imprisonment obtained alongside inequitable taxation and gross privilege in favour of the upper classes of nobility and clergy. Administrative inefficiency and an obsolete fiscal régime were added to these abuses and compounded by the lunatic incompetence of the French royal family. Economic and political bankruptcy inevitably ensued and in turn were succeeded by revolution which swept away the whole obsolete apparatus of privilege and attempted to build a new polity based on a new philosophy of government. The remnants of feudalism, serfdom and class privilege were uprooted and in their place were established principles of equality of taxation and a society based on individual, not hereditary, worth. Under the Declaration of the Rights of Man, the humanitarianism of the Enlightenment emerged in the doctrines of representative government, of freedom of speech, worship and press, of equality before the law, government by law and the protection of property from arbitrary confiscation.

To these Rousseauist views was added another powerful concept and a unique contribution of the French Revolution to eighteenth-century, as well as to more modern, thought – the idea of nationalism. Nationalism as we know it today had scarcely existed before this time; people tended to think of themselves as coming from a particular district, town, shire or fief, while the monarchs of the eighteenth century looked on their people less as French, German or Spanish nationals than as simply loyal subjects of his royal highness. Now the idea of nation was exalted – proclaimed through patriotic festivals and anthems, the raising of a national citizen army and establishment of nation-wide political, administrative, educational and other institutions. But mostly it manifested itself through a quasi-religious fervour in which devotion and loyalty to the French state were sworn and a mystical feeling of the destiny of the French nation was experienced. Thus the old idea of Bourbon glory was taken up and transformed so as to embody the whole French people, instilling them with the spirit of mission from which they were to experience such great satisfaction in bringing the fruits of French civilization to others in the world as yet denied these advantages.

In one important respect – in its handling of the institution of slavery – the French Revolution went well beyond the principles established by the political reformers in England and America. Eighteenth-century humanitarianism, concerned with the perfectibility of man, had been urging various social, ethical, religious and economic reforms leading to greater human liberty and happiness, and one of its leading objectives in this respect was the abolition of Negro slavery. Anti-slavery societies were formed in England, France and America, and religious groups, notably the Quakers, attacked slavery and forbade church members to own slaves or engage in the slave trade. Yet government action was slow to come. The revolutions in England in the seventeenth century had ignored the institution of slavery which was regarded at that time as a natural aspect of a plantation economy operating under mercantilist doctrine. The situation was later rectified within Great Britain itself through court action and an appeal to natural rights theory, but legalized slave trade lingered on until 1807, and slavery in the colonies was not abolished until 1834. In America both the Declaration of Independence and the Federal Constitution of 1787 were silent regarding the inhumanity of slavery, and it was left to later generations to assert this basic inconsistency of those documents. In France, however, through the Declaration of the Rights of Man of 1789 and subsequent legislation, slavery was abolished in the colonies while all colonials, former slaves included, were at once given French citizenship with every civil and political right pertaining thereto, and invited to send representatives to the government in Paris. Here indeed did men pursue the logic of democracy to its necessary end. Unhappily this expression of democratic principle did not survive the régime of Napoleon and slavery had to be done away with again and finally in 1848.

The government of Napoleon subtracted much from, and added little to, the liberal egalitarianism of the Revolution, but it did underscore one aspect of revolutionary governmental reform which came to be an important part of French thought. Government under the monarchy had been unsystematic to the point of chaos, involving a great array of local administrations, legal codes, tax schedules, civil and ecclesiastical districts, systems of coinage, standards of education and internal customs schedules, which not only lacked uniformity but frequently overlapped in powers and jurisdiction. The revolutionary government properly set about to replace confusion with order and established a new pattern of local government uniform throughout the land, instituted the metric system of weights and measures, and began work on legal reforms and a scheme for national education. To these developments Napoleon brought his own taste for a highly centralized, efficient administration directly responsible to Paris, and he was soon rewarded with thorough, quick, uniform administration of local government completely responsive to the dictates of the central régime. In addition he was able to conclude the codification already begun of French civil, criminal and commercial law, and to institute a state system of public instruction of identical content and standard in all parts of the country. Napoleon's passion for uniformity and centralization may have touched a responsive note in the French psychology, for his reforms were never subsequently altered in that otherwise politically fluctuating society, and centralized uniformity came to be a hallmark of French administration wherever it was found in the world.

3 The Rise of Nineteenth-century Liberalism

The age of the French Revolution and Napoleon brought changes not only to France but to all Europe. Much of the influence and character of the eighteenth century continued into the nineteenth, but already new forces were at work in the West which were changing Britain, for example, at least as profoundly as revolution had altered France. Perhaps the most important factor in bringing about this change was the rise of industrialism. Industrial development in England had been slowly gaining ground throughout the eighteenth century but it was not until after the Napoleonic wars that it became an outstanding factor in the economic, social and political life of the country. And not only did it begin to exercise profound material effect on a growing segment of the population, but it also caused fundamental changes in men's ideas.

The theory, if not the practice, of political liberalism had been worked out in the parliamentary revolutions of the seventeenth century, but even after the blow dealt her empire by the American Revolution, England clung to the economic conservatism of mercantilism. Bit by bit, however, the commercial and industrial classes found mercantile interference vexing and began to support the liberal ideas of the classical economists of the Adam Smith school. Smith and his followers preached free trade as more conducive to increased world production and exchange, urged

THE EUROPEAN BACKGROUND [27]

the abolition of colonies as an expensive impediment to economic expansion, argued for world peace and disarmament as a necessary prerequisite to an international economy of plenty and demanded a consequent reduction of the role of the state to the barest minimum necessary to ensure normal law and order. Gradually these ideas were translated into action. The protective tariffs on grain were repealed in 1846, and three years later England embraced a complete policy of free trade. Internally, the state was discouraged from interfering in any way with individual freedom of contract, with the natural laws of supply and demand regulating prices, wages and labour supply, and with the improvement of industrial working conditions which might tend to upset Malthusian formulas regarding population.

From economic liberalism, it was but a short step to politically liberal ideas. If the state should not interfere in the natural growth of commercial and industrial activities, it followed that the best government was an orderly government run in a business-like manner by business interests and limited in its activities to minor policing. Hence, despite the shudder of reaction to the excesses of the French Revolution and to the bloodletting of the Napoleonic wars, there was a persistent clamour for liberal political reform. In England it produced in 1832 an electoral law which effectively opened political power to the new industrialists who now united in control of the government with the old oligarchy of landowners and merchants.

The trends of political and economic liberalism were joined by a third strand of liberal thought—humanitarianism, which had survived virtually unchanged from the age of the Enlightenment. Belief in the goodness and perfectibility of man was, if anything, intensified in post-Napoleonic Europe, but now it was emotion and sentiment rather than cold reason which were felt to be the surer guides for mankind to a happier life. The idea of the perfectibility of man, understood through an appeal to the heart and spirit rather than through rational thought, led to changes in method and approach, but the objectives were the same. Just as in the eighteenth century there had been agitation for social reform such as the improvement of prison conditions, the growth of religious toleration, the institution of popular education and the abolition of Negro slavery, so in the nineteenth century did these movements continue to flourish. In England, eighteenth-century pressure on behalf of the Negro had ultimately found some outlet in the founding of the Freetown colony. During the early decades of the nineteenth century, reform brought more solid achievements, first in the abolition of the slave trade and then in the suppression of slavery throughout the Empire. One further element was added. Nineteenth-century romantic impulses resulted in a religious revival in Europe of evangelical character, and linked to this was a strong missionary movement designed to bring to peoples in far-off parts of the world not only the comforts of Christianity but the benefits of a higher European civilization.

However strong it may have been, the missionary movement in England was kept strictly private in character, for there were powerful and growing sentiments in that country against the efficacy of colonial possessions. The free traders argued that colonies were an unnecessary burden on the public treasury, that they led to ruinous wars and benefited certain groups only, while weighing on the nation as a whole. Better to cut loose the whole costly structure, maintaining a few scattered naval stations, and allow commerce to flow freely to the economic benefit of all. Of course, it was easy to uphold such doctrines in an England which had emerged in 1815 by all odds the predominant world power with total mastery of the seas and an industrial and commercial strength that no other nation could hope to match without recourse to a rigorously protective mercantilism. Nonetheless, despite the anti-imperial arguments and sentiment, the British Empire did not disappear; indeed it was strengthened and extended. But this extension seems to have been the result more of accident than design – the South African Cape Colony was acquired primarily as a naval station, Sierra Leone for the repatriation of freed slaves and Australia as a convict settlement, while expansion in India and the East Indies was mainly the result of individual, not national, initiative. It was, as has been said, an 'anti-colonial colonization'.[1]

Perhaps the dominant note in the romantic-liberal thought of France during the years after Napoleon was the influence of England. Admiration for British institutions, though an unusual turn of the Gallic mind, was not especially peculiar, considering the shattering impact of the English triumph over Napoleon and the reaction against Napoleonic militarism. After a brief flirtation with restored Bourbonism, France settled down in 1830 to the bourgeois monarchy of Louis Philippe which took on much of the colour of the middle-class government of Britain. Like England, France adopted a limited constitutional monarchy directed by industrial, commercial and land-holding groups. Government, while encouraging some public works, assumed the classic laissez-faire

---

[1] Klaus E. Knorr, *British Colonial Theories, 1570–1850*, 249–50; Henri Brunschwig, *Mythes et Réalités de l'Impérialisme Colonial Français, 1871–1914*, 10.

position of non-interference in economic activities, although in the face of an insistent demand for protection by a youthful industrialism a system of tariffs was maintained for a time in opposition to British free trade policies, remaining in effect until 1860. Foreign policy, though somewhat ambivalent, was essentially anti-imperialist and pacifist.

French preference for a government representing essentially bourgeois interests and restricting its activities to the minimum necessary for the preservation of law and order cannot be completely explained, however, in terms of admiration for Britain. Except for a few tiny remnants, the old French Empire was gone, and there appeared to be no great enthusiasm within France to acquire another. Colonies were regarded as an inconsequential factor in the French economy, and their possession evoked little enthusiasm within France itself. Moreover, a considerable body of public opinion, pointing to the burden of colonial administration and the expense of foreign wars, argued against foreign involvement. Yet, like England, France found itself slowly, almost against its will, acquiring the beginnings of a new colonial empire.[1]

The explanation lies to some extent in the French character and in French history. The old empire before the Revolution had been built in a considerable measure to feed the pride and elevate the prestige of the Bourbon kings. But the notion of the glory of France through imperial aggrandizement survived the Revolution, revived briefly under Napoleon, and now was still to be found undernourished but alive in the bourgeois monarchy of Louis Philippe. There were those who argued that France needed to restore her national prestige by rebuilding her navy, and a navy required bases where provisions could be obtained and crews given a period of rest. Hence even if colonies were uneconomical, they were necessary aspects of the revival of French hegemony in the world, aimed at disputing with Britain her control of the seas. Moreover, the French Revolution and the rise of Napoleonic power had in themselves greatly stimulated the sense of French national pride and this first manifestation of modern nationalistic spirit had by no means perished in the defeat at Waterloo. French nationalism, that spiritual communion in the knowledge of the superiority of French civilization, implied the obligation to share this greatness with other people. The aim was not only to colonize them, but also to teach them French culture and assimilate them into the French nation. The missionary zeal of the British humanitarianism of the day may not have been as well developed among the French, but their feeling for cultural

[1] Brunschwig, *op. cit.*, 21–2.

mission was clear and strong and far more self-conscious than with the English. If, therefore, the dominant note in France was anti-colonial, there were enough forces at work to bring about a modest renascence of empire. Senegal, regained in 1817, was cultivated in a desultory fashion, but it was not abandoned and its territory was gradually extended. Reunion in the Indian Ocean was thus recovered about the same time and equipped for use as a naval station. Years of indecision in Algeria ended finally in conquest during the 1840s, and somewhat later there were the beginnings of imperialist moves in Indo-China under Napoleon III. Still, the prevailing mood in France at this time was far from chauvinistic.[1]

4 The Roots of Nineteenth-century Colonial Policy in Britain and France

As France and England became increasingly involved in West Africa during the nineteenth century, each brought its own ideas, prejudices, national beliefs, religious convictions, philosophic systems, political institutions, economic experiences and other viewpoints distilled from centuries of antecedent activities in Europe. These ideas, which were to have a profound effect on African thought, were essentially similar whether French or English, but national character and history resulted in certain parochial distinctions which ultimately were to have important manifestations in Africa.

Not unexpectedly, each nation presented a many-faceted, sometimes paradoxical image. From the great Revolution, France brought the ideas of political liberty which guaranteed freedom of speech, worship and conscience and abolished arbitrary rule, of the equality of men in the pursuit of happiness, and of the mystical fraternity of all men seeking a better world. But with revolutionary liberalism came also Napoleonic centralism which organized, controlled and limited men's actions to the point of a greater efficiency but a vanishing freedom. From the Revolution also came the outburst of national feeling which carried the conviction that all men were entitled–indeed, obliged–to seek national independence as a vehicle for achieving political liberty, economic plenty and social equality. Yet French nationalism stood for the superiority of French culture and encouraged Frenchmen to assimilate other people and to teach them to ignore and despise their own culture and history.

[1] *Ibid.*, 10–16.

THE EUROPEAN BACKGROUND

France was well endowed with the humanitarian spirit of the eighteenth and nineteenth centuries and sought to fulfil this impulse by assisting the people of Africa and other parts of the world in achieving a better life. However, the very idea of the helping hand implied a sense of cultural superiority and a humiliating unhumanitarian condescension. France had long entertained ideas of imperial glory which were scarcely less powerful in the nineteenth century than they had been in the seventeenth and eighteenth. Still, France had been basically a continental, politically introspective, power, and so she continued. Finally, France never brought the degree of economic commitment to her colonial policy that other powers, notably Britain, did. Nonetheless, French colonial ideas born during the ascendancy of centralized monarchy and mercantilist theory, were never quite equal to eliminating a mercantile spirit which placed the interests of the colony an inevitable second to those of the metropole.

For her part, Britain brought convictions rooted in her political liberalism, her industrial revolution, her humanitarianism and her pragmatic turn of mind. British political experience was based on the idea of government by the consent of the governed, and British efforts in West Africa were long aimed at preserving the integrity of local states there. But her experience with widespread political chaos in West Africa during the nineteenth century served to confirm her conviction that in the final analysis only Englishmen were capable of self-government, and such an attitude was to be echoed in the British colonial administration of West Africa. Britain had built her first empire on commercial supremacy and by the first half of the nineteenth century she had added world industrial supremacy as well. The economic motive was paramount and decisive, and commercial profit was everything. Notwithstanding, it was England who secured the abolition of the slave trade, it was British philanthropists who founded the Freetown colony, and it was the London and Edinburgh missionary societies which took the lead in helping the peoples of Asia and Africa to achieve their image of a better life.

The humanitarian activities of the English missions were justifiably praiseworthy. Their workers laboured intelligently and diligently, not only to bring spiritual salvation, but to educate, to instruct and to improve the daily lot of people who were essentially strangers and whose betterment could offer nothing more material than a sense of brotherhood and personal satisfaction. Yet, these same missionaries ended up by corrupting their vision of selfless help–stooping to indulge in mission politics and imposing a régime of cultural imperialism which went a long way towards undoing the good they had achieved. Last of all, the Englishman prided himself on his lack of cultural chauvinism and his indifference as to whether or not the colonial people were drawn to adopt aspects of Anglo-Saxon civilization. Leaving aside the possibility that such insouciance was the most extreme degree of self-esteem, it is nonetheless a fact that many Englishmen of the time never ceased to point to the superiority of the British way of life and to assert their unshakeable belief that the world could only hope for general improvement proportionate to its degree of adoption of superior British standards.

Such were the attitudes of West Africa's major colonizing powers during the nineteenth century. What was the African response?[1]

[1] Knorr, *op. cit.*, 246–7.

2 The Eighteenth-Century Forerunners

1 *African Expressions of Europe's Enlightenment*

The career of Ottobah Cugoano was unusual but not unique. Of the millions of Africans transported as slaves from West Africa to the Americas up to the end of the eighteenth century, a considerable number managed to gain their freedom. Some came originally as indentured servants and liberty followed their contracted period of labour. Others were manumitted through philanthropy, while still others managed to set aside enough earnings to purchase their freedom. In the United States alone it was estimated that by 1790 there were 60,000 freemen; similarly, a substantial body of free Negroes and mulattoes developed throughout the West Indies and South America during the eighteenth century, and a number of these attained wealth, influence, and in some cases, slaves of their own.

Like Cugoano, there were those who learned to read and write. A few of these gained distinction as pedagogues and aesthetes, leaving testimony of their activities and attitudes towards the times in which they lived in the form of personal memoirs or other literary forms. There was, for example, the celebrated Phillis Wheatley, sold as a slave in Boston during the mid-eighteenth century, who blossomed as a poetess under the encouragement of a benevolent master and helped brighten Washington's early days as commander of the revolutionary armies in America with a poem dedicated to his valour and success. There was Ignatius Sancho, the indefatigable writer of letters and admirer of the novelist Laurence Sterne, born of slave parents on a ship headed for the West Indies. He eventually settled in London where he was able to indulge a love of literature and the theatre in combination with a weakness for gaming and dining, his modest literary accomplishments gaining him some notice as a minor figure in the London coffee-house set of the eighteenth century. Scholarship of distinction was represented by Anton Wilhelm Amo, a native of the Gold Coast and never a slave, who came to Europe under missionary auspices. He then remained to complete an education in which he mastered six languages including Hebrew and Greek, and lectured for a number of years in the field of philosophy at several German universities. Amo returned to the Gold Coast only at the end of his professional career; two other natives of that region, Jacobus E. Capitein and Philip Quaque, initiated a pattern which became common during the nineteenth century by going to Europe for early training which led to the Christian ministry and eventual assignment to West Africa. There they assumed direction of local educational establishments as their lifetime work.[1]

In each of these examples, the African came under the strong influence of a body of western, Christian ideas transmitted through schooling, language and ordinary day-to-day contact with the world around them. Quaque and Capitein, trained in European mission schools, offered their own students much the same curricula they had received. Amo responded to his Dutch and German education by teaching and adding his own refinements to the body of western philosophy with which he was concerned. Phillis Wheatley has been criticized by Negroes for having modelled herself on Alexander Pope while failing to introduce into her poetry more than the slightest awareness of her origins. As for the bon-vivant, Ignatius Sancho, the most evidently African characteristic of the edition of his letters is the engraving of their author's likeness in the frontispiece.

Yet, for all their European orientation, these Africans never forgot their origins; indeed, their turning from African ways was eloquent testimony to the fact. Quaque and Capitein returned home for the very purpose of teaching their countrymen skills and standards they believed would improve the African's lot. Amo used his western scholarship to demonstrate similarities between European and African civilization, thus weakening western arguments stressing the theological and 'natural' status of African slavery. Recent literary critics have professed to see more awareness of an African and Negro personality in the poetry of Phillis Wheatley than was once thought to be present. At any rate the

[1] Critical and biographical literature on Phillis Wheatley is abundant. See, for example, John W. Cromwell, *The Negro in American History*, 77–85, and Arthur P. Davies, 'Personal Elements in the Poetry of Phillis Wheatley', *Phylon*, vol. XIII, no. 2, 191–8. For Sancho, see *Letters of the Late Ignatius Sancho*. W. E. Abraham, *The Mind of Africa*, 128–30, deals with Amo. See also F. L. Bartels, 'Philip Quaque, 1741–1816', *Transactions of the Gold Coast and Togoland Historical Society*, vol. I, pt. 5, 153–77, and Bartels, 'Jacobus Eliza Capitein, 1717–1747', *Transactions of the Historical Society of Ghana*, vol. IV, pt. 1, 3–13, as well as *The Gold Coast Aborigines*, Jan. 8, 1898.

THE EIGHTEENTH-CENTURY FORERUNNERS [35]

pattern was to become a familiar one in West Africa as European influences touched, then penetrated, then spread into West Africa during the years of the nineteenth century and into the twentieth. Even at this initial stage there was evidence of the tension and balance between acceptance and rejection – the desire to introduce apparent improvement and to reform indigenous institutions which seemed decadent or primitive, poised against the need to retain some sense of contact with the African past, the African land and the African spirit threatened with destruction by alien forces.

2 The Afro-European Attack on Slavery

Of all the institutions with which the eighteenth-century African, Europeanized or not, was concerned, the chief was the institution of slavery. Cugoano wrote a whole book dedicated to that theme, apparently his life's sole literary output, and two years after this work appeared, another was published in which the theme of African slavery played a prominent part. This was a narrative autobiography by Olaudah Equiano stressing the adventure and travel in far-off places, a popular theme in that age. It had the additional attraction, however, of having been written by an African slave who had not only suffered many close escapes from personal destruction, but at the same time managed to earn his freedom, establish himself professionally and develop the skill of writing to a facility that each reader was invited to witness for himself. Throughout the recitation of adventure, however, were sprinkled both explicit and implicit condemnations of slavery which placed this volume with that of Cugoano as important early African judgments of certain aspects of European civilization and their effect on Africa.

Equiano, or Gustavus Vassa as he was baptized, suffered the typical fate of so many West African children victimized by the slave trade – kidnapped by strangers while unattended in his village, and hurried off to a coastal place to be sold to a European slaver. At that, Vassa was luckier than most. Surviving the Atlantic passage, he eventually came into the possession of the proprietor of a trading vessel and for the next thirty years he was more or less continuously sailing the high seas. The life was hard but no more so than for a freeman; young Vassa soon learnt to become a competent seaman; and when a subsequent master permitted him to profit from personal trading, Vassa used the opportunity to save the forty pounds necessary to purchase his freedom. After manumission he continued to follow the sailor's life which inevitably had taken him to exotic places where he experienced many adventures. He was present at the siege of Louisbourg in 1758, later participated in an abortive attempt to sail to the North Pole, and experienced many narrow escapes from shipwreck and the predatory designs of slavers ever eager to recapture an able-bodied former slave. He was, however, more than a mere sailor. The ambition that led to freedom also brought ultimate literacy and a rising position in the Negro community of London. When the expedition to repatriate the Black Poor of London was organized, it was Vassa who was named commissary steward. In the confusion which characterized the fumbling start of the expedition, Vassa was dismissed amidst charges and counter-charges of mismanagement, and his book was in part written as an apology for his role in the affair. In the main, however, it was a tale of adventure and a personal success story, spiced with illustrations and admonitions to his European audience on the evils of slavery.

On the question of African slavery the ideas of Cugoano made effective cause with the experiences of Vassa. The former developed powerful theoretical arguments against slavery and the slave trade, basing his position on theological, humanitarian and practical grounds. The latter limited himself to everyday examples of the cruelty, barbarousness and inefficiency of the slave system, but in so doing he lent authenticity and immediacy to Cugoano's reasoning.

Since the apologists for the institution of slavery regularly based its legitimacy on scriptural authority, Cugoano devoted a substantial portion of his assault on the slave system to demolishing its theological defences. The common contention was that the curse of Noah condemned the descendants of Ham to be servants of servants. Further, there was the precedent of the slavery of Israel in Egypt and the sanction of servitude included in the law of Moses. Cugoano attacked these arguments with force and ingenuity. In the first place, he pointed out, there had never been any inference of inferiority among the people of God. All came from the same source and the same blood, all were brothers descended from the same father. The present inhabitants of the world had sprung from the family of Noah, quickly dispersed over the earth, and had ultimately come to acquire distinguishing physical features such as colouring, or different ways of living in response to variations in environment. But, insisted Cugoano, 'it may be reasonably, as well as religiously, inferred, that He who placed them in their various situations, hath extended equally his care and protection to all; and from thence, that it becometh unlawful to counteract his

THE EIGHTEENTH-CENTURY FORERUNNERS [37]

benignity, by reducing others of different complexions to undeserved bondage'.

This was but the opening salvo. The assertion that the curse of Noah in the family of Ham justified African slavery, Cugoano continued, was simply bad history and faulty biblical interpretation. The curse had descended only on the families issuing from Canaan, the youngest son of Ham, and consequently had no effect on Ham's other issue. There was no doubt that the curse had taken full effect, for the Canaanites became a wicked people who paid for their licentiousness and idolatry with many calamities, but their land of Canaan was in Asia, not Africa. It was the people of Cush, Ham's first son, who ultimately emerged in East Africa as the Ethiopians, and Ham's other two sons, Mizraim and Phut, were the progenitors of races that settled in Egypt and North Africa. These people of Africa had no connection with Noah's prediction; the colour of their skin was a mark of environment, not a sign of slavery.

The fact that Moses had permitted slavery among the Israelites added no force to the argument, Cugoano continued, for slavery with the Jews had been quite a different affair from the harsh and bloody servitude later visited by the European on the African. Modern slavers in the West Indian trade, he said, were no more than thieves and so were the slave owners—they cheated the slave of his freedom and reimbursed him not at all for his labour. The Jews, on the other hand, had practised a form of voluntary indenture, which violated neither the natural liberties of men nor the concepts of equity and justice as they were then understood. It was just as reasonable for one man to contract with another to be his bond servant as it was for two men to agree on a partnership in business, one perhaps providing the capital and the other the management. One individual might agree to pay another's debts in return for labour and service; the essential difference was that the agreement was freely entered into by both sides, the period of servitude was temporary and the slave had rights and privileges as well as obligations. Even the Canaanites, though reduced to hewers of wood and drawers of water, were no worse off than poor working people in a free country—they were supplied with the necessities of life and were free to leave their employment at any time they chose. How different was the lot of the African slave in the West Indies, suffering under the barbarous fiat of British law. The Canaanites 'were not hunted after, and a reward offered for their heads, as it is in the West-Indies for any that can find a strayed slave'. But with the modern slave system, 'he who can bring such a head warm reeking with his blood, as a token that he had murdered him—inhuman and shocking to think!—he is paid for it; and, cruel and dreadful as it is, that law is still in force in some of the British colonies'.

With such reasoning Cugoano moved momentarily from theological to humanitarian considerations, but he quickly returned to his main argument based on Christian doctrine. Holy writ, he contended, was no compendium of casual commentary but a body of knowledge precise and purposeful in conception, designed to give man a deeper understanding of the will of God. A good example was the query of the prophet, Jeremiah, 'Can the Ethiopian change his skin, or the leopard his spots?' What was this, demanded Cugoano, but a means for showing man that he has no power to change his own nature, black with sin, any more than an individual can change his outward appearance. The evil inherent in every man, the blackness of his original sin, and the spotted character of his transgression can be cleansed only through the blood of Jesus, 'wherein all the stains and blackest dyes of sin and pollution can be washed away for ever, and the darkest sinner be made to shine as the brightest angel in heaven'. The importance of skin colour was therefore not intrinsic but symbolic. Introduced by God to teach man the wickedness of his nature, its insignificance was purely metaphorical, and 'the external blackness of the Ethiopians, is as innocent and natural, as spots in the leopards; and ... the difference in colour and complexion, which it hath pleased God to appoint among men, are no more unbecoming unto either of them, than the different shades of the rainbow are unseemly to the whole'.[1]

Having introduced the element of religious symbolism, Cugoano was ready for his final argument. Far from sanctioning slavery, the bondage of the Jews in Egypt and the punishment of the Canaanites were introduced precisely for the purpose of establishing the idea of God's omnipotence, and the need for mankind to conquer the weakness of sin. The illustrations were emblematic, not literal:

When God ... brought his Israel out of Egypt and temporal bondage, it was intended and designed thereby, to set up an emblematical representation of their deliverance from the power and captivity of sin, and from the dominion of that evil and malignant spirit, who had with exquisite subtilty and guile at first seduced the original progenitors of mankind. And when they were brought to the promised land, and had gotten deliverance, and subdued their enemies under them, they were

[1] Ottobah Cugoano, *Thoughts and Sentiments on the Evil and Wicked Traffic of the Slavery and Commerce of the Human Species*, 29–32, 33–8, 40–2, 45–7.

to reign over them; and their laws respecting bond-servants, and other things of that nature, were to denote, that they were to keep under and in subjection the whole body of their evil affections and lusts. This is so declared by the Apostle, that the law is spiritual, and intended for spiritual uses. The general state of slavery which took place in the world, among other enormous crimes of wicked men might have served for an emblem and similitude of our spiritual bondage and slavery to sin; but, unless it had been admitted into the spiritual and divine law, it could not have stood and become an emblem that there was any spiritual restoration and deliverance afforded to us. By that which is evil in captivity and slavery among men, we are thereby so represented as Israel to have dominion over sin, and to rule over and keep in subjection all our spiritual enemies. And, therefore, any thing which had a seeming appearance in favour of slavery, so far as it was admitted into the law, was to shew that it was not natural and innocent, like that of different colours among men, but as necessary to be made an emblem of what was intended by it.

As for the Canaanites:

The extirpation... out of their land, was so ordered, not only to punish them for their idolatry and abominable wickedness, but also to shew forth the honour of his power, and the sovereignty of him who is the only potent one that reigneth over the nations; that all men at that time might learn to fear and know him who is Jehovah; and ever since that it might continue a standing memorial of him, and a standard of honour unto him who doth according to his will among the armies of heaven, and whatever pleaseth him with the inhabitants of the earth. And, in general, these transactions stand recorded for an emblematical use and similitude, in the spiritual warfare of every true Israelite throughout all the ages of time.[1]

Now was Cugoano ready to follow negative injunction with positive precept. Not only was there nothing in scripture to warrant the enslaving of the black people or any others, but such an institution was a gross perversion of the law of God founded in love. This law commanded two loves—the love of God and the love of one's neighbour as oneself. God created man in His image and taught mankind the meaning of love arising out of the unity of nature and blood. It was only with the appearance of the enslavers of man that the jarring notes of envy and hatred appeared, and oppression, injury, and slavery were introduced as servants of sin and the devil. It was incumbent upon the good man, the man of honour, to scorn and to oppose this base instinct:

The noble philanthropist looks up to his God... as his only sovereign; and he looks around on his fellow men as his brethren and friends; and in every situation and case, however mean and contemptible they may

[1] *Ibid.*, 48–51.

seem, he endeavours to do them good: and should he meet with one in the desert, whom he never saw before, he would hail him my brother! my sister! my friend! how fares it with thee? And if he can do any of them any good it would gladden every nerve of his soul.[1]

It is possible that Cugoano may have received assistance in England towards the development of his theological argument. There is some evidence that he could not have sustained authorship unaided;[2] in any event, it seems doubtful that anyone without long training in a Christian seminary and firm grounding in the legalistic complexities of biblical exegesis would have been able to mount the refined and intricate reasoning presented. Nonetheless, whether or not he received assistance, he certainly must have subscribed to the basic principle he enunciated, as would any African of his time who had experienced the European-dominated slave system he was attacking.

Kinship with patterns of European humanitarian thought, however, was characteristic of the whole of Cugoano's tract and was readily apparent as well in Vassa's book. Both works were published at the time that the anti-slavery forces were organizing for their assault on the slave trade and both authors must have been well known to the abolitionists and in a position to exchange ideas with men like Granville Sharp and Thomas Clarkson. Only two years before the publication of Cugoano's volume in 1787, Clarkson had submitted his prize-winning essay on slavery at Cambridge University just as Wilberforce was undergoing the religious experience which led from drawing-room dilettantism to a dedicated determination to outlaw the slave trade. It was in 1787 that Sharp, fresh from his success in securing the abolition of slavery in the British Isles, was arranging for the colonization of Sierra Leone with which Vassa was actively associated. The same year the abolitionists formed their committee 'for procuring such information and evidence, and publishing the same, as may tend to the abolition of the Slave-trade', and in 1788 and 1789 the formal debate on the slave trade in the House of Commons was opened under the leadership of Wilberforce. For the abolitionists the philosophical foundations of their campaign consisted of Christianity, commerce and colonization, to which Cugoano and Vassa subscribed enthusiastically while adding one or two refinements of their own.[3]

[1] *Ibid.*, 60–1.
[2] See Christopher Fyfe, *A History of Sierra Leone*, 13.
[3] Reginald Coupland, *The British Anti-Slavery Movement*, 57–85; Thomas Clarkson, *The History . . . of the Abolition of the African Slave Trade*, I, 255; Cugoano, *op. cit.*, 100.

External influences aside, Vassa's approach to the slavery issue was more conventional, less sophisticated, than Cugoano's. Early baptized, he later experienced a deep conversion after a long period characterized by doubts over his personal adequacy to be in communion with Christ. When at last his dilemma was resolved, he felt the desire to bring the benefits of his experience to his less fortunate brethren living in Africa and made application to the Bishop of London to be invested as a missionary so that 'he may be a means, under God, of reforming his countrymen and persuading them to embrace the Christian religion'. Nevertheless, he made no effort to direct an attack on slavery based on Biblical authority. A man of action, not of contemplation, he mounted his best argument against slavery by describing outrages, brutality and indignities witnessed during his many years of travel in the West Indies and the southern ports of America.[1]

As with most Africans who had been subjected to slavery, Vassa first encountered the barbarity of its practices on the slave ship taking him to America. He soon knew the fear of the strange surroundings and harsh customs—the agony and indignity of floggings, the misery of being chained in the suffocating atmosphere below decks, the despair that made suicide preferable to the pain of punishment and the pangs of hunger—all leading to the terrifying experience of the slave auction which in turn culminated in the cruelty of the overseer and the anguish of the arbitrary separation of families for ever. He saw men suspended by their wrists and flogged, others mutilated, branded, weighted down with chains and irons, still others tortured in various fashions for trifling offences. One who let a pot boil over was beaten until his bones were broken. Another had his leg hacked off for attempting to escape. A slave who sought to poison an overseer was half hanged and then burned alive. Negro women were in constant danger of assault; yet Africans who consorted with white women were subject to the most severe reprisals—one who had been connected with a common prostitute was 'staked to the ground, and cut most shockingly, and then his ears cut off bit by bit'.[2]

These vicious practices, related by Vassa with a restraint which only added to their impact, also led him to wonder at the carelessness as well as the inhumanity of the slave owners. Not only were slaves injured in the manner described but so often were they poorly housed and fed

---

[1] Gustavus Vassa, *The Interesting Narrative of the Life of Olaudah Equiano or Gustavus Vassa, the African*, II, 139–61, 229–30.
[2] *Ibid.*, I, 70–87, 206–9, 212–15.

that they fell ill and became not an asset but an economic burden. In Barbados, a slave population of 80,000 needed to be replenished at the rate of 1,000 annually in order to make up for normal losses, and conditions on that island were justly considered to be the best in the West Indies. Nor were conditions any better for the free Negroes. In some respects they were worse, for freemen were constantly under the threat of being deprived of their liberty, always open to insult and theft without hope of redress or prospect of legal justice. The whole system was not only inhuman and contrary to the Christianity professed by its perpetrators; it was literally insane:

Are slaves more useful by being . . . humbled to the condition of brutes . . . No. When you make men slaves you deprive them of half their virtue, you set them in your own conduct an example of fraud, rapine, and cruelty, and compel them to live with you in a state of war; and yet you complain that they are not honest or faithful! You stupefy them with stripes, and think it necessary to keep them in a state of ignorance; and yet you assert that they are incapable of learning . . . that they come from a climate, where nature . . . has left man alone scant and unfinished . . . An assertion at once impious and absurd. Why do you use those instruments of torture: Are they fit to be applied by one rational being to another? And are ye not struck with shame and mortification, to see the partakers of your nature reduced so low? . . . But by changing your conduct, and treating your slaves as men, every cause of fear would be banished. They would be faithful, honest, intelligent and vigorous; and peace, prosperity, and happiness would attend you.[1]

The evils that Vassa described, Cugoano explained. He was most grateful to the European for having introduced him to 'some little learning' and the divine revelation of the Christian religion, but he was obliged nevertheless to assert that it was Christian Europe which was responsible for the villainous ruffians who encouraged the commerce in their fellow creatures as though they were but beasts in the fields. Clearly, under principles of universal natural rights, no man ought to enslave another, yet here was Europe, the source of humanitarian principles, taking the lead in pursuing the barbarous traffic. Beginning shortly after the voyages of Columbus, the Spaniards instituted their American conquests with rapine, injustice, avarice and murder, destroying the great Aztec and Inca empires through treachery, and subsequently plundering them and slaughtering their people. Finding the need for free labour to work their new settlements and having finished off the local populations, they turned elsewhere for help and it was not

[1] *Ibid.*, I, 211–12, 215–16, 225–7, 251.

THE EIGHTEENTH-CENTURY FORERUNNERS [43]

long before the nations of Europe were infesting the coast of West Africa:

> The European depredators and pirates have not only robbed and pillaged the people of Africa themselves; but, by their instigation, they have infested the inhabitants with some of the vilest combinations of fraudulent and treacherous villains even among their own people; and have set up their forts and factories as a reservoir of public and abandoned thieves, and as a den of desperadoes, where they may ensnare, entrap and catch men. So that Africa has been robbed of its inhabitants; its free-born sons and daughters have been stole, and kidnapped, and violently taken away, and carried into captivity and cruel bondage. And it may be said, in respect to that diabolical traffic which is still carried on by the European depredators, that Africa has suffered as much and more than any other quarter of the globe. O merciful God! when will the wickedness of man have an end?[1]

Europe in its wisdom and enlightenment should have been the defender, not the attacker, of the African, said Cugoano. Particularly was this true of England which, despite the advanced state of her people, had come to acquire a greater share in 'the iniquitous commerce' than all the other nations of Europe combined. Unfortunately, the people of the British Isles, far from helping, were as deeply involved as the citizens of England's overseas colonies. The British monarch, far from taking the lead as a humanitarian, was no better than his royal brothers in Europe who made no effort to suppress the trade. The British parliament, far from extending its constitutional protection to include the African as well as the Englishman, seemed to share in the ill-gotten profits of the slave system. Was it not the British nation that stood guilty of the grossest amorality through the infamous case of the slave ship *Zong* whose captain in 1781 jettisoned 132 sick slaves in mid-ocean like so many cattle and who was subsequently vindicated in the courts on the grounds that slaves had the same legal status as livestock? Cugoano's moral indignation was matched only by his certainty that retribution could only follow such calculated inhumanity:

> But again let me observe, that whatever civilization the inhabitants of Great-Britain may enjoy among themselves, they have seldom maintained their own innocence in that great duty as a Christian nation towards others . . . when they saw others robbing the Africans, and carrying them into captivity and slavery, they have neither helped them, nor opposed their oppressors in the least. But instead thereof they have joined in combination against them with the rest of other profligate nations and people, to buy, enslave and make merchandise of them,

[1] Cugoano, *op cit.*, 13, 30, 78–84, 92–3.

because they found them helpless and fit to suit their own purpose, and are become the head carriers on of that iniquitous traffic. But the greater that any reformation and civilization is obtained by any nation, if they do not maintain righteousness, but carry on any course of wickedness and oppression, it makes them appear only the more inconsistent, and their tyranny and oppression the more conspicuous . . . . by some way or other every criminal nation, and all their confederates, who sin and rebel against God, and against his laws of nature and nations, will each meet with some awful retribution at last, unless they repent of their iniquity. And the greater advantages of light, learning, knowledge and civilization that any people enjoy, if they do not maintain righteousness, but do wickedly, they will meet with the more severe rebuke when the visitation of God's judgment cometh upon them.[1]

This moralistic, humanitarian view of the slave system constituted a powerful argument to the liberals of the eighteenth-century Enlightenment. Cugoano and Vassa were well served in placing emphasis there, as were the European abolitionists themselves. Like the abolitionists, however, the two Africans had a practical argument as well. Slavery, they contended, was simply an uneconomical system. This idea was pure Adam Smith who had argued in the *Wealth of Nations* that free labour was cheaper than slave labour. Cugoano took up the argument. He pointed out that the labour of freed slaves in the sugar islands would be just as valuable as it had been under servitude; the only loss from manumission would devolve on the iniquitous slave dealers who deserved no better fate. Indeed a free people, intelligent and industrious, would soon convert barren land to fruitfulness through their art and their labour. Liberty, hand in hand with Christianity, would 'diffuse its influences first to fertilize the mind, and then the effects of its benignity would extend, and arise with exuberant blessings and advantages . . . every thing would increase and prosper at home and abroad, and ten thousand times greater . . . advantages would arise to the state, and more permanent and solid benefit to individuals'.

Though more lyrical, this argument was somewhat less persuasive than Adam Smith's dry assertion that free labour was cheaper than slave labour because the entrepreneur was not obliged to concern himself with the cost of its welfare, but Cugoano went on to another point which was to become a major argument of the abolitionists and later of the evangelist missionaries who attempted the regeneration of the West African during the nineteenth century. This was the view that the abolition of slavery would be the beginning of a fruitful trade be-

[1] *Ibid.*, 106, 110–12, 116–17.

tween England and Africa in which a growing African market would consume European manufactured goods as western civilization spread, while providing Europe in turn with a wide range of useful products drawn from the fertile soil of Africa by an enterprising free native yeomanry. Gustavus Vassa was more specific and more eloquent than Cugoano on this same point. In 1788 he wrote to the Secretary of State suggesting that the abolition of slavery would lead directly to a dramatic expansion of the African trade. The continent abounded in riches, and its already vast population promised to double every fifteen years. Once western civilization had been achieved, if on the average each African bought but five pounds worth of clothing and household goods each year from European merchants – what 'an immensity beyond the reach of imagination!'[1]

The case was overwhelming. On theological, humanitarian and economic grounds, logic called for the abolition of slavery and the end of the slave trade. Emancipation in the colonies could be carried out by immediately freeing all slaves who had laboured seven years or more for their masters and who had acquired 'any competent degree of knowledge of the Christian religion, and the laws of civilization, and had behaved themselves honestly and decently'. Others might continue with their masters up to such portion of seven-year periods of service as were yet unfinished but they would be entitled to humane treatment and would be provided with appropriate instruction in the Christian religion. Thus, Cugoano concluded, 'they would become tractable and obedient, useful labourers, dutiful servants and good subjects; and Christian men might have the honor and happiness to see many of them vying with themselves to praise the God of their salvation'.[2]

Beyond this, many former slaves thus educated might be encouraged to make their way back to Africa where they could busy themselves instructing others. To cap the process, a squadron of British war vessels should be sent to Africa to put a stop to slaving, and the British coastal factories could be reformed from 'a den of thieves ... into shepherd's tents'. All these proposals would not only rehabilitate a continent but would reaffirm the pre-eminence of British majesty and English philanthropy:

Should the noble Britons, who have often supported their own liberties with their lives and fortunes, extend their philanthropy to abolish the

[1] *Ibid.*, 121–2, 133–4; Vassa, *op. cit.*, II, 262–7. See Vassa to Lord Hawkesbury, Mar. 13, 1788, quoted in Christopher Fyfe, *Sierra Leone Inheritance*, 109–10.
[2] Cugoano, *op. cit.*, 130–2.

slavery and oppression of the Africans, they might have settlements and many kingdoms united in a friendly alliance with themselves . . . as well as . . . the happiness of being useful to promoting the prosperity and felicity of others, who have been cruelly injured and wrongfully dealt with. . . . And as Great-Britain has been remarkable for ages past, for encouraging arts and sciences . . . if they would take compassion on the inhabitants of the coast of Guinea, and to make use of such means as would be needful to enlighten their minds in the knowledge of Christianity, their virtue, in this respect, would have its own reward. And as the Africans became refined and established in light and knowledge . . . the fair Britons would have the preference with them to a very great extent; and, in another respect, they would become a kind of first ornament to Great-Britain for her tender and compassionate care . . . Due encouragement being given to so great . . . a noble undertaking, would soon bring more revenue in a righteous way . . . than ten times its share in all the profits that slavery can produce; and such a laudable example would inspire every generous and enterprising mind to imitate so great and worthy a nation, for establishing religion, justice, and equity to the Africans, and, in doing this, would be held in the highest esteem by all men, and be admired by all the world.[1]

3 *Some Misgivings Concerning Negro Colonization in Sierra Leone*

Despite their position as critics of slavery and prominent members of the Negro community in the British Isles, both Cugoano and Vassa treated Granville Sharp's colonization scheme in Sierra Leone with considerable suspicion. Their suspicion rested on the execution, not the conception, on doubts over the good faith of its agents, not on any misgivings about the saintlike Sharp and his philanthropic colleagues. Vassa's disillusionment was based on his experience as commissary for the expedition. Shortly after his appointment, he thought he detected irregularities which he reported to the authorities, only to be accused in turn by the expedition's leader, and ultimately dismissed from his post. Whatever the merits of this disagreement, Vassa was not far off the mark in criticizing flaccid leadership, inadequate supplies, and poor timing which brought the settlers to African shores lacking necessary discipline and incapable of coping with the rains that made effective cultivation impossible. His valedictory was an expression of regret over the failures of the venture which, 'however unfortunate in the event, was humane and politic in its design'.

Cugoano was less charitable. He was quite ready to congratulate the worthy and liberal philanthropists who had originated the plan and the

[1] *Ibid.*, 132–5.

British government which had supported it, but he feared for its practicality. No treaty had been concluded with the indigenous people to secure a clearly defined tract of land, while administrative shortcomings had led to serious delays threatening the health and welfare of the expedition. More than all this, however, was the basic distrust of the blacks in England of any adventure which might put them once again within danger of re-enslavement. Consequently many Negroes in England chose exile from their native land in preference to the risk of recapture by the slave dealer. Practical freedom in Britain was apparently preferable to theoretical independence in Africa. 'Doth a fountain send forth at the same place sweet water and bitter?' Cugoano wanted to know. 'Can it be readily conceived that government would establish a free colony . . . nearly on the spot, while it supports its forts and garrisons, to ensnare, merchandise, and to carry others into captivity and slavery.' It was not the last time Africa was to question the consistency of Europe's intentions.[1]

Nonetheless, some of the Black Poor did go, and the colony of Sierra Leone, however halting in its beginnings, did survive. And with its survival there opened a new era in the history of West Africa and its intellectual developments.

[1] Prince Hoare, *Memoirs of Granville Sharp*, 374–5; Vassa, *op. cit.*, II, 241–50; Cugoano, *op. cit.*, 138–42.

3 The Founding of the Sierra Leone Colony

1 *Granville Sharp Experiments in Philanthropy on the West African Coast*

Through the medium of the British anti-slavery movement, the humanitarianism of eighteenth-century Europe found a major philanthropic outlet which was profoundly to affect the subsequent course of Africa's history. In England, the impulse for reform led first to the termination of slavery at home in 1772, next to the abolition of the slave trade throughout the Empire in 1807, and finally to the determination to stamp out the trade completely wherever it might be encountered. These decisions in their turn led quickly to developments with far-reaching implications for the peoples of West Africa.

The first development came quickly with the founding of Granville Sharp's Sierra Leone colony in 1787. It was Sharp whose compassion, dedication and determination had brought about the end of slavery in England, forcing Lord Mansfield's decision to free James Somerset in 1772, but the same elevated principles and humanitarian attitudes now had to be brought to bear a second time. For the very decision bringing freedom brought also unemployment and destitution to some of the freed slaves, and these were joined by others drifted into extremity—chiefly stranded sailors and soldiers demobilized after the War of American Independence. Soon there were several hundred of these homeless Africans in the London streets. A relief committee was formed and Sharp himself helped many with private philanthropy, but it was clear that some more permanent solution would be needed. After considerable discussion a plan was evolved to send the Africans to Sierra Leone where they might found an independent colony. Public and private funds were solicited, recruits were gathered, an expedition outfitted, and in the spring of 1787 a group of over four hundred set sail for West Africa. Included were approximately one hundred women, many of them English, but there were Negresses as well. The party also contained a few European artisans and professional men. Predominantly African, it was nonetheless a group well accustomed to European ways.[1]

Sharp's contribution to the colony involved considerably more than good will and a measure of financial support. For some years he had been thinking of a settlement on the coast of Africa, and his ideas had progressed to the point where he had in mind a specific system of government and land ownership providing for mutual privileges and obligations among free citizens based on ancient principles of social compact. When the colonists left England, they took with them a set of regulations which were in fact a constitution establishing them as an independent community. It was the nearest thing to representative self-government that any European colony in West Africa was to see for one hundred and seventy years.

Sharp's scheme was worked out in meticulous detail. The Province of Freedom, as he was fond of calling the colony, was to direct its affairs through the agency of individual householders. The community would be divided into groups of twelve households and each head of house would automatically become a municipal officer or tythingman. Eight groups of twelve households represented by ninety-six tythingmen would be led by an elected hundredor, two chiefs of fifty, and one town clerk to round out the number of one hundred government officers for each municipal unit. These hundred citizens would constitute the common council of the colony until such time as growing community size forced some form of elective representation. They would also form the core of the militia, the hundredors becoming the captains, the two chiefs of fifty acting as lieutenants, the clerks as commissaries, and the tythingmen as non-commissioned officers and line troops. To these could be added other common soldiers drawn from among indentured servants, apprentices and lesser male members of households.

Together the hundredors and tythingmen were to elect their governor and judges and serve as jurymen. Minor offences were punishable by fine, and Sharp provided a complicated system of penalties graduated in proportion to income and degree of delinquency which he hoped would maintain a healthy exchequer, making other means of taxation virtually unnecessary. Where taxes were levied, however they would be payable in units, not of money, but of labour, for the whole economy

[1] Christopher Fyfe, *A History of Sierra Leone*, 13-19.

of the colony was to be based on labour. All goods would be valued in terms of eight hour day-labour units, and there would be no inflation or fluctuating currency, Sharp argued, with this substantial, stable basis for exchange. More than that, such a monetary system elevated labour to its proper position in the community by placing the man who worked with his hands in a position of essential dignity. When Sharp spoke of labour, he of course meant free labour. True to the tenets of the humanitarian economics then emerging in England, he pointed out that slavery was not only a corrupter of men and a manufacturer of injustice; it was also inefficient and expensive. Slavery would therefore have no place in the Province of Freedom, although indentured servitude was permissible under certain circumstances. Finally, land was to be distributed by lot, all were to have the same amount of land, and there would be community tracts reserved for public services.[1]

If all this fell somewhat short of democratic republicanism based on universal suffrage – for only the householders could vote – it also was an impressively liberal constitution reflecting the best traditions of eighteenth-century Enlightenment thought. Unhappily, it was at the same time thoroughly utopian, as the settlers soon demonstrated. Sharp's models came from ancient Israel, the first Christian churches and the Saxon kingdoms of England; the key was frankpledge, an early English legal form which bound members of a community in mutual aid and surety to keep the peace. To the untamed West African coast all this had no particular relevance. No doubt the colonists, many of them recent slaves and most of them familiar with the rudiments of British constitutional guarantees, were eager for the opportunity to govern themselves, but they were sadly lacking in the necessary experience. In any event the time and place were ill chosen for democratic experiments. Self-government implies self-discipline and of this commodity there seems to have been little. Law enforcement machinery was ineffective, the settlers were unable to agree very long on any one leader, many drifted into idleness, while others lost heart and the will to work. Soon, the looting of stores and the trading away of supplies for food replaced the more constructive work of building shelter and planting crops. Natural calamities added their measure of misfortune. The soil proved infertile, and the heavy rains brought killing fevers which reduced the original population by over one-third within a year. It had been assumed by Sharp and the philanthropists in London that

---

[1] Granville Sharp, *Short Sketch of Temporary Regulations*, 3-72; Prince Hoare, *Memoirs of Granville Sharp*, 265-7, 345, 521-2.

repatriated African stock would automatically adapt to its natural environment and develop a healthy community of free liberal-minded yeomen, but the colonists, long removed from Africa or never having known it, strangers to agriculture, lacking skill in many of the necessary crafts, and accustomed to either total authority or none, let freedom drift into licence and self-government into anarchy. The destruction begun by disease was finished by a combination of ineptness, discouragement and a hostile environment. Sharp sent a relief vessel with provisions and recruits in June 1788, but the end was foredoomed. Settlers continued to die or to wander off to work for the slavers in the region. In November 1789, the town was destroyed by a neighbouring chief and the remainder of its population scattered.[1]

Even before news of the disaster had reached England, Sharp was moving to stabilize the venture through incorporation, and this procedure was speeded up when word of the colony's destruction arrived. In 1791 the Sierra Leone Company was established by Parliament, but in this act the tone, and to some extent the purpose, of the enterprise were markedly changed. Sharp had been unable through his own modest resources to maintain the colony, but in turning to others he was obliged to renounce personal control and to give ground on some of his philanthropic objectives and principles of government which were not unreasonably considered visionary by many of his new colleagues. The new enterprise of one hundred subscribers passed over the highminded but romantic Sharp in choosing a chairman for its Court of Directors, announced that henceforth philanthropy would have to share the company's attention with the promotion of profitable trade, put an end to impractical schemes for self-government, and reorganized the system of land distribution and ownership.[2]

Under the act of incorporation, the colony and its lands were ceded to the company which was empowered to establish a government responsible to its directors, not to the settlers. Henceforward, the government would reside in a council of eight including a chief officer or superintendent, all chosen by the directors. The council was to be responsible for defence, justice, finance, trade and agriculture, as well as the affairs of company employees, administered as distinct from those of the settlers. The superintendent, a first among equals on the council, commanded the militia and acted as the colony's representative with

[1] *Ibid.*, 320–4, 329–32; Fyfe, *op. cit.*, 19–25; C. B. Wadstrom, *An Essay on Colonization*, II, 220–4.
[2] Hoare, *op. cit.*, 347–50, 358, 362, 364; 'An Early Constitution of Sierra Leone', *Sierra Leone Studies*, no. XVIII, Nov., 1932, 43–4.

native chiefs, directed the deliberations of the council and carried out its decisions.

Thus the experiment in representative responsible government ended, but the settlers were by no means deprived of all political and civil rights. Trial by jury was to be maintained, capital punishment was for all practical purposes banished, and there was established the right of appeal to the company directors for any settler questioning a decision by the council. Provision was made, moreover, for settler participation in what was somewhat vaguely referred to as 'internal legislation', but the exact nature of that participation was left to the future. The system of tythingmen and hundredors, however, was drastically revised so that these officials were to function henceforward primarily as peace officers, though they did salvage the right to recommend legislation for action by the council. All settlers were required to sign a declaration pledging allegiance to the new government and expressing willingness to be ruled by its laws. Slavery continued prohibited, and the council was cautioned to take care in guarding against any trace of racial prejudice.[1]

Land policy, which was to become the crux of a fundamental dispute between settlers and the company, was defined in terms of twenty-acre lots for each colonist, ten for his wife, and five for every child. A plan was drafted laying out town housing in single-acre lots, but water frontage was reserved for eventual disposal by the directors. It was understood by the company, if not by the settlers, that the land would not be granted in fee simple but that quitrents would be charged on all parcels, but this was meant more as a property tax than as a means for establishing residual ownership with the company. The original settlement had been called Granville Town; the new one was to be staked out adjacent to the old and named Freetown.[2]

2 The Ordeal of the Nova Scotians

As matters developed, the new regulations of the Sierra Leone Company had little more than academic interest for the original settlers. An agent of the company, sent out in 1791 to reassemble and re-establish them, could locate only about fifty, but by this time negotiations for a large body of new settlers from Nova Scotia were well under way; prospects were thus bright for the colony's renascence, not only on a scale much

---

[1] *Ibid.*, 42–77.
[2] *Ibid.*; *Substance of the Report Delivered by the Court of Directors of the Sierra Leone Company . . . 1794*, 5; Wadstrom, *op. cit.*, II, 228–9.

larger than ever but through the medium of a group of settlers whose history and circumstances ideally suited the humanitarian principles and practices of their abolitionist sponsors in London.[1]

As with the case of the London Black Poor, the Nova Scotians were Africans—for the most part former slaves from the American colonies who had escaped during the War of Independence, joined the British forces fighting in America, and served out the period of the war as soldiers and sailors. When peace came in 1783, they were not returned to their owners as the treaty stipulated; instead, it was suggested that as former servicemen they be mustered out and awarded a free passage to Nova Scotia where they would be given substantial tracts of land and farming equipment as a basis for permanent settlement. Such an attractive offer was accepted with enthusiasm, but theory, unhappily, was not so easily translated into practice. There were thousands of loyalist immigrants in Canada and good farm land was scarce in that glacier-scoured country. Many Negroes received grants but often these were in remote, uncleared areas. Others were forced to wait several years, landless and unsettled. More than this, all had come from warmer colonies and found the northern winters severe.[2]

There were other factors to which former slaves might naturally be sensitive. Slavery still existed in Nova Scotia and there was some disposition on the part of white slaveholding loyalists to lose sight of the distinction between a slave and a freedman, especially when it was felt by some that existence in that cold inhospitable land could not be maintained without the assistance of slaves. Loyalist slave owners who arrived in Nova Scotia from the southern colonies often found the cost of maintenance to be high; consequently in times of food shortage, they were inclined to let their slaves loose to forage for themselves and in some cases to die of hunger in the streets along with similarly unfortunate free blacks. Those who survived were likely to be reclaimed after several years of freedom and sold to new masters in the United States.[3]

Other forms of prejudice and persecution were common practice. Discrimination was frequent in land distribution—one observer reported that no more than ten per cent of the three thousand Negroes who migrated to Nova Scotia ever received what had been promised them,

---

[1] A. M. Falconbridge, *Two Voyages to Sierra Leone during the Years 1791-2-3*, 63.
[2] G. Halliburton, 'The Nova Scotia Settlers of 1792', *Sierra Leone Studies*, n.s., no. 9, Dec., 1957, 16-17; Anthony Kirk-Greene, 'David George: The Nova Scotia Experience', *ibid.*, n.s., no. 14, Dec., 1960, 97-9.
[3] Wadstrom, *op. cit.*, II, 230-1; Halliburton, *op. cit.*, 17, 19.

and those who remained behind permanently in Canada ended up more often than not as tenants, farming land that others owned. The choice waterside lots were exclusively reserved for the whites who in turn made the Negroes pay fees for the use of their wharfs. Upon their arrival in Canada, the Negroes were set to work building new towns for the immigrants, both white and black, for they were obliged to live separately as a segregated community. There were bad relations with the white ex-servicemen who on one occasion destroyed a number of Negro homes because they resented the Negroes accepting lower wages; yet it was the white community which forced lower pay scales, unwilling to accord former slaves the same treatment as free whites. There was also religious persecution mixed with racial discrimination. David George, the industrious minister of the Negro Baptists, was beaten, run out of town and his house destroyed by a large mob, and on another occasion was pursued by an angry crowd, furious that he had had the effrontery to baptize a white woman. Religious unrest was not always racial, however, for George was later set upon by a group of Negroes who resented his activities.[1]

Gradually despair and disillusionment replaced bright hope. Former slaves were particularly sensitive over matters of land ownership, for to them a freehold guaranteed the free man, and the discrimination of the government in giving precedence to the claims of white loyalists was threatening them with landlessness and a share-cropper's fate. To the Negroes, only recently freed, this was but slavery renewed in another form. Leaders of the African community like David George submitted for a time to the various persecutions visited upon them, but soon they were casting about for some means out of their dilemma. Finally, after several years of fruitless waiting, one of the Nova Scotians, Thomas Peters, journeyed to London in 1791 in search of some sort of redress. Through Sharp, Peters was soon in touch with the Sierra Leone Company and arrangements went swiftly forward to bring those Nova Scotians who so desired to Sierra Leone as settlers. Greatly cheered by the offer which included passage to Africa and the promise of plots of free land, almost twelve hundred joined the expedition which sailed from Halifax in January 1792, arriving off West Africa two months later. It was a moment full of hope. 'There was great joy to see the land', David George reported. 'The high mountain, at some distance from

[1] Kirk-Greene, *op. cit.*, 99–100, 103–4, 108–9; John Rippon, *The Baptist Annual Register*, I, 479–80; Diary of John Clarkson, quoted in E. G. Ingham, *Sierra Leone After a Hundred Years*, 100, 135.

Free-town... appeared like a cloud to us.' And they fell to work at once with spirit and industry, clearing the land, unloading supplies, and staking out their future homes.[1]

It was not long before the bloom of new opportunity faded before fresh frustrations and rising suspicions. The task of establishing quickly over one thousand people on uncleared land was virtually insuperable and was further complicated both by inefficiency and dishonesty on the part of some of the company employees, and by the ravages of fever and dysentery. Surveying and clearing went forward slowly and it was not until eight months after landing that the first tracts were allocated. Worse still, waterfront sites were reserved for the company, and because of the limited terrain the Nova Scotians were obliged to accept four-acre plots in lieu of the promised twenty. Moreover, many of these were far removed from the town site or situated on steep unprofitable slopes.

Perhaps, however, the difficulties were as much psychological as physical, traceable to long years of conditioned response to persecution. By the time the settlers reached Africa, their hunger for private ownership of land had become little short of an obsession. Many had lived lives like David George–born a slave, turned runaway as a result of brutal treatment, enduring long years of precarious existence as a fugitive, finally reaching apparent safety and comfort in Nova Scotia only to find that all was illusion. Discrimination continued to plague them, and the vision of the small snug self-sufficient farm still remained maddeningly just beyond reach. Even when the prospect of a new life in Africa finally materialized, the government and permanent residents of Nova Scotia did what they could at the last moment to discourage migration, for they had grown accustomed to a cheap and plentiful labour supply. Stories were circulated about the dangers of the transatlantic passage, and John Clarkson, the company agent who came to Canada to recruit and to arrange the passage, reported that the government, though outwardly cordial, was in fact hostile to the mass exodus. David George, eager to free his Baptist congregation from its abject position, found it expedient to negotiate with Clarkson secretly for fear of an attack on his life. Thus the émigrés brought with them convictions and prejudices ingrained through their long unhappy conditioning under slavery and their frustrating stay in Nova Scotia.[2]

One disquieting rumour had persisted in Nova Scotia. It was said

---

[1] *Ibid.*, 43, 100; John Clarkson Notebook, 'Remarks Halifax', Clarkson to Laurence Hartshorne, Aug. 4, 1793, Clarkson Papers; Rippon, *op. cit.*, 483.
[2] Halliburton, *op. cit.*, 19; Kirk-Greene, *op. cit.*, 108–9; Rippon, *op. cit.*, I, 473–83; *The Philanthropist*, no. 15, vol. IV, 106–7.

that the Sierra Leone Company was expecting to charge quitrents for its land in Africa. Indeed this was no rumour for the company had always hoped to indemnify itself primarily through an annual land tax which was felt to be equitable, and easily assessed and collected. What seemed fair to the company directors conjured up in the minds of the settlers images of renewed exploitation, and before sailing they had to be publicly reassured by Clarkson whose instructions contained nothing specifically relating to land rents and who assumed, wrongly as it turned out, that charges and obligations imposed by the company would involve no more than maintenance by the settlers of their own charitable and educational institutions. Upon arrival in Sierra Leone, bitterness and disillusionment once again overtook the Nova Scotians. Not only were their tracts small and inadequate, but it appeared that they might also be subject to the unpopular quitrents. Clarkson, who had been named superintendent of the council and later was made governor with full authority, was obliged to exercise great tact combined with sympathetic understanding in order to preserve morale and unity of purpose. 'The Nova Scotians', he wrote, 'are naturally suspicious and easily alarmed . . . they have been deceived and ill-treated through life . . . and seeing no probability of getting their lands, they began to think they should be served the same as in Nova Scotia, which unsettled their minds, and made them suspect everything and everybody.'[1]

As long as Clarkson remained, he was able to hold the colony together in good order. He promised alternative plots to those who felt they had not received their due, and on his own initiative renounced the company claim to water frontage. Moreover, he strictly enforced company regulations with regard to racial discrimination – another source of dissatisfaction on the part of the Nova Scotians. When sailors on company vessels abused the settlers, he had them flogged publicly. 'These people', he explained, 'have delicate feelings, and just ideas of right and wrong . . . they are very suspicious of the conduct of white people, particularly when they are attacked in an arbitrary way.'[2]

Clarkson was right up to a point. The settlers had endured a great deal in the form of broken promises and unfulfilled obligations; yet it was the present and future as much as the past which was to shape their attitudes and actions in Sierra Leone. For all their difficulties, the Nova Scotians seem to have been remarkably even-tempered. Wary of

---

[1] *Ibid.*, 105–7, 262–3; H. Thornton to J. Clarkson, Dec. 30, 1791, Clarkson Papers; John Clarkson Diary, Ingham, *op. cit.*, 42–3.
[2] *Ibid.*, 71, 100, 143.

white men's conduct they may have been, but their naturally open and free manner made them easily approachable by any European who took the trouble to try. David George, a substantial citizen and leader of an important group within the community, was constantly cited by Europeans as a sober, industrious, honest and faithful man of God, and many others might have laid claim to similar testimony, for the Nova Scotians were on the whole a deeply religious people whose overriding recreation, throughout all adversity, was religious worship. Services were held daily, and according to at least one observer, far into the night, and the people amazed visiting European clergy with the simplicity and zeal of their religious beliefs and with their complete lack of bigotry which enabled ministers and parishioners alike to place Christian fellowship above sectarian considerations. 'There is a warmth in their devotions to which we seem strangers', observed one visitor. 'They have such a flow of spirits in prayer, that I am sometimes afraid they will hurt themselves.' Such religious fervour only became superheated on the rare occasions that there appeared to be a threat to freedom of worship; normally it spent itself in celebrating divine praises. 'Their tunes have a great variety of music in them, and they are sung so well, that I do not remember to have ever heard such melody. In prayer, every one kneels; many utter the word *Amen* to most of the petitions, while others are using different expressions.' In church or out, the settlers presented a handsome appearance–the men in their loose blouses and trousers of nankeen, the women in their bright muslins, their turbaned headdresses often topped with beaver hats or straws.[1]

What Clarkson failed correctly to assess was the unfortunate effect which both he and the London philanthropists had on the actions and attitudes of the settlers. Clarkson, gentle-hearted and sympathetic, suffered with the colonists over every wrong imposed upon them, and went to great lengths to dispel their sense of injustice and to provide them with whatever material necessities he felt them entitled to. In a certain sense, however, his sympathy lacked understanding, and may have been designed more to serve self than to assist the settlers. Essentially he treated the Nova Scotians like the children of an indulgent father who moved mountains for their benefit but who never granted them the sanction of adulthood. 'So long as you treat us like children we shall behave like children', another African was to remark years later,

---

[1] *The Evangelical Magazine*, IV, 419–21; Rippon, *op. cit.*, I, 484; Falconbridge, *op. cit.*, 201; Viscountess Knutsford, *Life and Letters of Zachary Macaulay*, 143–5, 149–50; Governor and Council to Chairman of Court of Directors, July 30, 1796, C.O. 268/5.

but the comment was relevant to Governor Clarkson's policy. Full of self-conscious self-pity over his exertions on behalf of his wards and convinced of their helplessness without him, he never trained them for independence, substituting kindly paternalism and fatherly advice for the less accommodating demand that they learn to work things out for themselves.[1]

Under these circumstances the Nova Scotians came to adore Clarkson and to run to him with their troubles as the one loving and understanding person who solved all problems. However, when he left the colony at the end of 1792, less than a year after arrival, they were ill-prepared for the cooler brand of philanthropy to which they were thenceforward subjected. Not that the directors of the Sierra Leone Company were insensitive to the needs and aspirations of the settlers or unaware that they might be guiding the destinies of an historic venture. 'We mean [to do] full justice to the free blacks from Nova Scotia', the directors informed Clarkson and his council,

giving them the enjoyment of British rights, and fulfilling every expectation we have raised in them ... we are determined to co-operate ... in endeavouring to render their persons and their property safe, their industry productive, their character respectable, their condition in life more and more improvable, and their future days happy. We consider them the foundation of our colony.

And earlier, Henry Thornton, the chairman of the directors, informed Clarkson that 'this enterprise is a most important one. The lives of those whom you carry with you are ... an affair of great consequence ... the happiness of Thousands and Millions of our fellow creatures seems to depend upon a little virtue to be exercised by a few individuals.' Yet these fine sentiments were delivered with an abstractness which seemed to confuse self-righteousness with human understanding, and a preoccupation with material considerations which confounded humanitarianism with the profit motive. Clarkson was lectured from London on the theory and the practicalities of colonization, and when he finally departed, he was replaced by men determined from the start to place the interests of the company above all others and in the process to put an end to the coddling of colonists.[2]

---

[1] J. Clarkson to I. DuBois, July 1, 1793, to Richard Crankepone, July 27, 1793, Clarkson Papers; E. W. Blyden, *Christianity, Islam and the Negro Race*, iii–iv.
[2] Directors to Governor and Council, July 12, 1792, quoted in Ingham, *op. cit.*, 116; H. Thornton to J. Clarkson, Dec. 30, 1791, T. Clarkson to J. Clarkson, Jan., 1792, William Wilberforce to J. Clarkson, Apr. 27, 1792, Clarkson Papers.

THE SIERRA LEONE COLONY

Long years of persecution followed by a period of overindulgence, which in turn was succeeded by authoritarian rule, led straight to trouble. Although the settlers inevitably divided among themselves, reflecting differences in temperament, personal opinion or religious persuasion, they maintained over the years that followed an essentially united front of growing opposition to the company. Immediately after Clarkson's departure, there was an unpleasant incident connected with the land issue. The new governor, William Dawes, concentrating on building the colony's defence to the neglect of the land survey, tried to appropriate a small portion of one settler's plot to accommodate a palisade. There followed a violent public dispute between the settlers and the governor in which they not only refused to yield any land for any purpose but demanded the tracts still coming to them. When the governor objected to their incivility by threatening to leave the settlement, with one voice they urged him on his way. 'Go! go! go! we do not want you here, we cannot get a worse than you.' And shortly thereafter when new lots were at last ready, the settlers refused to move because these plots did not include the water frontage promised by Clarkson. To the Nova Scotians, the commitments of their champion were being deliberately repudiated and their rights as free citizens compromised. 'Mr. Clarkson promised in Nova Scotia that no distinction should be made here between us and white men; we now claim this promise, we are free British subjects, and expect to be treated as such; we will not tamely submit to be trampled any longer.'[1]

Suiting the action to the word, they sent a delegation to London to exercise their constitutional right of appeal over the head of the government to the company directors. Their petition reviewed the now-familiar ground—arbitrary rule and inordinate delays in allocation of land, to which was added the newer complaint of the company's economic monopoly in Freetown. The petition summed up the settler position with a simple eloquence, 'Health and Life . . . is very uncertain and tho we have not the Education which White Men have yet we have feeling the same as other Human Beings and would wish to do everything we can for to make our Children free and happy after us.' Kept waiting inconclusively for weeks, the petitioners finally exploded in annoyance, 'We expected to have had some more attention paid to our complaints, but the manner you have treated us, has been just the same as if we were *Slaves*, come to tell our masters of the cruelties and severe

---

[1] Isaac DuBois Diary, Jan. 25, Feb. 7, 1793, Clarkson Papers; Falconbridge, *op. cit.*, 202–3, 205–6.

behaviour of an *Overseer*.' Privately they warned Clarkson, 'We are afraid if the Company does not see Justice done to us they will not have Justice done to them.'

This was almost prophetic. Less than a month later back in Freetown, a fire broke out and destroyed the company store ship anchored in the harbour. However just, the response of the disenchanted Nova Scotians showed little sense of community responsibility. Many settlers did try to fight the fire but many others were content to let it burn. 'Some [rejoiced] in the calamity as a just judgment of heaven on their oppressors. Some said it was but right that the goods, withheld unjustly from them by the Governor and Council should be destroyed, and that their sinister aim should thus be frustrated.' These comments were made by Zachary Macaulay who soon was to become governor of the colony and whose sense of justice seems to have been about equal to that of the settlers. 'A fire happened in town to-day', he continued, 'and rather singularly the sufferers were almost all of the number who rejoiced in the *York*'s destruction. No man who had a spark of humanity in him could rejoice in their loss, but I confess I could not help feeling less grieved at its falling on those who had shown such a total want of charity.'[1]

With the governorship of Macaulay which began in 1794 on a temporary intermittent basis, became permanent in 1796, and continued until his departure in 1799, the lines between the settlers and the company clarified and hardened. For their part the Nova Scotians felt more misunderstood and persecuted than ever and gradually a hard core of extreme opposition to company authority took shape and began to gain influence among the settlers. In Macaulay, the company had a representative who never entertained the slightest doubt in the rightness of his opinions and actions and who deplored the lack of discipline which had grown up as a result of Clarkson's permissive administration. Intelligent, inflexible, chilling in manner, he was equally adept at employing superior force or irrefutable logic as the occasion demanded, so that the settlers invariably ended up the worse for their encounters with the governor and succeeded only in adding to their growing sense of frustration.

When they came to him to seek protection for some escaped slaves, he shocked them by questioning their right to give asylum to what was

---

[1] Perkins-Anderson petition, Oct. 30, 1793, Anderson and Perkins to J. Clarkson, Nov. 9, 1793, Clarkson Papers; Falconbridge, *op. cit.*, 265; Knutsford, *op. cit.*, 55–7.

THE SIERRA LEONE COLONY [61]

essentially private property. When some of them became involved in an acrimonious exchange with the captain of a slave ship, Macaulay dismissed them from their jobs, faced down a resultant riot, and arrested its ringleaders for trial in England. To Macaulay the issue was no less than the survival of the colony which could not prosper in a state of tumult and disorder. To the colonists, this was another example of high-handed, unsympathetic administration which upheld slave traders in their disputes with the settlers, and discharged those who had the backbone to stand up for their rights and fight for the dignity of the black race.[1]

For a time the settlers and the government closed ranks during the sack of the colony by a French fleet in 1794. Even here disputes arose. Some of the colonists had salvaged company supplies during the occupation by the French forces and were unwilling to return them after the enemy had sailed away. Though ready to pay a salvage fee, Macaulay demanded the return of what was still company property. The settlers grumbled that the few things involved had been bestowed on them by the French. They had taken the trouble to protect the property; consequently it now belonged to them. There was no question of the larceny of which they were unjustly accused.[2]

A year later at the annual election of the hundredors and tythingmen, Macaulay took the occasion to lecture these officials on their civic responsibilities and to comment more generally on what he regarded as the fundamental misunderstanding of the Nova Scotians over ownership of property and the relationship between the colony's government and governed. The company, not the settlers, he pointed out, owned Freetown and its land. The government was responsible to the company, not to the settlers. The colonists were freemen,[3] but this did not carry the licence to treat company property as their own, to interfere with measures for municipal defence, to question the company's free right to engage and discharge employees and to determine their wages and working conditions, to assume that health and education services were rights rather than privileges, or to default on personal debts to the company. The authorities had faithfully discharged their obligations to the people. The settlers were free, they were treated scrupulously on

---

[1] Knutsford, *op. cit.*, 42–4, 55; Sierra Leone Council Minutes, June 16, 18, 20–23, 30, 1794, C.O. 270/2; I. Anderson and L. Jordan to J. Clarkson, June 28, 1794, Clarkson Papers.
[2] Knutsford, *op. cit.*, 77–8; L. Jordan *et al.* to J. Clarkson, Nov. 19, 1794, Clarkson Papers.
[3] It is worth here noting the difference between the term 'freedman', meaning a manumitted slave, and the term 'freeman'.

a par with white men before the law, their civil rights were protected, they had jobs and land. If the land allotments were not what the settlers had initially expected, there had been more than adequate compensation in economic aid, educational and medical facilities. If the people still wanted their full land grants, let them agree to the quitrents they had avoided for so long.

The lecture continued remorselessly as the men shuffled in embarrassed silence. Finally one or two spoke up. Would it not be better if the governor dropped his severity, substituting mercy, equal justice, and kindness to his children? The response was icy, devastating:

I scarce know what to reply. If by kindness you mean personal Civility, if by kindness you mean hearty wishes and earnest endeavours to promote your happiness, I find no room to accuse myself of unkindness. Whom have I abused? Whom have I treated among you with harshness and severity, to whom have I returned railing for railing? To whom have I spoken unkindly? . . . But if by kindness you mean giving away the Company's property without any measure but your own fancied notions of your deservings, you must excuse me. I am content to be looked on as unkind and cruel.

Articulate, logical, commanding, Macaulay carried the day. His audience was defeated as usual in this unequal test of strength, but it was less convinced, more resentful than ever, 'for we yet do not know upon what footing we are upon whether to be made Slaves or to only go by the name of Freedom'.[1]

From this point the gap widened steadily between the determined, implacable governor and the unregenerate, unrepentant settlers. The core of the dispute was land and the quitrent. The governor's power lay in his authority as the chief of state and the company's representative, while the settler discontent concentrated its strength in their representatives, the hundredors and tythingmen. By law these were primarily peace officers, but custom had long permitted them to recommend legislation to governor and council, and over the years they had seen numerous recommendations converted into law. With them had originated ordinances against loose and disorderly conduct or language in the public streets. They initiated laws governing the price of bread, the naturalization of new settlers and the surveying and upkeep of roads and streets. Under the governor's watchful eye, they drafted their own working rules and orders, and carried out their basic function of policing the colony and settling minor disputes. More and more, however, they came to be regarded as the unofficial, yet consequential, spokesmen of

[1] Sierra Leone Council Minutes, Mar. 7, Apr. 21, 28, 1795, C.O. 270/3.

THE SIERRA LEONE COLONY

the people, and increasingly they felt obliged to speak out on the issue of land rents.[1]

As long as the company contented itself with proclaiming the principle of quitrents without exercising the right of collection, all went reasonably well. The settlers were co-operative in helping with the construction of fortifications, and there was enough interest shown in new agricultural ventures to raise a cautious optimism within the government. In 1796, however, a majority of hundredors and tythingmen were elected opposed to the company, and almost at once it was announced that the quitrents, long postponed, would now be inaugurated, with interest to be charged on any unpaid portion. Tempers rose again but the overall response was mild. Some few left the colony in disgust to set up afresh elsewhere, but the protest of the hundredors and tythingmen reflected more a sense of injury than outrage:

We are to inform you that we have left Lands to come here in expectation to receive Lands in the same condition as we received them in Nova Scotia. But we find it to the Contrary of that, for we find that the Company says the land is theirs. Sir if we had been told that, we never would come here on that condition ... Sir we are astonished why the Company could not tell us after three years we was to pay a shilling per acre. Sir we are deceived by some misunderstanding for the Company says that the land is belonging to them and if it is theirs, there is the Lands they may take it if they think proper in so doing. Sir this dispute is on account of the Rents for if the land is not ours without paying a shilling per acre, the lands will never be ours, no not at all.[2]

Macaulay was not deceived by this apparent mildness. Already there had been rumours of potential revolt and the governor had taken precautionary measures for defence, warning that things would go hard for insurrectionaries. Wisely, however, he made no effort to collect the rents for 'so wayward, perverse and unreasonable is the Majority of the Settlers, that we see no way of effecting ... regular payment but by force'. His astute combination of forcefulness and conciliation prevailed, but no real solution to the impasse had been achieved. It was clear that as soon as the rent issue was reopened, so surely would trouble follow.[3]

Slowly, inexorably, the situation drifted out of hand. The company

---

[1] Sierra Leone Council Minutes, Mar. 2, 7, May 12, June 9, Oct. 12, 1795, Mar. 13, 1797, C.O. 270/3, 4.
[2] Governor and Council to Chairman and Court of Directors, July 13, 1795, May 16, 1796, C.O. 268/5; Knutsford, *op. cit.*, 158; Boston King to J. Clarkson, June 1, 1797, Clarkson Papers; Sierra Leone Council Minutes, Jan. 4, Aug. 17, 1797, C.O. 270/4.
[3] Knutsford, *op. cit.*, 175-6; Governor and Council to Chairman, Court of Directors, Jan. 22, 1798, C.O. 268/5.

once again insisted on quitrents, then once again reversed itself. The hundredors and tythingmen became more excessive in their demands, arrogating the right to appoint judges, and claiming that only they possessed the legislative power to represent the Nova Scotians with whom ownership of the colony's land rested exclusively. In the spring of 1799, the tough-minded, sure-handed Macaulay left for home and was replaced by the milder, inexperienced Thomas Ludlam. In London, the company, though recognizing the need for a forceful policy, hesitated to act decisively since it had never received its colonial charter following the parliamentary action of 1791. In Freetown, the hundredors and tythingmen, more and more led by extremists, moved towards open revolt, making plans for taking over the government, and justifying themselves in accusations of white men's injustice. 'We are willing to shew that we cannot get justice from the white people', they complained to Ludlam and his council. 'Because it is for their own ends they expects gains Because we are ignorant. . . . I am sorry to see that the White people strives to blind the eyes of the Simple which we have seen them endeavoured from our youth.'[1]

In September 1800 the hundredors and tythingmen precipitated open revolt by posting their own laws publicly, proclaiming that all settlers were to be guided by these ordinances, and restricting the jurisdiction of the governor and council henceforward to the company's private affairs. Most of the Nova Scotians, though resentful over their treatment, were unwilling to go as far as armed insurrection, but neither could they be relied upon for active military support of the government. Thus the loyalist position was rendered precarious and the future of the colony cast in doubt, when an incredible storybook intervention saved the situation. At the crucial moment into Freetown harbour sailed a ship carrying 550 Maroon settlers–Jamaican Negroes, former slaves, who had been deported to Nova Scotia from their homeland in 1796 and then sent on to Sierra Leone at their own request. Having no stake in the local issue and with a long history of their own involving successful guerrilla opposition to legal authority, they nonetheless readily came to the aid of the hard-pressed Ludlam who, with this substantial assistance, quickly subdued the rebellious Nova Scotian faction. In the legal action which followed, the ringleaders were banished and two were executed. Rebellion, actual or potential, was finished in the colony of Sierra Leone.[2]

[1] *Substance of the Report . . . of the Sierra Leone Company*, 1801, 1–9; Sierra Leone Council Minutes, Sept. 10, 1799, Mar. 4, 1800, C.O. 270/4, 5.
[2] Sierra Leone Council Minutes, Sept. 26, 1800, 'A Narrative of the Rebellion', C.O. 270/5.

3 The End of an Era

It is difficult to assess the extent to which the Nova Scotians were influenced by traditional British ideas of the rights of freemen to tax themselves through their own representatives. Surely, having fought in the War of American Independence, they must have been aware of the complaint of those other colonists regarding unrepresented taxation. Yet, their essential interest was land, not political power. All their complaints over the years were formulated in terms of rightful ownership of land withheld, which thrust them back into a condition akin to the slavery that had once oppressed them. Concern for political power, constitutional rights, and the responsibilities of elected representatives arose only after the land dispute had become acute. Furthermore, once subdued, the Nova Scotians became politically listless. The long struggle ending in failure had left the settlers emotionally exhausted and no longer equal to another effort. The company's charter arrived shortly after the end of the rebellion, and with it came the end of the hundredors and tythingmen. Henceforth, the colony was to be governed by the governor and his council without settler participation, let alone interference, and it was to be another sixty-three years before Sierra Leoneans were offered even a nominal voice in their government through appointment as minority, unofficial members of a newly constituted legislative council. No voice of opposition was raised to this new arrangement.

This sudden loss of virility had its economic and social ramifications as well. Still steadfast in their opposition to quitrents, the settlers all at once replaced their passion for land with total indifference, and they freely let their land claims go by default rather than pay the hated tax. Even when the rents were discontinued, the settlers would not move back to the land. Many of the best farmers had been among those banished, and most of those who remained now preferred to work in Freetown as labourers and artisans. Perhaps, as has been suggested, the long years of frustration had led to a permanent suspicion that sooner or later the Europeans would always deprive them of their lands. Perhaps, unconsciously, they had begun to develop a taste for urban dwelling on European standards. They had been town dwellers, some in London, others in Canada, and all had long been exposed to European language and culture. Their religious institutions had long-standing attachment to European churches. The expressed policy of the company, moreover, was to introduce European civilization to Africa through the

Sierra Leone settlers, and to that end their children had been provided with European schooling. Thus they were tending to become a black community in Africa, but exclusive from the indigenous population in manners, dress and language, considering themselves closer in spirit to their British sponsors than to the Africans who surrounded them.[1]

The infusion of Maroon immigrants did little to alter this trend. They followed their loyal action against the Nova Scotians by co-operating in a successful campaign against some local tribes, then established themselves as peaceful citizens with full respect for the law, completely abandoning their former warlike habits. Though they maintained their cohesiveness and but slowly gave up long-standing customs such as polygamy, they gradually fitted into the European pattern of the colony. Their relations with the Nova Scotia settlers remained correct, if not cordial, and like them they turned their backs on farming, preferring work in town as labourers and artisans.[2]

In twenty years the colony had progressed from a precarious day-to-day existence to the status of a secure community of approximately two thousand inhabitants with a stable government and an adequate economy. It had also moved from an independent nation to a European colony. It was, however, the end of an era. In 1806 the company requested that its government be transferred to the British crown. The following year the slave trade was abolished and Britain, needing a base of operations in West Africa, took control of the settlement in 1808. From then on Freetown was to become a centre for the repatriation of thousands of liberated African slaves, and its subsequent history and the quality of its way of life were substantially altered.

[1] N. A. Cox-George, 'Direct Taxation in the Early History of Sierra Leone', *Sierra Leone Studies*, n.s., no. 5, Dec., 1955, 31–4; *Report . . . of the Sierra Leone Company . . . 1794*, 69–70; Arthur T. Porter, *Creoledom: A Study of the Development of Freetown Society*, 34.
[2] Fyfe, *op. cit.*, 88–92, 99–100.

4 The Establishment of France in Senegal

1 *The Effects of Early French Colonization*

The early history of the French colony of Senegal bears little immediate resemblance to the founding of Freetown in Sierra Leone, yet despite substantial differences in detail, the broad outlines of the two are not so dissimilar. Both involved a European presence on the West African coast, and the emergence of a local population which had absorbed a large measure of European social and cultural patterns, establishing them as its standards for everyday activity. The influence of these communities on the hinterland was at first negligible. Neither was greatly interested in the interior except for its commercial potential, but in the long run both were to become key centres through which European influence, standards and institutions were funnelled into the heartland of West Africa. French and British colonization differed in many ways, philosophically and practically, but the essential fact of both was that throughout the nineteenth and early twentieth centuries they introduced western modes of thought and action which ultimately touched off the political and economic revolutions which have characterized mid-twentieth-century Africa.

The beginnings of French colonization were not particularly impressive. Early Portuguese presence along the upper Guinea coast was giving way to the Dutch by the end of the sixteenth century, but by mid-seventeenth century it was France and England who were vying with each other in the area. St. Louis was established by France at the mouth of the Senegal in 1659 and Goree was captured from the Dutch in 1677, while at approximately the same time the British were installing themselves at the entrance to the Gambia River. But French administration was erratic and progress was fitful. The merchant companies charged with directing the posts were inefficient, the trade in slaves, ivory and gum though considerable, was disappointing, and during the eighteenth century, growing British sea power made it increasingly difficult for France to supply and hold her West African possessions. Between 1693 and 1815, France lost Goree to the British on four different occasions and St. Louis was given up three times, only to have them subsequently restored by treaty, the last time at Vienna in 1815.

Unlike Sierra Leone, the French establishments were frankly commercial. The island of Goree, nestled close to shore just below Cape Verde, was a useful place where ships heading for the West Indies could be refitted, but its main function was to serve as a gathering point for the slaves brought in from the coastal trading posts to the south. Around 1700, it was a miserable, unprepossessing place, with a small garrison of French soldiers and sailors manning two badly designed and maintained forts surrounded by a collection of nondescript huts. On the eve of the French Revolution, the situation had improved somewhat, for the population had risen to approximately 2,500, including a small French contingent and some 500 free blacks and mulattoes, the rest being household slaves. There was also a considerable, though fluctuating, population of transient slaves on their way to plantations in the West Indies.[1]

The local population of Goree came originally from the near-by mainland, mostly from the Lebou people, a Wolof-speaking group located just south of Cape Verde, who in 1790 had successfully revolted against their regional overlord, the Demel of Cayor, and set up an independent republic under French protection. For more than two hundred years their women had intermarried with the Europeans—Portuguese, Dutch, French and English—who had occupied the island at one time or another. The result was a native population consisting both of free blacks called *gourmets* and mulattoes known as *habitants*, for the most part converted to Christianity and in the process of becoming Europeanized. They owned numbers of household slaves, full-blooded Africans known as *captifs* who were treated as members of the family and rarely sold away and who, in many cases, had been converted to Christianity by their masters. The *gourmets* and *habitants* were primarily artisans and traders. Traditionally, the men wore a loose shirt and three-quarter trousers made of a coarse cotton cloth dyed blue or cocoa brown, a palm straw hat and sandals. By the time of the resumption of French influence after 1817, however, this costume was being replaced by metropolitan

---

[1] Abdoulaye Ly, *La Compagnie du Sénégal*, 265; André Villard, *Histoire du Sénégal*, 70–1.

styles, even as local languages were giving way to the everyday use of French.[1]

More colourful were the women of Gorée. These *signares*, tall and stately, had a well-deserved reputation for beauty. Slower than the men to adjust to European ways, they had their own style of dress which featured a variety of colour and texture. They affected long gowns of rich brocades made up of a number of different coloured cloths and added bright cotton headdresses tied in the traditional sugar-loaf style. Quantities of gold jewellery completed an impressive picture as the exotic forerunners and prototypes of today's women of Senegal. It was they who made the alliances with the Europeans who came to Gorée and it was they who laid much of the groundwork for the subsequent wealth and prestige of the mulatto population. Over the years the custom developed that a departing European husband was obliged to leave his children with his wife along with adequate property to provide for his deserted family. Consequently the majority of *signares* came to possess substantial numbers of *captifs* who served their mistresses in fine, richly appointed houses. There was no stigma attached to these common law marriages; on the contrary, they were prestigious as well as lucrative, and once a spouse had departed, his wife was free to marry again or to withdraw into the ease of her wealth and position. It was not uncommon for a retiring French official to leave to his replacement not only his job and his house but also his wife and family, an arrangement which well suited the quiet life in a colonial outpost lacking most of the social and recreational amenities to be found in the metropole.[2]

This predominantly mulatto group of Gorée, absorbing French ideas of European civilization and making them their own, was matched by the rise of a mulatto population in St. Louis of similar make-up and genesis. The island of St. Louis, about a dozen miles up from the mouth of the Senegal River, was not a very likely place to found a trading post despite the fact that it controlled deep penetration of the interior for several hundred miles via a major drainage system. The Senegal, for all its navigable miles, emptied into the sea over a bar whose constantly shifting channel, tricky shallows and difficult currents made possible the passage of only the smallest of sea-going vessels, and only those when provided with an experienced pilot and a measure of luck. Nonetheless, the settlement slowly developed. The initial fortifications

---

[1] Villard, *op. cit.*, 72; Abbé P.-D. Boilat, *Esquisses Sénégalaises*, 5–9, 42–5.
[2] *Ibid.*, 5–9, 221–7; J. P. L. Durand, *A Voyage to Senegal*, 115–18; L. L. C. Faidherbe, *Le Sénégal*, 99.

consisted only of a modest brick and limestone enclosure containing a chapel, a small garden and the slave baracoons. Despite official interdiction, the small French garrison of less than fifty lived mainly outside the walls, sharing the grass huts of the native women. The island, which was not two miles long and only a few hundred yards wide, was sparsely inhabited by local people and by groups of itinerant traders from the interior. Slaves from up river were a major commodity but so too was gum provided by the Moorish peoples living on the north bank of the Senegal.[1]

By 1800, St. Louis had expanded into a community of 7,000, including 2,400 *habitants* and *gourmets*, almost 700 Europeans, and more than 3,000 *captifs*. Its wide, flat, sandy streets contained a much enlarged fort, a hospital, a church and about twenty brick houses with limestone facing, along with a substantial number of round wooden thatched-roof huts. The city had a luminous, shimmering character which softened the sharp outlines of buildings and gave rise to a magic, dream-like atmosphere. This was caused by the sand blown up from the surrounding dunes, which hung in a thin haze over the white buildings eventually to drift down on to the roadways and roofs.[2]

In St. Louis the same custom of common law marriage between European and *signare* had given rise to a growing half-caste population in the process of adopting French manners and language. Unlike Goree, however, St. Louis was much more of a Muslim city. Most mulatto *habitants* and many of the free black *gourmets* were Christian, but many *gourmets* were Muslim, the exponents of each religion living peaceably side by side in the same community. Moreover, the swelling number of traders from the interior were normally Muslim, as were the *captifs* who were not encouraged to become Christian since in St. Louis it was felt that no Christian should be a slave—hence no slave should be permitted to become a Christian.[3]

The freemen were merchants and traders, and each summer during the rains they deserted the small city and took their craft far up the river to the Galam in search of ivory, gum and slaves. In their energetic pursuit of commerce, they as often resisted French-imposed mercantile limitations on their economic freedom and in 1791, on the plea of the *habitants*, a policy of free trade was finally inaugurated. Some years later, when one of the governors arbitrarily accorded commercial priori-

[1] Ly, *op. cit.*, 263–74.
[2] Durand, *op. cit.* 115–18; Villard, *op. cit.*, 71; Report of M. Huzart, Apr. 13, 1822, N.A.S. Q 16.
[3] Boilat, *op. cit.*, 209–13.

ties upstream to a particular group of merchants, there was a brief but effective revolt; he was summarily removed from office and packed off to Goree. The influence of the local people was such that on the eve of the Revolution in France it was decreed that the mayor of the city be a man of colour. As for the *signares*, they enjoyed the same wealth and prestige as those of Goree, and during the nineteenth century their fortunes laid the basis for important matches between local families and impecunious but adventurous Frenchmen.[1]

When the Revolution broke out in France in 1789, therefore, though the hundreds of thousands in the hinterland of Senegal remained untouched by Europe, there had emerged a small population with modest wealth based on up-country trade, with a growing addiction to the habits and customs of the metropole, and with some measure of spirit in preserving its rights against official irregularities. To this beginning, the Revolution brought not only the idea of freedom and equality for all men, but the offer to share the fruits of the new democracy France was building. The slave trade was terminated and slavery abolished. Full French citizenship was accorded to the people of Senegal, former slaves included, and an invitation was tendered to send representatives to Paris. That there was a substantial lack of realism in this hasty policy seems to have been overlooked at the time, both in France and in Senegal. The *habitants* of Goree and St. Louis petitioned for an end of the mercantile restrictions imposed by Paris, and joyfully subscribed an unsolicited sum of money in 1793 to help defend the 'motherland' from foreign invasion. The title of 'citizen' was welcomed by those more often accustomed to treatment as inferiors, and soon the registers announced the births of young Scipios and Robespierres, sons of Mamadou, Abdoulaye or Moctar. For its part, the new government in Paris proceeded to grant rights to thousands of Africans who little understood them and who, in any event, stood no opportunity of exercising them, cut off as they were from Europe by the English fleet which first stifled their trade and then occupied their country.[2]

Even the second thoughts which were had by the Revolutionary government in Paris had little effect on the Senegalese who were bent on becoming, not free and self-governing, but French citizens with full rights, privileges and responsibilities equal to those of citizens dwelling

---

[1] Christian Schefer, *Instructions Générales données de 1763 à 1870 aux Gouverneurs . . . en Afrique Occidentale*, I, 170, 175–7, 206; *L'Afrique Occidentale*, June 26, 1897.

[2] Villard, *op. cit.*, 66; Schefer, *op. cit.*, I, 171; Georges Hardy, *La Mise en Valeur du Sénégal, de 1817 à 1854*, 10.

within France itself. In 1790, the right to vote was abrogated for the slaves freed under the Declaration of the Rights of Man, and the same year private property was guaranteed in the colonies thus opening to question the validity of a manumission which deprived anyone of his former property in slaves. The following year the franchise of both blacks and mulattoes was further restricted. Most of this manoeuvring reflected pressures originating in the plantation colonies of the West Indies and had little immediate relevance to Senegal, but when Napoleon came to power, the whole movement towards freedom and equality came to an abrupt end for all colonials. Slavery and the slave trade were reinstituted in 1802 and men of colour were denied entrance into France. The French civil code forbade mixed marriages and the right of white fathers to recognize mulatto children. But by this time citizens in the metropole had also lost most of their rights; only their equality and fraternity–minus their liberty–remained.[1]

2 France Steps Up Her Civilizing Mission

Eighteen hundred and seventeen, the year France reassumed control over her West African possessions, marked the beginning of a new era of French colonization in Africa. The colonial empire of the *ancien régime* had been based frankly on adding to the prestige of the Bourbon royal house and on supplying slaves for the sugar islands in the West Indies. Now, a generation after the demise of Louis XVI, the Bourbons were back on the throne, but during the turbulent years since 1789, France had been subjected to a thorough-going revolution and military dictatorship, and the country and the royal house that ruled it were something quite different from what they had once been. Actually the mood of the country had become clearly anti-colonial and was to remain substantially so for more than fifty years. The slave trade was finished and the French government was determined that it should not be revived. Doctrines of free trade were in the air opening to question the economic utility of colonies. The humanitarianism and romanticism of early nineteenth-century Europe argued equally that the duty of the more developed races was to bring the benefit of their civilization to the less advanced peoples of the world, but not in order to subject them—rather to make them free and self-sufficient. Yet, from this point forward, an articulate, self-conscious philosophy of colonization gradually

[1] Schefer, *op. cit.*, I. 180, 185, 189; Lamine Guèye, *Étapes et Perspectives de l'Union Française*, 21–6; Guèye, *De la Situation Politique des Sénégalais Originaires des Communes de Plein Exercice*, 10–11.

emerged, and French presence in West Africa became permanent. France, like Britain, found herself becoming involved in a colonial empire precisely at the time when she was least disposed to do so.

What developed in West Africa—in 'Senegal and her dependencies', as the colony was called at this time—was a policy made up of indecision, error, inaction and contradiction, of too much government and not enough, but a policy withal which kept France firmly and increasingly in control and which, for all its weakness, never contemplated or approached abandonment and withdrawal. The forces which maintained French control in Senegal and offset official and unofficial disinterest within France were several, and interrelated.

First, perhaps foremost, was the continuing belief in the revolutionary doctrines of 1789. Metropolitan France might be in the grip of political reaction, but the spirit of democratic egalitarianism still dominated the French heart, at least in principle, and combined with revolutionary fraternalism—the impulse to share the fruits of French culture with others—in a sense of mission to help what were regarded as the less fortunate parts of the world. To Colonel Schmaltz, the first governor to assume control of the colony after its return by the English, went elaborate instructions defining the importance of this civilizing mission, and his successors consistently received similar directions. Towards the mulattoes of St. Louis and Goree, already well along the road to assimilation into French culture, there was to be continued equality with Europeans. The practice of choosing a creole mayor for St. Louis and Goree would be maintained, looking to the day when an African might qualify. The mayor should continue to have direction of the police, and it was suggested that several of the high court judgeships at St. Louis and Goree be held by distinguished mulatto members of the community. Great care had to be exercised, moreover, to avoid any suspicion of the sort of racial discrimination which had become characteristic of the French colonies in the West Indies.[1]

Towards the less westernized segments of the population, a benevolent paternalism was deemed appropriate. In place of the slave trade, the French hoped to develop an agricultural economy based on a free peasantry. 'The political and moral part of the enterprise', announced the government in Paris, 'consists of introducing gradually among the Senegalese, a civilization based on free labour and a more fruitful agricultural economy, on education and peace.' Using lands obtained through negotiation, not through force, the government planned to establish

[1] Schefer, *op. cit.*, I, 290, 303, 350, 421.

farming communities where slavery would be outlawed. It was recommended that prisoners, *captifs* from St. Louis and Goree, domestic slaves from the tribal areas and free blacks be employed as agricultural labourers. The slaves would be freed at once on condition that they agreed to a fourteen-year indenture. Thus a free, though largely landless, labour supply would result. We must 'bring to the people of Senegal with their new needs and responsibilities, a taste for work, and through work to lead them to a civilization which can thus spread far into the interior of Africa.' Christianity, which uplifted moral standards and ennobled character, would be extended, along with means for improving the health of the indigenous population. 'The prime mover of the new colony must be European culture driven by French energy, becoming through example, through persuasion, and through the appreciation of new achievements, the soul of the African.'[1]

Related to the civilizing mission of French culture was the common belief of most Frenchmen that they somehow have a peculiar talent for colonization. The people of Senegal, it was said, had long exhibited a gay and easy-going manner that ill matched the régime of the aloof and dour English. Hence, according to France's most careful student of this period of Senegalese history, the Senegalese were delighted with the return of the French in 1817. 'Our character', he added, 'which otherwise presents grave defects and often compromises our best colonizing efforts, at least offers to the blacks certain attractive traits: freedom without arrogance, a spirit of intimacy, the ability to understand different points of view, the constant desire to adapt ourselves to the viewpoint and wishes of the people.' All this helped to establish a bond between the colonized and the colonizer, but there was something more. Before the Revolution, France and the overseas empire had been two separate entities and the latter existed solely to serve the mercantile needs of the former. With the second empire it was different, at least in theory. A new idea of colonization began to take shape–a French empire of which the metropole was but a part, not the centre. France no longer possessed an empire, she was an empire, and the people of France overseas could look forward to the day when they would all be equally French, the Senegalese farmer just as much as the Burgundian peasant.[2]

A third factor operating to bring forth a more articulate forceful

---

[1] *Ibid.*, 256–7, 262–3, 283–4, 299, 375.
[2] Hardy, *op. cit.*, 10–11; R. Delavignette and C. Julien, *Les Constructeurs de la France d'Outre-Mer*, 12–28.

colonial policy was the simple desire for profit. Humanitarian regard for the spread of French civilization was all very well, but if it could be combined with economic advantage, so much the better. Laissez-faire principles guiding international trade and colonial administration were excellent in theory, but to the French mind the logic of mercantilism was irresistible. The proposed plantation system which would replace slavery as the economic basis of the colony was designed to concentrate on products that were scarce or expensive in France, thus in effect placing the colony once again in a mercantile relation to the mother country. When the French resumed control of the administration of Senegal, one of the first things they did was to forbid the entry of foreign commerce, thus reinstituting the cardinal mercantile doctrine of a closed circuit between the metropole and its subsidiary colonies. Clearly this neo-mercantilism did not square readily with the new assimilationist ideas of empire; nonetheless, the primacy of metropolitan interests continued to dominate French colonial policy right down to the mid-twentieth century when emergent African nationalism forced fundamental political, if not economic, changes.[1]

In pursuit of the policy of converting Senegal into a plantation economy, agricultural surveys were made, treaties were concluded to obtain territory in the Walo, a region bordering the Senegal River not far from St. Louis, experimental farms were established, tracts of land were granted to concessionnaires, and arrangements were explored to obtain an indigenous labour supply. The emphasis was to be on cotton, indigo, coffee, vegetable oils and other products which France was obliged to import at great expense. The point clearly was to enrich the home country—to develop a classical mercantile colony which would provide hard-to-obtain raw materials for home consumption or for France's infant manufacturing interests, while offering a market for French goods. 'You are to create for France', the governor was instructed in 1822, 'a colony which will furnish her at least in part with products for which she is dependent upon foreign sources and which offers a substantial outlet for the products of her industry and manufactories.' In fact, the venture was not a success. The examination of the possibilities of local soils and climate was superficial and unrealistic, the plan was over-ambitious and under-supported, little account was taken of indigenous social and cultural ways, and the French government was unwilling to take responsibility for the military conquest which was a

[1] Schefer, *op. cit.*, I, 269; Gov. Gerbidon to Minister, Aug. 25, 1827, no. 133, N.A.S. 2B11.

necessary prerequisite to any such externally-imposed basic social-economic changes. Even before the fall of the Bourbon Restoration and the succession of the July Monarchy in 1830, these fanciful agricultural experiments had been abandoned and the colony fell back once again on its riverain commerce in gum and a few subsidiary products.[1]

Despite this flurry of mercantile activity, the colonial trade amounted to little in the French economy of the day, but there was still another reason why at least a small body of opinion in France continued to press for an active colonial policy. This was the long-standing need of the French character for national prestige. The precedent was the earlier empire designed to glorify the Bourbons, but subsequent to that had come the varying fortunes of French power during the period of the Revolution and the traumatic years that saw the primacy of Napoleon followed by total defeat and eclipse by Britain. The road back to national self-respect lay in naval parity with England and this meant refuelling stations about the world in strategic locations. What if these colonies did not pay for themselves in produce and markets? Was it not enough that they were means through which the power and prestige of France might shine forth the world over?[2]

Thus, French colonial policy in Senegal wavered and stumbled. There were many who found colonies useless, wasteful, even dangerous, but there were others who saw them as outlets for economic and humanitarian activities, or as means for establishing the greater glory of France. That there was ambivalence in policy cannot be doubted, but a good deal of the weakness of French administration in Senegal at this time may be ascribed less to confusion over objectives than to unwillingness to pay the price for carrying them out—in money, in time, in patience and in work. Basically, France was interested in establishing a prosperous economy rooted both in an internal free trade which would help the native African to economic stability and in a cultural tutelage leading him to eventual assimilation as a Frenchman overseas. The instructions of the French government to its governors were always clear—to do away with the slave trade, to deal with the tribes of the interior by negotiation rather than by force, to move towards the abolition of slavery, to press forward a policy of assimilation as quickly as practicable, to make such profit as possible from trade or from plantations, and broadly 'to instil in these people a high opinion of the wealth, the

---

[1] Schefer, *op. cit.*, I, 300, 375. A detailed account of the plantation experiment in Senegal is contained in Hardy, *op. cit.*, 25–249.
[2] Brunschwig, *Mythes et Réalités de l'Impérialisme Colonial Français*, 10–16.

power, and above all, the benevolence of the French; to do everything, in a word, to prepare the way for eventual penetration of their territory, and to extend gradually through commerce a civilization from which France will be able to reap the brightest advantages.'[1]

3 And the Africans Respond

The bourgeois government of Louis Philippe brought no dramatic change of policy. Notoriously parsimonious, it offered the struggling colony a minimum of economic assistance, but it had come to power on a wave of revolutionary liberalism; hence there was a restatement of the principles of 1789 in the colonies. French citizenship, cast into doubt since the days of Napoleon, was once again proclaimed. In 1830, it was decreed that 'in the application of the Civil Code, a colony is considered as an integral part of the metropole'. Three years later this was made explicit. 'All persons born free or having legally acquired their freedom, enjoy in the French colonies: 1. civil rights; 2. political rights under conditions prescribed by law.' Thus, all freemen in the French-controlled areas of Senegal–Goree, St. Louis and a few other coastal stations, as well as a handful of trading posts up the Senegal River–were once again declared French citizens with all rights and privileges of that status.[2]

What kind of response did the African community in Senegal make to French culture and colonial administration? Politically the reaction was mixed. There is no question that the people of St. Louis, Goree and the other French points had been impressed by the offer of political equality which came from the Revolution. Moreover, they were proud to point out that initial French penetration had resulted from treaty between equal parties, not from military conquest. Even when reaction swept most reforms off the books, their devotion to France never faltered. Napoleon might become an object of scorn, but France herself was not doubted. The Senegalese, in their own eyes, were always a special case where mutual affection with the French brought mutual loyalty and mutual aid. Not only did Senegal offer material assistance to the Revolution, but in later years it was her soldiers, the celebrated *tirailleurs sénégalais*, who helped France ultimately to conquer the interior–the Sudan, Dahomey, the Congo, Chad, Morocco and other areas. It was

[1] Schefer, *op. cit.*, I, 258.
[2] Decree of Nov. 5, 1830; Law of Apr. 24, 1833.

therefore no wonder to the Senegalese that France was so ready to grant them French citizenship with all its prerogatives.[1]

But there was a curiously unreal, hypothetical quality to these political rights. For her part, France ruled in Senegal during the years of the Bourbon Restoration with autocratic paternalism which permitted no real democratic participation, whatever lip service there may have been paid to popular rights. The governor was absolute and was advised, but not directed, by an administrative council of appointive members, and there was no such thing as popular elections. For example, during the British occupation of Senegal, the custom had been for the mayors of St. Louis to be elected by an assembly of citizens and thus to be responsible to the people as well as to the colonial administration. The French saw no reason to continue this procedure. They wanted a mayor who would explain government policy to the people and keep the administration informed as to local needs and demands but he had to be the government's man; hence he was appointed by the governor and no longer elected by his constituency.[2]

After the 1830 revolution in France, some progress towards greater local control over the economic and political life of the country was demanded and secured by the mulattoes and freed Africans of St. Louis and Goree. Agitation for the establishment of representative assemblies had started as early as 1822, but later the forerunner of a local chamber of commerce was instituted, and during the 1840s assemblies were finally established for both Goree and St. Louis, remaining in existence up to 1848.[3]

Perhaps the attitude of the Senegalese with their orientation towards French culture and their identification with French citizenship was best illustrated by Gabriel Pellegrin, a trader and public officer who flourished during the first quarter of the century, and who was head of one of the most important mulatto families of St. Louis. Pellegrin first came into prominence in his youth as a rebel filled with revolutionary zeal who took a leading role in the 1802 insurrection which successfully unseated Governor Laserre, appointed to his post under Napoleon. Although freedom of commerce within the colony had been in effect since the early days of the French Revolution, the governor arbitrarily instituted a trade monopoly, conferring exclusive rights on a company in which he held a major share. This was too much for merchant

---

[1] Guèye, *Situation Politique*, 6–9.
[2] Schefer, *op. cit.*, I, 409; Gov. Roger to Minister, Nov. 12, 1823, N.A.S. 2B8.
[3] Information supplied by Dr. H. O. Idowu of Nigeria.

interests both in France and Senegal and an investigation was ordered. Before anything came of it, however, Pellegrin and several other mulattoes joined with some French to take direct action. Organizing a body of two hundred blacks, and to the cry of 'Long live the Convention! Long live Robespierre!'–a slogan which though somewhat out of date by 1802 indicated the degree of revolutionary fervour still alive in the colony–they arrested the governor. Dragged naked through the streets in the middle of the night, he was brought to Pellegrin's house, there pistol-whipped and threatened with assassination by the young creole, and shipped off to Goree which was at that time in the hands of the English.

Pellegrin and his fellow mutineers were never brought to justice, possibly because the case against the governor was clearcut even though the action was illegal, possibly because there was widespread dissatisfaction with Laserre's activities. Some years later, however, Pellegrin again found himself in difficulty with the authorities, this time over suspected co-operation with the British during their occupation of St. Louis. Nothing was ever proven, nor was an alleged involvement in a raid carried out in 1819 by the Moors on plantations in the Walo. Quite possibly Pellegrin was innocent of these later accusations, but in any event his early career hardly seemed an ideal preparation for his eventual emergence as a model of loyal French citizenship. Yet, by 1823, he was the administration's enthusiastic choice as mayor of St. Louis. The governor, Baron Roger, went out of his way to extol Pellegrin's moderation and trustworthiness, his common sense and deep knowledge of local affairs, his enthusiastic support of the plantation scheme in the Walo, his loyalty to king and government, and his consistent avoidance of any cabals and intrigues. Pellegrin's influence with the people of St. Louis and its environs and his position as head of the city's most influential family made him a natural choice, not only of the governor, but of his fellow citizens as well. To Roger, Pellegrin was the sort of man who could be very dangerous if he were in opposition to the administration; hence it was the best part of discretion to have him as a member of the official government family.

Roger's confidence was not misplaced. As mayor, Pellegrin directed under gubernatorial fiat colonial activities on the Senegal. In this, he enjoyed substantial success, commanding respect both among the citizens of St. Louis and the people along the river. Intelligent, liberal-minded yet firm, he constantly pursued the basic interests of the colony in working for the freedom of the Walo from Moorish interference.

Many years later the name of Gabriel Pellegrin was still held in great esteem among the people. By middle age, therefore, the youthful rebel and enthusiastic supporter of the principles of 1789 had become a popular and effective official of the Bourbon Restoration, settling down on the side of law and order and developing his position as one of the major gum traders up the Senegal River.[1]

It was indeed commerce which was the guiding passion of the *habitants*, absorbing their interest and shaping their destiny. When the slave trade was abolished, the people of Goree suffered a severe economic depression which they succeeded for a time in overcoming by developing trade in other commodities along the West African coast in the direction of Sierra Leone. Yet when Dakar and Rufisque rose to prominence later in the nineteenth century, Goreeans were unable to compete and, the island being ill-suited for non-commercial pursuits, it drifted into permanent eclipse. St. Louis was more fortunate. Gum continued to be in great demand in Europe as a sizing and dye-fast for textile manufacturing, and thus provided a plausible substitute for slaving. But gum was a crop subject to the uncertainties of the weather and other limitations on agricultural production, and because the enthusiasm of the people of St. Louis for trade sometimes exceeded their commercial skill, there were consequent economic complications.

Essentially the difficulty lay in the superabundance of aspirant traders in proportion to the amount of business available. Each summer the Senegalese would set forth up the river—for by custom direct participation in the trade was closed to Europeans. Some would take goods on credit from merchant houses in St. Louis, others merely acted as agents for these houses. In good years when there was a plentiful supply of gum, and warfare had not closed off the trade, there was reasonable opportunity for profit. But in years when the harvest was slight, the traders had an uncontrollable tendency to dump their goods for what they could get, which usually meant ruin for some and a measure of loss for all.

After a bad year, the traders were willing to abandon their free trade policies and would form a joint stock company which fixed prices and supply, and planned its marketing operations with care and foresight. If such a regimen succeeded in stabilizing the market and bringing back profits, the temptation would soon be too much and there would be a

---

[1] P. Cultru, *Histoire du Sénégal du XV Siècle à 1870*, 287–9; Gov. Roger to Minister, Nov. 12, 1823, N.A.S. 2B8; Frédéric Carrère and Paul Holle, *De la Sénégambie Française*, 272.

demand to return to free trade, for these people were incorrigible economic individualists, and such a move usually had the backing of the laissez-faire government in Paris. There were good arguments on both sides. Free trade engendered resourcefulness and expanded possibilities, while blocking monopoly control by a few big dealers, but monopoly also made careful planning possible and met the controlled merchandising of the Moors with a control of its own. So the argument continued, fluctuating with the success or failure of each year's trade and reflecting the ambivalence and excessive passion of these people for commerce. As with the settlers of Sierra Leone and Liberia, they avoided at all costs a farming life, preferring to exist through trade, and to live, if necessary to decay and to perish, in the city.[1]

It was the failure of the French government to recognize this traditional repugnance for agricultural pursuit which was a major cause for the breakdown of the plantation experiment. To encourage participation, the government introduced a series of bonuses or bounties to be paid on the amount of land under cultivation. This inducement, in addition to the promise of free land, brought forth an ample number of Senegalese and French applicants who proceeded to establish plantations along the river on the plots assigned. But alternately the river flooded the crops and the dry interior winds seared them, dykes were badly constructed and failed to hold back the flood, farm buildings were too lavishly designed, and labour was badly recruited. The resultant harvests were catastrophic. Nothing daunted, the planters duped the government inspectors by falsifying their labour accounts and passing off as genuine bogus cotton and indigo plants, and so they continued for a time to collect their premiums. It was not an edifying spectacle— the ingenuousness of the government and the indifference and cynical dishonesty of the planters. It did, however, illustrate the popular dislike of farming and the fact that the people of Senegal were still a long way from giving serious regard to the economic development of their homeland.[2]

By 1830 the local customs of the mulatto group were dying out. The men now dressed in the French mode; both women and men were usually found fluent in the French language; the children attended French schools and were often sent to France for more advanced

---

[1] Eugène Saulnier, *La Compagnie de Galam au Sénégal*, 45–53; Gov. Pujol to Minister, Nov. 29, 1834, N.A.S. 2B16; Schefer, *op. cit.*, I, 366–7; Carrère and Holle, *op. cit.*, 345.
[2] A. Raffenel, *Voyage dans l'Afrique Occidentale*, 21n; Schefer, *op. cit.*, I, 394; Gov. Jubelin to Minister, July 25, 1828, N.A.S. 2B12.

study; and most creoles were devout Christians. When the French civil code was instituted in the colony in 1830, the common law marriages of the *signares* began to give way to European-style, church-supervised marriages. Intermarriage with Europeans continued, however. Though it is usually stated that there was no racial prejudice in Senegal at the time, as indicated by the commonality of European-African marriages, the constant warning of the French government to its administrators to avoid at all costs the possibility of discrimination raises the question as to whether it was in fact totally absent. The depressing example of the West Indian colonies always was in the mind of white and black alike, and at least some of the Senegalese feared 'the arrival of Europeans by whom they felt threatened with humiliations, to which they were unaccustomed, similar to the sort of thing which in the West Indies comes from colour prejudice.'[1]

Important and influential though the *habitants* were, they were far outnumbered in the cities by the African population consisting of *captifs* or household slaves, a small but growing number of freedmen who made a living as artisans or labourers, and a shifting population of tribal Africans who came to town to trade or to work and eventually perhaps to return to their home villages in the interior. French culture and influence touched these people but slightly. The *captifs* still wore the native dress of loose cotton trousers and blouse for the men, and a knee-length cloth for the women. The few who were manumitted often continued to work for their former masters in town or were indentured to the plantations up the Senegal River. Most spoke Wolof or some other native language, and only a sprinkling found their way into the modest primary schools in Goree and St. Louis.

In Goree there were Christian *captifs* but in St. Louis by far the largest share of the population remained Muslim; hence not only were its background and language African, but its religious scruples and ethical practices were hostile to western ways. Although the Muslims in the cities were encouraged to enrol in the French schools, few cared to expose themselves to the infection of Christianity and the threat of conversion. The Muslims sent their children to Koranic schools conducted by marabouts, but this led only to Islamic religious instruction and addiction to non-western standards, which resisted assimilation into the French way of life. This rejection of French education and culture was a source of continuing irritation to the administration which regarded the people as living in a state of intellectual and moral

[1] Boilat, *op. cit.*, 209–13, 221–7; Schefer, *op. cit.*, I, 320 n.

stagnation that could only hold up the economic development of the country. Still, the status and attitudes of these people may not have been too vastly different from those of the peasants and artisans of contemporary France, only recently emerged from feudalism, for the most part illiterate, and strangers to political democracy and equality of economic opportunity.[1]

As little as French civilization affected the pure-blooded Africans living in the cities, it had even less impact on the Africans of the interior. The people up country were organized into independent tribes, few of which came under direct French influence or control. The commerce in gum was conducted at trading posts along the Senegal with the great Moorish nations living on the north bank of the river. These powerful tribes not only were able to dictate the terms of exchange by treaty but exacted special duties from the traders of St. Louis as a prerequisite to commerce. Moreover, they frequently disrupted normal trade through warfare which French military expeditions were unable to suppress until the days of Faidherbe in the 1850s. Similarly, the lands which the French put into use in the Walo during the great plantation experiment, were obtained through treaty from the independent local tribes who carefully reserved the best tracts for themselves, ceding only inferior land for which they had no use. This in part accounted for the failure of the plantations, but an additional factor was the implacable hostility of the local people. Over a period of several years, only four or five villagers were willing to take employment on the plantations and these were quickly dissuaded by their compatriots. Far from wishing to emulate what the government had hoped would be impressive demonstrations of superior western agricultural techniques, the indigenous Africans ignored the French except for occasional sabotage to the irrigation dykes. The dream of training a peasantry schooled in European agricultural methods remained but a European dream.[2]

The Lebou Republic of Dakar, though longer under French influence, was scarcely less refractory, and the people of the region only began to react to French political pressure and cultural influence after the establishment of the city of Dakar in 1857. The republic had maintained its independence over the years by playing the French off against the Demel of Cayor, and the Lebou fishermen found considerable profit

---

[1] Boilat, *op. cit.*, 10–18; Report on schooling to Gov. de Gramont, n.d., [1846–1847], N.A.P.O.S. Senegal X, 3 bis; Gov. Roger to Minister, Apr. 15, 1824, N.A.S. 2B9.
[2] Gov. Gerbidon to Minister, Aug. 25, 1827, no. 131, 132, 133, N.A.S. 2B11, Gerbidon to Minister, Oct. 10, 1827, N.A.S. 2B12.

and diversion from their more prosaic everyday occupation in plundering French shipwrecks washed up on the shores of Cape Verde. The only evidence of Europeanization came in the case of one eliman or chief marabout of Dakar, Diop by name, who flourished between 1830 and 1850, and who spiced a career devoted to organizing pillaging expeditions against stranded French shipping by consuming quantities of absinthe and white wine of which he was fond and which were supplied him secretly by the French missionaries in the area.[1]

In 1848 another revolution shook France and its effects were quickly felt in Senegal. Once again the slaves were freed, once again the Senegalese dwelling within the areas of French administration were offered the right to vote, and once again the colony was invited to send a representative to Paris. Nevertheless, though slavery was finally ended, achievement once more fell short of expectation, for the right to representation was soon removed by the autocratic régime of Louis Napoleon. To some observers this was just as well, for they regarded the newly-freed slaves and urban labourers as largely incapable of understanding the workings and significance of a western democratic election. Few could speak or read French, and all instructions had to be translated into Arabic and Wolof. Scarcely anyone know his correct age or birthplace, and records of these data were non-existent. Most African electors quickly came under the domination of former masters, for the most part mulattoes, who used their influence to gain their own political ends. Thus, subservient to a French government but unassimilated into French civilization, they found themselves the political and economic servants of the mulatto oligarchy which dominated Senegalese life during the second half of the nineteenth century.[2]

[1] Jacques Charpy, *La Fondation de Dakar*, 58–9; Boilat, *op. cit.*, 42–5.
[2] Gov. Duchateau to Minister, Oct. 12, 1848, N.A.S. 2B7.

5 The Liberian Experiment

1 *The American Humanitarian Effort in West Africa*

There is a rough parallel between the early histories of Sierra Leone and Liberia. Both were founded to solve a Negro problem at home. Both were the fruit of humanitarian concern with slavery and the slave trade. Both were conceived as centres where commercial profit might be co-ordinated with the regeneration of former bondsmen. Both endured great difficulties at their outset with inexperienced leadership, native hostility, and a relentless environment taking cruel toll in lives and threatening the existence of the infant settlements. The similarities are natural, emerging from similarities of circumstance. Only later, after the middle of the nineteenth century, did essential differences become apparent – differences set in motion by differences of conditions in the colonizing countries.

The British experience, begun privately by abolitionists, was later sustained by a reluctant home government, and, through the humanitarian, mercantile, and imperial forces operating throughout the century, grew slowly as an influential outpost of European civilization in West Africa. The American settlement, responding to different factors at work in the United States, remained a private venture, undernourished and precarious. America was preoccupied with the political and economic development of its own continent, and had little concern for imperial adventures in Africa. The Negro problem in the United States, moreover, was of a complexity and magnitude which precluded simplistic solutions through colonization, and rocketed on to the disaster of the American Civil War and its aftermath. Liberia was largely ignored by white and Negro Americans alike and cast off to find its way in national independence it was ill-equipped to sustain. Sierra Leone became in time an important centre from which flowed western social and economic doctrine, Victorian morality and Christian thought to serve the coastal communities of West Africa, and to bind them in closer unity within the British colonial system. Liberia, *per contra*, came in her weakness to develop a certain symbolic strength as a rallying point for African cultural and political independence. It was no accident that Edward Blyden chose Liberia as his home and the centre for his ideas on a new African civilization. Blyden, the greatest of nineteenth-century West African nationalists whose life work contributed so much to the spirit of African independence, recognized Liberia as small, weak and impecunious, constantly threatened with annihilation. Yet he also saw her as a free and independent Negro state in West Africa, equal in her sovereignty to the great powers of Europe, and a constant reminder that the black man, even under the worst of circumstances, was fully capable of governing himself.

Like Sierra Leone, Liberia began its existence both as a haven created by humanitarian interests for black men unwanted in a white country and as a means for the introduction of Christian civilization to the aboriginal African. A number of factors, however, gradually set the two colonies on divergent courses. In the first place, the dimension of the Negro problem in America was totally different from that encountered in London and Nova Scotia. The logistics facing the British philanthropists were defined in terms of hundreds whereas the American Negro who might require aid was reckoned in the order of hundreds of thousands. In 1800 there were 108,000 freemen in the United States out of a total Negro population of one million. Ten years later the number of free Negroes had risen to 186,000 against almost 1,200,000 slaves. By 1820 there were over 233,000 freemen and 1,500,000 slaves.[1]

These were formidable statistics, particularly in a country with a total population of only 5,300,000 in 1800, 7,240,000 in 1810, and 9,638,000 in 1820. Not only did they carry the complications of large numbers and great expense, moreover, but they reflected the complexities of the Negro and slave question which was already laying its heavy hand on the American psyche. Substantial communities of free Negroes in northern cities created social and economic problems which many felt could only be solved through mass migration, but the main debate over the fate of the Negro in America centred in the border states which contained both slaves and freemen in quantity. In states like Virginia and Maryland, sentiment for manumission and colonization fought constantly with a pro-slavery attitude, and the adherents of African repatriation were further divided between those who favoured it on

---

[1] United States Bureau of the Census, *Negro Population in the United States, 1790–1915*, 53.

abolitionist grounds and those who merely wished to be rid of elements regarded as dissident and an encouragement to slave rebellion.[1]

Nor were the Negroes in America themselves united in their attitude towards Liberia. Some were glad enough to try their fortune in a new country, particularly in circumstances such as the aftermath of the Nat Turner rebellion of 1831 when they were subjected to outbursts of anti-Negro activity. For the most part, however, the free Negroes much preferred to remain as they were in the only home they knew rather than to submit to the risks of a dubious adventure in the African wilderness.[2]

In time further complications came to plague the colonization movement. During the 1830s sharply rising prices for slaves in the cotton states of the lower South offered an attractive alternative to schemes for Negro repatriation and the border states soon became major exporters, not of free Negroes to Africa, but of slaves to the plantations of the Gulf area. At the same time anti-slavery sentiments within the country developed a serious ambivalence with the rise of the abolitionist movement headed by William Lloyd Garrison. While some philanthropists continued to regard colonization as the most humane solution to the Negro problem, a growing force of abolitionists attacked the movement as a deception designed expressly to perpetuate the institution of slavery by drawing off free Negroes from the population. As abolitionist criticism became more strident, moreover, southern reaction hardened into an increasingly rigid defence of slavery, and support in the states of the upper South for African colonization declined accordingly.[3]

Complex cross-currents of this order could only mean chronic difficulties for the colony of Liberia. Financial assistance from America was erratic and insufficient. By 1866 private philanthropy and the Federal Government had disbursed almost $5,000,000 on behalf of Liberian colonization, but most of this money went directly to defray expenses for the transportation and establishment of colonists, so that Liberia herself was forced to subsist on a trifling income collected from import duties, port taxes, ship licensing and other minor sources. Furthermore, the United States government, sensitive to the powerful political forces at play in the domestic slavery issue, avoided any direct and official endorsement of the colony. Liberia therefore lacked sovereignty since it was but the colony of a private philanthropic agency, the American

---

[1] Charles I. Foster, 'The Colonization of Free Negroes in Liberia, 1816–1835', *The Journal of Negro History*, vol. XXXVIII, 1953, 41–4; P. J. Staudenraus, *The African Colonization Movement, 1816–1865*, 28–32, 104–16.
[2] *Ibid.*, 32–4, 179–80, 188–93.
[3] Stanley M. Elkins, *Slavery*, 211–12.

Colonization Society, and when the need for clarification of its political status eventually became acute, Liberia was allowed to drift into independence, poverty-stricken and neglected.[1]

By contrast, Britain provided adequate if not lavish support for its Sierra Leone colony, which also differed from Liberia in another important respect. The use of Freetown as a rehabilitation centre for liberated Africans meant that by the middle of the nineteenth century tens of thousands of recaptives had been added to the settler population, a strain which had an important influence on the country's economic and social development. Up to 1866 Liberia had received fewer than 6,000 recaptives to supplement its 13,000 emigrants from America. Consequently the population remained small, and was further weakened by being dispersed among several scattered communities. Not until 1830 did the number of colonists exceed 1,000, and it was another twenty years before the population rose towards 3,000. Such a lack of manpower was not irrelevant to problems of developing a sturdy economy and a stable government.[2]

2 *Constitutional Government on the Liberian Coast*

Difficulties abounded from the very beginning. The first colonists arrived off Cape Mesurado early in 1822 after an unsuccessful attempt to plant a settlement on Sherbro Island. They found a narrow promontory, heavy with jungle and brush, a hot humid climate, and a hostile indigenous population which had been dragooned into ceding the Cape but which was now determined to drive out the newcomers. It was the Sierra Leone experience all over again. Labouring through the spring and summer rains, the small group of less than one hundred settlers struggled for survival–ill-disciplined and indifferently led, weak with fever and half-starved, hampered by the terrain and harassed by the local people. In August another fifty settlers arrived along with a white American, Jehudi Ashmun–an impecunious unsuccessful young man with vaguely missionary inclinations who had come to seek his fortune in West Africa. Suddenly Ashmun found his calling in the crisis of the failing settlement. When the authorized agents of the

---

[1] Charles H. Huberich, *The Political and Legislative History of Liberia*, I, 42–3, 637, 785.
[2] *Ibid.*, I, 41, 435, 726, 819; R. R. Kuczynski, *Demographic Survey of the British Colonial Empire*, I, 101–2; J. D. Hargreaves, 'African Colonization in the Nineteenth Century: Liberia and Sierra Leone', *Sierra Leone Studies*, n.s., no. 16, June, 1962, 194–8, 199–201.

THE LIBERIAN EXPERIMENT [89]

Colonization Society virtually deserted the colony, Ashmun unilaterally assumed command, rallying the settlers and directing military preparations with such skill and thoroughness that when the expected native attack arrived a few months later, the embattled settlers won two smashing victories, and ended once and for all the threat of annihilation. Weak though it was, the colony of Liberia had been established.[1]

The external danger thus reduced, the colonists found themselves less responsive to leadership, however inspired. Ashmun for a time left Liberia when the settlers objected to what they regarded as a discriminatory distribution of land. Building and clearing went forward slowly, fever continued to take its toll in illness, and all authority virtually ended with Ashmun's departure. Nevertheless there was halting progress. The differences between the colonists and the administration were eventually patched over through the grant of a greater degree of local participation in government, and the manpower and material resources of the settlement were strengthened when the parent American Colonization Society dispatched ships with additional settlers and provisions.[2]

Ashmun returned, and his vigorous administration now began to show results. He conducted a careful survey of the Cape Mesurado lands, encouraged house raising and the establishment of farms, further strengthened his fortifications, installed harbour facilities, and constructed a number of public buildings in the township which had been named Monrovia. By treaty he extended the colony's control to 150 miles of coast above and below the Cape, and arranged for further settlements inland from Monrovia along the St. Paul River. As agent for the American Colonization Society, Ashmun was limited in authority to securing the health and welfare of his charges, and his responsibilities towards the United States government did not go beyond providing rehabilitation for the small number of recaptives brought in by occasional American naval patrols. He interpreted his mandate with great liberality, however, and was soon conducting successful punitive expeditions against slave factories along the coast, a process which also led to the suppression of several legitimate commercial stations and the substitution of trading posts under Liberian sponsorship.

Trade was but part of Ashmun's plans for economic development, for he was convinced that the colony would prosper in the long run

---

[1] Huberich, *op. cit.*, I, 144, 199-213; E. W. Blyden, *A Chapter in the History of Liberia*, 7-12; William Innes, *Liberia*, 37-76.
[2] Huberich, *op. cit.*, I, 296-9, 316-22.

mainly through the production of its own wealth in the form of staple crops. The colonists were of another mind, however, and concentrated their attention on bartering with the native Africans, a pastime they found much more to their liking than the drudgery of farming. The result was an insubstantial economy, and excessive reliance on imports both from up country and overseas. Nevertheless, despite the slow start in agriculture, Liberia had shown some evidence of becoming a successful colonial venture by the time Ashmun finally left Africa in 1828.[1]

Subsequent progress was much less spectacular, for dynamic leadership of the sort provided by Ashmun was necessarily infrequent. In one interesting respect, however–the establishment of constitutional, representative government–the community made rapid strides. As free Negroes or former slaves in the United States the colonists had at least had the opportunity to observe the workings of representative government, and even the Negro's status as a citizen had occasionally been recognized in some northern communities. It is not surprising, therefore, that soon after their arrival in Africa the immigrants were demanding and receiving political and constitutional privileges well beyond anything which obtained in the other West African colonies. All trace of representative government had disappeared in Sierra Leone with the abortive insurrection of the Nova Scotians in 1800, while democratic institutions in the communities of Senegal were made more nominal than real by persisting French paternalism. In the case of Liberia, however, the directors of the American Colonization Society seem to have assumed the eventual establishment of local self-government patterned after American models.

In 1820 the Board of Managers of the Society drafted a constitution for the first settlers which, while autocratic on its face, gave promise of increased liberality at a later time. Ultimate political authority was clearly retained by the Society which appointed an agent to be solely responsible for day-to-day administration. No provision was made for a representative legislature, and all judicial functions were exercised by the agent. Subsequent changes in the constitution were permitted only with the consent of the Society's directors.

Such provisions left the settlers with few prerogatives but did not mean they lacked constitutional safeguards. First of all, the mere existence of a written constitution emphasized that this was to be a limited government by law, with specific powers defined and specific rights assured. Secondly, all settlers were accorded Liberian citizenship

[1] *Ibid.*, I, 343–60, 363–7; Staudenraus, *op. cit.*, 150–7.

which carried 'such rights and privileges as are enjoyed by the citizens of the United States'. Presumably this article referred to civil rights like freedom of assembly, guarantee of jury trial, or restriction of unreasonable search and seizure, as set forth in the American Bill of Rights, since the privileges of elections and parliamentary government were clearly not included. Thirdly, slavery was forbidden and common law, as practised in the United States, guaranteed. Finally, it was decreed that, though the Society possessed all residual power in the colony, this condition would continue 'until they shall withdraw their Agents, and leave the settlers to the government of themselves'. It was evident that ultimate self-government was contemplated.

That these provisions were considered unsatisfactory was reflected to some extent by chronic unrest among the colonists, although their dissatisfaction appeared to be caused more by economic than constitutional factors. The agitation which had led to the temporary departure of Ashmun, for example, was brought on chiefly by disagreements over the distribution of town lots in Monrovia, the colonists charging favouritism and arbitrary allocation of choice sites for public purposes, and claiming that the maximum time granted for improving the land was unreasonably short. Nevertheless in 1824 when the managers responded to the complaints of the settlers, they offered not only a more flexible land policy, but significant political concessions as well.

Under the revised plan of government, the agent of the Colonization Society still retained sovereign power, but he was now to be assisted by a vice-agent chosen by the agent from among three candidates nominated by the colonists. The vice-agent, who in the circumstances was certain to be a Negro colonist, became the chief officer of the settlement in the agent's absence, and along with two other nominees approved by the agent, made up a council to advise the agent on government policy when requested. Finally, two justices of the peace appointed by the agent were to assist him with his judicial functions.[1]

These provisions, which went into effect during Ashmun's administration, established a relation between governor and governed roughly analogous with that existent at Freetown during the days of Zachary Macaulay. Important additional concessions followed, however. In 1834 the number of elective councillors was raised to six, and the council was given the power of legislating money bills and 'such laws as they may deem necessary for the general welfare'—in effect, total legislative authority. Any bill vetoed by the agent could be repassed by unanimous

[1] Huberich, *op. cit.*, I, 300–7, 317–19, 326–7, 331–5.

vote in the council, although the Board of Managers still retained the right of ultimate review. A few years later the colonists were invited to submit their recommendations for further constitutional reform, and in 1839 a new constitution was drafted, submitted to the Liberians, and duly ratified.

Patterned on American models, the constitution of 1839 provided a government approximating those of the Organized Territories of the United States. The colonial council was to be elected by universal suffrage and apportioned according to population. Its acts were subject as before to the veto of a governor appointed by the Society, but his veto could be overridden by a two-thirds vote of the legislature. Provision was made for a popularly-elected lieutenant-governor, Liberia was proclaimed a commonwealth, and the governor, though virtually under the control of the Society, was legally defined as an officer of the commonwealth and obliged to swear support for its constitution. A separate judiciary was established, and the executive and legislative branches were separated in principle, although in practice the fact that the governor was chief justice as well as the presiding officer of the council rendered this separation largely hypothetical. Ultimate governmental authority rested with the Colonization Society through its power to revoke acts of the council, but by submitting the constitution to the settlers for ratification, the Society had apparently taken the significant constitutional step of establishing a government of law based, not on fiat, but on the consent of the governed.[1]

This constitution guided the Liberian state until total independence came in 1847, but long before that moment the citizens of Liberia had been able to exercise an important influence in their own government. The first vice-agent under the régime of Jehudi Ashmun was a colonist, Lott Cary, who took over the administration when Ashmun finally returned to America in 1828, and thus became the first Negro to fill the post of chief executive officer. Another important colonial officer was John Russwurm, a West Indian who abandoned his career as a prominent abolitionist in the United States when converted to the cause of colonization, and who in 1829 emigrated to Liberia where he edited the *Liberia Herald* and filled various government posts. Perhaps the most important and influential settler of this colonial period was Joseph J. Roberts, a freedman from Virginia who emigrated to Liberia in 1829 and was soon head of a successful trading firm. His many exertions on behalf of Liberia included diplomatic and military activities and in 1841

[1] *Ibid.*, I, 456, 649–65.

THE LIBERIAN EXPERIMENT [93]

as lieutenant-governor he became chief of state when the governor, Thomas Buchanan, died. Roberts was confirmed as governor and continued in that post until Liberia became independent in 1847. Thereafter he enjoyed a long and distinguished career as president of the republic, serving intermittently in that office until shortly before his death in 1876. Aside from outstanding individuals like Roberts, there were many other settlers in public life. Since there were virtually no whites in the colony, all posts other than the appointive governor were filled by Negroes, and with the administration of Roberts even that office became permanently closed to outsiders.[1]

3 The American Negro Settler as Political Theorist – Hilary Teague

One of the most prominent of Liberia's early patriots was Hilary Teague. Like Roberts, Teague was born in Virginia, from whence his clergyman father brought the family to Africa in 1821. By the time of his arrival in Liberia, young Teague had already absorbed a liberal education and had developed religious enthusiasms which appeared to be leading to missionary work as a member of the Baptist Church. In time he did serve as minister of a Baptist congregation in Monrovia, but his chief interests over the years were to be political and journalistic. In 1835 when Russwurm left Monrovia, soon to become the governor of the independent Maryland settlement at Cape Palmas, Teague succeeded him as editor and proprietor of the *Liberia Herald*. His wide-ranging interest in both the internal and external political affairs of the country was given outlet through his editorial columns as well as through a number of official appointments in the government. In 1835 he became Colonial Secretary and four years later acted as clerk of the convention which presented the views of the colonists to the Colonization Society regarding constitutional reform. Though staunch in his loyalty to the Society, Teague was a leader of the independence party in Liberia, playing an important role in the drafting of the Declaration of Independence, in the debates of the Constitutional Convention of 1847, and in the subsequent movement for ratification. After independence, Teague served as senator in the Liberian congress, terminating his association with the *Liberia Herald* in 1849 in order to devote his full attention to public affairs. He held the position of Secretary of State at the time of his death in 1853.[2]

[1] Harry Johnston, *Liberia*, I, 150, 185; Staudenraus, *op. cit.*, 191.
[2] Huberich, *op. cit.*, I, 549, 848–9; *Liberia Herald*, Dec. 31, 1847, Aug. 31, 1849, Sept. 18, 1850, Feb. 2, Apr. 6, 1853.

As an editor, Teague helped maintain the high level of journalism which was evident throughout West Africa during the nineteenth century. His paper, which appeared variously as a monthly and semi-monthly, was weakest in its news coverage which was filled out with quantities of copy from foreign–chiefly American–journals. In his editorials, however, Teague was free to comment on local affairs and to try to shape opinion on the pressing issues of the day–economic development, native affairs, colonization from America, the slave trade, national independence and the complexities of local politics. Teague managed as well to introduce a number of special features in a paper which had to do multiple duty as source of news, moulder of public opinion, advertising medium and literary instrument. A regular column of verse, for example, reflected Teague's interest in that medium, for he had a local reputation as a poet and was the composer of the Liberian hymn of independence. From his pages comes the appealing image of a country editor, working under trying conditions but devoted to his elevated conception of the press as the servant as well as the educator and protector of a free society:

To perpetrate an editorial, he seats himself–not in the cushioned boudoir of the literate idler . . . but in a little sooty apartment of six by eight. Beneath his dingy foolscap a portion of deal . . . on an empty barrel . . . At his side an inkstand . . . the small end of a cow's horn–on his left a quiver of quills rifled from the upper surface of a porcupine . . . .

The boy comes for copy. . . . he thus begins. 'The press, the omnipotent press, is the most powerful engine which it has ever been the lot of mortals to possess. It is the scourge of tyrants . . . the Palladium of civil liberty. . . .'
'There is no cassado for breakfast, sir.'
'Well go and get some and don't bother me.'
'I have no money, sir. . . .'
'Can't you borrow some?'
'No sir: I've tried . . .'
'Well, go and collect some money. . . .'
'Mr. —— says he has no money . . . Mr. —— says he don't like the paper now . . . Mr. —— says your paper is scurrilous. Mr. —— says there is too much religion in it and too little politics. Mr. —— says there is too much politics and too little religion . . .'
'That will do . . . call again in an hour for copy. . . .'
'The ram has gnawed the roller, sir.'
'Well, cast another.'
'We have no molasses, sir.'
'Well, shut up the office, and go to dinner.'[1]

[1] E. W. Blyden, *From West Africa to Palestine*, 104–5; *Liberia Herald*, Mar. 17, 1842, Aug. 26, 1847.

Commentary of this sort, so reminiscent of the flavour of American frontier conditions during the same era, underscored the essential struggle for survival of the infant community, a subject continually in the forefront of Teague's editorial thinking. Again and again he returned to questions of the economy—how it could be strengthened, how dependency on outsiders, either in the form of American or indigenous native producers, could be minimized. The essential question was whether the wealth of the country should be based in commerce or whether local agricultural production should be the foundation of the economy. The opinion of colonizers in Europe and America at the time was overwhelmingly in favour of agriculture. Their reasoning was complex, in part involving interest in African raw materials, but also reflecting both a philanthropic desire to replace slaving with legitimate commerce and a conviction that trade was essentially uneconomic since it did not produce tangible wealth as agriculture did. In the case of Liberia, the Colonization Society directors, while applauding early expansion of trade, came increasingly to deplore the corresponding neglect of farming. As colonial agent, Ashmun had urged the importance of agriculture, and subsequent administrators in turn reported their concern over the halting progress in this direction. In 1834 it was estimated that, aside from family truck gardens and a twelve-acre coffee plantation, there were not fifty acres under cultivation throughout the colony.[1]

There is no doubt that the settlers shared little of this enthusiasm for husbandry. Despite—or perhaps because of—the fact that many had come from farms and plantations in America, there was little inclination to resume the heavy toil of farming even though land was plentiful. Instead a lively commerce by itinerant merchants and pedlars developed with the people of the interior and this exchange was supplemented by more ambitious ventures in coastal and river trade as well as international commerce, chiefly with America. In 1831, forty-six vessels visited Liberia and at about the same time the colony's imports and exports were estimated at $80,000 and $120,000 respectively. Thus, the experience of the settled communities of Senegal and Sierra Leone was repeated as the attention of the colonists remained almost exclusively concentrated on trade. Even the ruse of the bogus plantation was practised—Lott Cary's pose as the owner of a non-existent coffee plantation being reminiscent of the machinations of the counterfeit planters of St. Louis during the time of Baron Roger.[2]

[1] Huberich, *op. cit.*, I, 364–6, 418, 445.
[2] *Ibid.*, I, 423, 436; Staudenraus, *op. cit.*, 152.

Teague was thoroughly out of sympathy with these developments. He argued that prosperity could never come to a community which produced nothing, which had to import most of its provisions including foodstuffs, which exported only those local products such as camwood, ivory and palm oil harvested by the Africans of the interior, and which had little control over its exports and imports for want of a Liberian merchant fleet. Commerce made a people look abroad to the neglect of their own country, he felt. While it arranged the importation of certain improvements, it also brought vices along with a fatal reliance on unstable exchange which could suddenly shift, leaving the unwary nation destitute.

For Teague, if true independence were ever to be achieved in Liberia, there would have to be substantial local agricultural production—arrowroot, ginger, pepper, coffee and palm oil, along with such processing of crops as was locally possible. To prove his point Teague, in cooperation with several other entrepreneurs, began a soap manufactory designed, as he explained, to provide soap at reasonable prices, to make a profit for those who had exhibited this initiative, and to help cut down the drain of currency abroad. Teague also hoped for an inflow of foreign investment which, combined with Liberian labour and initiative, could assist local production and help build a prosperous country.[1]

Once the economy had been launched on a constructive course, Teague saw prospects for the end of the continual crisis in government finances. Too long the treasury had been in extremity. For example, the revenue of the commonwealth in 1845 was a mere $8,853, and this represented an increase of $678 over the preceding year. Income, deriving primarily from import duties, permitted only the most trifling disbursements—judiciary, $918; legislature, $378; prisons, $1,044; and public improvements, $2,486. At the year's end the treasury showed a balance of $989; in 1844 it had been only $201. Such figures bore eloquent testimony to the extreme weakness of the administration.

Teague's proposed solution for a chronic insufficiency of state revenue was a government monopoly of tobacco imports. A fifty per cent retail mark-up added to a one-third *ad valorem* duty on other goods would easily provide the necessary funds. Not only that, by regulating and ensuring a steady volume of goods, such controls would enable Liberian merchants to extend their operations, thus bringing greater local profits. These were utopian proposals. Without the means for

---

[1] *Liberia Herald*, Aug. 31, 1842, May 31, 1845, Feb. 19, June 4, 1847, Nov. 24, 1846; Wilson Armistead, *Calumny Refuted by Facts from Liberia*, 31–6.

enforcement, there was no hope of imposing the suggested reforms. The Liberian treasury continued its hand-to-mouth existence, culminating in the crisis of 1871 when President Edward J. Roye negotiated an international loan on terms highly unfavourable to Liberia, thus complicating the country's finances for many years thereafter.[1]

Liberia's difficulties were political as well as economic, a circumstance which Teague and other leaders recognized full well. First of all, as the colony for all its weakness became more securely established, local political differences arose, partly among the several communities which made up the nation, partly between rival factions for political power, and partly against the authority of the Colonization Society. Chronic dissatisfaction with the government of the Society periodically erupted in rioting, and occasionally resulted in major political incidents such as the departure of John Russwurm in 1835 and the banishment a few years later of John Seys, an American Negro minister with political pretensions who had hoped to supplant the administration of the Society with his own government. Teague deplored these outbursts, defending the work of the Society which he recognized as the country's major support and attacking its critics, particularly Seys who was a regular target of the *Liberia Herald*.[2]

Teague's loyalty was to the Colonization Society, not to the United States government which had studiously ignored the struggling settlement over the years. Yet when the question of the authority of the colony was brought into question along with the sovereignty of the Society under international law, Teague appeared ready to desert the Society, and approached the government at Freetown over the possibility that Liberia might join Sierra Leone as a dependant of Great Britain. Whether he made this overture on his own responsibility or by direction, it was an interesting alternative to national independence which Teague was later to support so fully. The positions were not necessarily inconsistent. Teague wanted a strong state, preferably with American help, but if that were not possible, then with British assistance. Failing that, Liberia would have to strike out on her own, seeking strength as she could through self-help and philanthropic aid, and thus fulfilling her mission as an outpost of civilization struggling against the slave trade and helping to regenerate the indigenous African. Once independence was achieved, Teague spoke confidently of extending Liberian

---

[1] Huberich, *op. cit.*, I, 784–5; *Liberia Herald*, Feb. 5, 1847.
[2] Huberich, *op. cit.*, I, 470–1, 482–3, 728; Johnston, *op. cit.*, I, 184; see for ex. *Liberia Herald*, Aug. 31, 1843.

hegemony along the coast in an effort to eradicate slave factories, a development which he saw as complementary to the work of British and French anti-slavery patrols.[1]

Teague's views on the relations between Liberian settlers and the peoples of the interior stressed native assimilation into western culture under settler tutelage and leadership. When Liberian independence had been secured and the slave trade eliminated, he visualized the new country turning to another, perhaps nobler task – 'through this colony as a channel, to regenerate this continent'. It was important, therefore, that the aboriginal Africans be dealt with fairly – that they receive appropriate compensation without fail for lands ceded to the settlers, and that in all cases they be encouraged to remain in the immigrant communities to learn the ways of civilization. In Liberia, said Teague, the oppressed of America would thus join hands with the uncultivated natives of Africa and together they would build a new nation:

> In the absence of any other place where we may rest ... our weary feet, we have adopted this as our home – the home of our posterity and the asylum of each of our persecuted race as shall be so fortunate as to escape from the land of degradation. Our object is to form a regular community to be gradually matured into a nation. It is manifest that the most ready way of effecting this object is, by elevating the character and enlightening the minds of the natives preparatory to incorporation in the body politic to swell our number and augment our strength. ... Hence it follows that the true interests of the colonists and natives are ... the same; and it should be one among our first objects to convince them of the fact.[2]

Unhappily, this point of view seemed scarcely in tune with sentiments expressed in the Liberian Declaration of Independence of which Teague was the essential author, and with several provisions of the Constitution of 1847 supported by Teague. Independence for Liberia had come about largely as a result of the unwillingness of foreign states, chiefly Britain, to recognize either the American Colonization Society or its African colony as a sovereign nation. The Society therefore agreed to Liberian independence and presented the country with a new constitution which was duly debated by a ratifying convention elected in Liberia. Teague was one of the delegates. Active in discussion, he made his chief contribution, however, when he submitted a draft Declaration

---

[1] Teague to W. Fergusson, Sept. 16, 1841, C.O. 267/166; *Liberia Herald*, Feb. 28, 1849, Sept. 18, 1850.
[2] *Liberia Herald*, Sept. 21, 1842, Sept. 5, 1845, Oct. 16, 1846, May 18, 1849.

of Independence which, with some modification, was finally adopted by the convention along with the Constitution.

In form the Declaration resembled that composed by Jefferson seventy years earlier, but in content there was little in common. Whereas the American statement proclaimed the right of revolution against tyranny supported by an inventory of royal excesses, the Liberian Declaration was essentially a listing of the reasons why the Negroes had left America, the land of their persecution. Since the new constitution already provided an instrument of government for an independent state mutually agreed upon, the Liberian Declaration had little of the relevance and urgency of its better-known predecessor. For its part, the Constitution also revealed certain similarities with the Constitution of the United States. Both Declaration and Constitution, however, contained provisions which defined the relation of the resident Africans to the settlers and to the new independent Republic of Liberia in such a way as to throw into question the assurances of equality and partnership between settler and indigenous African so often proclaimed by the editor in his *Liberia Herald*.

First of all, in the Declaration of Independence, Teague appeared to be talking exclusively about the emigrant Negroes from America. In discussing the grievances of the Liberians, he referred only to the injustices of the racial system in the United States which prompted the 'people of the Republic of Liberia [who] were originally the inhabitants of the United States of North America' to make their home in West Africa. Thus presumably the indigenous African was not included in Teague's definition of 'the people of the Republic of Liberia', and occupied some other position than the settlers in the social and political structure of the state. What this position was became somewhat clearer in the definition of civil and political rights set forth under the Constitution. 'The great object of forming these Colonies, being to provide a home for the dispersed and oppressed children of Africa, and to regenerate and enlighten this benighted continent, none but persons of color shall be admitted to citizenship in this Republic.' This seemed at once to include the indigenous Africans technically as 'persons of color', but to exclude them in so far as the purpose of the colony was to benefit the immigrant Negro, not the native of the soil. Moreover the term 'benighted continent' appeared to imply an inferior status for the local people—an indication that they would not readily receive citizenship rights solely and simply on the basis of their colour.

Such indeed was the case. During the commonwealth period between the constitutions of 1839 and 1847, neither the liberated nor the indigenous African was considered to be a citizen, but both could acquire citizenship by naturalization provided they had remained in the colony for a minimum of three years and had 'abandoned all the forms, customs, and superstitions of heathenism, and . . . conformed to the forms, customs, and habits of civilized life'. Since the Constitution of 1847 provided that all previous legislation would remain in force, this law of 1841 became the basis on which the citizenship of the native African of Liberia was determined.[1]

Clearly, Teague and other American Liberians conceived of co-operation between the settler and the native African only on terms that the latter adhere to the western social and cultural standards introduced by the immigrants. The American Negro population would automatically provide leadership for the country to which the others might respond and it was assumed that this leadership and its values were superior to anything available locally. In theory this amounted to a type of assimilation-association policy not unlike that later evolved in the French colonies. In practice, it meant the establishment of colonial rule by an oligarchy in which only a small number of native-born Africans could hope to qualify for membership. Indeed, one major channel by which the African could proceed from alienage to citizenship was the system of apprenticeship widely practised at the time. Under legislation passed during the colonial period and maintained under the republic, native children could be bound out to settlers with the understanding that they be taught a trade along with reading, writing and simple arithmetic. Hence the acquisition of citizenship frequently came to mean the prerequisite of an indenture. As for the rest of the native inhabitants, the Liberian supreme court ruled in 1862 that they were subjects of the state to be ruled by the law of the land without rights of citizenship because of 'the peculiar situation of the natives in their mode of living, their depth of ignorance and their incapability to understand the workings of civilized governments'. In some cases, however, a degree of local government was retained by treaty. It was a system of government akin to the protectorates and colonial régimes which the European powers imposed in West Africa, and it was one with which American Liberian settlers like Teague fully concurred.[2]

[1] Huberich, *op. cit.*, I, 828–32, 852–64, 865–6, II, 1030, 1051–2.
[2] *Ibid.*, I, 527–9, II, 866–7.

4 The American Negro Settler as Philosopher of African Regeneration – Alexander Crummell

By mid-century the tiny settlement of Liberia had established itself – an autonomous republic of Negroes from America, politically frail but independent, economically undernourished but slowly gaining strength. The capital, Monrovia, situated on the high slopes of the Mesurado promontory, had lost the forbidding military aspect which had characterized it in the days of Ashmun, and was now a modest community of broad grassy streets laid out with gridiron precision. The houses were of clapboard and stone, styled after American models, spaced well apart and giving out an air of repose as though the inhabitants were at home asleep. Since the streets had been surveyed but not surfaced, they were the favourite grazing ground for herds of small African cattle that, along with long-haired sheep and goats, prospered on the abundant growth of grass that covered these thoroughfares. Truck gardens were a common sight since most citizens, whatever their occupation, raised a certain amount of their own food; hence cabbages, yams and pineapple contested the ground with orange, banana, or paw paw tree. Evidence of more formal agriculture could be seen near by as well, in the form of coffee plantations, some of the trees having been planted along the borders of the streets themselves. Church buildings had been in evidence from the first days and were constantly being augmented as the population slowly expanded. This was a religious people who brought their forms of worship with them – the highly charged Methodism and Baptism of the American rural south.

Beyond the town, the Cape rose to a summit of three hundred feet from which a magnificent view could be had of both sea and land. On the ocean side were usually to be seen the Kru fishermen, their long black canoes bobbing regularly out of sight on the surface of the undulating sea, and at certain times of day fleets of them paddling rhythmically as they brought the day's catch to shore. Back on the landward side beyond the town of Monrovia, the terrain dropped down to near sea level and was covered with a dense tangle of tropical rain forest little disturbed by human cultivation. About five miles to the north of Monrovia lay the mouth of the St. Paul River, a broad estuary which gave easy access to the interior. Along the St. Paul, smaller communities had taken form – Caldwell, White Plains, Millsburg, New Settlement and others. Like their parent, they were neatly laid out usually with a single street along the river edge lined with the same quiet well-kept houses. Here, agriculture was the major activity with particular emphasis on coffee and sugar.

There were other settlements as well, strung out along three hundred miles of coast from Cape Mount to the north-west of Monrovia down to Cape Palmas where the West African coast breaks its gradual southeastern descent and turns eastward. At Cape Palmas, the colony of Maryland was a smaller replica of Monrovia and was still independent of the larger settlement, remaining aloof until 1857 when a native war almost wiped it out. In between the two were other settlements, the product of various colonizing ventures from the United States. Like Maryland, they had begun their existence separate from the larger colony but they very early found that union was necessary for survival and thus it was that Bassa Cove, New Cesters, Greenville and others joined with the Monrovia settlements to form the Commonwealth of Liberia in 1839. Having originated independently, all these settlements maintained towards one another an attitude of chronic suspicion which erupted periodically as in the dispute between Bassa Cove and Mesurado over the ratification of the Constitution of 1847.

In 1850, for all its weaknesses, Liberia appeared in many ways to be the most developed and promising of the West African colonial ventures. Its major advantage was in its population, small in numbers but consisting of individuals long accustomed to western culture, on the whole a sober Christian people deemed capable of planting in Africa a civilization which European philanthropists agreed was the necessary basis for Africa's regeneration. To be sure, Freetown was much larger but its population consisted largely of unreconstructed recaptives, and Senegal suffered from the limited numbers of its educated population. The stamp of American standards was strong on the Liberians. They not only brought with them the character of their religious worship and the style of their architecture, but aspects of daily life and habits of thought. The men dressed in severe broadcloth, and the women, who sometimes disturbed the Baptist austerity of a strait-laced Hilary Teague, indulged their weakness for finery with silk gowns of the latest fashion imported from America. When the Liberian government was formed with a constitution based on an American model, it soon occupied legislative halls where the members lounged and chatted during debates, aiming at the ubiquitous spittoons in the best tradition of the American congressmen of the day. Indeed, the Liberian settlers, many of whom were mulattoes in any case, hardly regarded themselves as Negro by comparison with the indigenous people surrounding them, while these latter invariably referred to the settlers as white men.[1]

Imports from America during these mid-century years were not only in terms of the commerce in ideas, institutions and customs. Immigrants continued to arrive in a small stream and occasionally a new group of arrivals contained an individual who was to be of more than routine interest to the new community. The outstanding example was Blyden who appeared in 1851, a young man of nineteen soon to make his presence known at the beginning of a long career devoted to West African cultural and intellectual development. Two years later another important émigré arrived from America when Alexander Crummell came to Liberia to make his home.

There was a certain superficial resemblance in the careers of these two men who were now attracted to Liberia from America. Like Blyden, Crummell was a clergyman; both, moreover, had experienced the difficulty of a black man trying to obtain an education in *ante-bellum* America. In this respect Crummell was the more fortunate. Born in New York City in 1819 of a freedman mother and a Temne father who had emigrated to the United States, Crummell found his schooling interrupted for a time when a segregationist mob put an end to the academy he was attending in New Hampshire. Other opportunities later presented themselves, however, and he was able to train himself for religious orders which were conferred upon him by the Episcopal Church in 1844. Crummell was only the second Negro to be so invested and he soon found it difficult to build a parish which would pay its way. Finally he went to England, took a degree at Cambridge University, and in 1853 arrived in Liberia, having decided to emigrate largely for reasons of health.

Crummell remained in Liberia for twenty years, becoming a Liberian citizen, and aligning himself conspicuously with those who favoured a policy of Negro emigration from the Americas to Africa. His own intellectual interests and educational background were such that it was natural that he and Blyden would gravitate towards each other. Not only were there certain similarities—and some differences—in their thinking over questions such as African colonization, racial purity, the function of Liberia or the civilizing role of religion in Africa, but they were

---

[1] For a picture of life during the early years of Liberia, see Johnston, *op. cit.*; Huberich, *op. cit.*, I, 396–7; George T. Fox, *A Memoir of the Rev. C. Colden Hoffman*, 207–14; Winwood Reade, *The African Sketch-Book*, II, 249–61; F. Harrison Rankin, *The White Man's Grave*, I, 37–8; the *Liberia Herald*, for ex. Feb. 24, 1842; William Innes, *Liberia*, 150.

long-time colleagues on the faculty of Liberia College in Monrovia. Eventually there was a falling out between the two men at the time that Blyden was forced to Freetown in 1871. Shortly after that Crummell himself was caught in political cross-currents and left Liberia permanently to return to the United States. During his later years he was Rector of a successful Episcopal church in Washington, and a tireless commentator on Negro affairs both in Africa and America. Physically a tall man of frail aspect, in his later years he developed a marked patriarchal appearance which matched both his reputation as a leader and spirited defender of the Negro community in America and a man who stood for Negro accomplishment in education, science and the arts. Characteristically, he founded in 1897, the year before his death, the American Negro Academy designed at once to promote scholarly and artistic advance and to develop an intellectual leadership among Negroes in the United States. Crummell was among those nineteenth-century Negro nationalists who were convinced that his race would never gain full acceptance until Negroes were making important and fully recognized contributions to the world's enlightenment.[1]

Alexander Crummell arrived in Liberia, a Christian priest reared and educated in the West, yet the member of a persecuted race he was determined should free itself from its Christian, western oppressors. His was the familiar dilemma of the Negro–eager to bring western cultural and material attainments to the advantage of his people but mistrustful of the source of these accomplishments, instinctively reaching out to Africa as a clergyman and a Negro while still despising it as a barbaric wilderness. Clearly he saw that the fates of Africa and the West were already completely interdependent. The question was how this interrelation might best be utilized to serve the African race.

First of all, said Crummell, there must be no shallow sentimentalizing about the respective positions of Africa and Europe on the scale of civilization. Although Europe once lived in barbarous ignorance, she had long since attained a degree of civilization which could only be admired by those less fortunately placed. Crummell's personal experience was limited to America and Britain and he consequently tended to equate western accomplishments with Anglo-Saxon political philosophy and the literary potentialities of the English language. For him

[1] John W. Cromwell, *The Negro in American History*, 130–8; 'Crummell Memorial Rectory, Sketch and Appeal', Crummell Papers; *Lagos Weekly Record*, Dec. 30, 1911; 'List of Authors Quoted with Short Biographical Sketches', Bruce Papers; E. W. Blyden to H. Venn, Sept. 16, 1871, C.M.S. CA1/o47.

the history of the English nation was the saga of a strong and proud people whose energy and resourcefulness had led them to worldwide conquest through commerce and force of arms, but whose Christian discipline transformed pride into philanthropy and whose love of liberty brought forth government by law and the guarantee of man's basic right to worship his own God, to be judged by his peers and to speak the truth without fear.

Wherever Englishmen went, Crummell continued, they brought improvement to the lot of the less fortunate. In New Zealand and South Africa they sought the regeneration of the aboriginal, in Canada they worked for the preservation of the decaying Indian, while in the United States the English spirit was the basis for a mighty religious impulse which was demanding the abolition of Negro slavery. In West Africa, English humanitarianism had already abolished the slave trade, and rehabilitated the freed slave by teaching him how better to live in the world and to prepare himself for the glories of the world to come. Peace had been introduced to a land of chronic unrest, and an improved economy through European skill and knowledge had made the establishment of peace more than an end in itself. Hence, education, Christianity, commerce and government by law had all been brought to Africa by European effort to the eternal benefit of the African.[1]

Compared with this western accomplishment, said Crummell, Africa displayed only ignorance, idolatry, licentiousness and godlessness. Not that the African people were intrinsically evil; on the contrary, Crummell knew them from personal experience to be remarkable for their symmetry, strength and beauty—a healthy, vigorous, industrious race, hospitable and honest, but weighed down by superstitious paganism and incapable of their own regeneration. Here was the nub of the matter for this American-trained clergyman. Help from the West was needed, and particularly help in the form of Christian conversion. For centuries Africa had been cut off from civilization by desert and ocean, left to decay in her own ignorance, subject only to the baleful influence of Islam with its attendant bloodshed and slavery.

If this were somewhat fanciful history, it was also orthodox missionary doctrine which Crummell was enunciating. Furthermore, he went on, no rude and heathen people such as those inhabiting West Africa could be expected to raise themselves unaided. For centuries Africa had remained a spiritual desert until the advent of Christianity in a few short

[1] Alexander Crummell, *The Future of Africa*, 9–54, esp. 22–5, 122–3; Crummell, *Africa and America*, 312–22.

generations had spread civilization along the coast and prepared to carry its message of hope into the interior. Through Christian missionary enterprise, the slave trade was abolished, churches and schools established, legitimate commerce encouraged, and political stability introduced. Nonetheless, said Crummell, the salvation of Africa would come in the final analysis, not through the white man, but through the westernized Negro.

The white man, for all his accomplishments, had many serious drawbacks – he had an ambiguous record regarding slavery and, because of physical limitations, he could not hope to remain long enough in an African environment to effect more than a bare beginning to the work of redemption. What Africa needed instead were men whose history, blood, sentiments and aspirations placed them in sympathetic proximity to those who were to be saved. 'It is evidently *not* the intention of the Almighty that the white man with stained and gory hand, shall have the honour and the blessing of saving Africa', Crummell concluded. 'This sacred glory is reserved, as compensation, to the offspring of this race who themselves have been suffering the sad inflictions of servitude in foreign lands. The children of Africa, scattered abroad in distant lands, are the indigenous agency – the men ... who are yet to accomplish the large and noble work of uplifting Africa from degradation.'[1]

Crummell's arguments had thus prepared the ground for his support of the new Negro states in West Africa – Sierra Leone, and particularly Liberia. For him, the thousands of settlers from America who had migrated to Liberia were to be the forerunner of a great imperial dream. It was they who would gather the willing natives together to teach the skills and meaning of productive labour, to introduce the elements of civilization and to bring home the blessings of Christianity. Through organized modern government and scientific knowledge, commerce and industry would summon forth the riches of the land and make the people prosperous. Already there was encouraging evidence of healthy development. Crummell pointed to the expanding production of Liberian coffee, to the great potential of sugar, cocoa and cotton. Already there was a lively trade in ivory, gold, cloth and palm oil. Those who settled in Liberia would be able to achieve both a sense of mission and a handsome profit, building a new and rewarding life for themselves

---

[1] Sermon on missionary activities in West Africa, Description of Africa and its people (MS C 23), Sermon on civilization in Africa (MS C 37 vol. C), Sermon on Redemption of Africa, Crummell to ?, Aug. 15, 1864, Crummell Papers. See also Crummell, *Africa and America*, 433–53.

THE LIBERIAN EXPERIMENT

while they helped the natives to participate in the partnership of democratic government.[1]

Such assertions by Crummell were highly misleading to say the least, for he was well aware of the true state of affairs in Liberia, racked by internal dissension, woefully underpopulated with skilled settlers, lacking capital for the economic development he described so glibly, and saddled with a weak régime unable and unwilling to bring about an effective partnership between the settlers and the indigenous population. Crummell and Blyden had been members of a commission sent to the Americas in 1861 to encourage emigration to Liberia, so that Crummell's easy assertions were more sales talk than sober conviction.

A more candid assessment of the situation in Liberia took place in 1870, a short time before Crummell returned to America. Speaking before an Independence Day gathering, he suggested that a great deal of Liberian weakness could indeed be traced to a shortsighted native policy. The Liberian settler had yielded to a false sense of superiority and ignored the native, neglecting through education to train him into productive co-operation with the immigrants. The result was a waste of local manpower and resources, a costly reliance on imported goods and chronic unrest in the unsettled interior. Crummell's admonitions were well taken, but his solutions were anti-climactic. While advocating closer attention to the needs and wants of the indigenous population, he proposed a paternalistic administration in the form of a policed protectorate, suggesting at the same time that Liberia herself might benefit similarly through the establishment of a protectorate over her territory by the United States government.[2]

Crummell displayed more imagination if not more judgment in his image of what Liberia ought to strive towards as a member of the world community. All men, he said, are ultimately dependent upon one another's efforts, and so it was with nations. Liberia might be a new, small, weak arrival among the community of states but she too had a contribution to make to the prosperity of mankind. First of all, Liberia could provide high-quality commercial products including coffee, sugar, cinnamon, hemp, flax and indigo. Secondly, and more important, Liberia had the opportunity to give the world an example of outstanding morality and rectitude in government, a democracy directed by the

[1] Address made for recruitment of American Negro settlers in Liberia, 'The Progress and Prospects of Liberia', Crummell Papers; Crummell, *The Future of Africa*, 133–7, 221–45; *Africa and America*, 421–3.
[2] *Ibid.*, 169–98.

highest dictates of honesty and honour. Such high-minded sentiments with their faint echo of Blyden might have been admissible as the expression of a new country's aspirations had they not been so out of tune with the realities of Liberian circumstances. Charity requires that they be dismissed as the excesses of independence-day oratory.[1]

Yet there was the nucleus of an idea in Crummell's hyperbole. Like Hilary Teague, Crummell was convinced of the need for the development of local industry and had engaged in at least one business venture to that end. Moreover, his hopes for Liberia were closely linked with his belief in the destiny of the black race, and this in turn rested on unmistakable achievement, on the ability of the black man to create something of quality—whether it be speciality crops or political philosophy—recognized and desired by the other peoples of the world. In this, Crummell anticipated the aspirations of the people of independent mid-twentieth-century Africa.

Throughout his life Crummell was the tireless defender of Negro accomplishment, now citing the familiar biblical arguments, now marshalling statistics on birth rate, education, commercial activity or other evidence of material advance. For, despite all his admiration for western civilization, particularly the Anglo-Saxon variety, in his central thinking he came down squarely for a valid and unique Negro identity as an integral, essential part of the world community.

This was illustrated by his stand on African colonization and the American Negro. Although he was a long-time supporter of the settlement of westernized Negroes in Africa, he did not consider colonization as the solution to the Negro problem in the United States. It could only be a partial answer because of the vast numbers involved, but, said Crummell, if colonization was not the answer, absorption was an even more absurd suggestion. 'Races have their individuality', he went on. 'That individuality is subject at all times to all the laws of race-life. That race-life, all over the globe, shows an invariable proclivity, and in every instance, to integration of blood and permanence of essence.' Thus not only was there the practical problem of integrating millions of Negroes into a white American population, but there was the psychological barrier imposed by the instinct of each race for survival and for the assertion of its own unique characteristics. In pursuing this line of argument Crummell was often accused, like Blyden, of being prejudiced against mulattoes. This was probably unfair. He felt racial purity to be natural, but in the instances where he was critical of mulattoes

[1] *The Future of Africa*, 81–8, 90–6.

he insisted it was not their colour but only their practice of passing as white men when convenient which he called into question.[1]

While enunciating a theory of racial exclusiveness, Crummell thought he saw in the Negro character elements which were both gratifying and disturbing:

> The mind of our people seems to be a hot-bed of rich, precocious, gorgeous . . . plants . . . I think I discover in it all that permanent tropical element which characterises all the people whose ancestral homes were in the southern latitudes . . . I find no fault with this tendency and bias. . . . The aesthetic tendency is a grand and opulent capital, wherewith to commence the work of responsible life and duty. It serves, up to a certain point, to deliver a people from the control of the gross and vulgar.

Love of beauty without counterbalancing masculine characteristics, however, lacked the forcefulness and robustness necessary to achievement in a race:

> It is all . . . mere unrestrained spontaneity; and spontaneity, valuable as it is, requires the restraints and limitations which come from the judgment, and which can only be furnished by imperial faculties of moral and mental nature, the conscience and Reason. . . . No people can be fed on flowers. Aesthetics, while indeed they give outward adornment, and inward delicate sensibility; tend but little to furnish that hardy muscle and grim fibre which men need in the stern battle of life; nor next do they beget that tenacity, that endurance, that positive and unwavering persistence, which is the special need of a new people.

Thus Crummell seemed to be sounding a note of what later came to be known as negritude, but in this case it was negritude rejected.[2]

For Crummell, therefore, as well as for Hilary Teague, it was the standards of the West even more than the genius of Africa which were required to ensure the success of Liberia and the prosperity of the people of West Africa. They were not alone in this sentiment. East of Liberia in the Gold Coast, another West African nationalist, Dr. James Africanus Horton, was in the process of reaching similar conclusions.

---

[1] Agreement between Crummell and E. S. Morris, Talk before the Bethel Historical Society, Crummell Papers; *West African Reporter*, Aug. 18, Dec. 1, 1883; Crummell to J. E. Bruce, Apr. 7, 1896, Jan. 21, 1898, Bruce Papers; Crummell, *Africa and America*, 39–57.
[2] Address before the students of Lincoln University, Crummell Papers.

6 Africanus Horton and Independence in West Africa

1 Ambivalent British Colonialism in West Africa

During the early decades of the nineteenth century, British policy in West Africa was uncertain and contradictory, reflecting the diverse pressures exerted upon it at home. Committed to a laissez-faire philosophy towards colonies in general, the English government sought to minimize its presence along the West African coast and to reduce the expenditures incurred on behalf of its settlements there. At the same time, the decision to abolish the slave trade in 1807 gave rise to expensive enforcement machinery and led to the support of Sierra Leone as a rehabilitation centre for recaptive Africans. Moreover, increasing missionary and mercantile interests in Africa were able to command substantial political support at home with consequent pressure on the government to extend its authority in West Africa.

The net result of these conflicting influences was a vacillating course which edged gradually towards a deepening entanglement in the affairs of West African people. Possessing at the beginning of the century only a few coastal footholds scattered from Senegambia to the Gold Coast, Britain by 1880 had come almost by accident to complex commitments in the Gambia, Sierra Leone, the Gold Coast, and what was later to become Nigeria. The Gambia remained a small trading post closely limited by surrounding French territories, but when Britain tried to exchange it with France for holdings contiguous to Sierra Leone, the move was defeated by local Gambian mercantile interests. The Freetown colony not only served its purpose as a community for liberated Africans but developed commercial activities of its own which eventually were to force England to consider the logic of controlling the trade of the interior country. Similarly, initial contacts at Lagos and in the Niger Delta area led step by step to involvement with the peoples of the Yoruba and Ibo country and beyond.

INDEPENDENCE IN WEST AFRICA [111]

Nowhere was the ambivalence of British policy more pronounced and more demoralizing to the local people than on the Gold Coast. Fluctuating relations with Ashanti, with the coastal states and with the Dutch and Danish posts, along with periodic changes in the type of government by which the British trading stations were administered, left the indigenous coastal people bewildered and disillusioned as to British friendship and support. As the nineteenth century opened, the Gold Coast fortified factories were under the control of a privately chartered company of merchants, then subsequently became the responsibility of the colonial administration based in Sierra Leone. In 1827 Britain decided to withdraw its officials from the Gold Coast and there followed another period of private administration which ended in 1843 with the resumption of direct government.

These confusing changes were paralleled by inconsistencies in the treatment of the Fanti and Ga states on the coast and the Ashanti kingdom of the interior, which further eroded confidence in the British. Strong policies were followed by weak without apparent reason, and military and political objectives rarely seemed to coincide. Though the administration of George Maclean on behalf of the trading companies during the 1830s brought a marked improvement, its effect was temporary for it did not remove the essential uncertainties of the British position, always more responsive to pressures in England than to circumstances on the Gold Coast. The resumption of direct control in 1843 had been meant to strengthen British presence on the coast and was followed shortly by the Bond of 1844, an agreement with a number of Fanti communities which outlawed 'human sacrifice and other barbarous customs', and gave jurisdiction to British courts for certain types of crimes originating in the territories surrounding the forts. Sovereignty remained with the Fanti governments, however, and subsequent British administration in the Gold Coast being neither resourceful nor consistent, faith in British protection continued to deteriorate. When in 1863 the Ashanti invaded the coastal region without provoking any opposition from the government in the forts, the coastal people virtually abandoned hope of ultimate British assistance. Two years later a special committee of the House of Commons gave official indication of England's growing disinclination to remain in Africa by recommending that all settlements in West Africa be abandoned except the useful and successful rehabilitation centre of Sierra Leone. Such a suggestion, after two hundred years of English presence on the Gold Coast, caused widespread repercussions among the coastal states, particularly the Fanti, who found themselves facing not only the prospect of dealing with future Ashanti invasions without allies, but also the necessity of achieving effective political and military union against a common enemy.

2 The Emergence of Africanus Horton

The response of West Africa to the 1865 report of the Select Committee of the House of Commons found its most forceful, constructive and articulate voice in the person of James Africanus Beale Horton, a young African doctor who had graduated from medical studies at the University of Edinburgh in 1859, accepted a commission as a Staff-Assistant Surgeon in the British Army, and returned to his native West Africa for duty. Horton combined a taste for authorship with his medical interests, finding time to publish a number of works on West African geography, climate and disease, as well as a second body of writing dealing with a broad range of social, economic and political questions touching both traditional societies and the colonial states in West Africa. These latter efforts by Horton were in direct response to the issue of independence raised by the Select Committee's report, and consisted essentially of a series of detailed suggestions as to how the Committee's conclusions might be implemented through the establishment of modern independent nations in West Africa.

The 1865 report had to a considerable extent been precipitated by conditions on the Gold Coast, and some of Horton's recommendations related specifically to the Fanti Confederation which was the attempt of the Fanti people to form an independent state in anticipation of eventual British withdrawal from the Gold Coast. Horton's ideas, however, went far beyond the problems of a single nation to embrace all of British West Africa. His army duties took him to many parts of the coast where he had the opportunity to familiarize himself with the people and their institutions and to assess their particular qualifications for independence. Beyond this he was able to set forth a number of premises and principles concerning Africa and her people against which he placed his particular recommendations. Horton's ideas were therefore much more than just a blueprint for Fanti independence. They were meant to have a universality at least throughout British West Africa, and it is in this larger context that they are best understood.

In many ways Horton was typical of his times. The abolitionist movement in Britain, looking forward to the eventual development of westernized Christian communities in West Africa, sought through evangelization and education to create the beginnings of an African middle class patterned on an English prototype. Promising young Africans like Horton were early identified and given educational opportunities which enabled them to assume positions at the head of the new movement. In such a way a native Christian pastorate was developed, and similarly a West African merchant class slowly took shape. Training in a broad range of fields, including medicine, would be needed, for it appeared unlikely to the abolitionists that Europeans could or would long remain on the coast once the slave trade had been exterminated and progressive self-sufficient communities established. Thus when the British Army became concerned about the training of African doctors for service in West Africa, the missionary schools were able to recommend qualified candidates. In such a way Horton found himself embarked on a career in medicine.

Horton's father was a recaptive from Iboland who, after rescue by the British protective squadron, had settled in one of the villages outside Freetown, earning a modest living as a carpenter. Africanus was born in 1835 and eventually found himself attending the Church Missionary Society Grammar School and Fourah Bay College in Freetown, graduating from the latter in 1853. It was at this point that Horton and two others were chosen for medical training on the recommendation of the C.M.S. authorities. Four years of study brought certification as M.D. in 1859 and resulted in the publication of his thesis, *The Medical Topography of the West Coast of Africa*. Assigned to the army medical service immediately after graduation, Horton spent the next twenty years at various stations from the Gambia to the Bights, retiring finally in 1880 with the rank of Surgeon-Major. Most of his billets, however, were in the Gold Coast, where, for example, he served with distinction in the campaign which the British conducted into Ashanti in 1873-4.

During the brief years of retirement, Horton returned to Sierra Leone and busied himself chiefly in the promotion of commercial ventures. An advocate of economic development directed by West Africans, he became interested in Gold Coast gold mines and argued for railroad construction to provide quick access to the mines from the coast. In 1883 he founded the Commercial Bank of West Africa in Freetown explaining that credit facilities, always scarce along the coast, were particularly needed by small merchants, traders, commercial farmers and industrious young men in need of capital for developmental purposes. This enterprise had no opportunity to prove its value, however, for Horton died only a few months after its opening, and with his death and the liquidation of his estate, the bank was obliged to close.[1]

3 Horton and Scientfic Racism

Horton's death at the premature age of forty-eight cut short his exertions on behalf of economic enterprise in West Africa, but his complete views on African civilization had already been set forth in his writings fifteen years earlier. In 1865 he published a pamphlet, *Political Economy of British West Africa*, briefly examining aspects of national development in the colonies of British West Africa. Three years later there appeared Horton's major work, *West African Countries and Peoples*, which embodied and expanded *Political Economy* and presented his fully developed ideas on West African societies. Finally, in 1870 the *Letters on the Political Condition of the Gold Coast* completed his commentary by applying his concepts of African independence to the specific case of the Fanti Confederation.

Like most nineteenth-century Africans educated on western principles, Horton accepted the standards he had absorbed in Europe as the unchallenged basis on which African accomplishment and shortcomings might be examined. Unlike most of the educated élite, however, he reached conclusions which argued for a substantial degree of African self-reliance and divorce from Europe. In this respect he most resembled Edward W. Blyden who was to follow Horton's lead by calling for independent initiative and character on the part of the African. The resemblance should not be overstressed, for where Blyden's logic led him to the idea of a unique African personality, Horton saw African independence primarily in the mastery by Africans of the philosophy and techniques of a European civilization which he conceded to be superior to anything which had been produced by indigenous African societies. The principle of racial equality he strongly and ably defended, but his reasoning rested not on Blyden's complementary nature of the world's races, but on his own belief in the ability of all races to absorb and utilize with equal facility the greatest achievements that civilized communities had been able to produce through the ages.

Horton began his argument where it had to begin – in a thoroughgoing

[1] *The West African Reporter*, Jan. 15, 1881, July 1, 1882, Mar. 10, Oct. 20, 1883; J. Horton to H. Venn, Sept. 20, 1860, C.M.S. CA1/0117; George Shepperson, 'An Early African Graduate', *University of Edinburgh Gazette*, no. 32, Jan., 1962, 23–6; J. A. B. Horton, *Physical and Medical Climate and Meteorology of the West Coast of Africa*, x; *The African Times*, Dec. 1, 1882.

attack on the assumptions of Negro inferiority which were being broadcast by racial anthropologists in mid-nineteenth-century Europe. The assertions were only too familiar. It was claimed that African mental development ceased with the onset of puberty whereupon the adult Negro manifested characteristics of senility and a female personality. He began to show a marked preference for sensual pleasures such as dancing and music-making; he retreated to a child-like belief in the supernatural powers of inanimate objects; he became indolent, apathetic and obstinate like an old man; and he resembled the female in his preoccupation with children, family and home. Essentially an imitator, he was unable to create, but was skilled at repetitive exercises if disinterested in the steady application of labour.

Physically the African was deemed repulsive—short and heavy-boned with hollow chest cavity, heavy facial features and a protruding pithecoid jaw. No better were the mulattoes whose unpleasant aspect worsened with age and matched a barbarous nature born of their bastard origin. Physically weak, the mulattoes were defined as the most immoral people on earth, making up for their inferiority by treachery and guile. Most of the men found employment as soldiers, but the women to their shame were almost entirely enlisted into prostitution.[1]

Horton had no difficulty in exposing such pseudo-scientific absurdities. Disciplined in biology and trained to combine objective observation with deductive-inductive logic, he pointed out first of all that the racial anthropologists rarely troubled themselves to gather their data first-hand. He himself had examined thousands of Negroes in Africa and not once did the alleged physical characteristics manifest themselves; indeed in such matters as skeleton structure and physiological maturation there were no discernible differences between the races of man to match the substantial differences between man and the lower primates. His own observations, moreover, had been confirmed repeatedly in tests by others.

It was clear, Horton continued, that the racialists were not only neglecting to perform their own experiments but were indulging in the fallacy of establishing an outstanding example of one race as the standard against which the most depressed specimens of another race were compared. Such scientific techniques were contemptible, unworthy of serious attention, said Horton. There simply was no scientific evidence of physiological and mental differences based upon race. 'I claim the

[1] J. A. B. Horton, *West African Countries and Peoples*, 37, 40-2, 53-4; *The African Times*, Apr. 23, 1866.

existence of the attribute of a common humanity in the African or negro race . . . there exist no radical distinctions between him and his more civilised *confrère* . . . . the amount of moral and intellectual endowments exhibited by him, as originally conferred by nature, is the same, or nearly so, as that found amongst the European nations.'[1]

There were, however, social and cultural distinctions to be accounted for. To begin with, Horton the cultural Eurafrican, was ready to concede primacy to European over African civilization. Many native African societies were circumscribed by ignorance and poverty, superstition and disease, while others had made substantial progress in improving their material lot. Still, none could be compared in their advancement with the peoples of Europe. But, Horton continued, this did not mean essential racial disparities, only differences in historical development. Did not the Romans report that Britons had painted their bodies, worshipped crude idols, lived in hollow trees and made the poorest slaves because of their ugliness and stupidity? Yet they had not been condemned to eternal darkness. The elements of civilization were introduced into the primitive world of the ancient Briton who in the long struggle of almost two millennia had finally attained the standards of eminence of which he was now justly proud. Meanwhile, said Horton, by the time of Britain's period of barbarism Africa had long since been a centre of learning and literature. The Greeks came to Africa in search of knowledge; Africa gave the world many of the most eminent fathers of the early Christian church; and it was Africa which helped preserve a large share of the learning of the ancient world when Rome was overrun by barbarian hordes. Once great, the people of Africa were eventually replaced by others as custodians of man's cultural treasures. Nations rose and fell, almost as if by law. Was it not reasonable to suppose that Africa's turn might come again?

The proudest kingdom in Europe was once in a state of barbarism perhaps worse than now exists amongst the tribes chiefly inhabiting the West Coast of Africa; and it is an incontrovertible axiom that what has been done can again be done. If Europe . . . has been raised to her present pitch of civilization by progressive advancement, Africa too, with a guarantee of the civilization of the north, will rise into equal importance. . . . We may well say that the present state of Western Africa is, in fact, the history of the world repeating itself.

What was more, Horton pointed out, with technological improvements in transportation and communication, Africa's regeneration would be

---

[1] *West African Countries*, 29, 37, 42–6.

far more rapid than the centuries of slow struggle which had characterized the emergence of Europe from the dark ages of her own barbarism.[1]

Historical interpretations of this sort, however, described rather than explained. It was necessary to search out the reason that lay behind the long ebb and flow of historical movement. To Horton, the explanation was obvious—differences apparent among the races of the world arose solely from the impact of external factors, in short, from environment. The history of the Negro race, said Horton, was a splendid example of the direct effect of environmental factors on cultural achievement. Depressed into slavery, the Negro like anyone else became brutalized, unresponsive, depraved. Yet in spite of the savage treatment to which he was subjected, and unlike the Indian in America, he had the stamina to survive and even to multiply. On the other hand, given the opportunity to rehabilitate himself, he quickly showed his aptitude for absorbing the benefits of civilization. The recaptives of Sierra Leone were a good case in point. They arrived in Freetown naked and abject, but after a few months of supervision were able to make substantial progress. They learned to read and write; they cultivated their own land and mastered a useful craft; they replaced ancient superstitions with Christian worship; and they began to guide their actions towards each other on the basis of Christian ideas of justice, charity, fraternity and equality. Soon, Horton continued, they were extending themselves into large-scale mercantile enterprise, building substantial homes, importing the elements of a civilized daily life, expanding their capacity for education and responding to man's basic desire to manage his own political affairs.[2]

In stressing the importance of environment, Horton seems to have hypothesized an inheritance of biological traits through the repeated impact of environmental factors. This Lamarckian approach in a pre-Mendelian era he illustrated in several ways. In West Africa, for example, he suggested that excessive tropical heat brought on a progressive darkening of the skin, which over generations was transmitted to offspring. Horton did not go to the extent of attributing mental qualities to the inheritance of characteristics shaped by environment but he did propose that certain Negro physical characteristics were caused by external factors when reapplied countless times. In particular he cited the custom of African mothers in carrying their babies 'doubled up...

---

[1] *Ibid.*, 1–11, 30–1, 66–8; *The African Times*, Apr. 23, 1866; Horton, *Letters on the Political Condition of the Gold Coast*, i–ii.
[2] *West African Countries*, 28–9, 51–2, 60.

for hours at a time, their head and face pressed in the concavity of the back, the hands and feet twisted up . . . Is this not a system', Horton asked rhetorically, 'which, when persistently acted on, in the young and delicate frame, must lead to fearful deformity?' Possibly more serious was the debasing practice of forcing young girls to petty merchandising and heavy field work. In this way they fell into habits of coarse and filthy speech, of licentious conduct, and of vagrant tastes which ill fitted them for eventual domestic responsibilities. But even worse than the effect on moral character were the inherited consequences in physical deformity. 'I have noticed that girls who have been exposed to hard labour in a nation, are generally the most ill-formed', Horton observed, concluding sadly, '. . . this acting prejudicially from generation to generation, leads to those abnormal developments for which anthropologists of this age have so much denounced a whole race.'[1]

If therefore racial improvement could be effected through an altered environment, it followed for Horton that a concerted effort by Africans and European philanthropists would succeed in introducing the elements of civilization to Africa and help to establish independent communities comparable with Europe's own. All the factors pointed in the same direction. Europeans could not for reasons of health live permanently in Africa. The African race was celebrated for its ability to survive and the African for his powers of adaptation to alien cultures. Great progress had already been made in a few short years by a handful of missionaries in the introduction of Christian civilization. It was necessary therefore that the rising generation of West Africans work hard to consolidate and extend the gains already made, once the process of regeneration had been started by European initiative.[2]

Above all, Horton admonished, there must be no concession to the 'jejune and barren generalization' of the racial anthropologists that 'British civilization and Christian influences have demoralized the native African—that, in fact, these institutions were the chimera of a mistaken philanthropy', and that it was a serious mistake to introduce the African to European cultural influences. Observers like Captain Burton claimed that traditional African states such as Benin were tough and honourable though crude, whereas the liberated Africans of Sierra Leone were immoral prating knaves whose malign influence tended to depress the rest of West Africa.

[1] Horton, *Physical and Medical Climate and Meteorology of the West Coast of Africa*, 66–9; *West African Countries*, 57–8.
[2] Ibid., 73–4, 176, 273–7.

This was a highly prejudiced view, Horton insisted, put forward by a notorious antagonist of the Negro towards whom he was invariably 'personally abusive, turgidly illustrative, and illogically argumentative'. No doubt, there were rogues in Sierra Leone as there were anywhere in the world, Horton continued, but there were many estimable citizens whose good works far outweighed the shortcomings of the few. The recaptives had spread along the coast, occupying positions of trust in both the civil and military services, and helping to encourage economic growth through their energetic merchandising. Their industry and sense of adventure were just the characteristics needed for West African development; in this respect Horton thought they much resembled the English who had spread throughout the world in search of economic gain and had brought their civilizing influences with them. He could only hope, therefore, that European philanthropy would not flag, that Englishmen would not become snared in the trap. 'If we can find men here who oppose the preaching of the Gospel', Horton warned, 'how much more must we expect to find men strongly in opposition to matters that will raise the African to a people.... I am certain that the [English] Government will not allow individual prejudices to prevent them from continuing in this most noble undertaking.' Rejecting Burton, Horton could no more easily accept Blyden's contention that the European rule of Sierra Leone had throttled the development of civilization in that country. To a man of Horton's thinking, Blyden's view was but Burton's view, with vice turned to virtue.[1]

Having established the primacy of environmental factors and the need for western Christian civilization in West Africa, Horton proceeded to explain how this process might be carried out. Naturally much depended on economic development, an area in which Africa had no need to lag. The African was acquisitive by nature, said Horton, anxious to save and ambitious to rise in the world. The Sierra Leone merchant class was already demonstrating the innate African propensity for trade, and it was to be hoped that to commerce might also be added the fruits of agriculture. With the exception of certain pockets like the arid Accra plain, the soil of West Africa was rich and could sustain a wide range of valuable crops. Aside from palm products and cotton, Horton urged special attention to coffee, tea, indigo, pepper and cloves. Better methods of husbandry added to hard work would develop the

---

[1] *Ibid.*, 27, 41, 61–2, 269–70; R. F. Burton, *Wanderings in West Africa*, I, 266–8; Horton, to Resident and Members of the Educational Committee of the War Office, May 13, 1862, C.M.S. CA1/0117.

immense riches of the country. Beneath the surface were the precious metals, which could be of much value in rehabilitating West Africa and particularly so when brought forth through local enterprise.[1]

In the final analysis, however, Horton's chief agent for African development was education, and in this area it would seem that his views were in large measure a reflection of his personal experience. Having himself risen to a position of influence and responsibility through educational opportunity, Horton was steadfast in urging expansion of school systems. He had scarcely returned to West Africa at the conclusion of his own medical studies when he was proposing to the authorities the establishment of an introductory medical school in Sierra Leone which might precede final training in Britain. Students already proficient in the classics and mathematics would receive instruction in anatomy, physiology, chemistry, natural history, pharmacy, hospital practice, as well as the botany of Africa. The school would be under the direction of an African doctor, and at one time Horton suggested himself for the post. The advantages were evident–West African medical services would gradually become the responsibility of educated African doctors who, native to the coast, would remain in the area working in sympathetic harmony with the people, and conducting long-range research in tropical medicine. As it happened, Horton's proposal was not seriously considered, for the authorities had reached the conclusion that African doctors were unacceptable both to the Europeans and to the educated Africans on the coast. Horton's medical competence was never questioned but his own career was complicated by racial prejudice and this in turn led to a decision to discontinue the systematic training of native African physicians.[2]

Horton's demand for medical training, however, was but a part of larger educational objectives. 'The improvement of the West Coast of Africa', he argued in pressing the British government for his medical school, '... can never be properly accomplished except by the educated native portion of the community ... the more the educated portion of the inhabitants is increased, the more will the rise of the other portion be made evident and the more so will impartial judges be able to prove the capabilities of the African.' Thus it was not surprising to find Horton advocating broad advances in several aspects of education. At one time he had been instrumental in the establishment of a school for

[1] *West African Countries*, 22; *The African Times*, May 23, 1864, Jan. 2, 1882.
[2] *West African Countries*, 46–50 n.; C. O'Callaghan to Director General, Army Medical Dept., Dec. 13, 1861, E. Lugard to Horton, June 19, 1862, C.M.S. CA1/0117.

native children, and after his death it was revealed that his will contained provision for the endowment of a secondary school to be devoted primarily to the sciences. In 1870 Horton, who had been complaining about the poor schools in the Gold Coast, was invited by the government to submit plans for their reform. His response was a scheme involving a system of primary schools in the principal seaport towns, an academy at Cape Coast for teacher training, a higher quality staff, and a board of education with citizen representation. In the day schools the curriculum would consist of English grammar, arithmetic and geography. The high school would add elementary Latin and Greek, geometry, botany, mineralogy and music. As with Horton's proposals for medical education, this plan was given a rough reception, not on its merits but because of political stresses arising out of the Fanti Confederation movement.[1]

At various times Horton made other suggestions in the field of education—for example his proposals for vocational training—but his outstanding contribution was his scheme for a university in West Africa. As early as 1862 he had recommended such a move and was probably the first public figure in West Africa to do so. What he urged was a university staffed by recognized authorities, to be located centrally in Sierra Leone but to serve and be supported by all the colonies. Its curriculum was to include classics, English language and literature, modern European languages, Hebrew, history, philosophy and education. In addition, special attention was to be given to the physical sciences and mathematics 'which are closely connected with our daily wants and conveniences . . . and cure many defects in the wit and intellectual faculties'. There were practical considerations as well:

Africa is considered as one of the richest mineral-producing countries in the world . . . The fields and forests in Africa abound with vast commercial and medical plants of untold importance and whom have we to work steadily at their discovery . . . none but persons whose native stamina has fitted them supremely to encounter the pernicious influences of the climate. The minute geological stratification of the coast has never yet gone through the scrutinizing investigation of a master geologist . . . The study of physiology and chemistry . . . is entirely unknown to natives on the coast . . . Do we not find that the greatness of civilized countries, depend on the development and practical application of these studies. And to whom then must Africa look for the

---

[1] Horton to President and Members of the Educational Committee of the War Office, Nov. 13, 1863, Horton to H. Venn, Dec. 7, 1864, C.M.S. CA1/0117; Fyfe, *A History of Sierra Leone*, 472; *Letters on the Political Condition of the Gold Coast*, 142–6, *The Gold Coast Leader*, Sept. 10, 1904; A. Kennedy to Earl of Kimberley, Jan. 25, 1871, C.O. 96/87.

ultimate development of her vast resources, and in what school are the majority of those who would be called upon to act their part in regenerated Africa be taught?[1]

4 A Blueprint for West African Independence

These were the basic conditions which Horton felt were prerequisite to political independence. The people of West Africa were physically and intellectually qualified to take their place among the civilized communities of the world. British philanthropy had introduced the advantages of the West, and those Africans who had been exposed had demonstrated the progress that could be made in a few short years. Westernization through economic development and education would soon take firm root, and West Africa under the leadership of its educated classes would be ready for independence. To Horton, this was the message contained in the report of the Select Committee of the House of Commons, and he was prepared to add substance to the Committee's recommendations by offering specific suggestions as to the type of political organization best suited to the character of these emerging communities.

Horton began his survey with the Gambia which he felt to be least prepared for political independence, not so much because of a want of capacity for self-government but because of a need for material development. The colony was small and sparsely populated with people of different tribes lacking common interests and loyalties; it was composed of a number of small isolated villages along the Gambia River which would have great difficulty in defending themselves against the attacks of the energetic surrounding tribes. It needed, therefore, a consolidation of these communities into larger defensible units, the encouragement of cotton, indigo and fibres to supplement the ground-nut trade, a schooner which could double as warship and river trader, an improved school system, a savings bank with limited commercial functions and better public health facilities. Once the colony's economy had been assured and its safety secured against attack, the time for independence would have arrived. In this case, the most appropriate form of government would be a monarchy with the king chosen by universal suffrage.[2]

Horton pointed out that, although Liberia had already provided a successful experiment in West African self-government, it was Sierra Leone which had shown the most promise for self-direction. The Free-

[1] *West African Countries*, 201-4, 213-14, 257; T. J. Thompson, *The Jubilee and Centenary Volume of Fourah Bay College*, 54-6.
[2] *West African Countries*, 81-6, 230-42.

town colony had begun life uncertainly with the immigration of the Maroon and Nova Scotian settlers, but these people had long since been supplanted by the sober and substantial liberated Africans in whose hands the future progress of Sierra Leone clearly rested. They were an energetic people—talented in commerce, law-abiding, prosperous and eager for education. Already 22 per cent of the Sierra Leone population had schooling compared with only 13 per cent in England and 16 per cent in Prussia. The colony had excellent harbours and navigable rivers, and an abundance of produce for export. Of course, a good deal still needed to be done—public works designed to facilitate trade, the encouragement of agriculture which still lagged because of its association in the minds of the people with slave labour, improved public health facilities in the cities, and particularly a more vigorous policing policy in the interior to protect the lives and property of Sierra Leone merchants. For Sierra Leone, Horton recommended a monarchy, the ruler to be chosen by universal suffrage but backed up by a popularly elected assembly with membership limited by property and educational qualifications. In addition there would be an upper chamber of senators chosen by the king, either for life or for an extended term. Internal stability would be the immediate domestic programme of the administration, and annexation of neighbouring territories for the protection and support of Sierra Leone merchants would constitute an initial foreign policy. The result would be a strong independent constitutional monarchy ready to take the lead in African regeneration:

It is evident that there is growing at Sierra Leone an enlightened population, and that under the fostering care of the mother Government the people can, within a short time, be left to govern themselves; that with an enlightened monarch, elected by universal suffrage, and an efficient legislation, the African element, so essential to African civilization, will receive a powerful impetus to intelligent progress, and then will Sierra Leone be able to compete with Liberia in virtuous emulation towards progressive civilization, and in endeavours to raise their much-abused race and country in the scale of civilized nations.[1]

Far down the coast in Yorubaland the situation was somewhat different, but not without promise. To begin with, Horton took issue with those who indicted Britain for high-handed and unnecessary intervention in the annexation of Lagos. Lamentable as was the use of force, he felt the results achieved more than offset the arbitrary means adopted. It was, after all, British administration which had been responsible for

[1] *Ibid.*, 12–19, 28–9, 87–8, 97–103, 199–229.

the cultural advance of Lagos, the increase of commerce, the improvement of sanitary conditions, the intellectual development of the people and the civilizing effect on neighbouring kingdoms. Horton stated without hesitation 'that it was the greatest blessing that could have happened to Lagos and the whole of the Yoruba . . . that such a responsible, civilized, and powerful government should have at that opportune moment commenced her regeneration. . . . Lagos is . . . a star from which must radiate the refulgent rays of civilization into the interior of the Yoruba . . . Country.'[1]

The importance of Lagos lay, therefore, not only in the fact that a major West African port had been exposed to westernizing influences, but that the Yoruba country behind with its energetic intelligent people and its rich resources also stood to gain in several important respects. In the first place, said Horton, the occupation of Lagos meant its end as a slave port, and would indirectly lead to a decline of warfare and slave raiding among the Yoruba up country. This in turn would free the energies of the people for peaceful trade in the many agricultural products which came from the rich land.

Furthermore, a European presence at Lagos would have useful political effects. For some time, educated Africans from Sierra Leone had been migrating back to their homeland in the Yoruba country and numbers of these had settled in the booming town of Abeokuta. While they had already rendered great service to the traditional governments in Abeokuta, it was chiefly after the arrival of Christian European power in Lagos that these educated immigrants had initiated radically different and important changes in the local structure of government. Under the leadership of George W. Johnson they had reformed the administration and sought to control trade between Abeokuta and Lagos in an effort to secure a steady revenue and to modernize the inefficient government of the traditional authorities. It was true that in 1867 there had been an outbreak against Christian missionaries in Abeokuta in which Johnson had been implicated, but this was caused by over-zealous heathen chiefs and hopefully would not constitute a permanent setback. Abeokuta, said Horton, was a natural capital for a united Yorubaland, but as yet the country was too undeveloped economically and too disordered politically, to be ready for independence and unity. Perhaps some day Abeokuta could be the chief centre of a strong power, but until that time it was well that the stabilizing influence of British power remained on the coast.[2]

[1] *Ibid.*, 158-9.   [2] *Ibid.*, 166-70.

Horton admittedly had spent only a brief time in Lagos and probably had never visited the Yoruba country. Judging from his comments about the Ibo, his knowledge of these people was similarly restricted. He classified as Ibo all the people living east of the Niger and south of the Benue as far as Old Calabar. Though there were local variations in language and appearance, he hypothesized a strong Judaic element in the population, introduced at an earlier date, probably as a result of the pressures exerted by the Muslim invasions in North Africa. Indeed, Horton suggested, it was likely that these Hebrew immigrants were remnants of the Lost Tribes of Israel, and he saw strong characteristics in Ibo language and religious practices to support this view. Thus, though the Ibo comprised numerous independent tribes, there was a unifying national spirit which might serve to bind together a progressive independent nation at some future time. Since the main buttress of the economy would be the export of local products, Horton thought the capital of such a state ought to be a port town like Bonny. For chief executive he recommended an elected king, preferably an outsider because of local jealousies. State revenue could most easily be raised through the regulation of trade. True to form, Horton proposed an extensive school system and sytematic encouragement of agricultural production. Because the people were not advanced in terms of European civilization, Horton thought the monarchy ought to be absolute, not only for effective rule, but to encourage the smaller interior Ibo groups to gravitate to the main seaboard government for protection, thereby encouraging the development of a large unified nation. Finally, every effort should be made to encourage the immigration of educated foreigners, for Horton believed no nation was capable of civilizing itself, while among the imitative Ibo such a move would doubtless be useful. With a promising start along these lines, Horton concluded, the eventual emergence of a mature progressive Ibo empire would be assured.[1]

5 *Horton and British Policy on the Gold Coast*

If the 1865 report of the Select Committee had been stimulated largely by conditions on the Gold Coast, it was on the Gold Coast that Horton's suggestions for political independence came closest to realization. First of all, the Committee's report seemed to say to the Gold Coast people that Britain was withdrawing its influence from the country. Then in 1868 the Dutch and English exchanged a number of their forts which

[1] *Ibid.*, 171–98.

had been interspersed among one another, primarily to increase administrative efficiency and establish unbroken stretches of coast under the authority of each state. However, this move upset the power balance among the coastal states and with Ashanti, thus stimulating the Fanti to consider independent united action. When Horton's *West African Countries* appeared later in the same year, it was a direct answer to questions already being asked as to how the local people might deal with local problems through unity and co-operation and without British assistance which had been uncertain in the past and promised greater uncertainties in the future.

Horton offered a formula for the Gold Coast similar to his recommendations for the other West African communities. Most of the Gold Coast people he regarded as backward by European standards, but the transfer of territory between the Dutch and British had opened the possibility for the formation of strong states under British suzerainty, and such states could provide the basis for eventual independent progressive nations. Moreover the need was immediate, for unity was compelled by the constant threat of Ashanti invasion. In the west, therefore, the Fanti communities might form a monarchy with the king either elected or nominated by the British governor. What was more important was that he be a ruler of wisdom and learning-in short, an educated African-and that he have the assistance of an advisory council consisting both of responsible chiefs and members of the educated class in the coastal towns. In the east the general formula was the same though the details differed somewhat. Horton recommended a republic with Accra as its capital, suggesting that in place of a king there be a president nominated by the colonial administration and ratified by popular vote. As with the Fanti kingdom, the essential character of the state was to be strength and unity, and Horton expressed the hope that local chiefdoms might gradually vanish before the greater efficiency of constitutional government. Immediate independence could not be possible in light of local political divisions, particularly among the Fanti; consequently it was necessary that British authority remain on the coast to protect and advise, else 'confusion, massacre, and bloodshed would be the inevitable result'.[1]

Because of the vagaries of British policy, Horton saw serious difficulties in the realization of his recommendations. What was needed was a clear, strong and consistent policy, but what had developed instead was a succession of contradictions and paradoxes. First, there were

[1] *Ibid.*, 124-7, 135-8, 151.

proclamations to the effect that British authority did not extend beyond the confines of the forts, but this was quickly followed by arbitrary fines for alleged offences committed outside the forts. Next, there was a bewildering succession of governors—seven within the five years 1862–1867—with each incumbent more intent upon the pursuit of his own plans than on developing consistent and constructive objectives for the country. Finally, the territory beyond the forts had long been regarded as a protectorate brought into being by agreement between England and the coastal nations—equally sovereign states; yet the freedom and sovereignty of these local states had been compromised by the Dutch-English transfer of territory which took place without so much as a formal notification for the governments affected.[1]

Indeed, said Horton, British policy had for some years been nothing short of appalling. The people had been told repeatedly that they could expect no assistance from the British against Ashanti attack, and the military record seemed to bear this out. When this abdication of responsibility was followed by the exchange of British and Dutch forts, the Fanti quite naturally resolved to band together in a defensive league to protect themselves against further Ashanti invasion. Under these changing circumstances, Horton urged the British administration to re-examine its objectives and re-employ its resources towards the eventual establishment of strong independent African states on the coast.

He made a number of specific suggestions. First of all, Horton recommended governors of tact and resolution who could act with firmness but whose judgment would always be rooted in common sense and directed to further the interests of the local people. Secondly, he suggested that total Dutch withdrawal from the coast would be desirable in light of the unrest created by the transfer of the forts and the consequent fear by the Fanti that the Dutch might permit an Ashanti attack on the coastal communities. Further, Horton made his usual plea for the expansion of educational opportunity. Finally, he reminded the administration that if political and social progress were ever to take place in the interior, it would have to come by means of machinery along the lines of the Fanti Confederation which had been formed at the time of the Dutch-English transfer. Such a union would overcome ancient feudal confusion; it would bring unity against outside attack; it would introduce the beginning of efficient, modern government; it would bring a healthy alliance of chiefly authority and educated African; and it would

---

[1] *Ibid.*, 243–5; *Letters on the Political Conidtion of the Gold Coast*, 22, 26–7.

create an efficient national treasury. Hence the British government would be well served to encourage a free people in their search for efficient government in the interests of peace and plenty in the land.[1] These recommendations quickly became obsolete before the march of events. Despite the views of the Select Committee of the House of Commons, the realities of British presence on the Gold Coast pointed to increasing, not decreasing, involvement. The disinclination of successive British administrators on the ground to refrain from interfering in local affairs, the transfer of the remaining Dutch forts to Britain in 1872, and the growing realization in London that only British power could deal effectively with Ashanti, all militated against Horton's proposals. The Fanti Confederation, which had taken shape along lines suggested by Horton, ran into immediate opposition from the British administration, and Horton was accused of having been a ringleader in the confederation movement and an opponent of the original British-Dutch territorial transfer. With the campaign against Ashanti in 1873-4, the British policy solidified. Instead of countenancing a local federation as the prelude to independence, Britain proclaimed a protectorate and colony in the Gold Coast wherein she would henceforth exercise full governmental powers. With this move, even the dream of independence expired.[2]

6 *The Significance of Africanus Horton*

It is difficult to judge how much Horton may have entertained serious hope for the establishment of successful independence movements in West Africa, and how much he was preoccupied merely with laying down guide lines for a distant future. Viewed as a blueprint for action, his proposals lacked practicality, limited as they often were by insubstantial, inaccurate information and fanciful notions of human motivation and political behaviour. His plans tended towards the grandiose schemes of the dreamer, and there is evidence that he allowed himself to be swayed by dreams even when the information in his possession should have dictated different conclusions. For example, his proposals for the establishment of medical training in West Africa lacked realism under the circumstances of growing racial prejudice of which Horton was only too well aware. Again, his application in 1872 for the position

[1] *Ibid.*, 24–31, 73–90, 136–67.
[2] David Kimble, *A Political History of Ghana, 1850–1928*, 222–63; A. Kennedy to Earl of Kimberley, Jan. 25, 1871, C.O. 96/87.

of administrator, the chief executive in the Gold Coast, revealed a nature impervious to the running of the tides of official British opinion.

Viewed from another perspective, however, his arguments may be regarded as the ideals of an African nationalist, living well ahead of his time, far enough ahead perhaps to grasp the vision of the future. His proposals for a West African university were remarkably prophetic of what finally emerged, more so than the recommendations of later advocates including the formidable Blyden. If he failed to anticipate some of the details of subsequent state formation in West Africa, he certainly caught the substance of the dream of independence, and forecast to a remarkable degree the events that followed—colonial tutelage, the widespread intrusion of European influence, the rise of an educated westernized leadership, and the ultimate marriage of alien and native culture and institutions in the free nations of West Africa which emerged in the mid-twentieth century.[1]

[1] J. Pope Hennessy to Earl of Kimberley, Oct. 24, 1872, C.O. 96/94.

7 Mid-Century Freetown: The African Bourgeoisie

1 *The Liberated Africans in Sierra Leone*

Even in its earliest days, the Sierra Leone colony that was to produce Africanus Horton had begun to take on some of the characteristics of the English Protestant middle-class society which had brought it into being. The Nova Scotians certainly had their differences with the administration of the Sierra Leone Company, but these were a reflection of their unhappy history, not a fundamental repudiation of a social system. The settlers were Christian in their faith and in their moral, ethical outlook, and they accepted Britain as their saviour as well as a standard for social and political behaviour. They saw little or no kinship with the people of the native tribes surrounding them; these were but rude savages into whose dismal world an element of civilization had been introduced through the medium of the colonists from Nova Scotia.

The Nova Scotians were few in number even with the addition of the Maroons, and it may be doubted that the Freetown community could have grown and prospered had it not been for another and far more important immigration which followed from another source. The abolition of the slave trade in 1807 was accompanied by enforcement through naval patrols, and before long British cruisers were intercepting slave ships off the West African coast and confiscating their cargoes. The problem of how to deal with these rescued slaves was solved by converting the colony of Sierra Leone into a rehabilitation centre where slaves were deposited, emancipated and resettled. The great majority of them chose to remain in Sierra Leone so that in a few short years the size and the make-up of the population of Freetown and the network of villages which grew up around the city were greatly changed. Though statistics are not always complete and accurate, it is estimated that up to 1845, more than 75,000 slaves were put down and emancipated at

THE AFRICAN BOURGEOISIE [131]

Freetown, and by the middle of the century Sierra Leone contained over 40,000 of these liberated Africans. Most of them came from the Slave Coast to the east—Hausa, Ibo and a scattering of others, but chiefly Yoruba, for the civil wars which broke out afresh among the Yoruba people in 1821 soon brought substantial numbers to the baracoons at Lagos and Badagry, and for the fortunate, to ultimate capture by the British protective squadron and a new life of freedom in Sierra Leone.[1]

Though the Sierra Leone colony was turned over to the British crown in 1808, the abolitionists continued for some years to maintain a preponderant voice in its administration. Through the African Institution the leaders of the defunct Sierra Leone Company could advise a government little interested in its newly-acquired possession, while missionary societies established themselves in the colony to begin the task of Christian conversion. Consequently the new immigrants, fresh from an alien African way of life, were subjected immediately to new influences from the West, and beginning a new life from scratch, they were willing to do so with standards suggested by those who had delivered them from a life of slavery. English was attempted as a lingua franca, the elements and the spirit of Christianity gradually took hold, and the old way of life was correspondingly weakened. Most of the newcomers began as labourers or apprentices to traders and artisans in Freetown or as members of the farming communities which surrounded the city. In time, those with the requisite energy, enterprise or good fortune rose to become petty traders and small shopkeepers while others, even more successful, developed careers as shippers or merchants, possessing spacious houses filled with furniture from Europe, substantial holdings of real estate and a growing stature as leading citizens in the community. Some were early recruited by the English missionary societies for theological training which occasionally led to teaching as well as the ministry. Eventually other professions made their appearance, particularly law and to a lesser extent medicine. Everywhere Christian worship became standard, and European schooling was much sought after so that a degree of literacy spread quickly, particularly among the children.[2]

A contemporary account gives a fair picture of the aspirations and achievements of these early recaptives:

... a leading feature in the character of the liberated Africans is their great love of money. But this, though remarkable, is by no means of that

[1] R.R. Kuczynski, *Demographic Survey of the British Colonial Empire*, I, 96, 101.
[2] A. B. C. Sibthorpe, *The History of Sierra Leone*, 52–6; Christopher Fyfe, *A History of Sierra Leone*, 305. See below, pp. 266–9.

sordid nature which induces the miser to hoard up his wealth for its own sake. On the contrary, their whole surplus means are devoted to the increase of their domestic comforts and the improvement of their outward appearance of respectability. A comfortable house is the first great object of their desire. For this they are content to labour at any sort of work, and turn themselves diligently and cheerfully to any honest means of earning money. . . . Of the liberated Africans as a body, it may with great truth be said that there is not a more quiet, inoffensive, and good humoured population on the face of the earth. Of their religious spirit it is not easy . . . to form a decided opinion, but I know that their outward observance of the Sabbath-day is most exemplary. On that day the passion for amusements is altogether laid aside, and the whole body of the people are to be found at one or other of the churches or chapels, which abound in the colony.[1]

At first the recaptives suffered the fate of all immigrants-to be despised, ridiculed and exploited by those who had preceded them. Thus were the newcomers treated by the Nova Scotian and Maroon settlers, but their numbers and their energy more than made up for initial shortcomings so that by mid-century, in scarcely more than a generation, it was the liberated Africans, not the settlers, who were the colony's economic and social sinew and who were producing the present and future leaders of the Sierra Leone community.

2 *The Educated African and Economic Development*

The fundamental ethic which came to characterize the Freetown of the liberated Africans was essentially the same as that which governed the standards of the colony's godfathers – the abolitionist and humanitarian reformers of Victorian England. These latter, recruited from among the rising commercial and industrial segments of the British population, were confirmed in the efficacy of a free economy which prospered through the initiative and industry of England's business leaders, and which enabled these same community leaders to indulge in good works such as the regeneration of the primitive African. Taken over in Sierra Leone, this philosophy produced traders and merchants who became sturdy lay members of the local Protestant churches, and who were interested in establishing a bridgehead of European liberal Christian culture in West Africa, from whence through trade and missionary activity the rest of the continent might gradually be brought under the benign influence of the civilization they themselves had embraced.

---

[1] William Fergusson quoted in T. F. Buxton, *The African Slave Trade and Its Remedy*, 373–4.

THE AFRICAN BOURGEOISIE

Called 'assimilation' in Senegal where it was consciously practised as such, this policy unconsciously pursued in Sierra Leone succeeded in producing 'educated Africans' virtually indistinguishable in their standards of behaviour, in their ethical and moral judgments, in their economic goals and in their attitudes towards the African hinterland, from the Englishmen who had been responsible for their training and who were their inspiration.

Such men were conspicuous among the more successful merchants. John Ezzidio was one of the earliest examples, a Nupe recaptive who arrived in the colony in 1827, who rose by his own exertions to become a prominent merchant and Wesleyan lay preacher, and who was the first African to be appointed to the new Legislative Council formed in 1863. Others included Emmanuel Cline, a successful Hausa real estate operator, and William Henry Pratt, an Ibo businessman who like Ezzidio was also a lay preacher in the Wesleyan Church. This process, started early, continued into the second generation—witness William Grant, born in Sierra Leone in 1831 of Ibo stock, who rose through ability, self-help and hard work in the best traditions of the time to become one of Freetown's leading businessmen and devoted churchgoers. Grant was a respected figure in Freetown society, listened to not only by the people of the colony but by its government as well, which was more than happy to have him join Ezzidio as an unofficial member of the Legislative Council in 1869.[1]

By no means all the representatives of this rising African bourgeois society were merchants; there was a small but important professional class and a growing number of civil servants, some occupying high posts in the local government. Neither were they all necessarily recaptives, for some of the most influential were West Indians who had made their way to Sierra Leone for various reasons and had remained to pass important years of their lives there. What they did hold in common, however, was belief in the importance of individual initiative, of personal rectitude, of social responsibility and of the necessity for leading Africa out of the darkness of her ignorance through the medium of western Christian civilization.

An early though representative member of this class was William Fergusson who in 1845 was appointed governor of Sierra Leone, the first Negro to hold such a post in the Freetown colony. A West Indian by birth, Fergusson had studied medicine at Edinburgh University and

---

[1] Fyfe, *op. cit.*, 231–2; see also Fyfe, 'The Life and Times of John Ezzidio', *Sierra Leone Studies*, n.s., no. 4, June, 1955, 213–23.

began his long career in West Africa in about 1814 after qualifying as an army physician. Joining the colonial establishment a year later, he ultimately rose to the position of senior military medical officer, and then in 1841 he was made acting governor. For a time he was used to fill the gaps between permanent appointments to the governorship arriving from England, but finally Fergusson was elevated to that post in his own right, serving throughout 1845 until ill health forced his retirement. Altogether he was in charge of the colony's affairs for a total of two years, during which time, though aware that he was on trial as a black man uniquely placed in such a high position, he conducted a vigorous though judicious administration.[1]

In his early years Fergusson had been a protégé of the African Institution and consequently was well known to its secretary, Zachary Macaulay, and to other prominent abolitionists. How much influence they may have had on his thinking is not known, but his observations concerning the economic development of Sierra Leone closely paralleled early abolitionist ideas on that subject and were of assistance to Thomas Buxton in Buxton's crusade to bring about the end of the slave trade by offering indigenous chiefs more lucrative commercial alternatives. Fergusson, however, began his argument not with Buxton's indigenous societies but with the liberated Africans of Sierra Leone. Greatly admiring them for their industry, he nonetheless felt they had concentrated their efforts far too exclusively on commerce to the neglect of other pursuits, notably agriculture. The health of the colony, he was convinced, depended upon diversification, and a proper balance between trade and agriculture. There were many crops to be encouraged – cotton, arrowroot, coffee, pepper and palm products. The recaptives needed only the encouragement and instruction of model farms and marketing aids to convert their natural energies and efficiency to the successful pursuit of commercial agriculture. Not only would this development contribute to the sound growth of the colony, he wrote to Buxton, but it would create a market for agricultural labour which would draw off the slaves of the native tribes, thus helping at once to spread Christian civilization and to put an end to the slave trade that was keeping the native trapped in his depressed social and economic state.[2]

Economic inducements were only part of Fergusson's native policy, however, the rest being a vigorous diplomatic and military offensive

[1] Gov. C. MacCarthy to Earl Bathurst, July 22, 1815, C.O. 267/40; Fergusson to Lord Stanley, June 1, 1844, Feb. 7, 1845, C.O. 267/184, 187.
[2] Buxton, *op. cit.*, 367, 374–9; Fergusson to Lord Stanley, Jan. 30, 1842, May 18, 1845, enclosures, C.O. 267/175, 187.

designed to discipline refractory chiefs who harboured slave dealers and to open up the interior for trade and the acquisition of farmland for interested recaptive settlers. Such thinking was orthodoxy itself in Freetown and closely paralleled British philanthropic views on the need for penetration beyond the coastal tribes to the great nations of the continental interior. Similarly, Fergusson's vigorous support of local education found ready assent within the colony. He urged educational assistance by the British government and equated a growing desire for education among the recaptives as a sign of their reaching out for the British standards set before them. 'It will, at no remote date', he wrote the Colonial Office, 'be the means of establishing a new, a most important, and influential grade in the Society of Sierra Leone. Among which, the husbands, the wives, and the domestic intercourse of the middle classes of England will, for the first time, find representatives in Western Africa.' The people were hungry for education, he added; what was more they were achieving a state of affluence wherein they were beginning to be able to afford it.[1]

During Fergusson's incumbency, there was an unusual amount of population movement in and out of Sierra Leone. In 1839 the first of a series of voyages brought recaptives back to their homeland in the Yorbua country, a development of profound significance for that part of West Africa. At the same time, British men-of-war continued to capture slavers and deposit their cargoes at Freetown for disposition. These immigrants were warmly received by the liberated Africans for the uncharitable reason that they welcomed a cheap labour supply. For the same reason newly freed recaptives were solicited in the West Indies where the plantation slave had been replaced by a free wage earner, thus complicating the labour market for plantation work. Official policy encouraged migration to the Indies and Fergusson followed his instructions in this respect, but he did not sympathize with this development. Rather he favoured the movement down the coast which he felt reflected that excellent African characteristic–love of homeland–and furthered the laudable objective of spreading Christian civilization into other parts of West Africa.

Mostly, however, Fergusson was disturbed by the social dislocations which these migrations brought to Sierra Leone. Ideally, he would have preferred an end to all immigration so that the colony might achieve social stability and moral strength. Too often newly arrived recaptives were reduced to virtual household slavery, the women and children

[1] *Ibid.*; Fergusson to Stanley, Aug. 26, 1844, Feb. 13, 1845, C.O. 267/185, 187.

particularly suffering, while their social innocence merely encouraged indolence and licentiousness among the older inhabitants:

> I have long regarded the farther importation of Liberated Africans into this Colony as a moral millstone round the necks of its people. By placing easily within their reach the means of obtaining gratuitous labour, idleness is engendered . . . as, at length, to become an inveterate habit. By means of the apprentices, their own children are relieved of the necessity of performing domestic and other offices . . . Many of the creole-born children, therefore, arrive at adult age, not only unaccustomed to labour, but disinclined to it, and actually incapable of working. The constant renewal of the barbarous element . . . perpetuates barbarous habits and customs, and greatly retards the sustained progress of improvement.'

Thus Fergusson, for all his admiration of the liberated Africans, was early voicing a criticism which was later to gain much currency, particularly towards the turn of the century: to the effect that the Sierra Leone creoles – as the descendants of recaptives, Nova Scotians and Maroons were by then called – somehow were effete, unequal to the rigours of building a modern civilization in Africa.[1]

Under the circumstances it was hardly a fair criticism. The problem of the creoles was the classic one of developing an economy *de novo* with small resources and few skills. They lacked capital and the means for its accumulation. In the early days few were educated, illiteracy was high and ignorance and superstition were everyday limitations. Furthermore, the colony possessed neither a fertile soil nor mineral resources. The people fell to trading naturally, but their almost total preoccupation with a commerce involving petty transactions and a low profit margin was not well designed to bring the necessary wealth with which investment in a more diversified economy might have been attempted. At all times there were those in the colony who clearly saw their needs and urged appropriate solutions: diversification into productive agriculture, pacification of the interior in the interests of trade, better education more particularly designed for the particular needs of African development, the prosecution of a favourable trade balance and the encouragement of European investment. All these things were repeatedly suggested along with the advice that it was up to the people of Sierra Leone themselves to effect the necessary revolution through industry, application and co-operative enterprise.[2]

[1] Fergusson to Stanley, Jan. 30, 1842, enclosure, Nov. 26, 1845, C.O. 267/175, 189.
[2] See for example, *The Independent*, May 13, 1875; *The West African Reporter* May 7, 1881.

Analysis and exhortation were relatively easy, but there were also those who acted on the advice they gave. Such a one was William Grant, who was only approaching early manhood when William Fergusson became governor, but who in his generation was to provide an example of what the creole community could accomplish when intelligence was propelled by industry. Grant was self-made – perhaps that was the secret of his success. Fergusson obtained him a post to study marine engineering when he was only fourteen but his frail constitution would not sustain the rigours of a life at sea. Thrust early, therefore, upon his own resources with only a minimum of formal schooling, he nonetheless rose speedily from a clerical post with a European firm to the point where he was soon managing the office force, and manoeuvring himself into a position to inaugurate his own mercantile establishment. Over the years his business grew, encouraged by the energy and sound judgment of its founder who possessed the vision to educate himself with wide reading in literature and history. His near contemporary, James Johnson, had ample opportunity as a young minister in Freetown to observe Grant. 'His well informed mind,' recalled Johnson years later, 'his depth of thought, his cultivated and refined intellect were due chiefly to himself; to his natural powers, his love of learning, his ambition to excel, his faithful diligence and earnest perseverance.'[1]

Self-made and self-generating, Grant was a man more of action than of reflection. Though he was motivated by firm, carefully cultivated principles, these were more often than not the product of the thought of others. Because of his prominence as a merchant, his attractive appearance and engaging manner, his genuine desire to help his people and his community, and the steady sober application he brought to each task, he became widely respected within the government as well as among the creoles; hence his opinions, borrowed or not, carried more weight than had they been sponsored by a more thoughtful but less influential man.

One who influenced Grant's thinking was his contemporary, Edward W. Blyden, who by the 1870s was already working out his theories of a unique Negro culture and African personality. Blyden with his powerful and original mind developed concepts of racial equality and the importance of Africa's contribution to world civilization which gave eloquent expression to what a patriot and humanist like Grant instinctively knew to be right. Grant was particularly attracted by Blyden's insistence upon a carefully conceived educational philosophy as a means to the realization

[1] *Ibid.*, Feb. 25, Aug. 5, 1882.

of Africa's potential. Blyden argued that the African had long suffered from an overdose of European education which was never designed to bring out the black man's qualities and which therefore left the African at a disadvantage when compared and competing with the European.

Many Africans at the time saw the strength of Blyden's educational thinking as an answer to the criticism often voiced in Europe that somehow the African was basically inferior, that the proof of inferiority was not the tribal African living in his primitive world but the educated African who, despite the advantages heaped upon him by European philanthropy, still could not seem to measure up to ordinary standards of civilization. A parochial version of this contention was voiced by the Sierra Leone governor, Sir Samuel Rowe, when he observed in 1877 that the 'educated and semi-civilized' African always patronized the native living in the bush when indeed the merits of the two were reversed, for 'those who, inferior in the possession of white men's knowledge, are generally far superior in courage and endurance'. *The West African Reporter* which Grant had founded in Freetown shortly before this incident affected agreement with the governor, then remarked acidulously that possibly the difficulty lay in a type of training for Africans which was imitative rather than creative and which as such tended to emphasize the white man's failings rather than his virtues. Summing up, the *Reporter* served notice that, whatever else, the West African did not lack wit. 'We need a different system of education... if ever we are to rise above the contempt of such clear-sighted and statesmanlike criticism... Our defects... cannot be inherent and incurable, if it be true that the natives of the interior—our blood relations—who have not enjoyed the benefits of our "civilization" show to so much better advantage. The deficiency must be in the process by which we have attained to this unsatisfactory result.'[1]

The lesson was clear for all to see. The advantages of European civilization were of doubtful value to the African. A different man from the European, he could rise to the heights only through the medium of his own institutions. Grant himself stated the case in clearest terms:

There is a great difference between the Negro and the white man... He is capable of doing anything that a white man can do. But... to get him to do that you must educate him by himself.... He must be educated to carry out a proper and distinct course for himself.... He fancies by the sort of education that you give him, that he must imitate you in everything—act like you, dress in broad cloth like you—and have his

[1] *Ibid.*, July 18, Aug. 1, 1877.

tall black hat like you. Then you see the result . . . when he comes to act within himself as a man he is confused . . . But if he is properly educated you will find him of far greater assistance.[1]

Essentially Grant had two things in mind. First of all, he urged a basic change in curriculum away from the conventional literary education which emphasized European culture and values and ignored Africa. The mission schools had long served the colony most effectively, he pointed out, but the time had come for reassessment and new directions, for fresh leadership and greater skills, which would meet African, not European, needs. He urged that the grammar school of the Church Missionary Society be reorganized and its faculty strengthened, and that the society's seminary at Fourah Bay be extended to include a broader curriculum serving the entire community, not merely a small number of theological students. Secondly, with primary and secondary education focused on the needs of Sierra Leone, Grant followed Blyden's lead in suggesting the addition of a university at the apex, an institution designed to provide teaching and research in fields relating to Africa where students from all over West Africa could come for study, and where the intrinsic qualities of the African character would come to flower. Neither Blyden's artful arguments nor Grant's sturdy support could bring about the desired university development, however, although Fourah Bay was soon expanded to include a broader student body and the school was affiliated with the University of Durham in England.[2]

As a leading Freetown merchant, Grant was deeply concerned with the economic development of the colony and towards this end he advocated three essential steps – the opening up of the hinterland to legitimate trade, the diversification of the economy through emphasis on agriculture and the processing of agricultural products, and an increase of capital investment from Europe.

In 1874 Grant was recommending the extension of British political control in order to provide customs jurisdiction inland. The next year on behalf of three hundred merchants, shopkeepers and traders, he presented Governor Rowe and the Colonial Office with a petition urging British penetration of the interior on a broad front, arranging either through purchase or treaty for rights which would enable the colony to strengthen long-standing commercial ties with the tribes of the back country. Grant and the Freetown business community agreed that such

[1] *Ibid.*, Jan. 14, 1882.
[2] *Ibid.*, Aug. 5, 1882; Grant to C.M.S. Secretary, Oct. 1, 1874, C.M.S. CA1/023.

a policy would increase colonial prosperity and revenue, bring peace to the land, put a final end to the slave trade, and spread Christianity and western civilization throughout the peoples of the interior. The British administration, however, was reluctant to add to its overhead and extend its military involvement on behalf of an unimportant colonial population. Rowe dismissed the petition as a manoeuvre of creole traders too idle to stir out of Freetown in search of business, and the Colonial Office made no more than vague promises to explore the matter further. When, some twenty years later, England had become involved in a more active role in the country behind Freetown, it was too late, for the French had by then laid effective claim to all but the small enclave which became the final British possession of Sierra Leone.[1]

Successful merchant though he was, Grant gave strong support to that undying dogma, introduced with the first settlers and nurtured over the years by missionary doctrine, that the prosperity of the colony was linked to agriculture and that an economy based exclusively on commerce could never hope to achieve a healthy and independent maturity. There was plenty of good farming land in the immediate vicinity of the colony, said Grant, where the government already exercised sovereignty. All that was needed was manpower and the will to work. As with all the others, so with Grant it was but a vain dream. At one point he suggested that immigration by American Negroes be encouraged for their long experience with cultivation. No armchair theoretician, he characteristically took up farming himself, late in life, undertaking to start a demonstration sugar plantation, and planning the introduction of a mill to process his sugar and to encourage its growth by others. Whether through optimism or salesmanship, he was enthusiastically professing at the time of his death in 1882 that the creoles were at last turning from trade to farming and he predicted the early appearance on the market of West African cotton for the mills of Manchester, and West African coffee and cocoa for the breakfast tables of Britain.[2]

To ensure this happy transformation, Grant urged British capital investment in Sierra Leone, not as an act of philanthropy, but as a sober decision on behalf of sound financial practice. Late in 1881, only a few weeks before his death, he assured an audience in London of the exciting prospects of investment:

[1] *The West African Reporter*, Aug. 1, 1877; *The Sierra Leone Weekly News*, Aug. 29, 1885.
[2] Grant to E. Hutchinson, Jan. 29, 1877, C.M.S. CA1/023; *The West African Reporter*, Aug. 6, Sept. 3, 1881; *Proceedings of the Royal Colonial Institute*, XIII, 75, 88–9.

We hope that this discussion to-night will . . . encourage capital in going to the country, because it would do a great deal to assist not only the Negroes, but to introduce much of the manufactured goods which you have in this country, and at the same time open the eyes of the capitalists of England to the fact of the existence of this new and profitable field for the investment of their money. Sierra Leone is the central point, and she must be the point where you have to penetrate into the interior of Africa.

To his compatriots he counselled the cultivation of a scrupulous business ethic as a means to the encouragement of foreign capital:

Among an essentially trading people who are nevertheless young in commercial enterprises, and are comparatively of limited capital, the permanent and healthy success in their speculations depends on a higher commercial morality, strictness in keeping promise, and an honest and even superstitious regard to render to every man his due; for these are the conditions for inspiring and securing confidence and credit which for them must supply the stead of capital.[1]

To his London audience, Grant was of course playing the persuasive salesman, stressing his strong points and trying to eliminate the weaknesses in his case. As he continued with his talk, he was at pains to congratulate the English people for their gratuitous kindness towards Africa. 'The Negro . . . feels grateful to the English people . . . he looks upon them as a father . . . and he reveres them as one who is superior to himself.' Britain has sacrificed fortunes and untold lives to assist a downtrodden race, and for what? The tall graceful speaker paused. 'Nothing', he continued at last. 'You gain nothing from us. You simply do it as an act of justice and . . . kindness . . . And I as a representative Negro, stand here and bow down my head in token of reverence to this nation for my people and my country.'

Such remarks were calculated to soften, and they did not fail to bring forth an enthusiastic response from the audience. Despite the practical merits of this line of argument, however, Grant was completely serious. He meant every word. He had always been impressed by the record of British philanthropy. Were not he himself and many others good examples of what it could and did accomplish for Africa? Nevertheless the educated African was beginning to suffer a basic ambivalence in his attitude towards the West. Genuine admiration and gratitude there certainly were, but there was another side, a hot blinding resentment which burst forth periodically over the sense of moral superiority and the essential selfishness which characterized so much of the European humanitarian

---

[1] *Ibid.*, 89–90; *The West African Reporter*, Apr. 21, 1880.

[142] MID-CENTURY FREETOWN:

effort in Africa. This was how Grant's *West African Reporter* expressed this feeling, in commenting upon Africa's commercial relations with Europe:

> It continues to be a standing blot upon the intercourse of Europeans with Africa, that every steamer that comes to the coast . . . brings in large quantities of that which is comparatively worthless to be exchanged for that which is valuable and useful. . . . If the articles given were simply worthless but harmless gew-gaws in exchange for articles of value, the morality of the transaction would even be reprehensible, but how much more when the articles are not only of trifling value . . . but often positively destructive. They take home that which builds them up in wealth, often leaving to the African that which impoverishes and destroys him. It is a sad reflection that, in many cases, European commerce has left its African customer as naked as it found him . . . they will never secure a footing in Africa for their ideas of civilization, until the commercial relations between the high-toned, enlightened European and the 'savage' African, are placed upon a more equitable basis. But so long as demijohn follows demijohn of rum . . . no reinforcements of missionaries and no homilies from professional philanthropists, on the blessings of European civilization will avail anything.[1]

3 The Educated African as Christian Clergyman

A strong attraction to Christianity had been one of the chief characteristics of the early Nova Scotia settlers in Sierra Leone, and Christian thought and practice continued to dominate Freetown society throughout the nineteenth century. Considering the early philanthropic beginnings of the colony and its continued utilization as a depot for the rehabilitation of recaptives, it was a natural consequence that European missionaries would find Sierra Leone an attractive area for work. First of all, there was the task of converting the indigenous African himself. Next, there were souls to be saved among the recaptives pouring into Freetown harbour, a labour which became increasingly inviting since the liberated Africans proved to be so much more receptive to Christianity and western culture than did the villager in the hinterland, still comfortably and firmly attached to his own customs and institutions.

The missionaries began arriving in the years after the collapse of the Nova Scotian insurrection and the abolition of the slave trade. Although their primary objective was conversion, as missionaries they were also concerned with the training of local ministers in order that missionary personnel and resources might be freed to move on to new areas and

---

[1] *Ibid.*, Jan. 14, 1882, Feb. 11, 1880.

THE AFRICAN BOURGEOISIE

new problems. The strategy of the Anglican Church Missionary Society, for example, called for the establishment of a self-supporting African church in Sierra Leone, led by African pastors who in turn might develop their own corps of African missionaries for service in the interior or down the coast where fresh labours beckoned. The work was necessarily slow at first. Schools had to be inaugurated for literacy and basic education, and a sharp eye kept for the few promising recruits in whom further training might be profitably invested. In the beginning candidates for orders were sent to London for study, but later a seminary was founded at Fourah Bay which eventually produced the large share of those West African clergymen who played influential roles in Sierra Leone and in the Anglican missions of Yorubaland and the Niger territory.

Samuel Ajayi Crowther, explorer and missionary who was as well West Africa's first Negro bishop and most distinguished churchman, was also the first and most distinguished alumnus of Fourah Bay, having been enrolled in its initial class in 1827 even before it had achieved seminary status. Others included James and Henry Johnson, whose main work was to be performed in the Nigerian missions, and T. B. Macaulay, Herbert Macaulay's father, who married one of Crowther's daughters and eventually settled in Lagos where he founded and became first principal of the C.M.S. Grammar School. Many remained in Sierra Leone. Two of the earliest were Thomas Maxwell and George Nicol who, like Crowther, were obliged to journey to England for their professional training. Nicol married another daughter of Crowther, devoting his long life to the native pastorate in Sierra Leone broken only by a tour as colonial chaplain in the Gambia. There were still others such as James and William Quaker, Moses Taylor, and G. J. Macaulay. James Quaker was another who studied at the C.M.S. college in London, returning to become principal of the grammar school which the C.M.S. founded in Freetown in 1845 at the time that Fourah Bay was directed to the training of candidates for orders. G. J. Macaulay, pugnacious and disputatious by nature, found himself in the thick of many a battle which developed over the years out of the strains of establishing in the colony an Anglican communion independent of European authority.

As might be expected the African clergy of Sierra Leone divided among themselves on a number of issues, but all were deeply imbued with a sense of mission—almost of destiny—which they felt divine fortune had placed in their hands. Given the opportunity of conversion to Christianity and introduced to the advantages of western culture through western education, they saw themselves as God's instrument in bringing the same advantages to the mass of their fellow Africans. James Johnson, at first assigned to a Freetown church, laboured incessantly for the spiritual and material betterment of his parishioners, agonizing over signs of backsliding and rejoicing with those who confirmed their commitment to Jesus. James Quaker, associated with the grammar school from its inception, worked a Spartan regimen for over thirty-five years, teaching a wide variety of subjects virtually singlehanded, caring for the spiritual and material needs of his students, and supervising the administration of the school–all this effort performed with a high sense of dedication and achievement.

Macaulay, Nicol and others were similarly motivated–troubled by the sometimes slow progress of conversion, worried by problems of financial support or concerned with devising ways for bringing Christian worship more forcefully into their communities, but always glorying in the progress recorded and unshaken in their conviction that Africa's salvation was in their hands. Ready they were to give the European missionary full credit for a splendid beginning. 'How many souls and bodies have been made "free indeed"; how many homes have been cheered; how many hearts have been filled "with joy unspeakable and full of glory", by the early and tearful labours of the agents of the Church Missionary Society', James Quaker asserted amidst general agreement in 1866. Yet the response had already been contained in Nicol's valedictory as he set out for England to his seminary studies over twenty years earlier. 'What is my object ... I have no other end in view but the glory of God ... the salvation of my soul and that of my fellow creatures. ... I am deeply convinced ... that if Africa could be raised from its present degraded state of barbarism, superstition, and vice, to any equal with the civilized world, recourse must be had to the native agencies. Africans themselves must be the principal harbingers of peace.'[1]

Such a view fitted very closely with the policy of the C.M.S. which had been speedily moving towards the independent native church in Sierra Leone, finally inaugurated in 1862. The native pastorate, as the church was called, soon comprised ten parishes with the prospect that others would follow as soon as they became able to support themselves. Proud of this development, the local African clergy took sober account

[1] For James Johnson, see below, chap. 14. James Quaker to Henry Venn, July 22, 1854, C.M.S. CA1/0178; G. J. Macaulay to Venn, Dec. 26, 1867, May 13, 1871, Macaulay Journal for the Half Year ending Sept. 30, 1860, C.M.S. CA1/0141; *C. M. Intelligencer*, 1866, 349–50; Geo. Nicol to J. Warburton, Apr. 12, 1844, C.M.S. CA1/0164.

THE AFRICAN BOURGEOISIE [145]

of responsibilities as well as achievement. For them it was a heart-warming sign of Africa's coming of age that a purely native church superintended by African ministers was at last a reality. But there was much to be done. The native pastorate was not only responsible for the religious needs of its people; there were social and commercial problems which had to be solved in order that the pastorate might be sustained. The nagging question of a broadening economic base could be evaded by the church no more than by the government, and the pastorate must do its part to encourage diversified agriculture and to seek out new plants for experimental cultivation. Moreover, the native church was now in the same relation to West Africa that the church in England originally had been. It too was obliged to take up the missionary burden, to train the workers, to maintain the stations in far-off places, and thus 'to fertilize the distant parched countries' of Africa through Christ's joyful message.[1]

Of course, this separation from the parent church, the African ministry assured the C.M.S., though real enough, was essentially outward and nominal. The native pastorate would always be closely bound to its parent, not only by the Gospel but by the feelings of respect, affection and gratitude born of the past and the hope of continuing guidance and counsel in the future. Such an expression of sympathy was more theoretical than actual, however, for in fact the relations between the native pastorate and the English missionaries in Sierra Leone were marked more often than not by antipathy and mutual recrimination. Whatever the merits of the various charges, the missionaries sometimes found it difficult to share authority with African colleagues or felt their efforts no longer appreciated, while the Africans, jealous of their newly independent status, were quick to take offence at real or imagined invasions of their authority.

Typical of the sort of unpleasant incidents which sometimes occurred was a disagreement which flared briefly but hotly between G. J. Macaulay and one of the missionaries, G. R. Caiger. When Macaulay was assigned to a parish near Freetown, he accused Caiger of refusing him occupancy of the mission house on the grounds that residence there would somehow contaminate a dwelling where a white missionary might again be assigned at some future time. 'Strange inconsistency', announced an anonymous writer in the local press who might have been Macaulay himself, 'Mr. M. is quite fit to take charge of the *Church of*

---

[1] *C. M. Intelligencer*, 1862, 128; Report of the Sierra Leone Native Church Pastorate ... 1868, C.M.S. CA1/09.

God . . . but let him but tread the outer court, and it becomes forever polluted.' Macaulay eventually apologized for the whole incident, but not before he had delivered himself of a torrid indictment of the racial intolerance of Europeans. 'What other thoughts could have entered my mind', he wrote Caiger, '. . . but that you hated my colour and would not regard me as a man and as a brother.' And he went on to express his dismay at such a show of prejudice from a man whose whole calling proclaimed the knowledge that all men were made of one blood under God.

Impetuous and quick-tempered, Macaulay was probably wrong in this particular instance although in general there was legitimacy in his complaint. It was at this time that injudicious, half-informed accounts of the capabilities of the educated Africans of Freetown were beginning to appear from European travellers and government officers like Captain Richard Burton, who flayed the missionaries as well as their protégés with easy generalizations and superficially plausible anthropological arguments which had the effect, among others, of setting the missionaries and the African clergy against each other. Essentially, however, the differences between the European missionaries and their African colleagues were a matter of control over local church policy. The ordinarily mild Nicol became involved in disputes with the missionaries concerning the closing of an orphan asylum outside Freetown and a right of way on Nicol's property near Fourah Bay College. Further friction occurred over the appointment and subsequent dismissal of Edward Blyden who had been engaged by Henry Venn to preach to the Muslims but who was released almost immediately, possibly for an alleged scandal in Liberia, possibly because of his pro-Muslim views, but with missionaries and native pastors differing sharply over the case. The missionaries became so convinced that the African clergy were engaged in a systematic campaign to be rid of them that a series of public and private denials was deemed necessary. Nicol assured the readers of the *African Times* in London that relations with the missionaries were excellent and that he was sure the colony would need their intelligent guidance and skilful experience for years to come. Privately, Quaker wrote to Henry Venn, denying that there was a movement to be rid of European assistance. 'The general feeling here is that all the Europeans *who do not love the Africans* should go away', he reported, but all others were more than welcome.[1]

[1] G. J. Macaulay to G. R. Caiger, Sept. 10, 1866, C.M.S. CA1/0141; Fyfe, *History of Sierra Leone*, 334, 352; M. Taylor, J. Cole *et al*. to Nicol, Sept. 14, 1868, C.M.S. CA1/0164; J. Quaker to Venn, Sept. 14, 28, 1868, Nov. 15, Dec. 24, 1871, C.M.S. CA1/0178; *The African Times*, Sept. 23, 1868.

The African ministers had been sympathetic to Blyden over his dismissal by the C.M.S., but on another matter he was the source of differences within their body. His views on the validity of Muslim culture in Africa were by implication part of his growing attack on the effectiveness of European missions. Such a position disturbed the more conservative ministers who were further shocked by Blyden's insistence that European educational philosophy and curricula ill suited African needs and should be replaced by a system more directly responsive to the qualities of African genius and the requirements of African society. His ideas for an African university, which excited William Grant, upset traditionalists like George Nicol and James Quaker, who also had little sympathy for Blyden's provocative newspaper, *The Negro*, which was the Freetown vehicle for most of his views. To Quaker it was madness to alienate the European source and inspiration of so much African progress just at the moment when a measure of independence had been achieved, and more assistance to that end would be sorely needed. The 'Negro race question and the general tone and spirit of the *Negro* newspaper have separated Mr. Blyden and myself,' he wrote to mission headquarters in London. 'I have told him that Israel is not to be delivered by killing the Egyptians . . . Africa still stands in need of all the aid she can get from British philanthropists in order to rise to her proper standard in the scale of humanity.'[1]

While James Johnson, G. J. Macaulay and many other creoles found Blyden's opinions highly stimulating, to a veteran clergyman like George Nicol they often seemed like insubstantial innovation replacing solid accomplishment. It was true, Nicol admitted, that Africans wanted their own university so that their sons and daughters might be properly educated, but it was a European education that they sought. 'I refer not here to the strange scheme that has been proposed,' he explained:

The native gentlemen feel that they want a good substantial English school under well qualified English and native masters, where their sons will enjoy all the advantages of a complete English education. . . . I am sure this is what the intelligent portion of the community wants. They understand nothing about an institution where 'race feeling', and 'the national idiosyncrasies' etc. etc. will be developed or respected. . . . We want an English school to be established in Sierra Leone.'

And to carry out his conviction, when no university became established

[1] J. Quaker to Venn, Oct. 28, 1872, to E. Hutchinson, Apr. 15, 1873, C.M.S. CA1/0178.

in West Africa, Nicol sent his son to Cambridge to study for the ministry.[1]

While there were differences between factions among the African clergy, there were also tensions between the creole pastors and their congregations. Independence of C.M.S. control was not to be preempted as a monopoly of the priests of the native pastorate; the parishioners wanted their share of independence too. Furthermore, they were in a good position to enforce their demands because as independence brought financial responsibility for the churches, it was to their parishioners that the clergy were obliged to look thenceforward for their main source of income. For a while, the government helped with an annual £500 subvention but when that was terminated, the native pastorate found that almost one-third of its £2,000 yearly budget was still being supplied by philanthropic outsiders. The laity claimed that the reason for poor local support resided in the continued reluctance of the ministers to permit greater lay participation in church affairs. It was time for the clergy to show more flexibility towards their parishioners, for the experiment in independence of the native pastorate was an opportunity for the people of Sierra Leone 'to demonstrate to the world at large and also to those who ... are sceptical of our capabilities, that we have in us the germs of self-dependence'.[2]

A staunch defender of native clerical authority like G. J. Macaulay would yield nothing to such an agitation. Like James Johnson, Macaulay was ever watchful for signs that members of his flock might be slipping into heathenism and he saw no reason why people of such propensities should be entrusted with even a moderate share of direction in the affairs of God's church. Insisting that the issue of independence had been much overemphasized, he pointed out that virtually all the Anglican churches in the colony had long operated independently and that differences between pastor and congregation ought not to be played up by a hostile press out of all proportion to their significance. 'Is it fair', he demanded, '... to represent only the native pastors and their parishioners as two snarling dogs chained together and pulling in opposite directions? ... is it anything to be wondered at, if occasionally, nay "constantly", there should arise between people and pastor ... having the oversight of hundreds and thousands of people of different tribes and nationalities, the majority of whom are only verging toward Christian civilization, some misunderstandings ... springing many a

[1] Nicol to C. C. Fenn, Aug. 14, 1873, C.M.S. CA1/0164.
[2] *The West African Reporter*, Sept. 12, 1877, Aug. 11, 1880.

time from trifling incidents?' Macaulay's determination and aggressiveness were superior to his logic. There was a strong case in the argument that increased lay responsibility went hand in hand with increased lay financial support. Macaulay was able to hold his ground for the moment but a number of years later his congregation temporarily turned him out of his own church during the course of a dispute over the jurisdiction of the bishop of Sierra Leone which was complicated by these recurrent quarrels over church funds.[1]

4 The Educated African Scrutinizes Colonial Administration

The Victorian society of nineteenth-century Freetown would not have been complete without its reform element which, following the lead of similar movements in the West, proposed to guard popular rights against official tyranny, supported movements towards a broadening democracy, and came to the defence of the underdog on all issues. At mid-century, the unchallenged leader of this faction in Sierra Leone was William Rainy. A West Indian like Fergusson, Rainy had settled in Freetown, first as a civil servant and then as a barrister. Clever, energetic, quick and persuasive in debate, he was more than a match for most of the colony's legal and judicial elements, and this soon led to a comfortable law practice. Undeterred by official authority, he was constitutionally at home only while in opposition to the government, and so became the natural champion of those who felt they had grievances against the State. With his particular character and training, he could have been an important agent in bringing the people of the Sierra Leone colony forward in their drive to build a modern productive democratic community. As a reformer he might even have succeeded in dislodging the government both in Freetown and in London from its smug assumption that Africans, whatever their background and training, were unqualified for growing public responsibilities leading eventually to self-government. Unfortunately, though posing as the great democrat and champion of the oppressed, Rainy was essentially a self-seeker and a demagogue. Immensely popular with the people of the colony during his residence there, he produced a continual series of spectacular incidents designed to set right some egregious wrong, but usually all that was forthcoming was publicity for the name and activities of William Rainy. When he finally left after twenty-five exciting years, nothing was very much

[1] *Ibid.*, Sept. 19, Oct. 10, 1877; Macaulay to E. Hutchinson, Nov. 26, 1874, C.M.S. CA1/0141; Fyfe, *History of Sierra Leone*, 510-11.

changed and little accomplished. The task of African advancement was resumed by less spectacular but perhaps more competent hands.[1]

The pity of Rainy's career in Freetown was lodged in the essential illiberality and inefficiency of the colonial government poised against the fact that the creole community was beginning to produce representatives who could have learned much and contributed much through an apprenticeship of productive, meaningful public service. There was a need, therefore, to inject the kind of criticism introduced by Rainy. Unfortunately, in his hands it only angered the authorities and strengthened their conviction that the colony was not ready for reform as long as a man like William Rainy was an acknowledged leader.

In 1863, the Colonial Office introduced a new constitution in Sierra Leone, replacing the old governor and council by an executive council of senior aides and a legislative council comprising the executive council and three or four unofficial members. The unofficial appointees were all chosen by the governor, but it was understood that they were to represent the interests of the community. The legislative council was not a parliament; it did not initiate and debate legislation but rather acted as an advisory body to the governor in performing the legislative function. There was little danger of democratic insurgence. Though John Ezzidio was appointed an unofficial member, nominated to the governor by the merchants of Freetown who were requested to recommend a candidate, he was not a forceful representative and did not give trouble over official policy. The other unofficial members hardly could have been said to represent the creoles at all, and in any event there seems to have been no great popular interest at the time in the new constitutional change.[2]

Such a situation was made to order for one of Rainy's temperament. With a legal practice built up largely through mercantile actions against the government, he was already on bad terms with several members of the administration and eager for a chance to pay them back and pose at the same time as the protector of the weak and defenceless. Despite apparent reform, government in Sierra Leone was no more than a sham, Rainy thundered, an unexampled despotism directed by unchecked executive power, and all ironically sanctioned by those bastions of human freedom, English law and the English crown. To be sure there

---

[1] Rainy's activities are detailed in Fyfe, *History of Sierra Leone*.
[2] J. D. Hargreaves, 'Colonial Office Opinions on the Constitution of 1863', *Sierra Leone Studies*, n.s., no. 5, Dec. 1955, 2-10.

was a legislative council but its members were thoroughly submissive to the governor and only one could be said to reflect the people of the colony. Moreover, Rainy added slyly, the council, both as legislature and as the supreme court of appeals, sat privately, unwilling to permit public scrutiny of its deliberations.

Rainy never suffered for lack of a public platform. He organized several newspapers in Sierra Leone and one in London. More important, he gained the sympathetic ear of the *African Times*, the defender of West Africa in London, and acted as its Freetown correspondent. Hence his critical views received wide public circulation, while privately he forwarded complaints and petitions to the Colonial Office which challenged, on behalf of the Freetown community, the competence of the administration and which, when unanswered, eventually found their way into the columns of the pro-Rainy press.

Publicly, he called for an expansion of the legislative council to include influential leaders like William Lewis and T. A. Rosenbush—and William Rainy, the *African Times* dutifully added. In Paris, speaking at an anti-slavery conference in 1867 where he was the self-styled 'delegate of a broad and distant land ... the representative of the African race', he levelled his colourful delivery at the government in Sierra Leone which was oppressing his people:

Alas, I grieve to say that they have been legislated for by a council sitting with closed doors, and at a board where one of their race alone is allowed to take his seat. This star chamber is presided over by the governor of the colony. Within the last twelve months the native people have been deprived of the English bulwark of liberty—*trial by jury* ... Whilst they have advanced in every thing that could add to the dignity and the honour of a nation, they have been unscrupulously deprived of a right which they enjoyed in their primitive and less worthy state of political existence, and yet they are to be told that they are unfit for self-government by the very party who deprived them of the elementary school wherein to learn the noblest of all sciences.

Rainy complained to the Colonial Office that the government in Freetown practised racial prejudice, suspending a Negro judge who found damages against a European, retaining white officials in office despite dishonesty and incompetence, and interfering with jury trials in civil cases by permitting executive review of damages assessed. Called upon for explanations, the administration grumbled that Rainy was a troublemaker who rallied to every dubious cause, allied himself with a journal which specialized in attacks upon the government, and all in all 'made himself conspicuous by his unscrupulous advocacy of what he termed the rights and privileges of the native races'.[1]

Trouble-maker he may have been but, unfortunately for the government, Rainy was able to make his case in several particulars. He pointed out that violations by shippers of customs regulations were tried before officials appointed by a governor who stood to collect a personal share out of any resultant fines. He protested the appointment of two officials to judicial posts, one as chief justice of the colony, on the grounds of incompetence in the first case and licentious personal conduct in the other. He questioned a colonial budget which allowed £14,000 for policing but only £292 for education. 'It is impossible to exaggerate the deteriorating influences exercised upon any colony where such a glaring contrast exists', he warned. '. . . It is the contrast between moral persuasion and physical force—between mental culture and rude control.'

All this had the plausible ring of half truth. Clearly the regulations on customs seizures needed reform. The government offered no argument on this account and repealed the offending legislation. The matter of the judicial appointments was less clear, however, partly because Rainy seems to have been motivated by the hope of appointment as chief justice himself, and partly because these were interim appointments, so understood by the authorities who were well aware of the deficiencies of the individuals involved. As for the educational budget, Rainy neglected to mention what everyone knew—that there was no need for heavy government expenditure because the schools had long been the chosen responsibility of the Christian missions in Sierra Leone.[2]

These matters related, however, to another and more serious charge which caused a widespread furore within the colony. This was the question of jury trials. Trial by jury had been the one constitutional relic which had survived from the days of Granville Sharp's Province of Freedom, but over the years it had come under increasing criticism. It worked well enough in criminal cases but was said by its opponents to give rise to prejudiced verdicts in civil suits with juries invariably finding for creoles, particularly those suing Europeans for damages arising out of personal assault. Whatever the merits of these arguments, the government first permitted assessors appointed by the governor to

---

[1] Christopher Fyfe, 'The Sierra Leone Press in the Nineteenth Century', *Sierra Leone Studies*, n.s., no. 8, June, 1957, 230; *The Sierra Leone Journal*, Dec. 23, 1865, Col. Chamberlayne to Edward Cardwell, Jan. 18, 1866 and enc. C.O. 267/287; *The African Times*, Apr. 23, June 23, 1869; *Special Report of the Anti-Slavery Conference held in Paris . . . 1867*, 49.

[2] Rainy to Duke of Buckingham, Apr. 24, July 6, 9, 10, Aug. 22, 1867, C.O. 267/292; *The African Times*, July 23, 1867.

review damages allowed by juries in civil cases; then tried unsuccessfully to pass an ordinance compelling plaintiffs in assault cases to post bond for court costs. These measures proving insufficient, an act was pushed through the legislative council restricting trial by jury entirely to criminal cases.

The reaction was immediate and intense. Petitions to the Secretary of State in London pointed out that this action was contrary to the ancient rights and liberties of British subjects, that it was a clear case of legislation on behalf of the privileged few, and that it had been engineered through the council in a flagrantly unparliamentary fashion. The defenders of the act argued that it actually protected litigants from racial and tribal jealousies, and obviated inequitable judgments handed down by juries confused by obfuscating lawyers. Freetown was a small community, the litigants were invariably known to the jurors and such an act would minimize the possibility of bribes and other forms of pressure.

Rainy had no monopoly of complaint in this controversy but as usual he led all others in the variety and intensity of his objections. In addition to the above arguments, he protested that the law was passed to allow Europeans to beat their servants with impunity, that it was urged by a governor notoriously antagonistic towards Negroes and that it was drafted by a chief justice who for twenty-five years had never criticized the jury system until this sudden change of mind just before his retirement on a life pension. Such an about-face was more than strange coming from a man, of African blood himself, who could so unexpectedly after a quarter of a century 'form so degrading an estimate of his own race and blood'.

The new jury ordinance was upheld in England and the governor soon left Sierra Leone on regular transfer to another post. Rainy sped him on his way with a mock description of a remorseful man conducting a losing debate with his conscience over his ill deeds. Would he not have to confess that he had seriously impaired the liberties of unoffending citizens, while giving them bad government through unqualified appointments? Would he not in self-reproach say, 'I found this colony enjoying the bulwark of English liberty—trial by jury, and, aided by a coloured ex-Judge... I took from her that sacred right'.[1]

With the arrival of a new governor, there was for a time cordiality between Rainy and the administration, but when the governor insisted

---

[1] Blackwell to E. Cardwell, May 19, Nov. 21, 1866 and enclosures, C.O. 267/287; *The African Times*, Nov. 23, Apr. 23, Aug. 23, Dec. 23, 1867; *The African Interpreter*, Feb. 2, 1867.

on following his own judgment rather than being advised by Rainy, relations deteriorated. The flamboyant barrister continued to pose as reformer, but in a manner which still did not quite ring true and seemed to contain more self- than public-interest. Yet much of his criticism was just. He brought suits against the unpopular African Steamship Company, protested against poor prison conditions and excessive, illegal sentences, complained that the house tax in Freetown was inequitably weighted to the disadvantage of the poorer landholder, urged economy in government and more efficient courts and continued to deplore the narrow representation of the legislative council and the lack of jury trials. When the annual subvention of the government to the native pastorate was attacked, he sensibly suggested that it be removed from the governor's discretion rather than abolished, for such a move could only bring an overall weakening of religion in the colony. Yet he forcefully opposed a State church, arguing that freedom of worship was at stake.[1]

As usual no great changes resulted from these exertions. Rainy continued to enjoy public acclaim as he regularly protested his devotion to the causes of human liberty and African advance. A few years passed in this fashion, then Rainy fell ill and in 1871 sailed for Europe to repair his health. He was expected to return once recovered, but he never came back. The colony settled back into a quieter routine, neither better nor worse for the absence of its champion.

[1] *The African Times*, July 23, Oct. 23, Nov. 23, 1868, July 22, Oct. 23, Nov. 23, 1871; *The African Interpreter*, Apr. 24, 1869.

8 The Évolués

1 *The Assimilationist Views of Abbé Boilat*

Like Sierra Leone, the coastal communities in Senegal faced an adjustment to European influences. In French eyes, reoccupation of Senegal in 1817 and the conversion of the land into a productive colony involved, among other things, plans by the colonial government for a system of public education. If the efforts of the people were to be co-ordinated behind the development of an ambitious agricultural experiment, the common language of French would have to be learned. If an augmented productivity for the country was to be achieved, better methods of farming would be needed along with substantial numbers of trained craftsmen. If the stultifying atmosphere of Islam was to be replaced by the higher morality of a Christian order, some educational counterpoise was essential to offset the Koranic schools of the region. Nevertheless, early educational policy, like the initial economic plans of the administration, lacked sufficient force and direction to reach the anticipated objectives. For almost fifteen years an undernourished educational establishment was maintained, limited in extent to primary education, hampered by inadequate direction and confounded by the difficulty of introducing French as a language of instruction. Not until 1841 did a more vigorous policy emerge with the introduction of missionary-directed schools in Goree and St. Louis, and even these establishments had little effect on the total population since enrolment consisted mainly of the Europeans and Christianized mulattoes living in the coastal cities.

During 1822–3, Mother Anne-Marie Javouhey visited Senegal and Sierra Leone on behalf of the teaching and nursing order, the Sisters of St. Joseph of Cluny, which she had founded in 1807. During her stay in Senegal, Mother Javouhey was able to persuade the authorities regarding the importance of schools for girls, which were shortly thereafter instituted on a modest scale by members of her order in both St. Louis and Goree. At the same time, concerned about the long-range problem of developing an indigenous body of trained educators, she proposed that a number of young Senegalese be entrusted to her care for study in France which would lead eventually to their return to Senegal as teachers for the local schools. Laudable though the idea was, its execution met with various complications in the form of illness, death and the disinclination of parents of some of the young students to be separated for long years from their children. In the end the original group was reduced by attrition to only three who in 1838 completed their secondary education and turned to training for the priesthood. In 1841 they were ordained and early in 1843 two of them, the abbés Moussa and Boilat, were back in Senegal preparing to launch a new educational venture, a secondary school in St. Louis.[1]

Both the experiment and its authors suffered an interesting, albeit unhappy, existence during the life of the school which began with much promise and enthusiasm but which soon encountered difficulties leading to its ultimate dissolution in 1850. The project was in fact the idea of Governor Bouet-Willaumez who directed the affairs of the colony briefly in 1843 and 1844, and whose plans included the inauguration of secondary education to be devoted to the study of Latin, history, geography, mathematics and graphic design. Governor Bouet and his young helpers, Boilat and Moussa, were persuaded that the youth of Senegal ought to be developed in a manner similar to that of France, that assimilation into French culture could best be achieved through the rigours of classics and mathematics as they were taught in the metropole. This view conflicted with the educational philosophy of the order of the Ploermel Brothers who had been placed in charge of the elementary schools a few years earlier, and who were convinced that fundamental literacy, the rudiments of practical science and arithmetic and the inculcation of western precepts of hard work, honesty, truthfulness and sobriety were much more realistic bases for education in the Senegal of their day.

At first all went well. Boilat was able to begin with thirty-four students and by the end of his first year he had an attendance of forty-seven, all progressing well in response to his energetic direction and enthusiastic instruction. Gradually difficulties arose, however. When Bouet was replaced as governor, the college lost its highly-placed support, and those who followed were less convinced of its utility. The Ploermel Brothers were angered by what they felt to be an infringement upon

---

[1] Georges Hardy, *L'Enseignement au Sénégal de 1817 à 1854*, 39–45, 62–3; Gov. Roger to Minister, Aug. 24, 1824, no. 194, N.A.S. 2B9.

THE ÉVOLUÉS

their prerogative, and they complained that Boilat and Moussa were raiding their students to fill the rolls of the college. In Paris, the colonial ministry was not persuaded that an emphasis on Latin instruction was what was needed for Africa, and reacted much more favourably to the less ambitious Ploermel educational objectives. After the first enthusiasm had worn off, there were doubts over the quality of instruction; worse still, there began to be questions regarding the competence and moral rectitude of the direction. Moussa left the college under a cloud almost at once and he was followed by Boilat in 1845 when the latter was assigned to parish duties in Goree. Boilat was replaced by the Abbé Fridoil, the third of the three young priests, but his tenure soon terminated on an anti-climactic note, and by 1849 the college existed in name only, having no longer either students or faculty. The next year it was merged with the primary school system directed by the Ploermel Brothers and secondary education in Senegal was at an end, not to be taken up again for another thirty years.[1]

No doubt it was too much to expect three young inexperienced priests to succeed with an educational venture which was as premature as it was difficult to institute. The charges of immorality and wrong-doing, however, were somewhat more difficult to assess, especially since they appeared to be largely circumstantial. Moussa was said to suffer from habitual alcoholism which severely limited his reliability and caused the administration to urge his reassignment in France. Fridoil encountered financial difficulties while directing the college, a situation which may have been due to an essentially impractical nature, for he was later accused of chronic personal indebtedness which led eventually to a complete moral disintegration. Boilat was strongly suspected of licentious conduct; at any rate he fell under popular censorship as a voluptuary although he was never subjected to public prosecution for lack of adequate evidence. Despite a promising beginning, therefore, this early French effort at assimilation was disappointing to its sponsors.[2]

Disappointing perhaps, but not unproductive. While still at the college, Boilat had begun collecting materials on the customs and languages of the people of Senegal and in 1843 he arranged for three of

[1] Bouet to Minister, Mar. 29, 1842, N.A.S. 2B22; Report of the Chief of the Administrative Service, Dec. 31, 1843, Gov. Thomas to Minister, Sept. 5, 1844, Minister to Gov. Bourdon-Gramont, Sept. 4, Nov. 6, 1846, Minute of Administrative Council, Nov. 30, 1848, N.A.P.O.S. Senegal X bis; Boilat, *Esquisses Sénégalaises*, 276–7. The affairs of the college are discussed in Hardy, *L'Enseignement au Sénégal*, ch. IV.

[2] Gov. Baudin to Minister, Feb. 21, 1848, no. 77, N.A.S. 2B27; Hardy, *L'Enseignement au Sénégal*, 72–4.

his young pupils to accompany a government expedition to the interior so that they might have an opportunity for a first-hand study of the land, its inhabitants and its resources. When he moved to Goree, Boilat found that his duties included the establishment of mission stations in the Serer territory to the south where he was able not only to fulfil his religious responsibilities but to indulge his interests in studying the people and their way of life. All this extracurricular activity resulted in 1853 in the publication of *Esquisses Sénégalaises* in which Boilat analysed the sociology, mythology, languages and customs of a number of indigenous nations in Senegal, adding sections on the geography, history and economy of the country. In addition he traced the impact of Europe on Senegal from earliest times, and explained the nature of the mulatto communities of St. Louis and Goree which had arisen as a result of the European presence. He discussed in detail his stewardship of the college at St. Louis along with his philosophy of education for Africa, and offered a number of suggestions as to how the affairs of the colony might be expanded and improved. Finally, an artist of unusual accomplishment, he produced a companion volume containing some two dozen colour portraits of the inhabitants of Senegal drawn from life sketches and providing rare and vivid evidence of their physical appearance and way of life. Like the journals of Bishop Crowther, Boilat's *Esquisses* offered not only an unusual picture of a part of Africa as seen by one of her own people, but it gave an equally unusual insight into the social thought of one of the early educated Africans of the nineteenth century.

The analogy to Crowther is not inappropriate. Both were of the same generation. Both were taken by European missionaries and exposed to a western education which terminated in the priesthood. Both returned to Africa to put their training to effect in aiding their fellow Africans through Christian conversion and European education. Each had pronounced ideas regarding the religious, political, economic and pedagogical development of his respective part of West Africa, and the opinions of each in these areas were profoundly influenced by the training he had received during his European residence.

The key to Boilat's philosophy of African development was simple assimilation. He had spent over fifteen formative years in France totally immersed in French culture. When he emerged he was a thoroughly westernized African, dedicated to the idea that only through absorption of the Christian culture which he had acquired in France could his Senegalese compatriots hope to put barbarism behind them and master the achievements of a higher civilization. Put in terms of education, assimilation meant first of all learning the French language in all its beauty and subtlety and using it to the exclusion of all other tongues. When Boilat first returned to Senegal, he was struck by the excellent instruction in French which the young girls were receiving in the schools of Goree and St. Louis and yet, despite the efforts of both teachers and pupils, these students somehow lacked 'that gentle piety that characterized young persons of their age in France. They enjoyed listening to sermons and reading religious lessons, and yet nothing seemed to touch them and to bring them to experience the goodness which the love of God brought to innocent souls'. Sorely puzzled, Boilat continued to search for some blemish in the apparently blameless lives of these students. At last he could find but one thing—the continuing habit of speaking Wolof outside the classroom.

To Boilat this was no trivial matter. He put the case before the parents of the school children, assembling the evidence and examining the ramifications of what he regarded as an incomplete policy of French language instruction—incomplete because progress at school during the day was compromised by the laxity of parents who permitted their children to converse in Wolof after school hours. Without a firm grasp of French, asked Boilat, how could the students master the intricacies of their other studies? History would degenerate into a memory exercise involving meaningless terms, geography would be transformed from an informative science into an insupportable bore, astronomy, which showed man the glory and majesty of God, became but a sequence of absurd and barbarous formulae, and mathematics remained far beyond the reach of all. More than all this, young girls imperfectly trained in French would suffer from imperfect religious training as well, for the refinements of Christian doctrine could not be transferred through the crude medium of an African language. They would miss the beauties of their prayers and hear of the heroic acts of the saints with cold indifference. Who could doubt that missionary efforts in the land suffered because of the limited extent to which French was used? And what of those women who spoke it fluently? Did they not show greater refinement, deeper wisdom? Was their society not more sought after, and as mothers did they not exercise an admirable influence on their children? Through the use of French they were able to begin the task of civilizing and converting their servants; in the wake of this good work came a reduction of vice—theft, falsehood, hypocrisy and immorality—and in its place were substituted learning and culture. 'You see ... all the moral riches which your children will gather from studying French', Boilat concluded. 'Put your hand to the task . . . I am persuaded that after having witnessed their labours and their success . . . they will become for you an object of joy, of hope, of consolation.'[1]

Basic literacy in the French language was, therefore, an essential, but it was not an end in itself. Beyond mere literacy lay the training of a native leadership competent to assume widening responsibilities in the direction of local affairs, and it was towards this goal that Boilat's college was directed. As effective as the elementary schools were, they prepared individuals only to be petty clerks in commercial or government offices. More important for Senegal, Boilat insisted, was a local institution devoted to secondary education offering instruction comparable with that available in France and preparing the way for further training leading to positions in the army and navy, marine and mechanical engineering, education, the church, medicine and pharmacy. Those who might wish to follow careers in the riverain trade would at any rate possess an education which enabled them to carry on their affairs with efficiency. With the establishment of Boilat's college, therefore, would be made available a corps of trained Africans qualified to explore the interior country, to man the necessary military and administrative posts up the Senegal River and along the coast, to undertake research in such areas as tropical medicine, combining western remedies with those of native doctors, or to carry on in any of a variety of important duties within the colony. Then would Senegal flourish, materially and morally:

What a glorious future is in prospect for Senegal! With education you will see the flowering of commerce, science, art, religion, and above all, an improved morality. You will see the fall of all those gross, if not dishonourable, ways known as *the custom of the country*. You will witness the disappearance of all those absurd superstitions born of that silly deplorable gullibility with which most of the population deludes itself.[2]

Boilat was a Catholic priest and his religious persuasion necessarily coloured his view of the state of morality in Senegal. With regard to the population of the tribes in the interior, it was a question of total ignorance sustaining individual superstition and social immorality which in turn supported devil worship and belief in the power of demons. The worship of evil spirits had once been widespread throughout the world, he said, but with the extension of Christianity devil worship had been proportionately reduced. It was still practised widely in Senegal, however, and there were many witnessed accounts of people fallen under

[1] *Esquisses Sénégalaises*, 9–18. [2] *Ibid.*, 227–38, 477–9.

1. Gustavus Vassa   2. Alexander Crummell

3. Monrovia *c.* 1840

4. Freetown in 1856

5. George Nicol

6. Africanus Horton

7. Bishop Crowther

8. Gaspard Devès

9. St. Louis in 1865

10. Edward W. Blyden

11. James Johnson

12. Lagos Marina c. 1885

13. Cape Coast c. 1890

14. Samuel Lewis

15. S. R. B. Attoh-Ahuma

16. John Mensah Sarbah

17. C. C. Reindorf

18. J. E. Casely Hayford

19. Henry Carr

20. Lamine Guèye

21. Herbert Macaulay

22. Blaise Diagne

the spell of spirits who had enslaved them and caused them to perpetrate mischievous prodigies. Boilat himself not only believed in the existence of these evil spirits but reported having witnessed a young woman thus possessed who remained completely beyond help until Boilat himself was able to attach a holy medal to her head thus forcing the spirit to release his victim and flee. 'Was this a possession, an obsession, or a simple epilepsy?' asked Boilat. 'It is not for me to decide', he concluded, but it was clear that in his opnion he, with the aid of the Virgin Mary, had wrested a soul from the toils of the devil. On another occasion Boilat attempted to test the occult powers of one of the many itinerant marabouts who made their living by divination. In this case the marabout was successful, not only reading Boilat's thoughts but predicting a future event with remarkable accuracy. The reason was not far to seek, confirming Boilat's worst fears; indeed the man admitted quite openly that his ability to read the future came directly through consultation with the devil.

As much as Boilat feared the alliance of the marabouts with evil spirits, he found the temporal influence of these Muslim holy men infinitely worse. In addition to their supernatural adventures, they constituted a major hindrance to Christian conversion and were largely successful in preventing Muslim children from attending the French schools in preference to their own Koranic institutions. In these latter establishments, said Boilat, the children learned only to memorize passages from the Koran and to perfect the art of begging so that when they grew up they had no choice but to become illiterate mendicants. Boilat wanted to deal with this disgraceful situation by closing all the marabout schools and forcing the parents to send their children to the French institutions which might, in deference to the needs of the Muslims, establish courses in Arabic. In time the desired results would occur – the children would learn to speak and to read French; with literacy would soon come an impatience to be baptized, and then these young people would be on the road to becoming good Frenchmen and good Catholics in all their heart and soul. But this could only be achieved by a constant struggle to rid the land of its evil virus:

It is Mahomet, it is his absurd and retrograde religion which has destroyed everything. . . . a religion established by force, which promises sensual delight as a reward to its converts, cannot help but spread rapidly: the state of dishonour, stupidity, servitude, corruption into which have been plunged all the people subjected to the law of Mahomet is demonstrably evident.[1]

[1] *Ibid.*, 207–8, 232, 447–55.

Boilat's anxieties over native immorality aided and abetted by Muslim cupidity were supplemented by other problems arising mainly within the creole community of St. Louis and Goree. These mulattoes were practising Christians but only up to a point, for ancient usage had already made legitimate a marriage custom which enabled Europeans living temporarily in the country to unite with members of the *signare* class in a form of common law marriage carrying no social stigma. Although this custom had begun to die out after the French civil code was put into effect in the colony in 1830, it had still been enough of a commonplace at the time of Boilat's return to Senegal to cause him to raise his voice in concern. As Boilat described them, the marriage arrangements were conducted openly and according to well established procedures, but for him local usage was no substitute for the Christian marriage ceremony. Couples so united were denied the sacraments of the church and few appeared willing to legitimize their 'marriages in God's word', as they were called, by subsequent ceremony within the Church. 'What suffering for the parish priest', Boilat lamented,

when having catechized and prepared young people of both sexes for their first communion, to see suddenly passing under his window even as his young neophytes were learning to appreciate the value of piety and the sacraments, a great procession of Europeans and *habitants* leading triumphantly a lamb dragged from his flock. What could he say? What could he do? Nothing but to pour out his grief before his God, and to spill his bitter tears on the holy altar. Was this to mean that priests and nuns were condemned to rear the youth in their charge only to provide concubines for the colony's potentates?

Fortunately not. When Boilat and his fellow African priests arrived in Senegal during the early 1840s, they set about to rectify the situation. In the space of a few short years they had, through perseverance, succeeded in legitimizing most of the irregular marriages and had established holy matrimony to the extent that within a ten-year period the old custom had for all practical purposes disappeared.[1]

The bulk of the *Esquisses Sénégalaises* dealt with descriptions of the indigenous people of Senegal, and in this respect Boilat's book paralleled in style and content the contemporary works of such men as Raffenel and René Caillié, Barth, Burton and Clapperton. He examined in detail the tribal economy and the degree of sophistication of traditional crafts; he reviewed socio-religious customs such as marriage, birth ceremonies and the respect for the dead; he described the daily life–clothing, physical appearance, hospitality towards strangers and the types of

[1] *Ibid.*, 221–7.

festivals practised; he analysed such matters as the state of government involving the role of the chief, the character of justice and the condition of household slavery; he explored the development of language and literature leading to concepts of African cosmology which to Boilat were better classified under the heading of native superstition. Most of the people of Senegal were carefully included – the Serer, Wolof, Fulani, Mandinka, Bambara, Sarakole, Tucolor and the Moorish tribes inhabiting the country along the north bank of the Senegal River. His point of view remained inflexibly Catholic and French, so that all things were measured by their degree of deviation from these western standards, but his descriptions were straightforward and dispassionate, and appeared to be accepted at face value by French geographers as substantial contributions to the body of scientific knowledge about Africa. Boilat's notes, sketches and anthropological specimens were gratefully received in France by the Geographical Society as welcome additions to the knowledge of African languages, literature and customs. They were especially acknowledged on behalf of the Society, moreover, by Baron Roger, the former governor of Senegal, who urged Boilat to continue his research, suggesting further exploration of Wolof, Mandinka, Fulani and Bambara manuscripts written in Arabic script.[1]

Boilat's descriptions of the interior tribes included, where appropriate, discussions of their history drawn from local tradition. Similarly, he treated the history of the evolving communities of Goree and St. Louis as part of his description of their culture and society. As with his anthropological observations, Boilat's historical analyses were coloured by his commitment both to French civilization and the Roman church, so that he must be regarded not so much as an historical scholar as an advocate of a particular point of view who used history to underscore his arguments. His discussion of the early European contacts with West Africa, therefore, dealt almost exclusively with the activities of Portuguese priests in proselytizing the local people, and when he focused on the classical times of the late Roman Empire, it was to point to the riches of Africa's ancient culture as exemplified by the early Church fathers. His whole concept of African history was rooted in the view that there had once been great scholars in Africa who had added to the world's knowledge and helped preserve it. Only with the destructive and barbarous force of Islam did Africa fall into long ages of darkness, but she was destined once again to rise through the agency of her initial strength – the Christian church:

[1] *Ibid.*, 245–54.

This land of Africa, today so barbarous, so savage—forgive the expression, it is a friend who addresses you—this corner of the world least known and until this moment forsaken, has had its moments of glory and prosperity. Many centuries before our time, she produced the world's foremost luminaries; fathers of the Church whose scholarly works still excite our imagination. They were Africans just like us—St. Augustine, the greatest scholar of his century, the famous Tertullian, St. Cyprian, and so many others in whose veins flowed African blood. These were universal men; all the sciences were familiar to them.

If this view of African history was somewhat limited in its perspective, it shared with the writings of other African intellectuals in the nineteenth century its element of pride in Africa's accomplishments, and its vision of a future revival of the greatness of the African people.[1]

Boilat's observations on the state of affairs in the colony of Senegal were not limited to mere description. He had his suggested remedies which might more quickly set the country on the road to material prosperity and spiritual rehabilitation. Education was only part of his programme, for only frustration could result from the training of leadership without plans for a sound economy, political stability and the establishment of moral and ethical standards necessary as foundations for the material structure of Senegalese society. Boilat's comments regarding political development were limited to the observation that France had sent Senegal no fewer than fourteen governors between 1843 and 1850, each with a new policy of his own, but the implication was clear that progress on all fronts required careful planning and the time under a single executive to see policy from conception to execution, and from execution to maturity. Boilat wrote in 1853; others were also concerned, for the substance of his criticism was soon met with the appointment of Faidherbe who remained as governor of Senegal for almost a decade.

The recommendations for economic rehabilitation which Boilat put forward were much more detailed and came under two categories. In the first place, he felt, it was necessary to diversify and extend the economy beyond the gum trade on the Senegal River. In Baron Roger's time, there had been the effort to cultivate the Walo through plantations devoted chiefly to cotton and indigo. This experiment had, however, come to a disastrous end largely because of what Boilat regarded as the immoral, dishonest conduct of certain colonists who preferred to defraud the government for a few years rather than build a sound agricultural economy in a productive land. It was argued at the time that alternative drought and flood combining with hot dry winds made impossible the

[1] *Ibid.*, 231-2.

THE ÉVOLUÉS

culture which Roger had instituted. This view, insisted Boilat, was incorrect. The Walo was a fertile land where, with proper attention and hard work, indigo, cotton, ground-nuts and castor oil plants could thrive. The experimental garden at the town of Richard Toll had demonstrated, moreover, that many other plants could be cultivated in Senegal—coffee, sugar, cloves, senna and various temperate zone fruits, in addition to the indigenous palm products and citrus fruits. Boilat himself had raised cotton plants in his own garden without difficulty; both cotton and indigo were native to the country and required no especial care. Thus, with ordinary cultivating methods, these crops could be made to thrive, and it was only human failing that was holding back the country from a full realization of the riches that lay in the bountiful land.[1]

The second aspect of Boilat's economic plan was complementary to the first. Diversification in a variety of farm products suggested an end to the popular preoccupation in the ruinous gum trade on the Senegal River. Virtually all the *habitants* of St. Louis were involved in the trade which was demonstrably risky and an unstable base on which to build a strong economy. Year after year the traders made their way up the river to barter their goods for the gum gathered by the Moorish tribes. Sometimes the trade was strictly regulated by government decree and sometimes it was free, but more often than not the superior merchandising ability of the Moors in addition to the uncertainties of the weather meant that profits were unpredictable at best, and a stable market difficult to achieve. For Boilat it was clear that the economic life of the colony ought not to be ransomed to such an uncertain commerce; the gum trade needed drastic reduction in quantity and what was continued would have to be by all standards strictly regulated so that through co-operative marketing the mercantilism of the Moors might be neutralized. Then at last might end the spectacle of 'the colony . . . reduced to agony'. Over the years, said Boilat, 'the traders had ruined themselves, and most had been obliged to sell out, losing their houses, their boats, their slaves, and the money of their wives, while others felt the necessity to drown their sorrow in drink'.[2]

If agriculture were to be pursued once again and the gum trade reduced and regulated, there would be the need for an intelligent, well-trained labour supply to replace the *captifs* freed by the emancipation act of 1848. Here again Boilat had a positive suggestion. We need, he said, men accustomed to heavy work under tropical conditions but who

[1] *Ibid.*, 275–6, 326–45.   [2] *Ibid.*, 470–3.

can also qualify as skilled farmers and craftsmen. We want men who have been exposed to the benefits of western civilization, who are good Christians, who are interested in developing a freehold of their own, and who are already able to speak French. Where could such ideal workers be obtained? From the West Indian sugar islands.

In the Antilles, Boilat went on, there was a surplus of labour occasioned by the end of slavery throughout the empire. Thus there were workers in the islands who would be glad to trade their skill against a passage to Africa and the opportunity to farm their own lands. Once in Senegal, they would be provided by the state with a free homestead and the necessary tools, and could quickly set about building their homes and raising sugar cane, ground-nuts, coffee and cotton. Their farms would serve as models which would attract both the citizens of St. Louis and Goree and the natives of the inland country. As Africans they would be well received by the local people and they in turn would wish to teach their African brothers not only their technical skills, but the French language and the Christian faith. Soon a healthy yeomanry would arise with products for the markets of Europe and a growing capacity in turn for the consumption of European goods.[1]

So much for the material life of the colony. Boilat, the missionary priest, did not neglect the rehabilitation of the spirit. In order to provide for religious development, Boilat offered the interesting suggestion that Franciscan missions be established in the country. Essentially his reasons rested on the similarity between the way of life of the Franciscans and of the Muslim marabouts. For all his dislike of marabouts and what they stood for, Boilat was quite prepared to admit their hold over the people and he was shrewdly able to assess the reasons therefor. The marabout was the supreme man of God, preoccupied with prayer and the instruction of the young, an ascetic who flourished on privation and sought out mortification of the flesh. He fasted rigorously, and deprived himself of sleep to devote his time to prayer. He gathered about him no worldly goods and subsisted on the charity of the people. He went everywhere in his simple austerity and was everywhere received as the representative of God on earth. So might it be with the Franciscan monk. He too specialized in itinerant teaching, in piety, in poverty and in prayer. His austerity was celebrated, his fasting as rigorous as that of the marabout, his clothing as coarse, and his worldly possessions as few. How then could the Senegalese, already impressed with the piety and other-worldliness of the marabout fail to respond to these simple

[1] *Ibid.*, 474–7.

THE ÉVOLUÉS

devout monks? They would be equally regarded as saints, their teaching would be equally attended and they would ultimately succeed as well as the marabout in bringing their message before the people. The true religion of Jesus would do the rest. Conversion and baptism would necessarily follow. Boilat was able therefore to view the future with optimism:

Is this country lost forever? Most assuredly not. Senegal possesses innumerable resources. All that is needed to make her one of the most prosperous of colonies is the desire. The means are very simple, and I have no doubt that all who wish for the best, who desire the interest of France and her commerce, of the civilization of these people and the propagation of the Catholic faith, will readily understand the plan I propose.[1]

2 Paul Holle and French Domination of the Senegal

The Abbé Boilat linked all his plans for the regeneration of his country and his people to absorption of French culture and adherence to the church of Rome. As a priest his views tended to revolve around religious conversion, but essentially his doctrine was a classic example of French assimilationist philosophy. Despite his anthropological and linguistic studies, he tended to overlook local African accomplishments, interests and values in his zeal for bringing to Africa the benefits of western civilization. In this insistence on the absorption of French culture, however, he was far from being alone, and it is fair to say that few of his suggestions or criticisms would have raised any opposition among the evolved creole and pure-blood population of the St. Louis and Gorée of his day. Indeed, where evidence of their opinions has survived, it has fully supported the views of the young priest. Of much the same bent of opinion, for example, was the mulatto government administrator and soldier, Paul Holle – the defender of Medina and one of Senegal's early national heroes.

The name of Paul Holle is not normally associated with the development of ideas in West Africa. A creole born in St. Louis, he was a young man at the time that Baron Roger instituted his plans for agricultural development in the Walo, and was employed by Roger, along with other young creoles, to help administer the programme. Later, Holle served in St. Louis as a tax collector, but his major career as explorer and soldier began in 1840 when he was appointed commander of the

[1] *Ibid.*, 473–90.

frontier post of Bakel on the Senegal River. Such a post involved considerable responsibility for it was several hundred miles upstream from St. Louis in the heart of the unpacified Tucolor country. His appointment was in part a matter of government policy to put troops under African direction whenever possible, and he soon proved to be an able commander and administrator and remained at Bakel and other near-by posts continuously for the ensuing fifteen years. Thus it was that in 1855 when El Hadj Omar began to focus his attention on the French forces on the Senegal, Governor Faidherbe established a new fort at Medina and shortly thereafter Holle was dispatched to command its garrison.

Two years later, in 1857, these antagonistic worlds of Africa confronted each other–Holle the assimilated mulatto at the head of a small force of fifty-six African and seven European soldiers holding Medina as an outpost of western civilization in the African wilderness; El Hadj Omar leading his Tucolor armies in a holy war to bring Islam triumphant to Senegal and to rid the land of the infidel. In mid-April the attack came; Holle defended the fort brilliantly against El Hadj's initially heavy assaults, then settled down to endure a four-month siege which virtually eliminated his supplies and reduced the garrison and its several thousand refugees to the point of starvation. Somehow the defenders managed to hang on and when the summer rains permitted Faidherbe to ascend the river and raise the siege, he found the flag still flying over the battered fort. The defenders could not have held out much longer. Their ammunition had been reduced to two rounds per man, fuel had long since given out and food was so scarce that when Faidherbe arrived and drove off El Hadj's forces, the people rushed out to devour the grass outside the walls. Yet under Holle's direction, morale had been excellent. He had planned to blow up the fort if El Hadj succeeded in forcing an entry, but mostly he maintained an unruffled concern with the present. 'Why bother returning their fire?' he admonished his soldiers. 'Don't we already have enough corpses around the walls?' And he took the trouble to post on the main portal a placard designed to taunt the Muslim enemy with the inscription, 'Long live Jesus! Long live the Emperor. To conquer or to die for God and Emperor.'[1]

This was the typical romantic gesture expected by France of her soldiers fighting for God and country in exotic far-off places, and Holle's

---

[1] Hardy, *La Mise en Valeur du Sénégal*, 138; P. Cultru, *Histoire du Sénégal du XV Siècle à 1870*, 339–43; *Annales Sénégalaises de 1854 à 1885*, 128–41; Gov. Charmasson to Minister, Sept. 20, 1840, no. 298, N.A.S. 2B18, 13G165, 166, *passim*; Faidherbe, *Le Sénégal*, 181–96.

image has survived in just this form of the brave soldier defending with stubborn skill what he held dear against the forces of darkness which threatened his world. There indeed the image might have been fixed had it not been for the fact that Holle was something more than a simple soldier; like the Abbé Boilat, he was an articulate defender of his way of life, and he added to his skills of military persuasion the more peaceable argument of authorship. Two years before the attack on Medina, he published jointly with a French civil servant, Frédéric Carrère, a treatise entitled *De La Sénégambie Française* in which both men sought to describe the African colony and its people and to set forth a series of suggestions for its future development.

Superficially their book was another in the series of quasi-geographical, quasi-anthropological studies of Africa appearing commonly during the nineteenth century and designed to entertain or to instruct a European audience on the characteristics of an exotic foreign land. Actually, in this case it was much more a tract criticizing the shortcomings of French colonial policy in Senegal since 1817, and suggesting specific remedies for the regeneration of the colony. In broad outline the message of the two authors was simple and straightforward. Holle and his colleague did not feel that France understood fully the importance of Senegal. Here was a potentially rich and important land held up in its development by the ignorance, superstition and religious bigotry of the local population. France, for her part, the embodiment of a higher civilization, was the means by which the people of Senegal could be freed from their limitations and conducted on the road to material and moral betterment. It behoved France, therefore, to replace her former vacillating colonial policy with a positive programme, forceful and energetic, carefully designed in detail and clearly aimed at specific goals. Carrère and Holle undertook to show what that programme ought to be.

First of all were the backwardness of the people and the potentialities of the country. The people of the interior were primitive, living by and large in a state of feudalism, but under proper conditions they were amenable to French rule and guidance. At the same time the country possessed riches for the most part untapped. The river trade in gum could easily be supplemented by other products such as ground-nuts, there were unexploited gold mines in the interior, and agricultural regions, particularly the Walo, awaited the proper cultivation of a variety of crops which might be exchanged in the markets of Europe.

Little progress in any of these directions could be expected to occur, however, until several specific steps were taken. The trouble with French policy, Holle and Carrère insisted, was that it had not been strong enough. Between 1840 and 1855, for example, there had been nineteen governors of Senegal. Estimable men they may have been, but they could accomplish little when they were replaced before their first experimental months had ended, and their successors in turn were forced through the same procedure. Like Boilat the two authors pointed out that it took time to learn local customs and languages on which to base sound policy. The governors, moreover, tended to be drawn from the ranks of naval officers who, competent enough in their own sphere, were not usually well suited to civil administration.[1]

Linked to short gubernatorial administrations was a weak policing policy. Though the agricultural experiment in the Walo conducted by Baron Roger had failed through lack of interest in farming by the commercially minded people of St. Louis, the failure of the Walo was also attributable to the subsequent military domination of that territory by the Moors. This had once been a prosperous land, well-populated and fruitful. But the Moorish tribe of Trarzas had overrun the Walo and France had failed to check their advance which had ultimately extended as far as the Cayor. Thus this rich country had been laid waste, emptied of its inhabitants, and dominated by despair, terror and uncertainty. All this could have been prevented by a vigorous French intervention. 'If, as was our right and our duty', said Holle, 'we had prevented the Moors from violating their promises and devastating the Walo, this unhappy country would not have fallen into the state of depression and degradation in which we find it today. We ought to blame ourselves, for through our indifference, we are experiencing the unhappy effects.' What was needed was a policy of restricting the Moors to their own territory on the north bank of the Senegal River. In this instance they would either learn to settle down to a peaceful existence as farmers or they would fall victim to famine and French military action. Whatever the choice, said Holle, the Africans who loved the soil would be free once again to return to their fields, and the land would prosper as it had before, under French suzerainty. To assure all this, France required a policy of energy and perseverance, qualities which Holle felt the new governor, Faidherbe, possessed in abundance.[2]

Strong military action was going to be needed on another count, the co-authors announced. The trade on the Senegal River could never hope to flourish until peace was secured along its course. Already a

[1] *De la Sénégambie Française*, 100, 341.   [2] *Ibid.*, 89-90, 94, 99, 105-6.

number of fortified points had been established as trading posts and Holle himself had been instrumental in the negotiations leading to the location of a fort at Sénoudébou in the 1840s. But Holle could clearly see trouble arising in another quarter. For some years he and his colleagues had marked the activities of the Tucolor marabout El Hadj Omar and they were convinced that he was aiming at a holy war designed to rid the country of the French. Possessed of rare ability and energy, the young Omar had early developed a religious zeal which resulted in a pilgrimage to Mecca in 1825. On his return, his tireless preaching soon brought him a reputation as a holy man, a growing following and material support which he consistently converted into arms. His doctrines comprised a stricter application of the precepts of Islam, conversion of the infidels and the overthrow of the petty chiefdoms in the country. When he met the French governor in 1847, he protested his desire for peace, but Holle who was present at the meeting was not persuaded. 'It was already clear at that time that under the mask of religious proselytism he sought to create a vast empire in Senegambia.'

Back and forth across the interior, El Hadj continued to preach and gradually the Africans came to feel that under the leadership of this holy man the end both of Moorish oppression and the tyranny of their own chiefs was in sight. By 1855, El Hadj felt himself strong enough openly to appropriate supplies from the French post at Medina, justifying this action on the grounds that the French had refused to provide him with arms in the past and that Christians were standing in the way of his holy war. 'Now I will be avenged by force', he vowed, 'and I will not stop until your tyrant [the governor] sues for peace and submits to me.' These words were not lost on Faidherbe who moved quickly to fortify Medina and other posts along the Senegal. Neither were they lost on Paul Holle:

> Without any doubt, El Hadj intends to create a vast empire . . . he wishes above all to collect . . . the various tributes which we are now paying to the chiefs on the left (south) bank. . . . to be tolerated the infidel will have to buy through large payments the goodwill of the true believer. Once master from the Cayor to the Kaarta, he would close the river with a word; he is an enemy who must be destroyed. Doubtless the war with the Trarzas is important, but the ambition of El Hadj is much more of a threat to the future of this colony.

This tough-minded estimate, written in 1855, did not even give El Hadj the credit for conducting an honest holy war. Clearly, Paul Holle possessed an ideal psychological equipment for facing warrior marabouts, and his frame of mind was to stand him in good stead two years later when the two met at Medina.[1]

The antipathy which Carrère and his African mulatto colleague, Paul Holle, bore towards El Hadj Omar was not entirely based on personal dislike or suspicion. Quite aside from personalities, they entertained a lively antipathy for the Muslim faith which they felt preached religious war and kept the local people in a state of barbarism. Once again the fault could be traced to a lack of vigorous French administration. Far from trying to influence the people away from Islam, the authorities had allowed the marabouts free reign in the pursuit of their activities. The result had been an almost complete rejection among the Senegalese people of the French language, western civilization and the Christian faith. The marabouts controlled the education of children from their earliest years, teaching them to ignore French culture and to distrust the French schools. They dominated the African population of St. Louis, encouraging ignorance and superstition among the people and milking them of their meagre income in return for all sorts of false charms and nostrums. This situation would never improve until the movements and activities of the marabouts were sytematically regulated – their residence in the capital city, and their authority over births, deaths, marriages and civil disputes – so that the Africans might begin to turn to the French law for protection. At the same time positive action was needed in the form of western education, a lay school in each quarter of St. Louis with compulsory attendance. There the primary aim would be clear: *'to force the children to learn to speak French'*. Only through strong measures could the slow evolution of a backward people be speeded up:

At first they will resist with that inertia which is characteristic of their race, but if we force them we will succeed. The Muslim, and particularly the black, only respects force: we believe in using it in moderation but it will have to be used. There will be no results without pressure. Let it be applied gently, but steadily. Let us have no more talk of toleration and religious freedom. These principles perhaps have value in countries where human reason, developed to the point of self-restraint, is able to invoke freedom of conscience without violating the law. Here, however, we must not forget that we are dealing with races of crude instincts, taught by a brutalizing religion. Furthermore, if we reflect that all primitive societies have passed through this stage of government by force, we can accept the propriety of a force applied with intelligence and moderation.[2]

[1] *Ibid.*, 163–5, 191–208, esp. 207–8.   [2] *Ibid.*, 355–63, esp. 360.

The views of Carrère and Holle on the economic development of the country were also linked with the idea that the French government lacked a clearly defined and executed colonial policy. First of all, the agricultural experiment in the Walo had suffered for lack of official comprehension that the people of St. Louis, both mulatto and black, were traders to the marrow of their bones and would never take to the sedentary life of cultivator. Next, the administration had pursued a series of attempts to stabilize the gum traffic on the Senegal. Regulation was tried in various forms and free trade was instituted for a time, but none of these schemes was more than palliative, and the commerce suffered in the face of the organized bargaining of the Moors who continued to control the supply of gum and who were able to dictate the price structure through economic monopoly backed by the threat of military action. To Holle, long experienced on the river, force was the only solution. Once the power of the Moors was broken, there would be no more trouble at the trading posts and bargaining could be conducted by the St. Louis merchants in free competition. Nevertheless these merchants would have to understand that the rough and ready days of the gum trade had come to an end with the establishment of peace. Henceforward, a sophisticated merchandising carried on by educated, hard working, scrupulously honest traders would have to replace trickery and brute force:

> Let these young men to whom the future belongs, imbue themselves with the French way of doing things, let them never forget that it is through patience, probity, reliability, and diligence that they can gain the confidence of investors, and after having proven themselves as faithful agents, wise and thrifty, they will become in their turn skilful businessmen.[1]

To this sober bourgeois formula Holle and Carrère added the plea for diversification through introduction of ground-nut culture and its by-products into the economy of the colony. This would not only broaden the economic base of Senegal, but it would also free metropolitan refineries from reliance on foreign supplies and rejuvenate the French merchant marine. There were widespread areas throughout Senegal where ground-nuts could be made to thrive; all that was needed was the willingness to invest time, labour and money in crop production and in greatly improving the capacity and speed of the river craft so that an increased tonnage could be handled cheaply and efficiently.

---

[1] *Ibid.*, 343–54, esp. 353.

Here again it was the same story—the need for a more energetic colonial policy emanating from Paris.[1]

It was in connection with economic development and overall French colonial policy that Carrère and Holle offered their most surprising suggestion regarding manpower. The Abbé Boilat had recommended the return to Africa of the freed slaves of the French West Indies as the nucleus of an independent yeomanry. Holle and his colleague proposed reversing the procedure. The end of slavery in the colonies, they pointed out, had created a shortage of labour in the Antilles which the government had sought in vain to overcome. These islands were necessary to the prosperity of the mother country; why could not sufficient labour be found from among the freed slaves of another of France's children, the colony of Senegal? It would be simple to send ships down the coast collecting former slaves, helpless and facing almost certain death through neglect by their recent masters. These would be shipped to the sugar islands for ten-year indentures. At the end of that period, the government would select some to remain in the islands, subject to their consent, while the others would be returned to Senegal and given a homestead in the Walo. Thus would be created a body of skilled farmers, accustomed to effective labour, Christian in faith and French in culture. They would be able to instruct their neighbours in their more sophisticated agricultural techniques and would form the vanguard for the march of civilization into the interior of the country.

Holle was aware that some squeamish souls might shrink from this somewhat arbitrary enforced migration with its overtones of the slavery just ended. One had to look at the large picture, however. If human progress came through worldwide intercourse and experience, was not Africa's future bound up in major migrations of this sort? This was not the time for faint measures:

Can it be denied that the black race, stricken with a mysterious curse, has been from the beginning of time subjected to humiliation and oppression? With the help of two generous nations, this unhappy race has now begun to get a glimmer of better days, to occupy a little place in mankind's moral sun. Why stop at this point? Why hesitate because of timid scruples? Who believes that if Africa is abandoned to herself, civilization will easily penetrate there, that if a strong hand does not force the breach, this mysterious continent will by herself attain the respect of mankind? . . . Away with such dreams. . . . Let France, going to the heart of the matter, institute the suggested migration which,

[1] *Ibid.*, 149, 380–8.

though immediately profiting the colonies in the west, would ultimately turn to the advantage of the black race and of Senegal.[1]

The pattern was clear. What Senegal needed was hard-headed planning by an interested France whose philanthropy would coincide with enlightened self-interest. The destinies of the two countries were forever interlocked and the benefits to Senegal, following the lead provided by an enlightened cultivated France, were unlimited:

We would like, and we believe our hopes are not Utopian, to see St. Louis the centre of an important commerce salutary to the people engaged in it and profitable to our industry. We would like to see the spirit of France, symbol of the best and most noble civilization, gradually penetrate this country which until now has suffered under a crushing barbarism, and infiltrate the customs of these peoples with whom the moral light has flickered so uncertainly. Finally, we would like to see a triumphant Christianity, that mother of progress, forming the base and the apex of a structure whose creation would add to our national glory. It is far from our thoughts that Senegambia be conquered by force of arms. Material conquest is bootless, but force and moral action ought to be in the hands of the most competent and clearsighted. It is essential that we who are helping these people to a better future, protect them against their oppressors and against themselves.[2]

3 More French than the Frenchman

When Faidherbe became governor of Senegal in 1854, he quickly set about with characteristic energy to solidify and extend France's foothold in Africa. He pacified much of the interior and laid the groundwork for further military conquest which he clearly saw was the first necessity of a profitable and stable commerce. He instituted a system of public works designed to open up the country and improve the economy. He established the Bank of Senegal, redesigned the city of St. Louis, and arranged for the founding of Dakar. He encouraged education on a scale previously unessayed and reformed French administrative and military efficiency. Frenchman though he was, he saw that good government could not come through ignorance of the local people and their ways, and he placed knowledge and respect for local language, custom and religion at the foundation of his colonial policy. He sought to introduce European civilization, but not at the expense of local beliefs and culture. He provided schools for the sons of chiefs and saw to it that lay schools were available to the Muslims of St. Louis who feared the religious biases of the Catholic mission schools. He instituted

[1] Ibid., 372–6, esp. 373–4.   [2] Ibid., 368–9.

western vocational training, but his solicitude for Islamic customs led him to inaugurate specially constituted Muslim courts.

In comparison with the moderate Faidherbe, Abbé Boilat the African priest and Paul Holle the creole soldier seem more inflexibly French than the Frenchman. They saw little reason for studying local custom and language except better to find ways for ruling, no point in tolerating a degenerate Islam which was fit only to be stamped out. They sought total assimilation into French culture, total rejection of Africa's traditional way of life. Yet they were Africans, not Europeans, and their ultimate interest was in African development, not in European ascendancy. To be sure they looked to France for cultural, economic and political guidance, but it was essentially the society, the economy, the polity of Senegal which claimed their allegiance. The appeal to France for help was always in terms of African development. They wanted Christian conversion because they believed this would be a benefit to their own people. They sought economic development, not for the trading houses of Bordeaux or Marseilles but for the merchants of St. Louis. They urged war on the interior tribes not to further French imperialism but to encourage a new civilization in Senegal. In this regard they anticipated the Senegalese who came after them in the nineteenth and twentieth centuries, who in their turn continued to regard mastery of French culture and institutions as the basis for the cultural and political development of Senegal.

9 British Assimilation along the Niger: Bishop Crowther

1 *The Bible and the Plough*

In the early years of the nineteenth century, the possibility of a modern Nigerian state could scarcely have been deduced from the political configurations and social patterns to be found at the time in that area of West Africa. Political, social and cultural groupings gave little hint of later amalgamation; warfare, isolation and separatism, not cohesion, were the hallmarks of the day.

Furthermore, the prospect of European cultural influence appeared remote as the century opened. Orientation tended to be northward and inward, beginning with the great states of the savannah preoccupied with their dynastic and religious differences, but including the fratricidal Yoruba, the decaying power of Benin, and the Ibo people, shut off from the sea by the slaving city states of the Niger delta. Yet in little more than one hundred years, the whole pattern had changed. Britain had established herself in Yorubaland, Benin had fallen, the Niger country was occupied and the northern territories were conquered. The foundation for a modern Nigerian state had been established.

During the nineteenth century the impact of Europe on the Nigerian peoples came in two different ways. Essentially the impulse was economic—first the demand for slaves and then, when the traffic was abolished by Britain in 1807, a gradual substituting of other products, chiefly palm oil to lubricate the machines of the new industry of the West. In time there followed a desire to penetrate to the interior in search of bigger, richer markets and the movement led eventually to military action and, along with other factors, to final political control.

But Europe entered the Nigerian world in another, more particularly African, way. Most of the Yoruba, Ibo and other recaptives released in Freetown settled down to build a new life in Sierra Leone. Not all were so adaptable, however. Some found it difficult to make their way in a strange land without capital and lacking technical skills. Others chafed over the paucity of good land, and all felt the open hostility of the Nova Scotian and Maroon settlers. Women were necessarily scarce; consequently it was difficult to put down roots. By 1839, therefore, while a considerable population of liberated Africans was permanently settled in Sierra Leone, there were those who longed to return to their homes in the east, despite the dangers of the voyage and the possibility of reenslavement. In that year the first emigrants shipped from Freetown to Badagry, and these were quickly followed by others who proceeded down the coast as far as Old Calabar, establishing substantial communities in ports like Lagos and Badagry, and fanning out into the interior to centres such as Abeokuta where they were often united once again with families from whom they had been separated many years before. Within a short time several hundred had made the trip back down the coast and the migration continued through the 1840s and 1850s until the repatriates probably numbered several thousand.[1]

These wanderers come home again could scarcely fit back unchanged into their old ways. Some were complete strangers, children of the original slaves, who had never known their ancestral land. Their elders, in any case, after years of absence in another land, shaped by another environment, converted to Christianity in many cases, fluent and possibly literate in English, accustomed to western food, dress, lodging and customs, returned in varying degrees with new standards, new ideas, new tastes and new values acquired during their residence in Sierra Leone. And consciously or unconsciously they were bound to impress these new ways on their old communities, forcing the traditional and the conservative to adjust, grudgingly or willingly, to these ideas and customs from overseas. Thus it was that the repatriates from Sierra Leone added their measure in opening up their motherland to European influence.

There was, however, another important factor which made of the African returning from Sierra Leone not merely an accidental vehicle for the casual introduction of European influences, but in a number of important cases a conscious, organized, trained agent dedicated to promoting western culture and institutions in the territories of West Africa. This was the anti-slavery and missionary movement in England. And more particularly it was the ideas and the activities of two of the move-

[1] Christopher Fyfe, *A History of Sierra Leone*, 212–13, 317–18; R. R. Kuczynski, *Demographic Survey of the British Colonial Empire*, I, 135–7.

ment's leading exponents and most successful practitioners—Thomas Fowell Buxton and Henry Venn.

The thinking of these men was fixed by their determination to put an end to slavery for all time. Although both the slave trade and slavery throughout the British Empire had been abolished by 1834, it seemed clear that the law and the fact were not the same, that the trade had not been stamped out as expected by the combination of naval patrols in West African waters and international treaty. If anything slaving was on the rise, responding to the continuing demands of plantation owners in the Americas and stimulating to greater exertion the evasive ingenuity of the African middleman and the slavers themselves. New methods were needed, therefore, and it was Buxton who supplied the theoretical framework for a different, extended anti-slavery policy.

It was simplicity itself. In order to put an end to the slave trade, Buxton argued, it was necessary only to provide the indigenous African suppliers with a more lucrative substitute, to replace slaving with legitimate commerce. When it was demonstrated to the Africans that greater profit would result from keeping their manpower at home, using it for the development of more valuable agricultural products, the source of supply would quickly dry up and the trade would be ended. What was needed, therefore, was exploration of the great waterways leading to the interior of Africa to be followed by treaties with the chiefs of the inland nations providing for direct trade between those people and Europe. Britain, for example, would undertake to establish trading posts and agricultural stations, not on the coast but far inland, and at these centres commerce would be conducted while the people were instructed in useful crafts and techniques of crop production. British ships would institute a more rigorous patrol of the coast and British arms would keep the peace in the interior. Since Africa was known to have an unhealthy climate for Europeans, the burden of manning these new stations would fall on the many Africans who had become civilized and christianized in the West Indies. And tying the whole structure together would be the beneficent influence of the Christian mission, leading the African to understand not only the blessings of western civilization, but teaching him to enjoy the bliss of a higher Christian moral order.[1]

Thus, Christian humanitarianism was to join hands with sound practical business methods and western scientific agriculture to

---

[1] J. Gallagher, 'Fowell Buxton and the New African Policy, 1838–1842', *The Cambridge Historical Journal*, vol. X, 36–43; Thomas Fowell Buxton, *The African Slave Trade and Its Remedy*, 299, 306, 491–2, 511.

regenerate Africa. As it happened, Buxton's proposal received a severe reversal with the disastrous expedition which was sent to explore the Niger in 1841 as a prelude to establishing the inland stations he had described. But the idea, despite the immediate setback, did not end there. It was adopted, refined and developed in the imaginative mind of Henry Venn, and subsequently put into effect by that energetic individual who in 1841 had become secretary of the Church Missionary Society.

Venn carried Buxton's philosophy to its logical conclusion. If Africa was to be regenerated, what better agency was there than a sober, hard-working, Christian middle class and what better model for success than Venn's own Victorian England? What Africa needed was a middle class of merchants, industrialists and scientific farmers capable of building up the local economy, re-investing surplus profits, and making effective use of local manpower to feed expanding commerce, agriculture and industry. For ignorant chiefs presiding over primitive states barely subsisting on the edge of famine, the slave trade was an invitation to sell off surplus population which only depressed stagnant economies and local living standards. But in the hands of a middle class, labour could be the basis for increased production and an expanding purchasing power. New products should be grown—indigo, arrowroot and particularly cotton—and processing plants developed so that a healthy and profitable exchange between the new Africa and industrialized Europe might develop to the benefit of both. In the process slavery would automatically wither away and die.

To be sure, outside help would be needed in the initial stages, first to protect the system against interference by the old slaving interests, then to provide funds for investment in new industries and for research in new crops, to build the necessary schools for the training of the new bourgeois leadership, and to instil the Christian moral and ethical standards which were the foundations of the whole structure. This help would be available through British governmental protection, through British economic aid and through the Christian missions which would take the lead in education and religious instruction. When the local economy had been sufficiently developed, when an adequate middle class had emerged to direct its own affairs, and when a strong local church had established itself to deal with the spiritual needs of the African community, outside assistance might cease and a healthy modern independent African society, after the successful model of Victorian England, would be the result. Such a system was already taking shape in the Sierra Leone colony, and Venn saw the prospect of all West Africa blossoming in similar fashion, possibly through the aid of the Sierra Leoneans themselves.[1]

2 *'Africa for the Africans alone is . . . ignorance'*

The missionary view of Africa's future, with some variations, became the prevailing view of a number of important African leaders during the second half of the nineteenth century. The first and most influential of these was Bishop Samuel Ajayi Crowther.

Crowther's career has always intrigued the romantically-minded and inspired those who enter life with few advantages and great expectations. His story is well known—the young village boy, Ajayi, captured during a slave raid arising out of the Yoruba wars, forcibly separated from home and family, taken into domestic slavery, then sold to Portuguese traders and loaded on a slaver; the miraculous appearance of two British men-of-war who took his vessel and freed its occupants; and the eventual arrival and emancipation at Freetown. He was only in his early teens when all this took place, the capture in 1821 and the eventual debarkation at the sanctuary of Sierra Leone in June 1822. His career had thus far been characterized by adventure and extremely good fortune; now the good fortune continued but romantic adventure was replaced by hard work and slow steady achievement.

At Freetown he proved quick and intelligent, diligent and amenable to discipline. Taken under the wing of the missionaries of the Church Missionary Society, he responded well to their training, learned to read and write, and was baptized Samuel Crowther in 1825. By 1827, after a brief stay in England, he was enrolled in the C.M.S. training institution at Fourah Bay from whence he graduated to become a school teacher in mission and government schools in and around Freetown. Slowly gaining recognition as a substantial member of the Yoruba community of Freetown and impressing the missionaries as a sober and down-to-earth but high-minded Christian, he was invited to join the Niger expedition of 1841 at the conclusion of which he produced his factual and eloquent *Journal*. Two years later he was in England where he was ordained and in 1845 he went to Abeokuta as a missionary, one of the early Sierra Leone emigrés to go home again.

The ensuing years were crowded. Two more voyages up the Niger

[1] J. F. A. Ajayi, 'Henry Venn and the Policy of Development', *Journal of the Historical Society of Nigeria*, vol. I, no. 4, 331–42.

in 1854 and 1857 followed a visit to England in 1851 where he helped Venn promote his policy for the economic and moral regeneration of Africa through partnership between the missions and the British government. The expedition of 1857 was expressly for the purpose of establishing inland missions along the Niger, and stations were begun at once at Igbebe at the confluence of the Niger and the Benue, and at Onitsha. Others were to follow, and it was soon apparent that administration of these posts would require a West African diocese under its own bishop. The choice was obvious. Henry Venn's policies had always rested on the idea of a Christian-educated indigenous population with its own native leadership. Who could better give that leadership than the man who had three times ascended the Niger, who had founded the missions on its banks, who was a close student of African languages, among other things translating several books of the Bible into Yoruba, and who in thought and action was the outstanding example of Venn's westernized, Christianized African bourgeois? In June 1864, Crowther was consecrated as Bishop of the territories of West Africa beyond the British Dominions.[1]

Rescued from slavery by the British navy, educated by English missionaries, protégé and close friend of the influential Henry Venn, Crowther predictably developed ideas of Africa's renascence which followed closely those of his teacher. And it was necessary that this be so for he was the primary agent for carrying out Venn's policies, devoting his life and his professional career to the achievement of those purposes. To understand Crowther's career in thought and deed, therefore, it is essential to understand this deep debt and close attachment to the West, so close indeed that it is often difficult to realize that after all Crowther was an African and not an Englishman. Without identification, much of his public commentary and private correspondence might easily be mistaken for the observations of any of the various English missionaries who were his colleagues in West Africa during the mid-century years.

Viewed from another perspective, his philosophy was a reflection of personal character. Small in stature, unobtrusive in appearance, and shy in manner, he was a simple unaffected man—not so much unselfconscious as selfless, modest rather than uncertain, meek though fearless. Surviving photographs invariably show him in an attitude of calm repose, his heavy features impassive, his eyes thoughtful and infinitely

---

[1] J. F. Schon and S. A. Crowther, *Journals of the ... Expedition up the Niger in 1841*, 371–85; J. F. A. Ajayi, *Christian Missions in Nigeria, 1841–1891*, 26–7, 32–4, 72–3.

sad. His frail appearance belied a strong constitution which held up against illness throughout a very long life, and enabled him to work tirelessly for long hours year after year. His capacity for work also reflected an unshakeable sense of duty and a devotion to the principles on which his career rested. His correspondence is voluminous – long letters, thick diaries and journals carefully copied out in the late hours of days crowded with the events they related. Intelligence there was aplenty reflected in the painstakingly recorded, yet lively and vivid, accounts of tribal customs, native dress, linguistic variations and topographical phenomena. His courage had an element of doggedness to it – his unfaltering determination to make his missions succeed despite sometimes catastrophic reverses is nothing less than admirable as is the near-ecstatic quality of his religious faith in the face of adversity.

Patient in manner, on the whole dispassionate in judgment, yet even he in his elevated spirit sometimes succumbed to fatigue or discouragement. There must have been many times when the people in the mission villages drove him to distraction; still one feels that the not infrequent comments in his papers regarding such matters as the venality of the natives, the primitive quality of their institutions, the shortcomings of their personal hygiene, the superstitions of Muslims, or the treacherousness of chiefs were something less than the Christian charity and understanding he professed. One looks in vain, moreover, for a lightness of touch, an occasional spark of humour to relieve the sober, almost sombre manner. His writings reveal very little self-expression of opinion, perhaps too little for they also lack the image of a creative incisive mind at work, the kind of mind which can somehow meet each new problem with a new solution, taking old ideas and reshaping them to fit altered circumstances.

Crowther's strengths and weaknesses thus were at war, both helping and hindering his attempts to establish the western Christian society he believed so fully was necessary for the temporal and spiritual salvation of Africa. His tireless unswerving efforts were ideally suited to the early years of exploration, the founding of the mission stations and the slow work of nurturing these infant establishments to strength and self-sufficiency. Later, his innate humility and his unfailing devotion to the English missionary movement robbed him of the necessary independence of judgment and toughness of character to deal with subordinates who undermined his authority or to discipline those members of his clergy who were weak or refractory. When the time came for a change of policy and a new direction in which to lead the people of West Africa who ever looked to him for guidance, he was unable to provide that leadership. Perhaps by that late hour he was too old and set in his ideas; yet the suspicion remains that, despite his studious manner, he was essentially an unreflective person, better at carrying out the ideas of others than at developing his own. Be that as it may, he was a remarkable man; certainly the most remarkable to come out of West Africa in his generation.

Following the lead of Henry Venn, Crowther was a wholehearted supporter of the doctrine of 'the Bible and the plough'–the phrase popularized by Buxton–the idea that the regeneration of West Africa lay in economic development through sound business methods and spiritual salvation through Christian conversion. Whether speaking of the Yoruba, the people of the Niger delta, or the inland tribes along the great waterways, Crowther hammered away at the possibilities of economic rehabilitation through improved agricultural methods and technical training. The old trade in ivory and the farming of palm oil from uncultivated trees in the forest was not sufficient for the new Africa, however satisfactory it might be to the European merchants on the coast. There were infinite possibilities in other products–ground-nuts, tobacco, indigo, arrowroot, cayenne pepper and ginger. Particularly promising was cotton which could be successfully grown in Africa and which, if so developed–though Crowther did not say so–would help relieve British manufactories of dependence on cotton production from America.

The vast majority of the people, said Crowther, were farmers already; they lacked only the guidance and knowledge to try new products. With cotton culture might be combined the preliminary processing of ginning and baling for shipment to the mills in England. Thus an adequate supply of craftsmen should be developed to supplement the farming population and to this end technical schools were needed, doubly valuable in that they inculcated sound habits of industry as well as the skills of a useful trade. Not long after he arrived at the Abeokuta mission, Crowther recorded in his journal:

> The people here are industrious farmers and active traders; they want a model farm before them, to teach them . . . how to improve their land: they also want a market opened to stimulate them . . . Sugar cane can be grown here . . . Tobacco plant is indigenous, what is wanted is only the act of curing it; when this once can be done . . . the slave trade will receive a heavy blow.

Fifteen years later he was saying much the same thing about the Niger missions:

> The country abounds with produce; labour is cheap: if the youths are only taught to prepare them for European markets our work is done.... Let us improve the country from its own resources.

Given economic growth and establishment of the necessities of life, a Christian community could flourish:

> When trade and agriculture engage the attention of the people, and with the gentle and peaceful teaching of Christianity, the minds of the people will gradually be won from war and marauding expeditions to peaceful trade and commerce.[1]

For all the talk of economic development, Crowther was first and last a priest and a missionary, and he never lost sight of the primary goal which was to convert heathens and to save souls. 'I regard industry as a necessary, though a secondary, part of missionary labours', he informed the clergy in the Niger Mission in 1866, '... we have acted consistently with our profession by introducing the Gospel and the Plough... Both have worked hand-in-hand—the Gospel primarily; Industry as the handmaid to the Gospel.' It was an error to think that first emphasis had to be placed on temporal things, that Christianity would automatically follow upon the teaching of mechanical arts which heightened material comfort through better houses, more plentiful food, improved medical care and more adequate schooling. The world's history was enough to belie this doctrine; one had but to look at the material advantages emerging from western industrial civilization and to wonder at the spiritual poverty which accompanied those advantages. The road to salvation and spiritual satisfaction lay elsewhere:

> If we confer with flesh and blood; if our weapons are carnal... we cannot expect otherwise but a reaction upon ourselves... But when we go out at the command of Jesus to preach the Gospel to the heathens as Christ's faithful soldiers and servants, having no other objects in view but the glory of God and the salvation of souls, we need not fear.[2]

Christian evangelization, therefore, was to be the primary objective but the agent, wherever possible, was to be the African, not the European. Returning from his voyage up the Niger in 1854, Crowther was convinced that the time was ripe for the introduction of Christianity in that territory. Who would make the most effective missionaries?

---

[1] Crowther's Journal ending June 25, 1847, C.M.S. CA2/031; *C.M. Intelligencer*, 1857, 199–200, 1871, 93–4.

[2] 'Charge delivered on the Banks of the River Niger', 1866, quoted in D. C. Crowther, *The Niger Delta Pastorate Church*, 165–6; *C.M. Intelligencer*, 1875, 86.

The people are willing to receive any who may be sent among them. The English are still looked upon as their friends, [but] . . . God has provided instruments to begin the work, in the liberated Africans in the Colony of Sierra Leone who are the natives of the banks of this river. . . . It would be of very great advantage if the colony-born young men were introduced by their parents or countrymen to their fatherland . . . They are brought back to their country as a renewed people, looked upon by their countrymen as superior to themselves, as long as they continue consistent in their Christian walk and conversation . . . It takes great effect when returning liberated Christians sit down with their heathen countrymen, and speak with contempt of their own former superstitious practices . . . all which they now can tell them they have found to be foolishness, and the result of ignorance . . . The services of such persons will prove most useful in the introduction of the gospel of Jesus Christ among the heathens.[1]

Actually, in time and out of experience, Crowther came to alter this view. He had originally thought of drawing his mission aides from among the educated African youth of Sierra Leone, Gambia and the Gold Coast—this 'civilized African . . . carrying the English habits and language with him . . . the only hope of improving the interior . . . introducing a superior race of negro blood'. But the training college at Fourah Bay was unable to provide adequate numbers and, in any event, those who were recruited proved to be 'conceited educated young men on whom one cannot rely, and who at any unexpected moment may desert the work and leave one in the lurch'. Crowther eventually favoured a humbler practitioner—the middle-aged Christian from Sierra Leone who was literate but not highly educated, who understood the Bible well enough to be catechist and evangelist but who did not require a long period of preparation for field work. Such individuals would be respected by chiefs and elders because of their age and exemplary behaviour and because of their superior knowledge and experience, while their devotion to the word of God and their familiarity with hard work and harsh living conditions made them ideally suited to bear up under the privations of missionary life. This view corresponded closely with that of Venn who felt that the native teacher should be more advanced than his countrymen but not so far as to be out of touch with them.[2]

Thus Crowther ratified the Buxton-Venn thesis that westernized

---

[1] *Ibid.*, 1864, 234–5; S. A. Crowther, *Journal of An Expedition up the Niger and Tshadda Rivers . . . in 1854*, xvi–xviii.

[2] *Ibid.*, xi, xii; Crowther to Venn, Feb. 8, 1862, Crowther to C.M.S. Parent Committee, Mar. 30, 1870, C.M.S. CA3/04A; Ajayi, 'Henry Venn and the Policy of Development', *op. cit.*, 334.

Africans were in the long run superior to European missionaries, better adapted to the rigours of tropical living and competent evangelists when properly trained. But Crowther added a corollary of his own. Not only were African teachers, catechists and ministers likely to prove superior, but one should not lose sight of the values of indigenous African customs and traditions which, far from contradicting the teachings of Christ, would make those doctrines more vivid and meaningful to the native African:

Christianity has come into the world to abolish and supersede all false religions, to direct mankind to the only way of obtaining peace and reconciliation with their offended God. . . . But it should be borne in mind that Christianity does not undertake to destroy national assimilation; where there are any degrading and superstitious defects it corrects them; where they are connected with politics, such corrections should be introduced with due caution, and with all meekness of wisdom.

There was much value in community associations and traditional recreational forms so long as they were not immoral or indecent. Fables, story telling, proverbs and songs fell into this category. So too did religious terms and ceremonies which helped to convey the message of the Scriptures:

If judicious use be made of native ideas, their minds will be better reached than by attempting to introduce new ones quite foreign to their way of thinking. . . . Many awkward native habits will gradually be dropped and others more comfortable will be introduced . . . till the state of society will be imperceptibly improved without forcing it. When once Christianity has taken a firm hold among the people, then will follow in its train many attendant blessings.[1]

Crowther also saw value in the use of African languages, both for preaching and for translation of the Bible and other religious texts. Here again he followed closely the thinking of Henry Venn. The reason was primarily one of expediency–for the widest dissemination of Christian doctrine, African languages would have to be used, but there were psychological advantages as well. Crowther's early preaching in Freetown, for example, had been in Yoruba, and this had greatly pleased the local population. Throughout his life he was a close student of African languages, and his diaries are filled with linguistic notes. At various times he published Yoruba, Nupe and Ibo grammars, and at Venn's urging did a number of scriptural translations into Yoruba. For the Yoruba and Niger missionaries he advocated mastery of whichever

[1] Crowther's Charge at Lokoja, Sept. 13, 1869, C.M.S. CA3/04A.

languages were necessary for their work among Hausa, Ibo, Yoruba, and Nupe. 'The employment of four such powerful native languages will be a mighty lever which the combined forces of the heathens and mohammedans shall not be liable to withstand... the word of the Lord shall run and be glorified.'[1]

At various times he also advocated the study of Arabic by missionaries, pointing out the asset of missionaries able to read passages from the Bible in Arabic and to use that language with greater facility than could the Muslims of Africa themselves. Like most Christian missionaries, Crowther was troubled by Islam which he encountered everywhere, apparently virile where Christianity struggled, often failing, sometimes enjoying modest success. His criticisms of Islam were the usual ones. In addition to the purely doctrinal objections regarding the nature of Christ, there were serious sociological shortcomings. Crowther genuinely believed that Islam like the indigenous religions was based on—indeed encouraged—the ignorance and superstition which contributed their measure of keeping the African people in a depressed state. Islam relied on charms, 'scraps of paper to sooth the fancy of the ignorant', whereas Christianity practised enlightenment through education. Islam was autocratic, placing women in an inferior position to be imposed upon at will while Christianity practised equality of all before God. Islam was essentially cruel, condoning the slavery which the Christians had come to Africa to eradicate. Islam was obscurantist, refusing to allow the Koran to be rendered in any language but Arabic, but enlightened Christianity was eager to share the teachings of the Old and New Testaments through translations by people like Crowther himself. Finally, Islam condoned that ultimate horror of the mid-Victorian clergy, polygamy, which 'enslaved the female population... and made many to be miserable victims to the carnal lust and depraved appetite of one man'.[2]

Crowther's views on Islam were something less than doctrinaire, however, for he was no armchair theologian, raising his hands in holy horror at the thought of false prophets and spurious doctrines. He recognized the virtues of Islam—for example, its monotheism, and its abolition of idols and human sacrifice. He was in constant contact with Muslims whom he saw not as demons but as men, albeit misguided, and he never lost an opportunity to speak with them, gently persuading, quietly trying

---

[1] Crowther to Venn, Feb. 8, 1860, C.M.S. CA3/04A.
[2] S. A. Crowther and J. C. Taylor, *The Gospel on the Banks of the Niger*, 55–6; Crowther's Journal for the Quarter ending Sept. 25, 1846, CA2/031; Crowther to Venn, Dec. 3, 1859, C.M.S. CA3/04A; D. C. Crowther, *op. cit.*, 174.

to convert. He writes of many such conversations in which his listeners often admitted the superiority of Christianity, but he also speaks of the great difficulty of achieving ultimate conversion of Muslims. He was less charitable towards heathen religion which he regarded as a system designed by the elders and priests to keep the population subdued by playing on ignorance and superstition. On his frequent trips up the Niger he constantly deplored the depressing effects of tribal rites, nor was he any more forbearing with his own Yoruba:

> People in this country are harassed within and without by unjust war and kidnapping, as well by the superstitious belief in the power and influence of false gods, and the craftiness of the priests. The priests rob the people of their cloths, money and other property by promising the credulous populace peace, health, children, and money.... Instead of peace, they have continual war, instead of health they are as sickly and subject to death as any other persons; a great many of their women are without children ... instead of being rich they are continually impoverished ... still they cannot see that the worship of these things is vanity and vexation of spirit.[1]

In general Crowther shared the European view of Africa as 'this long benighted continent', shrouded in darkness that could only be dispelled through the introduction of European civilization. This was no unqualified condemnation, however, failing to make distinctions among peoples and places. The Yoruba, for instance, he regarded as industrious farmers and shrewd traders, saddled with their share of ignorance, bigotry and selfishness to be sure, but the victims more of faulty leadership than of innate meanness of character. By the people of the interior along the Niger and the Benue, he was continually appalled, especially by the primitive state of their way of life. He speaks constantly of filthy villages, crowded with dilapidated huts lining crooked muddy evil-smelling streets; of people whose only clothing was a scrap of dirty rag; of meals made of rotting meat; of wretched disease-ridden individuals scratching the ground with primitive farming implements and placing their faith for a bountiful harvest on useless charms and ornaments. In the north where the Fulani and Hausa predominated, conditions were better; for example, clothing of a graceful design was widely used. But such clothing and such habits of sanitation!

Notwithstanding the pride of the people on account of their flowing dresses ... they go about in them in a most filthy and disgusting state;

---

[1] Crowther and Taylor, *op. cit.*, 171; Crowther's Journal ... ending Sept. 25, 1846, C.M.S. CA2/031.

they are never washed from the time they are made and put on to the time they are worn threadbare, and they are the receptacles for all kinds of vermin ... Even their ablutions are an abomination ... a description of them would insult the pure heart of a Christian.

Soap and water existed in quantity but washing was avoided since, he was informed, clothes so treated merely became dirty again.[1]

It was for the people living on or near the coast, particularly those of the delta states, that Crowther reserved the full expression of his frustration and disappointment. This point of view certainly fitted the prevailing opinion among missionaries and others[2] that the inhabitants of the coast, long brutalized by the slave trade or corrupted by the less savoury aspects of western culture, were beyond redemption. Centres like Lagos and Badagry, said Crowther, contained few individuals of genuine religious conviction, and most of their congregations were formed not by natives of those towns but by immigrants from the interior. In Ado and Ijebu the missionaries were completely shut out, while at Abeokuta heathenism had gained the day when the missionaries were expelled in 1867. Worst of all, however, were the old slaving towns of the Niger delta, and here Crowther's long experience with persecution and backsliding, barbarism and debauchery go a long way towards explaining the unrestrained severity of his observations. New Calabar troubled him by its discouraging weakness for showy material display. The women particularly were addicted to elaborate clothing and copious jewellery, while some of the chiefs managed to bedeck their hats with as much as £480 worth of jewellery and coins. When it came time to pay the modest school fees of the missions, however, the people complained of excessive charges and threatened to remove their children from class. At Bonny where the Christians suffered severe persecution, Brass and Akassa the situation was no better:

The minds of the people are very low ... it is very difficult to raise them above the things of sense, such as eating and drinking, and an insatiable desire to get all they can without labour. Hence cupidity, covetousness and selfishness prevail to an incredible degree. The principle of charity is foreign to their ideas. . . . To give of their substance to another without receiving an equivalent in return is a sacrifice which this people cannot make without deep feeling of mortification ... On the other hand they are very avaricious.

[1] See, for ex., Schon and Crowther, *op. cit.*, 289–90, 304; Crowther, *Journal of an Expedition up the Niger and Tshadda Rivers*, 102; Crowther and Taylor, *op. cit.*, 227–8.
[2] See the views of Edward W. Blyden, pp. 221–2, 223.

And withal, 'They are passionate and revengeful . . . The propensity to theft may be classed as an instinct'.[1]

For all the disgust and heartbreak contained in these judgments, Crowther could not turn his back on these people, nor could he fail to find some good to remark. Though robbed during one of his voyages up the Niger, he still protested that dishonesty was rare in that area. The villagers in the delta, despite their shortcomings, he thought were ambitious, intelligent and shrewd bargainers with a great capacity for learning. The expulsion of the missionaries from Abeokuta was not pure wickedness but could be explained in part by the malign influence on the inhabitants of misguided advisers from Sierra Leone. The best method for dealing with the superstitions on which much of the difficulty rested was a gentle application of Holy Scripture:

Avoid ridiculing the idolators and abusing them as stupid. . . . Assure them that you point out their mistakes into which they have been led by their forefathers by the unerring word of God given to direct mankind in the right way. In this way you will find an entrance into their hearts and reasoning powers; for many of them are reasonable men: but if they are ridiculed and abused as stupid, they will become obstinate and furious.[2]

There was no doubt in Crowther's mind that a considerable share of the responsibility for the African behaviour he deplored belonged to Europeans—first the slavers and later the traders dealing in legitimate commerce, whom he saw as essentially immoral, irreligious types setting bad examples and encouraging the Africans in their superstitious ignorant ways. What is more, they conspired to keep the missionaries out of the interior for they wished to maintain their monopoly of the Niger trade, and they felt this monopoly rested on exclusion of western culture and religion which might educate and uplift the population, and ultimately free the people of foreign exploitation. Yet Crowther remained devoted to his British ties. African though he was, he could not escape the influence of his missionary training. For example, he inadvertently refers on one occasion to England as 'home'. During one of his Niger voyages, his journal comments on the cosy appropriateness of a Christmas celebration complete with roast fowl and pudding, green decorations and, of course, a holy service, all pleasantly reminiscent of a

---

[1] *C.M. Intelligencer*, 1871, 57–8, 1875, 246, 250; Crowther to Edward Hutchinson, Apr. 30, 1878; Crowther's Charge at Lokoja, Sept. 13, 1869, C.M.S. CA3/04A.
[2] Schon and Crowther, *op. cit.*, 299–300; *C.M. Intelligencer*, 1875, 247; Crowther to Venn, Dec. 3, 1867, C.M.S. CA3/04A; Crowther's Notes on African Superstition for the Gaboon Conference in 1876, C.M.S. CA3/013.

traditional English Christmas. When the news of the capture of Sebastopol in 1855 reached Lagos, he was as thrilled as any Britisher, observing, 'England's success is our preservation and prosperity, her failure is our ruin'. In the negotiations for the cession of Lagos to Britain in 1861, it was Crowther who played an important role in persuading the reluctant King Docemo of the wisdom of placing himself and his people under British protection.[1]

All this, however, was more than sentimental. Crowther quite reasonably regarded England as the West's most progressive nation—preeminent in her industrialization and wealth, a leader in the development of representative democratic government, the home of so much of the world's missionary movement, and a centre of cultural, aesthetic and educational progress. He was convinced that Africa could not hope to develop without outside aid; this being so, was not Britain the most appropriate agent for providing that aid? In 1869 while addressing his clergy of the Niger Mission, he dwelt at length on the question of Africa's ability to make her way without the assistance of others. The question was already being mooted. Africanus Horton had just made his plea for West African independence; in Abeokuta the Egbas had expelled the missionaries and adopted a firm line with the British in Lagos; while the controversial ideas of Edward Blyden were beginning to be heard in the cities of West Africa. Crowther had no doubt as to where the future of Africa lay and he expressed himself in clear and unmistakable terms. Europe, Asia and America were far ahead of Africa in development, yet they still found much profit in the help of missionaries. Was it not the height of foolishness for Africa, far less developed as she was, to reject the needed aid and take doubtful refuge in isolation?

If we have any regard for the elevation of Africa ... our wisdom would be to cry to those christian nations which have been so long labouring for our conversion, to redouble their christian efforts for the evangelization of this continent. ... we (Africans) can act as rough quarry-mends, who hew out blocks of marbles from the quarries, which are conveyed to the workshop, to be shaped and finished into perfect figures by the hands of the skilful artists. In like manner native teachers can do, having the acquaintance with the language in their favour, to induce their heathen countrymen to come within the reach of the means of grace and hear the word of God. What is lacking in good training and sound evangelical teaching, the more experienced foreign missionaries will

---

[1] Crowther to Edward Hutchinson, May 10, 1876, Crowther to H. Wright, Jan. 21, 1878, C.M.S. CA3/04A; D. C. Crowther, *op. cit.*, 166; Crowther and Taylor, *op. cit.*, 141–2; Crowther to J. Chapman, Nov. 6, 1855, C.M.S. CA2/031; Crowther to Venn, Feb. 8, Mar. 8, 1862, C.M.S. CA3/04A.

supply, and thus give shape to new churches in heathen countries. . . . Africa has neither knowledge nor skill to devise plans to bring out her vast resources for her own improvement; and for want of Christian enlightenment, cruelty and barbarity overspread the land to an incredible degree. Therefore to claim Africa for the Africans alone, is to claim for her the right of a continued ignorance to practise cruelty and acts of barbarity as her perpetual inheritance. For it is certain, unless help came from without, a nation can never rise much above its present state.[1]

It was, however, not just missionary help that Crowther sought. He wanted nothing less than the concurrent participation of the British government complete with diplomatic representation and military force. Letters went back to Venn, who heartily approved this point of view, and to others after Venn's death urging more vigorous governmental action. A British resident in the delta area, and a British gunboat on the Niger, were for Crowther the necessary means for peace and progress. Without these aids there was danger of a reversion to the slave trade through collusion between unscrupulous slavers and the venal natives of the delta. As early as 1841, treaties had been concluded with peoples along the Niger, abolishing the slave trade and human sacrifice and laying the groundwork for economic and moral regeneration. The biggest part of the job had already been done, Crowther argued; all that remained was a small additional effort following up the initial moves. With British consular and military presence on the Niger, the great river would be opened to commerce, the tribes which were friendly and interested in improving their world would be given the support they deserved, hostile tribes would be properly chastened and the expansionist ambitions of other powers such as France would be blocked. Such a viewpoint anticipated Sir George Goldie by twenty years.[2]

3 *The Decline of Bishop Crowther—End of an Era*

The death of Henry Venn in 1873 marked the beginning of the end of Bishop Crowther's influence, and not long thereafter began the long decline from a position of prime importance in determining Anglican mission policy in West Africa to an ultimate impotence and repudiation. There had always been those among the C.M.S. missionaries who questioned the wisdom of Venn's policy in establishing a native African

---

[1] Crowther's Charge at Lokoja, Sept. 13, 1869, C.M.S. CA3/04A.
[2] Crowther's correspondence contains many expressions of such sentiments. See, for ex., Crowther to Venn, Nov. 11, 1860, Aug. 30, 1862, Oct. 18, 1867, Crowther to Gov. H. S. Freeman, Mar. 2, 1863, Crowther to David Hopkins, Aug. 22, 1878, C.M.S. CA3/04A.

church and clergy based on an economically productive African congregation. Once Venn was gone, this critical view gained currency and as it did, Crowther's authority over his diocese was eroded away bit by bit. At first there were questions raised over the probity and moral rectitude of members of the Bishop's missionary staff. In some cases, the accusations may have been justified; in others they were perhaps excessive, but underlying the whole process was a fundamental scepticism over the competence of the Negro race for leadership. Europeans had always questioned Negro capabilities, but by mid-nineteenth century expressions of doubt had reached the status of a dogma which conveniently supported the military conquest and political domination of Africa that followed during the several decades leading up to the First World War.

Doubtless a more determined man than Crowther would still have been caught up and submerged by irresistible events, but his own mildness of disposition, personal modesty and charitable nature made the task that much easier. Though he defended his workers, his efforts lacked vigour. An aging humanitarian, he did not possess the ruthlessness to chastise and so gained the reputation of conducting a flaccid administration. To the new generation of English missionaries, he was just another example of African shortcomings – not dishonest or immoral, perhaps, like his subordinates, but inefficient and wanting the necessary qualities of leadership. When his competence was questioned, instead of fighting he concurred and thus secured his downfall. 'I know my place as a negro', he wrote in 1884, adding, 'The Europeans are better managers, their actions and report will be better confided in both out here and in England. We shall be content to work under their direction as in former years.' Amazingly, the old man – for he was then about eighty – offered to go out into the field once more as a missionary to found new stations, but such a suggestion was not taken seriously. Instead, step by step, his mission was divided, his helpers were suspended or transferred and his authority circumscribed, until by 1891 he had been stripped of all practical control over his diocese. Later in the same year he died.[1]

If Crowther came in time to be out of tune with his European missionary colleagues, his humility and deference to European standards no longer sufficed for the new generation of Africans. This was the very generation which had been trained by Crowther and his co-workers to

[1] Jesse Page, *The Black Bishop: Samuel Adjayi Crowther*, 370-1; Ajayi, *Christian Missions in Nigeria*, 206-55.

emulate western ways and to aspire to European Christian standards. But with education came knowledge and the power of discrimination, while the shift in European thought from the humanitarianism of the anti-slavery movement to the arrogance of colonialist theory soured and disillusioned many an African who had begun by accepting and ended by questioning what Europe had to offer. Crowther had always seen the fallacy of European racial prejudice, but had been unwilling or unable to raise a vigorous and serious opposition. This task was left to those who came after, and so it was that the development of African ideas passed on to others.[1]

[1] Crowther to H. Wright, Feb. 28, 1876, C.M.S. CA3/o4A.

10 Indigenous African Nationalism: Reversible Johnson

1 *African Resistance to Europe*

The westernized assimilationist views of Bishop Crowther were not acceptable to all West Africans even in the days of his greatest influence. First of all, there were the millions of indigenous peoples inhabiting the vast reaches of the continental interior who had little awareness or understanding of the outside forces which were pressing in upon them. There were, moreover, the chiefs and kings who had met the European but who preferred, for reasons of their own, to continue to live much as they always had. But there were other Africans who, like Crowther, had seen a good deal of European culture, who lived to a greater or lesser degree by European standards, who appreciated much of European civilization and yet who looked with suspicion upon European motives and questioned the desirability of the African following blindly whither Europe beckoned. These men were ready, indeed eager, to borrow aspects of European culture which they felt might be useful to the cause of African development, but they stubbornly resisted the spread of foreign control, turning aside the persuasiveness of the missionary, the blandishments of the merchant or the political pressure of the consul, while striving to preserve local territorial and institutional integrity.

2 *The Egba Challenge British Power in Yorubaland*

One of the most unusual examples of early West African resistance to Europe came in the person of George W. Johnson of Abeokuta. Johnson appeared abruptly one day in Abeokuta in mid-summer of 1865, and remained to place the stamp of an original mind on his contemporaries and to gain among their descendants a measure of immortality as an early patriot. He was known at once as Reversible Johnson, a nickname which was later explained to have arisen in appreciation of his refined political tactics in gaining support from many, sometimes unlikely, quarters while pursuing his objectives. Contemporary accounts provide a more casual reason—he had invented a printed handkerchief with contrasting patterns on each side which was much favoured for its versatility as a lady's head-dress. Hence 'Reversible'; but trivial though the reason, it fitted a pattern of a bizarre and unconventional character whose apparent eccentricity both confused his adversaries and served to mask his basic objectives.

Johnson had come originally from Sierra Leone where he was a tailor by profession, but characteristically it was an exotic factor—his prowess with the native flute—that first brought him attention and the opportunity to do something beyond the routine. When Prince Alfred visited Freetown in 1860, he was enough impressed with Johnson's playing to bring him back to England for formal musical studies. Johnson, who was then in his early thirties, returned to Africa three years later after having concluded his training and tried his hand unsuccessfully in a Liverpool business venture. Briefly he appeared in Lagos and Abeokuta, assessing the prospects for a living and, finding them to his liking, he quit Sierra Leone for good and settled in Yorubaland. This was no random choice of a footloose wanderer prospecting for a better stake. His people had come originally from Abeokuta, for Johnson was an Owu, a member of that Yoruba subgroup which had finally taken refuge in Abeokuta many years earlier after having been routed and their city destroyed when the civil wars erupted in 1821. This lineage may explain his mixture of purposefulness and eccentricity, for the Owu were said to be stubborn and courageous as well as proud in spirit if somewhat unconventional in their morals.[1]

Johnson's initial interests were commercial but his talents were political, and within three months of his arrival he had begun to attract notice on the local political scene. This in itself was a revealing measure of the man, for politics among the Egba were a tissue of complexity, confusing and repellent to the uninitiated. The situation was further complicated, moreover, by the intricate alliances arising from the Yoruba wars and the presence of the British in the newly-formed colony of Lagos.

The Egba people had arrived at the site of Abeokuta in 1830, refugees from burned-out, gutted villages, a series of quasi-independent groups driven from their traditional homes and banded together in common

---

[1] S. A. Maser Journal, Oct. 24, 1865, C.M.S. CA2/068; *Lagos Weekly Record*, Sept. 16, 1899; Ladipo Solanke, *A Special Lecture Addressed to Mr. A. K. Ajisafe*, 70; Samuel Johnson, *History of the Yorubas*, 206.

defence only in response to the extreme peril of their situation. In the ensuing years they managed to live with one another out of the necessity of beating back the attacks of warlike neighbours, but despite adversity the city was never able to transform itself from a collection of discrete townships into an organic metropolis, and the lines of internal authority remained tangled and tenuous. Governmental functions were divided among the different Egba groups after a fashion, but real power was illusory and tended to rest more on personality than on legal sanction. Add to this the shifting relations and alliances among the Yoruba as the civil wars progressed and the dangerous threat to the Egba flank by a rapacious slave-hungry Dahomean kingdom, and the problems of Abeokuta living uncertainly in a parlous world were as easy to visualize as they were difficult to solve. The final complication was that of the European who was indirectly involved in the outbreak of civil war because of his demand for slaves, who had arrived at Abeokuta as a missionary some years after its founding to introduce new and confusing standards of social behaviour, and who now was making his presence felt ominously at Lagos and on the adjacent coast. Here indeed were circumstances to challenge the resources of a master politician.

By the time Johnson arrived in Abeokuta in 1865, relations with the English at Lagos had deteriorated from relative cordiality to a state of virtual warfare. British occupation of Lagos as a colony in 1861 had come from a desire to stamp out the slave trade and to stabilize and encourage legitimate commerce with Yorubaland and the regions beyond. To the Egba, however, the annexation smacked more of territorial aggression, while the English policy of opening up the interior appeared as a direct blow to Abeokuta's commercial position and a threat to her security. When the British proposed installing a consul in Abeokuta, the offer was refused, for consulship had preceded annexation in Lagos, and it was but a short step of reasoning to see the same fateful sequence for Abeokuta.

Relations continued to deteriorate, weakened by Egba suspicion and internal weakness and by British desire to see the country pacified. To the British administration, the Egba were obstructionists concerned with maintaining the trade in slaves and in perpetuating unrest in the interior. In the final analysis Abeokuta might have to be coerced if peace were ever to be achieved. The British therefore blockaded the coast to prevent supplies from proceeding inland to Abeokuta, and in 1865 smashed the Egba siege of the town of Ikorodu in an effort to push a trade route through to Ibadan. The Egba, for their part, long accustomed to being surrounded by enemies, became more confirmed than ever in their xenophobia, and thus attempted to tighten their control over the trade routes from the coast.[1]

The English were a new and difficult force in Yorubaland. To contain their apparently aggressive moves, the Egba clearly needed strong centralized authority at home and the ability to understand, to assess and to meet western diplomatic machinations. In the past the missionaries had helped in relations with the authorities in Lagos but now confidence in the missionaries was melting away as suspicions of English motives mounted. At the same time the chronic Egba inability to agree among themselves on a central government and a unified policy had been further aggravated when the ruling alake died in 1862, for there had been no agreement on a successor and the government was being conducted under the regency of the prestigious but ineffective bashorun, Shomoye. Hence as Johnson arrived on the scene, these two things were clearly needed – a firm central authority and the ability to deal effectively with the British. Johnson set about to provide both.

Rallying a number of Sierra Leone émigrés resident in Abeokuta, he succeeded in persuading the bashorun to establish the Egba United Board of Management with the bashorun as president and with Johnson as executive secretary. This at once replaced missionary influence with the government, for Henry Townsend, the C.M.S. representative at Abeokuta, had up to that time been serving as the bashorun's secretary and amanuensis. The Board was not, and was not designed to be, a complete government in itself; its chief purpose was to act as a kind of foreign ministry, particularly in relations with Lagos. Its objectives, however, involved basic political changes for Abeokuta from a loose federation to a more highly organized modern state with a central seat of power and modern administrative machinery drawn from western models. Johnson hoped to establish customs posts which would regulate and protect trade and provide the income necessary to operate the government. 'The Board of Management', he announced, 'is established on purpose to direct the Native Government, forward civilization and promote the spread of Christianity, together with the future protection of the property of European merchants and British subjects.' The protection of commerce would be accompanied by the guarantee of Christian moral and ethical procedures:

---

[1] S. O. Biobaku, *The Egba and Their Neighbours, 1842–1872*, 64–78; G. W. Johnson for Shomoye and Asalu to S. Blackall, Feb., 1866, C.O. 147/11; J. Glover to Earl of Clarendon, Feb. 7, 1866, F.O. 84/1265.

Knowing Abeokuta to be the very centre for commerce and fortune, and the place where Christ's Gospel has already been most firmly planted, it is the intention of this newborn Government to ring the bell round . . . to aid in spreading the same far and wide among the surrounding tribes.

But the crux of Johnson's policy involved a vigorous course of action in relation to the Lagos government. From the Egba point of view, the British had been guilty of aggression in annexing Lagos, they were violating the neutrality they expressed by sending arms through to the Ibadans, and they were encroaching on Egba territory and interfering with Egba commerce between Abeokuta and the coast. Thus, said Johnson:

[English] efforts to civilise and Christianise Africans by sending missionary after missionary can have but very partial success until they become convinced that something more is wanted besides sending missionaries and putting men-of-war in the water, and that is to encourage the forming of a proper Government among educated Africans which must go hand in hand in the great work. Alas . . . to open the doors for civilisation and Christianity in these parts of Africa, the Lagos Government must put away all hostile spirit.[1]

In standing up to Lagos Johnson was assuming heavy and dangerous responsibilities for, despite the anti-colonialism of Westminster expressed in the 1865 House of Commons report of the Select Committee on Africa, the government of the Lagos colony was under particularly vigorous direction at this moment. The lieutenant-governor was John H. Glover, an energetic administrator who combined belief in direct action with the conviction that the Egba were determined to rid the area of the English presence in order to reinstitute the old slave trade. Peace and free intercourse with the inland towns were his objectives but his means for achievement did not preclude the use of force. It was Glover who had routed the Egba before Ikorodu early in 1865, and over the next several years he was to press Johnson and the Egbas unceasingly in his effort to gain regular commercial access to the interior.

Glover was not the man to let things drift. Following the Ikorodu incident, he instituted a partial blockade of Egba territory, imposing a duty on goods between Lagos and Abeokuta, and enforcing it with his own constables. Then sweetening an otherwise unpalatable policy, he negotiated a regular postal service between Lagos and Abeokuta and provided most of the machinery for its operation. One of its first fruits

---

[1] S. A. Maser Journal, Oct. 24, 1865, C.M.S. CA2/068; *The African Times*, Oct. 23, 1866; Johnson to Glover, July 18, 1867, C.O. 147/13.

was a warning to the Egba that a Dahomean attack was being planned against Abeokuta, a warning for which the city was duly grateful.[1]

But Johnson was neither cowed nor lulled by Glover's tactics. Objecting strenuously to the policy of blockade and tariff, which also involved rough treatment for Egbas who fell into the hands of the Lagos constabulary, Johnson first cut off intercourse with Lagos and then, reopening trade, imposed a counter-duty of his own levied on goods leaving Abeokuta for Lagos. This was part of his plan to obtain for the Egba government a steady source of income, but the move immediately involved him in difficulties at home. He originally had secured the backing of the bashorun and other important leaders but when his custom duty was announced opposition developed, both among the chiefs who traditionally governed trade and with those sections of the city controlling the gates and the commerce on the Ogun River. Additional troubles developed as Johnson sought to unite the city behind a new alake, and here again he was thwarted by the unwillingness and inability of the people to countenance the strong central authority which effective government required.[2]

The war of nerves quickened. Johnson moved to block trade bypassing his custom control by establishing another check point on the Ogun below the city, but this immediately stimulated Glover to suggest negotiation of the Egba-Lagos boundary, at the same time placing his constables in territory below Abeokuta which the Egba claimed as their own. The news soon came back that the constables were molesting Egbas on the road. Johnson responded with vigour. Under no circumstances would Abeokuta consider discussion of boundaries which were already quite clear. The territory down to the coast with the exception of the island of Lagos was subject to Egba government; furthermore, the constables were illegally occupying foreign soil. 'I am strongly requested to notify to your Excellency that in receipt of this letter, you will please cause such *Constables to be removed* from the Several Stations of the Egba Territories *in order to prevent inconveniences* and to keep peace between the Two Governments.'[3]

It was soon apparent what inconveniences Johnson had in mind.

---

[1] Glover to H. Townsend, Mar. 6, 1865, C.M.S. CA2/04; Glover to Townsend Sept. 10, 1865, G. W. Johnson Papers.
[2] Bashorun to Glover, Sept. 18, Oct. 20, 1865, G. W. Johnson Papers; Johnson to S. Blackall, Mar. 6, 1866, F.O. 84/1265; *The African Times*, Oct. 23, 1866; J. B. Wood to Venn, May 2, Aug. 1, 1867, C.M.S. CA2/096; Townsend to Venn, July 27, 1866, C.M.S. CA2/085.
[3] J. Gerard to Johnson, July 8, 1867, Johnson to Glover, July 18, Sept. 7, 1867, G. W. Johnson Papers; Johnson to Glover, Sept. 19, 1867, C.O. 147/13.

Glover apologized for the conduct of his constables but failed to order their removal. 'The Chiefs and people of Abeokuta', Johnson informed him, 'are not satisfied that Constables should be still on the roads. The Bashorun has been obliged ... to press and keep back hundreds of ... war boys ... but too ready to go after the Constables.' Now it was Glover's turn to explode. The constables would not be removed. They were there at the request of the people of the area who demanded and needed protection. Writing directly to the bashorun, he lashed out at Johnson, describing him as a renegade British subject, implying that he had illegally used the bashorun's staff of office to legitimize his dispatches, and stating that any threatening move on British territory would go badly for the Egbas and reduce Johnson in British eyes to the status of a felon liable to conviction and possible execution. At the same time Glover announced that he would recognize no further communications from Johnson as a representative of the Egba government.[1]

Apparently the postal service, at any rate, was operating smoothly for the dispatches flew back and forth. Glover wanted to reopen the boundary question, suggesting as a basis for discussion that roughly the inland half of the area between Lagos and Abeokuta be considered neutral, the implication being that the lower region down to the coast already belonged to Lagos. He then introduced a new note – that messengers travelling from the Emir of Nupe to Lagos had been waylaid in Abeokuta and murdered. Johnson could give as good as he received. 'It is [not] the custom of the Aku tribes in these parts of Africa to murder messengers who may be sent from one king to another', he announced with magisterial dignity, adding, 'And your request that the Egba Government must get another person to write letters for this Government ... is considered by the Bashorun, Chiefs, and people of Abeokuta, *as a dodge mixed up with bad* – a request so arbitrary ... as if the Bashorun was to write ... requesting Her Britannic Majesty to change the Secretary of State.'[2]

Johnson had successfully faced down Glover. His position as an authorized officer of the Egba government was impeccable; for his part Glover clearly had no business telling Abeokuta who its ministers might be. He was soon repudiated by his home government in England which

[1] Gerard to Johnson, Sept. 20, 1867, Johnson to Glover, Sept. 24, 1867, G. W. Johnson Papers; Johnson to Glover, Oct. 17, 1867 enclosed with Glover to G. N. Yonge, Oct. 19, 1867, C.O. 147/13; Glover to Bashorun, Oct. 2, 1867, Nigerian National Archives, CSo8/5. See below, pp. 383–6, for discussion of the Eleko affair and another alleged misuse of a traditional native staff of office.

[2] Glover to Bashorun, Oct. 2, 1867, Nigerian National Archives, CSo8/5; *The African Times*, Jan. 23, 1868.

deplored the description of Johnson as a felon, and insisted that Glover withdraw to the original boundaries of the Lagos colony. But by this time enormous anti-European pressures had built up within Abeokuta. Whatever responsibility Johnson may have had in their development, it was clear that he was right about the growing excitement of the war boys and that the city was in considerable measure behind his strong stand against Glover. While the constable incident was still being argued out, rioting broke forth in Abeokuta on Sunday, October 13, 1867. The immediate objectives of the rioters were the Christian churches which were forcibly closed by large agitated mobs which roamed the streets throughout the day. Churches were looted and some were destroyed, most missionary homes were plundered and damaged, and some parishioners were attacked. The outburst was over in a day but the churches remained closed during the ensuing weeks and finally, one by one, the missionaries left the city. For the time being the missions in Abeokuta were finished.[1]

At first the causes appeared obscure. The rioting had seemed spontaneous and unplanned but there was evidence during the day that the mobs were being led, albeit loosely. From where did they get their directions and what was behind it all? Although stunned by the event, the missionaries were certain that the bashorun had at least acquiesced in a plan to close the churches but that its active author was Reversible Johnson himself. Johnson and his colleagues from Sierra Leone who made up the Board of Management were described as half educated, semi-civilized, unprincipled men who abandoned themselves to polygamous, idolatrous, sinful lives and then, guilty over their fall from what they knew to be a moral upright life, turned on the missionaries and duped the ignorant heathens into a show of lawless force. Some, and Bishop Crowther was one, looked more deeply and saw a long-standing though inchoate conspiracy between the Egbas and the Ijebu people to the east to drive out the Europeans and reinstitute the old slave trade. Few were inclined to connect the incident with the actions of Glover and his constables along the Abeokuta-Lagos Road, though Johnson insisted repeatedly that the closing of the churches–though not the rioting–was a reprisal in response to the deployment of the constables.[2]

[1] Biobaku, *op. cit.*, 82–3; *C.M. Intelligencer*, 1868, 5–8.
[2] *Ibid.*, 1868, 64, 1869, 36; S. Crowther to Venn, Dec. 3, 1867, C.M.S. CA3/04A; Wood to Venn, Nov. 11, 1868, C.M.S. CA2/096; R. B. Hone to Duke of Buckingham, Feb. 17, 1868, Glover to Blackall, Jan. 17, 1868, C.O. 147/14; Johnson to Glover, Oct. 17, 1867 enclosed with Glover to G. N. Yonge,

There was no question but that Johnson was involved in the breach of peace. He seems to have tried to instigate an outbreak by suggesting that missionaries were obliged by biblical authority to move on to new territories approximately every twenty years, and it was scarcely to be doubted that it was his influence which caused the bashorun to order the closing of the churches. Shortly after the riots, he was attacked by a group of Egba Christians who resented what they regarded as his arrogant satisfaction in inspecting the wreckage of one of the church buildings. Johnson's tactics were not often straightforward and his movements were usually masked, but his motives were perfectly open and quite consistent with the policy he had been pursuing ever since his rise to power. In pursuit of his 'civilized form of government', he had pressed hard to thwart Glover's expansionism in the south and when it appeared inexpedient to loose the Egba forces against Glover in direct action, it was a not illogical step to let the war fever work itself out against the European missionaries who, in the Egba view, as white men must have been privy to Glover's policy. It was Glover and the constables, Johnson insisted, who were responsible, and this he maintained to the end of his days. In his papers is contained the original dispatch in which Glover questioned the legality of the custom house and suggested settlement of the Lagos boundary. Years later Johnson wrote at the top of this letter, 'N.B.–Heathen uprisen at Abeokuta in the year 1867 October 13–through misunderstanding between the two Governments originating through this despatch of 8 July 1867.'[1]

The immediate crisis faded away. The missionaries had departed and were not permitted to return, while the Lagos government was quiet, chastened by the repudiation of the British Colonial Office. But for Johnson his central difficulty remained and was soon to become intensified. The faction-ridden Egba still had no alake and existing divisions were deepened when the bashorun died in 1868, taking to his grave the personal prestige which had given his government some measure of cohesion and power. Eventually in 1869 an alake was chosen but his influence was restricted and the city remained fragmented. Johnson's policy continued unchanged–to work for cohesion and a strong united front in opposition to the English in Lagos. Tactics were an expedient, and for a time he sought the help of Glover in support of his customs

---

Oct. 19, 1867, Johnson to Glover, Oct. 31, 1867, enclosed with G. N. Yonge to Duke of Buckingham, Nov. 13, 1867, C.O. 147/13.

[1] W. Moore to C.M.S. Parent Committee, Oct. 28, 1868, C.M.S. CA2/070; *The African Times*, Sept 23, 1868; Gerard to Johnson, July 8, 1867, G. W. Johnson Papers.

house, but soon the two old adversaries were once again in violent opposition. Gradually Johnson evolved a plan for an effective coalition government in Abeokuta. The city would be divided into four townships, each with its king who would administer his own territory. Overall jurisdiction would rest with an oba, Prince Oyekan, but this plan had no hope of success. Oyekan was merely the candidate of one faction; moreover, powerful groups within Abeokuta continued to oppose Johnson's attempted establishment of an exclusive customs policy for goods proceeding to Lagos.[1]

Reflecting the vagaries of Egba politics at the time, Johnson's influence rose and fell alternately, but he seems to have been able to maintain some measure of control over the Egba posture towards Lagos. When Glover reinstituted his constable policy, it was Johnson who voiced the protest. To the chronic complaint of the Egba-Lagos boundary he added another old Egba demand – that Lagos subjects be restrained from inducing domestic slaves to escape from Abeokuta to Lagos where they were ironically often resold to other towns in the interior. In 1872, when Governor Pope Hennessy protested to the alake that the Lagos road was again closed, Johnson was again spokesman for his community. The whole trouble, he pointed out, dated from the time that the Egba territories below Abeokuta were illegally occupied and the constables installed. Since that time the occupation had continued while the administrator, Glover, complicated the internal government of Abeokuta, sowing discord and jealousy by sending official letters now to this chief, now to that one, instead of recognizing the legally constituted Board of Management:

In conclusion, I am authorized ... to notify your Excellency that considering all such wilful Trespass in the Egba Territories, apart from the evil actions practised in the said lands, is a breach of Confidence, which can never again be replaced for peace and goodwill towards the Queen's Government in Lagos inasmuch as such authority of *might* for *right* against the peace of the Egba Nation has no other end in View than of War & Bloodshed.[2]

This attitude was a bit unfair to Glover, considering the deep cleavages within Abeokuta, but Johnson was fighting for survival on a number

[1] Johnson to Glover, Oct. 27, 1869, G. W. Johnson Papers; Johnson to Glover, Oct. 2, 1869, Gerard to Ogundipe *et al.*, May 14, 1870, C.O. 147/15, 18; H. T. H. Cooper to Johnson, Feb. 2, 1870, Nigerian National Archives, CS08/5; Johnson's manifesto, 'Africa Shall Rise', 1872, G. W. Johnson Papers; Biobaku, *op. cit.*, 85–90.
[2] Johnson to Glover, Feb. 17, 1871, S. Crowther to the Earl of Kimberley, Feb. 6, 1872, C.O. 147/20, 23; Johnson to Pope Hennessy, May 20, 1872, G. W. Johnson Papers.

of fronts. It was not just political unity at home or a question of national honour. There were strategic practicalities as well. The secretary of the Board of Management had intelligence that both Ibadan and Dahomey were planning new attacks on Abeokuta, encouraged by supplies of arms from the outside. Glover had already armed the villages to the south which the Egba considered as fiefdoms by right of conquest, and letters from Ibadan to Lagos had been intercepted urging Glover to open a road to the interior so that arms might flow through. What then was Johnson to think of Glover's persistent efforts to communicate with Ibadan? 'Thus you see the evil of the Ordinance by the Govt. of Lagos', he informed the editor of the *African Times*, '. . . supplying Guns etc.'[1]

Whatever the specific reasoning behind Johnson's actions, they all reflected his determination to build a unified government strong enough to deal with Glover's aggressiveness. 'I have from the beginning done all I could to get all of us united in carrying out the good of a Civilized form of Government in this our father Country', he announced to a correspondent in Lagos, adding later that all territories occupied by Lagos would have to be given up as a prior condition to the reopening of the roads to the interior controlled by the Egba and the Ijebu:

Forced by the powerful weapons of Civilized Government, Heathen Egbas and their Children will eat Grass from bush to bush, instead of given up their lands to the French, or any other nation. . . . I must here solemnly confess that your new Governor . . . must fail to find success here, and be looked upon by the Egbas, as an enemy! and a Glover!! should he insist holding on to Egba Lands–Ebute Metta.

Johnson's syntax may have lacked polish but there was no mistaking his meaning. As he remarked much later in retrospective view of these unsettled times, 'You will observe . . . that I have done all I could possibly have done for our Unity'.[2]

For the moment, it was not enough. Lagos had been held off and Glover was replaced in 1872, but internal division within Abeokuta continued and in the midst of the feuding and infighting, Johnson lost influence and was ousted. In 1877, however, the alake died and two years later Prince Oyekan was elected alake. Not long thereafter Johnson was back in Abeokuta still striving for unity under a 'civilized government'. For a few years the old fire flared again. Johnson reinstituted his

[1] Johnson to F. Fitzgerald, Apr. 8, 1872, G. W. Johnson Papers.
[2] Johnson to W. P. Richards, Nov. 25, 1872, Jan. 17, Feb. 5, 1873, G. W. Johnson Papers.

customs programme and drafted a number of patriotic ceremonies under the heading 'Africa Shall Rise', which combined pageant with the idea of Egba nationhood, national independence and territorial integrity. He designed an Egba national flag and composed a hymn to National Unity which began, 'How good and how pleasant, when Egbas agree, Bound closely together, in firm Unity'. He formally renounced his British citizenship and changed his name from George W. Johnson to Osokele Tejumade Johnson. George W., he explained, was a foreign and a slave name. Osokele was a good Egba name and Tejumade, meaning 'highly dignified', had been given him at birth.[1]

Despite these renewed efforts, Johnson was swimming against the tide of the times. The Egba were as hopelessly split as ever and British influence was fast leading towards control of Yorubaland. In 1893 Governor Carter made his celebrated journey through the interior which established for all practical purposes a British protectorate over the Yoruba country, although Abeokuta was able to maintain nominal independence for another twenty years. By this time, however, Johnson was in exile once more in Lagos, living out the remnant of a shattered dream. His valedictory was a ringing manifesto under his old slogan, 'Africa Shall Rise':

A man who loves his country, and doing good for its elevation, has indeed fulfilled to some extent, one great law of the Creator ... doing a universal good for the benefit to humanity ... The Nation cannot long obey those who have no right to command ... and a solid peace will not be restored, till the people have been consulted, or made to see their error; that there is but one acknowledged and recognized Government in Abeokuta ... and this is—The *Egba United Board of Management*—issued from the National Sovereignty ... which Board ... rising above the egotism of parties ... is a power ... whose Authority you can vouch; not only to heal the present ... wounds on our Trade, but to reopen your hearts to hope, and to bring back Industry, Concord, and Peace, to the bosom of the authorities, and peoples of Lagos and Abeokuta.

This was in 1898, and the next year he was dead. Nevertheless the ideas which he promoted—national cohesion and freedom sustained by a modernized political authority—were to be a major theme of African leaders during his times and after and have established the person of George Osokele Johnson as one of the first nationalists in West Africa.[2]

[1] A. K. Ajisafe, *History of Abeokuta*, 139; Oath of Allegiance to the Alake of Abeokuta, Notice to be published, May 1, 1885, G. W. Johnson Papers.
[2] Manifesto 'Africa Shall Rise', G. W. Johnson Papers.

11 The First African Personality: Edward W. Blyden

1 *The Dilemma of Acceptance and Rejection*

Of all the individuals in West Africa who wrestled during the nineteenth century with the problem of the identity of the African, Edward W. Blyden, sometime citizen and public servant of the republic of Liberia, stands out as by far the most arresting figure. Countless West Africans throughout the nineteenth century and into the twentieth were forced by circumstance or induced through preference to deal with the intrusion of western ideas and institutions, the application of western political power, the introduction of western custom, western economic patterns, western religion, western government and western moral and ethical codes. Their reactions were widely various. There were the unassimilated Lebou of Dakar, and there were the highly adaptable creoles of Freetown. On the Oil Rivers the trading chiefs were quick to respond to European economic interests but slow to absorb European Christian ethics and morals. The Yoruba of Abeokuta welcomed the English missionaries in 1842 only to expel them twenty-five years later. Reversible Johnson himself was a complex of ambivalence towards Europe.

The degree of involvement and the extent of reaction were closely related to the proportion of European contact, and since circumstance dictated that those most familiar with the West were those best equipped to deal with its intrusive presence, there tended initially to emerge African leadership which accepted western standards as axiomatic, which discounted African institutions when they did not meet these western standards, and which urged in varying degrees African absorption of western thought and western institutions. This was the position of the mulattoes of Senegal, or to a somewhat lesser extent, the creoles of Sierra Leone. Later there were leaders like Bishop Crowther, who urged basic westernization but with sympathetic attention to African customs.

Still later there was a sharp reaction in which the African, rebuffed by the European in his effort to assimilate western culture, began to assert his Africanness, first through clothing, language, ceremony and custom, and then through direct political activities. The breakaway churches in Nigeria at the end of the nineteenth century were just one manifestation of this first movement. The agitation of nationalistically-minded newspapers in Sierra Leone, the Gold Coast and Nigeria, the increasingly sharp criticisms of government policy by the unofficial members of the legislative councils of those colonies, or the rise of African political groups such as the Young Senegalese are all instances of the second development.

Although these stages differed in the degree and kind of their reaction to European ideas, there were few exponents of each who had examined and digested all the implications of their position in relation to the West. The initial acceptance was essentially a spontaneous emotional response to what was new, exciting and seemingly superior. Little attention was given at the time to the problem of preserving that sense of cultural integrity which makes one group secure in its manhood, while another gropes for its values or remains uncertain and unfulfilled, sustained only by the borrowed standards of others. The eventual anti-western reaction which followed was equally charged with emotion, and similarly lacking in any profound reflection over the ultimate consequences of such action for the material and the spiritual vigour of African civilization.

There were of course some exceptions. There were those who were genuinely troubled by these matters, who attempted to provide answers to the question of what the future African society was to be and ought to be. Essentially they were searching for a philosophy of life which might resolve the conflict between African and European standards by accepting from Europe what appeared beneficial to Africa while preserving the best of the traditional African way of life. This was not as easy as it sounded. If Crowther, James Johnson and the other native African missionaries were convinced of the efficacy of British Victorian Christianity, they were faced with the task of isolating those Sabbath values from the weekday vices which accompanied them. If they came to feel that there were aspects of African civilization which should be preserved–family responsibility, a sense of religiousness, and sympathy with nature–how were these to be preserved without carrying over such unhealthy customs as human sacrifice or household slavery?

Each individual in his time worked out his own version of the problem and its solution. For full-scale assimilationists like the Abbé Boilat, the problem was simple and the solution simplistic. For others who came later or saw the issues more clearly, the awareness of complications brought correspondingly more sophisticated efforts at solution. In most cases, however, the response was a pragmatic reaction to a pressure applied from the outside and was usually partial and inconsistent. Only one man in nineteenth-century Africa was able to see the problem in its entirety and this man was Edward W. Blyden. It was Blyden who tried and succeeded in fashioning a total philosophy of Africanness which not only had great appeal for his contemporaries, but for future generations of Africans as well. It was Blyden who re-established the psychic and emotional sense of security of the African in the face of Europe's intrusion with a brilliance that foreshadowed to a remarkable degree African thinking in the mid-twentieth century when another generation of Africans, achieving political independence from Europe, sought economic and cultural independence as well.

2 *The Emergence of a West African Patriot*

Blyden's most active years spanned roughly the half century preceding the outbreak of the First World War, that is, the period of major initial European penetration and control of Africa. His ideas, therefore, were no feeble product of hothouse theorizing – he was right in the middle of the essential political issues of his day and his suggestions, whatever their merit, had a sense of immediacy which constituted not only a specific African reaction to European pressures, but a source of inspiration to thoughtful Africans plagued by the same questions which he was attempting to answer.

Blyden was born in 1832 in St. Thomas, one of the Danish West Indies. His parents were pure African, possibly of Ibo descent; in any event he tells us that they were very devout and that his mother was responsible 'more than any other earthly cause' for the religious aspirations and literary tastes which he came to develop. As a boy he showed high scholastic interest and aptitude, continuing his studies part time after he had been apprenticed to a tailor, and showing a developing linguistic ability by mastering Spanish during a two-year residence in Venezuela. By his early teens he had come under the surveillance of a Presbyterian minister from the United States who guided Blyden's religious instruction and who eventually sent the young man to America in 1850 that he might continue his studies in that country.

This venture ended in failure, thwarted by the deep racial prejudice of the day which made it impossible for Blyden to gain admission to an appropriate institution. Whatever the effect this unhappy affair may have had on his future attitudes the reaction was certainly not simple, and one sees little evidence of later points of view or prejudices directly traceable to this incident. In another sense the occasion was momentous, however, for out of it came the opportunity provided by the New York Colonization Society for Blyden to carry on his studies in Liberia. So it was that the young man proceeded to Africa later in that same year, initially to complete his education but eventually to become the leading statesman-philosopher of Africa in his generation. He made quick progress at the Presbyterian high school in Monrovia, once again exhibiting linguistic prowess by mastering Greek and Latin. More remarkable, he taught himself Hebrew in his spare time in order that he might satisfy his desire to read the Scriptures in their original form. Before long he was teaching and occasionally directing the activities of the school. In 1858 he became its principal, and the same year was ordained a minister of the Presbytery of West Africa. Three years later he was made professor of Greek and Latin at the newly-founded Liberia College.[1]

Blyden soon began to show evidence of unusual abilities. In 1861 the Liberian government sent him to America to recruit settlers as the result of which a group of émigrés eventually began a settlement on the St. Paul River. At about the same time he began his well-publicized correspondence with William Gladstone in which he took the interesting position that there was no essential difference between the northern and southern states in America since oppression and segregation of the Negro existed similarly in all parts of the country. Even at this stage, Blyden was basing action on clearly-formulated policy. His willingness to work on behalf of Liberian colonization rested on the conviction of American racial discrimination of which he had much painful personal experience, and on the belief that the Negro race could achieve physical and cultural independence only in Africa in unencumbered pursuit of its own native genius. No race, he explained, could reach its fullest self-expression under alien circumstances. 'I believe nationality to be an ordinance of nature; and no people can rise to an influential position among the nations without a distinct and efficient nationality. Cosmopolitanism has never effected anything.' The Negro in America would

---

[1] E. W. Blyden, *Liberia's Offering*, i–iii; *The Lagos Weekly Record*, Feb. 24, 1912.

always remain oppressed and dominated by foreign ideas. Only in Africa could he draw strength from his native soil and demonstrate to himself and to the rest of the world that he was a man among men:

> We must *prove* to our oppressors that we are men, possessed of like susceptibilities with themselves; by seeking after those attributes which give dignity to a state; by cultivating those virtues which shed lustre upon individuals and communities; by pursuing whatever is magnificent in enterprise, whatever is lovely and of good report in civilization, whatever is exalted in morals, and whatever is exemplary in piety.[1]

Blyden's early pronouncements on behalf of Liberian colonization set a life-long pattern, for he was to return to Liberia and her prospects again and again throughout a long life. Already he was a leading educator in his adopted country and was soon to serve as Liberian Secretary of State. At the same time, however, his career was beginning to exhibit that larger dimension which transcended the limits of the small West African republic, which made him a personage of international reputation, and a citizen, not just of Liberia, but of all Africa, eventually establishing him as a spokesman for all members of the Negro race. He had already travelled to America and Europe and met some of the leading English statesmen and philanthropists. In 1866 he visited Egypt and the Middle East where he acquired his familiarity with Arabic and began to develop his appreciation of the Muslim faith. In 1871, he quit Liberia for Sierra Leone, and while he returned to Monrovia many times over the ensuing years, he may be regarded from that time forward as an African rather than as a Liberian. It was thus that the people of English-speaking West Africa came to regard him, it was in that wider context that his views about African civilization were most appropriately examined, and it is still in this larger dimension that he is most fruitfully studied today.

3 Edward W. Blyden and the Philosophy of Negritude

Blyden lived through an age when the African continent was not only being subjected increasingly to military conquest and political control but the African people were being told that they were basically inferior racially and culturally, and consequently their subservient position was natural and proper. European expressions of superiority came in various forms which began with appeal to biblical authority and ended with

---

[1] *Ibid.*; *Liberia's Offering*, iii–iv, 27, 63–4; Wilbur D. Jones, 'Blyden, Gladstone and the War', *The Journal of Negro History*, vol. XLIX, 1964, 57–8.

what passed at that time for scientific reasoning. Whatever the method, the conclusions were the same—mankind was divided into different groupings or races which were easily distinguished each from the other by physical characteristics such as skin colour or bone structure, or by cultural traits including language and social custom. These traits were not only analysed, but they came to be compared, race against race, and finally to be ordered into a hierarchy from good to bad or high to low. In describing such a hierarchy, standards of beauty and truth had to be invoked and invariably the standards chosen were those of the individual who was pursuing the study. Since most of the investigators at the time were Europeans, it was not surprising that their studies reached the conclusion that the white race or sometimes some subdivision—in British anthropological circles the preferred subgroup was Anglo-Saxon—was clearly the most advanced. Consistently the Negro was relegated to the bottom of the scale.[1]

Blyden knew by instinct and experience that such conclusions were nonsense, but European ideas and ways of thinking had long since become an integral part of his mental and psychological apparatus so that when he sought to refute these racist doctrines, it did not occur to him to scrap the whole structure with its network of unconscious assumptions which so completely prejudiced the case. In effect a psychological Eurafrican, Blyden began by accepting the racial theories of European anthropologists with their division of the world's races according to cultural and physiological characteristics, and then proceeded with great skill to present theological, historical, anthropological and sociological arguments to show that the conclusions of a European racial superiority were simply not tenable.

He argued thus. It was quite true that the races of the world differed—this was clearly apparent in the physical and cultural distinctions manifested. What was untrue was that there was a necessary scale of achievement which placed once race above another. Like Africanus Horton, Blyden discovered European anthropologists attempting to demonstrate European superiority by examples of African slaves, brutalized and debilitated, compared with representatives of the intellectually élite of Europe. This sort of sophistry deceived no one. The races were not better or worse; they were simply different. Shaped over the ages by the force of environment, each race gradually developed characteristics peculiarly its own. Each excelled in certain pursuits and was less successful in others. It was therefore bootless and irrelevant to compare

[1] See Philip D. Curtin, *The Image of Africa*, esp. 363–87.

racial capabilities on some sort of competitive scale—they were as irreconcilable as skew lines.[1]

It was much more to the point to recognize and exploit the complementary character of the world's races. Blyden, who was a deeply religious man but no narrow sectarian, viewed each race as an integral part of the godhead, each contributing its own unique share of God's nature, and each therefore essential to complete the unity of the divine:

> Each race sees from its own standpoint a different side of the Almighty. ... It is by God in us, where we have freedom to act out ourselves, that we do each our several work and live out into action, through our work, whatever we have within us of noble and wise and true. What we do is, if we are able to be true to our nature, the representation of some phase of the Infinite being. ... As in every form of the inorganic universe we see some noble variation of God's thought and beauty, so in each separate man, in each separate race, something of the absolute is incarnated. The whole of mankind is a vast representation of the Deity.

Therefore, he argued, 'we cannot extinguish any race either by conflict or amalgamation without serious responsibility.'[2]

From this basic premise, Blyden was able to draw a whole series of important corollaries. If the races were equal and complementary, it followed that each had its own culture to contribute to the totality of human civilization. Any attempt by one race either to adopt or to destroy the culture of another was a wicked and immoral presumption for, 'Every race ... has a soul, and the soul of a race finds expression in its institutions, and to kill those institutions is to kill the soul—a terrible homicide.' This position firmly established the validity of civilization as it had developed in Africa, making it possible for the African to pursue his time-honoured and time-tested philosophies, cosmologies and customs secure in his knowledge of their intrinsic merit. Indeed, it was incumbent upon the African to take care not to become involved in an alien culture, for in this fashion, said Blyden, he could only lose the vision of his own racial genius, wasting his energies in fruitless pursuit of unnatural foreign ways:

> We must start out ... fully recognizing ... that the customs of all peoples ... are due largely to the influence of race and climate and that while these customs may sometimes be modified to advantage by wise and judicious external agency, they cannot be wholly or indiscriminately eradicated without the most serious mischief—without leaving a void

---

[1] Blyden, *African Life and Customs*, 8–9; *The African Times*, July 22, 1865.
[2] Blyden, *The African Problem and the Method of Its Solution*, 22–3.

which nothing can supply and in consequence of which disintegration and demoralization must take place.[1]

What were these elements of African culture—racially unique, and not only necessary for the survival of the African, but an important facet of a universal civilization? First of all, Blyden cited the fundamental communality of African life. Society in Africa was supported at bottom by the institution of the family. All men and women married, and all took part in the basic human process of continuing the human race. 'The foundation of the African Family', he pointed out, 'is plural marriage ... this marriage rests upon the will of the woman, and this will operates to protect from abuse the functional work of the sex, and to provide that all women shall share normally in this work with a view to healthy posterity and an unfailing supply of population.' There was no spinsterhood, no prostitution, no women wasted or unfulfilled. At the same time, women were protected from the exhausting effects of excessive childbearing by polygamy which provided each mother with a period of repose and recuperation without compromising the basic law of life to 'multiply and replenish'. We have developed in Africa a practical eugenics, Blyden insisted, 'whose operation extends back over centuries producing continuously a vigorous and prolific race of men and women ... without which ... decay and death stare the African in the face'.[2]

Beyond the family, Blyden pointed to the community, characterized by co-operation and mutual aid. This was the result of no accident; rather it came from centuries of experience and the workings of a faultless logic. Among the Vai people there was a revealing proverb, 'What is mine goes; what is ours abides'. Thus in African society the land and water belonged to everyone to be used equally by all for obtaining food, clothing and shelter. No law of property existed so sacred that anyone could be made needlessly to suffer hunger or exposure. There was no individualistic competition which separated people into antagonistic classes constantly struggling with each other, the one to keep its excessive luxuries, the other to obtain the bare necessities of life. There was no need for the cheerless homes for the aged, the dehumanizing workhouses, or the charity hospital wards of the West, since the weak, the aged, the incurable, the helpless and the sick were all cared for in the comforting, affectionate atmosphere of the family. In the rare

---

[1] Blyden, *West Africa Before Europe*, 140; *The Lagos Weekly Record*, May 25, 1901.
[2] *African Life and Customs*, 10-25.

instance where the family failed, responsibility was quickly assumed by the village. In the same way theft was virtually unknown in an Africa where all had their social rights, and where for each there existed a sufficiency to satisfy life's basic wants.[1]

For Blyden the whole African approach to the idea of wealth was radically different from that which obtained in Europe. Europeans never ceased talking of the dignity of labour but it was usually the millionaire who spoke of it thus; to the worker it was more likely to be just plain drudgery. In Africa, however, there was no sharp distinction between work and play, or put another way, the African found ways of converting work into a pleasurable productive pastime. When a job had to be done, the whole community turned out with supplies and music and proceeded to sing and dance its way through to the successful conclusion of each particular chore. Occasionally, Blyden admitted, there were Africans who, having been educated in the European way, managed to accumulate considerable wealth by western competitive methods but who then tried, only to fail, to apply these individualistic methods to Africa:

> Some . . . spent thousands of pounds and devoted years of labour to this enterprise . . . built large substantial houses with the idea of making permanent centres for their work, but all, without exception . . . failed. Their habitations are now tenanted by bats and other noxious vermin. . . . They do not succeed because they violate the law of African life and growth. . . . They do not imply the *We* of communal life. They are competitive Organizations not only to promote their own but to circumscribe the prosperity of others. . . . they threaten the life of others; and this Africa will not allow.[2]

African emphasis on communal life was rooted in another typical characteristic of the African—his sympathetic communion with nature. After all, said Blyden, it was observation of nature's rhythm of productivity and recuperation which had provided the model of procreation leading to this 'vigorous and prolific race of men and women'. It was nature, moreover, which suggested the collective pattern of life and work adopted so successfully in Africa. From the termite the African learned to develop a co-operative, rather than an egotistical or individualistic, industrial system; from the same industrious insect came the design of the circular dwellings of Africa, and it was said that the anthill was the prototype of the great pyramids of Egypt. Thus the African in his appeal to nature tended to approach man in his perfect state.

[1] *Ibid.*, 29–44.
[2] *Ibid.*, 48–9; *The Lagos Weekly Record*, Aug. 1, 1908.

Where he failed, it was usually where he had been interfered with by alien influences. He lived out of doors, never overburdened by clothes, freely bathing each day in near-by streams, using the whole book of nature for his school. 'His real work', said Blyden, quoting the Book of Job, 'is to speak to the earth and let it teach him—to dress the garden and to keep it.'[1]

If communion with nature helped determine the shape of the African's society, communion with God characterized his spirit, for Blyden saw in the African psyche a more pronounced religious sense than was evident in other peoples, particularly those of Europe. He argued first of all that religion had originated in Africa, spreading north and east to Egypt and then on to Asia. Africa had been, moreover, the refuge of those great modern faiths—Judaism, Christianity and Islam, protecting them during their period of consolidation before they spread themselves over the surface of the earth. Much later, in modern times, Africans had shown much attraction to Christianity and Islam which, thus encouraged, had taken root in all parts of the African continent. What all this reflected in the African people was a long-standing religious sense of high refinement. Traditional religion in Africa had always been based on the concept of a single divinity, but one which was attended, through pantheism, by a hierarchy of spirits and forces which brought all nature within the compass of God's essence. African society was also closely integrated with religion, not only in the concept of a single community comprising the living, the ancestors and the unborn, but in the intimate relation between religious thought and practice, and the workaday world of seedtime and harvest, of birth and death, of government and justice, of love, of art, of all things.[2]

By necessity and very likely by design, Blyden set forth these somewhat idealized versions of African society and religion partly to correct what he felt were serious errors in European anthropological analyses of African culture, but more particularly to give the African a sense of worth and self-respect, a pride in himself, in his race, in his way of life, and in the role he had played and would play in the history of world civilization. This last was important. It was not enough to have a culture the intrinsic merits of which were comparable with those of other races. It was essential that Africa also make positive contributions to the progress of all mankind, contributions which could only come through the unique genius of the African.

[1] *African Life and Customs*, 9, 29–30, 51.
[2] *Ibid.*, 62, 68–73; Blyden, *Africa's Service to the World*, 4–8.

Already Africa had made great and memorable contributions to the march of civilization. 'If service rendered to humanity is service rendered to God, then the Negro and his country have been during the ages ... tending upward to the divine.' Blyden followed this assertion with a full bill of particulars. Africa had been the cradle of civilization: two great religions had been fostered there; so had science and much of art—witness the great pyramids, still a marvel in the modern world. Africa had provided shelter for the Jews and sanctuary for the child Jesus, and later it was an African, Simon of Cyrene, who helped Christ to carry the Cross. Egypt and North Africa in their time had been the granary of Europe, and now it was Africa which was again assisting Europe as market and source of raw materials. The hallmark of these accomplishments was, not glory, but service:

Africa's lot resembles Him also who made Himself of no reputation, but took upon Himself the form of a servant, and, having been made perfect through suffering, became the 'Captain of our salvation'. And if the principle laid down by Christ is that by which things are decided above . . . that he who would be chief must become the servant of all, then we see the position which Africa and the Africans must ultimately occupy.[1]

So much for history. What of the future? Here, said Blyden, was where the fundamental African qualities of sympathetic harmony with nature and close communion with God combined in what might yet be the greatest racial gift to mankind in its upward struggle towards civilization:

During all the years which have elapsed since the commencement of modern progress, the African race has filled a very humble and subordinate part in the work of human civilization. But the march of events is developing the interesting fact that there is a career before this people which no other people can enter upon. There is a peculiar work for them to accomplish, both in the land of their bondage and in the land of their fathers, which no other people can achieve. With the present prospects and privileges before his race—with the chances of arduous work, noble suffering, and magnificent achievement before them—I would rather be a member of this race than a Greek in the time of Alexander, a Roman in the Augustan period, or an Anglo-Saxon in the nineteenth century.[2]

The list was long of great nations which had led the human race forward—Egypt with the scientific marvels of her ancient tombs, Phoenicia, the teacher of the secrets of navigation, India, where phil-

---

[1] *Ibid.*, 7–12. [2] Blyden, *The Prospects of the African*, 7.

osophy had been born, Greece, the source of artistic and aesthetic development, and Rome from whence came law and the knowledge of political organization and power. But what of the Negro? Surely, 'God has something in store for a people who have so served the world . . . and we may believe that out of it will yet come some of the greatest marvels which are to mark the closing periods of time.'

Africa may yet prove to be the spiritual conservatory of the world. . . . When the civilized nations, in consequence of their wonderful material development, shall have had their spiritual perceptions darkened and their spiritual susceptibilities blunted through the agency of a captivating and absorbing materialism, it may be that they may have to resort to Africa to recover some of the simple elements of faith.

The world had not yet witnessed 'the forging of the great chain which is to bind the nations together in equal fellowship and friendly union, I mean the mighty principle of Love . . . Many are of opinion', Blyden insisted, 'that this crowning work is left for the African. . . .'

Perhaps there is no people in whom the religious instinct is deeper and more universal than among Africans. And, in view of the materializing tendencies of the age, it may yet come to pass that when, in Europe, 'God has gone out of date' . . . or when that time arrives in the development of the great Aryan race . . . 'when the belief in God will be as the tales with which old women frighten children, when the world will be a machine, the ether a gas, and God will be a force', then earnest inquirers after truth leaving the seats of science and the 'highest civilization', will take themselves to Africa to learn lessons of faith and piety; for 'Ethiopia shall stretch forth her hands unto God'.[1]

Thus, from his principle of the races of mankind as different but complementary facets making up God's infinite perfection, Blyden had deduced his doctrine of the importance of African civilization. Further, he had suggested the prospect of future African contributions to world progress to match those contributions of Africa's past, and perhaps to exceed the weight of accomplishment of the other races of the world. Other interesting conclusions also found their source in his same principle. If the races were co-equal but distinct in their character, might it not follow that they were best able to develop their own genius when isolated from one another? Blyden thought he saw more than the dictates of logic in this conclusion, for there seemed to be good empirical evidence to illustrate his contention.

First of all, Blyden asserted, there were vast differences in the

---

[1] *Ibid.*, 7–9; *Africa's Service to the World*, 16.

characteristics of the world's races, particularly between the Negro and the Caucasian. Where the Negro was sympathetic, morally profound, in tune with nature and with the community of the spirits, the European was didactic, physically and mentally strong, materialistic, accomplished in the sciences and politics, preoccupied with the improvement of his immediate environment, and ever inclined to dominate other races that they might better serve his purposes. Often this led to salutary ends. In Africa it had brought the end of the slave trade, and substituted peace for warfare. In Blyden's view, European powers such as France, Germany and Belgium were largely responsible for opening up the country to reviving commerce, building great cities, introducing much needed medical advances and eliminating local political unrest that the people might put their full energies into improving their economies and enriching their social order. Britain too had effected vast changes in the few years she had been on the West African coast. Who could not recall the horrors and atrocities of the slavers once infesting the coast and not thrill at the changes from spoilation and bloodshed to English Christianity and philanthropy, English statesmanship and commercial enterprise? Surely, said Blyden, the European occupied 'an indispensable and a beneficent place. . . . He is God's ruler, God's soldier, God's policeman to keep order; and order is Nature's first law, without which nothing can exist. The man who produces order where chaos previously reigned is a second creator.'[1]

Looked at in another light, however, European racial characteristics appeared less attractive:

Can we refer the want of Aryan success among foreign races to the original idiosyncrasy impressed upon the races in their cradles, and fitting each for a specific work? It would seem that the tendency of the West Aryan genius is ever to divorce God from His works, and to lay great stress upon human capabilities and achievement. Man is an end, not a means. The highest man is the highest end to which all things else must bow. The aggregate must bend to the individual if he is superior to other individuals in intellectual or pecuniary might. The more favoured race must dominate and control the less favoured race. Religion is to be cherished as a means of subserving temporal and material purposes . . . There is now no more direct communion with or inspiration from God necessary or possible. Everything now depends upon man.

---

[1] S. A. Coker, *The Rights of Africans to Organize and Establish Indigenous Churches*, 13–14; *African Life and Customs*, 9; *West Africa Before Europe*, 13–17; *The African Problem and the Method of Its Solution*, 16–17; Blyden, *The Return of the Exiles and the West African Church*, 6; Blyden, *Report on the Falaba Expedition*, 14; *Proceedings at the Banquet in Honour of Edward Wilmot Blyden*, 39–41.

Everything else is within his grasp. He may even by searching find out God. Material progress is the end of the human race. . . . Presbyterians from Scotland, Episcopalians from England, Puritans . . . all went to foreign shores with high and earnest purpose, but they were hampered in the attainment of any philanthropic result by their race-intolerance and impracticable narrowness. They aimed at securing material aggrandisement at any cost. . . . The human soul – the immaterial – was of secondary and subordinate importance.[1]

In such circumstances, Blyden insisted, the black race might well question the wisdom of too close association with the white. Would not the dominating white once again bend the Negro to his will and use his labour for selfish purposes? Had not the European already perverted the concept of Christ's agony from suffering for the salvation of others to forcing others to suffer for Europe's advantage? Was there not considerable evidence along the coast of West Africa that, despite certain advantages, the European presence had brought only physical and moral degeneracy where once there had been moral and mental virtue, physical and intellectual vigour? And in America, could it honestly be said that the African aping the white man's ways was any more than an outcast in his adopted land? Leaving moral judgments aside, was it not so that in terms of climate and geography Europe was best left to the European and Africa to the African? 'It is a truth at which not only we ourselves but thinking foreigners are arriving', Blyden remarked, 'that Africa is to be civilized and elevated by Africans – not merely because of the physical adaptation but on account of the mental idiosyncrasy of Africans. Not only on account of the colour of the Negro but because of his psychological possibilities and susceptibilities.'[2]

When one penetrated to the continental interior yet untouched by the taint of European contact, one left the weak, degenerating people of the coastal areas and encountered a completely different type of man, 'superior tribes, who have many of the elements of civilization'.

There are . . . the great Mandingo and Foulah tribes, who are Mohammedans, and the principal rulers of central Africa, extending their influence nearly across the Continent. They have schools and mosques in all their towns, and administer their government according to written law. There is a steady and improvable element in their barbarism, which is leading them to develop the idea of a national and social order. They read constantly the same books and from this they derive that

---

[1] Blyden, *Christianity, Islam and the Negro Race*, 278–80.
[2] Coker, *op. cit.*; *Proceedings at the Banquet in Honour of Edward Wilmot Blyden*, 41–2; *Christianity, Islam and the Negro Race*, 43–4; Blyden, *A Chapter in the History of Liberia*, 31.

community of ideas, and that understanding of each other . . . which gives them the power of ready organization, and effective action. There is a simplicity and sincerity about them—there are features of purity and sobriety in their society which will fit them to receive and welcome certain aspects of higher civilization. . . . Without the aid or hindrance of foreigners . . . they are growing up gradually and normally to take their place in the great family of nations—a distinct but integral part of the great human body, who will neither be spurious Europeans, bastard Americans nor savage Africans, but men developed upon the base of their own idiosyncrasies, and according to the exigencies of their climate and country.[1]

Clearly, the logic of Blyden's argument was leading him to occupy an explosive and controversial position—the adoption by the people of the world of racial exclusiveness involving both physical segregation and biological purity. Although he may not have been the first to advocate such views—after all, racial segregation was implicit in the schemes of repatriation of Negroes in Sierra Leone and Liberia—his was the first African voice to suggest such a position, and because of his eloquence and his prominence, he was able to command a respectful hearing, if not universal acceptance, among his people. To Blyden, however, the conclusion of the argument was inescapable. The races were separate but equal. When they came together they tended one to dominate and confound the other, to confuse moral objectives and to depress social standards. Consequently, the best procedure was to keep them physically apart.

Blyden particularly pointed out the Negro in America as the horrible example of what happened to the African race when removed from its natural environment and forced to dwell in an alien land. First there was slavery which even in its rare humanitarian moments treated the Negro like a helpless child. Then followed physical freedom but with a spiritual bondage which was as crippling to the soul as the heavy labour on the plantations had been exhaustive of the body's strength. Negroes in America subjected to western education found themselves cut off from their cultural roots and grafted on to a foreign way of life through which they could never reach natural flower. Hence the American Negro was being transformed into a cultural freak:

From the lessons he every day receives, the Negro unconsciously imbibes the conviction that to be a great man he must be like the white man. He is not brought up . . . to be the companion, the equal, the comrade of the white man, but his imitator, his ape, his parasite. To

[1] *The Prospects of the African*, 5–6.

be himself... is to be nothing.... Every intelligent Negro, in the lands of his exile, must feel that he walks upon the face of God's earth a physical and moral incongruity.

But there were in America some Negroes who had escaped the conditioning of western education, and these pure untrammelled specimens not only endured racial segregation, said Blyden, they welcomed it. 'The Negro properly educated – I mean educated on the basis of his own idiosyncrasy – never complains against such discrimination. The racial feeling is strong within him; he understands, and is glad to have a place apart. It is only those who have been trained as White men in the schools and in the church who grieve at these discriminations.'[1]

Voluntary racial segregation was one thing, but Blyden was prepared to take an even more revolutionary step. It was not only the properly educated Negro who saw the problem with greater clarity; even more, it was the Negro of pure-blood who, because he was racially pure, was able better to understand the validity of African culture and to strive for his right to live as a pure bred African under undiluted African conditions. In America the coloured or half-caste Negroes shunned the opportunity to return to Africa and aspired instead to acceptance in the white man's world. To Blyden, the best that could happen to these racial cripples was to be absorbed by either the black or the white race. In West Africa it was the mixed creoles along the coast who were decaying and effete in comparison with the pure nations of the interior. Even within the continental mass there were distinctions to be drawn resulting from racial mixing. For example, the great Samori was a pure-blooded Negro; thus it was that at the height of his conquests he sought to surrender his territory to British rule because, said Blyden, the Negro is by nature a peaceful man disinterested in political ascendancy. El Hadj Omar, on the other hand, and other Tucolor infected with white blood, became the leaders of a series of fanatical explosions and destructive holy wars.[2]

As a natural consequence of his doctrines of racial segregation, Blyden advocated throughout his long public career the recolonization of Liberia by the former African slaves in America. Citing Thomas Jefferson's comment that the white and black races could never hope to live together in America in equal freedom, Blyden unceasingly drew attention

---

[1] *Christianity, Islam and the Negro Race*, 44; *The Lagos Standard*, Oct. 24, 1906.
[2] *Ibid.*; *The Lagos Weekly Record*, Apr. 27, 1895; Blyden, *The Significance of Liberia*, 33–4; *West Africa Before Europe*, 88–90. Blyden's views on miscegenation were not emphasized in his writings for fear of offending influential mulattoes, white philanthropists, and others who did not share his views.

to the great possibilities awaiting the courageous immigrant in the small republic on the West African coast. 'My heart is in Liberia and longs for the welfare of Africa', he cried. Here in this charming country, 'the garden spot of West Africa', with its beautiful hills, its mountain streams and its fertile acres, the people would come and bring forth the wealth of the land. The forests would be felled, roads built, streams bridged, cities raised, fields sowed and quarries mined. The exiles would return, join forces with the sturdy native stock, and build a great Negro nation, great because it would be true to the African genius and instinct. Blyden was never more poetic than when singing the praises of his ideal and idealized African dream. 'I am kindled into ecstasy as I contemplate the future of that infant nation . . . The hills . . . covered with flocks, and the valleys with corn; the increase of the earth . . . fat and plenteous . . . Language fails . . . Imagination itself is baffled . . . and pauses with reverent awe before the coming possibilities.'[1]

Such hyperbole may have been required to bolster flagging spirits, for Liberian fact remained far short of Blydenesque fancy. Throughout his life Liberia was continually plagued with problems of uncertain leadership and a faulty economy, of political weakness and financial instability. Worse still, the settlers from America consistently ignored the necessity of Blyden's major thesis and refused to merge and make common cause with the indigenous tribes, preferring to treat them as uncivilized savages unqualified to participate in the operation of a modern state and certainly no fit object for intermarriage. Furthermore, to the chronic disappointment of hostility between settler and native tribesman were added occasional personal complications arising out of local political differences, so that from time to time Blyden found himself an enforced exile from his adopted country–the very example chosen by him to prove his racial theories.

But Blyden felt that he knew precisely where the fault lay–that the difficulty was not with any shortcomings inherent in his basic theory of race but with the Afro-Americans corrupted by alien cultural standards and weakened by their mulatto inheritance. He therefore continued until his death to press for his Liberian colonization scheme, for 'it represents an important principle, and may be made the instrument of a great work'. As an independent African state, Liberia was in position to demonstrate to the sceptical world what African civilization could accomplish, given the opportunity:

[1] *The Liberia Herald*, Aug. 18, 1852; *The African Problem and the Method of Its Solution*, 11–12, 20; *Liberia's Offering*, v; *The Prospect of the African*, 19–20.

It is the only spot in Africa where the civilised Negro–the American Negro without alien supervision or guidance–is holding aloft the torch of civilisation and the symbol of Christianity, endeavouring to establish government on principles recognised by the civilised world and ... international relations with the leading nations; a country to which thousands of Africa's descendants in the Southern States are looking as the only place where they can obtain relief from their difficulties and a field for the unhindered cultivation and untrammelled development of their peculiar gifts as a people.[1]

There was some inconsistency in this position, not only the displacement between racial theory and practice, but the contradiction implicit in demanding the creation of a purely African culture with tools largely drawn from western experience. In the first place, the settlers would be westernized Negroes, but more than that, Blyden expected them to come equipped as experienced farmers and mechanics, teachers and doctors, familiar not only with the workings of western science but capable of dealing with political and economic problems in western terms, replacing heathenism with Christianity, introducing English as the lingua franca of West Africa, and in sum establishing American civilization in the land. In 1891 he was suggesting to a Lagos audience the military and political benefits which would accrue to the Yoruba country through the introduction of one hundred thousand American Negroes. A few years later he was advocating the systematic introduction to Liberia of two hundred and fifty Negro families a year comprising carefully selected professional and technical experts. Here indeed imagination had far outdistanced reality.[2]

There was another aspect of Blyden's African philosophy which involved not so much inconsistency as the necessary complication of a sophisticated mind at work. This was his attitude towards religion. Trained as a Christian minister, Blyden also gave bent to his scholarly interests and linguistic aptitude by studying and mastering Arabic, and with this came the opportunity for a growing familiarity with the riches of Islamic literature and thought. By the time he arrived in Sierra Leone in 1871, he had already visited Egypt and the Holy Land and become much impressed with Africa's Muslim connections. In Sierra Leone his interests were given free reign for he came initially to teach Arabic in the C.M.S. college at Fourah Bay and, when that project

---

[1] Blyden to Henry Venn, Sept. 16, Oct. 15, 1871, Apr. 17, 1872, C.M.S. CA1/047; *The Significance of Liberia*; *The Lagos Weekly Record*, Nov. 2, 1895, June 13, 1908; *Christianity, Islam and the Negro Race*, v.
[2] Blyden, *The Problems Before Liberia*, 11; *The Return of the Exiles and the West African Church*, 23; *The Sierra Leone Weekly News*, Aug. 5, 1899.

collapsed, he remained as a government agent dealing with the Muslim tribes of the interior. Much later he was to be instrumental in encouraging Islamic schools in Lagos, but throughout his life wherever he was, he maintained a lively respect for Islamic culture and institutions. In Freetown he was attracted by the sobriety, independence, intellectual curiosity and open-minded attitude of the Muslims, and when he visited the interior he encountered the same characteristics. 'I was not a little surprised to find so much literary cultivation and intellectual activity', he reported, adding dryly his gratification 'at the exhibition . . . witnessed of capacities and susceptibilities altogether inconsistent with the theory that dooms such a people to a state of perpetual barbarism or of essential inferiority to the more favoured races.'[1]

This admiration for Muslim civilization was matched by a growing impatience with Christian missionaries who, with few exceptions, condemned Islam out of ignorance, reinforcing Blyden's own judgment that the bigotry and narrowness characterized the accusers, not the accused. Institutionalized Christianity, moreover, seemed so frequently to appear in Africa as the agent of slavery, racialism and colonial domination:

An Imperial race is incompetent to maintain the simplicity of the Nazarene, and diffuse His teachings . . . It is not the business of imperialism to make *men* but to create subjects, not to save souls, but to rule bodies. . . . How is Christianity, bearing on its back the burden of its caste prejudices, the liquor traffic, and its ethical intolerance, ever to make way among these people?

For its part, Islam revealed a totally different philosophy, stressing tolerance instead of prejudice, and human dignity in preference to racial discrimination:

The Mohammedan religion . . . seeks for the real man, neglects the accidental for the essential, the adventitious for the integral. Hence it extinguishes all distinctions founded upon race, colour, or nationality. To the African . . . the religion of Islam furnishes the greatest solace and the greatest defence. . . . The foreigner never fails to respect him when he presents himself with the badge of the faith of Mohammed.[2]

All this sounded like straightforward advocacy of Islam over Christianity, but it was not as simple as all that. Blyden was a practising Christian and looked on Christianity as the highest form of religious experience.

[1] Blyden to Venn, Aug. 24, Sept. 6, Oct. 28, 1871, C.M.S. CA1/047; *Report of the Falaba Expedition*, 2.
[2] *West Africa Before Europe*, 65, 73–5; *Christianity, Islam and the Negro Race*, 281.

The trouble lay not with the basic teachings of Christ, but with the inept interpretation of Christian principles by European churches and missionary societies. They had allowed the idea of the brotherhood of man to be corrupted into doctrines of human slavery, and had preached a morality on the Lord's day that was ignored, if not defied, during the rest of the week. For Blyden the Muslims were closer to basic principles, but their faith was still but a stage leading upward to the perfection of the Christian ideal. In 1891 he wrote, 'I believe Christianity to be the ultimate and final religion of humanity. Indeed I believe that it has always been and always will be the system which raises mankind to the highest level.' However, he went on to say:

I believe that Islam has done for vast tribes of Africa what Christianity in the hands of Europeans has not yet done. It has cast out the demons of fetishism, general ignorance of God, drunkenness, gambling, and has introduced customs which subserve for the people the highest purposes of growth and preservation. I do not believe that a system which has done such things can be outside of God's beneficent plans for the evolution of humanity.

A dozen years later he seemed to have gone a good deal further. 'These are the views I am now teaching', he announced, 'that Mohammedanism is the form of Christianity'—the locution is an interesting one—'best adapted to the negro race.'[1]

As one so completely dedicated to the renascence of a purely African culture, Blyden devoted a great deal of thought to the type of education appropriate to African needs. Not surprisingly, he consistently advocated practical training to meet the material requirements of African society combined with an emphasis on the cultural values of that society in order to strengthen its full African character. Ideas of racial exclusiveness transferred to educational philosophy emerged in the form of a brand of cultural nationalism similar to what was being practised concurrently in Europe on behalf of Anglo-Saxon ascendancy, Gallic superiority, or dreams of the ancient glories of the Teutonic knights. Blyden simply offered the African version of this process, suggesting that it might be more profitable to study the life of Toussaint L'Ouverture than that of Admiral Nelson, to retain the ancient classics but to combine them with Arabic and the native languages of Africa, or to emphasize the art, music and literature of the African peoples in preference to that of a foreign western culture.[2]

[1] *The Lagos Weekly Record*, Dec. 3, 1892; *West Africa*, Aug. 22, 1903.
[2] *The Sierra Leone Weekly News*, Apr. 25, 1903; *Christianity, Islam and the Negro Race*, 100–6.

A fundamental of Blyden's educational policy was the creation of a centre of higher learning in West Africa itself. Ideally it was to be located inland, the better to establish free uninterrupted contact with the educated leadership of the interior tribes while at the same time avoiding the disruptive influences of low foreign ideas found on the seaboard. The major reason for a university in Africa, however, was to avoid the necessity of Africans studying abroad, for when they did so, invariably they imbibed foreign ideas which ill equipped them for leadership within Africa. The tendency was uncritically to imitate European thinking and to conform to European standards. In Europe, the teachers and the books, the viewpoints and the subject-matter, were all centred on Europe. One learned only what Europeans thought, and saw the world only with a European perspective. Often the African student was taught that Africans were heathens and fools and that only Europeans exhibited the proper standards of personal and civic virtue. Africans learned to turn their back on the accomplishments of the great African nations, and to allow the history of Africa to be written by others. The inevitable result was a thin and disappointing stream of poorly educated Africans untrained in self-respect, unqualified to deal with the problems of their own society, and lacking the necessary instinctive, sympathetic response to the rhythmic pulse of Africa. Unable to understand their own culture and to help their own people, they were equally helpless in explaining Africa to outsiders, unable to reveal the African racial character and aspirations to those who sought to help.[1]

Blyden's great hope for a West African university was never realized in his lifetime. Liberia College, with which he was long associated as professor and president, suffered from weaknesses inherent in the political and social structure of the Liberian nation, and colonial administrations in other West African territories were a long way from being persuaded as to the need for such a centre. In 1872 Blyden's recommendation to the sympathetic governor, Pope Hennessy, for a university in Sierra Leone led no further than an affiliation between Fourah Bay College and Durham University in England. Almost a quarter of a century later he was urging upon another British governor, Sir Gilbert Carter, the establishment of a training college in Lagos which would embody most of his educational philosophies. His curriculum began with practical vocational studies such as surveying and engineering, adding classical languages and mathematics for their well-known virtues in disciplining the mind and the basic teaching of Christ

---

[1] *The Lagos Weekly Record*, May 2, 1895; *West Africa Before Europe*, 144.

for its moral and ethical values. The biology, geology and geography of Africa would also be studied for their relevance to the future activities of the students. All this provided in an African context would not only save time and money in offering much needed training; it would also preserve African moral and intellectual integrity along with African racial purity and instincts. British administrators, perhaps more interested in a corps of vocationally skilled Africans than in Blyden's educational philosophy, showed initial interest in the scheme, but it was not adopted at the time.[1]

It was appropriate that Blyden, an African nationalist, should speak forcefully regarding education in Africa. Similarly, it was appropriate that Blyden, Africa's most formidable student of African affairs, should place his scholarship at the disposal of his major objective—the re-establishment of the dignity of the African race—by his insistence on a long and distinguished history for the people of Africa. European travellers who visited only the coastal areas of West Africa tended to the conclusion that African culture was rudimentaty and African history non-existent, that everything worthwhile in Africa had been obtained from Europe. Actually, said Blyden, history taught that the Negro's residence in Africa was long-lived and his accomplishments in ancient times, illustrious. Blyden cited biblical evidence to show that the Negro was a very early resident of Egypt. He had arrived there a descendant of Ham through Cush and Nimrod. It was the Cushites who were responsible for the Tower of Babel, and many generations later they employed this same architectural talent in raising the great pyramids at Gizeh. If this was not sufficient evidence of a major Negro role in ancient Egyptian history, there was the Sphinx with its obviously African physiognomy representing one of the great Pharaohs, and the later testimony of Homer, and of Herodotus who spoke of the woolly-haired Ethiopians, 'the tallest and most beautiful of men ... the associates and the favourite of the gods'.

In more recent times, Blyden argued, the Negroes migrated from Egypt across the interior of the continent, emerging eventually on the Guinea coast. The process was a long one during which changes in climate, food and mode of living brought about a physical and intellectual decline. The major factor in the disintegration of the people of the West African coast, however, was the slave trade introduced by Europe in

---

[1] *Proceedings at the Banquet in Honour of Edward Wilmot Blyden*, 55–6; *Correspondence Between Edward W. Blyden, LL.D., and His Excellency Sir Gilbert T. Carter, K.C.M.G.*; *The Sierra Leone Weekly News*, Oct. 7, 1899.

the sixteenth century. This institution upset the peaceful industry of the people and substituted disruptive war. Cut off from the great independent nations of the interior, the coastal people degenerated to the pitiful condition which had plagued them thereafter. It was natural, therefore, that Blyden chose to emphasize the greater glories of an earlier golden age:

> The ancient Egyptians and Ethiopians were . . . clearly of the Black race. . . . I would much rather trust Herodotus than the whole tribe of modern commentators on his writings . . . Herodotus, writing in the simple innocence and candour of an unsophisticated eye-witness, affirms that the Colchians must have descended from the Egyptians *because* they have black skins and woolly hair. He celebrates the Egyptians as the greatest of men, and civilisers of the world . . . Homer bears similar testimony of the Ethiopians.[1]

4 The Impact of Blyden on West Africa

It was a sultry evening in Lagos on January 2, 1891, and it was warm in the densely crowded assembly hall of the Breadfruit Church schoolhouse. The room was filled with the city's leading citizens, and despite the uncomfortable atmosphere, there was an air of expectancy which transcended any annoyances of material discomfort. On the dais about twenty people were seated. In the chair was Sir Alfred Moloney, the governor of the colony. Near him were members of his official family, but most of those on the platform were representatives of the professional and commercial élite of Lagos–the merchants R. B. Blaize and J. S. Leigh, J. Otumba Payne, chief registrar of the colony, James Johnson, pastor of the Breadfruit Church, C. J. George, member of the legislative council, the physician, Dr. John Randle and others. Moist in their heavy black broadcloth suits, they exchanged quiet comments among themselves and with the stranger who was seated near them. He was a man apparently in the prime of life, probably in his late fifties. His large face and dark features reflected a healthy vigour under his thick grizzled hair. He seemed grave, his bearing dignified.

In the audience people were chatting in low tones, neighbour with neighbour, but conversation was desultory for all were waiting for the moment when the evening's proceedings would begin. Finally the governor arose and silence fell. He spoke briefly and quietly, and then

---

[1] Blyden, 'The Negro in Ancient History', *The People of Africa*, 1-34; Blyden, *From West Africa to Palestine*, 104-9, 114; *Christianity, Islam and the Negro Race*, 224; *The Significance of Liberia*, 6.

the stranger stood to face the audience. Stranger he was in appearance to many, for this was his first visit to Lagos. Yet there were few in the room who had not read at least some of his many works and responded to their stimulating authority. The applause died down at last and he began to speak. Head bowed, his manner unassuming, he expressed his profound delight at the opportunity to address the people of Lagos, for he had long been impressed with the progress of their great city. He was especially gratified at the opportunity to speak to them this night because he wished to discuss a subject in which the government and people of Lagos had shown much interest. His voice was soft and musical but it easily filled the room, and there was already in it a faint note of excitement as the speaker began to develop one of his favourite themes. Edward W. Blyden was about to speak on the subject of the return of the exiles—the Negroes of America—to their home in Africa.

Blyden spoke for about an hour that evening—eloquently as always, and with marked effect on his audience. Then suddenly he turned to another and unrelated subject. 'Events now transpiring have roused thinking minds among the Christian natives along the coast to establish a Church of their own', he began, and immediately there was a low but excited murmur of response. 'This present ecclesiastical arrangement, with its foreign props and supports . . . can neither be transmitted nor transferred. . . . The time will come, and not in any distant future, when our foreign patrons will withhold their patronage . . . then, do you think our children will be able to maintain these alien and artificial arrangements?'

This was a bold beginning, but in fifteen minutes it was all over. Blyden had suggested nothing less than religious independence for West Africa from the Christian churches of Europe. A few months later, a small group seceded from Breadfruit Church and formed the independent United Native African Church, the first clearly independent church to be established in West Africa.[1]

There were of course many other factors which led to the decision of these few parishioners from Breadfruit to take their historic step. For a number of years there had been growing dissatisfaction through West Africa with the tight missionary control of church activities. Others besides Blyden had criticized the European missionaries and had hinted at secession, among them no less an orthodox churchman than James Johnson himself. Bishop Crowther had sustained for some

---

[1] *The Lagos Times*, Jan. 3, 10, 1891; *The Return of the Exiles and the West African Church*.

time a growing resistance to his authority from among his English missionaries, and this development no doubt had had its effect. Perhaps more than anything else, however, West Africans were becoming increasingly disturbed by evidence of a European cultural arrogance combined with the extension of political power and economic control. The more militant of them, urged on by men like Blyden, were asserting a brand of African nationalism which, if it could not manifest itself in political nationalism, could at least sublimate that drive through an independent church movement. Yet, for all these factors, it was Blyden who was the catalyst, Blyden whose influence was probably decisive. What was it that made this man such a powerful force throughout West Africa?

Blyden never commanded more than a small personal following in West Africa, but the influence of his ideas was widespread. First, Blyden was one of the earliest African leaders to gauge correctly the European tendency towards domination of Africa and to take exception to this development in a way which later reflected with great accuracy the misgivings of a small but growing number of West Africans. Since the greatest doubts about European encroachment took place precisely in the cities along the coast where European influence was strongest, the educated articulate leadership within these cities was at once most persuaded by Blyden's arguments and in position to convince in turn substantial numbers of their own countrymen slowly beginning to throw off the traditional influences of the village government and way of life. Blyden, moreover, was not only among the first African nationalists; he was by far the most forceful and effective–indefatigable in propounding his message in the public press, in the pulpit, through educational media, to European and African alike, on three different continents. Finally, Blyden took the trouble to work out a complete and consistent philosophy of Africanism which dealt with all aspects of African life and which contained demonstrable connections among those aspects. It did not matter that the system was sometimes illogical, sometimes rooted in dreams rather than in reality; it had the ring of plausibility. More than that, it was an exciting declaration of faith in Africa and her people, reflecting needs and aspirations which resided in many an African heart too timid or too inarticulate to enunciate what was felt to be true.

Blyden had been trained by western missionaries but he was never dominated by them as were Crowther, James Johnson and so many of the African church leaders of the day. Blyden received and absorbed the best of European education and in his day was a learned man by any conceivable standard, completely capable of dealing with European civilization on its own terms. Beyond his scholarship, however, he had developed that rare and ultimate result of ideal education–the ability to think creatively, imaginatively and independently. Consequently, he was not often limited by prevailing conventions, attitudes, prejudices or shibboleths.

In a larger sense, his plea transcended the Africa of his day. What he demanded was nothing less than the re-establishment of human dignity, lost momentarily and in need of restoration in Africa, but more generally lost to all mankind. For he knew that when a part suffered, all suffered. Some of his ideas appear strained one hundred years later–his notion of racial exclusiveness, for example–but there was no distortion in his view of basic humanity with its need for charity and love, for humility and compassion. It is not surprising, therefore, that his ideas have generated an appeal to the African of the twentieth century even as they did to his contemporaries.

12 The Politics of Assimilation in Senegal

1 *French-African Culture in the Senegal Communes*

The French colony of Senegal, even in the active days of Faidherbe, was limited in practical extent to the coastal communities and to the points in the interior controlled by the French army. This meant Goree and its new neighbours the settlements of Dakar and Rufisque, the handful of armed posts along the Senegal River and the city of St. Louis. It did not include in any *de facto* sense the vast stretches of the back country which Faidherbe's African battalion, the *tirailleurs sénégalais*, could penetrate at will but could not hold. It did not even mean the Cayor, lying along the coast between Dakar and St. Louis, peopled by tough and refractory Wolof who successfully resisted pacification until the mid 1880s. Indeed, although French policing had finally gained a definite upper hand by 1890, the country settled down to a full colonial status with reluctance, so that occasional military expeditions were necessary well into the early years of the twentieth century, particularly in the Casamance country to the south of the enclave of British Gambia.

Nevertheless, the governorship of Faidherbe had been decisive in changing Senegal from a precarious coastal foothold into a substantial colony which was to provide the foundation for the vast French conquests of the Sudan at the end of the nineteenth century. After conquest, moreover, came a fundamental change in the tone and tempo of life in Senegal – a change conditioned by an expanding and stabilized trade, the physical alteration of the country through such improvements as railroads, telegraph lines and enlarged port facilities, the rapid growth of urban life and the final establishment of French political institutions in the coastal communes of Goree, Dakar, Rufisque and St. Louis.

It was St. Louis which was the queen city during these changing years; the other centres were hamlets by comparison. In 1879, the year that Senegal at last obtained her general council and settled down to sending her deputy regularly to the parliament in Paris, Dakar was after twenty-five years of existence a disappointing village of 1,500 inhabitants, Rufisque, slightly junior, had only 1,200 inhabitants, while ancient Goree possessed but 3,000 and was well along her descent into quiet picturesque decay. St. Louis was quite another matter. Already over two hundred years old, she had a population of 16,000 and was the acknowledged centre of commerce and banking for the colony as well as the administrative capital and social centre. To be sure, St. Louis had her limitations born of her unpromising location on a small island near the virtually unnavigable mouth of the Senegal River. Within a short lifetime Dakar and Rufisque would overtake her both in population and in economic importance, but during these early years of the French Third Republic, when both democratic republicanism and colonial expansion were ideas in the ascendancy, St. Louis was the symbol of France's success in both areas, self-confident and ebullient in her new growth, yet graceful and self-contained through her long years of maturity.

The character of the city had been changing from the day of Faidherbe who had characteristically introduced alterations to meet the demands of the times. The streets were still laid out wide and straight, but now all but the northern tip of the island was occupied. Paving had replaced the old sandy roadbed on major thoroughfares in the middle of town, and in the central part of the island government buildings formed an imposing nucleus. The old fort had given way to the attractive governor's palace and to the executive and legislative offices which dominated the central square with their modified classicism. Near by were the church and the barracks, and not far were the homes and shops of the principal merchants. A colonial architectural style had developed in St. Louis which was characteristic, yet somewhat reminiscent of the West Indies, of Freetown, as well as of New Orleans in America. Many of these private structures were single-storeyed, but the more pretentious had a second floor which overhung the first with a balustraded veranda. The ground floor was normally devoted to the commercial establishment while the second storey served as a living area. Normally these houses surrounded a central court in which were contained the servant quarters along with quiet gardens where flowering shrubs and fruit trees flourished in the hot sun. It was said that these buildings with their brick construction and white limestone facing were copies from architectural styles prevalent in southern France from whence came most of the metropolitan merchants living in St. Louis. Their second storey verandas not only provided an attractive decorative embellishment, but were popularly resorted to by their occupants where the evening breeze could be enjoyed at day's end while admiring the fading glow of the sunset and chatting with friends before dinner.

At either end, the island gradually took on a more typically African appearance as the big white houses gave way to the traditional round straw huts. Here the density of population was much greater, and so too were the noise and bustle of people carrying on their everyday activities, half inside their dwellings and half in the streets and outdoor compounds. The big houses belonged in the main to the several hundred members of the French and creole population, but the large bulk of the city's Africans had long since left the island proper for the suburbs of Guet N'Dar and N'Dar Tout on the Barbary peninsula, and Bouetville on the island of Sor which flanked the isle of St. Louis on west and east respectively. Here in these adjacent neighbourhoods the quiet of the city's centre which seemed to fill Europeans with melancholy was replaced by a more typically African effervescence. Guet N'Dar was a particularly lively market, perched on the narrow tongue of sand separating St. Louis from the Atlantic. There the Moorish caravans from up the Senegal congregated, and a variety of goods were for sale, ranging from gold jewellery to gazelle droppings, from annotated old Korans to sour milk. There were the marabouts with their followers, the ubiquitous beggars, the tethered camels, the refuse underfoot—all the noise and confusion, the laughter and the shouted arguments, the brilliant colour and the play of odours, the jostle and the bustle of a native African market.

The isle of St. Louis was connected with both Barbary and Sor by bridges, and special dykes had been constructed to prevent flooding during the high water season of the rains. These improvements had been instituted by Faidherbe, the engineer, but modern engineering had not succeeded in solving the problem of drinking water, especially in the dry season when the inadequate reservoir system yielded a predominantly brackish water supply. Neither had the engineers been able to tame the treacherous bar at the harbour entrance, a failure which in the end was to condemn St. Louis to an enforced decline as commerce gradually shifted to the more convenient accommodations at Dakar. But that was to be a somewhat later development.

When the traveller left St. Louis and proceeded upstream to the trading posts along the Senegal, a completely different world became

ASSIMILATION IN SENEGAL

evident. The river was navigable only during the rainy summer months, and the trade in gum was necessarily seasonal. When travel was possible, the trip into the interior revealed a wild landscape, a great bare plateau dotted with occasional palms and baobabs. The yellow stream wound its way through the wilderness, lined by mangroves in which monkeys romped, and punctuated by occasional villages and caravan sites. The few French posts – Dagana, Richard Toll, Podor, Mantam – were modest to the point of austerity. Podor, for example, was little more than a fort located on the river's edge, an uninviting, uncomfortable centre scorched in the great heat of the tropical sun. A single waterfront street containing a few mournful houses was backed by a large African town divided by wide straight streets with each quarter surrounded by thick fortified wooden fences, protection against attack by man or wild beast. The country was indeed wild. Not many years before, in Faidherbe's time, the soldiers at Richard Toll had shot elephant in the river opposite their post, and lion took steers from the Fulani herds gathered just outside St. Louis. In the Cayor, the last independent chieftain, Lat Dior, was still holding the district as an independent principality, succumbing to French arms only in 1886 shortly after the completion of the Dakar-St. Louis railroad which he had sought to prevent.

But by 1879 in St. Louis a modern Africa was taking shape. A local bourgeoisie was emerging, the frequent balls and festivals during the season reminiscent of at least provincial France. The city had her own commercial bank which was taking the lead in directing the economy of the colony, the railroad connecting her with Dakar was soon to be finished, a government newspaper-gazette had been a weekly occurrence for some years, and representative democratic government was an established institution, following the model of regional divisions and urban centres in metropolitan France.[1]

2 *The Emergence of Creole Political Power*

The unique blend of theoretical democracy and practical autocracy with which France had governed her colony of Senegal over the years began to clarify itself to a certain extent after the proclamation of the

[1] Information on St. Louis has been gathered primarily from Carrère and Holle, *De la Sénégambie Française*, Boilat, *Esquisses Sénégalaises*, Faidherbe, *Le Sénégal*, R. Pasquier, 'Villes du Sénégal au XIX Siècle', *Revue Française d'Histoire d'Outre-Mer*, vol. XLVII, 1960, 387-426, and Pierre Loti, *Roman d'un Spahi*. Population figures are from the census of 1877, N.A.P.O.S. Senegal VII, 48. See also P. Cultru, *Histoire du Sénégal du XV Siècle à 1870*, 358-61, and André Villard, *Histoire du Sénégal*, 162-3.

Third Republic in 1870. The year of revolution, 1848, had brought the final manumission of the slaves and at the same time universal male suffrage had beein reinstituted. Although Senegal had long since possessed an administrative council, its membership was appointive and its powers purely advisory, so that the right to vote had to be made effective in other ways. For a brief time this was achieved when electoral lists were drafted throughout France and her colonies, and Senegal was given the right to elect a deputy to the assembly in Paris. In the autumn of 1848 an election took place, the seat being contested by no less imposing figures than the former governor, Bouet-Willaumez, and Victor Schoelcher, the celebrated abolitionist from Alsace who was in the mid-passage of his long life devoted to fighting discrimination against the Negro. The contest, however, was won in a lively campaign by a mulatto merchant from St. Louis, Durand Valentin, who easily succeeded with the support of the African vote. Two years later another creole, John Sleigth, became deputy by the same formula when Valentin resigned his seat, but shortly thereafter the establishment of the Second Empire put an end to such democratic exercises.[1]

In 1871 Senegal once again sent a deputy to Paris and, though the privilege was temporarily suspended four years later, it was reinstituted on a permanent basis in 1879. That same year the first territorial general council in Senegal was formed with powers and functions based on those of the general councils of the departments of the metropole. Elected by universal suffrage, the council had legislative responsibility for local administrative and financial matters but it was explicitly decreed that there was to be no authority to levy import duties, no power of decision as to the location of ports and markets and no control over affairs in the territories under military government. In addition to these important limitations was the ultimate veto by the colonial ministry in Paris. France was taking no chances with runaway democracy in Africa.

Nevertheless, in deference to French theories of assimilation, other steps were soon taken to bring the colonial administration further into conformity with local government in France. In 1872, St. Louis and Goree were made into fully incorporated municipalities with their own municipal councils, the infant community of Dakar sharing this power with Goree. In 1880 Rufisque was similarly incorporated, and in 1887 Dakar and Goree were separated, thus finally bringing into existence the so-called Four Communes of Senegal. General council, municipal

---

[1] Gov. DuChateau to Minister, Oct. 20, Nov. 29, 1848, N.A.S. 2B27; *L'Ordre*, Oct. 12, 1851, in N.A.P.O.S. Senegal VII, 44d.

councils and deputy were all elected by universal suffrage, and voting rights were defined to extend to all who could show proof of residence of five years in the communes. Thus for practical purposes most of the African residents of the Four Communes became bona fide voters along with the French and creole groups. The administrative council was maintained as before, but henceforward the manner for choosing its membership was liberalized. Hence in theory at any rate, Senegal had a partly representative government which, whatever its limitations, was to be much more far-reaching than anything attempted in the British colonies until after the Second World War, and was to provide the local citizens with the opportunity for genuine political activity and development.[1]

The politics which emerged from 1879 onward were complex and subtle, reflecting a variety of local and metropolitan pressures. First of all, there were the powerful commercial interests of the mercantile establishments of Bordeaux. These were represented by French agents but also by important creoles having business connections with Bordeaux. Next, there were mulattoes and a scattering of Africans controlling local trading houses which competed, on the whole indifferently, with the Bordeaux merchants. Thus the small European community generally made common cause with certain of the mulattoes against other mulattoes in contention over the local export-import business. Creole divisions were not based solely on commercial competition, however. Personal rivalries and long-standing quarrels between prominent creole families added stresses and pressures which found expression in political action not to be explained by a purely economic determinism.

Two other groups were prominent in the political picture—the African population of the communes and the colonial administration. Broadly speaking the administration tended to support the objectives of the Bordeaux commercial interests, partly through predisposition as metropolitan Frenchmen, partly through long devotion to mercantilist ideas as to the role of colonies, and partly because the European merchants were in a position to influence colonial policy both in Paris and in St. Louis. At the same time, the administration in Senegal never lost sight of its own identity and objectives, for it was essentially concerned with orderly government, both of the settled communities and of the interior, and it sought to please, not the mercantile interests of Bordeaux, but the ministry in Paris. As for urban Africans, they were an important

[1] Decree establishing the General Council, N.A.P.O.S. Senegal VII, 31a; Gov. Brière de l'Isle to Minister, Jan. 22, 1879, N.A.P.O.S. Senegal VII, 23b.

element in local politics for it was their vote which determined elections, but they were on the whole illiterate and politically inexperienced so that they gained little from their power and were constantly controlled and used by the creoles.

Finally, there was the ministry in France, sensitive to metropolitan political pressures but concerned with colonial government in the larger context of France's total overseas empire. Engaged in a continuing review of each governor's administration, the ministry had the job of reconciling Senegalese and metropolitan influences and fitting them into an articulated colonial policy which would contribute to a successful French international diplomacy.

Because the creoles by tradition, by wealth, by occupation and by education dominated the African community, they at once took control of the elective positions in Senegal. They held the office of deputy almost without a break down to the eve of the First World War, controlling it directly or sponsoring the occasional European incumbent. Similarly their influence on the general council and municipal councils, while varying over the years, was always important and frequently overwhelming. Had the creoles presented a united front, they would have constituted a formidable political force to confront both the Europeans and the colonial administration. Their inability to co-operate, however, made it relatively easy for the agents of the Bordeaux houses to support competing creole groups and thus to pursue political objectives favourable to the economic interests of their employers.

As for the colonial government, while it too was obliged to treat creole power with respect, it was infrequently embarrassed by creole politicking. The administration, thoroughly aware of its ultimate responsibility to the parliament in Paris and not to the general council in St. Louis, entertained a classic suspicion of democratic processes and expressed continuing doubts over the political maturity of both the creole leaders and the African electorate. It directed the affairs of the colony largely unruffled by the more or less continuing state of exasperation of the creoles in the elected assemblies who tended to regard the government as unresponsive and arbitrary.

Beyond these cross-currents generated by the thrust of economic, social, administrative and personal considerations, were a number of cultural factors linked to France's assimilationist policy for her colonies. The official French position regarding colonies was rooted in the idea of a worldwide community of Frenchmen who shared the benefits of French language and culture. Theoretically there was no duality between France in Europe and France overseas—French institutions and traditions applied equally everywhere. Thus Senegal could have its Four Communes which were governed in a manner identical—or at any rate almost identical—with communes in the metropole. This view, emanating from France itself and serving as one of the bases for guiding the policy of the controlling Ministry of the Navy and Colonies, was not shared by the administrative hierarchy in Senegal. By and large, the governors and their staffs looked on assimilation as premature as long as the majority of the population could not read and write French, and as long as it lacked any working concept of the ideas of French civilization, the moral standards of Christian worship, and the theory and practice of democratic responsible government. Consistently over the years, successive governors complained that ignorant natives offered no reasonable basis for elective government, and could only fall victim, as they consistently did, to the corrupting influences of the local creole population.[1]

As for the creoles, they subscribed wholeheartedly to French assimilationist philosophy, and along with a small number of educated Africans, provided a Senegalese example of an African community consciously committed to standards of French culture. The mulattoes looked on France as the mother country and considered themselves as true sons of the Revolution, fully equal to those born on French soil. In this respect their attitude towards the pure-blood African community was mixed, however. The native tribesmen of the interior were both customers and an enemy to be subdued. The African people of the cities were former slaves and present servants, but they were also Senegalese entitled to the opportunity of evolving into Frenchmen. The city African, moreover, was a voter to be cultivated with tact or coerced with threat or bribe, an ignorant Muslim to be despised or a potential Christian to be converted.

Over and above these considerations, the delicate and complex parochial divisions within the creole community made difficult any consistent attitude towards the African population, towards the administration, towards European economic interests, or towards principles of assimilation. Consequently, there were continual contradictions in individual views and sudden modifications in position. Finally, the creoles were faced with the essential problem of the educated African

[1] See Gov. Baudin to Minister, Aug. 19, 1849, N.A.P.O.S. Senegal VII, 44c; Gov. Valière to Minister, Aug. 22, 1874, N.A.P.O.S. Senegal VII, 55; *Moniteur du Sénégal*, Nov. 24, 1879; Gov. H. Lamothe to Minister, Nov. 17, 1894, N.A.P.O.S. Senegal VII, 34d.

in nineteenth-century West Africa–the reconciliation of loyalties both to home and to Europe. Concern for local economic interests was very frequently accompanied by less material feelings of local pride, while devotion to French standards was often qualified by a shadow of distinction between the *we* of Senegal and the *they* of the metropole.

3 The Art of Political Opposition– Gaspard Devès and Jean-Jacques Crespin

In these early years of the Third Republic, the creoles of Senegal gained legislative experience and a growing political authority, making use of the votes of the urban Africans to achieve their ends. In this respect, two of the most interesting, if not always the most successful, creole figures were Gaspard Devès and Jean-Jacques Crespin.

Devès and Crespin made a good team. The former was the son of a St. Louis *signare* and a French father. The elder Devès had sailed for Senegal on the ill-fated *Medusa* in 1816, but had survived the agonizing ordeal of shipwreck eventually to arrive safely in Africa to take up residence in St. Louis. Perhaps it was fortitude and good luck which had pulled him through this initial crisis, but during the ensuing years the young émigré built a successful career as a trader in gum and established the house of Devès and Son as one of the leading mercantile firms of St. Louis. His son carried on the business in his turn, and by the 1870s the firm was thriving and powerful with important connections with several of the larger interior kingdoms, a big African clientele and a solid reputation as the only local enterprise able to deal with the Bordeaux firms on equal terms. When the opportunity for political expression came, Gaspard Devès was quick to take advantage thereof, serving at various times in the administrative council, and as a municipal councillor and mayor of St. Louis. Devès was interested in politics as a means to achieve his commercial objectives, these being the monopolizing of as great a proportion as possible of the interior trade. He reasoned that a strong political showing would not only have its effect on policy in St. Louis but, more important, would convince local chiefs that it was to their advantage to deal with the house of Devès because of its influence in the government. His policy yielded results for he had longstanding agreements with the Moorish tribe of the Trarzas, and had virtually converted the Cayor into a private market through the highly dubious practice, as it was described in government circles, of supplying Lat Dior and other chiefs with arms while stirring them to oppose French authority.

Tough-minded, hard-working and possessed of a sympathetic understanding for the psychology of the indigenous African, Devès had long espoused the African cause as a matter of principle, although his detractors were inclined to attribute his attitude less to philanthropy than to a feeling of personal discrimination because of his own colour. Whether or not this judgment was justified, it was evident that Devès required no compensation through public acclaim; indeed, he concentrated on political control rather than political office. Consequently, he came to rely increasingly on his colleague Crespin as the nominal leader of what nevertheless continued to be known locally as the Devès party.[1]

Popular, articulate and choleric, Jean-Jacques Crespin was a splendid counterpoise to the shrewd and substantial Gaspard Devès. Born in 1837, Crespin spent several years of his early adult life engaged in trade along the Guinea coast, and in 1862 married an English girl from Matacong Island. About 1872 he returned to St. Louis where he established himself as a solicitor, but soon he was engaged in local politics in association with Devès. Crespin was able to gain a considerable following among the people of St. Louis through his consistent advocacy of the rights of the African for whom he was a self-appointed spokesman and through his persuasive and forceful public speaking. During the 1870s both he and Devès served on the administrative council as nominees from St. Louis where Devès was mayor and Crespin his deputy. In 1879, the Devès party decided to run Crespin for the seat of representative from Senegal in the parliament at Paris and from that point until his death in 1895, Crespin was a major political figure in the colony—a perennially unsuccessful candidate for colonial deputy, but serving at various times in the general council and the municipal councils and late in his career as mayor of St. Louis.

Crespin's close association with Devès had led to the marriage of his daughter to one of Devès's sons, and the two men worked closely together throughout the years until a falling out not long before Crespin's death broke up their long partnership. Crespin was an ideal associate from Devès' point of view, for his personal popularity and disputatious manner combined with that unyielding hostility towards the administration which was the cornerstone of their politics. His activities earned him the wholesome dislike of several governors whose

[1] Gov. Lamothe to Under-Secretary of State for Colonies, Jan. 16, 1891, N.A.P.O.S. Senegal I, 91.

censure ranged from a mere questioning of Crespin's judgment to an expression of serious doubts over the independence and honesty of his opinions and actions. 'Crespin is ambitious and impecunious', reported one critic, 'and he does not hesitate to gain and maintain popularity by giving the worst advice to the natives ... But Crespin is only a straw man for the Devès clan, a puppet whose strings are controlled by others, the docile instrument of the party he appears to direct.'[1]

On the whole, Devès and Crespin experienced considerable frustration over the years in their attempts to dominate local politics. They were usually able to gain seats on the general or municipal councils but rarely did they control those bodies, and rarer still were they able to seize the supreme prize – the position of deputy to the French parliament in Paris. Energetic and resourceful in soliciting the urban African vote by fair means or foul, they achieved no advantage over their adversaries, for all were guilty of chronic irregularities – bribery, illegal registration, intimidation, false counts, double voting and improper influence by election officials. It was only during the brief term of the French Admiral Vallon as deputy that Devès was able to exert any clear political control, manipulating the patronage for a time and taking over the municipal council in St. Louis. Even then, Devès eventually lost his influence with Vallon who maintained an independent policy in Paris during the last part of his term.[2]

There were other ways of exerting influence, however; Crespin and Devès also made good use of the newspaper as a device for political and economic advantage. In 1885 and 1886, two journals were founded, *Le Réveil du Sénégal* and *Le Petit Sénégalais*, under a European editor and director who had previously been head of the government press. It is difficult to know precisely how closely these papers reflected the opinions of Devès and Crespin, but Devès was known to be the principal backer, Crespin frequently wrote for the columns of *Le Réveil*, and both papers consistently supported the policies of the Devès-Crespin party. The inauguration of these two papers was a shrewd move for at the time there were no journals in Senegal except the official gazette, *Le Moniteur du Sénégal*, which had been founded by Faidherbe and which

[1] *Ibid.*; *Journal Officiel du Sénégal*, Jan. 5, 1895; A. Fitzjames to S. Fortescue, July 21, 1863, C.O. 267/269.
[2] Lamothe to Minister, Nov. 17, 1894, N.A.P.O.S. Senegal VII, 34d; Gasconi to A. M. Berlet, Feb. 9, Mar. 28, 1882, N.A.P.O.S. Senegal VII, 46c; *Le Réveil du Sénégal*, Nov. 15, 1885; J. J. Crespin *et al.* to Gov. Quintrié, May 8, 1888, N.A.P.O.S. Senegal VII, 60a; Vallon to Under-Secretary of State for Colonies, Dec. 4, 1889, Gov. Clément-Thomas to same, Mar. 9, 1890, N.A.P.O.S. Senegal VII, 7 bis.

ASSIMILATION IN SENEGAL

was largely limited to official announcements. The policy of both journals was so extreme, however, as frequently to border on libel, and after a couple of years both disappeared following legal action. Nevertheless, they constituted an important public voice for Devès and Crespin, strident in tone, frequently actionable in content, but entertaining and influential.[1]

As might be expected of those whose interests were primarily commercial, Devès and Crespin based their programme and their ideas on economic factors. These factors, in turn, reflected the struggle between the local Senegalese traders and the mercantile houses of Bordeaux. One of the main bones of contention was the trade in gum up the Senegal River, long the monopoly of the Senegalese, but more recently the object of growing activity by merchants from France. In 1842 the trade on the Senegal had been exclusively reserved for freeborn Senegalese with previous commercial experience on the river. Access was specifically denied Europeans. During the time of Faidherbe, however, a policy of free trade had permitted the agents of French commercial firms to trade directly in gum and, according to Devès, the results were detrimental to all concerned, Senegalese and French alike. Speaking in the administrative council in 1878, he gave a clear statement of his objections to the free trade policy which was still in effect and still bringing economic ruin to the country:

Under the 1842 ordinance, the Colony had ... about 180 traders each employing a boatful of local roustabouts, and this went well since each trader was able to pay his creditors and have a small profit for himself. But since the importer has come to operate directly in the River ... the number of traders has fallen from 180 to 22, and the operation of the gum trade has become more and more burdensome for the importers and for the Colony.... so long as the trader had only other traders for competition, he always paid his bills and safeguarded the profits of the importer who had advanced him his merchandise; but the day the importer decided to combine his own profit with that of the trader, the latter was ruined and with him disappeared his profit. Direct competition between importers was thus established, and the results as we all know are more and more disastrous. An intermediary is therefore necessary, and it is not the number of traders but the introduction of the importer in the affairs of the River which is ruining the operation of the gum trade.

And at the same session, Crespin in his colourful fashion explained the ways of the Bordeaux merchants. 'These gentlemen', he pointed out,

[1] R. Pasquier, 'Les Débuts de la Presse au Sénégal', *Cahiers d'Etudes Africaines*, vol. II, no. 3, 1962, 480–5; Gov. Genouille to Minister, Nov. 13, 28, 1886, N.A.P.O.S. Senegal I, 76; *Le Petit Sénégalais*, Dec. 30, 1886, Apr. 14, 1887.

'wish to milk Senegal dry... why taxes... why a decent water supply? These privileged individuals wonder, while savouring their Médoc, why we must have drinkable water.'[1]

Crespin had no need for wondering; he knew where the trouble lay. For him, the colony had been completely subordinated to the commercial interests of Bordeaux against whose influence the ministry in Paris was powerless. It was Bordeaux merchants who were able to set election dates in Senegal at such a time that most of the St. Louis traders were absent up the river and thus unable to prevent the election of a Bordeaux-controlled deputy. It was the Bordeaux merchants who arranged the tax schedule in such a way as to permit the export of their goods duty free, despite the dislocation this brought about in the colonial budget. Crespin had just been overwhelmed in the election for deputy in 1879 and his natural gift for invective had taken on an additional sharpness. 'If the power of Bordeaux money and Bordeaux thinking dominates the next elections as it did the last, I will have nothing to do with them.' Crespin was speaking before the administrative council and had already been reprimanded by the governor, Brière de l'Isle, for turning the council into a political forum. But Crespin insisted on his right to speak out. 'It is heart-rending, but Bordeaux influence is stronger than ever. No one contests the legitimate power of money. But why does it insinuate itself into political matters, even into the administration?... It is unheard of! The influence I am fighting is as illegal as it is disastrous in its effects.'[2]

Devès and Crespin pegged their fight against the economic and political pressures of Bordeaux on the principle of protecting the rights and the livelihood of the small creole and African traders of Senegal, but clearly there was a large element of self-interest involved. Devès was the only St. Louis firm large enough to compete with the Bordeaux companies; consequently, if the latter had been excluded from direct participation in the riverain trade, Devès would have been able to enjoy a virtual monopoly. This policy of exclusion had worked well in the Cayor, for example, where Devès had succeeded in developing close ties with Lat Dior and other chiefs to the virtual elimination from the Cayor market of all effective competition. Thus, just as Devès fought to exclude Europeans from the river, so he tried to maintain his primacy already established in the Cayor against the efforts of Bordeaux to break in.

[1] Administrative Council, Apr. 14, 1878, 269, 270, N.A.S.
[2] Administrative Council, July 28, 1879, N.A.P.O.S. Senegal VII, 33a, 35a.

When the railroad from Dakar to St. Louis was completed in the summer of 1885, it was clear that the quasi-independent status of the Cayor would soon have to give way to direct French administration. The way was opened in 1886 when the reigning king, Samba Lawbé, was killed in a skirmish with French troops and Lat Dior fell in the course of a subsequent action. The Cayor was annexed, and immediately Devès' two papers began a savage attack on Governor Genouille. All through the autumn of 1886, the journals mounted a campaign of increasing criticism of the governor. He had acted hastily, they said, and with much too great a display of force. Samba Lawbé was not killed in a legitimate action but cut down in an ambush. The trouble with France was that she had a tendency towards chauvinism, her sense of patriotism easily degenerated into bloodletting and an aggressive stance towards the very people she tried to cultivate. The governor, moreover, was incompetent and incapable of constructing and directing a reasonable and articulated policy in the interior:

In the Cayor, the Governor's policy has no name: made of expedients inspired by . . . scornful sentiments for the people and the king who in his eyes are not men but objects . . . This policy has halted commerce in the country and seriously compromised its interests, adding to the present crisis another complication . . . Will the Cayor, placed under our protection, be better administered and produce as much as in the past? We hope so with all our heart, but when we see the state of material and spiritual misery which has characterized the Walo since our annexation . . . with the inhabitants moving to the Moorish side of the River to improve their lot, we can only doubt the future of the Cayor.

There is no doubt that this journalistic campaign greatly irritated the governor who was goaded into using the *Moniteur* to answer the charges levelled at him, and who grumbled to the ministry in Paris that he should be given special powers to deal with the two papers. The ministry counselled a calm approach adding significantly that Genouille was responsible to Paris, not to local public opinion. In the end the policy of annexation and direct administration was maintained and Devès' privileged position in the Cayor came to an end.[1]

The position of Crespin and Devès regarding the Cayor was a special case arising from their particular influence with the Cayor chiefs. Normally they criticized the administration which they accused of lacking vigour in stamping out the last vestiges of an indigenous

[1] *Le Petit Sénégalais*, Oct. 14, 1886; *Le Réveil du Sénégal*, Nov. 14, 1886; Genouille to Minister, Nov. 28, 1886, Under-Secretary of State for Colonies to Genouille, Dec. 1886, N.A.P.O.S. Senegal I, 76.

independence which barred commercial penetration of the interior. Two local chieftains in particular, Abdul Bubakr in the Futa Toro and Mamadu Lamine along the far reaches of the Senegal River, were singled out, for they had long threatened French control of the Senegal. Lamine almost took Bakel from its French garrison in 1886, and both he and Bubakr were finally subdued only with great difficulty after long hard campaigns.

Le Réveil and Le Petit Sénégalais continually complained over what they regarded as weak half-measures. Crespin pointed out in several issues that religious fanaticism was combining with ignorance and barbarism to hold up progress in the interior. More generally the two papers called for a build-up of military strength along with the determination to act quickly and decisively. Only then could matters be settled once and for all. 'France cannot shrink from this struggle of civilization against barbarism, of freedom against slavery, from this ennobling competition among civilized nations . . . for the happiness of the slaves we are going to free, for the prosperity of civilized nations through new markets . . . in a word, for the happiness of humanity.'[1]

Hence the attitude of Devès and Crespin towards the Africans of the interior tribes was pragmatic, shifting with the economic pressures, and made up of a large portion of commercial self-interest combined with a modest amount of humanitarian regard for less fortunate brethren. Much the same attitude characterized their view of the Africans of the Four Communes who were wooed as prospective voters before the day of election and scorned by a defeated party as ignorant barbarians after the votes had been counted. During the campaign for deputy in the autumn of 1885, Le Réveil was all solicitude for the Muslim native vote and attacked the opposition leaders unceasingly on the grounds that their apparent concern for the African in the communes was nothing but hypocrisy. After Crespin had been defeated, the paper returned to its old position that the assimilation of the African should proceed but slowly, in proportion to his apparently limited capacity to absorb French language and culture and his reluctance to drop the stultifying religion of Islam.

There were three things wrong with Senegal, announced Le Réveil—yellow fever, clericalism, and the native vote. By giving the franchise to these non-naturalized French, France had allowed the spirit of her laws to be violated. The Romans had awarded the privilege of citizenship only in company with the responsibilities of taxation and military

[1] Le Réveil du Sénégal, Aug. 2, 1885, Aug. 15, 29, Sept. 19, 26, 1886.

service. In Algeria, France had done the same with the Jewish population with complete success. In Senegal, on the other hand, the franchise had generously been granted without assessing the consequences, and the people had accepted the privilege but refused to measure up to the responsibilities of assimilation.[1]

Such a policy was leading to national ruin. The conquerors became the subjects and the slaves ruled the masters. St. Louis had fallen into the hands of semi-clad natives who filled the air with an incessant thumping of drums and shrewish howling, and who promptly set upon anyone who dared to remonstrate. Moreover, good government was becoming increasingly difficult because of the folly of native members of the municipal councils. Not long before, the mayor of St. Louis had sought to obtain appropriations for the construction of a new and unnecessary city hall. He found himself stymied until two native councilmen arrived, their robes floating about them. Then he knew he could carry the day:

> These assemblymen are little versed in administrative affairs. The difference between state enterprise and private competitive bidding means little to them. . . .
> 'Now let's see, so-and-so, are you voting for competitive bidding or for public works?'
> 'What's that—bidding? What's that—public works?'
> 'That's not the question; we (the mayor and his friends) have voted for state construction, and you?'
> 'Ah, so do I!'
> 'And you, so-and-so?'
> 'I don't understand. What's the question?'
> 'Public construction or competitive bidding.'
> 'In connection with what?'
> 'The city hall, of course!'
> 'Ah, competitive bidding.'
> 'There is no question of bidding. I tell you we have voted for state construction.'
> 'Very well, the same for me.'

And so the game is played. And that is how our most serious affairs are treated . . . Is this not a shameful spectacle? Does not this one incident show the danger of granting universal suffrage to natives without the strictest of guarantees?[2]

To most creoles the root of the matter was the Mohammedan faith. It was Islam that created and encouraged ignorance and fanaticism. It was Islam that resisted the march of civilization. It was Islam that was

---

[1] *Ibid.*, Sept. 13, 20, Nov. 1, 29, 1885.
[2] *Ibid.*, Dec. 6, 1885, Jan. 3, Oct. 3, 1886.

holding back the primitive African from the fruits of French language and culture. As a religion it may have been characterized by a great intellectual flowering at one time, but it had long since become the refuge of closed minds and xenophobes who extolled ignorance and gloried in reaction. As a result, Muslim countries were backward, lacking education and science, intellectually empty and incapable of absorbing a new idea. Strong action was necessary to check the long slide of Africa into the abyss of ignorance. Instead, the government actually encouraged the Muslims—creating special courses in Arabic, assisting in the study of the Koran, giving Muslims their own tribunals and making them French citizens and voters.[1]

The complaint was a familiar one, and so was the solution. What the colony needed, *Le Réveil* continued, was more and better schools which Muslims would be forced to attend in order to learn French language and ways and to become responsible citizens. For those who had ability, additional training in France should be available so that Africans returning home would not only have absorbed the essence of true civilization but would be able to act as missionaries of French culture, helping to spread it to the natives of the interior:

Let us always strive to fight ignorance, that social canker and cause of revolutions. Let us teach the natives to understand the advantages of schooling. Let us make them men so that they never forget France and the immense sacrifices she has made and continues to make for her colony in Africa. Then, in the future, when thanks to education the language and name of France will shine forth over all West Africa, their hearts will beat in unison with ours for the love of the French fatherland.[2]

There was, however, another and perhaps even better means of persuasion. The application of French military conscription to the colonies was being seriously discussed at this time, both in France and overseas. To many observers in Senegal, here was a superb opportunity to help Africans to rid themselves of their primitive ways, to absorb French culture, to learn the meaning of frugality and hard work, and to qualify for the citizenship which France had bestowed upon them. Upon contact with the industrious youth of Europe and in response to barracks discipline, the mulatto population would lose its easy-going manner and substitute the qualities of ambition and thrift. The African, too, in danger of becoming spoiled by excessive solicitude on the part of France, would gain immeasurable benefits. After a few years of

[1] *Ibid.*, Sept. 6, Nov. 15, 1885; *Le Petit Sénégalais*, Feb. 24, 1887.
[2] *Le Réveil du Sénégal*, Jan. 17, June 27, July 25, 1886.

military service, the primitive would have disappeared. He would now speak French with ease, he would have developed a taste for work and would know what it meant to save. He would think and plan for the future which he formerly ignored. And he would be proud of his title of citizen of France, blessing the European who had made him worthy of it.

That this was an expression more of hope than of fact was reflected in the widespread disinterest among the African population at this time in performing compulsory military service. There was considerable consternation in St. Louis, for example, when it was announced that Senegalese troops might be used by France in Dahomey, the reaction dying down only when the report turned out to be false. The creoles, however, were lined up solidly behind conscription as a means for binding France and Senegal closer together and as an educational device leading to more effective assimilation. Speaking in the general council, Crespin put the position plainly. The people of Senegal, he said, did not want to stand back while compatriots from France came to defend their soil in Africa, sometimes to die of wounds or disease. They wanted to share the obligations of military service which balanced the privileges of citizenship. There was, however, the Muslim problem, and here Crespin was willing to be flexible. Strict Muslims feared that their religious practices might be compromised by military service. Provision should therefore be made to guarantee their right of worship during army service, said Crespin. If then they still persisted in rejecting the obligation to serve France in the army, they would have to give up citizenship and voting rights, reverting to the status of French subjects. At the same time there should be a tightening of the electoral law which permitted any African to come to the communes from the countryside and establish citizenship merely through a five-year residence. The choice should be made, Crespin declared. 'I consider it indispensable that all who wish to exercise the right to vote must first establish the authenticity of their French citizenship.' Other creoles, however, rejected any concession to the Muslims. For them, military service and the franchise were irrevocably linked. All who served in the army would have to be governed by the French civil code, and those who refused would be obliged to forfeit their right to vote. There could be no exceptions for Muslims. 'It is only by following this route that we will arrive at complete assimilation with France, for if the proposed categories were allowed, this would . . . sow division and perhaps hate between the diverse sections of the population around us.' And the council voted down Crespin's suggestion, going on record as supporting total unequivocal military conscription.[1]

Crespin had his political successes and failures, but he was more often than not able to carry others with him in the general council. Always active in debate and forceful in argument, he usually had some comment on most matters which came up for discussion. Now he would be urging the repair of a bridge in Goree or the extension of a street in Rufisque; now he was arguing for increased educational opportunities for Africans in preference to Europeans. Here he would rise to encourage greater use of the port facilities of Dakar and Rufisque; on another occasion he would debate the merits of street lighting in St. Louis or call the administration to account for its budget policy. Most of his remarks were concerned with affairs in the Four Communes—schools, public works, hospitals, water supply or the administration of justice. Invariably he was critical of the administration, finding fault with its conduct of affairs in the interior and its stewardship of local matters in the communes. Typical was his complaint before the general council in 1889 that a reorganization of the Senegal courts had resulted in a shortage of qualified judges and a consequent devolution of important judicial functions on ill-qualified administrative officials. When the director of the interior protested against this aspersion on the impartiality of his officers, Crespin flared characteristically. 'By what right do you contest my freedom to speak out, to say what I think, as my proper responsibility? I concede you but one right ... the right to answer me.' It was the activities of men like Crespin which moved governors to complain that the councillors were irresponsible parliamentarians who neglected their prescribed duties, interfered in matters which did not concern them and used the legislature improperly as a political forum.[2]

Though understandable, this was hardly a fair analysis. Quite aside from traditional executive suspicion of legislative authority was the ambivalent position of the mulattoes of Senegal. They were Africans and interested in the welfare of their own land. Yet they were committed to French assimilation and identified themselves in spirit with the metropole. Their commercial interests were closely integrated into the French economy, but they felt that intrinsic in the system was discrimination in favour of Bordeaux. Their devotion to ideas of French civilization made them despise unreconstructed Africans, particularly

[1] *Ibid.*, Aug. 16, 30, 1885; Gov. Clément-Thomas to Under-Secretary of State for Colonies, Apr. 16, 1890, N.A.P.O.S. Senegal VII, 60a.
[2] See *Conseil Général*, 1882–94, esp. 1889, session extraordinaire, 137–47; Gov. Quintrié to Minister, Apr. 6, 1888, N.A.P.O.S. Senegal VII, 32c.

Muslims, but they always entertained some hope that eventually the African population would join them in embracing Franco-Christian culture. Hence they could both exploit the African and hope for his regeneration; entertain a patriotic love for the mother country of France and carry on incessant harassment of the French colonial administration. Later, in the early decades of the twentieth century, when the Africans of Senegal finally seized the opportunity for education and assimilation, they too came to occupy this same position in relation to France, and the old creole ambivalence towards Europe was extended to a wider African population. Finally, in the full flood of African nationalism in the mid-twentieth century, though new worldwide forces made a strong impact on Africa, the ambivalence remained, altered in degree and in emphasis but unchanged in essence. This was the Eurafrican movement of negritude.

13 The African Historian in West African Thought

1 *Early Historical Writing in West Africa*

It is a characteristic of growing national self-consciousness that a people requires a sense of its past. Thus it was that the rise of nationalism in Europe during the nineteenth century was marked by a vast production of historical literature dedicated to showing that this or that nation sprang from illustrious antecedents, and counted in its history at least one era of ascendant glory. Though the facts of the past were what they were, the need was of the present—to provide a sense of roots, of continuity, of cohesion and of mission, and to dress all these in the language of heroes and epics, of great deeds and broad contributions to civilization.

As with the nations of Europe, so with the people of Africa. Traditional African societies had of course long practised their own versions of history. Lacking the convenience of written documentation, they had nonetheless the common need of mankind to know who they were and from whence they came. To meet this requirement they developed the technique of recording their past orally, committing it sometimes to the informal tale told by the evening fire, sometimes to a highly trained professional court linguist whose full-time occupation it was to remember to perfection such information as genealogies, legal precedents, particular historical incidents, royal successions or the organization of clans. In some cases this information was couched in the form of poetry, in others it consisted of obscure symbolic language. It could range in substance from unadulterated myth, through highly partisan versions of specific events, to straightforward listings of royal lineage. In all cases, however, it was the history of a people—the memory of these particular traditional societies, serving highly important legal or political needs such as the establishment of chiefly succession or the right of land ownership, or more generally providing entertainment and a feeling of social cohesiveness and accomplishment.

As modern African nations began to take shape and, more particularly, as they approached the prospect of national independence, like the people of Europe they felt a growing need for a greater sense of their past. What was required was history which would not only bring into view the roots of nations and of the African race, but hopefully might rediscover ancient glories and broad contributions to the march of civilization long lost in the mists of time. During the 1950s, therefore, a few Africans began to insist that a fuller understanding of the world's history and Africa's role therein required a new appraisal written by the African himself. Slowly there emerged a small but growing body of African historians trained in the techniques of modern historical scholarship, intent upon studying Africa's past from an African point of view and reviewing Africa's long-standing relations with adjacent continents through their own fresh perspective.

Africa's mid-twentieth-century historical renascence was, however, not the first attempt by the educated Europeanized people of West Africa to deal with Africa's past. As early as 1850 attempts were being made to examine the history of the African continent and people, and these continued and increased during the second half of the nineteenth and into the twentieth century as West African intellectual leadership grew and as an African nationalistic awareness emerged in response to Europe's own historical pretensions. The first in the field was the Abbé Boilat whose *Esquisses Sénégalaises*, published in 1853, was a source of anthropological, geographic and sociological information based in part on observation of the tribes in the Senegal territory and in part on historical materials. Boilat collected oral traditions and mythology as a necessary background to the understanding of the contemporary life of the traditional societies, and he used history to explain the shape of the mixed creole communities in the coastal centres of Goree and St. Louis. More than that, Boilat, as an African thoroughly assimilated into Franco-European culture, composed his historical observations in part to illustrate the point that Africa had possessed a rich civilization in ancient times, and that in her future she would rise again through the medium of French culture and the Church of Rome.

The use of the historical argument for ulterior purposes also characterized the work of Edward Blyden. Blyden never wrote formal histories as such, but his wide reading in Biblical and classical scholarship frequently provided an historical argument to underscore the dignity and accomplishments of the African people. Throughout his writings he was at pains to cite the Negro contribution to ancient Egyptian civilization, to suggest the role of the black man in Old Testament history, or to explain that the subsequent decline of the African people was due to a complex series of environmental factors to which the European slave trade applied the finishing touches.

There were other nineteenth-century Africans who, though they were not professional historians in the modern sense, attempted systematic histories of Africa designed to instruct their countrymen concerning the shape of their past. These men wrote full-scale histories based on documentary sources, but also attempted to make effective use of the oral traditions of the people. Hence they foreshadowed, both as to objective and technique, the work of contemporary African historians. As with Africa's present generation of historians, they were seeking to reassess the past of their people from the point of view of the African who had experienced that past, in order that later generations might not only know the flow of events but, more particularly, would know with what emotions and reactions their ancestors greeted those events. There were not many of these pioneers during the latter part of the nineteenth century, which makes their surviving work all the more interesting and relevant to a study of intellectual developments in the West Africa of their day. Three individuals stand out in particular. They were the Sierra Leonean schoolteacher, artist and amateur botanist, A. B. C. Sibthorpe, Samuel Johnson who devoted twenty years to the writing of his monumental *History of the Yorubas*, and the Gold Coast missionary, Carl C. Reindorf.

2 *African History written for and about Africans – C. C. Reindorf*

Reindorf completed his *History of the Gold Coast and Asante* in 1889 after thirty years devoted to the slow and careful accumulation of material. He proved himself to be no idle chronicler, but rather a self-conscious, purposeful historian who wrote to fill an informational gap, whose techniques were based on a thoughtful analysis of the task before him and the tools at hand. Reindorf had a surprisingly modern and prophetic view of national history. His title had been chosen with care for he wanted not only to describe the activities of Accra, the first kingdom of the Gold Coast, but also of its second kingdom, Fanti, 'the land of history . . . poetry and enlightenment', as well as of Ashanti which ultimately came to be the leading power in the land, for 'the histories of both countries are so interwoven'.

Having settled his history's dimension, Reindorf turned next to authorship, explaining that no foreigner could do justice to the subject for want of the ability to acquire and assess the traditions of the land. 'Hence it is much more desirable that a history of the Gold Coast and its people should be written by one who has not only studied, but has had the privilege of initiation into the history of its former inhabitants and writes with true native patriotism.' Finally, there was the question of purpose:

If a nation's history is the nation's speculum and measure-tape, then it brings the past of that nation to its own view, so that the past may be compared with the present to see whether progress or retrogression is in operation; and also as a means of judging our nation by others, so that we may gather instruction for our future guidance. When such is not the case with a nation, no hope can be entertained for better prospects.[1]

In order to achieve an authentic narration of events as the people of the Gold Coast had experienced them, it was necessary to make use of the traditions of the country, and during the course of his research, Reindorf interviewed over two hundred individuals, comparing and testing the traditions they provided in order to arrive at an undistorted view of his subject. In addition he consulted such written works as were available to him, lamenting that he was denied access to the colonial records which would have greatly simplified his task in substantiating dates and other information. The *History* which emerged covered a span of more than three centuries from approximately 1500 to 1860. It dealt primarily with the political and military events described in the local traditions, but there were occasional sections devoted to such matters as the structure of government, the relations of the pagan priest class to the native state, or the practice of agriculture and crafts. It is not always an easy history to read for it consists in large part of a maze of detailed information liberally sprinkled with individual and place names, and presented in chronological order without much attempt to sort out and select the more important or relevant material. Clearly, Reindorf strove for an objectivity which he often achieved, for his descriptions of events tally substantially with other accounts. And certainly he realized his basic purpose of writing an African history for

---

[1] C. C. Reindorf, *History of the Gold Coast and Asante*, iii–vii.

and about Africans, for the essential difference between his and other histories dealing with the same events is largely one of perspective – they treating the subject from the European view and Reindorf treating it from the African.

Yet Reindorf had his biases. He was a mulatto of Danish descent, but ancestors on both sides of his family came from the Ga people of Accra, and his account of the Accra men rarely lost an opportunity to set forth their virtues:

> By nature the Akras are mild and inoffensive, yet unconquerable, independent and not easily governed. Wherever an Akra man goes, he is not only respected on account of his national prestige, but by his personal abilities and qualifications, able to endure any hardship and privation thrice better than any one of another tribe. In wars, in travellings, in voyages, in times of epidemic, they are divinely more preserved than any other nation. When two or three Akras would die in any of the above emergencies, the loss of any other tribes in their company is counted by dozens.

Reindorf explained that the religious and political institutions of the Ga resembled those of the ancient Hebrews, thus placing them in a more advantageous position than their neighbours to be converted to the higher blessings of Christianity. Because of their military prowess, the Accra had never been conquered by their traditional foes, the Twi; indeed the warlike Ashanti entertained a long-standing affection for the Ga people, possibly because 'they never provoked other people to war, and were inoffensive to the Ashanti'. Thus, according to Reindorf, in 1824 when the Ashanti were attacking Cape Coast, they discovered that the Accra were in the lines, having been brought there at the instance of the Europeans, and with this information the Ashanti king immediately broke off the engagement and retired to Kumasi. Two years later at the pivotal battle of Katamanso, it was the Accra who were conspicuous in bravery and magnanimous in victory:

> The name of 'Akra' now became famous; their influence spread far and wide, and they were respected everywhere. Their former enemies, Fantes, Akems, Akwamus, and Akuapems, bowed to them, respected them, and their prestige was even acknowledged at Asante and Dahome. They obtained riches by traffic in distant countries, and strangers came down to the coast for the purpose of commerce. . . . Well done! Victorious Ga, Thou great and durable Akra.

Yet, adds Reindorf, the Ga were not by nature rulers and they let slip the opportunity at the time to impose a system of tribute on the chiefs who owed them allegiance.[1]

Reindorf was more dispassionate in his comments concerning the Fanti, and of the Ashanti he reported the usual testimony of ferocity in battle and bloodiness of disposition, of bravery combined with barbarous cruelty. When the Ashanti controlled foreign territory, their rule lay heavy on the land, and they 'ground down the people with the most barbarous tyranny'. Extortion was common, attractive wives were always liable to requisition, the mere mentioning the king's name was punished by fine, leaders were put to death and large segments of the population enslaved, cities lay sacked, and poverty resulted everywhere. That such a situation was permitted to exist, said Reindorf, was in considerable measure the fault of the Europeans who pretended to protect the people against the Ashanti but who in fact rarely interfered with their activities. During the eighteenth century the coastal tribes were too weak and too evenly matched to maintain a secure peace; the result was that 'pillage, manstealing, and murder prevailed in every district. If the European governments of the Danes, Dutch, and English then established on the coast had not become demoralized and weakened by the slave trade, such general disorder could easily have been checked. The poor people they pretended to protect, were so far protected, alas for their own benefit.'

For Reindorf, therefore, slavery was at least in part responsible not only for the unsettled political situation in the Gold Coast but for the uncertain and vacillating policy of the Europeans. Speaking more generally, Europe seemed always to bring trouble to Africa. Reindorf quoted an African proverb, 'Never a musket bursts in Europe and wounds one in Africa.' With the arrival of the westerners, petty warfare became constant in response to the disputes among the Europeans whose parochial wars were soon extended to the coast of West Africa. When at last the slave trade was outlawed after 1807, the local people still found no relief. Rescued from the barbarities of slavery, they were thenceforward subjected to the harsh measures of enforcement. British policy towards the Ashanti, moreover, lacked consistency. During the early years of the nineteenth century, one British governor, Colonel Torrane, agreed to defend Assin against the Ashanti, then when he realized his forces were insufficient, he betrayed the Assin chiefs to the

---

[1] *Ibid.*, 22-4, 114-16, 177, 197, 210-19. See A. B. Ellis, *A History of the Gold Coast of West Africa*, 181-5, and W. W. Claridge, *A History of the Gold Coast and Ashanti*, I, 386-91 for other versions of the battle of Katamanso.

Ashanti and allowed many of the people to be enslaved by the Fanti. A number of years later confusion of authority between agents of the British crown and of the British Company of Merchants occupying Cape Coast led to gratuitous insult of the Ashanti by the English authorities. This in turn brought on a stoppage of trade, 'and the whole territory was a scene of lawless violence'. The essential problem, Reindorf pointed out, was that the Europeans were not basically interested in Africa, but only in their own commercial affairs. As the Ashanti king properly remarked over the Assin affair, 'From the hour governor Torrane delivered up Cheboo, I took the English for my friends, because I saw their object was trade only, and they did not care for the people.'[1]

Nevertheless, for Reindorf, Africa and Europe were inextricably bound up with each other, for it was Europe which had brought the uplifting influence of Christianity to West Africa and it was Europe which would have to assist in raising African civilization from its barbarous ways. War and plunder, kidnapping and pillage, slavery and extortion had devastated the land and depopulated whole districts. People were bought and sold like cattle, captives were incinerated when no slave market was found for them, the victims of the constant warfare—women, children, the aged—expected no mercy from their conquerors, the sick and wounded committing suicide, mothers killing their babies to prevent capture or abandoning them in the bush in their headlong flight from death and slavery. Now as Reindorf was writing late in the century, the British had finally broken the Ashanti hold on the country, peace was in the land, and the people could look with optimism to future progress under British guidance:

> We are fully content to be under the sway of our most blessed sovereign because, when we cast our glance on all the colonies under England, we see great improvement. Even in those colonies where our brethren have been dragged to as slaves, but were made free by England, great improvements have been made . . . We . . . entertain all hopes that . . . our time is not far distant when we also shall be elevated from our degradation. We therefore look to England, we look to the English people . . . to help us on.[2]

Already important progress had been made in introducing Christianity and curbing the effects of a primitive paganism. If the effects of early Portuguese proselytizing were difficult to trace, the efforts of later missionaries were full of promise. Before their arrival, 'the whole

---

[1] Reindorf, *op. cit.*, 128, 145, 146–7, 151–2, 171, 174–6; Joseph Dupuis, *Journal of a Residence in Ashantee*, 263 n.
[2] Reindorf, *op. cit.*, 163, 283, 311, 315.

country was lying in an Egyptian darkness of barbarism and superstition'. Now under mission leadership, polygamy and household slavery were subdued, education introduced and paganism tottered. Only in Ashanti, where fear of the king deterred the people, did Christianity gain but slowly. All the same, Reindorf insisted, African progress could not be tied too completely to outsiders for, in the final analysis, the people had to develop self-reliance and learn to make the most effective use of the richness of the native soil and the skill of the native hand. The land was fertile and produced many fine crops. The people had learned the art of fishing, they knew how to work iron and gold, how to manufacture salt and how to weave. Other pursuits had been introduced by the European, including teaching, trade, bookkeeping and a number of skilled crafts. Yet instead of pressing forward in improving the expertise they already possessed, there were many who saw their future only in emulating the westerner. Farmers who used their profits to engage in trade instead of improving their farms, fishermen who turned from a lucrative occupation to a commerce of questionable value, educated Africans who insisted on being only clerks or traders, all failed to grasp the essential quality of progress in civilization. 'We have every facility to become monied men, respectable men,' Reindorf complained, 'if we only give up the false notion of civilization which we aim at, and turn to our rich soil, and work with our own hands.'[1]

Not only was the problem one of neglecting what Africa had to offer; it was also an excessive zeal to become as much like the European as possible. The women of the Gold Coast tried to live like English women, refraining from working and mistaking the mere use of European dress for the wearing of true civilization. Educated Africans patronized their uneducated compatriots, divorcing themselves from their own people and associating only with the white man. All that this achieved was an inhibition of progress:

This want of principles in us Africans . . . that those who have got education in Europe look down on our own brethren who were educated in the country, is the sole cause of the unimproved state of the country. . . . Our brethren are too low to keep our society. We say, no! There are people, although educated in the country among the mass, who are respectable, behave respectably, who could be selected to form a society if we don't despise them. . . . Let the better classes among us diffuse their better qualifications, their Christian and moral qualifications, into the rest, and then a change will certainly take place on the Gold Coast.[2]

[1] *Ibid.*, 220, 228, 242-3, 272, 280-1.
[2] *Ibid.*, 281-2.

Here then was the classic ambivalence of the educated West African towards Europe. Reindorf wanted the advantages of European, Christian civilization for his people, but he recognized the dangers of a total cultural assimilation which smothered native character and initiative while failing to replace it with a way of life that would be meaningful in the West African context. In his final assessment, Reindorf somewhat reluctantly concluded that the African would have to make the best of an inevitable European occupation. In describing the British government which replaced the Danes in Accra in 1850, he explained some of the difficulties of adjustment. Under the Danes, native law and custom had by and large governed local administration, but with the English, a new set of legal principles and procedures had to be learned. This became particularly odious when the government sought to levy a poll tax for purposes of local finance. Initial acquiescence, though grudgingly given, was soon converted into opposition over what were regarded as arbitrary methods of collection, and a severe and inequitable rate. In the ensuing negotiations, the British maintained a restrained firmness while the African reluctance deepened to the point of revolt. Confusion, misunderstanding and lack of vigorous African leadership followed; a leaning towards coercion by the British brought forth an African counter towards violence, and finally a rebellion broke forth which was only subdued by force. Fortunately the loss of life was light, but there was extensive property damage and each chief was obliged to give a son or nephew to the government as hostages against future outbreaks. For Reindorf, the moral was clear. 'Oh, that we were wiser in time, that we did not kick against the pricks!' It was the Christian missionaries who first returned to the towns and induced the people to rebuild their houses. It was to England that the Gold Coast would henceforth have to look for its destiny:

> Rule, supremely rule, Britannia, rule
> Thy acquired colony on the Gold Coast! . . .
> Superstition will then flee far away,
> And Christianity will rule supreme![1]

3 *African History as Social History — A. B. C. Sibthorpe*

The Reverend Reindorf was not the only African historian with a weakness for versifying. In the third edition of his *History of Sierra Leone*, A. B. C. Sibthorpe adorned the flyleaf with this motto:

[1] *Ibid.*, 329–41.

> Read Sibthorpe once, and still persist to read;
> Sibthorpe will be all the First Books you need.

And in *The Ten Lost Tribes*, he informed the reader that,

> The joys of earth are nothing worth,
> If you cannot read Sibthorpe.

Here the similarity ended; even in these brief lines emerges a different character whose puckish, humorous self-regard is poised against Reindorf's ponderous solemnity.

A. B. C. Sibthorpe—the initials, an abbreviation of the splendid Aaron Belisarius Cosimo, were adopted possibly by the subject himself, so accurately does it reflect his rococo flamboyance. He was born during the 1830s, probably near Benin, coming to Sierra Leone as a recaptive while still a youth and living out his long life as a schoolmaster in one or two small villages located outside Freetown. His origins were obscure and his life was outwardly quiet; it was only through his writing that the effervescence of an irrepressible spirit burst forth. He seems to have regarded himself as of royal blood, and in any event, the possessor of rare artistic and scholarly talents designed to instruct and uplift his fellow men. His artistic endeavours were extracurricular but not without recognition. At a local exhibition in Freetown in 1865, by his own admission, he 'astonished both strangers and citizens in the triple capacity of painter, sculptor or engraver, and modeller', his renditions of artificial fruits deceiving all viewers. Subsequently he did portraits of the governor of the time, Samuel W. Blackall, and of the well-known barrister, William Rainy. Twenty years later he tells us his work dominated a colonial exhibition held in London, and for this achievement he received a bronze medal from the Prince of Wales and a modest cash price from the Sierra Leone government. In his day, Rainy had tried unsuccessfully to find a means for Sibthorpe to study abroad, but failure did not upset the artist, 'because Sibthorpe is a child not of patronage but of Providence; the civilized world will know him hereafter.'[1]

Art was yet an avocation, and Sibthorpe had other pursuits. In 1868 he published a geography of Sierra Leone, and studied phrenology, subsequently examining several local clergymen including James Johnson, G. J. Macaulay and James Robbin. Next he mastered photography and then began a concerted study of local plant life which yielded a

---

[1] Sibthorpe, *The History of Sierra Leone*, 81–2, 103; P. E. H. Hair, 'A Reference to A. B. C. Sibthorpe', *Sierra Leone Studies*, n.s., no. 18, Jan., 1966, 69–70.

variety of species which he considered to be of commercial value–among others, alum, gum, rubber, indigo, nutmeg, chocolate, guttapercha, senna and sassafras–to all of which he appropriately affixed the name of their cataloguer. Well towards the end of his life he was planning scientific and literary works to supplement his *History*. He hoped to bring forth a study of 'Endemics and Epidemics of Sierra Leone', 'The Botany of Sierra Leone and West Africa', 'Sibthorpe's Fables', and 'Sierra Leone, Its Scenes and Society, Fifty years Ago', but nothing came of these ventures.[1]

Sibthorpe managed to keep his *History* from becoming pedantic, mainly through the medium of his humour which was always available to introduce a light note. His frequent references to his herbal discoveries must have been only semi-serious, and he tells of his pranks as a schoolboy with enthusiasm and relish. When Reindorf reported plagues of locusts, he quite naturally registered his dismay at the devastation. So too did Sibthorpe, but not before launching into a short treatise on the succulence of locusts, comparing later specimens with those he had eaten in his youth, suggesting how they might be chosen for maximum tenderness, and then how they might be properly prepared for the table. In another place, concluding a serious section on labour problems and changes in the municipal government, Sibthorpe suddenly announced, 'Freetown is a wonderful city. It has three governments, but four governors.' On another occasion his description of Freetown society was punctuated by:

Three things are too wonderful for me in Sierra Leone marriages–yea, four: A good wife never lasts; separated pairs ever live; a grand marriage portends quick separation; and a professional dancer or a drunkard (not a drinker) has the best of wives.

Here indeed was social philosophy to go along with social history.[2]

Still, through superficial eccentricity ran a strain of stability that led to sound achievement. As a youth Sibthorpe excelled in the grammar, geography, history and Bible studies offered at the missionary school he attended, and so was encouraged to proceed to more advanced studies leading to enrolment in Fourah Bay seminary. From there he was diverted from the ministry to teaching, in which occupation he remained for the rest of his life. His *History* appeared first in 1868 along with the *Geography* and both were accorded a warm reception. A thousand copies were sold within a month, a number were exported to France and

[1] *The History of Sierra Leone*, iv, 85–8.   [2] *Ibid.*, 119, 171, 217.

America, most schools in the colony adopted them as texts, and students read them widely. Each was revised and reissued twice, the *History* appearing last in 1906 and the *Geography* one year earlier. From time to time, Sibthorpe published supplementary material in the local press, and in 1909 his final work, *The Ten Lost Tribes*, appeared. This last was a short treatise attempting to link the Yoruba recaptives in Sierra Leone with the lost tribes of Israel, but composed in such a confused and disjointed style as to suggest some deterioration of the powers.[1]

Sibthorpe's occasional contributions to the newspapers frequently contained thoughtful historical observations such as the following remarks on the difficulties of research and composition:

There never yet was an author who did not deceive himself, and consequently deceive others, as to the period at which his labours would be completed. The stupid, the thoughtless, and the malignant ... consider as intended for the purpose of deception the erroneous estimate which authors are thus apt to form. They either cannot or will not be taught that ... no man is at all hours capable of thinking deeply, or of clothing his thoughts in an attractive dress; that he who is dependent on his reputation for existence ought not to be compelled to hazard it by crude and slovenly efforts, the product of haste. That he who draws up a narrative from widely scattered, numerous, and conflicting documents must often, in painful research and in balancing evidence, spend more months than he has calculated on spending weeks. That the discovery of a single paper ... may compel a writer to modify, to arrange, and even to cancel much that he had supposed to have received his last touches. And, therefore, that the delay which has been a proof of literary indolence, is so frequently and so unfeelingly an object of censure, ought rather in many cases to be rewarded with praise, because it is a duty which an author conscientiously ... performs to society and to truth.[2]

Sibthorpe's reputation as an historian, however, rests ultimately on his *History of Sierra Leone*. Designed in its first edition as a catechism of questions and answers, it appeared subsequently in narrative form, but in a style which tended to make it more chronicle than history. The text was divided into sections corresponding to the tenures of the several governors, and the immediate discussion was necessarily limited to events which occurred during each particular administration. Paragraphs were headed with descriptive titles such as Memorable Events, Wars,

---

[1] *Ibid.*, 85–6. Sibthorpe's life and activities have been examined with care and affection by C. H. Fyfe in 'A. B. C. Sibthorpe: A Neglected Historian', *Sierra Leone Studies*, n.s., no. 10, June, 1958, 99–109. See also Sibthorpe, *op. cit.*, 164–73.
[2] *The Sierra Leone Weekly News*, Feb. 24, 1894.

Names of Note, and Administration. A surprising amount of information was crowded into these categories but they were often uneven in quality, and they sadly lacked a sense of historical development, an attention to relations of cause and effect, and an organization of materials drawn together from different times to illustrate important movements unnoticed when viewed as isolated events.

Sibthorpe possessed little of Reindorf's self-conscious historicism or nationalism, but this did not mean he lacked a basic philosophy of history:

Write not such work as will stand in a library silently for ages, moved only to be dusted and catalogued . . . and gazed at, occasionally, by men as ignorant as I am . . . Indeed, unless a man can link his written thoughts with the everlasting wants of men, so that they shall draw from them as from wells, there is no more immortality to the thoughts and feelings of the soul than to the muscles and bones. . . . One thing is certain, that it is the historian that gives duration to kingdoms and empires, puts them as individual portrait before rising generations to scan their good and bad deeds, and learn from their misfortunes, the punishment of evil, and the peaceful reward of righteousness. In short, without the historian every kingdom is but Jonah's gourd, grow in the dawn and perish with the twilight. History is the soul of empires.[1]

In writing his history, the Sierra Leone schoolmaster was motivated in part by a teacher's need for adequate materials, but also by his feeling that the reader might be both entertained and instructed:

Considering the pleasure and interest with which the public in general read histories of foreign nations, and finding that everyone in the colony has not the privilege of hearing or reading the history of his father's or mother's nation; and as we have been compelled by fortune and nature to become one people or nation, of mixed generation, on this soil – I have endeavoured to give in a condensed form the history of the place we now inhabit.

In Sibthorpe such modest objectives were an asset for they enabled him to indulge his natural gaiety and his artist's instinct for local colour uninhibited by any overriding sense of mission. What emerged, therefore, was social history of vividness and verisimilitude which brought forth the early years of Freetown in all their tropical brightness and projected the people and their way of life with a sure hand.[2]

In the early days of the colony, as Sibthorpe described them, the settlers copied European dress, but as with the women of Senegal, so those of Freetown revealed a weakness for quantities of gold, coral and

---

[1] *Ibid.*, Feb. 18, 1893. [2] Sibthorpe, *op. cit.*, v.

glass jewellery which were worn as rings, bracelets, necklaces and earrings as well as in the form of a special girdle of beads that jingled from the waist. The men performed the crafts—sawyers, carpenters and masons—while the women often acted as nurses for the Europeans and as laundresses. The diet was essentially European, the lingua franca a pidgin English, and the chief recreation of the women was 'the all ravishing dance... called a Koonken'. Dancing must have been a widely practised pleasure for during the administration of Sir Charles MacCarthy, a sharp rise in government expenditures was described by a local citizen, 'Macarthy live—much dollar, much laugh', at which Sibthorpe commented, 'He ought to have added "more dance".'

Nearing mid-century, Freetown had taken on a more cosmopolitan look in Sibthorpe's narrative. The descendants of the original settlers continued to dress much like the Europeans, and the liberated Africans tended to imitate the settlers and the whites. There were, however, the stately dark Wolof women who glided by in their mantillas, while Kru labourers from Liberia clad only in loincloths jostled white-clad Fulani in the busy, crowded streets. The English lived in open veranda houses through which wandered an unending succession of tradesmen and their relatives, for to deprive them of access was considered a breach of form. The whites enjoyed riding for recreation but the old settlers were still addicted to the Koonken, while the later-arriving Aku favoured the ceremonial aspects of their marriages, birthdays and funerals.

Prices about 1840 were low. Cattle could be obtained for as little as £3 a head and chickens for 4s. 4d. apiece, beef was only 4d. a pound, and eggs 1d. each. Fully equipped schooners were often auctioned for £200 and one was actually obtained for only £130. These prices probably accounted for the early ability of Aku traders to institute shipping services for their compatriots back to Yorubaland. Imported foodstuffs were expensive, however, running 30 per cent above the European market, and wages were not sufficient for the needs of the average worker. Senior government salaries ranged from £800 to £2,000 a year, but apprentice carpenters and masons could make only 1s. 1d. a day which was the same wage received by common labourers. There was a serious shortage of machinery in the colony. There were not enough clocksmiths to keep the church tower clocks in repair, the government wharf lacked a crane for unloading, and carts, carriages, wagons, even wheelbarrows, were rarities. Heavy labour rested exclusively on the broad backs of the Krumen.[1]

[1] *Ibid.*, 27–8, 36, 51–2, 57–9.

Sibthorpe continued to provide glimpses of Freetown society down to the early years of the twentieth century at which time he was observing among other things that creoles and Europeans were neglecting their Sunday religious responsibilities in favour of sport, that the population was more than ever cosmopolitan and entirely devoted to the pursuit of money, and that most people preferred walking to horses, bicycles or carriages. Such comments were usually more than idle gossip, however. One major theme which runs through the *History* and which much of Sibthorpe's social reporting was designed to illustrate, was that the Nova Scotian settlers were an unhealthy factor in the colony's history. Early addicted to rebellion, they gradually sank into a lethargy, allowing the liberated Africans to monopolize the manual labour of the colony. 'But this was the beginning of ruin', observed Sibthorpe, 'because... they and their children became comparatively idle, and flattered themselves with an overweening self-importance.' False standards led to decline and an empty show of progress:

The Nova Scotians saw with chagrin and envy themselves sinking into oblivion... Instead of competing with those whom they deemed their inferiors, the Nova Scotians, with a few exceptions, withdrew from the field of industry in disgust, some transporting themselves back to America, some embarking in petty mercantile pursuits... others, without much thought of the future, living upon the money acquired in their 'golden age'.

That the virus of indolence ultimately infected other parts of the population may be inferred from Sibthorpe's description of Freetown society in 1875:

A stranger beholding Freetown groaning with palaces, and splendour in marriage festivals, and left fingers of males glittering with gold... would scarcely believe that the Colony has no commercial resources, no developed latent riches, and no manufactures. Yet it is a fact worthy of observation that these riches never descend to the third generation of the same family; in most cases they end with the founders themselves, or are squandered with the second.[1]

The Maroons, 'a race... neither religious nor educated', received scarcely better treatment–'that Maroon body... invaded by open violence, or diminished by quick decay'. For Sibthorpe it was rather the liberated Africans–the Akus of Yoruba descent, the Ibos and other recaptives from the tribes to the east–who had through hard work and sober application preserved and increased the prosperity and happiness

---

[1] *Ibid.*, 13–15, 28, 50, 88, 220–1.

of the people. These recaptives were to be found in all levels of society – indefatigable and productive. The most recent arrivals lived modestly as farmers or unskilled labourers, 'a harmless and well-disposed people ... industrious and frugal'. Those that prospered and advanced became small traders and craftsmen – tailors, cobblers, blacksmiths, masons, carpenters – and above all these were the successful merchants with their European houses and furniture, their small libraries, and the 'general air of domestic comfort ... which, perhaps, more than anything else, bore evidence of the advanced state of intelligence at which they had arrived'. Finally, there were the largest merchants whose substantial wealth reflected 'the acuteness of their understanding and their improved moral condition', and whose outstanding ability and talents were frequently utilized on petty, grand and special juries. 'I have dwelt long on the character and condition of the "captives",' Sibthorpe continued,

because to their rising importance and dawning enterprise we must look for the ultimate welfare of the Colony. The Europeans are too insignificant in numbers, and too migratory, to be considered an important item in the future advancement of the settlement; their tastes and interests lie in England, to which all intend to return before they die. The Kroomen profess no sympathy with others, and are merely a succession of visitors; whilst, of the permanent residents, the settlers are in the last stage of decay; and such of the Foulahs, Mandingoes, and Jalloffs as are content to dwell here for a time have little stake in a community of infidels or unbelievers. The liberated alone remain to enlarge, progress, and to enjoy the full benefits of this noble district.[1]

There can be no gainsaying Sibthorpe's love of his 'noble district'. It was the failure of the settlers from Nova Scotia to develop the material and spiritual prosperity of the land which brought down his scorn, just as it was the diligence of the recaptives in developing the country's resources which led to their commendation. The British, too, were judged by what they contributed to local progress. Sibthorpe was sympathetic towards the activities of the early Sierra Leone Company whose government had striven to demonstrate the viability of a free black state, enduring the slanders levelled at the undertaking and the 'exaggerated representations of the unhealthiness of this part of the coast'. Organizations like the philanthropic African Institution were congratulated for their exertions 'to introduce ... the arts of civilization and social improvements'; governments and official policy were criticized or commended depending on how they measured up to Sibthorpe's

[1] *Ibid.*, 27, 52–7; *The Ten Lost Tribes*, 7.

standards of achievement. Sir Arthur Kennedy was therefore 'a Governor indeed [who] laboured for the security and happiness of his subjects'. At other times Sibthorpe saw lack of systematic planning in Whitehall which left governors to pursue personal and often conflicting policies, with results, as in Senegal, of drift and lack of solid progress. Other evidence pointing to successful British policy was given full credit, however. Sibthorpe was quick, for instance, to express gratitude for the splendid work of the English naval forces in stamping out the slave trade in West African waters.[1]

Hence Sibthorpe wrote his history from an African point of view, although his view was the somewhat specialized perspective of the Freetown creole. African though he was, moreover, he was a Europeanized African, writing from unconscious assumptions of an Afro-European cultural base. His educational background, his style of writing, his literary allusions, his automatic unthinking classification of the interior tribes as 'natives' and 'the enemy', all made him sound like a European. When he extolled the civilizing work of the English philanthropists he meant European civilization with its western education, Christian worship, and the encouragement of Puritan ideas of thrift and hard work. But in these partialities he was not unlike so many of the educated West Africans of his times.

4 The Moralist as Historian—Samuel Johnson

The ancient Oyos or Yoruba proper were very virtuous, loving and kind. Theft was rare as also fornication . . . Friendship was more sincere. Children were more dutiful . . . and inferiors respectful . . . Now, as formerly they are remarkably patient of injuries . . . They are characteristically unassuming in their manners and submissive to their superiors. They are very shrewd at driving bargains . . . No nation is more remarkable for cautiousness . . . but when an opportunity offers for asserting their rights . . . they are never slow to embrace it. . . .

Intercourse with other nations has caused various forms of vice to creep in among modern Yorubas or Oyos; their natural timidity and submissive spirit have produced a degeneracy of manners so as to be considered essentially lacking in straightforwardness . . . Yorubas as a whole are social, polite, and proverbially hospitable. Licentiousness is abhorred.

In this fashion did Samuel Johnson describe his own Oyo countrymen in *The History of the Yorubas*. Coming from the pen of a professed

---

[1] *History of Sierra Leone*, 16–17, 19–20, 68–72.

patriot, the assessment was reasonably balanced. To be sure it ignored the quarrelsome myopia that placed local pride above national cohesiveness and immediate gain over ultimate objective. It overlooked the bloodthirsty cruelty that held life cheap and presented a calloused indifference to human suffering. It was silent regarding a bankruptcy of statesmanship which turned a nation from peace and progress and condemned it to a century of civil war which the Yoruba people could not halt even at the point of total emotional and physical exhaustion. Yet these are traits which at times have darkened the character of all peoples; along with the occasional incidents of heroism and self-sacrifice, warfare generates the worst passions in the best of humankind, turning loose destructiveness and brutality and encouraging the annihilation in a few short months or years of civilizations that have been painfully brought into being over generations and centuries. Johnson was well aware of this. Indeed his whole history was an indictment of the failure of Yoruba culture, the futility of barren policy, and a deprecation of 'the spirit of tribal feelings and petty jealousies now rife among us'.[1]

At first sight, Samuel Johnson might have seemed an unlikely author for the broad panorama of Yoruba history in its social and cultural complexity, its strenuous politics and lusty war-making. Like Reindorf, he was missionary-trained and had dedicated his life to the quiet persuasion of the heathen to the principles of Christian faith which he upheld. His family had long been under the influence of the Anglican missionaries, first in Sierra Leone where Samuel was born in 1846, and later in Ibadan. Two of his three brothers found careers within the Anglican Church in West Africa, his elder brother Henry serving as an archdeacon both in Sierra Leone and on the upper Niger. Samuel Johnson, shy and self-effacing, was content at the conclusion of his formal education to remain in Ibadan as schoolteacher and catechist, and it was only later in life that he was finally ordained and posted to Oyo as pastor. His reports and journals sent regularly to C.M.S. headquarters in London reflected the image of a gentle humble man. Occasionally he forwarded accounts of the warfare that continually swirled around him, but his main preoccupation was preaching and converting. We see him going forth into the streets, enduring the jibes of unbelievers, engaging Muslims in theological argument, agonizing helplessly over the maltreatment of slaves and exalting in the occasional sign of conversion:

[1] Samuel Johnson, *The History of the Yorubas*, vii, 101–2.

Went out for open air preaching. . . . I saw a young man sitting alone under an odan tree; and from his look I perceived he was under some bodily ailment. . . . I tried to speak to him kindly, and told him we are all messengers of peace, a friend, and not a foe. Gaining his confidence I proceeded to speak with him telling him the cause of our unhappiness which is sin, and how it was introduced into the world. I went on practically showing how peace of mind cannot be obtained by sacrifices. His attention was now fixed, and his eager glistening eyes tell of conviction. . . . May the words spoken be a word in season.[1]

Nevertheless Johnson's very gentleness led him to abhor the war which was part of his daily life, to study the political issues that had brought conflict to the country, to look to the past for historical causes, and thus bit by bit to collect the raw materials for his history. And over all these factors prevailed 'a purely patriotic motive, that the history of our fatherland might not be lost in oblivion . . . Educated natives of Yoruba are well acquainted with the history of England and with that of Rome and Greece, but of the history of their own country they know nothing whatever! This reproach it is one of the author's objects to remove.'[2]

After years of study, what finally emerged was a massive text setting forth in exhaustive detail the complexities of Yoruba political and military history. Beginning with the mythological past, Johnson proceeded to historical times sustained by quantities of oral evidence patiently gathered and sifted, but the bulk of his work was concentrated in the nineteenth century, the actual period of the Yoruba civil wars. Johnson did not neglect the social and cultural life of his people, devoting his early chapters to religion, government, village life, customs and law, to say nothing of a lengthy introductory section dealing with the Yoruba language. In his discussion of national origins, he stressed the Egyptian and Middle Eastern antecedents of the Yoruba as stated in their traditions. The Yoruba people sprang from Lamurudu, or Namurudu, which he thought to be a variation of Nimrod whose descendants, the Phoenicians, settled in Arabia and were subsequently driven to Africa by religious persecution. He pointed out the Egyptian character of Ife art, and suggested that at one time the Yoruba might have lived in Upper Egypt as Coptic Christians; hence Yoruba knowledge of the stories of the creation, the flood, and other familiar Biblical tales.[3]

[1] J. F. A. Ajayi, 'Samuel Johnson, Historian of the Yoruba', *Nigeria Magazine*, no. 81, June, 1964, 141–6; *The Lagos Weekly Record*, May 4, 1901; Samuel Johnson Journal Extracts, Apr. 3, 1870, Half year ending Dec., 1874, Jan. 18, Oct. 18, 1876, C.M.S. CA2/058.
[2] Johnson, *op. cit.*, vii.   [3] *Ibid.*, 5–7.

Mythology and oral tradition, however, were not the main contributors to Johnson's *History*. He himself was a daily observer and active peacemaker during the final phase of the wars between 1877 and 1893, and it is his projection of this stage of Yoruba history–the vivid descriptions of skirmishes and sieges, the exact portrayal of the immolation of heroes or the fate of poltroons, the agonizing appraisal of faulty statesmanship and inadequate generalship, the chronicling of ultimate exhaustion of land and people–that has most completely captured the critical attention of the reader, and gives greatest insight into the historical judgments of the author.

Always modest, Johnson managed in the main to submerge his opinions beneath the surface of his narrative. Only on occasion did he allow himself the luxury of an editorial aside regarding the folly of a certain course of action or the wisdom of some particular leader. Yet there was no hiding his basic point of view, and the key to his attitude was peace and the brotherhood of mankind. Implicit in the *History* was the futility of warfare, the narrowness of parochialism and the stupidity of arrogance. As special messenger for the British in Lagos, Johnson worked ceaselessly to bring the wars to an end, enduring frustration and setback, but always patiently and faithfully doing what he could to bring the sides together, to soften differences, and to explain the prospects of peace. Most of his conclusions and judgments appear coloured by his passion for a settlement which would free his people from the tyranny of the wars. When at last the end was in sight, his description of the popular reaction was like a great release of dammed-up emotion, the cool fresh draught of relief expressing as much the sentiments of the author as those of the people he described:

> To the vast majority of the common people it was like the opening of a prison door: and no one who witnessed the patient, long-suffering, and toiling mass of humanity that week by week streamed to and from the coast with their produce . . . could refrain from heaving a sigh of gratification on the magnitude of the beneficial results . . . The first night . . . large fires were lighted, and all the men and women sitting round, spent the hours in recounting their sufferings and losses for years . . . They continued thus far into the night, and occasionally raised loud huzzahs for the merciful deliverance, and the prospect of freedom of trade, and the discharge of their debts which the long period of . . . war had imposed upon every individual in the interior countries.[1]

Johnson was an Oyo and much of his adult life was spent in Ibadan,

---
[1] *Ibid.*, 466, 482, 508, 558, 568, 614, 623.

so that it is not surprising to find his estimate of the Yoruba character largely conditioned by geography. The Oyos he took for granted to be the essential Yoruba and the core of a great empire that might again be united under the Alafin of Oyo. The Ibadans, long-time associated with Oyo and holding off with courage and skill innumerable alliances designed to crush them on the field or to starve them through attrition, were similarly treated with a sympathetic pen. On the other hand, the Egba and Ijebu to the south were invariably criticized by the otherwise dispassionate Johnson. Although tribal differences doubtless explain this antipathy in part, it is quite possible that the tactics of the southern tribes in seeking to deprive the Ibadans of supplies were regarded by the peaceful Johnson as a needless and senseless extension of the war he so profoundly wished to see terminated. In any event, Johnson portrayed the Egba as treacherous allies who, in the case of the siege of Ijaye by the Ibadans, lured the starving children of their Ijaye allies into the Egba tents, then carried them off to Abeokuta as slaves. Perfidious as friends, they were pusillanimous as foes, ever lacking the courage to quit the security of their walls while facing the armies of Dahomey. Yet these were the people who felt obliged to interfere with Ibadan's legitimate efforts to find coastal trading outlets.[1]

Like the Egba, Johnson asserted, the Ijebu were kidnappers and slavers who preyed on innocent commerce passing through their territory from the north to the coast. The least of their vices was a galling conceit with which they patronized other Yoruba, particularly the Oyo. In commercial transactions they were invariably dishonest, backing up their bare-faced frauds with threats and assault for the victim who deigned to protest. Worse still, continued Johnson, they were highwaymen and extortionists, and frequently found sadistic amusement in flogging travellers at their toll gates. Unlike other Yoruba they would show no respect for age or station, and their treatment of Oyo women involved kidnapping and false arrest with the usual unpleasant results. The Ijebu repeatedly interfered with Johnson's journeys as peace emissary, and their last bid of defiance to the British in 1892 was a needless extension of hostilities which were finally ended to the intense relief of the whole country. The only qualification of Ijebu intransigence which Johnson would allow—and it was an important exception—was his admission that their unwillingness to open the roads leading to Lagos was in part motivated by a desire to prevent the country from being taken over by the Europeans.[2]

[1] *Ibid.*, 344, 354, 363, 485, 650.   [2] *Ibid.*, 570-1, 611-12.

Countryman from the interior that he was, Johnson was unimpressed by the westernized Africans of Lagos. He found them ill informed about conditions in Yorubaland, and he was consequently scornful of their repeated and clumsy efforts to influence the policies of the inland tribes:

The interior ... was so little known that the people living at ease and security at Lagos had no idea of those arduous circumstances of life that moved men resolute and brave to protect their interests by the sinews of their own right arms. Probably there were not half a dozen men in all Lagos, certainly not among the 'influential' personages—so-called—who knew the exact state of things prevailing in the interior, or we would have heard less of the 'influence' which the ex-king of Lagos or the Awujale of Ijebu Ode was able to exert with the heros of a Homeric struggle, incapable as they were to intervene with a force or to guarantee safety for an hour; nor was it apparent by what means they could sheath the sword of men who meant business.[1]

It was towards the English in Lagos that Johnson directed his warmest appreciation, an attitude which reflected in part the British-trained clergyman, but more particularly the patriotic Yoruba searching for an agent of peace. In speaking of the entry of the missionaries into Abeokuta in 1842 and 1843, Johnson mentioned the ancient tradition in the land that ruin and desolation would spread from the interior to the coast, and that the forces of light and restoration would one day enter the country from the coast inwards. Was not the arrival of the missionaries the beginning of prophecy's fulfilment, he asked. Later, when the first real progress towards peace was made, he noted that it was the British who took the initiative. Their efforts at first may have missed success due to inexperience and lack of a forceful policy, but with the arrival of the vigorous Governor Carter, the task was brought to a speedy and successful conclusion. The 'refractory and irreconcilable Ijebus' were quickly subdued, the Egba brought into line, and the interior settled during Carter's journey through Yorubaland in the early months of 1893. 'The Governor's mission to the interior was a complete success from every point of view,' exclaimed the exultant Johnson, 'and he deserved all the ovation given him with one accord by the Colony. He had a right royal progress through the town ... the mass of the crowd was like a moving sea of humanity shouting welcome at the top of their voices.'[2]

In Johnson's estimate Carter's success was as much a personal triumph for the governor as a success of British diplomacy. Not only

[1] *Ibid.*, 482–3.   [2] *Ibid.*, 296, 584–6, 613, 626, 633.

did Carter bring final peace and institute the programme of roads, railroads and other internal improvements which so greatly stimulated the economy of the country, but he exercised an unfailing tact and politeness that more than won over the people to acquiescence in British rule:

> Two traits in Governor Carter impressed the chiefs and people . . . One was the unfailing deference usually paid to native rulers, and the non-encroachment upon their rights. The result of this was the almost entire absence of bullying and belittling by subordinate officers which generally brought about disorganization of Native Governments, and other evils consequent thereupon. The other was the Governor's intuitive and almost unerring judgment of character and his sense of justice. The country was prosperous in those days.[1]

For Johnson, then, peace and progress came to be associated finally with British rule:

> With the establishment of the British Protectorate a new era dawned upon the country. . . . When we have allowed for all the difficulties of a transition stage, the disadvantages that must of necessity arise by the application of rules and ideas of a highly civilized people to one of another race, degree of civilization, and of different ideas, we should hope the net result will be a distinct gain to the country. But that peace should reign universally, with prosperity and advancement, and that the disjointed units should all be once more welded into one . . . that clannish spirit disappear, and . . . that Christianity should be the principal religion in the land . . . should be the wish and prayer of every true son of Yoruba.[2]

5 Forerunners of Modern African Historiography

These early African historians broke new ground with their work; yet, despite their innovations—their emphasis on an Afro-centric view of history, and their use of oral tradition as a source for serious historical scholarship—they were essentially reflecting attitudes common to the African communities from which they had sprung. A. B. C. Sibthorpe's divorcing the tribal African from the inhabitant of the Freetown area was an expression of prevailing opinion in the Sierra Leone colony. As a thoroughly westernized African, Sibthorpe followed a way of life and formulated viewpoints much like those of his fellow citizens. The hope set forth in his *History* that his country might follow the lead of Christian, western civilization would have aroused little controversy among his readers whose education and background were much the same as his.

[1] *Ibid.*, 634-5. [2] *Ibid.*, 641-2.

For Sibthorpe a prime agent in shaping his philosophy and way of life was the religious education he received in the mission schools, a training which also had its effect on the two Christian ministers, C. C. Reindorf and Samuel Johnson. The histories of Johnson and Reindorf were less thoroughly committed to western thought and ways, however, perhaps because the people about whom they were writing had long possessed a virile culture and a clear sense of history. The Sierra Leoneans were authentic Africans but they were immigrants, not natives of the land; it was, after all, one of Sibthorpe's stated purposes to help shape a Sierra Leonean nationality. But Yoruba traditions were long-lived and the Yoruba way of life had its own integrity, while the nations of the Gold Coast exhibited a similar brand of military, political and cultural toughness. With Johnson and Reindorf, therefore, the emphasis was placed on absorbing the best of European civilization while still preserving ancient and honourable African traditions. Such a view had considerable currency among their contemporaries.

There were other similarities among these pioneer historians. As individuals they showed considerable variety in personality, interests and literary style – it would be difficult to find historical writing further apart than Sibthorpe's genially discursive style and Reindorf's heavy prose, or two personalities more unlike than the sprightly Sierra Leone schoolteacher and the quietly self-effacing Samuel Johnson. From the viewpoint of historical objectives and philosophy, however, these three were very much alike and, what is more, in this respect they anticipated to a remarkable degree those present-day students of Africa's new history. In their several ways, they were searching for a better future for their people, utilizing the reconstruction of a neglected and discounted past to lead to necessary reform through introduction of more effective institutions from other civilizations, or renascence of traditional African culture in its ancient glory and strength.

While there is no gainsaying the influence which European education and culture had in shaping the careers and the opinions of Sibthorpe, Johnson and Reindorf, it would be an error to underestimate the primary importance of Africa. Reindorf and Johnson were concerned with reviving the past of their people precisely in order to build permanently into the popular mentality a sense of pride in age-old accomplishment as the basis for a new African nationalism. Sibthorpe presented a clear picture of a society seaching for legitimacy as an authentic modern African state, and employed history to help secure that end. The use by Johnson and Reindorf of oral tradition and African mythology was a necessary and appropriate source of information about the African past, but it also was important in that it removed these essentially African historians from the main stream of nineteenth-century western historiography and established them as the founders of a new African school of historical scholarship. Finally, these Africans were determined to view their history as seen not by the outsider but by the African himself. In such ways did they anticipate Africa's historians of the mid-twentieth century who were also to be concerned with the idea of African identity and national progress based on the achievements of those who came before. For they well understood the truth of Gladstone's celebrated dictum, 'Unhappy are the people who cut themselves from their past.'

14 The Dilemma Resolved: Bishop James Johnson

1 *A Puritan of the Old School*

Bishop Samuel Crowther lived at a time when it was relatively simple to reconcile devotion to Christianity and the West with love of Africa and its people. To Crowther these were complementary concepts. Christian conversion, European education and a westernized economy would yield in a generation or two a core of African Christians led by native pastors who could carry on the work of evangelizing Africa, spreading literacy through a missionary school system, and raising the productivity of the land as a prelude to the emergence of modern Christian independent African nations. In his later years Crowther saw his dream of Africa's progress turn to a nightmare of frustration and disillusion, and his death came at a time of profound crisis over the question of religious independence. It was left to others, therefore, to attempt the difficult reconciliation of Christian humanitarianism with European colonial government, of African acceptance of western civilization with African desire for self-expression and cultural fulfilment.

The problem of effecting this reconciliation became the life work of James Johnson, Crowther's successor as the leader of Nigeria's Christian community and one of the most influential minds of his day in West Africa. Johnson's position in the development of African ideas is particularly interesting and important—first, because he flourished at a time when basic conflicts between Europe and Africa were commanding a fresh examination by the African of his relation with the West; second, because of Johnson's influential position in the African community; third, because Johnson himself was a complicated, difficult personality whose vigorous standards of individual behaviour and moral rectitude were often at war with concepts of Christian charity, and whose intense love of his European religion was poised in uneasy balance against his passionate devotion to the African race.

Like Crowther and like so many westernized Africans in Yorubaland during the late nineteenth century, Johnson was an Aku, a Yoruba transplant in Sierra Leone who later returned to his home country to live and work. While still a youth, Crowther had endured and survived the shattering experience of enslavement and repatriation at Freetown. Johnson's early years were much more placid and conventional. His parents may have been repatriated slaves, but Johnson was born in a quiet village outside Freetown some time between 1835 and 1840, and his boyhood years appear to have been uneventful. At the age of nine, however, he was converted to Christianity, and shortly after secured the conversion of his backsliding parents. This early display of religious zeal and missionary skill was followed by a successful period of schooling in the C.M.S. grammar school in Freetown. When, in 1855, he read Buxton's *Slave Trade and Its Remedy*, he knew he had found his calling. He promptly enrolled at Fourah Bay, and four years later was made catechist under the tutelage of a European missionary. In 1863 he was ordained a minister in the Anglican Church and assigned to a Freetown parish.[1]

Even at this early stage in his career, the picture of an unbending ascetic was already emerging – a Puritan of the old school whose love of God approached antipathy for mankind, a humourless intense man with a self-discipline that transformed physical forcefulness into religious zeal, and a devotion to religious formalism that tended to overlook the humanity of Christ. Holy Johnson, he was soon called by his contemporaries with the economy and accuracy of well-constructed epithet. His reports back to the C.M.S. in London at this time referred constantly to the godlessness of the Freetown community – the bad influence of the soldiers, the drunkenness, obscene language and lewdness in the streets, the immorality of the women whose downfall, he solemnly explained, was due to their devotion to colourful dress. Johnson's standards of female behaviour were touchingly naïve, born apparently of total inexperience. Shortly after his ordination, he sought to get married. What he wanted, he explained to Henry Venn in soliciting Venn's advice and assistance, was a sober pious girl who would not disgrace him and his church, an educated girl who would be qualified to hold female class meetings and visit the sick. For these somewhat

[1] *The Lagos Weekly Record*, May 26, 1917; *C.M. Intelligencer*, 1900, 249–50, 307.

unusual wifely qualifications, he explained, he had already located one candidate, but unfortunately the lady died in England, sent there by Johnson to train for missionary work. It is interesting to note that not until 1895, more than thirty years later, did Johnson finally marry.[1]

Such superheated views were bound to bring a perversion of Christian love. An early report condemning the usual signs of idolatry and frivolousness among the people of his district, ended on what Johnson evidently considered a more cheerful note:

Visited Susan Davies and found her covered with sores all over – a perfect skeleton – almost blind from ophthalmia, sitting literally in ashes in a dark room. But bad as was her condition, miserable as was her appearance, she enjoyed a happy communion with her Jesus ... and hoped soon to enter into the rest provided by him for her.... It certainly does afford a Christian visitor no little degree of pleasure and satisfaction in his round to meet up with distressed or dying persons who possess a practical knowledge of Jesus.[2]

There was, however, another side to the matter. Johnson worked hard with his people, visiting the sick, bringing help and comfort where he could, holding impromptu services in the streets, like Crowther preaching in Yoruba, and always trying to convert the uninitiated and to redeem backsliders. That this unceasing activity was appreciated by his congregation is reflected in the innumerable expressions of gratitude tendered him by souls thus saved. He was, moreover, an early champion of the nascent cultural nationalism which caught the imagination of the people of Freetown during the early 1870s, at which time he joined forces with Edward W. Blyden in a call for greater use of African customs, African traditions, African thought and African languages. Too long, he insisted, his countrymen had accepted the European judgment of the African as a member of an inferior race. Actually, African literature, art, history, social patterns and economic systems, like those of Europe, were shaped by geography and climate; being different did not necessarily make them inferior. It was time for the African to realize his worth and to achieve a spiritual independence that matched the end of physical slavery:

What is esteemed by one country polite, may be justly esteemed by another rude and barbarous ... God does not intend to have the races confounded, but that the Negro in Africa should be raised upon his

---

[1] Johnson to ?, Apr. 13, 1864, Johnson to the C.M.S. Committee, May 26, 1870, Johnson to Venn, Dec. 20, 1864, C.M.S. CA1/0123; *The Lagos Weekly Record*, Apr. 27, 1895.

[2] Johnson to Venn, Dec. 20, 1864, C.M.S. CA1/0123.

own idiosyncrasies. . . . we, as a people, think more of everything that is foreign, and less of that which is purely native; have lost our self-respect and our love for our own race, are become a sort of non-descript people . . . There is evidently a fetter upon our minds even when the body is free; mental weakness even where there is physical strength, and barrenness even where there appears fertility.[1]

Thus early were formed deep convictions regarding Africa's need both for Christian conversion and for African cultural self-expression, views which became increasingly difficult to put into consonance as British economic and political imperialism rubbed and chafed African sensibilities, bringing forth an ever more forceful assertion of Africanness. On the one hand, Johnson's rigid adherence to mid-Victorian morals and ethics gave rise to contempt on his part for many native customs in conflict with his rather bleak view of Jesus. However, though thoroughly committed to the Venn-Crowther version of the 'Bible and Plough', he found his progress blocked by British divines and British proconsuls and his people relegated to apparent subservience in perpetuity. Hence his militant demands for the assertion of African cultural freedom. Superficially this nationalist position resembled that of Blyden who doubtless influenced him, but much more than Blyden he was trapped by the logical dilemma of the westernized African poised between acceptance and rejection. Whether he was more influential with his contemporaries than Blyden is problematical, but in his own personal efforts to bring Africa and Europe together in his own mind, he may well have typified more than any other leader of his day the essential dilemma of his people.[2]

2 *The Struggle to Reconcile Africa and Europe*

Johnson left Sierra Leone in 1873 for Lagos and the Yoruba mission where he laboured in various capacities until 1900. In that year he accepted the commission of assistant bishop in charge of the Niger delta and Benin territories, remaining in that post until his death in 1917. During this long term of forty-four years he refined his philosophy of

[1] Johnson C.M.S. reports, Mar., 1865, Apr., 1868, C.M.S. CA1/0123; *The West African Reporter*, June 23, 1880; *The Lagos Training College and Industrial Institute, Correspondence between Edward W. Blyden, LL.D. and His Excellency Sir Gilbert T. Carter, K.C.M.G., Governor and Commander-in-Chief of Lagos and Its Protectorates.*

[2] The details of Johnson's career are set forth in E. A. Ayandele, 'An Assessment of James Johnson and his Place in Nigerian History (1874–1917)', Part I, *Journal of the Historical Society of Nigeria*, vol. II, no. 4, Dec., 1963, 486–516, and Part II, *ibid.*, vol. III, no. 1, Dec., 1964, 73–101.

a Christian Africa, developing the guide-lines necessary for leading his people to the better world he saw for them.

As a Christian missionary, Johnson's first duty was to gain converts and to save souls, and as a devoted mission worker he saw much need in West Africa for the blessings of Christian civilization. In Lagos where he served many years as pastor of St. Paul's Breadfruit Church and at Abeokuta where he spent a brief but stormy period in charge of the C.M.S. Yoruba mission, Johnson noted widespread evidence of the evils of heathenism and idolatry. Ignorance, superstition and disease were endemic and long-standing custom condoned, nay encouraged, slavery and polygamy. Warfare and political anarchy were the standard conditions in the interior, and to all this the European had added the baneful effects of gin and rum drinking which, '. . . unchecked, will work for Africa a far greater and more serious evil than the Trans-atlantic slave-trade with all its hellish horrors'. The people on the coast had degenerated furthest for, though heathens, they practised their religion but loosely and to a man of Johnson's psychology and moral standards, even heathenism was preferable to godlessness. In Lagos they lived in hot, airless, haphazardly constructed houses which were crowded and dirty, a constant source of fire and threat of serious epidemic. They subsisted on trade at which they were very skilled, but long association with slaving had made them calloused while exposure to gin had had its inevitable effect. In Johnson's view, their business transactions were based on a credit system which was an open invitation to crime.[1]

The situation up country was scarcely better. Abeokuta was a sprawling slovenly town lacking civic planning or minimum sanitation facilities, and without the necessary policing to put an end to chaos, overcrowding and the threat of disease. Ibadan was more of the same except that, war being the chief occupation of the city, the inadequacy of municipal sanitation was compounded by the water of the rivers polluted by dead bodies. Only when one came to the smaller villages could the missionary raise his hopes. Here the people welcomed the higher morality and educational advantages of the Christian visitor. Poor and oppressed they were and perhaps too preoccupied with pleasures of the flesh, but they also longed for a peaceful, quiet, secure life. Only the hostility of their chiefs held them back from embracing the missionary's message.[2]

[1] *C.M. Intelligencer*, 1875, 76; 1878, 552.
[2] *Ibid.*, 1878, 90, 168, 544-5.

No doubt the hard-working missionary slowly and painfully making converts was pressed for reasons why progress was so slow, and human frailty tended to place the blame not on the subject but on the object of missionary activity. To be sure, Johnson admitted, the Yoruba moral system taught religiousness, reverence for ancestors and authority, filial piety, chastity, truthfulness, honesty and kindness. But the Yoruba were also proud and vain, given to selfishness, vengefulness, anger and jealousy. These in turn had led to the slavery, polygamy and warfare which were ruining the country. Moreover, a tradition-bound society was static and reactionary:

> Respect for the authority of rulers assumes an obstructive form. . . . Wisdom swells only with the ancient and the aged . . . There is no inquiring disposition, no stir of thought. I question very much whether the present race of Yorubans can produce the nice, rich, and wholesome parables and proverbs, full of moral lessons for which the language is remarkable, and are at once its charm and its beauty. They indicate keenness of observation, quickness of mind, readiness to distinguish things that differ, and draw comparisons. Listlessness, impatience to listen, and devotedness to pleasure are common.

And, he added sourly, 'there is more drinking of native beer than is good.'[1]

There were, however, all manner of Yoruba and it was the Egba of Abeokuta whom Johnson, whose mother was an Ijebu, found most trying. Fund raising was especially difficult. The people were notoriously close-fisted 'except it be in things that promise them popularity'. They combined a grasping disposition with a natural reliance on others and an irresolution which eroded self-respect and discounted straightforwardness and plainness of speech. As with others, Johnson noted the inability of the Egba to submit to any kind of authority so that liberty quickly degenerated into licence. He found his missionary agents difficult to control, a situation which reflected not only natural contrariness but a faulty understanding of the dignity of their position and office. This insubordination sorely troubled Johnson:

> I am sensible of the responsibility I incur by accepting the appointment the Society has given me, the experimental character of such appointments at present and the important questions involved in it in regard to Negro capabilities . . . It is not at all true as some would represent it that Africans do not readily submit to authority exercised by their countrymen and that every Negro holding an authority may be expected

---

[1] James Johnson, *Yoruba Heathenism*, 51; *C.M. Intelligencer*, 1878, 92.

to make the position of his fellows uncomfortable, but much depends upon people's native character, education and other circumstances and the Egba mind is no admirer of subordination and order.[1]

There was another main source of difficulty – the returning immigrants from Sierra Leone. On the whole Johnson found the Christian community of Abeokuta quiet, neat and clean. Slavery and superstitious offerings appeared to be on the decline. Yet spiritual life was low and religion was a thing of Sunday ritual rather than daily practice. Part of the fault rested with the Sierra Leone men who with their education and background should have been a source of strength to the church. Instead, they more often used their European training to gain power among their heathen friends, lapsing into the use of household slaves and the practice of polygamous, idolatrous ways. Very likely it was these customs of the country which had lured these unprincipled men back to Yorubaland in the first place. 'Their influence has been great', Johnson mourned, 'and has borne much evil fruit.' The situation in Lagos was substantially the same. Backsliding was a constant problem, particularly with regard to adultery, and it was more often than not the educated long-standing Christians and the repatriates from Sierra Leone, rather than recent heathen converts, who were the chief offenders.[2]

When Johnson left Freetown, he came to Lagos to serve briefly as pastor of the Breadfruit Church, but he soon was posted to Abeokuta to try and regain control for the C.M.S. of its missions which had been lost at the time of the expulsion of the missionaries in 1867. Since that time local African clergy had carried on, but reports had it that there were moral and doctrinal lapses along with ineffective administrative and financial management. As an African, Johnson was perfectly free to stay in Abeokuta and, as a trusted African member of the C.M.S. missionary force, he was considered eminently qualified to pursue this work. Difficulties developed, however, which soon found Johnson under sharp attack. In the first place, the state of affairs in Abeokuta was such that there would be inevitable resistance to the type of administration he introduced. He was already well known for the rigid discipline he imposed on his parishioners, commanding rather than urging, instructing rather than suggesting. Such inflexible discipline was not likely to be well received in the individualistically-minded city of the Egba; moreover, they had already carried on for a decade without the

[1] Johnson to H. Wright, Aug. 2, Sept. 18, 1879, C.M.S. CA2/o56.
[2] *C.M. Intelligencer*, 1876, 53; 1877, 425–6; 1878, 546–8

interference of missionaries. Why should they be expected to welcome renewal of outside interference?[1]

It soon developed that they did not, least of all from Johnson. He had been instructed to tighten the financial administration of the parishes looking to eventual independence from C.M.S. support, and his vigorous action soon had contributions increased many fold, but this type of reform was secured only at the expense of a rising opposition among the parishioners. More than this, the old missionary bugbears of polygamy and domestic slavery were still being practised among the Christians, not only by the people themselves but by their clergy as well. Johnson counted thirty-five slaves and ten pawns held by three of the C.M.S. agents, and moved to eradicate the evil with his characteristic energy and determination. This was more than the Egba, Christian and heathen alike, could bear, and for a time Johnson lived under the threat of assassination. The C.M.S. authorities, alarmed over developments, first urged caution and tact, and finally recalled him to Lagos early in 1880, suggesting that his rigid leadership had failed to gain the necessary moral influence within the community.[2]

The recall was bitterly resented by Johnson who had worked tirelessly for the Christian betterment of this section of his people, and who had good extra-religious reasons for opposing his removal:

Why should the Society withdraw me from my position when with a little more help from it, it would have prevented another feather being added to the crown of those who are very fond of preaching up Negro incapacity for independent trust, a doctrine which the Society I believe stands pledged to disprove, and save Negroes anxious to prove this in themselves or see it proved in others for the good of native Christianity, the country and race, from disappointment and despondency?

What had he done to deserve such treatment? 'You emphasize the need of *love*,' he cried, 'that the want of it has occasioned me difficulties. . . . I have been very much misjudged.' He had worked for years giving comfort to the poor, the sick and the dying, sticking to his post, following orders, and always trying to help those in need. And now he was told he was void of love:

[1] J. O. Lucas, *Lecture on the History of St. Paul's Church, Breadfruit, Lagos*, 32–3.
[2] Johnson to Wright, Aug. 2, Sept. 18, 1879, Johnson to J. A. Maser, Jan. 28, 1880, C.M.S. CA2/o56; *The African Times*, Nov. 1, 1879, Jan. 1, Apr. 1, 1880. It has also been suggested that Johnson's recall was on more than the merits of the situation in Abeokuta, that he was an early victim of the shift in C.M.S. policy from using African clergy to placing Europeans in charge of the African stations. See Ajayi, *Christian Missions in Nigeria, 1841–1891*, 238, 260.

At the risk of losing my life, at the risk of being beheaded or shot down dead like a dog in the streets I faced the danger ... saving thereby the credit of native, of duty and the Society's work. ... but the only recompense I have received ... is a temporary forfeiture of my trust, disgrace and the loss of reputation.

There was some justice in his complaint, though characteristically he had managed to confuse love with courage and a sense of duty.[1]

Back at Lagos, Johnson resumed his old seat at Breadfruit Church where he remained for the next twenty years, not idly and contentedly, but vigorously pursuing the theme of African cultural integrity and development which he had voiced at various times in the past and which had contributed heavy overtones to his protests over his treatment at Abeokuta. A few years after his return he spoke out in his pastorate report, criticizing the essential foreignness of Christian religious practice in Africa and urging that the universality of Christ's teachings be projected through more essentially African rites and ceremonies. The pastorate was native in name but not in character, he explained. The sentiment and language of its services were foreign, from foreign teachers came the organization of the church, the prayers, the hymns of praise, and even the music which carried the hymns. Africa had long-developed religious experiences and rituals of its own. Was it not time that these were brought into use?

Native Christians breathe not yet those spontaneous native breathings which had marked their devotions in heathenism with the sounds of which the houses of worshippers, the sacred groves, the open fields, the hills and the valleys had very frequently resounded, which though idolatrous ... showed ... a firmness and vigour of faith not unworthy of man's religious nature, and which were the genuine conception of and spontaneous offspring from native hearts and had identified their religion with their existence and regarded it as their own invaluable possession.

And, as if to illustrate his contention, he began arbitrarily to baptize babies with African names, ignoring the wishes and protests of his congregation in his characteristically tactless fashion.[2]

An African form of Christianity was only part of a larger pattern of African assertion to counter the European culture which threatened to engulf and destroy native African civilization. This could manifest itself in a variety of ways, some of them superficial on the face, but no less important in what they did to the inner self. Johnson never tired of

[1] Johnson to Wright, Feb. 9, 1880, C.M.S. CA2/o56.
[2] *The Lagos Weekly Record*, Oct. 27–Nov. 3, 1917; Lucas, *op. cit.*, 26–8.

ridiculing the use of European dress and social custom, partly on the grounds that it was inappropriate, uncomfortable and unhealthy in the tropics, but also because it involved a basic loss of respect, both respect for self and respect from westerners:

> There is too much made by young men and young women of European forms of dress, of senselessly high and stiff collars, corsets and hats and boots and silk and other attractive dresses suitable or unsuitable to us in this our hot African climate . . . as if they confer any importance on us, and as if we would challenge respect from Europeans . . . the treatment which is meted out to us Africans . . . is very very far inferior to that which was usually accorded to us in former years . . . It reads . . . a clear despisal of us as a people and of our Race in spite of the English costumes with which it appears many of us would challenge respect from the white man.[1]

It was not a question of African inability to master European ways; there were many examples of westernized Africans, said Johnson, distinguished in their professions by western or any other standards. One needed only to point to the example of Bishop Crowther with his pioneering missionary work, to Blyden of worldwide reputation and to his Liberian countrymen, Alexander Crummell and Hilary Teague, whose inspiring teachings had done so much to raise the aspirations of Africans everywhere. There were Africanus Horton, scientist and patriot, Samuel Lewis of Freetown whose distinguished public service had led appropriately to knighthood, and James Quaker, Babington Macaulay and Captain James Davies who had done so much to further education in West Africa. Johnson might have added his own name to this list, as well as many others, but the point had been sufficiently made.[2]

Neither was it a question of denigrating European customs that they might not appear superior to things African. It was simply that they were often inappropriate to Africa and brought harm when adopted without discrimination. It went deeper than just the matter of hats and shoes and coats. Repeated contact of varying degrees of personal intimacy had grievously injured the African living on the coast of West Africa. And look what happened when foreign institutions were introduced into a purely African community–for example, the billeting of Negro soldiers in villages or towns that had no previous experience with standing armies, and knew nothing of adultery and illegitimacy. There was, moreover, good reason to suspect the wisdom of black-white

---

[1] *The Lagos Weekly Record*, Oct. 27–Nov. 3, 1917.
[2] James Johnson, *Address Delivered At Wesley Church, Olowogbowo, Lagos, 19th July 1903 in Honour of the Late Sir Samuel Lewis*, 5–6.

intermarriage. African life, customs, language, religion and philosophy had their own integrity. If the races were blurred, would not these values lose focus as well? Such a view came very close to Blyden's opinions regarding miscegenation, but there was one important distinction between the thinking of the two men. Both insisted on the basic role of religion in African life, but where Blyden thought of the term in its broader, lower-case definition, Johnson equated it universally but always in terms of Christian universality. 'Our only difference is this,' Blyden complained, 'he seems to identify Religion with European Theology.'[1]

The core of Johnson's position, however, was thoroughly consistent with the ideas of Blyden and some of the other African leaders of his day. It was essentially the argument later adopted by the exponents of the negritude philosophy of the mid-twentieth century. Said Johnson, the African in his struggle for self-improvement had reached out for the help of European civilization, but in the process he had sustained serious injury and perhaps in the long run had lost more than he had gained. He gained a measure of what was called civilization, but with this achievement he found that the man—the genuine man—had disappeared. 'The African is not there,' he said, 'and the European whom we think we imitate is not there.' What is left? 'Nothing.' Europe had grown great on its own customs, but imitating them did not necessarily make Africa great. Indeed African accomplishment could only be achieved by adhering to the ancient faiths of Africa, the old traditions, the proven customs, and the religious, ethical and moral codes tested time out of mind and found fully sufficient unto the need.[2]

Such a position suggested views as to the education of the African similar to those expressed by Blyden and other pronounced African cultural nationalists. Johnson's reasons were theoretical, designed to conform to this early expression of negritude—'We have for a long time now been contending . . . for a teaching and training that shall not destroy our Native African idiosyncrasies and that will not Europeanize us.' It had indeed been a long time. Over thirty years earlier he had said the same thing, adding, 'The injuring or destroying of such peculiarities is among the greatest calamities that can befall a nation.' But the reasons were also practical. Education for the African was better performed in Africa—it was cheaper and there were problems of health

---

[1] *The Lagos Weekly Record*, Aug. 4, 1900; E. W. Blyden, *African Life and Customs*, 64.
[2] *The Lagos Weekly Record*, May 2, 1896.

and cultural estrangement for those who went to Europe for their training and tarried too long. Curricula should be suitable to the needs of the country, and the establishment of schools in West Africa not only provided this education but also gave valuable experience to Africans in managing their own affairs. Schooling should be conducted, wherever possible, in the local language, not to satisfy cultural vanity, but because students would not then have to delay their advancement until English or some other foreign language had been sufficiently mastered. In Sierra Leone where the lingua franca was a pidgin English, Johnson insisted that this was an appropriate vehicle for instruction. In the Niger delta, he pointed out, one of the main reasons why education had proceeded so slowly was the misguided insistence of the local chiefs that instruction had to be given in English. As for Arabic, it should by all means be learned so that Islam might better be understood and combated.[1]

Here was the essential paradox. Johnson was at once wholly committed on the one hand to orthodox European Christianity and on the other to what was becoming orthodox African cultural nationalism. How was the contradiction to be reconciled, the dilemma resolved? For Johnson the solution was simple although there were few among his African followers who understood him thoroughly at the time. Quite clearly he viewed Christianity-orthodox European Christianity, including its Anglican version-as the only true and universal religion. As such it was just as African, just as Asian, just as American as it was European. There was no contradiction in Johnson's mind between Christianity and the assertion of the personality of the African as there was, for example, in the thinking of Edward Blyden. Christianity, introduced into Africa by Europe, was a great step forward, and Africa was grateful to Europe for this gift. The next step was for trained native clergy to get ahead with the great and good task of converting a whole race while those already enjoying the infinite blessings of Christian conversion prepared themselves for the independent management of their own religious affairs. First, financial responsibility and then self-government, he insisted. If an 'institution is maintained by certain individuals, control of its affairs should rest entirely on those who contribute towards its maintenance, and they should be able to call it their own and lavish upon it all the cares they can'. But-and here is where there was confusion in the minds of some of Johnson's contemporaries-

---

[1] Blyden, *African Life and Customs*, 63–4; *The Lagos Weekly Record*, Apr. 22, 1899; *The West African Reporter*, Jan. 23, 1880; *C.M. Intelligencer*, 1902, 126; Johnson to E. Hutchinson, Apr. 29, 1875, Mar. 6, 1876, C.M.S. CA2/056.

true independence was to come in communion with the mother church in England. It was an error, he said,

> to think that the aspiration of the church in West Africa is to cut herself loose altogether, under the influence of a restless impatience and perhaps dislike, from the church to which under God she owes her existence, which has expended much in life and money upon her and from whose greater Christian experience and other higher advantages she may yet gain much to promote in her a higher, larger and richer development.... I would respectfully ask all who are interested in the stability of the Christian church in ... West Africa generally to pray earnestly for and otherwise help to promote the reunion of the divided.[1]

That was in 1903, but long before that time doubts and misunderstandings had arisen within the African community, particularly in Lagos, as to both the future of European-related churches in Africa and the role of James Johnson in providing his people with the leadership they desired and needed in religious affairs. Johnson's unequivocal views concerning an African ethos had been well publicized for years, so that when in 1891 the crisis of Christian leadership came to a head, there were many who assumed that he was the natural person to take the lead in breaching the impasse and providing his people with the independent African church he had seemed to be advocating for many years. In the 1880s, as European economic and political interests in Africa increased, there was a corresponding change in missionary tactics from the Venn policy of African churches led and supported by Africans, to European-directed and -controlled churches. It was this shift that had brought on the harassment of Bishop Crowther's administration of the Niger missions and ended in his fall and the reorganization of the Niger Delta Pastorate as an independent church within the Anglican communion in 1892. But even before that event, a growing wave of dissatisfaction within Lagos had burst forth in the establishment of the Ebenezer Baptist Church in 1888, the first independent Ethiopian church in Nigeria, and then in 1891 in the even more significant first breakaway from the Anglican parish at Breadfruit. If the basic cause was the growing paternalism of the mother church in England, the immediate trigger was Blyden's celebrated appeal to the people of Lagos to establish an African church truly independent of European connections. Johnson was instrumental in inviting Blyden to Lagos and had for many years responded enthusiastically to Blyden's ideas, but

---

[1] *The Lagos Weekly Record*, Oct. 27–Nov. 3, 1917; *The Lagos Standard*, Jan. 14, 1903.

although he agreed with much of what Blyden had to say on religious questions, he differed fundamentally on the issue of severing connection with the founding, parent church in England. Thus when part of the Breadfruit parish seceded in 1891 and formed the United Native African Church, Johnson stayed behind with the remainder of his parish.[1]

Again in 1901 an even larger group cut free from Breadfruit to found the African Bethel Church, and again Johnson held back. There were clearly those among the African Christian community of Lagos whose thinking had taken them well beyond Johnson's position. In commenting on the event, the *Weekly Record* stated their point of view admirably:

Religion . . . may be one thing for the European and another thing for the African . . . The deep religious earnestness of the African shows that he is not far removed from the desired relationship with God, while his life in contrast with his would-be teachers, exemplifies in its practice that spirit of love and human brotherhood which Christ taught . . . We regard the local movements to set up independent native Churches and obtain the full play of nationality in religion, as really a . . . movement towards a purified African 'Heathenism' through and by which God has been revealed . . . to the African and through which only the African on his part, is able to develop the spirit of God that is in him.[2]

Johnson knew, however, precisely what he was doing even though, as Henry Carr later remarked, he did not make his ideas explicit enough. Christianity and African integrity were in Johnson's view completely consistent, while 'divisions, separations and secessions do not make for strength . . . they rather promote and perpetuate weakness'. Yet one is drawn to the conclusion that there was more to the matter than this. Somewhere in Johnson's psychology was the inability or unwillingness to step out on his own. Like Crowther of a generation earlier, he was too closely tied emotionally to the C.M.S. and the Anglican communion in England to break clean. It was a subtle thing, for he was quite capable of standing up to the full majesty of the British imperial government when the occasion demanded. His spirited defence of the Ijebu in the legislative council against all the authority and prestige of Governor Carter was proof enough of that. Where the Church was concerned, however, he always adhered in the end. At the C.M.S. centenary celebrations in 1899, he gave eloquent expression to this essential submission:

I bring with me . . . the greetings of children to their parent . . . The

[1] J. F. A. Ajayi, *op. cit.*, 254, 267–8; Blyden, *The Return of the Exiles and the West African Church*.
[2] *The Lagos Weekly Record*, Feb. 22, 1902.

Church Missionary Society has vindicated the claim . . . of the Negro to the brotherhood of humanity. . . . The Church Missionary Society has . . . proved that the Negro is not the ape and the brute that he was thought to have been, but that . . . he can hold his own with almost any other person in the world. . . . We . . . desire to be upheld by you. And . . . we desire that whilst you exercise paternal interest . . . and parental care . . . you will so arrange affairs here for us that we may acquire a stronger sense of responsibility . . . that the whole body of Native Christians may realize the Church to be their own . . . this Church supporting itself, this Church expanding itself, this Church governing itself, this Church looking to you, as to a parent, for counsel and advice, this Church enfolded by you in your bosom.[1]

Thus towards the end of his career, Johnson was drifting away from the main stream of nationalist thinking in West Africa but at the same time he was moving towards a reconciliation between Europe and Africa which for him at least was consistent and satisfactory. In 1891 and 1901 he turned his back on the breakaway movement and remained with the Anglican communion. Yet when the C.M.S. sought to reorganize the Anglican church in West Africa and asked Johnson to serve under a European bishop of Western Equatorial Africa as assistant bishop in charge of the Niger Territories Mission, he declined the offer repeatedly because, 'I did not think that that was what the Native Church needed.' He viewed the move as a retrogressive step after the administration of Bishop Crowther, and was reported to have refused the proposal with characteristic bluntness – 'Assistant Bishop to whom?' he wanted to know.[2]

But this did not end the matter. During the 1890s, the Delta Pastorate Church resumed its relations with the C.M.S. and requested that James Johnson be named bishop to head its affairs. In 1900 Johnson accepted the post of assistant bishop which he had initially refused twice, 'with the understanding . . . that I would be at liberty after consecration to seek to promote the independence of the position and office'. What this meant was that he was free to labour for financial independence leading to self-government for his diocese within the Anglican communion. It also meant that his would be one of several West African bishoprics under African leadership and similarly independent and self-supporting. All would be united in one great West African church, an independent African episcopate guided by Africans in communion with the Church

---

[1] Lucas, *op. cit.*, 28–9; *The Lagos Standard*, Jan. 14, 1903; *The Lagos Weekly Record*, Dec. 5, 1891, Oct. 15, 1892, July 1, 1893; *C.M. Intelligencer*, 1899, 425–7. See also E. A. Ayandale, *op. cit.*, *Journal of the Historical Society of Nigeria*, vol. III, no. 1, Dec., 1964, 95.
[2] Lucas, *op. cit.*, 26–8; *The Lagos Weekly Record*, Dec. 1–15, 1917.

of England. His last years were devoted to this task and he was hard at work raising funds for his African Bishoprics Endowment Fund when he died.[1]

In this way Johnson saw Christianity and African civilization brought closer together. Africa needed Christianity in its pure form and so the African church had to remain within the orthodox communion. Yet, if there was to be a true concord, there had to be reciprocity and so universal Christianity was obliged to prove its flexibility and accommodate itself to varying local conditions. In his later years, therefore, Johnson began to propound virtual heresy, particularly on the delicate subject of polygamy. Throughout his career he had been one of the strongest voices among the African clergy in condemning polygamy. It was wrong, he said, because polygamy contravened divine law. 'If polygamy is immoral in Europe, it is immoral in Asia and Africa also . . .'

It is admitted on all hands that polygamy is a serious hindrance to the growth of population; that it enervates the man, makes him a slave to his passions, robs him too often of mental vigour, debases and brutalizes him, and degrades and humiliates woman. It is known to be a prolific source of family feuds . . . Is not polygamy then a physical and a moral evil?[2]

These remarks were made in 1894 but many years earlier Johnson had raised with understanding sensitivity the question of how the church was to deal with heathen second wives of backsliding polygamous Christians. They were adulterous only in a technical sense and were following deep-seated customs in a society where all women were given the opportunity to marry and bear children. Was it right to refuse them baptism when they earnestly desired to be brought into the church? By the time of the C.M.S. centenary in 1899, he was beginning to have serious doubts over the practicality of a rigid enforcement of monogamy:

We go amongst the Heathen. We preach to them the Gospel. They are touched. They see the evil and folly of Heathenism, but they think that the Christian life is too high for them. They think monogamy is too high for them. They will not break up their families because they wish to be Christians. They say that they know that Christianity is a superior religion to Mohammedanism; they see it, but the demand made upon them is too high, and for that reason they make this compromise: they go to Mohammedanism.

From that point he was said to have begun to distinguish between people who were born Christian and heathen converts who already had

[1] *Ibid.*, Dec. 1–15, 1917, Jan. 5–26, 1918; *C.M. Intelligencer*, 1902, 790.
[2] *The Lagos Weekly Record*, Mar. 17, 1894.

families which could not be destroyed and scattered through the rigid application of a law ill designed to accommodate the realities of African society.[1]

Johnson's motives were probably less humanitarian than tactical, more concerned with the actual and potential loss of converts to Islam than with the personal problems of individual families. A few years later when he had pushed his position further in support of polygamy, his preoccupation appeared to be solely with missionary losses to a competing faith. In 1908, at the Pan-Anglican Congress in London, he delivered a paper entitled 'The Relation of Mission Work to Native Customs' in which he made careful distinction between those traditional customs which might be acceptable to Christianity and those which could not be tolerated. The latter included many barbarous practices which the missionaries had long struggled against in West Africa—human sacrifice, infanticide, ordeal by witchcraft and torture. But other customs, the employment of tattooing and tribal marking, for example, were harmless and did not violate Christian precepts. As for domestic slavery, so fiercely attacked by Johnson in Abeokuta thirty years earlier, it might best be left to the 'quiet ameliorative influence of the missionary's teaching' until, with the help of a friendly government, it could be removed. The giving of names, native dress, marriage ceremonies and even polygamy called for a 'treatment different from that which the Christian missionary has generally accorded to them'. Though ultimately 'the aim of Christianity ... is to re-establish everywhere the original form, Monogamy', there was the immediate necessity of considering the possibility of admitting polygamous heathen inquirers into the church because, by denying them, the church was pushing them all to Islam. In his later years, therefore, Johnson not only wished to bring Africa to Europe by maintaining the Anglican connection but he also hoped to Africanize Christianity by liberalizing the church's position on polygamy, one of the major issues which was to contribute to the rise of independent churches in Africa.[2]

A curious man. Rigid and unyielding to a fault, this fierce old Puritan hardly seemed a good choice for bringing divergent European and African ideas into confluence. Yet this is what he accomplished, and with greater success than any other of his time. There were many contemporaries who did not accept his position, but few who did not

---

[1] Johnson to H. Wright, Nov. 12, 1877, C.M.S. CA2/o56; *The Lagos Weekly Record*, Feb. 2–9, 1918; *C.M. Intelligencer*, 1899, 427.

[2] *The Nigerian Pioneer*, Aug. 3, 1917; *The Lagos Weekly Record*, Aug. 7, 21 1909.

respect it and in the end come to welcome him as the great patriot he was:

His love for the Christian religion and the Anglican Church was intense, but so deep also was his love for his race and so intense his religion that all natives of West Africa from the Gambia to Nigeria, whatever their religious persuasion, regarded him as their type of a great, patriotic and Christian African.[1]

[1] *The Lagos Standard*, May 23, 1917.

15 Sierra Leone: The Twilight of the Creoles

1 *'Whither are We Drifting?'*

The Sierra Leone experiment had begun on a note of high idealism and great expectations – a sanctuary for freed slaves, a new home for the dispossessed, a noble effort in Christian humanitarianism, and then a base from which a whole continent might be regenerated. Yet almost from the first there had been a concurrent note of doubt and a sense of ultimate failure. In the early days, it had arisen in the gap between the idealism of men like Granville Sharp and John Clarkson and the practicalities of planting a community on the West African coast consisting of individuals totally unprepared by any education or experience for achieving success. In retrospect, it was no wonder that achievement fell short of expectation; rather the wonder was that the experiment worked as well as it did. Nevertheless, at the time, there was always implicit in the activities and pronouncements of a hardheaded and exacting administrator like Zachary Macaulay the conviction that the settlers were thoroughly unqualified to govern themselves, and would remain so for a long time to come.

Even when the fortunes and the make-up of the colony changed during the first half of the nineteenth century, there continued this reluctance on the part of a paternalistic government to permit genuine self-expression and self-control in government by the people of Sierra Leone. If the measure of political and social maturity was mastery of western culture and a show of independence and energy, then the liberated Africans of mid-century Freetown might have felt they had come a considerable way in proving their fitness for self-government. Had they not revived the sagging spirits of the colony no longer sustained by the original settlers? Were they not in a short generation building a sturdy Christian church in a substantial mercantile community? Did they not now export their christianized, westernized native clergy and merchants for the rehabilitation of the rest of West Africa? Would not the dream of the European philanthropists for African regeneration ultimately rest on the exertions of the people of Sierra Leone, the keystone to civilization in Africa?

The answer came in a growing chorus of European-expressed doubt. The cultural veneer was thin, it was said. Pagan rites kept breaking through recently and imperfectly acquired Christian practice. Furthermore, the establishment of the legislative council in 1863 had led to embarrassments, first in the unexpected appearance of a creole on the council, and then in the encouragement it gave to an unsavoury adventurer like William Rainy. As for the economy, stability continued to elude a people who would only trade, who would not apply themselves to the effort of creating substantial wealth through agricultural production.[1]

As the century moved to a conclusion, European reservations steadily mounted. The anthropological commentaries of Richard Burton and others appearing in the 1860s set a pattern alleging that the unreconstructed African of the interior possessed a superior culture and more substantial moral and ethical standards than his urbanized cousin on the coast who had grown effete in the process of absorbing western ways. This view was adopted increasingly by colonial administrators who preferred dealing with a tribal African unencumbered by an understanding of the theory and practice of British constitutional government, rather than with the educated African who might be well versed in English law and capable of using it against unpopular or vagrant official policy. When the protectorate was established over the interior of Sierra Leone in 1896 and two years later there were uprisings against the hut tax imposed on the tribes, the governor, Frederic Cardew, placed the blame squarely on the people of Freetown who he was certain had encouraged rebellion through an irresponsible press and through the activities of creole traders up country. From that point forward, Cardew's policy precluded the appointment of creole officials so that, by the eve of the First World War, they had been substantially replaced by European officers within the senior colonial establishment.

Over the years, therefore, the European attitude towards the educated African had gradually stiffened, forming itself more or less along the lines expressed by A. B. Ellis, long a resident military commander in West Africa:

[1] J. D. Hargreaves, 'Colonial Office Opinions on the Constitution of 1863', *Sierra Leone Studies*, n.s., no. 5, Dec., 1955, 2-10.

THE TWILIGHT OF THE CREOLES [299]

The Sierra Leone negro is the most insufferably insolent and ostentatiously vain and arrogant of his species. It is natural that the negro should think himself of some consequence. He sees a large fleet kept up for the purpose of preventing his countrymen being carried away into slavery; he knows that the colony of Sierra Leone is maintained principally for the benefit of his liberated compatriots; he sees and mixes with shoals of missionaries, who are sent out for his spiritual welfare, and being besottedly ignorant, he imagines that since white men take so much trouble about him he must be a person of immense importance ... It is all very well for people in England to insist upon the coloured inhabitants of the colonies being treated as the equals of the Europeans ... they never have to mix with the negroes; they have not to endure their insufferable insolence, their ostentatious vanity, and their overpowering odour.... It is a very strange circumstance that no class of men who have lived among negroes, except missionaries, consider them the equals of Europeans.

There were a few exceptions, the argument ran on—people like Bishop Crowther, James Johnson and Samuel Lewis—but for the most part the educated Africans were of a low order, lower even than the tribal African. After all were they not a mongrel collection of petty traders, petty journalists, and doubtful pastors of religion, the offspring of slaves, as Sir Harry Johnston put it, 'descended from the sweepings of West Africa'?[1]

Much more surprising than a growing European prejudice towards the educated West African was a parallel lack of faith by the Freetown population in its own destiny. Beginning with the collapse of the Nova Scotian uprising in 1800, there were repeated demonstrations of self-doubt by word or action, in the long run surely more erosive to a sense of racial and community esteem than adverse European opinion. The police action which subdued the settlers from Nova Scotia was followed immediately by a manifestation of total emotional fatigue. Vigorous demands for land were suddenly replaced by a weary indifference to fate and the future and, in time, by an empty illusion of superiority over the liberated Africans who followed them into the colony. It was as though the Nova Scotians had sought out failure as an act of will, gathering some perverted pleasure in their self-destruction and the consequent scorn heaped upon them by the very receptives they themselves held in contempt.

The process did not end there, however. The liberated Africans in

---

[1] Christopher Fyfe, *A History of Sierra Leone*, 334-5, 579-80, 615-17; A. B. Ellis, *West African Sketches*, 149-50, 153-4; *Proceedings of the Royal Colonial Institute*, XX, 90-111.

their turn seemed incapable in their own eyes of building a society which would flourish and demonstrate to other Africans the magic formula for success. Why did not their community expand more rapidly? Why were wealth and culture so elusive? Why did each generation have to rebuild, for want of a firm foundation supplied by their forebears? Where were the goals, the aspirations? What fatal flaw was slowly forcing European opinion from cordiality to scorn? After one hundred years of effort the colony could show an economy precariously based on a petty commerce by individual merchants whose businesses died with them. Where was the imagination for major development through cultivation of local products and export on a scale to compare with Europe's best?

During the closing decades of the nineteenth century, the sense of malaise increased and gave rise to repeated expressions of concern. To some it was a deadly, destructive indolence, a chronic aversion to labour, particularly manual labour. 'If Africa is to raise her head,' they insisted, 'that desirable end must be brought about by Africa's sons, who must lay aside their vanity, and disembowel the hidden riches of Africa's soil.' Others were less certain, more speculative. 'Whither are we drifting?' they asked:

We have contemplated the future of a Settlement planted originally with the most philanthropic object, with a programme based on the liberal principle of training its inhabitants to manage their own affairs and for the spread of civilization and Christianity to the dark places around. We have seen the programme followed in its entirety to a certain period with every promise of success. Then we have observed a change ... the picture has become blurred ... the aspirations of its inhabitants treated with contempt, and ... a too perceptible evidence of the want of that cordial feeling of united effort ... between the rulers and the ruled ... we have discovered ... an aggregate of units, called a community thoroughly dissatisfied and discontented ... crushed, pursuing a nameless something which leads to no permanent improvement.

Still others searched for the truth in the depths of African character, positing a genetic flaw which robbed men of their virility and cut leaders off in their prime. When in 1882 William Grant died suddenly at the age of fifty-one, followed within a few months by James Quaker at fifty-three, Grant's *West African Reporter* asked what caused this attrition by premature death. 'Is it possible that an excessive effeminacy, and unlimited sensual indulgence may tend to shorten life? Is it also possible that fast living among the liberated African descendants may aid in producing this early mortality?'[1]

If Europeans were becoming contemptuously certain of African inferiority while troubled creoles searched for explanations rather than questioning European assumptions, Edward W. Blyden saw no difficulty in reconciling the European indictment with a promise of African achievement, though only at the expense of the creoles themselves. The trouble, said Blyden characteristically, lay in the African's unquestioning acceptance of European cultural values and institutions. By embracing western cultural standards and allowing himself to be educated along western lines while he cut himself off genetically and psychically from the well-springs of his own culture, the Freetown creole had unwittingly allowed himself to be transformed into a caricature Englishman. To Blyden, this was nothing less than racial suicide, and fully deserved at that. When Samuel Lewis died in 1903, Blyden was among the many who expressed their genuine admiration both for Lewis as a man and as a powerful influence for good in West Africa. Yet Blyden could not avoid the opportunity presented to enunciate once again his principle of creole degeneracy:

I cannot close this utterly inadequate tribute to a great African personality without referring to a sad lesson suggested by the comparatively early physical decadence and death of Sir Samuel, viz., the incompatibility of the current European civilization with the best and most enduring interests of the natives of Africa. . . . There is no sign which emphasizes this serious fact more than the rapidity with which the leading educated natives are passing away, in many cases quite young and in others before or just as middle life has been attained.[2]

The fallacy in the analyses of Blyden and the European critics of Sierra Leone lay, not in conjuring up a non-existent problem, but in making assumptions as to the problem's cause which conformed to preconceptions more snugly than to the evidence before their eyes. It was clear enough by the opening of the twentieth century that the colony of Sierra Leone was failing to fulfil the role of pacesetter in African rehabilitation which the humanitarians had earmarked for her. What was not so clear was that this failure was due to any innate inferiority of the African character, or that creole association with

---

[1] *The Independent*, May 13, 1875; *The Sierra Leone Weekly News*, Apr. 28, 1888; *The West African Reporter*, May 7, 1881, June 3, 1882.
[2] H. S. Wilson, 'The Changing Image of the Sierra Leone Colony in the Works of E. W. Blyden', *Sierra Leone Studies*, n.s., no. 11, Dec., 1958, 136–48; *The Lagos Standard*, Aug. 12, 1903.

European culture had somehow led to fatal mental and physical weaknesses. On the face of it, the argument of longevity collapsed beneath the evidence of long-lived creoles. If William Grant or even Lewis were dead before their time, George Nicol lived to be over eighty and G. J. Macaulay just missed that figure. Blyden himself, a splendid practising sample of the europeanized African he criticized so severely, died in his eightieth year and was fully active up until a few years before. As for virility of thought and action, there were those among the citizens of Sierra Leone who, if prematurely dead, had managed to pack their short lives with creative achievement. Certainly Lewis was one of these, as was William Grant. So too was Ernest Parkes who helped the administration fashion British policy towards the tribes of the hinterland at the time that the protectorate was established. Again, there was the example of George Guerney Matthew Nicol, Reverend George Nicol's son, who had already evidenced a lively mind and a vigorous personality before death cut short his promising career.

2 *In Defence of Creoledom – G. G. M. Nicol*

The younger Nicol had taken his degree at Cambridge with a view towards a career in the ministry, presumably to follow in the family tradition of missionary service. Religiously inclined though he may have been, his brand of theology was more in consonance with the thinking of militant native clergy like James Johnson than with the conservative tradition exemplified by his father and by Bishop Crowther, his grandfather. Upon his university graduation he was offered a post by the C.M.S. but at a level inferior to that of the society's own protégés. To this Nicol was unwilling to agree, much to the distress of old Bishop Crowther. He finally became a minister in the native pastorate of Sierra Leone, but his health had long been frail and in 1888 he died, while still in his thirties and only a few years after his ordination.[1]

Before death overtook him, however, he was able to deliver himself of a few interesting observations regarding African civilization and the future of Sierra Leone. In 1881, while attending a meeting of the Royal Colonial Institute in London, Nicol was found mildly agreeing with the opinion expressed by another speaker to the effect that West Africa could not hope to exist without European supervision and guidance.

---

[1] G. G. M. Nicol to H. Wright, May 22, 1880, to E. Hutchinson, June 10, 1880, C.M.S. CA1/0164; G. Crowther to F. E. Wigram, May 6, 1882, C.M.S. G3A3/01; *C.M. Intelligencer*, 1888, 731.

THE TWILIGHT OF THE CREOLES [303]

'In that opinion I entirely concur', he remarked, but his words were not a simple acquiescence in the implication of African inferiority. 'Can you exist without communication with France, Germany, Austria, America, and other parts of the world?' he asked, continuing, 'You live by one another.' And so it was with all peoples.[1]

At the time he spoke, Nicol had recently completed a brief treatise on the future prospects of the Sierra Leone colony, the burden of which was to subdue the sneers of European critics while attempting to calm the rising doubts of his own countrymen. What was the matter with Sierra Leone? Nothing that a little show of courage could not conquer. Nothing that would not disappear as soon as the white man abandoned his unreasoning prejudice. In the first place, said Nicol, it was a slander to call the creoles descendants of slaves. Descendants of freemen they were, as were all God's people. Enslaved they had been, which reflected more on the captor than the captive. Eventual emancipation came, therefore, not as a gift but as a belated recognition of man's inalienable right to be free, the discharge of a moral obligation and the triumph of justice over oppression and wrong.

With freedom at last secure, what was next needed in Sierra Leone was respect, respect from others and respect from self. The European thinks we are already insufferably conceited, Nicol went on. Why? Because we refuse to be spat upon, and fail to fall to our knees and give thanks for gratuitous cuffs and a few friendly kicks. Our forefathers had suffered many indignities – their rights violated, their manhood trampled, their wills broken. As a result, the new generation was reasserting what had been crushed in their grandfathers. If this were insolence and pride, said Nicol, it came as a direct consequence of the oppression forebears had endured.

Nicol's arguments were designed to meet directly the defeatism manifested by some of his countrymen. He had no doubts about the steel in the African character, and the determination to succeed in the world of white men's standards. Let us not be cozened, Nicol urged, by European talk about the lazy African happily basking in the sun, worshipping his wooden fetishes, and idling his life away in ignorance. When Africans did not show to advantage, it was more than likely the result, not of faulty incentive or intelligence, but of inferior European instruction. Worse still, Nicol added, there had long been a lack of clearly formulated educational policy, leading to aimless drift. All this

[1] *Proceedings of the Royal Colonial Institute*, XIII, 92–4; *The West African Reporter*, Jan. 14, 1882.

could be banished by unifying education under government supervision and, more particularly, by making it clear that those Africans so educated could anticipate the exciting prospect of direct service to their country through their training just terminated. And, concluded Nicol, 'when the authorities ... wish to decide whether we are fit for this or that post, let not their [standard] be race or nationality ... A fairer test should be sought in *character and attainments*. If they do this ... it would give our education at once an object and aim. There would be a sudden bound and impetus from our present uncertain existence.' Sierra Leone would then go steadily forward, not in frustrated solitude but in fruitful collaboration with her British friends and helpers.[1]

3 *Samuel Lewis and Education for Citizenship in Freetown*

Nicol's observations had all the enthusiasm and idealism of youth. Doubtless they inspired their author, and perhaps others in Freetown were attracted by their expression of hope and confidence. Had he lived, Nicol might have had the opportunity to test them, and possibly to convert them into agents for the African renascence he sought. As it was, the attempt fell to others to make of Sierra Leone the centre and source of the new eurafrican culture of which the philanthropists had long dreamed. By far the most important of these was Samuel Lewis.

Lewis was naturally endowed with the necessary qualities. In an age when Europeans and most educated Africans assumed that mastery of European culture was the hallmark of the successful African, Samuel Lewis impressed both English and African observers. 'As English as the English themselves', pronounced the former, bestowing their highest praise. 'He had by his achievements ... challenged universal respect', proclaimed the African, enjoying the warmth of reflected esteem. '[He] contributed very largely to convince many and sceptical Europeans that ... the African and Negro would in spite of the depressing influences of centuries of ignorance and barbarism upon him, hold his own with the European.'[2]

Lewis made no self-conscious effort to cultivate western qualities in order to impress the European with the African's adaptability. He was by nature the sort of man who appealed to the Englishman of the

[1] G. G. M. Nicol, *An Essay on Sierra Leone*, 9–20.
[2] J. J. Crooks, *A History of the Colony of Sierra Leone*, 312; *The Lagos Standard*, July 15, 1903.

Victorian era. As a schoolboy he had been a careful, thorough, diligent student, regular and punctual in his habits, not brilliant but persevering. He was no rebel, possessed of too great respect for authority to question prevailing standards, and he was quite content to work out his life within the framework which had been established for it. When his father, a Freetown merchant, suggested that Samuel follow him in the family business, Lewis was content. When a change of parental plans decreed a career in law, again Lewis made no objection. Yet within the conventional range of his activities, he showed uncommon ability. His studies in London were marked by prizes and honours, and when he returned to establish himself in Freetown, he quickly built up a substantial practice which was a fair reflection of his own high competence. A devoted Wesleyan like his father, he was a man of great moral strength, incapable of deviating from what he felt was right, and unflinching in meeting the consequences of such a course of action. If there was a touch of the humourless and self-righteous in his make-up, it was the price that had to be paid for serious, sober application, and devotion to the high standards he had set for himself.

These standards, in addition to an unquestioning belief in Christianity as the truest medium for the shaping of universal values, included a faith in British constitutional procedures as the most refined basis for government yet devised by man. Government by law characterized all his public actions and pronouncements. Justice could be achieved if men held to principles of what was right, and disputed them only through the machinery of the law which had been devised as a necessary substitute for force and deceit. When Lewis made use of the law, he did so with the confidence that it would indeed serve justice. Thus he was able when the occasions arose to take cases in defence of European against African interests, standing unflinching in the face of public disapproval. Thus, too, he could vote in the Sierra Leone legislative council for the curtailment of constitutional privileges when he thought they were being abused by his countrymen.[1]

He was from time to time accused by the creoles of being indifferent to Africa and her people. This was not so. In 1888 while Lewis was in England, he one evening attended a meeting of the Royal Colonial Institute in London where he heard Harry Johnston, the main speaker, deliver himself of a characteristic discourse on the essential inferiority of the Negro race. Lewis was quick to answer, his dry precise manner

[1] *The Lagos Standard*, July 15, 1903; *The Sierra Leone Weekly News*, Aug. 22, 1903; J. D. Hargreaves, *A Life of Sir Samuel Lewis*, 6–13.

appropriately in tune with his straightforward rebuttal. Begging exception to Johnston's 'displays of moral philosophy', Lewis pointed out that the people of Sierra Leone, far from being the lower slave order suggested by Johnston, were in fact frequently descended from the leading members of communities caught up in the slave wars; many moreover were Yoruba, an intelligent, industrious trading people much like the English. What saddened Lewis mostly, he concluded, was not the slur itself, which was an old blow, but the fact that such irresponsible talk might create doubts in the minds of the many good people whose help was offered to Africa and greatly appreciated by her inhabitants.

Basically, however, Lewis was moved not by African nationalism but by inner principles, by logic and by the weight of evidence. Sometimes those went for the African; sometimes against. Truth was to be served first; after that he was full of concern for his country and the future of Africa. His official career–in the legislative council, as sometime public prosecutor or judge, and as mayor of Freetown–was chiefly designed to serve the advancement of the Sierra Leone community. When he was knighted in 1893, he regarded it not as a personal honour but as a possible source of useful instruction for his people, and took the occasion to urge public careers on his countrymen governed by conscience, not by expediency. On all his legal briefs he lavished the most painstaking care. When questioned over this apparently excessive labour, his answer was characteristic, 'My friend, those who entrust me with their cases often have to pay me for my services from very hard earnings, and from the sweat of their brows. It is nothing but right that I also should work hard for them in return, serve them well, and do all in my power to promote their interest in the causes they entrust me with.'[1]

In the final analysis, his standards were western–Christian faith, English law and Victorian ethics; hard work, and a sober life of service in combination with a reasonable amount of individual profit. This was the way to personal fulfilment and national progress. He knew and admired Blyden and wrote the introduction to *Christianity, Islam and the Negro Race*, stating therein his conviction that, though Africa would need foreign assistance for some time, it was up to the African himself in the long run to develop his own land and shape his own destiny.

---

[1] *Proceedings of the Royal Colonial Institute*, XX, 90–117; *The Sierra Leone Weekly News*, July 29, 1893; James Johnson, *Address . . . In Honour of the Late The Hon. Sir Samuel Lewis . . .*, 7–8.

As expected he took polite exception to Blyden's thesis that Islam might be the instrument of Africa's regeneration, but there can be no doubt, from all that he stood for, that Lewis could never have subscribed to Blyden's theories of racial exclusiveness and Africa's need to divorce herself as fully as possible from the debilitating effects of western civilization. On the contrary, Lewis, the thoroughly assimilated African, using his European education and his westernized standards, sought the development of his part of Africa through the very medium of European civilization which Blyden had called into question.[1]

When William Grant died early in 1882, Lewis was selected to fill the vacancy on the legislative council as unofficial member. He held this position until his death in 1903, and during this twenty-one-year period was able to test theories of community participation in the affairs of government based upon study both of the British constitution and the law in the colony. Lewis's approach to the problem was far more sophisticated than the inflexible, doctrinaire opposition to the administration which had been advocated by men like William Rainy. Realizing where the power lay and aware that more might be accomplished through co-operation and joint effort, Lewis evolved practical procedures which, under the limitations of the day, permitted a moderate degree of community influence on public policy and established a relationship from which a genuinely responsible representative government might have evolved. From his first appearance on the legislative council, he played a highly constructive role, which broke down only in the last years of his tenure when circumstances no longer made true co-operation possible.

Actually his first suggestions concerning the legislative council antedated his nomination by a few years. As an observer and occasional substitute in the council before 1882, Lewis had been struck by the slow turnover of unofficial members. Only a small handful had served over the years since the formation of the council in 1863, thus preventing the development of a growing circle of community leaders with some practical experience in the affairs of government. Better to have short terms, said Lewis, extending to a larger number, than virtual life terms for only a few. At the same time, the government might appropriately increase the use of qualified creoles in official administrative positions, in an effort to reduce the inevitable waste and inefficiency occasioned by long European leaves and by illness or death among the British civil servants. But Lewis was no democrat. He did not recommend election of unofficial council members by what he regarded as a small

[1] E. W. Blyden, *Christianity, Islam and the Negro Race*, xii–xiii.

untried community of voters. Let them better be appointed, but at the same time, let the council meet regularly, not merely on the pleasure of the governor.[1]

Lewis was well aware that the legislative council was an advisory, not a legislative, body; further, that the unofficial representatives were a small minority which could always be outvoted by the governor's official members. Nevertheless, he regarded himself as an integral part of the governmental establishment, assuming that his advice and judgment were being solicited on their merits and would be acted upon to the extent that they proved tenable. He prepared himself thoroughly for the business of each meeting and his legal training made him at home with the parliamentary procedure employed. Consequently the administration applauded his active, thoughtful role in debate, and was particularly grateful for his workaday premise that the government ought to be supported unless circumstances dictated otherwise. By no means did this mean that Lewis was a captive of official policy. His remarks before the council constantly referred to the need for proper information and adequate time for study of proposed legislation, which he then proceeded to subject to the closest clinical inspection, pointing out flaws and recommending improvements with regularity. He was frequently on record, moreover, as reserving the independence of his vote and his right to criticize official policy.[2]

If Lewis but rarely stood forth in open opposition to the administration and even more rarely succeeded in altering its proposals, his careful study of issues and his parliamentary and legal skills were factors in keeping the government, up to and including the Colonial Office in London, very much alive to the need for sound argument and substantial fact with which to support particular lines of action. When on one occasion an ill-advised press censorship law was attempted, Lewis successfully forced its withdrawal. At another time he severely embarrassed Governor Rowe by criticizing Rowe's native policy in the interior, not on the merits with which he was, as it happened, out of sympathy, but because Rowe had neglected to consult the legislative council beforehand, thus reducing the council to the position of having to ratify *ex post facto* a money bill introduced by the governor. To Lewis, this was a clear usurpation of the legislative function by the executive power.[3]

[1] S. Lewis, *A Few Suggestions on the Wants of Sierra Leone*, 9–12.
[2] Legislative Council, May 23, 1892, Apr. 25, 1893, C.O. 270/31, 33.
[3] Legislative Council, Feb. 15, 22, Mar. 1, Apr. 16, 1884, C.O. 270/28; Aug. 25, 1886, C.O. 270/30.

Lewis was no less demanding of his constituents. As unofficial representative he willingly presented all petitions whether or not he sympathized with them, but he reserved the right to speak and vote for himself. Though he agreed that it was necessary to expand unofficial representation on the council beyond the two members then appointed – if one were absent, an unofficial motion could not normally be seconded and discussed – he also urged more popular interest and participation in governmental affairs through greater use of the constitutional privileges available to the people. 'I would point out to you', he told a group of Freetown traders, 'that, as an unofficial member of the Legislative Council, I have little better than yourselves the opportunity for influencing the policy of the Government. What is required is, after full discussion by the inhabitants of the views of policy which they think is best to be followed, to constantly remind the Government of those views by the constitutional method of laying them before the Government by petitions.' In effect, this was what he was doing as a member of the council.[1]

Lewis's favourite school for self-government, however, was embodied in his plan for a municipal council in Freetown with full-fledged elections of a representative local assembly responsible for the discharge of civic functions such as sanitation, lighting, markets, street cleaning and a municipal water supply. From the time he joined the legislative council, Lewis had been urging that the city be incorporated as a municipality, complete with mayor and municipal council with the power not only to administer local affairs, but to levy the necessary rates to underwrite the expenses of its programme. Such a development would not only offer an apprenticeship in self-government, but would also generate a higher sense of public spirit, undernourished in the past by lack of opportunity. Ever cautious over the dangers of an undisciplined electorate, however, Lewis initially proposed that the council be divided between members elected and those appointed by the governor, and he provided for a complicated franchise system which would have effectively eliminated any possibility of democratic excesses. As he explained to Governor Havelock at the time, 'Whilst it is desirable . . . to make the privilege of suffrage practically universal, in order to give a general interest in the proceedings of the municipality, some such device is necessary . . . for limiting the evils likely to arise from the exercise of a democratic privilege by a people not having yet the

---

[1] *The Sierra Leone Weekly News*, Sept. 18, Oct. 2, 1886.

necessary information and intelligence to use that privilege with assurance of safety'.[1]

That was in 1882. Ten years later a municipal ordinance largely formulated by Lewis finally passed the legislative council, the delay having been occasioned principally by lack of public enthusiasm for a city government which meant not only the granting of new political rights but also the responsibility of municipal support through new local taxes. Nevertheless, Lewis's cautious optimism was not entirely misplaced. In 1895 elections were held and the first municipal council of Freetown came into being with Lewis chosen by the council members as the first mayor. Lewis, in the role of mayor, conducted the council meetings as though he were indeed directing a class in civic government. He quickly organized departments for sanitation, street lighting, licensing and other matters; he instructed the councillors, none of whom had ever had experience in municipal administration, in mundane matters such as bookkeeping; he dominated the council's deliberations, insisting that speeches be strictly limited to the questions under discussion; and he managed through strong will, clever purpose and parliamentary skill to direct the council to adopt the plans he felt were most fruitful. All in all he gave the impression that he was ruling rather than merely presiding over the affairs of the city. Withal, a working municipal establishment slowly emerged, but even Lewis's strong hand was unequal to the task of making the townspeople face up to the problem of revenue. After five years, the municipal council had still not succeeded in formulating a rating scheme which would provide the income necessary to operate the city government, and the governor was thinking seriously of intervening to settle the matter himself. This shortcoming was in no way a reflection on Lewis who, in fact, had repeatedly pointed out the need for a responsible financial policy to avoid the intervention of the colonial administration. It was, however, a disappointing anticlimax to plans for a self-sufficient municipality, and added its share to the burden of frustration which Lewis was obliged to bear during his last years.[2]

Throughout his public career, Lewis held spirited and influential views on a number of matters affecting public policy, and important

[1] *The West African Reporter*, Sept. 1, 1883; Legislative Council, Sept. 13, 1892, C.O. 270/31.
[2] *The Sierra Leone Weekly News*, Aug. 31, Sept. 7, 14, 1895, Nov. 21, 1896, June 26, 1897; F. Cardew to J. Chamberlain, Jan. 10, 1898, enclosing Second Annual Minute of the Mayor of the City, Nov., 1897, C.O. 267/437; Cardew to Chamberlain, Mar. 28, 1900, C.O. 267/452.

among these was the chronically delicate issue of trial by jury. It had had a long history in the colony, beginning with the days of the Sierra Leone Company, erupting again at mid-century in time to arouse the easily outraged William Rainy, and in the last decades of the century once more appearing as a fundamental dispute between the government and the Freetown citizenry. The essential argument was the ancient one of civil responsibility versus licence, of individual freedom versus arbitrary power, the balance between constitutional safeguards and the government's need to protect itself. Over the years the authorities had complained that Freetown juries were easily influenced in favour of creole interests, and it was on the strength of that presumption that jury trials in civil cases were abolished in 1866. The matter was much less clear with regard to criminal cases, but pressure continued intermittently for a further curtailment of the jury system as a necessary step towards more effective, equitable government.

This was a particularly difficult issue for Lewis. On the one hand his deep commitment to the principles of English jurisprudence argued strongly for jury trials, and so too did his constant search for means to educate his countrymen towards responsible self-government. On the other hand, there was the first-hand experience with creole juries in several important cases where Lewis felt the weight of evidence had been cynically ignored and gross injustice thus perpetrated. As a result Lewis vacillated, reflecting the circumstances at particular moments, now supporting the jury system, now opposing it. Basically he favoured the extension of English constitutional law to the British colonies, including such safeguards as trial by jury, the clear right of appeal to higher courts, and the separation of the judicial and executive arms. He successfully opposed the attempt to censor the press of Freetown, first by attacking the provision for curtailment of jury trial in libel cases, and then by getting the bill itself quashed. On another occasion, however, after he had lost cases resulting from the corrupt behaviour of local juries, he acquiesced in legislation limiting jury responsibility, even to the extent of helping draft the enabling ordinance. Finally, however, when the government introduced a bill virtually eliminating juries except for capital offences, Lewis at first supported this action but later voted against it as an excessive and needless infringement of constitutional rights.[1]

[1] Lewis, *A Few Suggestions of the Wants of Sierra Leone*, 12–14; Legislative Council, Feb. 15, 22, Mar. 1, Apr. 16, 1884, C.O. 270/28; July 26, Aug. 2, 1895, C.O. 270/33; June 11, 17, 1898, C.O. 270/36; *The Sierra Leone Weekly News*, Sept. 7, 1898.

This last change of face came at a time of deep disillusionment with the administration and this may have had some effect on Lewis's judgment at the moment. In any event, his equivocal position on the jury issue not only brought a good deal of public criticism upon his head, but probably weakened in the long run the struggle of West Africans to salvage political and constitutional safeguards, for it was at this time that British West African administrations were beginning a broad attack on African partnership in government. In the Gold Coast the steady erosion of the native power had resulted by 1900 in the substitution of total British authority for the older conception of association in government between the British and the indigenous chiefs. In Nigeria, the establishment of protectorates in the south and the north culminated in the authoritarian régime of Lugard who instituted his greatly resented provincial court system with its use of administrative personnel for judicial functions. In Sierra Leone, the establishment of a protectorate over the interior in 1896 was marked by a sharp decline in the partnership of the British and the creoles in government, a decline reflected in Lewis's own loss of influence in the formation of official policy.

The hopes which Lewis entertained for a broader, more popular government in Sierra Leone were paralleled by a carefully formulated programme for colonial development which he urged as the basis for official policy. This involved two main lines of argument, the first relating to the economic improvement of the colony, and the second concerned with political adjustments necessary to bring about economic betterment. The economy of Sierra Leone, Lewis pointed out, rested on trade between Britain and the interior country, with the Freetown creoles acting as middlemen. Though the development of industry was an ultimate prospect, it belonged to a distant future; hence a broader base of economic activity would have to be served through agriculture. It would not be easy to develop local agriculture, said Lewis, partly because of poor soil and primitive methods of cultivation, partly due to inadequate education of the local population, but principally because of the shortcomings of British policy in the interior. Lewis did not criticize the creoles for turning to commerce. Many had tried farming but it was too difficult to gain a living from barren land without the advantages of modern scientific agricultural methods. Education in the colony, moreover, largely restricted in the mission schools to basic literacy with large doses of theology, completely ignored practical training in the pursuit of life's necessities. Until some form of instruction were made available to the broad mass of the population in how to till the soil, Lewis saw no hope for effective diversification of the economy into agriculture.[1]

Lewis thought he saw a solution to the problem of agricultural education in the establishment of an experiment station where research in improved methods of cultivation could be combined with demonstration of these techniques, a search for new marketable crops and a service offering cheap, efficient machine-processing of the produce of small-scale farms. As much as anything, said Lewis, the Sierra Leone farmer had to emancipate himself from the short-handled hoe and the machete, and learn techniques of rotation, mulching, pruning, shading, harvesting and the proper employment of fertilizer. The importance of the appearance of crops in marketing had to be understood, with emphasis on such things as colour, uniform size and standardized quality. Lewis recommended annual agricultural exhibitions where prizes might be awarded for achievement in a variety of categories. Like William Grant, he did not stop short at giving advice, but instituted his own farm where for years he experimented with coffee, tropical fruit, rubber, kola and livestock.[2]

Thus Lewis perpetuated the nineteenth-century belief both in the potential wealth of African agriculture and the need for something besides commercial activity as a basis for national prosperity. Echoing the pronouncements which had begun in the days of Baron Roger in Senegal and of the anti-slavery philanthropists in Sierra Leone, Lewis argued for the promotion of a commercial agriculture the success of which was contradicted by his own farming experience and the possibility of which he reluctantly began to doubt only towards the end of his life. Lewis's contemporary, Louis Huchard of Senegal, was at the same moment urging large-scale French investment in public works and agricultural diversification in West Africa as a means for meeting increasing world competition and a falling world price-structure during the 1880s, but Lewis and most Sierra Leoneans saw the financial problems of the colony largely in local terms. The economics of agricultural development and the improvement of trade were basically governed by conditions in West Africa, he said. Indeed, for the creoles

[1] S. Lewis, *A Few Suggestions of the Wants of Sierra Leone*, 4–7; Lewis, *Sierra Leone Association*, 14; Chalmers Report (Parliamentary Papers, 1899, vol. LX), II, 140.
[2] J. D. Hargreaves, *A Life of Sir Samuel Lewis*, 26–28; *The West African Reporter*, Nov. 4, 1882; Lewis to F. Cardew, July 31, 1894 enclosed in F. Cardew to G. Ripon, Aug. 9, 1894, no. 230, C.O. 267/410; *The Sierra Leone Weekly News*, Aug. 25, 1894.

the future of the whole experiment begun in 1787 was fatefully bound up with Britain's policy towards the native tribes of the interior.[1]

If Lewis's analysis of the Sierra Leone economy was incomplete, his assessment of the administration's interior policy was prophetically accurate. Whatever the economic base, Lewis contended, whether it were agriculture, commerce, industry or some combination of these, there could be no hope for fulfilment of the Sierra Leone dream without a forceful policy by the British government in relation to the indigenous inland tribes. The argument had behind it the force of history and the exigencies of circumstance. Why had England singled out Sierra Leone in the first place, he asked, populated it with a people rescued from slavery, and encouraged the idea of a centre from which the African schooled in western Christian civilization could extend to the rest of Africa the beneficent influence of a new way of life? Surely not to abandon the experiment once started, a tiny, feeble coastal enclave, uncertain in its political and economic power, and limited in its influence. The logic of the venture assumed the establishment of a community of educated Africans firmly secured by an economy rooted in legitimate trade and in agriculture. For the latter, extensive land was needed, while the former required good interior communications and, above all, peace in the country. The government could not repatriate tens of thousands of liberated slaves as the basis for a new social and economic order in West Africa, without facing the consequent moral obligation of a police action in the hinterland.

On the one hand, continued Lewis, there were the primitive ignorant tribes preoccupied with their petty parochial wars; on the other was the expanding power of France, concerned with capturing West Africa for her own economic and political aggrandizement. Unless decisive action were taken, tribal unrest would continue to impede the development of legitimate commerce to the detriment of British manufacture, and slaving would continue to thrive to spite England's highest philanthropic objectives. More serious still, unless decisive action were taken, France would establish herself throughout the back country and Sierra Leone would be reduced to an unimportant coastal foothold, helpless in the face of French power and influence. Despite these obvious threats to British interests in Sierra Leone, England did nothing because it was contrary to prevailing colonial policy. Now and then she made feeble attempts to reconcile her unrealistic policy with circumstances through

[1] Chalmers Report, II, 133–5; *Le Réveil du Sénégal*, July 19, 26, 1885.

expediencies such as the futile interior peace missions of Governor Rowe. Such exercises were useless and undignified, Lewis insisted, and could never impose peace on 'semi-barbarous aggressors'.

What was needed, he continued, was nothing less than annexation of an extensive area surrounding Freetown and the establishment of direct rule through appointed administrators. Though this was challenged by some in the colony as the imposition of a 'rum and gin civilization' on the unfortunate native, most creoles supported Lewis's strong stand. Pacification and domestication, the opening up of the interior through roads and railways, the encouragement of local agriculture and crafts, and the end of slave raiding and the gradual elimination of domestic slavery would result from a strong policy which in the long run would be of the greatest benefit to the indigenous African himself. Even a protectorate was no answer. To Lewis it was insufficient and it was dishonest. 'When you trick a people out of their country... you implant ... elements of insubordination ... However it may be expedient to hold as a protectorate, a large, civilized but weak power against the encroachments of more powerful neighbours ... such a relation ... cannot safely be formed with small, petty, and barbarous people.'[1]

Lewis's analysis and recommendations were based neither on knowledge of native customary law nor on first-hand experience in the interior. Unlike John Mensah Sarbah, his legal expertness rested exclusively in British systems, and unlike his countryman, Ernest Parkes, he was almost completely untravelled in the back country. His position therefore grew from his westernized view of the imperial mission, and was similar in reasoning to that of those other creole expansionists, the mulattoes of Senegal, and of the people of Lagos, weary of the Yoruba warfare which had so long hampered their trading activities with the interior. Unfortunately for Lewis and for Sierra Leone, by the time official policy had begun to line up with the Lewis point of view, it was already too late. British foreign policy, always more responsive to domestic and European politics than to conditions in the colonies, permitted the extension of French interest in the vast interior surrounding the Sierra Leone foothold, and by 1890 French hegemony was fully recognized. Hence, the establishment of the protectorate of Sierra Leone in 1896 merely ratified international boundaries already agreed upon. Sierra Leone was thenceforward limited to her present

[1] *Proceedings of the Royal Colonial Society*, XX, 113–17; *Sierra Leone Association, op. cit.*, 1–11, 24–34, esp. 33–4; Lewis, *A Few Suggestions of the Wants of Sierra Leone*, 7–9; Legislative Council, May 21, 1885, Nov. 2, 1887, C.O. 270/28, 30; May 30, 1894, May 5, 1895, C.O. 270/33.

dimensions and the stage was set for the final development in the eclipse of the creoles and the personal frustration of Samuel Lewis.

In 1893 Lewis was knighted on the recommendation of Governor Cardew in recognition of the many contributions Lewis had made to Britain and to Africa. 'This is significant,' rejoiced the *Sierra Leone Weekly News*. 'It is only a beginning . . . of the days when Africa will take her proper place in the ranks of those who not only produce, but whose productions are recognized as bearing the stamp of genuine merit and therefore of helpfulness to humanity.' At the banquet celebrating the occasion, others echoed these sentiments:

> We meet . . . to congratulate Mr. Lewis but also to congratulate ourselves. His appointment allays the suspicion which sometimes haunted the native element . . . that the Native inhabitants of the West African Settlements are British subjects by only a sort of imperfect title, that we cannot enter fully into the rights and privileges of British subjects of English birth and origin. Now that the Queen has admitted Mr. Lewis to the ranks of those of her subjects whom it pleases her to honour, it should prove to us that we are within the circle, possessing all the possibilities of Colonial British Subjects; and that all that is left for us to do now is to show ourselves loyal, patriotic, industrious and active in promoting the National as well as our individual interests.[1]

In fact it was more an end than a beginning, for the colonial government was gradually becoming disenchanted by what it regarded as continuing creole immaturity and irresponsibility in economic and political affairs. Partly this feeling rested on creole mismanagement and dishonesty within the government. Partly it related to the old issue of incompetent juries. Partly it found justification in the faltering beginning of the Freetown Municipality. Lewis himself soon encountered the chill of official disapproval and was accused of obstructive tactics when he fought a growing tendency by the administration to bypass the legislative council as an active arm of government. More generally, however, the movement away from local participation in government was part of the ground-swell of scepticism by colonial powers over the possibility of effective African partnership. In Senegal it was manifest in a challenge to the principle of assimilation and an effort to deprive the people of the Four Communes of their political and civil rights. In the British West African possessions it led to the establishment of effectively autocratic colonial administrations, and where these developments were resisted by the educated elements in centres like Lagos, Cape Coast or Freetown, it resulted in their being largely segregated from sources of

[1] *The Sierra Leone Weekly News*, June 10, July 29, 1893.

THE TWILIGHT OF THE CREOLES

political power and accused of ill representing the needs and aspirations of their untutored countrymen. As the twentieth century opened, it seemed to be closing the future on African hopes.

With this general deterioration of circumstances, it was but a matter of time before Lewis, with his long and distinguished career and his delicate sense of constitutional proprieties, should encounter serious official censure. The immediate cause was trivial—a land dispute in the interior—but it led to a fatal break between Governor Cardew and Lewis. Lewis, as counsel for one of the parties, tried to bring the case to settlement before the courts. The governor felt his authority challenged and used his position to enact legislation calling for administrative disposal of the matter. Lewis was bitter. This was virtually *ex post facto* legislation, jammed through the council with unpardonable haste and without supporting evidence. What had happened to constitutional government?

The question . . . raised [is] the important one of whether or not within this Colony the Law of the Executive Government [is] to decide the legal rights of parties. Every legitimate means should . . . be adopted not only to expose the evil of such an assumption of power by the Government but to prevent its successful exercise.

If . . . the decision of the Government founded upon evidence which it regarded as satisfactory [is] obligatory on Members of the Legislative Council, and . . . they [are] thereupon to ratify the action of the Government blindly not only without evidence but on the refusal to furnish the evidence within the possession of the Government . . . not only [is] the doctrine highly unconstitutional, but it [is] one under which no unofficial member would consent to serve on the Council.

It is 'the virtual assertion of a principle which is both unconstitutional and subversive of political independence', Lewis complained in his protest to the Colonial Office. Later Lewis summed up what he regarded as the deterioration of political rights in Sierra Leone. It was not so much the solid block of an official majority; rather it was the haste with which bills were being introduced, allowing no adequate time for study either by the unofficial members or by the public. There was no satisfactory arrangement for the publication of bills, and legislative sponsors repeatedly appeared unwilling to explain and clarify points in response to unofficial questions. 'In my view,' Lewis concluded, 'the position of the unofficial members of the legislative council within the past few years is a mockery.'[1]

[1] Fyfe, *A History of Sierra Leone*, 540–2; Legislative Council, May 9, June 24, 1892, C.O. 270/36; F. Cardew to J. Chamberlain, June 10, 1896, enclosure, C.O. 267/425; Chalmers Report, II, 146–7.

Despite these deep differences, Lewis continued to support the administration according to his principle of constructive criticism. When the government instituted a hut tax in the protectorate, Lewis was solidly behind the measure, expressing his delight over the new close association between the colony and the hinterland, and the prospect that the people of the interior would soon be exposed to 'the blessings of Civilization that are enjoyed under British rule'. When the hut tax massacres broke out two years later in protest against this assessment, Lewis was devotedly on the side of law and order. He continued firmly in his conviction that the protectorate was a necessary and desirable development. The uprising in his view was due, not to some flaw in policy, but to the tactical error of failing to devote sufficient care in explaining to the indigenous chiefs the purpose of the tax, and by not inviting their co-operation in determining the best way in which it might be administered. By this time, however, the breach between Lewis and the authorities was irreparable, and indeed had been widened by Cardew's conviction that the creoles themselves had been the major cause for the uprising. With this conviction ended the last hope for continuing creole influence in governmental affairs, and when Samuel Lewis died a few years later, the final symbol of creole partnership died with him.[1]

4 Ernest Parkes Proposes a Protectorate for Sierra Leone

Creole leadership in the colony was experiencing a mixed success of another sort during these same years, in connection with the development of the government's policy towards the indigenous tribes of the interior. The leading creole figure in this instance was J. C. Ernest Parkes. Parkes had come into a position of importance in the aboriginal affairs administration at precisely the moment that the colonial government was being forced through circumstances to assume a much more active role in the interior. Consequently, he was able to exert immediate and unusually strong influence on interior policy undergoing important changes involving the Africans of the tribal areas, the creoles of Freetown and the governments of France and England.

As a young man, Parkes had joined the colonial civil service in a minor clerkship. Moving ahead rapidly through several posts, he was brought into the newly-created Aborigines Branch in 1885. He very quickly

---

[1] Legislative Council, Sept. 8, 1896, C.O. 270/36; Fyfe, *A History of Sierra Leone*, 576; Chalmers Report, II, 140–5; F. Cardew to J. Chamberlain, May 28, 1898, C.O. 267/438.

distinguished himself as an intelligent, thorough and knowledgeable officer–tactful in his relations with the chiefs, completely trustworthy and loyal to the government. When the official government interpreter and liaison with the indigenous chiefs retired in 1888, Governor Hay at once recommended Parkes as Secretary of the Aborigines Branch. As head of what later became known as the Department of Native Affairs, Parkes was charged with maintaining communications between the chiefs and the governor. He looked after chiefs when they visited Freetown, accompanied governors on their expeditions up country, and provided them upon request with information and advice on tribal affairs.[1]

Information and advice were precisely what was demanded of him by a series of colonial governors, hard-pressed by a difficult and constantly shifting situation in the country beyond the immediate area of British jurisdiction. A number of factors were at play. First of all, there were chronic outbreaks of violence among the tribes based upon both ancient enmities and a search for new trading opportunities, frequently with slaves as the major commodity. These petty wars sometimes resulted in loss of life and property among creoles or others presumed to be under British protection. Secondly, there was the formidable Samori, ranging over a wide area in the interior, knitting together his Mandinka empire, spreading the gospel of Islam by the classic method of the sword, and coming into sharp conflict with the French power pushing eastward from Senegal into the Sudan. Samori had early selected Freetown as a major source of arms supply so that the colony was in no immediate danger. Nevertheless the peoples of the back country were in a continual state of alarm over the potentiality of a raid by Samori and his Sofa warriors, and trade suffered as a result of this unrest. The third factor was the unwillingness of the British government to become more deeply involved in the affairs of the hinterland, especially if this were to mean the additional expenses of military activity. The dilemma of the colony's administration in Freetown was to keep the peace by pure powers of verbal persuasion and without the aid of a police force in an area where it admittedly had no jurisdiction.

What developed was a policy of extensive trekking by Governor Rowe and his successor, J. S. Hay, in which they attempted the impossible task of solving long-standing disputes and soothing the fears of suspicious chiefs, merely by means of their presence and what moral influence they could bring to bear. The result was that new outbreaks soon replaced

[1] Fyfe, *A History of Sierra Leone*, 479; Chalmers Report, II, 26, 36; J. Hay to H. Knutsford, Nov. 19, 1888, no. 373, C.O. 267/372.

old, or old ones burst forth afresh under the stimulus of some new incident. In some instances these disturbances developed into raids on coastal towns in the British area, and consequently demanded some sort of reprisal. In any event the totally unsettled condition of the interior seriously upset trade and called down creole criticism on the administration to the point that in 1887 the Colonial Office finally allowed a limited extension of British influence by instituting travelling peace commissioners and a modest police force. This step proving insufficient, Governor Hay drew up a plan the next year which was approved in London and became the beginning of a stronger policy.

This new plan, which was drafted with the help of Ernest Parkes, provided for construction of a road connecting the navigable heads of the several rivers flowing to the sea to mark the boundary of British interest up country. This frontier line was to be patrolled by a force of creole and native African police, but Parkes recommended that the police be charged with responsibilities beyond mere patrol work, that they take an active role in suppressing crime and in preventing the passage of slave caravans to the interior. Later he even urged that they be permitted to move into the area beyond the road in order to deal with disputes involving British subjects, to break up the slave trade, and to establish closer relations with Samori. Like Samuel Lewis and so many creoles, Parkes saw the colony's economic future in terms of a peaceful interior, and to one like himself who knew the region from full first-hand observation, physical force was the only means by which peace could be effected. The results, however, would be worth the effort:

> With men of tact and discretion their influence would be incalculable in assisting the Chiefs in their difficulties by their advice, as well as influencing the people, as far as practicable, to cultivate their lands. The advantages of this scheme would also be that we would be in a measure giving the people from whom the produce comes, and our revenue is really derived, the protection to which they are entitled, and we would be taking up 'the burden we have shirked ... of keeping peace within that area which produces the revenue'.

To Parkes, the way to encourage trade and civilization was to surround the colony with tribes fully amenable to British influence.[1]

Parkes's views were typical of progressive creole thinking in the late nineteenth century. Having studied in England, he was thoroughly westernized, but his ideas had a practical ring to them, the product of a

[1] Fyfe, *A History of Sierra Leone*, 448–80; J. Hay to H. Knutsford, Nov. 7, 1888, C.O. 267/372; J. D. Hargreaves, 'The Evolution of the Native Affairs Department', *Sierra Leone Studies*, n.s., no. 3, Dec., 1954, 179.

THE TWILIGHT OF THE CREOLES

man who eschewed theorizing for experience. He had no doubt about the advantages of European education. For example, he joined Lewis and others who scoffed at the idea of pidgin English as 'the budding promise of a great language'; yet he was just as quick to criticize too literary an education for Sierra Leone, there being far too many in the colony, he felt, who could flourish the pen but were unable to drive the plough.

If in his early days Parkes advocated a strong frontier policy, he was objective enough to see the limitations of Sierra Leone–75,000 creoles of modest education and attainments backed up by one million tribal Africans living in a state of barbarism. All groups needed much help, and the tribal African particularly had to be assisted with crop production, for a poor country lacking natural resources would have to fall back on farming for its livelihood. Like so many other West Africans–for example, Blyden, William Grant, Abbé Boilat and Paul Holle–Parkes recommended the importation of skilled farmers from the Americas to establish a model plantation and perhaps to remain permanently, tempted by special land grants. Native Africans, employed at the plantation, would eventually return to their villages having absorbed new techniques of cultivation which Parkes hoped might become the technological base on which a series of agricultural communities would grow up in the hinterland.

Economics aside, Parkes never wavered in his belief that morally and ethically the indigenous African would be saved, not by Islam, but by Christ. It was Christianity which had planted all the consequential settlements in West Africa. It was Christianity which had abolished the curse of the slave trade. Where race prejudice existed within Christian communities, it did so as a disease spread by a despicable minority consumed with an abominable conceit and senseless pride. But true Christianity did not contain this evil. Still not yet widely known, it would one day root out all prejudice:

A time will no doubt come when its principles will be ... more generally followed and it should be the endeavour of the Negro to strain every nerve to rise higher and higher in moral and intellectual culture, those irresistible levers in the rate of progress, that must in time cause all prejudices to die out in one common Christian Brotherhood bent on the advancement of man. By this he may aid in the advancement of his race but not by advising the adoption of the religion of Islam or the following of its pernicious teachings.[1]

[1] *The Sierra Leone Church Times*, Aug. 20, 1884; *The West African Reporter*, June 28, 1884; *The Sierra Leone Weekly News*, Aug. 8, 1896.

Though Parkes initially recommended strong police action, he gradually began to change his position for several reasons. In the first place, he had become disenchanted both with the leadership and with the rank and file excesses of the frontier police. It was being urged by an overenthusiastic command that the Frontiers be used in a campaign of mass manumission which, in Parkes's eyes, would have raised far more problems than it settled. The tribal society and economy would be badly upset by the freeing of domestic slaves mistaken for slaves in transport to the Sudan markets, and the resultant glut of free labour in the colony would certainly lead to grave economic dislocation on the coast. He was not defending the institution of slavery, Parkes protested to his superiors, but household slavery was a thoroughly different matter from the intertribal slave trade. Based on ancient traditions of mutual privileges and obligations, it could only be ended gradually. 'The state of a so-called domestic slave is far better than that of a day labourer in Freetown', Parkes continued. 'He is housed and fed and clothed by his master for whom he works but 5 days a week the remaining two days he works for himself and his farm is always in better condition than his master's.' Furthermore, Parkes was certain that the chiefs could be trusted not to pass off caravan slaves as households. In all his experience he had never encountered this type of deception.[1]

Respect for the chiefs and their institutions and nervousness over the misdirected humanitarianism of the frontier police command were joined in Parkes's mind by growing doubts about the Frontiers themselves. Requiring discipline and direction, they were, through an insufficiency of officers, left largely to themselves to roam over a vast area, interpreting their orders as they liked and in the process taking advantage of their official position for personal ends. By 1893 Parkes had felt obliged to report a series of incidents in which chiefs had been gratuitously insulted and misused by the very agents sent to protect them. Asked for alternatives, he recommended a new approach to the administration of the back country.

Parkes had already drafted a plan for civil administration of the interior. He now proposed the formal establishment of a protectorate which in his eyes already existed in fact. The interior would be divided into five districts to each of which would be assigned a political agent or commissioner who would advise and assist the chiefs in their government, prevent slaving and witchcraft ordeals, bring the colony's law

[1] H. Knutsford to J. Crooks, June 18, 1891, enclosure, C.O. 879/36; F. Fleming to G. Ripon, enclosure 3 of Jan. 9, 1893, C.O. 267/400.

into effect against murder and theft, and supervise road clearing and improvement of agriculture. Once a year there might be a 'durbar' between the principal chiefs and the governor for the discussion of important matters affecting the country. Sensitive to London's attitude regarding colonial expense, Parkes proposed that the costs of administration be met by savings effected through a substantial reduction of the frontier police. Instead of a large force scattered across the interior, Parkes recommended small bodies under responsible officers to be located in strategic centres from which they could travel quickly to points of trouble. Gradually as peace settled over the land, the police could be further disbanded and replaced by a fully civil administration. 'The Government have shirked . . . responsibility long enough,' Parkes concluded, 'they cannot, I am afraid, shirk it much longer, as the march of events is fast bringing things to such a crisis that the consideration of some definite policy for the future cannot be much longer delayed.'[1]

It has been suggested that Parkes's protectorate plan and his disenchantment with the frontier police were partly the reflection of a struggle for power within the administration between his own Native Affairs Department and the frontier police, but there is no doubt that Parkes's criticisms struck home at basic weaknesses in the policies and organization of the Frontiers. In any event his suggestion for civil administration turned out to be ill timed for it appeared just as a new complication entered the scene in the form of a band of Samori's Sofa warriors withdrawing southward to escape French pressure and applying their characteristic fire-and-sword tactics to the country they traversed. Parkes's protectorate scheme was consequently turned down as an unwise reduction of the military at a time of particular unrest, and instead a campaign was mounted against the Sofa threat. Parkes's major criticism remained unanswered, however—that the government still had not faced the problem of a positive policy for the interior. He continued to press for a peaceful solution, possibly underestimating the Sofa menace, but swayed also by a high regard for the people he had come to know so well over the years:

I have always held . . . that in dealing with quasi independent native tribes living outside of British Jurisdiction efforts should always be made to . . . ascertain what may be their reasons for fighting between themselves and if possible arrange their differences amicably, but if this is impossible then to warn the side which the Government may consider

[1] F. Fleming to G. Ripon, Feb. 13, 1893 enclosing Parker protectorate scheme dated Nov. 18, 1892, C.O. 267/400; Chalmers Report, II, 48-9, 52, 561-2.

after impartial inquiry to be in the wrong that they are wrong and if they persist in wrong doing they will be punished. After this a punitive expedition may . . . be justifiable, but to send one upon people who have no quarrel with us and to whom we have never sent one word of warning . . . is unworthy of the high principles of the most civilized nation in the world.[1]

These remarks may not have been entirely ingenuous for they were meant to apply not only to the relatively peaceable local tribes but to the Sofas who, as Parkes well knew, were anything but gentle in their outlook on life. Parkes, the Freetown creole seeking an outlet to the interior for his cramped homeland, may well have been looking far beyond the immediate question of tribal unrest. If we attack the Sofas, his report continued, we may alienate Samori, leaving him to make peace with the French and to make war on the British. This in addition to French consolidation of their control of the inland trade routes would spell ultimate ruin for Sierra Leone. On the other hand, an alliance with Samori might rid the back country of French influence and leave to Freetown commerce the unimpeded penetration of the Sudan. Such a strategy would have fulfilled the most optimistic wishes of generations of Freetown creoles.[2]

A few years later the protectorate was established substantially along the lines Parkes had proposed, though sustained by a more formidable establishment of frontier police. The irony of the situation now became apparent, for with the protectorate there came into being a new provincial administration staffed by European officers who soon assumed the functions in relation to the indigenous authorities which Parkes once had fulfilled. When he died prematurely in 1899 he left behind him an administration rendered superfluous by the very policies he had laboured so hard to effect. His department was closed and, as in the case of Samuel Lewis, an end was brought to another of the few remaining channels of creole influence on the official conduct of the Sierra Leone government.[3]

5 *The Twilight of the Creoles*

The lives and works of men like George Guerney Nicol, Ernest Parkes and Samuel Lewis offered frail evidence to sustain a concept of creole

---

[1] J. D. Hargreaves, 'The Evolution of the Native Affairs Department', *op. cit.*, 179; F. Fleming to G. Ripon, Feb. 13, 1893 enclosing Colonial Office minute, C.O. 267/400; F. Fleming to G. Ripon, Dec. 16, 1893 enclosing Parkes memo to Fleming, Dec. 7, 1893, C.O. 267/404.
[2] *Ibid.*; Hargreaves, *op. cit.*, 181.
[3] Chalmers Report, II, 36; Fyfe, *A History of Sierra Leone*, 596.

THE TWILIGHT OF THE CREOLES

decline rooted in the theory of an exhausted virility, played out somehow in the hundred-year exertion of bringing Sierra Leone from the eighteenth to the twentieth century. Such an hypothesis, if occasionally appropriate to Renaissance princes, did little to explain the shortcomings of the Sierra Leone experiment, though by the early 1900s the creoles were clearly beginning to suffer an eclipse. The answer lay in another direction, not genetic and racial but circumstantial. In the first place, the creoles had undoubtedly grown soft from long years without commercial competition. When that competition arrived at the turn of the century, they were unable to deal with it effectively. They naturally found it difficult to meet the large-scale merchandising of British interests which moved into the colony once the railway offered easy access to the interior after 1900. At the other end of the financial scale, however, they were no more successful in facing the competition of the newly-arrived Syrian immigrants who worked harder than the local people, travelled farther, took a smaller profit, clannishly assisted one another, and gradually forced the creoles out of the Freetown retail trade. As newly liberated Africans, they had begun their businesses the same way many years before in the streets of the city and over the long inland trails and waterways. Now, fulfilling a fear expressed by William Fergusson sixty years earlier, they were no longer willing to work long hours and give up their ease, and so in the long run they lost the prosperity and ease they already had.

On the level of national development the problem was somewhat different. Here the shortcomings of Sierra Leone were rooted in the deficiencies of the colonial policy the creoles had opposed for so long. It was Samuel Lewis, more than any other man of his time, who had identified and explained this flaw in Britain's imperial design:

In Sierra Leone we . . . cannot understand why the English . . . should have rescued us from slavery, and given us the idea we were to become a great people, who should have opportunities for developing the resources of their country, and yet should leave us only a miserable strip of the coast. . . . What great things do you expect from such a miserable strip of country? We have long clamoured for larger room in which to develop ourselves, but we have been told the British people do not want more territory in these parts. . . . When the adjacent native chiefs offered more territory – rich territory – they were refused. The French then stepped in, and little by little took this territory. . . . I hate to think of such a thing. Instead of depending upon my own resources for a living, instead of tilling the ground and working the minerals of our own country, we may . . . be dependent on [England] to supply us with even the necessary means of governing ourselves. We shall have to ask [England] to pay taxes to keep up—what? What would become a sham of a Colony. It would merely serve . . . as a coaling station. I hate the idea.

But, as Lewis pointed out, when England finally awoke to the perils of the situation, it was already too late.[1]

[1] *Ibid.*, 613–14; *Proceedings of the Royal Colonial Institute*, XX, 115–17.

16 Nationalism on the Gold Coast

1 *British Authority Establishes itself on the Gold Coast*

During the 1860s, Africanus Horton had talked of ultimate independence for West African peoples, and on the Gold Coast the coastal states had taken a specific step towards unity and independence in forming the Fanti Confederation. British reaction, however, wrecked the Confederation movement, leaving the Fanti still disunited. At the same time the final transfer of the Dutch forts in 1872 had precipitated the Ashanti attack on the coast in an effort to maintain the rights to tribute from the town of Elmina.

Whatever the merits of these moves, however, British administrative indecision on the Gold Coast ended with the Ashanti campaign of 1873–4. The policy of withdrawal from Africa suggested by the Select Committee of the House of Commons in 1865 was now repudiated, and British authority was thereafter gradually but consistently extended in the land. Characteristic of the new policy was the proclamation in 1874 establishing a colony comprising the settlements of the Gold Coast and Lagos. Gone was the atmosphere of the Bond of 1844 negotiated between sovereign and equal powers. Occupation was now decided upon unilaterally in Whitehall, and once the decision was made, it was proclaimed by the British government without the formality of consulting the local chiefs. Indeed, such a step was specifically ruled out. Times had changed since the days of the Bond and negotiation between equals when equality no longer existed could only bring confusion, encouraging the illusion of an authority that had long since vanished. To be sure, tact was to be employed in explaining the nature and extent of British rule, but as to the reality of its presence there was to be no ambiguity. A protectorate was proclaimed for the territories beyond the forts and settlements, and the jurisdiction of the governor and his legislative council, already established in the Gold Coast colony, was henceforth to be equally operative in the protectorate.

Authority having thus been established, a listing of particular powers followed which left little doubt as to the completeness of British rule. Jurisdiction was to cover the preservation of civil peace and the protection of property, the administration of justice including indigenous courts, the settlement of disputes between local rulers, the development of education and religious training, the establishment of municipalities and the promotion of public health and sanitation facilities in towns and villages. The slave trade, human sacrifice, trial by ordeal, and 'other immoral, barbarous, and cruel customs' were abolished, and steps were to be taken to deal with domestic slavery. Finally the government was to meet its expenses through such taxes and duties as were from time to time deemed appropriate.[1]

In time other measures followed which steadily extended British control in all areas of legislative, administrative and judicial activity, and in the process laid increasing emphasis upon British governmental procedures and English law practice to the detriment of traditional native institutions. The courts were reformed in such a way as to make them more in keeping with British jurisprudence. Taxation, direct and indirect, was imposed. Land legislation was introduced to forestall exploitation of mineral and timber resources, but in the process indigenous customary land law was compromised. Attempts were made to reorganize municipal government in the interests of efficiency, but to the consequent weakening of the native authorities. Finally, at the turn of the century, the colony and protectorate were redefined as a colony at the same time that Ashanti was annexed, and the protectorate of the northern territories established. British rule was thenceforward complete over the Gold Coast.

2 *John Mensah Sarbah*
and the Defence of Traditional African Institutions

Britain's strength was such that there could be no question of resisting her governmental authority, but within the protectorate and colony much opposition to British rule developed during the last quarter of the nineteenth century. In his day, Africanus Horton had pointed out the inconsistencies between the resolutions of the 1865 Select Committee of the House of Commons and the aggressive policies of the British administration on the Gold Coast. Following in this tradition other educated Africans subsequently challenged the right of the British

[1] John Mensah Sarbah, *Fanti Customary Laws*, 268–83.

to govern, and demanded increased participation in their own affairs. Small in number, these men were energetic and articulate in argument. Some were successful merchants like James H. Brew, John Sarbah and J. W. Sey, and Brew was a particularly effective critic through the medium of his Cape Coast newspapers, the *Gold Coast Times* and the *Western Echo*. Of growing importance was a group of young lawyers returning from their training in England—particularly T. Hutton Mills, John Mensah Sarbah and J. E. Casely Hayford—whose mastery of the complexities of British law combined with a respect for traditional African institutions to enable them to contest British presence in their land on constitutional grounds. Casely Hayford's manifold activities included journalism along with the law, and he was joined by others with a bent for authorship, notably the transplanted Sierra Leonean, James Bright-Davies, who edited the *Gold Coast Chronicle* in Accra, and a Methodist clergyman, S. R. B. Solomon, whose fervent nationalism was reflected in the impassioned columns of his *Gold Coast Methodist Times*.

Not passion, but cool logic and careful scholarship were the weapons of John Mensah Sarbah, one of the most persistent and successful critics of colonial rule on the Gold Coast. At first sight it might have seemed strange that a man of apparently conservative disposition, trained in the law with its emphasis on precedent and historical process, preferring by nature long hours of research and reflection to an unstudied emotion-charged position on any issue—that this man should have become one of the leading opponents of British policy. In his personal habits and family life he was the epitome of the British middle class, while his standards of professional behaviour and thought were conventionally western. Mensah Sarbah was the son of John Sarbah, and the latter being not only a merchant but a schoolteacher and agent for the Wesleyan Mission Society, young Mensah Sarbah was early exposed to the full force of Victorian morality—church, school and counting house. Though his youth was spent at Cape Coast where he was born in 1864, he received his advanced education in Britain, finishing with three years of legal study which concluded in 1887 when he was called to the bar, the first African barrister so to qualify from the Gold Coast. In England he proved a hard-working serious young man, seemingly more steadfast than brilliant, any tendency towards gaiety melting before the seriousness of life and his sober approach to its problems. During the last few years of his residence in England his younger sister was also at school in Great Britain. A few of his letters to her have survived—now cautioning her on the care of her money in a strange country; now urging the constant search for self-improvement; now preaching the importance of correct English in the development of a young lady. Religious thoughts were always in the mind of this Victorian youth. 'How is the welfare of your soul?' he asked his sister on one occasion. On another he sent her his blessing, 'May God spare your life for good work . . . may you love Him more and more serving Him all the days of your mortal life.'[1]

This image of a pious, industrious student watching over the affairs of his young sister was only part of the picture, however. 'What we want in Cape Coast are men and women of action', he announced in one of his letters, adding that what was learned by those fortunate students living away from home must eventually be passed on to others back home for the good of all. As for Mensah Sarbah himself, he apparently regarded his education as beginning, not ending, with his Blackstone. Before leaving England he wrote at length to a member of Parliament criticizing the legal basis for British government on the Gold Coast and questioning its administrative efficiency. 'The fundamental principle of the British Constitution that taxation goes with representation is not only violated,' he concluded, 'but the large revenue of this once prosperous Colony is practically wasted in keeping up a staff of Government officials unnecessarily large and expensive, the legitimate needs of the people being absolutely neglected.' It was a student effort but already it contained the germs of a philosophy of Gold Coast nationalism which was later to emerge in full force in Mensah Sarbah's subsequent public activities and writings.[2]

Mensah Sarbah's legal training had indeed combined with his natural sobriety and moderation to produce a first-class critic of British Gold Coast policy. Attracted to historical causation, Mensah Sarbah studied the past of his people and found a vital society mature in its ethical, legal and political standards and well qualified through experience for self-government. At the same time he examined the successive intrusion of foreign powers, beginning with the Portuguese and ending with the English, and discovered a long record of power usurped. As legal scholar, he examined the laws and customs of the Fanti, and was impressed by their continuity and the necessity for taking them into account

[1] *The Gold Coast Chronicle*, Sept. 12, Nov. 7, 1892; Magnus J. Sampson, *Gold Coast Men of Affairs*, 212–13; John Mensah Sarbah to Evan Sarbah, July 23, Aug. 22, Dec. 22, 1884, Feb. 22, 1884(?), Sarbah Papers, Ghana National Archives.
[2] John Mensah Sarbah to Evan Sarbah, n.d., *ibid.*; Mensah Sarbah to A. McArthur, Feb. 15, 1887, C.O. 879/25, no. 333, 46–7; see also *The Gold Coast Echo*, Dec. 17, 1888.

if there was to be any meaningful latter-day colonial administration in the Gold Coast. To one of his temperament, it was folly to superimpose alien cultural, legal and political systems and expect them to work unless a substantial accommodation were effected with local institutions. As a student of Gold Coast constitutional history, he could only protest against the violation of treaties and the arrogation of authority by the strong over the weak, and ridicule the stumbling efforts at government by successive British administrations which ill understood the issues he had studied so long and carefully.

This love for historical scholarship produced intellectual values and standards of public ethics of a high order. Mensah Sarbah reported how, in the course of preparing one of his studies, he had quite by accident come across a number of important official letters, not through a search of government archives but by discovering one day a group of labourers feeding the fire by which they cooked their noonday meal with bundles of government papers which they had been permitted to dispose of in this fashion. 'It was the Gold Coast version of an old, old story', he lamented. '... Knowledge, through patient and frugal centuries, enlarging discovery, and recording it; Ignorance, wanting its day's dinner, lighting a fire with the record, and flavouring its one roast with the burnt souls of many generations.' But this was not the worst of it. He was able to save some of the papers through purchase but the rest were shortly thrown into the ocean for 'historical facts are often embarrassing in West Africa, and nothing so facilitates a spirited, indefinite policy as — a clean foolscap sheet of paper'.[1]

Mensah Sarbah's thoughts on the theories and practicalities of government in the Gold Coast were set forth in three formidable volumes dealing with Fanti constitutional law. Chief among these was his *Fanti National Constitution* which appeared in 1906 only four years before his premature death and represented a distillation of his mature views. In these several works his argument rested on analysis both of evolving indigenous institutions and their superstructure of covenants, treaties, agreements, judicial decisions, administrative acts and legislation. He was always the legal practitioner carefully preparing his brief. The method was historical—to seek the understanding of present institutions by tracing them back to their genesis. The tool was patient attention to detail—here laying bare the meaning of current administrative policy through examination of a neglected treaty, there illuminating an obscure indigenous practice through study of a long-forgotten custom.

[1] *Fanti National Constitution*, xi.

The result hopefully would be increased harmony between the government and the governed regarding their respective rights and responsibilities, and a diminution of the misapprehensions and suspicions which so often led to bad government.

A basic misunderstanding which early arose on the Gold Coast, said Mensah Sarbah, was the conviction of Europeans that African rulers in making treaties freely relinquished authority over their own people. This was ridiculous on the face of it, he continued, but in addition military conquest in Africa was normally followed by tribute, not by occupation and loss of sovereignty. When protection and suzerainty were arranged between two African nations, the rights as well as the duties of the protected were always carefully defined. It was usual for a protected community to maintain its internal governmental functions, exchanging some form of tribute to the overlord in return for its protection. As for the British, despite their long presence on the Gold Coast, they had never acquired any legal jurisdiction through cession, conquest or purchase of territory. The local chiefs had always understood that they were signing only military pacts with England involving temporary alliances in pursuit of common military objectives but never implying, let along conceding, loss of sovereignty and independence.

Mensah Sarbah cited a series of examples of authority arrogated. There was the case of King Aggrey, deposed and deported by the British when he claimed jurisdiction over territory adjacent to Cape Coast Castle. Aggrey was, after all, the legitimate king of Cape Coast, Mensah Sarbah insisted, and his removal from office rested not on legal sanction but on extra-legal force. Another example involved the custom which had arisen of relying exclusively on British courts in trying capital cases. This process had its genesis, said Mensah Sarbah, in the Bond of 1844. However, the practice of turning exclusively to British courts was no part of the Bond but merely a reflection of fear on the part of the people that they would incur official displeasure if they ignored the English tribunals and continued to utilize their indigenous courts.[1]

Moreover, there was the 1865 report of the Special Committee of the House of Commons which recommended that the people of West Africa be encouraged towards self-government; yet, Mensah Sarbah complained, this resolution was ignored by the British administration on the Gold Coast which made no effort to train individuals for independence, and which on the contrary smashed the Fanti Confederation and treated its leaders as conspirators and traitors. Still another instance came with

[1] *Ibid.*, 86–9, 90–2, 99; Mensah Sarbah, *Fanti Law Report*, 172.

the defeat of the Ashanti in 1874 when the colony and protectorate of the Gold Coast was proclaimed unilaterally by Britain. This was a most curious development, said Mensah Sarbah. In the first place, the campaign was against Ashanti, not against the coastal people; in fact, local troops were conspicuous in the assistance they lent the British. Furthermore, the assumption of power by Britain was claimed by usage—that is, in such matters as customs duties, administration of justice and legislation in general it was argued that authority had been uncontested for so long that *de facto* government had fallen to the British administration, a view which was hardly shared by the traditional authorities:

Gold Coast territory was not an uninhabited district settled on by British subjects, or an inhabited territory obtained by conquest or cession. Whether the inhabitants were taken to be half or wholly savages, they had their aboriginal tribal government, each regularly established, invested with the rights of sovereignty and exercising its powers. With these governments treaties were made from time to time. . . . A study of [these] treaties of friendship and protection existing between England and several Gold Coast rulers does not support the view that it was contemplated at least by these rulers and their people that they would be deprived of their judicial powers and other rights of sovereignty in course of time.[1]

Additional constitutional aberrations followed. In 1896 Ashanti was reoccupied by military action and subsequently annexed, along with all her protected tribes, as conquered territory. This was incomprehensible, said Mensah Sarbah, since once again the campaign had been against Kumasi, not against surrounding tribes with whom treaties of friendship and protection had been made shortly before, treaties guaranteeing the customs of the country and the sovereignty of the protected powers. Suddenly these guarantees were set aside, the chiefs told that their authority stemmed from the will of the British crown, and the people treated thenceforward as British subjects rather than protected aliens. Ultimately these opinions rested on superior force, concluded Mensah Sarbah, their logic coming from an indiscriminate application of principles of English jurisprudence to the alien conditions which obtained in West Africa. It was a sorry fate for people who had been faithful friends and protected allies of Britain for centuries.[2]

Yet these were political realities, and despite everything Mensah Sarbah had no doubt that the people of the Gold Coast would continue to follow their ancient traditions of trading and living with Great

---

[1] *Fanti National Constitution*, 104, 106–10.
[2] *Ibid.*, 111–14; *Fanti Customary Laws*, 288–91.

Britain. It thus behoved England for her part to take with renewed seriousness her responsibilities of stewardship:

> In these days of a new imperialism against aboriginal races, the English sojourner in tropical Africa should know that a sublimer function of imperial rule is to respect and encourage their sense of self-help and self-reliance; that for the mutual and permanent advantage of both alike (whether in developing the mutual resources of Africa, or in the assimilation of European culture) no obstacles should be put in the way of Africans to rise from a condition of mere passive subjection, to prove their undoubted capacity to discharge successfully their legitimate responsibilities, public and private.

This could best be done by taking full account of the assets of traditional African society and combining them in their most effective forms with the best of European institutions.[1]

Specifically, a major step in the direction of improved British-African co-operation was fuller participation by Africans in the colonial legislative council and greater attention in its deliberations to traditional patterns of legislative authority. The council, said Mensah Sarbah, tended to be overloaded with official members of the administration whose position made it impossible for them to exercise a free vote. Unofficial members, on the other hand, were limited in number and their opinions frequently ignored; yet it was the unofficial members who by their status as community leaders were best qualified to speak for and represent their community, and to give insight into local traditional precedent and custom which were so often ignored in the development of legislation on the Gold Coast.

Related to the question of the legislative council was that of municipal government. In England it had long been customary for taxes on real estate to be assessed in a municipality on the basis of what a reasonable rent might be on the property in question, less the cost of normal repairs. Municipal rates thus defined were levied by town councils elected by householders, the council president being chosen by its members. In the Gold Coast these procedures had no particular relevance. African property was held by family rather than by individual, and since rent was charged only of strangers, there was no proper basis for assessment of rent. Nevertheless, ordinances were passed on the British model except that representation was denied the people. Membership in the municipal councils was made up half of administrative officials who owned no

---

[1] *Fanti National Constitution*, 120; H. W. Hayes Redwar, *Comments on Some Ordinances of the Gold Coast Colony*, v–vi.

property and paid no taxes, and half of local inhabitants appointed by the governor, not elected by their constituents. Direct taxes on real estate were attempted despite the well-known aversion in West Africa to hut taxes, and chiefs were made liable to fines for failing to keep clean the open spaces in the municipality despite the fact that such chiefs were by definition ineligible for a seat on the council. To Mensah Sarbah it was small wonder that there had been little success in the incorporation of municipalities. It was just another example of the failure of government based on a failure to take account of local custom and tradition.[1]

Mensah Sarbah was quick to point out, however, that the African, particularly the educated African, shared responsibility with the European for good government. Because of his background and training, the educated African had a peculiar responsibility to see that chiefs and other traditional leaders were not belittled and discounted, but rather were instructed to a higher level of usefulness. To be sure, the educated African was in a difficult position, for both his unlettered brother and the European tended to suspect him of being in league with the other, but the very character of his equivocal situation could be a strength, for through it he would be able to utilize all the best features of both imported and national institutions on behalf of good government. On the one hand he served as a natural interpreter of the intentions of government to the chiefs and the people, while at the same time he could represent the needs and desires of the community to the government through his position as unofficial member of the legislative council.

This was a great responsibility, continued Mensah Sarbah, the more so for the many opportunities the educated African had to place self-service above service to his people. Doubtless there were those who sacrificed their people for their own advantage, but others were unjustly accused of deserting Africa, sometimes merely because of their preference for the white man's style of living. Nevertheless it was probable that excessive zeal in emulating European customs was unwise. Not only did it expose such educated Africans to inordinate expense on behalf of an unsuitable and spurious respectability, but it led to charges of African incapacity for European civilization and introduced false standards for the guidance of their untutored countrymen. What was needed was a national character 'racy of the soil', as Mensah Sarbah put it, developed by a system of education which would not only provide training in necessary skills but would produce men of self-respect, with

[1] *Fanti National Constitution*, 122–6, 140–5.

a sense of duty and a devotion to truth, a desire for freedom and a love of God.[1]

3 The Role of the Educated African in Colonial Government

For all his erudition, John Mensah Sarbah was no isolated academic. A practising lawyer and representative of his people, he was an active leader of the Gold Coast resistance to the encroachment of British power. It was not long after his return from study in England that he was able to make his first contribution to the nationalist cause. In 1887 the people of Cape Coast drafted suggestions for a municipal government, but these were quickly turned aside by the administration which substituted its own municipalities ordinance. This bill offered a council with a majority of elected members but called for revenue through direct property taxes. Opposition was immediate, couched in the form of a petition to the secretary of state. Many prominent and respectable citizens of Cape Coast supported the protest, among others John Sarbah, J. P. Brown, W. E. Pietersen and J. D. Abraham. Young Casely Hayford was also involved and John Mensah Sarbah was said to have been the petition's author.

The main line of his argument was typical. The ordinance ran counter to the whole structure of Fanti town organization, said Mensah Sarbah. The traditional hierarchy consisted of heads of households, ward leaders concerned with several families, and a council of elders and chiefs which governed the town. Officials were elected to deal with street cleaning and sanitary regulation. Thus all municipal functions were cared for by institutions in which all freeborn inhabitants had a stake. With the Ashanti War of 1873-4 came a social and political disorganization and consequent unrest and rioting. What was clearly needed, therefore, was municipal reform in keeping with changing conditions but rooted in time-tested native institutions. One of the major shortcomings of the proposed legislation, Mensah Sarbah continued, was its reliance on direct taxation, anathema to the people, where revenue from import duties would be acceptable and expedient. Here again there was ancient precedent, 'the principle that representation means taxation cannot be applied . . . For from time immemorial we have enjoyed representative institutions without such direct taxation . . .'

By granting us municipalities adapted to our needs . . . our native institutions reformed and reorganized will be established on a firmer

[1] *Ibid.*, 151, 238-9, 247-8, 250-3.

Renaissance, 18
  Senghor on, 18
Reunion Island, 30
Réveil du Sénégal, Le, 244, 247–8, 367
  on Muslims, 248–50
Richard Toll, 165, 237
Robbin, James, 263
Roberts, Joseph J., 92–3
Roger, Baron, 79, 95, 163, 164, 167, 170, 313
Rosenbush, T. A., 151
Rowe, Samuel, 138, 139, 140, 308, 315, 319
Royal Colonial Institute, London, 302, 305
Roye, E. J., 97
Rufisque, 80, 234, 235, 238, 366, 370, 392, 400
Russwurm, John, 92, 97

St. Louis, Senegal, 67, 69, 74, 75, 77, 155, 162, 163, 167, 175, 234, 238, 255, 346, 370, 392, 396, 400
  described, 69–70, 234–6, 237, 366
  mayors, 71, 73, 78, 79, 242, 243, 249
  traders of, 80–1, 165, 173, 245, 246
  Africans of, 172, 173, 236, 248–9, 393, 394
St. Paul River, 89, 101–2, 211
Samba Lawbé, 247
Samori, 223, 319, 323, 324, 374, 467, 478
Sancho, Ignatius, 33, 34
Sapara Williams, A., 376, 390
Sarakole, 163
Sarbah, John, 329, 336
Savage, R. A., 444
Schmaltz, J., 73
Schoelcher, V., 238
Science, western
  impact on Africa, 17, 459, 460
  impact on Europe, 17–18
Second Empire, France, 238

Senegal, 30, 71, 78, 90, 95, 163, 174, 234, 319, 345, 362, 366, 395, 435
  and economic development, 81, 164–6, 173, 313, 369, 413, 413 n.
  government under Third Republic, 238–9
  Administrative Council, 238, 242, 245
  Deputy, 238, 239, 240, 243, 244, 246, 248, 392, 400, 405, 411, 412
  General Council, 238, 240, 242, 370, 405
  municipal councils, 238, 239, 240, 242
  politics under Third Republic, 239, 244, 249, 413
  colonial administration, 239, 240, 241, 396–8, 405
  voting rights, 251, 396, 403–4
  Colonial Council, 405, 412
Senegal River, 69, 75, 77, 163, 170, 234, 235, 236–7, 248, 366
  trade along, 70–1, 80, 165, 171, 245
Senghor, Léopold S., 18, 414, 467, 469, 471, 477–8, 479, 480
  philosophic system of, 473–5
  and negritude, 475–6
Sénoudébou, 171
Serer, 158, 163
Seven Years War, 23
Sey, J. W., 329
Seys, John, 97
Sharp, Granville, 152, 297, 460
  and abolition of slavery, 40
  and Sierra Leone, 40, 46, 48, 50–1
  ideas of government, 49–50
Sherbro Island, 89
Shomoye, Egba bashorun, 199
Sibthorpe, A. B. C., 256
  life and character, 263–4
  observations on historical writing, 265, 266
  as social historian, 266–8

INDEX

Oluwa, Chief, 386
Omar, El Hadj, 168, 171, 172, 223, 366
Onitsha, 182
Owu, people, 197
Oyekan, Prince, 205, 206
Oyo, 270, 274, 347

Pacification of Interior
  urged by W. Fergusson, 135
  reluctance of British government, 140, 314–15
  urged by Paul Holle, 170–1, 173
  and Bishop Crowther, 193
  Devès and Crespin, 247–8
  Samuel Lewis, 314–15, 318, 320, 325–6
  and Lagos traders, 315, 350
  and Senegal mulattoes, 315
  and Sierra Leone 'creoles', 320, 324
  urged by J. P. Jackson, 350
Palm products and oil, 96, 106, 119, 134, 165, 177, 184
Pan-African Congresses, 405–6
  1911, 405, 449
  1921, 405–6
Pan-Africanism, 405, 406, 425, 444, 447–8, 449, 455, 471
Parkes, J. C. Ernest, 302, 315, 318–19, 365, 435
  on British interior policy, 320, 321, 323–4
  on indigenous peoples, 321, 322, 323–4
  on economic development, 321
  on Christianity, 321
  on frontier police, 322, 323
  on domestic slavery, 322
  protectorate plan, 322–3
Payne, J. O., 230
Pellegrin, Gabriel, 78–80, 466
Peters, Thomas, 54
Petit Sénégalais, Le, 244, 247–8, 367
Pietersen, W. E. 336
Pinet-Laprade, J., 366
Ploermel Brothers, 156–7
Podor, 237

[509]

Political Economy of British West Africa, 114
Polygamy, 66, 261, 286, 269
  advocated by E. W. Blyden, 215
  and James Johnson, 283, 285, 294–5
  and Henry Carr, 425–6
Pope Hennessy, J., 205, 228
'Positive Neutrality', 471
Pratt, W. H., 133
Présence Africaine, 476
Prince Alfred, 197
'Province of Freedom', 49, 50, 152

Quaker, James, 143, 144, 146, 147, 288, 300, 461–2, 464
Quaker, William, 143
Quaque, Philip, 34

Racial anthropology, 212–13, 298
Racial prejudice and discrimination
  Senegal, 82, 371, 394–5
  and Africanus Horton, 120, 128, 213
  and William Rainy, 151–2
  and Bishop Crowther, 195
  and E. W. Blyden, 211, 212–13
  in Gold Coast, 445
Raffenel, A., 162
Rainy, William, 263, 298, 307, 346, 462
  character, 149
  criticizes Sierra Leone administration, 150–2, 154
  and jury trials, 151, 152–3, 311
  and racial prejudice, 151–2
Randle, John, 230, 349, 376, 390
Reindorf, C. C., 256, 264, 271, 465
  his philosophy of history, 256–8
  use of oral tradition, 257
  discussion of Gold Coast people, 258–9, 277
  critical of Europeans, 259–60
  on European civilization, 260, 262, 277
  encourages African qualities, 261, 277
  as African nationalist, 277–8

National Council of Nigeria and the Cameroons, 389
Nationalism
  and French Revolution, 24, 29, 30, 76
  and Napoleon I, 29, 76
  and Abbé Boilat, 176
  and Paul Holle, 176
  and G. W. Johnson, 207
  and E. W. Blyden, 212, 232
  and historical writing, 254, 277-8
  and A. B. C. Sibthorpe, 269-70, 277-8
  and C. C. Reindorf, 277-8
  and S. Johnson, 277-8
  and James Johnson, 281, 287
  and Samuel Lewis, 306
  and John Mensah Sarbah, 330, 336, 340-1
  and Attoh-Ahuma, 341-2, 343, 344
  and J. P. Jackson, 350, 353, 355-6
  and Herbert Macaulay, 377, 384 et seq.
  and Henry Carr, 424-5, 426, 427, 428
  and J. E. Casely Hayford, 433-4, 436-41, 455
National self-determination, 442, 443, 445, 446, 447
Native Administration Ordinance, Gold Coast, 453, 454
Native Jurisdiction Ordinance of 1883, Gold Coast, 338
Native Pastorate church, in Sierra Leone, 142, 143, 144-5, 148-9
N'Dar Tout, 236
Negritude, 109, 253, 289, 394, 468, 476, 477, 480
  and ideas of E. W. Blyden, 212 et seq.
  and *Ethiopia Unbound*, 435
Negro, The, 147
Neo-colonialism, 471
New Calabar, 190
New Cesters, 102
New Settlement, 101

New York Colonization Society, 211
Nicol, George, 143, 144, 146, 147-8, 302, 461
Nicol, George G. M., 324
  defends 'creole' culture, 302-4
Niger delta, 110, 177, 184, 190, 193, 290
Niger Delta Pastorate, 291, 293, 357
Niger Expedition of 1841, 181
Nigeria, 110, 177, 384, 424, 443, 445, 446, 471
  colony and protectorate, 354, 355, 359
  legislative council, 365, 382, 389, 429, 432
Nigerian Council, 429
Nigerian Chronicle, The, 359
Nigerian National Democratic Party, 389
  founded by T. H. Jackson and H. Macaulay, 388
Nigerian Pioneer, The, 346, 429, 431
Niger River, 182, 189
Nkrumah, Kwame, 467, 473, 477
  political and economic ideas, 469-72
  downfall, 472
'Non-alignment', 471
Nova Scotians, 90, 123, 132, 142, 178, 266-7, 268
  origins, 53
  in Nova Scotia, 53-4, 55
  land hunger, 55, 59-60, 65
  character, 56-7, 59, 60, 65-6, 297
  critical of government, 60, 61, 62, 63, 130
  in revolt, 64, 299, 461
Nupe, language and people, 187, 347
  Emir of, 202

Ofori Atta, Nana, 451, 452, 454, 457
Ogun River, 201
Oil Rivers, 208, 374
Old Calabar, 125, 178, 423
'Old Town', Lagos, 347, 348

INDEX

Maryland, Liberia, 102
Matacong Island, 243
Matam, 237
Maxwell, Thomas, 143
The Medical Topography of the West Coast of Africa, 113
Medina, 168, 171
Medusa, shipwreck, 242
Mensah Sarbah, John, 315, 329, 341, 353, 376, 434, 435, 436, 463, 464
  his Victorian standards, 329–30, 331
  criticizes British Gold Coast rule, 330–1, 322–3
  constitutional interests, 330, 331, 332
  and indigenous institutions, 331, 332, 333, 339
  urges African participation in government, 334
  on legislative council, 334, 338, 341
  and 'educated Africans', 335–6, 340–1
  on municipal administration, 334–5, 336–7
  and native authorities, 337–8
  and land legislation, 339–40
  political philosophy, 340–1
  Africa and Europe, 340
Mercantilism, 22, 75, 394
Military conscription, Senegal, 250–1, 398, 401
  opposed by Africans, 251
  favoured by mulattoes, 251–2
  favoured by Africans, 398
Mills, T. Hutton, 329, 338
Millsburg, 101
Missionaries, 28, 31–2, 124, 131, 142, 163, 231, 275
  disliked by African ministers in Sierra Leone, 145, 146
  Franciscans suggested by Boilat, 166–7
  and African 'rehabilitation', 180–1, 184
  at Abeokuta, 191, 198, 199, 203, 204
  critical of Bishop Crowther, 193–4
  critical of African church leadership, 291
  attacked by J. P. Jackson, 357–8
Modernization, 376
  in Europe, 17–18
  in Liberia, 106–7
  concept among abolitionists, 112–13
  in Abeokuta, 124
  and missionary policy, 179–81, 184
  in West Africa, 458, 459, 468–9
  and Nkrumah, 469–70
Mody, M'Baye, 393
Molinat, Charles, 371
Moloney, Alfred, 230
Moniteur du Sénégal, Le, 244–5, 247
Monrovia, 89, 91, 93, 102, 211, 212, 346
  described, 101
Moore, E. O., 365, 389
Moors, 83, 163, 165, 170, 173, 242, 366
Moussa, Abbé, 156, 157
Mulattoes (creoles), Senegal, 73, 78, 81–2, 84, 162, 165, 167, 173, 208, 255, 367
  and colonial politics, 240, 399–400
  favour 'assimilation', 241, 375, 461
  attitude towards Africans, 241, 253, 370, 373, 394, 398
  favour military conscription, 251–2
  ambivalence towards France, 252–3, 367–8, 372
Municipal councils, Senegal, 238, 239, 240, 242

Napoleon I, 25, 28, 29, 78
  government under, 25, 30
  and French nationalism, 29, 76
  and colonial rule, 72
Napoleon III, 30, 84
National Congress for British West Africa, 443, 445–7, 448, 450, 451, 452, 455

Lewis, Samuel—*cont.*
  devotion to the law, 305, 311, 317
  defends African people, 306
  knighted, 306, 316, 357
  westernized standards, 306–7
  and E. W. Blyden, 306–7
  on legislative council, 307–9, 341
  and Freetown municipal council, 309–10
  as Freetown mayor, 310
  and jury trials, 311–12
  on economic development, 312–13, 315, 325
  and agriculture, 312–13
  on British policy in the interior, 314–15, 318, 320, 325–6
  and British colonial government, 317–18
Lewis, William, 151
Liberalism
  in England, 27
  and Herbert Macaulay, 379, 386
Liberia, 85, 93, 109, 122, 211, 212, 345, 356
  compared with Sierra Leone, 85–6, 88
  symbol of free Africa, 86
  American Negro disinterest in, 87, 88
  neglected in America, 87–8
  Constitution of 1847, 93, 98, 99, 100
  Declaration of Independence, 93, 98–9
  weak economy, 96–7
  sovereignty, 98
  citizenship, 99–100
  and indigenous Africans, 99–100, 224
  political weakness, 107
  colonization and E. W. Blyden, 212, 223–5, 231
Liberia College, 211, 228
Liberia Herald, 92, 93, 97
Liberian colonists, 90, 91, 95, 99–100, 107, 356, 461
  character, 102

and African 'regeneration', 106, 107, 224, 225
Louis Philippe, 28, 29
Ludlam, Thomas, 64
Lugard, Sir Frederick, 354, 383, 386, 416, 417, 418, 429, 431
  provincial court system, 312, 360, 362, 431
  and 'educated Africans', 359–61, 363, 364
  administrative reforms of, 360

Macaulay, G. J., 143, 263, 302, 461
  criticizes missionaries, 145–6
  and lay church control, 148–9
Macaulay, Herbert, 143, 346, 364, 365, 376, 428, 435, 465–6, 467
  early life, 377
  criticizes British colonial régime, 378–9, 418–19
  ideas and personal characteristics, 379–81, 382–3, 386, 391–2
  and Eleko controversy, 383–6, 418–19
  and land policies, 386–8
  and taxation, 388, 420
  and Nigerian National Democratic Party, 388–9
  feud with Henry Carr, 390–1, 415–16, 421, 422 n.
Macaulay, T. B., 143, 288, 377
Macaulay, Zachary, 91, 134, 460
  on Nova Scotians, 60, 297
  as Sierra Leone governor, 60–2, 63, 64
  character, 60, 62
MacCarthy, Sir Charles, 267
Maclean, George, 111, 439
Mali, 478
Mamadu Lamine, 248, 374
Mandinka, 163, 221, 269, 319
Mansfield, Lord, 48
Manumission
  in United States, 33, 86
  in French territories, 238
Maroons, 64, 66, 123, 130, 132, 178, 266–7, 268, 461
Martinique, 23

INDEX

and African nationalism, 207
Johnson, Henry, 143, 271
Johnson, James, 137, 143, 144, 148, 209, 230, 231, 232, 263, 299, 302, 346, 352, 382, 463, 480
   reconciliation of Africa and Europe, 279, 282, 290
   character and early life, 279–81
   as African nationalist, 281–2, 287
   and E. W. Blyden, 281, 282, 289, 290, 291
   as assistant bishop, Niger Delta and Benin, 282, 293–4
   critical of native African character, 283, 285
   on Yoruba character, 284
   assesses Egba character, 284–5
   and Sierra Leoneans in Yorubaland, 285
   in Abeokuta, 285–7
   favours African culture for Africans, 287–8
   questions European values for Africa, 288–9
   on African education, 289–90
   and language training, 290
   on Christianity in Africa, 290–1, 294, 295
   and independent African church, 291–2, 293
   on polygamy, 283, 285, 294–5
   on African customs, 295
Johnson, Samuel, 256, 465
   on Yoruba culture and people, 270, 277
   historical objectives, 271, 272, 273
   character and training, 271
   and Yoruba wars, 271, 272, 273
   criticizes Egba, 274
   criticizes Ijebu, 274, 275
   criticizes Africans of Lagos, 275
   pro-British attitude, 275, 276
   estimate of Governor Carter, 275–6
   as African nationalist, 277–8
Johnston, Harry, 299, 305–6
Judaic-Semitic connections, in West Africa, suggested, 125, 258, 265, 272
Justitia Fiat, 380, 384

Kane, Cheikh Hamidou, 476
Kanuri, 347
Katamanso, 258
Keita, Modibo, 479
Kennedy, Arthur, 270
Krumen, 101, 267, 269, 347
Kumasi, 258, 333, 437

Lagos, 124, 125, 131, 178, 190, 197, 199, 200, 205, 206, 228, 230, 275, 282, 283, 316, 345, 346, 350, 356, 359, 376, 383, 384, 390, 418, 435
   described, 347–9
Lagos Standard, The, 359
Lagos Town Council, 364, 365
Lagos Weekly Record, The, 292, 347
Lagos Weekly Times, The, 349
Lamarck, J. B., 117
Lamurudu, 272
Lat Dior, 237, 243, 246, 247, 374
Laye, Camera, 476
League of Nations, 405, 450
Lebou, people, 83–4, 208, 399, 400, 402
Legislative council,
   in Sierra Leone, 65, 133, 150, 298, 307–9
   and Samuel Lewis, 307–9, 341
   and John Mensah Sarbah, 334, 338, 341
   in Nigeria, 365, 382, 389, 429, 432
   in Gold Coast, 334, 338, 440, 442, 452
Leigh, J. S., 230
Lekki, 349
Letters on the Political Condition of the Gold Coast, 114
Lewis, Samuel, 288, 299, 301, 302, 324, 376, 378, 435, 464, 465
   characterized, 304
   early life and personal standards, 305, 306

Horton, J. Africanus B.—*cont.*
  on Yorubaland, 123–4
  on Ibo, 125
  Judaic connections in Africa, 125
  on Gold Coast, 126
  on British colonial policy, 126–8, 328
  significance, 128–9
House of Commons, Select Committee, 1865, 111, 112, 122, 125, 128, 200, 327, 328, 332
Huchard, Louis, 313
  editorial policy, 367–8
  economic ideas, 313, 369
  political activities, 370–1
  critical of French in Senegal, 371
  and native policy, 372
  attitude toward Africans, 373
Humanitarianism, 27–8, 31, 72, 105, 179, 460, 461
Hundredors and tythingmen, 49, 52, 61, 62–3, 64, 65

Ibadan, 200, 206, 271, 274, 283, 347, 351
Ibo, language and people, 110, 125, 177, 187
Ife, 272
Igbebe, 182
Ijayi, 274
Ijebu, 190, 203, 284, 292, 349, 351, 352
  criticized by Samuel Johnson, 274, 275
Ijebu Ode, 347, 351
Ijemo massacre, 361, 431
Ikorodu, 200
Imperialism
  French, 22, 23, 30
  British, 22, 23
Independent African church, 209, 291, 292
  and E. W. Blyden, 231
  and James Johnson, 291–3
Indigénat, 398
Indigo, 75, 107, 119, 164, 165, 180, 184, 369
Indo-China, 30, 410

Industrialism, 26, 96, 108, 180, 369
Interior, see Pacification of Interior
International Labour Organization conference on forced labour, 407–8
Islam
  influence on Africa, 17, 319
  in Senegal, 82–3, 155, 396, 397
  criticized by Boilat, 161
  criticized by Paul Holle, 172
  Bishop Crowther on, 188–9
  and E. W. Blyden, 212, 225–7

Jackson, John Payne, 347, 364, 435, 464
  idiosyncrasies, 349
  condemns Yoruba wars, 350–2
  urges native administration, 352–3
  on land policy, 354–5
  and racial mixing, 355–6
  cultural nationalist, 355–7, 358
  on Christian churches, 357–8
  and E. W. Blyden, 355, 358
Jackson, Thomas Horatio, 358–9, 431
  attacks Lugard's administration, 360–2, 364
  estimate of Lugard, 363, 364
  political agitation, 364–5
  and Nigerian National Democratic Party, 388
Jaja of Opobo, 374
Javouhey, Mother Anne-Marie, 155–6
Jefferson, Thomas, 99, 223
Johnson, Chris, 359
Johnson, G. W., 'Reversible', 124, 208, 462
  character and early career, 196–7
  and Egba United Board of Management, 199–200
  political acuteness, 199, 204
  political strategy, 199, 206–7
  and trade policy, 201
  opposes Glover, 201–3, 204–5, 206
  and anti-missionary riots in Abeokuta, 203–4

INDEX

Dutch on, 125, 127, 128
Danes on, 111
British colony and protectorate, 128, 327-8, 333
  legislative council, 334, 338, 440, 442, 452
  municipal administration, 334-5, 336-7
  native authorities, 337
  land regulation and ownership, 328, 338-9, 340, 440-1, 446
  Constitution of 1925, 443, 453
Gold Coast Aborigines, The, 342
Gold Coast Chronicle, The, 329
Gold Coast Leader, The, 342, 444, 449
Gold Coast Methodist Times, The, 329, 342
The Gold Coast Nation and National Consciousness, 342
Gold Coast Times, The, 329
Goldie, Sir George, 193
Goree, 67, 73, 74, 77, 80, 82, 155, 157, 158, 162, 163, 167, 234, 235, 238, 255, 366, 392, 400, 410
  as slave factory, 68
  population, 68-9
Gourmets, 68, 70
Grant, William, 133, 147, 300, 302, 307, 462
  character, 137, 141
  on European culture, 138-9, 141-2
  urges British penetration of interior, 139-40
  and agricultural development, 140, 313, 321
  encourages British capital in Sierra Leone, 140-1
Greenville, 102
Ground-nuts, 122, 165, 166, 169, 173, 366, 368, 369, 413 n.
Guadeloupe, 23
Guet N'Dar, 236
Guèye, Lamine, 412, 413, 414, 466, 467

Guinea, 369
Gum, 70, 80, 83, 169, 173, 237

Habitants, 68, 70, 71, 80, 82, 162, 165
Hausa, 131, 189, 347, 353
Havelock, A. E., 309
Hay, J. S., 319-20
History of the Gold Coast and Asante, 256, 257
History of Sierra Leone, 262, 264-6, 276
History of the Yorubas, 256, 270, 272
Holle, Paul, 462
  early career, 167-8
  at Medina, 168-9
  urges strong interior policy, 170-1, 173-4
  on Islam, 172
  and mandatory French language instruction, 172
  on Africans, 172, 174
  economic development in Senegal, 173
  on manpower, 174-5, 321
  assimilationist views, 176
  as an African nationalist, 176
Horton, J. Africanus B., 109, 130, 192, 288, 441, 462
  life and character, 112-14
  writings, 113, 114-22
  and economic development, 113, 119
  admires western civilization, 114, 118, 122, 124
  defends Negro race, 114-19, 122
  Lamarckian view, 117-18
  on education, 120-2
  and racial prejudice, 120, 128, 213
  and 'educated Africans', 120, 124
  advocates West African university, 121-2, 129
  and independence for West African nations, 122-5, 126, 129, 327
  on Sierra Leone, 122-3

[502] INDEX

Fanti National Constitution, 331
Fanti Public Schools Ltd., 342
Fergusson, William, Sierra Leone governor, 133–4, 137, 149, 325, 461
  favours agriculture, 134
  urges strong policy for interior, 135
  and African education, 135
  criticizes liberated Africans, 136
Forced labour, 407–9
Forest Bill, Gold Coast, 441
Four Communes, Senegal, 238, 239, 241, 316, 362, 413, 414
  African population, 239, 241, 248, 253, 375, 394, 395
  civil and political rights, 392, 396, 397–8, 401–2, 403, 407
  and decree of Faidherbe, 1957, 396, 397, 402
  and Blaise Diagne, 401–2, 403
Fourah Bay College, 113, 139, 143, 146, 181, 225, 228, 280, 416, 435
France
  under Bourbon rule, 23, 24, 25, 72
  under Louis Philippe, 28–9, 77
  expansionist ideas, 29–30, 319
  national character, 30–1
  and Revolution of 1830, 76
  and Revolution of 1848, 84
  and Third Republic, 235, 238, 242, 394
  and Second Empire, 238
  colonial ministry, 241, 247, 371, 405
Freeman, Thomas B., 461
Freetown, Sierra Leone, 67, 102, 104, 150, 235, 316, 346
  repatriation centre, 66, 130–1, 142
  society described by A. B. C. Sibthorpe, 266–8
  viewed by James Johnson, 280
  Samuel Lewis and the municipal council, 309–10
French citizenship
  for colonials, 25, 71, 77, 251, 393, 396, 398
  and Blaise Diagne, 401–2, 403, 414
French civil code, 77, 162, 251
  and special status for Muslims, 396, 397
French civilization, 29–31, 74, 167, 169, 172, 174–5, 240, 241, 250, 368, 395–6
French Empire, 365–6
  concept of, 74, 461
French language, 155, 159–60, 172, 240, 241, 250, 251
French Revolution of 1789, 27, 29, 72, 74
  ideas of, 24–5, 30, 73, 461
  influence in Senegal, 71, 241
Fridoil, Abbé, 157
Fulani, 163, 189, 221, 267, 269, 347, 355
Futa Toro, 248

Ga, people, 111, 258
  described by C. C. Reindorf, 258
Gambia, 110, 112, 234, 445
Gambia River, 67, 122
Garrison, W. L., 87
Garvey, Marcus, 406, 450
General Council, Senegal, 238, 240, 242, 370, 405
Genouille, Governor, 247
George, C. J., 230
George, David, 45, 55, 57
  on Sierra Leone, 54–5
Ghana, 478
Gide, André, 408
Gladstone, William, 278
  and E. W. Blyden, 211
Glover, John H., 200, 206, 348, 349, 365, 377
  policy toward Abeokuta, 200–2, 203, 205
  censured by British government, 202–3
Gold Coast, 33–4, 110, 111, 121, 125, 126, 127, 256, 257, 346, 353, 425, 435, 436, 446
  forts, 125, 127, 128, 327

INDEX

government and politics, 197, 199, 201, 204, 205, 206, 207
xenophobia, 198–9
Samuel Johnson estimate of, 274
judged by James Johnson, 284–5
Egba United Board of Management, 199, 203, 205, 206
Egerton, W., 378, 383
Eleko of Lagos, 374, 416, 420–1
  controversy, and Herbert Macaulay, 383–6, 418–19, 422
  and Henry Carr, 419–21
Ellis, A. B., 298–9
Elmina, 327
Emancipation from Europe
  cultural, 468, 476–7
  and economic development, 468–9
  and education, 477–8
Empire Resources Development Committee, 445
The Enlightenment, 27, 44, 50
  in Britain, 22, 23–4, 25
  in France, 22–3, 24–5
  in America, 23–4
Equiano, Olaudah, see Vassa, Gustavus
Eshugbayi, Prince, 420–1
Esquisses Sénégalaises, 158, 162–3, 255
Ethiopia Unbound, 433–4, 435
Europe
  influenced by scientific revolution, 17–18
  early impact on Africa, 18, 34, 459
  criticized on slavery, 42–4, 461
  nineteenth and twentieth-century impact on Africa, 177, 460–6
  and economic imperialism, 177, 325
  doubts over African ability, 138, 194, 212–13, 298, 303, 403, 418
  colonialist doctrines, 195, 232, 291
  racialism, 212–3
  Blyden's estimate of, 220–1

European civilization for Africa
  and Africanus Horton, 114, 118, 122, 124
  in Sierra Leone, 131–3
  value questioned by W. Grant, 138–9
  urged by Paul Holle, 169, 172, 174–5, 176
  theories of Henry Venn, 180–1, 460
  favoured by Bishop Crowther, 182, 186, 189, 191–3, 208, 209
  resisted, 196
  African ambivalence toward, 141–2, 208–10, 252–3, 262, 277, 282, 340, 367–8, 372, 374–7, 435–6, 449–50
  judged by E. W. Blyden, 220–1
  assessed by C. C. Reindorf, 260–1, 262, 277
  assessed by Samuel Johnson, 276, 277
  favoured by A. B. C. Sibthorpe, 276
  opposed by James Johnson, 281–2, 288–9
  and Ernest Parkes, 321
  and Mensah Sarbah, 340
  criticized by Attoh-Ahuma, 341–4
  and Henry Carr, 426, 428, 429
  and Casely Hayford, 436–7, 438, 440
  impact on West Africa, 458, 460–6
  search for emancipation and accommodation, 468, 476–7, 480
European Economic Community, 470, 471
Ezzidio, John, 133, 150, 462

Faidherbe, L. L. C., 164, 168, 175–6, 234, 237, 245, 365–6, 396
Fanti, people, 111, 126, 127, 256, 258, 259, 260, 327, 330, 347
Fanti Confederation, 112, 114, 121, 128, 327, 332, 452
Fanti Customary Laws, 344

Devès, Gaspard—*cont.*
  on gum trade, 245
  economic policies, 246
  critic of colonial administration, 247–8
  pacification of interior, 247–8
Diagne, Blaise, 373, 435, 464, 466, 467
  characterized, 392, 393–4, 400, 409–10, 414
  election of 1914, 393, 394, 400, 401
  political skill, 400, 403, 412, 413
  and colonial exploitation of Senegal, 400–1
  and French citizenship in Senegal, 401–2, 403, 414
  and African dignity, 402–4
  Commissioner of the Republic, 403
  and military recruitment, 403, 404
  and pan-African congresses, 405–6
  growing French orientation, 405–7, 409–11
  on forced labour, 408–9
  criticized in Senegal, 411–13
  and economic activities, 413, 413 n.
Dike, K. O., 478
Diop, Cheikh Anta, 478
Diop, David, 476
Diop, Eliman of Dakar, 84
Diouf, Galandou, 412, 413
Dislike of farming
  in Senegal, 81
  in Liberia, 81, 90, 95
  in Sierra Leone, 65, 81, 299
  in Gold Coast, 261
Docemo, and House of, 354, 374, 380, 390, 418–19, 428
Dodds, A.-A., 371
Domestic slavery, 261, 286, 295, 315, 322
D'Oxoby, Jean, 412
Du Bois, W. E. B., 405, 406, 450
Durham University, 228, 416

Easmon, J. F., 357
Ebenezer Baptist Church, 291
Ebute Metta, 206, 348
Economic development in Africa, 459, 460–1, 468–9
  and Senegal, 81, 164–6, 173, 313, 369, 413, 413 n.
  and Africanus Horton, 113, 119
  theories of T. F. Buxton and H. Venn, 179–81
  Bishop Crowther on, 184–5
  and S. Lewis, 312–13, 315, 325
  and Ernest Parkes, 321
  and Casely Hayford, 442, 445–6
'Educated Africans'
  supported by Africanus Horton, 120, 124
  in Sierra Leone, 132–3, 186
  criticized by Bishop Crowther, 186
  question European standards, 195
  influenced by E. W. Blyden, 232
  interest in African history, 255
  and taxation, 310, 330, 364, 443, 453
  question British colonial rule, 328–9
  Mensah Sarbah on, 335–6, 340–1
  in Lagos, 359–60, 390
  defined by T. H. Jackson, 363–4
  sensitivity of, 382, 417, 459–60
  and Gold Coast native authorities, 441, 451–4
  an exclusive social class, 456–7
  and European civilization, 460–6
Education
  and Africanus Horton, 120–2
  and W. Fergusson, 135
  encourages Aku repatriation, 135
  and W. Grant, 139
  in Senegal, 155–7, 160
  and E. W. Blyden, 227–9
  and James Johnson, 289–90
  and J. P. Jackson, 358
  and Henry Carr, 422–5
  and Casely Hayford, 446, 448–9
Egba, people, 192, 197, 198, 200, 203, 285, 348, 349, 351, 361

INDEX

Cotton, 75, 106, 119, 134, 164, 166, 180, 184, 369
Cour de Cassation, Paris, 396, 397
'Creoles', Sierra Leone, 136, 208, 298–302, 303, 305, 311, 312, 315, 316, 318, 320, 324, 325, 356
Crespin, J. J., 367, 370, 464
  character, 243–4, 252
  early career, 243
  political activities, 243, 244, 246, 248, 252
  critic of Bordeaux, 245–6
  critic of colonial administration, 247–8
  pacification of interior, 247–8
  on military conscription, 251–2
Crowther, Samuel Ajayi, 143, 158, 279, 280, 282, 288, 293, 299, 302, 357, 377, 462–3
  early career and education, 181–2
  Niger expeditions, 181–2
  devotion to western civilization, 182, 186, 189, 191–3, 208, 209
  Bishop of West African territories, 182
  attachment to Henry Venn, 182
  character, 182–4, 194
  programme for economic development, 184–5
  religious devotion, 184–5
  on native African missionaries, 185–6, 187
  on 'educated Africans', 186, 191
  and African customs, 187, 209
  student of language, 187–8
  attitude toward Islam, 188–9
  and heathenism, 189
  on character of indigenous life, 189–90, 191
  believes coastal people depraved, 190–1, 193
  critical of European traders, 191, 193
  charge of Lokoja, 1869, 192–3
  and European missionaries, 193–4, 231–2, 291
  on expulsion of missionaries from Abeokuta, 203

Crummell, Alexander, 288
  in United States, 103, 104
  compared to Blyden, 103–4
  on Negro progress, 104, 108
  Africa and the West, 104–6, 109
  on indigenous Africans, 105, 107
  on Liberia, 107–8
  on Negro colonization of Africa, 108
  on race purity, 108–9
  on Negro character, 109
Cugoano, Ottobah, 21–22
  attacks slavery, 35–40, 44–6
  indicts Europe for slavery, 42–4, 461
  and Sierra Leone, 46–7

Dagana, 237
Dahomey, 198, 201, 206, 251, 258, 412
Dakar, 80, 175, 234, 235, 238, 366, 367, 370, 392, 397, 399, 400, 402, 404
Danquah, J. B., 467
The Dark Child, 476
Davies, J. P. L., 288
Dawes, William, 59
Declaration of Independence, American, 25, 99
Declaration of Independence, Liberian, 93, 98–9
Declaration of the Rights of Man, 25, 72
De Graft, William, 461
De la Sénégambie Française, 169
Démocratie du Sénégal, La, 412
Department of Native Affairs, Sierra Leone (Aborigines Branch), 318–19, 323
  Ernest Parkes as secretary, 319
Deputy, Senegal, 238, 239, 240, 243, 244, 246, 248, 392, 400, 405, 411, 412
Devès-Crespin party, 367, 371
Devès, Gaspard, 346, 370, 464
  merchant of St. Louis, 242
  political offices held, 242
  character, 243

[498]

Christianity, Islam and the Negro Race, 306
Church Missionary Society, 113, 180, 271, 294, 302, 357
   grammar school, Freetown, 113, 139, 280
   and native pastorate church, 143, 144–5, 148
   grammar school, Lagos, 143, 377
   and E. W. Blyden, 146–7, 225
   and Bishop Crowther, 181–2, 193–4
   and Abeokuta mission, 199, 283, 285–6
   and James Johnson, 286–7, 292–3
Clapperton, Hugh, 163
Clarkson, John, 55, 56, 57–8, 59, 60, 297
   on Nova Scotians, 56
Clarkson, Thomas, 40, 460
Clemenceau, Georges, 403, 405
Clifford, Hugh, 364, 387, 442
Cline, Emmanuel, 133
Coffee, 75, 96, 101, 106, 107, 119, 134, 165, 166, 313
Colonial Council, Senegal, 405, 412
Colonial Office, London, 135, 150, 151, 204, 308, 317, 320, 439, 440
Colonial policy, British
   ideas of, 31–2
   effect on Africans, 67, 334
   ambivalence, 110–12, 126–7
   Africanus Horton advice on, 126–8, 328
   on Gold Coast, 111–12, 128, 312, 327–8, 330–40
   opposes penetration of interior, 140
   in Sierra Leone, 150–2, 154, 312, 314–15, 316, 317–18, 319, 323, 324, 325–6
   at Lagos, 198, 200–1
   in Yorubaland, 207
   in Nigeria, 312, 316, 350, 377–8, 390, 417
   and French expansion, 314, 315
   Mensah Sarbah on, 330–5, 336–7
   J. P. Jackson on, 350–4

INDEX

   T. H. Jackson on, 360–2
   and Herbert Macaulay, 378–9, 418–19
   and Henry Carr, 421, 426, 427
   favoured by Kitoyi Ajasa, 430–1
   attacked by Casely Hayford, 436–7, 438–41
Colonial policy, French, 30, 31, 68, 72, 73, 75
   effect on Africans, 67
   colonial representation, 71
   toward Senegal, 73–4, 76–7, 78, 169, 240, 371, 396–8, 405
   criticized by Paul Holle, 170, 173–4
   criticized by Devès and Crespin, 247–8
   assessed by Louis Huchard, 368–72
   and forced labour, 407–8
   defended by Blaise Diagne, 409–11
Colonial policy, land
   in Sierra Leone, 52, 54, 56, 62, 63, 64
   in Gold Coast, 328, 338–9, 340, 440–1, 446
   in Nigeria, 354–5, 386–8
   in Senegal, 399
Colonial policy, taxation
   in Gold Coast, 328, 336
   in Nigeria, 388, 420
Colonial policy, trade
   in Senegal, 70–1, 78–9, 394
   in Liberia, 89–90, 95
   in Sierra Leone, 140, 320, 324
   in Gold Coast, 439
Conakry, 404
Concession Ordinance, 1900, Gold Coast, 440
Constitution, American, 25, 91, 99
Constitution of 1925, Gold Coast, 443, 453
Constitution of 1847, Liberia, 93, 98, 99, 100
Constitutional government, Liberia, 90–2, 99–100

INDEX

Bond of 1844, 111, 327, 332, 439
Bonny, 125, 190
Bordeaux merchants, 239, 240, 242, 245–6, 368, 370, 372, 394, 395, 435
  and Blaise Diagne, 407, 411
Bouetville, 236
Bouet-Willaumez, L. E., 156, 238
Bourgeois standards, West Africa, 180–1
  in Sierra Leone, 131–3, 135, 136, 137, 141, 269, 461
  in Gold Coast, 329, 461
Brass, 190
Brazilians, 347, 348
Breadfruit Church, Lagos, 230, 231, 283, 285, 287, 291, 348
Brew, J. H., 329, 346, 376, 464
Brière de l'Isle, L., 246
Bright-Davies, James, 329, 359
British Company of Merchants, 260
Brown, J. P., 336
Buchanan, Thomas, 93
Burton, Richard F., 118–19, 146, 163, 298
Buxton, T. F., 134, 184, 186, 280, 460
  anti-slavery programme, 179–80

Caiger, G. R., 145–6
Caillié, Réné, 162
Calabar, 365, 388
Caldwell, 101
Cameron, Donald, 385, 386
Canada, 23, 53, 54, 55
Cape Coast, 121, 258, 260, 316, 346, 435
Cape Colony, South Africa, 28
Cape Mesurado, 88, 89, 101
Cape Mount, 102
Cape Palmas, 93, 102
Cape Verde, 68, 84, 366, 399
Capitein, Jacobus E., 34
Captifs, 68, 69, 70, 74, 82, 165
Cardew, Frederick, 298, 316, 317, 318, 435
Carpot, François, 392, 399, 405

Carr, Henry, 292, 376, 382, 390, 429, 464, 465–6
  and feud with Herbert Macaulay, 390–1, 415–16, 421, 422 n.
  as Resident of Lagos colony, 390, 416, 418–19, 422
  appearance and character, 415–16, 417–18, 421, 425, 426, 428, 430
  government service, 416–17
  African criticism of, 418, 421
  and Eleko question, 419–21
  on Africans, 421, 427–8
  on British rule, 421, 426
  as educator, 422–5
  on use of English language, 423
  as pan-Africanist, 425
  on African progress, 427, 428, 429–30, 465
Carrère, Frédéric, 169, 172, 173
Carter, Gilbert, 207, 228, 275–6, 351, 352
Cary Lott, 92, 95
Casamance, 234, 369
Casely Hayford, Joseph E., 329, 336, 342, 346, 376, 443–4, 463, 464, 467, 480
  character, 434–5, 449, 455–6
  education and early career, 435
  on European rule, 436–7, 438–41
  African culture and institutions, 433, 437–8, 439–40, 442, 449
  Africa's moral superiority, 438, 447–8
  on legislative council, 442, 443
  and National Congress for British West Africa, 445–7
  as pan-Africanist, 444, 447, 449
  ambivalence toward West, 449–50
  and E. W. Blyden, 448, 449, 450
  and native authorities, 451–5
Cayor, 68, 83, 170, 237, 242, 246, 247, 366, 369, 373
Central Native Council, Lagos, 385
Césaire, Aimé, 468
Christianity, 74, 105–6, 117, 131, 142, 175, 180, 184, 260, 287, 290–1, 295, 321, 437

Badagry, 131, 178, 190, 349
Bakel, 168, 248
Balewa, Sir Abubakar Tafawa, 477
Bambara, 163
Bannerman family, 346
Bannerman, James, 461
Barbary peninsula, 236
Barth, Heinrich, 163
Bassa Cove, 102
Benin, 177, 354
Benue River, 125, 182, 189
'The Bible and the Plough', 184, 282
Blackall, S. W., 263
'Black Poor', London, 21, 36, 47, 48–9, 53
Blaize, R. B., 230, 346, 349
Blyden, Edward W., 107, 108, 114, 192, 302, 346, 347, 376, 382, 435, 450, 480
   quoted, 19
   and Liberia, 86, 103
   compared to Alexander Crummell, 103–4
   differs from Africanus Horton, 119
   influences William Grant, 137–8, 147
   on education, 138, 139, 147, 227–9, 448
   in Sierra Leone, 146
   and Islam, 146–7, 212, 225–7
   philosophy of Africanness, 210, 214–17, 218–19, 228, 232
   early life and education, 210–11
   correspondence with Gladstone, 211
   Liberian colonization, 212, 223–5, 231, 321
   and American Negroes, 211–12, 222–3, 231
   doctrine of complementary races, 213–14, 218–19
   religious sense, 214
   on African institutions and values, 215–17, 281
   advocates polygamy, 215
   extols African communal life, 215–16
   African communion with nature, 216–17
   and Africa's religious sense, 217
   urges African self-respect, 217
   African contributions to civilization, 218–19
   African spiritual superiority, 219
   and racial exclusiveness, 219–23, 228, 233, 301
   on African character, 220
   estimate of European traits, 220–1
   prefers interior Africans, 221
   criticizes Christian missions, 226–7
   advocates West African university, 228
   on African history, 229–30, 255–6
   advocates an independent African church, 231, 291, 359
   influence on 'educated Africans', 232, 233
   and James Johnson, 281, 282, 288, 289, 290
   on Sierra Leone 'creoles', 301
   and S. Lewis, 306–7
   and J. P. Jackson, 355, 358
   influences Casely Hayford, 448, 449, 450
   ambivalence toward Europe, 463–4, 465
Boilat Abbé P.-D., 156, 157, 480
   and secondary education, 156–7, 160, 462
   assimilationist views, 158, 163, 167, 176, 210, 461, 466
   stresses French language, 159–60
   religious views, 160–1
   and indigenous Africans, 160, 162–3
   attacks Islam, 161, 163
   deplores common law marriage, 162
   cites Africa's history, 163–4, 255
   on economic development, 164–6
   and labour supply, 166, 321
   on mission work, 166–7
   as an African nationalist, 176

INDEX

Africans, liberated
  in Senegal, 84
  in Sierra Leone, 110, 117, 123, 130–3, 134, 135, 136, 177–8, 267, 268–9, 280, 299–300
  return home to Yorubaland, 178, 181
  in Yorubaland, 285, 377, 416
Afrique Occidentale, L', 367
Agbebi, Majola, 346, 376, 463
Aggrey, J. E. K., 376, 450
Aggrey, King, of Cape Coast, 332
Agriculture
  in Senegal, 73–4, 75–6, 81, 95, 155, 164–5, 173
  in Liberia, 90, 95, 96
  in Sierra Leone, 134, 140
  and William Grant, 140, 313, 321
  and Bishop Crowther, 184
  and S. Lewis, 312–13
Ajasa, Kitoyi, 346, 390, 429, 464
  compared with Henry Carr, 429, 431
  sceptical of democracy, 430
  favours British rule, 431
  on African languages and traditions, 432
Akassa, 190
Akem, 258
Aku, see Africans, liberated, Sierra Leone
Akuapem, 258
Akwamu, 258
Algeria, 30, 249, 395, 412
American Colonization Society, 87–8, 89, 90, 91, 92, 93, 95, 97, 98
American Negroes, 19, 86, 140
  attitude toward Liberia, 87, 88
  and African 'regeneration', 106
  and African colonization, 108
  and E. W. Blyden, 211–12, 222–3, 225, 231
Amo, Wilhelm, 33–4
Anglo-African, 346 n.
Anti-colonialism
  in Britain, 27, 28, 200
  in France, 29, 72–3
  in America, 85

Antislavery and Aborigines Protection Society, Lagos Auxiliary, 383
Anti-slavery squadron, British, 131, 135, 179, 181
Apapa land case, 386, 422
Arrowroot, 96, 134, 180, 184
Ashanti, people, 111, 112, 113, 127, 128, 256, 258, 259, 260, 327, 328, 333, 439
Ashanti War, 1873–4, 128, 327, 333, 336
Ashmun, Yehudi, 88–90, 91, 92, 95, 101
'Assimilation'
  French doctrines of, 29, 75, 238, 395
  in St. Louis, Goree, 73, 76, 81–2, 84
  in Liberia, 100
  in Sierra Leone, 132–3
  and Paul Holle, 176
  and Abbé Boilat, 158, 163, 167, 176, 210, 461, 466
  and liberated Africans, 178
  in Senegal, 241, 252, 316, 367, 395
  favoured by mulattoes, 241, 375, 461
  and Africans in Senegal, 253, 398
  and C. C. Reindorf, 262
  and S. Lewis, 306–7
  in British West Africa, 375–6
  and Blaise Diagne, 409–11, 414
  and Lamine Guèye, 414
  and West Africa in the nineteenth century, 460–6
Assin, 259, 260
'Association', 100, 411
Attoh-Ahuma, S. R. B., 329, 346, 434, 436, 463, 464
  personal traits and early career, 341, 342–3
  nationalist views, 341–2, 343, 344
  favours traditional customs, 343–4
  and European civilization, 344
Australia, 28
Azikiwe, Nnamdi, 389, 467–8, 477

Index

Abdul Bubakr, 248
Abeokuta, 124, 178, 181, 191, 192, 196, 197, 198, 199, 201, 205, 206, 208, 275, 283, 285–6, 347, 348, 354, 360, 416, 431
Abolitionists
  in Britain, 40, 85, 112–13, 132, 134
  in United States, 87
  and westernization of West Africa, 178–81
Aborigines' Rights Protection Society, 339, 342, 435, 440, 451
Abraham, J. D., 336
Accra, 126, 256, 258, 262, 435
Achebe, Chinua, 476
Adeniyi-Jones, C. C., 389
Administrative Council, Senegal, 238, 242, 245
Ado, 190
African Bethel Church, 292
African Bishopric's Endowment Fund, 294
African civilization
  Alexander Crummell on, 105
  Abbé Boilat on, 164
  Bishop Crowther on, 187, 189–90
  E. W. Blyden on, 215–19
  C. C. Reindorf on, 261, 277
  James Johnson on, 287–8, 295
  Mensah Sarbah on, 332, 333, 339
  Casely Hayford on, 433, 437–40, 442, 447–8, 449
  recent political and economic changes, 467
African-European trade, 44–5

African history
  and Abbé Boilat, 163–4, 255
  and E. W. Blyden, 229–30, 255–6
  traditional, 254
  and African nationalism, 255, 277–8
  as written by Africans, 256–8, 265, 266, 271, 272, 273, 278, 478
  and African identity, 478
African identity, 476–7, 478, 479, 480
African Institution, 131, 134, 269
African and Negro accomplishment, concept of
  Alexander Crummell on, 104, 108
  E. W. Blyden on, 217–19
  and S. Lewis, 316
  and J. P. Jackson, 358
  and contemporary Africa, 479
'African personality', 471
African press, 209, 345–7, 446, 464
  in Lagos, 360
  in Senegal, 367
African Times, The, 146, 151, 206
Africans, indigenous
  in Senegal, 83, 84, 172, 173, 398
  in Liberia, 97, 98, 99–100, 102–3
  Alexander Crummell on, 105, 107
  Abbé Boilat on, 160, 162–3
  Paul Holle on, 172, 174
  James Johnson on, 283, 285
  S. Lewis on, 314–15, 318
  in Sierra Leone, 319–20
  Ernest Parkes on, 321, 322, 323–4
  response to Europe, 374

BIBLIOGRAPHY

United States Bureau of the Census, *Negro Population in the United States, 1790–1915*, U.S. Government Printing Office, Washington, D.C., 1918.

Vassa, Gustavus, *The Interesting Narrative of the Life of Olaudah Equiano, or Gustavus Vassa, the African*, T. Wilkins, London, 1789. Heinemann, London; Praeger, New York, 1966.

Villard, André, *Histoire du Sénégal*, Maurice Viale, Dakar, 1943.

Wadstrom, C. B., *An Essay on Colonization*, 2 vols., Darton and Harvey, London, 1794.

Wauthier, Claude, *The Literature and Thought of Modern Africa*, Pall Mall Press, London; Praeger, New York, 1966.

Webster, James B., *The African Churches among the Yoruba, 1888–1922*, Clarendon Press, Oxford, England, 1964.

Winterbottom, Thomas, *An Account of the Native Africans in the Neighbourhood of Sierra Leone*, 2. vols., C. Whittingham, London, 1803.

Sampson, Magnus J., *Gold Coast Men of Affairs*, A. H. Stockwell, London, 1937.
Sampson, Magnus J., ed., *West African Leadership*, A. H. Stockwell, Ilfracombe, England [1949?].
Saulnier, Eugène, *La Compagnie de Galam au Sénégal*, Larose, Paris, 1921.
Schefer, Christian, *Instructions Générales Données de 1763 à 1870 aux Gouverneurs et Ordonnateurs des Établissements Français en Afrique Occidentale*, 2 vols., Larose, Paris, 1921, 1927.
Schon, J. F., and Crowther, S. A., *Journals of the . . . Expedition up the Niger in 1841*, Hatchard, Nisbet, Seeley, London, 1842.
Senghor, L. S., *Liberté 1, Négritude et Humanisme*, Le Seuil, Paris, 1964.
Senghor, L. S., *On African Socialism*, Praeger, New York, 1964.
Senghor, L. S., *Pierre Teilhard de Chardin et la Politique Africaine*, Le Seuil, Paris, 1962.
Sharp, Granville, *Short Sketch of Temporary Regulations for the Intended Settlement on the Grain Coast of Africa near Sierra Leone*, London, 1786.
Sibthorpe, A. B. C., *Bible Review of Reviews, The Discovery of The Ten Lost Tribes, Yorubas or Akus*, Clinetown, Sierra Leone, 1909.
Sibthorpe, A. B. C., *The History of Sierra Leone*, 3rd Edition, Stock, London, 1906.
Sklar, R. L., *Nigerian Political Parties*, Princeton University Press, Princeton, New Jersey, U.S.A., 1963.
Solanke, Ladipo, *A Special Lecture Addressed to Mr. A. K. Ajisafe . . . on Egba-Yoruba Constitutional Law and its Historical Development*, Ife-Olu Printing Works, Lagos, 1931.
Special Report of the Anti-Slavery Conference Held in Paris in the Salle Herz on the Twenty-Sixth and Twenty-Seventh August, 1867, London [1869].
Staudenraus, P. J., *The African Colonization Movement, 1816–1865*, Columbia University Press, New York, 1961.
Stock, Eugene, *The History of the Church Missionary Society*, 4 vols., Church Missionary Society, London, 1899–1916.
Substance of the Report . . . of the Sierra Leone Company, J. Phillips, London, 1794.
Substance of the Report . . . of the Sierra Leone Company, W. Phillips London, 1801.
Suret-Canale, Jean, *Afrique Noire Occidentale et Centrale, L'Ère Colonial, 1900–1945*, Editions Sociales, Paris, 1964.
Swanzy, Henry, ed., *Voices of Ghana*, Government Printer, Accra, 1958.
Thomas, I. B., ed., *The House of Docemo: Full Proceedings of an Inquiry into the Method of Selection of a Head to the House of Docemo*, Lagos, 1933.
Thomas, I. B., *Life History of Herbert Macaulay, C.E.*, Lagos, 1948.
Thompson, T. J., *The Jubilee and Centenary Volume of Fourah Bay College, Freetown, Sierra Leone*, Elsiemay Printing Works, Freetown, 1930.

Nigerian Progress Union, *The Nigerian Students and Henry Carr*, Caledonian Press, London, 1924.
Nkrumah, Kwame, *Africa Must Unite*, Heinemann, London, 1963; Praeger, New York, 1963.
Nkrumah, Kwame, *The Autobiography of Kwame Nkrumah*, Nelson, Edinburgh, 1959.
Nkrumah, Kwame, *I Speak of Freedom*, Heinemann, London, 1961; Praeger, New York, 1961.
Ojo-Cole, Julius, *A Collection of Yoruba Thoughts*, Nigerian Press, Lagos, 1931.
Osadebay, D. C., *Africa Sings*, A. H. Stockwell, Ilfracombe, England, 1952.
Padmore, George, *The Gold Coast Revolution*, Dobson, London, 1953.
Padmore, George, *Pan Africanism or Communism? The Coming Struggle for Africa*, Dobson, London, 1956.
Page, Jesse, *The Black Bishop: Samuel Adjai Crowther*, Simpkin, London, 1910.
Perham, Margery, *Lugard: The Years of Authority*, Collins, London, 1960.
Perham, Margery, *Native Administration in Nigeria*, O.U.P., London, 1937.
Porter, Arthur T., *Creoledom, A Study of the Development of Freetown Society*, O.U.P., London, 1963.
Présence Africaine, *Le Premier Congrès International des Écrivains et Artistes Noirs*, Présence Africaine, Paris, 1956.
Présence Africaine, *Deuxième Congrès des Écrivains et Artistes Noirs*, 2 vols., Présence Africaine, Paris, 1959.
Proceedings at the Banquet in Honour of Edward Wilmot Blyden, London, 1907.
Raffenel, Anne, *Nouveau Voyage dans les Pays des Nègres*, 2 vols., Chaix, Paris, 1856.
Raffenel, Anne, *Voyage dans l'Afrique Occidentale*, P. Bertrand, Paris, 1846.
Rankin, F. H., *The White Man's Grave: A Visit to Sierra Leone in 1834*, 2 vols., Bentley, London, 1836.
Rattray, R. S., *Ashanti Law and Constitution*, O.U.P., Oxford, England, 1929.
Reade, Winwood, *The African Sketch-Book*, 2 vols., Smith, Elder, London, 1873.
Redwar, H. W. H., *Comments on Some Ordinances of the Gold Coast Colony*, Sweet and Maxwell, London, 1909.
Reindorf, C. C., *History of the Gold Coast and Asante*, Basel, Switzerland, 1895.
Rippon, John, *The Baptist Register*, 4 vols., London, 1793–1802.
Roberts, S. H., *History of French Colonial Policy (1870–1925)* 2 vols., P. S. King, London, 1929, and Frank Cass, London, 1963.
Runner, Jean, *Les Droits Politiques des Indigènes des Colonies*, Paris, 1927.
Sainville, L., *Victor Schoelcher, 1804–1893*, Paris, 1950.

Kuczynski, R. R., *Demographic Survey of the British Colonial Empire, West Africa*, vol. I, O.U.P., London, 1948.
The Lagos Training College and Industrial Institute, *Correspondence between Edward W. Blyden, LL.D., and His Excellency Sir Gilbert T. Carter, K.C.M.G., Governor and Commander-in-Chief of Lagos and Its Protectorates*, Lagos Standard Printing Office, Lagos, 1896.
The Lagos Water Rate Scheme, Further Correspondence, Lagos, 1915.
Laye, Camara, *L'Enfant Noir*, Plon, Paris, 1953. Issued as *The Dark Child*, Noonday Press, New York, 1954.
League of Nations, *International Labour Conference, Fourteenth Session, Geneva, 1930*, vol. I, Geneva, 1930.
Letters of the Late Ignatius Sancho, J. Nichols, London, 1784.
Lewis, Samuel, *A Few Suggestions of the Wants of Sierra Leone*, Artisan Workshop, Freetown, 1885.
Lewis, Samuel, *The Sierra Leone Association*, T. J. Sawyerr, Freetown, 1885.
Loti, Pierre, *Le Roman d'un Spahi*, Calmann Lévy, Paris, 1893.
Lucas, J. O., *Lecture on the History of the St. Paul's Church, Breadfruit, Lagos*, C.M.S. Press, Lagos, [1946?].
Ly, Abdoulaye, *La Compagnie du Sénégal*, Présence Africaine, Paris, 1958.
Macaulay, Herbert, *An Antithesis . . . on the Public Lands Acquisition (Amendment) Ordinance, 1945*, Ife-Olu Printing Works, Lagos, 1946.
Macaulay, Herbert, *Henry Carr Must Go*, Lagos, 1924.
Macaulay, Herbert, *Justitia Fiat: The Moral Obligation of the British Government to the House of King Docemo of Lagos*, London, 1921.
Macmillan, Allister, *The Red Book of West Africa*, Collingridge, London, 1920.
Mensah Sarbah, John, *Fanti Customary Laws*, Clowes, London, 1897.
Mensah Sarbah, John, *Fanti Law Report of Decided Cases on Fanti Customary Law*, Clowes, London, 1904.
Mensah Sarbah, John, *Fanti National Constitution*, Clowes, London, 1906.
Moore, Gerald, *Seven African Writers*, O.U.P., London, 1962.
Moreau, Paul, *Les Indigènes d'A.O.F.: Leur Condition Politique et Economique*, Domat-Montchristien, Paris, 1938.
Morgenthau, Ruth S., *Political Parties in French-Speaking West Africa*, Clarendon Press, Oxford, England, 1964.
National Congress of British West Africa, *Resolutions of the Conference of Africans of British West Africa, Held at Accra, Gold Coast, from 11th to 29th March, 1920*, Electric Law Press, London, 1920.
Nicol, G. G. M., *An Essay on Sierra Leone*, T. J. Sawyerr, Freetown, 1881.
Nigerian National Democratic Party, *Address of Welcome . . . to His Excellency, Sir Graeme Thomson, K.C.B., Governor and Commander-in-Chief of the Colony and Protectorate of Nigeria*, Lagos, 1925.
Nigerian National Democratic Party, *Memorandum of Objections Against the Enactment of 'The Native Courts and Native Authority Extension Ordinance' and The General Tax Ordinance*, [n.p., n.d.].
Nigerian National Democratic Party, *Petition Against the General Tax (Colony) Bill, 1927*, Lagos, 1927.

BIBLIOGRAPHY

Gide, André, *Travels in the Congo*, University of California Press, Berkeley, California, U.S.A., 1962.

Guèye, Lamine, *De la Situation Politique des Sénégalais Originaires des Communes de Plein Exercice*, La Vie Universitaire, Paris, 1922.

Guèye, Lamine, *Étapes et Perspectives de l'Union Française*, Editions de l'Union Française, Paris, 1955.

Hardy, Georges, *L'Enseignement au Sénégal de 1817 à 1854*, Larose, Paris, 1920.

Hardy, Georges, *La Mise en Valeur du Sénégal de 1817 à 1854*, Larose, Paris, 1921.

Hargreaves, J. D., *A Life of Sir Samuel Lewis*, O.U.P., London, 1958.

Hargreaves, J. D., *Prelude to the Partition of West Africa*, Macmillan and Co., London, 1963.

Hoare, Prince, *Memoirs of Granville Sharp*, Henry Colburn, London, 1820.

Hodgkin, Thomas, *African Political Parties*, Penguin, Harmondsworth, Middlesex, 1961.

Horton, J. A. B., *Letters on the Political Condition of the Gold Coast*, W. J. Johnson, London, 1870.

Horton, J. A. B., *Physical and Medical Climate and Meteorology of the West Coast of Africa*, J. Churchill, London, 1867.

Horton, J. A. B., *West African Countries and Peoples*, W. J. Johnson, London, 1868.

Huberich, C. H., *The Political and Legislative History of Liberia*, 2 vols., Central Book Co., New York, 1947.

Hunter, Guy, *The New Societies of Tropical Africa*, O.U.P., London, 1962; Praeger, New York, 1964.

Ingham, E. G., *Sierra Leone After a Hundred Years*, Seeley, London, 1894.

Innes, William, *Liberia*, Waugh and Innes, Edinburgh, 1831.

Johnson, James, *Address Delivered at Wesley Church, Olowogbowo, Lagos ... in Honour of the Late The Hon. Sir Samuel Lewis, Knt., C.M.G., of Sierra Leone*, London, 1903.

Johnson, James, *Yoruba Heathenism*, James Townsend, Exeter, England, 1899.

Johnson, Samuel, *The History of the Yorubas*, C.M.S. Bookshop, Lagos, 1921.

Johnston, Harry, *Liberia*, 2 vols., Hutchinson, London, 1906.

Kane, Cheikh Hamadou, *L'Aventure Ambiguë*, Julliard, Paris, 1961.

Kimble, David, *A Political History of Ghana*, Clarendon Press, Oxford, England, 1963.

Knight, William, *Memoir of Henry Venn, B.D.*, Seeley, Jackson and Halliday, London, 1882.

Knorr, Klaus E., *British Colonial Theories, 1570–1850*, Frank Cass, London, 1963.

Knutsford, Viscountess, *Life and Letters of Zachary Macaulay*, Arnold, London, 1900.

Kopytoff, J. H., *A Preface to Modern Nigeria*, University of Wisconsin Press, Madison, Wisconsin, U.S.A., 1965.

Crowther, S. A., *A Grammar and Vocabulary of the Yoruba Language*, Seeley, London, 1852.
Crowther, S. A., *Journal of an Expedition up the Niger and Tshadda Rivers*, Church Missionary House, London, 1855.
Crowther, S. A., and Taylor, J. C., *The Gospel on the Banks of the Niger*, Seeley, Jackson and Halliday, London, 1859.
Crummell, Alexander, *Africa and America*, Willey and Co., Springfield, Massachusetts, U.S.A., 1891.
Crummell, Alexander, *The Future of Africa*, Scribner, New York, 1862.
Cugoano, Ottobah, *Thoughts and Sentiments on the Evil and Wicked Traffic of the Slavery and Commerce of the Human Species*, London, 1787.
Cultru, P., *Histoire du Sénégal du XV Siècle à 1870*, Larose, Paris, 1910.
Curtin, Philip D., *The Image of Africa*, University of Wisconsin Press, Madison, Wisconsin, U.S.A., 1964.
Delavignette, Robert, and Julien, C., *Les Constructeurs de la France d'Outre-Mer*, Editions Correa, Paris, 1946.
Delavignette, Robert, *Les Vrais Chefs de l'Empire*, Gallimard, Paris, 1939.
Deniga, Adeoye, *African Leaders Past and Present*, 2 vols., Tika Tore Printing Works, Lagos, 1915.
Deniga, Adeoye, *Nigerian Who's Who for 1922*, Lagos, 1921.
Deniga, Adeoye, *The Nigerian Who's Who for 1934*, Lagos, 1933.
Dia, Mamadou, *The African Nations and World Solidarity*, Praeger, New York, 1961.
Diop, Cheikh Anta, *Nations Nègres et Culture*, Présence Africaine, Paris, 1955.
Diop, David, *Coups de Pilons*, Présence Africaine, Paris, 1956.
Du Bois, W. E. B., *The World and Africa*, Viking Press, New York, 1947.
Dupuis, Joseph, *Journal of a Residence in Ashantee*, Henry Colburn, London, 1824.
Durand, J. P. L., *A Voyage to Senegal*, Richard Phillips, London, 1806.
Elias, T. O., *Nigerian Land Law and Custom*, 3rd Edition, Routledge and Kegan Paul, London, 1962.
Elkins, Stanley, *Slavery*, University of Chicago Press, Chicago, 1959.
Ellis, A. B., *A History of the Gold Coast of West Africa*, Chapman and Hall, London, 1893.
Ellis, A. B., *West African Sketches*, Tinsley, London, 1881.
Fage, J. D., *Introduction to the History of West Africa*, Cambridge University Press, Cambridge, England, 1956.
Faidherbe, L. L. C., *Le Sénégal*, Hachette, Paris, 1889.
Falconbridge, A. M., *Narrative of Two Voyages to the River Sierra Leone during the Years 1791-2-3*, London, 1802.
Fox, George T., *A Memoir of the Rev. C. Colden Hoffman*, Seeley, Jackson and Halliday, London, 1868.
Fyfe, C. H., *A History of Sierra Leone*, O.U.P., London, 1962.
Fyfe, C. H., *Sierra Leone Inheritance*, O.U.P., London, 1964.
Geary, W. N. M., *Nigeria Under British Rule*, Methuen, London, 1927, and Frank Cass, London, 1965.

'Extracts from a "Report of Surprise Visits to the Schools in the Colony of Lagos" ', Lagos, 1893.
Carrère, Frédéric, and Holle, Paul, *De la Sénégambie Française*, Firman Didot, Paris, 1855.
Casely Hayford, J. E., *The Disabilities of the Black Folk and their Treatment, with an Appeal to the Labour Party*, Accra, 1929.
Casely Hayford, J. E., *Ethiopia Unbound*, C. M. Phillips, London, 1911.
Casely Hayford, J. E., *Gold Coast Land Tenure and the Forest Bill: A Review of the Situation*, C. M. Phillips, London, 1911.
Casely Hayford, J. E., *Gold Coast Land Tenure and the Forest Bill, 1911: A Review of the Situation*, (Second Notice), C. M. Phillips, London, 1912.
Casely Hayford, J. E., *Gold Coast Native Institutions*, Sweet and Maxwell, London, 1903.
Casely Hayford, J. E., *The Truth About the West African Land Question*, C. M. Phillips, London, 1913.
Casely Hayford, J. E., *United West Africa*, C. M. Phillips, London, 1919.
Charpy, Jacques, *La Fondation de Dakar, 1845-1857-1869*, Larose, Paris, 1958.
Claridge, W. W., *A History of the Gold Coast and Ashanti*, 2 vols., Murray, London, 1915, and Frank Cass, London, 1964.
Clarkson, Thomas, *An Essay on the Impolicy of the African Slave Trade*, J. Phillips, London, 1788.
Clarkson, Thomas, *The History of the Rise, Progress, and Accomplishment of the Abolition of the African Slave Trade*, 2 vols., Longmans, London, 1808.
Coker, Increase, *Seventy Years of the Nigerian Press*, Daily Times, Lagos, 1952.
Coker, S. A., *The Rights of Africans to Organize and Establish Indigenous Churches, Unattached to, and Uncontrolled by Foreign Church Organizations*, Tika Tore Printing Works, Lagos, 1917.
Coleman, James S., *Nigeria, Background to Nationalism*, University of California Press, Berkeley, California, U.S.A., 1958.
Constitution, Rules and Regulations of the Nigerian National Democratic Party [n.p., n.d.].
Coupland, Reginald, *The British Anti-Slavery Movement*, O.U.P., London, 1933, and Frank Cass, London, 1964.
Cromwell, John W., *The Negro in American History*, American Negro Academy, Washington, D.C., U.S.A., 1914.
Crooks, J. J., *A History of the Colony of Sierra Leone*, Browne and Nolan, Dublin, 1903.
Cros, Charles, *La Parole est à M. Blaise Diagne*, printed privately, Paris, 1961.
Crowder, Michael, *Senegal, A Study in French Assimilation Policy*, O.U.P., London, 1962. Revised ed., Methuen, London, 1967.
Crowther, D. C., *The Establishment of the Niger Delta Pastorate Church*, Thompson, Liverpool, 1907.

Blyden, E. W., *Africa's Service to the World, A Pledge of her Successful Future*, Doulton, London, [1880?].
Blyden, E. W., *A Chapter in the History of Liberia*, T. J. Sawyerr, Freetown, 1892.
Blyden, E. W., *Christianity, Islam and the Negro Race*, 2nd Edition, W. B. Whittingham, London, 1888.
Blyden, E. W., *From West Africa to Palestine*, T. J. Sawyerr, Freetown, 1873.
Blyden, E. W., *Liberia's Offering*, J. A. Gray, New York, 1862.
Blyden, E. W., *The Problems before Liberia*, C. M. Phillips, London, 1909.
Blyden, E. W., *The Prospects of the African*, Imray and Doulton, London [1874?].
Blyden, E. W., *Report on the Falaba Expedition, 1872*, Government Office, Sierra Leone, 1872.
Blyden, E. W., *The Return of the Exiles, and the West African Church*, W. B. Whittingham, London, 1891.
Blyden, E. W., *The Significance of Liberia*, John Richardson, Liverpool, 1907.
Blyden, E. W., *West Africa before Europe*, C. M. Phillips, London, 1905.
Boilat, P. D., *Esquisses Sénégalaises*, P. Bertrand, Paris, 1853.
Brunschwig, Henri, *L'Avènement de l'Afrique Noire*, Armand Colin, Paris, 1963.
Brunschwig, Henri, *Mythes et Réalités de l'Impérialisme Colonial Français, 1871–1914*, Armand Colin, Paris, 1960. Issued as *French Colonialism, 1871–1914: Myths and Realities*, Pall Mall Press, London; Praeger, New York, 1966.
Buell, R. L., *The Native Problem in Africa*, 2 vols., Macmillan, New York, 1928, and Frank Cass, London, 1965.
Burton, Richard F., *Wanderings in West Africa*, 2 vols., Tinsley Bros., London, 1863.
Buxton, T. F., *The African Slave Trade and Its Remedy*, Murray, London, 1840.
Campbell, Patriarch J. G., *The First Conference of Africans of British West Africa*, Lagos, 1920.
Carr, Henry, *Diocesan Synod of Western Equatorial Africa, Report of Speech delivered in Synod, May, 1907*, Townsend, Exeter, England, 1907.
Carr, Henry, *Diocesan Synod of Western Equatorial Africa, Report of Speeches delivered in Synod, May, 1912*, Swan and Morgan, Newcastle-on-Tyne, 1912.
Carr, Henry, *General Report for the Year 1897 on the Schools in the Colony of Lagos*, Lagos, 1898.
Carr, Henry, *General Report for the Year 1898 on the Schools in the Colony of Lagos*, Lagos, 1899.
Carr, Henry, *Special Report on the Schools in Southern Nigeria*, Old Calabar, Government Press, 1900.
'Amendments desirable to make in "The Education Rules, 1891" ', Lagos, 1897.

BIBLIOGRAPHY

Afrique Occidentale', *Présence Africaine*, n.s., bimestrielle, no. 34–5, Oct., 1960–Jan., 1961, pp. 79–91.
Wilson, H. S., 'The Changing Image of the Sierra Leone Colony in the Works of E. W. Blyden', *Sierra Leone Studies*, n.s., no. 11, Dec., 1958, pp. 136–48.
Wilson, H. S., 'E. W. Blyden on Religion in Africa', *The Sierra Leone Bulletin on Religion*, vol. 2, no. 2, Dec., 1960, pp. 58–66.

5 BOOKS

Abraham, W. E., *The Mind of Africa*, Weidenfeld and Nicolson, London, 1962.
Achebe, Chinua, *Things Fall Apart*, Heinemann, London, 1958.
Adeniyi-Jones, C. C., *Address Given . . . at a Mass Meeting Held at Glover Memorial Hall, Lagos, on 1st October 1938*, Lagos [1938].
Adeniyi-Jones, C. C., *Political and Administrative Problems of Nigeria*, London [1928].
Ajayi, J. F. A., *Christian Missions in Nigeria, 1841–1891*, Longmans, London, 1965.
Ajayi, J. F. A., and Smith, Robert, *Yoruba Warfare in the Nineteenth Century*, Cambridge University Press, England, 1964.
Ajisafe, A. K., *History of Abeokuta*, Revised Edition, Richard Clay, Suffolk, 1924.
American Society of African Culture, *Pan-Africanism Reconsidered*, University of California Press, Berkeley, California, U.S.A., 1962.
Annales Sénégalaises de 1854 à 1885, Paris, 1885.
Armistead, Wilson, *Calumny Refuted by Facts from Liberia*, C. Gilpin, London, 1848.
Attoh-Ahuma, S. R. B., *The Gold Coast Nation and National Consciousness*, D. Marples, Liverpool, 1911.
Attoh-Ahuma, S. R. B., *Memoirs of West African Celebrities*, D. Marples, Liverpool, 1905.
Austin, Dennis, *Politics in Ghana, 1946–1960*, O.U.P., London, 1964.
Ayandale, E. A., *The Missionary Impact on Modern Nigeria, 1842–1914*, Longmans, London, 1966.
Azikiwe, Nnamdi, *Zik, A Selection from the Speeches of Nnamdi Azikiwe*, Cambridge University Press, England, 1961.
Balewa, Abubakar Tafawa, *Nigeria Speaks*, Longmans of Nigeria, Ikeja, Nigeria, 1964.
Bassir, Olumbe, ed., *An Anthology of West African Verse*, Ibadan University Press, 1957.
Biobaku, S. O., *The Egba and Their Neighbours, 1842–1872*, Clarendon Press, Oxford, England, 1957.
Birtwhistle, Allen, *Thomas Birch Freeman*, Cargate Press, London, 1950.
Blyden, E. W., *African Life and Customs*, C. M. Phillips, London, 1908.
Blyden, E. W., *The African Problem, and the Method of Its Solution*, Gibson Bros., Washington, D.C., 1890.

Johnson, G. W., 'The Ascendancy of Blaise Diagne and the Beginning of African Politics in Senegal', *Africa*, vol. XXXVI, no. 3, July, 1966, pp. 235–53.
Jones, Wilbur D., 'Blyden, Gladstone and the War', *The Journal of Negro History*, vol. XLIX, 1964, pp. 56–61.
Jones-Quartey, K. A. B., 'A Note on J. M. Sarbah and J. E. Casely Hayford: Ghanaian Leaders, Politicians, and Journalists – 1864–1930', *Sierra Leone Studies*, n.s., no. 14, Dec., 1960, pp. 57–62.
Jones-Quartey, K. A. B., 'Sierra Leone and Ghana: Nineteenth Century Pioneers in West African Journalism', *Sierra Leone Studies*, n.s., no. 12, Dec., 1959, pp. 230–44.
Jones-Quartey, K. A. B., 'Sierra Leone's Role in the Development of Ghana', *Sierra Leone Studies*, n.s., no. 10, June, 1958, pp. 73–84.
Keita, Modibo, 'The Foreign Policy of Mali', *International Affairs*, vol. 37, Oct., 1961, pp. 432–9.
Kirk-Greene, Anthony, 'David George: The Nova Scotia Experience', *Sierra Leone Studies*, n.s., no. 14, Dec., 1960, pp. 93–120.
Lynch, Hollis R., 'The Native Pastorate Controversy and Cultural Ethno-Centrism in Sierra Leone, 1871–1874', *The Journal of African History*, vol. V, no. 3, 1964, pp. 395–413.
Lynch, Hollis R., 'Edward W. Blyden: Pioneer West African Nationalist', *The Journal of African History*, vol. VI, no. 3, 1965, pp. 373–88.
Mauny, Raymond, Review of Diop's *Nations Nègres et Culture*, *Bulletin de l'Institut Français d'Afrique Noire*, vol. 22, 1960, pp. 544–51.
Mazrui, Ali A., 'African Attitudes to the European Economic Community', *International Affairs*, vol. 39, no. 1, Jan., 1963, pp. 24–36.
Pasquier, Roger, 'Les Débuts de la Presse au Sénégal', *Cahiers d'Etudes Africaines*, vol. II, 1962, pp. 477–90.
Pasquier, Roger, 'Villes du Sénégal aux XIX Siècle', *La Revue Française d'Histoire d'Outre-Mer*, vol. XLVII, no. 168–9, 1960, pp. 387–426.
Peyrat, Joseph, 'Un Congrès Pan-noir', *La Revue Indigène*, no. 151–3, Juillet–Août–Sept., 1921, pp. 133–45.
Sadji, Abdoulaye, 'Blaise Diagne', *Paris-Dakar*, Apr. 30, 1955.
Sadji, Abdoulaye, 'Souvenirs sur Blaise Diagne', *Paris-Dakar*, May 7, 1955.
Senghor, L. S., 'African-Negro Aesthetics', *Diogenes*, no. 16, winter, 1956, pp. 23–38.
Senghor, L. S., 'Some Thoughts on Africa: A Continent in Development', *International Affairs*, vol. 38, no. 2, Apr., 1962, pp. 189–95.
Shepperson, George, 'An Early African Graduate', *University of Edinburgh Gazette*, no. 32, Jan., 1962, pp. 23–6.
Soyinka, Wole, 'From a Common Backcloth: A Reassessment of the African Literary Image', *The American Scholar*, vol. 32, no. 3, summer, 1963, pp. 387–96.
Touré, Sékou, 'The Republic of Guinea', *International Affairs*, vol. 36, no. 2, Apr., 1960, pp. 168–73.
Wallerstein, Immanuel, 'La Recherche d'une Identité Nationale en

BIBLIOGRAPHY [483]

Nigeria, vol. 2, no. 4, Dec., 1963, pp. 486–516, and vol. 3, no. 1, Dec., 1964, pp. 73–101.

Balewa, Sir Abubakar Tafawa, 'Nigeria Looks Ahead', *Foreign Affairs*, vol. 41, no. 1, Oct., 1962, pp. 131–40.

Bartels, F. L., 'Philip Quaque, 1741–1816', *Transactions of the Gold Coast Historical Society of Ghana*, vol. IV, pt. 1, pp. 3–13.

Bartels, F. L. 'Philip Quaque, 1741–1816', *Transactions of the Gold Coast and Togoland Historical Society*, vol. I, pt. 5, pp. 153–77.

Blyden, E. W., 'Mohammedanism in Western Africa', *The People of Africa*, New York, 1871.

Blyden, E. W., 'The Negro in Ancient History', *The People of Africa*, New York, 1871.

Charpin, Henri, 'La Question Noire', *La Revue Indigène*, nos. 167–8, Nov.–Dec., 1922, pp. 275–85.

Cox-George, N. A., 'Direct Taxation in the Early History of Sierra Leone', *Sierra Leone Studies*, n.s., no. 5, Dec., 1955, pp. 20–35.

Davis, Arthur P., 'Personal Elements in the Poetry of Phillis Wheatley', *Phylon*, vol. XIV, no. 2, June, 1953, pp. 191–8.

Dike, K. O., 'African History and Self-Government', *West Africa*, nos. 1879, 1881, 1882, Feb. 28, Mar. 14, 21, 1953, pp. 177–8, 225–6, 251.

Fyfe, C. H., 'A. B. C. Sibthorpe: A Neglected Historian', *Sierra Leone Studies*, n.s., no. 10, June, 1958, pp. 99–109.

Fyfe, C. H., 'The Life and Times of John Ezzidio', *Sierra Leone Studies*, n.s., no. 4, June, 1955, pp. 213–23.

Fyfe, C. H., 'The Sierra Leone Press in the Nineteenth Century', *Sierra Leone Studies*, n.s., no. 8, June, 1957, pp. 226–36.

Foster, Charles I., 'The Colonization of Free Negroes in Liberia, 1816–1835', *The Journal of Negro History*, vol. XXXVIII, 1953, pp. 41–66.

Gallagher, J., 'Fowell Buxton and the New Africa Policy, 1838–1842', *The Cambridge Historical Journal*, vol. X, pp. 36–58.

Gwam, L. C., 'Dr. Henry (Rawlinson) Carr . . . 1863–1945', *Ibadan*, no. 17, Nov., 1963, pp. 3–8.

Hair, P. E. H., 'A Reference to A. B. C. Sibthorpe', *Sierra Leone Studies*, n.s., no. 18, Jan., 1966, pp. 69–70.

Halliburton, G., 'The Nova Scotia Settlers of 1792', *Sierra Leone Studies*, n.s., no. 9, Dec., 1957, pp. 16–25.

Hargreaves, J. D., 'African Colonization in the Nineteenth Century: Liberia and Sierra Leone', *Sierra Leone Studies*, n.s., no. 18, June, 1962, pp. 189–203.

Hargreaves, J. D., 'Colonial Office Opinions on the Constitution of 1863', *Sierra Leone Studies*, n.s., no. 5, Dec., 1955, pp. 2–10.

Hargreaves, J. D., 'The Evolution of the Native Affairs Department', *Sierra Leone Studies*, n.s., no. 3, Dec., 1954, pp. 168–84.

Hodgkin, Thomas and Schachter, Ruth, 'French-Speaking West Africa in Transition', *International Conciliation*, no. 528, May, 1960, pp. 375–436.

Ikoli, Ernest, 'The Nigerian Press', *The West African Review*, vol. XXI, no. 273, June, 1950, pp. 625–7.

The African Times, London.
L'Afrique Occidentale, Dakar.
L'A.O.F., Dakar.
La Démocratie du Sénégal, Dakar.
La Dépêche Coloniale, Paris.
The Economist, London.
The Church Missionary Intelligencer, London.
The Evangelical Magazine, London.
La France Coloniale, Dakar.
The Gold Coast Chronicle, Accra.
The Gold Coast Echo, Cape Coast.
The Gold Coast Independent, Accra.
The Gold Coast Leader, Cape Coast.
The Gold Coast Methodist Times, Cape Coast.
The Independent, Freetown.
The Lagos Daily News, Lagos.
The Lagos Standard, Lagos.
The Lagos Weekly Record, Lagos.
Liberia Herald, Monrovia.
The Nigerian Pioneer, Lagos.
L'Ouest Africain Français, Dakar.
Paris-Dakar, Dakar.
Le Petit Sénégalais, St. Louis.
The Philanthropist, London.
Proceedings of the Royal Colonial Institute, London.
Le Réveil du Sénégal, St. Louis.
The Sierra Leone Church Times, Freetown.
The Sierra Leone Weekly News, Freetown.
Le Temps, Paris.
West Africa, London.
The West African Mail, Liverpool.
The West African Pilot, Lagos.
The West African Reporter, Freetown.

4 ARTICLES

Achebe, Chinua, 'Where Angels Fear to Tread', *Nigeria Magazine*, no. 75, Dec., 1962, pp. 61–2.
'African Personality', *The Economist*, vol. 193, Nov. 21, 1962, p. 711.
Ajayi, J. F. A., 'Henry Venn and the Policy of Development', *Journal of the Historical Society of Nigeria*, vol. I, no. 4, pp. 331–42.
Ajayi, J. F. A., 'Samuel Johnson, Historian of the Yoruba', *Nigeria Magazine*, no. 81, June, 1964, pp. 141–6.
'An Early Constitution of Sierra Leone', *Sierra Leone Studies*, no. XVIII, Nov., 1932, pp. 26–77.
Ayandele, E. A., 'An Assessment of James Johnson and his Place in Nigerian History, 1874–1917', *Journal of the Historical Society of*

Bibliography

1 MANUSCRIPT SOURCES

Archives Nationales, Section Outre-Mer, Paris.
Archives Nationales du Sénégal, Dakar.
John Edward Bruce Papers, Schomburg Collection, New York.
Henry Carr Papers, University of Ibadan.
Church Missionary Society Archives, London.
Clarkson Papers, British Museum.
Colonial Office Archives, Public Record Office, London.
Alexander Crummell Papers, Schomburg Collection, New York.
Foreign Office Archives, Public Record Office, London.
Ghana National Archives, Accra.
G. W. Johnson Papers, University of Ibadan.
Macaulay Papers, University of Ibadan.
Nigerian National Archives, Ibadan.
Sarbah Papers, Ghana National Archives, Accra.

2 OFFICIAL PUBLICATIONS

Gold Coast, *Legislative Council Debates.*
Gold Coast Sessional Papers, no. VII, 1919–1920.
Journal Officiel, Chambre des Députés, Paris.
Journal Officiel du Sénégal.
Moniteur du Sénégal et Dépendances.
Nigeria, *Legislative Council Debates.*
The Nigerian Gazette.
Sénégal, Conseil Général, *Minutes.*
Sénégal, Conseil Colonial, *Proceedings.*
Sierra Leone, *Report by Her Majesty's Commissioner and Correspondence on the Subject of the Insurrection in the Sierra Leone Protectorate, 1898,* [Chalmers Report], London, 1899.

3 NEWSPAPERS AND PERIODICALS

The African Mail, Liverpool.
The African Messenger, Lagos.

4 *The Continuity of African History*

The aftermath of the Second World War had indeed brought great changes to West Africa, to all of Africa. Political independence, the beginnings of modern economic development, an African presence in international affairs, the social and cultural revolutions accompanying economic and political metamorphosis all testified to vast and accelerated change. Yet the change was not so much in direction as in amplitude, not qualitative but quantitative. Africa moved forward more resolutely than ever to take possession of the fruits of westernization even as she appeared to recoil from the West politically and culturally. Nonetheless the reaction against western ideas and institutions was carried on, as in earlier times, largely through the medium of western institutions and systems of thought. Even that most African of movements, negritude, stripped down to a manifestation of cultural nationalism, while Senghor's philosophic flights, for all their appeal to an African mystique, appeared to owe much of their inspiration to systems of European thought.

This was understandable—rooted in an historical process which had been unfolding for a century and a half. The rhythm of attraction to and repulsion from Europe—the desire for the fruits of western civilization balanced against the fear of cultural annihilation—continued to preoccupy African leadership as it had in the days of Abbé Boilat, James Johnson, or Casely Hayford. And the reaction in West Africa to the impulse of Europe was much as it had been in earlier times. There was the old urge for economic development on western lines, and there was the suspicion of European motives and the desire for some form of cultural emancipation. Senghor, the philosopher of twentieth-century Africa, conceived the theory of the complementary nature of the world's races, an idea which had been put forward a century earlier by Edward W. Blyden, the philosopher of nineteenth-century Africa. Thus it might be said that, as present-day Africa continues its search for a new civilization, it will rely not only on the West but also on those who began this work before them during the difficult days when the fruits of western culture were first introduced to the people of Africa.

advantages. Similarly, Modibo Keita has explained that one important advantage of technical aid offered by the nations of eastern Europe lies in the fact that it is not given in such a way as 'to injure the pride or offend the dignity of the receiving country, which is only too aware of its lack of means'. Sékou Touré has on occasion been particularly eloquent in explaining the African view:

Man, as a human being must fulfil himself. . . . This is the real moving force of African nationalism . . . What we want is to have laws that are the expression of our own people . . . An imposed system . . . is never valued as much as one that one had created for oneself. What is lacking is human dignity. . . . We want to be responsible for our own lives. One can always give one's brother good advice, but he may prefer to make his own mistakes. That is the African psychology.

He might have said, that is human psychology.[1]

Finally, African identity has been linked with the desire to contribute to the march of the world's civilization in a way which is universally recognized and acclaimed. This impulse shows itself again and again – in the effort to develop a uniquely African literature and art, in the efforts of Nkrumah and others to influence international power politics, in the doctrines of negritude, in the assertions of Africa's moral superiority. Its fullest, most universal expression has taken shape in Léopold Sédar Senghor's image of modern civilization as the complementary action of the races of the world. The African, says Senghor, vibrates with his intuitive knowledge of the universe. The westerner learns through the process of discursive reasoning. Each in its way is only a partial realization of man's humanity. Hence the traditions of Graeco-Roman civilization, of Aristotle and Descartes, must be combined with the African's sympathetic understanding in order to gain the fullest comprehension of the meaning of life. 'Each continent, each race, each people possesses the total characteristics of mankind. Up to the twentieth century, each cultivated only his own qualities, scorning the others and thus developing only a partial image of man: a segment of civilization. Now,' concludes Senghor, 'in the twentieth century mankind must co-operate, each people with all others, to build the true humanity: the *Civilization of the Universal.*' Then at last will both Africa and mankind fulfil their destiny.[2]

[1] Sir Francis Ibiem in *West Africa*, no. 1777, Mar. 17, 1951, 237; Chinua Achebe, 'Where Angels Fear to Tread', *Nigeria Magazine*, no. 75, Dec. 1962, 61–2; *The Economist*, vol. 193, Nov. 21, 1962, 711; Modibo Keita, 'The Foreign Policy of Mali', *International Affairs*, vol. 37, Oct., 1961, 435; Sékou Touré, 'The Republic of Guinea', *ibid.*, vol. 36, no. 2, Apr., 1960, 170.
[2] Senghor, *Liberté 1, Négritude et Humanisme*, 296–7.

same time, Senghor concludes, the study of Africa must go forward through attention to such subjects as tropical medicine, Arabic and Islamic civilization, or African languages and societies.[1]

The search for identity is also evident in the renascence of interest among Africans in their history. While this has occasionally led to disputed claims concerning African origins as in the work of Cheikh Anta Diop of Senegal, it has more generally released a substantial and growing body of research designed to appeal to past accomplishment as a basis for self-confidence in the present. Young, emergent nations, requiring the psychological buttressing of historical continuity, turn to the resurrection of forgotten heroes like Sundiata, the reassessment of leaders like Samori, the use of state names like Ghana and Mali evoking past glory on behalf of present national unity, or more generally continue attempts to push back the frontier of knowledge in the search for origins. To the Nigerian historian, K. O. Dike, African self-respect must emerge not only from material accomplishment but from cultural achievement. This must come from an appreciation of Africa's cultural heritage, a grasp of the two thousand years of history which has made the contemporary African what he is. 'Only when he comprehends himself and his heritage', Dike concludes, 'can he govern himself successfully, and ... that comprehension has to be more than instinctive.'[2]

The need to establish an African identity is perhaps most sharply exemplified by the African's sensitivity over the question of individual, national, or racial dignity. In their various occupations, Africans have continually stressed the importance of African pride in accomplishment, of the need to assert the independence of African opinion and world view, and in the insistence on strict observance of national sovereignty and equality within the community of nations. When Sékou Touré visited London in 1962, he demanded and received the strictest sort of state protocol. This was no petty indulgence insisted upon by the insecure leader of a small nation. Touré pointed out repeatedly in his meetings with the press that his primary objective was to gain respect for the African, not to obtain more obvious economic and political

---

[1] Balewa, *Nigeria Speaks*, 162; N. Azikiwe, *Zik*, 283, 289, 295–7; *On African Socialism*, 61; Senghor, *Liberté 1, Négritude et Humanisme*, 295.
[2] Cheikh Anta Diop, *Nations Nègres et Culture*; R. Mauny, Review of *Nations Nègres et Culture*, *Bulletin de l'Institut Français d'Afrique Noire*, vol. 22, 1960, 544–51; I. Wallerstein, 'La Recherche d'une Identité Nationale en Afrique Occidentale', *Présence Africaine*, nouvelle série bimestrielle, no. 34–35, Oct. 1960–Jan. 1961, 84–7; J. Ki-Zerbo, 'African Personality and the New African Society', American Society of African Culture, *Pan-Africanism Reconsidered*, 281; K. O. Dike, 'African History and Self-Government', *West Africa*, no. 1882, Mar. 21, 1953, 251.

Yet some African critics complained that, literary merit aside, these writings lacked authenticity in the artificial, parochial image of African life they evoked – quaint stereotypes of a pseudo-exotic Africa for the entertainment of the literary dilettante, avoiding the deeper insights into human experience which are the responsibilities of the genuine artist. This objection has been introduced chiefly by the Nigerian playwright, Wole Soyinka, who has registered the same complaint concerning the French African writers – painfully self-conscious in their negritude and in their negritude limited in their humanity. Soyinka has thus become one of the first representatives of contemporary Africa to practise the emancipation from Europe others have demanded. In urging that the African artist be first an artist and secondly an African, he has dispatched national self-consciousness by ignoring it, as few others have yet found possible. 'Only through the confidence of individual art', he insists, '... can the African emerge as a creature of sensibilities.... Idealization is a travesty of literary truth; worse still, it betrays only immature hankerings of the creative impulse.'[1]

Echoing Soyinka, Sir Abubakar Tafawa Balewa said 'I do not believe in African personality, but in human personality.' Still the effort has gone forward to establish an African identity and presence in the world, to make certain that African dignity is not discounted. This has been manifest, for example, in changing educational theories and practice. In the post-war years, West African universities have not only fought their way into existence, but have struggled incessantly, if not always successfully, to develop curricula designed to strengthen the new societies materially and to provide them with ethical and cultural objectives which make meaningful this material advance. Political leaders like Nkrumah and Azikiwe have complained of university curricula copied from European models irrelevant to African needs, and Azikiwe went to the extent of founding in Eastern Nigeria a university along lines he felt were essential to African development. Even the assimilated Senghor deftly turns the threat of absorption – 'we must assimilate, not be assimilated' – and speaks of studies in the schools from the primary level through the university fitted to the needs of African, not French, students. To be sure, this means utilization of the best that Europe has to offer; not, however, in the interests of a cultural imperialism but to assist the African to master the problems of the modern world. At the

[1] Henry Swanzy, *Voices of Ghana*; Dennis Osadebay, *Africa Sings*; O. Bassir, ed., *An Anthology of West African Verse*; Chinua Achebe, *Things Fall Apart*; Wole Soyinka, 'From a Common Back Cloth', *The American Scholar*, vol. 32, no. 3, summer, 1963.

territories negritude came to be closely associated with artistic and literary activity which in turn was bound up with the process of nation-making.

The doctrines of negritude became the preserve of a group of French-African post-war artists and critics who banded together to proclaim and promote its virtues. Most were writers–novelists, poets and essayists–for negritude for the moment found little expression in the visual or musical arts. Less subtle or less sympathetic than Senghor, these writers eschewed his Afro-European synthesis in favour of a straightforward cultural nationalism which portrayed Africa as virtuous and Europe as depraved, and stressed the unsavoury aspects of colonialism. Though not precisely the negritude expounded by Senghor, it was a natural and predictable product of the post-war period–a nationalist reaction to the humiliations of colonial rule. It showed itself in the gentle simplicity of Camera Laye's *Dark Child*, in the bumptious verse of David Diop, in the self-conscious debates of the Pan-African congresses held in 1956 and 1959 under the auspices of *Présence Africaine*, in the idealized African world described by the novelist Cheikh Hamidou Kane. Interestingly, a large share of negritude writing was produced in Paris, the permanent residence of most of its apostles, while its philosophical base was the same French existentialism which inspired Senghor's thought.[1]

In English-speaking West Africa, the concept of negritude never scratched deeply but the same search for cultural identity, the same resentment against European domination, was apparent. Early efforts at literary expression tended to evoke a romantic image of the African past, either through traditional tales of village life or through more directly patriotic verse. Only an occasional poem or short story dealt more searchingly with the difficulties of reconciling Europe and Africa. During the late 1950s and early 1960s, however, a group of Nigerian novelists developed a more systematic approach to the theme of acceptance-rejection of Europe, and in the very process raised in a new form the fundamental question of Africa's ultimate cultural independence from the leading strings of the West. In the works of Chinua Achebe and others were explored the many facets of Africa's struggle for self-expression in the face of European cultural and political domination, and implicit was the concept of an African intellectual and cultural integrity needed to give purpose to Africa's economic development and political independence.

---

[1] *On African Socialism*, 49; see Camera Laye, *L'Enfant Noir*, D. Diop, *Coups de Pilons*, Présence Africaine, *Premier Congrès International des Écrivains et Artistes Noirs, Deuxième Congrès* . . . , Cheikh Hamidou Kane, *L'Aventure Ambiguë*.

than the understanding of man's whole universe. In the theories of the French philosopher-scientist, Pierre Teilhard de Chardin, Senghor found the concept of a universe whose evolutionary development was governed by synthesis–nuclear, biological and social. All complex forms sprang from a communion of simpler elements; hence those factors contributing to synthesis were contributing to a higher complexity and ultimately to a higher civilization. But, said Senghor, it is precisely through co-operation and dialogue, through a collectivism of family, village and tribe that the genius of African culture has manifested itself. Since perfectibility was to be found only through the concept of co-operation, Senghor insisted, it was clear that Africa had much to contribute to the future progress of the world.

The races of the world are necessarily complementary, Senghor concludes. Europe and Africa are complementary, and together they can fashion a civilization more perfect than that which lies within the power of either world alone. Europe can contribute her scientific knowledge and her socialism; Africa her own ancient communism, her spiritual strength and her realization that in art is found the meaning of life. The result, says Senghor, will be a higher synthesis:

Our ideal is the creation of the Civilization of the Universal, in which our complementary differences will be fused and live on together in symbiosis. We know how easy it is to be partisan in this world of unbridled passions. We . . . remain partisans of progress, peace, and friendship. . . . We have chosen the African way to Socialism, which will be a synthesis of Negro-African cultural values, of Western methodological and spiritual values, and Socialist technical and social values. Man is the constant factor in all our calculations; we want to make him happier by setting him free from contradictions and from all forms of slavery; we want to put an end to his 'alienation' in the real world.[1]

The more particularly European aspects of Senghor's African philosophy have generally been overlooked in favour of negritude–that amalgam of sympathetic reason, artistic sensitivity, religious feeling, identity with nature and basic humanity which characterized in Senghor's mind the African's response to the world around him. To Senghor, art was a fundamental quality of negritude and culture was 'the basis and the ultimate aim of politics . . . the spirit of civilization . . . the very texture of society'. Here, indeed, Senghor was far from the pragmatists of British West Africa, and it is not surprising that in the French-speaking

---

[1] *Ibid.*, 30; *On African Socialism*, 5, 13, 49, 134–40; Senghor, 'Some Thoughts on Africa; A Continent in Development', *International Affairs*, vol. 38, no. 2, Apr. 1962, 190–1; Senghor, *Pierre Teilhard de Chardin et la Politique Africaine*, 64.

boundless. To know this new universe required techniques far removed from traditional western logic with its reliance on objective analysis in which the observer always remained separated from the observed. Indeed, said Senghor, the new method was the opposite of predication and critical realism:

> To know an object, it no longer suffices to see it, to dissect it, to weigh it, even if one has the most perfect precision instruments. One must also touch it, penetrate it from the inside . . . and finger it. To know a human fact, psychological or social, no longer means to investigate it with the aid of statistics and graphs, but to live it . . . This is what phenomenological or existential thought reveals, as it follows the path of Marxism and exceeds it while integrating it. In this school of thought, the real coincides with thought, the content of a statement coincides with the form in which it is expressed, philosophy blends with science, as art merges with existence, with *life*. There is more than coincidence here, there is *identity*. . . . Thus, knowledge is less a creation than a discovery, less a discovery than a rediscovery. More specifically, knowledge coincides with the essence of a thing in its innate and original reality, in its discontinuous and undetermined reality, in its life.[1]

Europe's latter-day discovery of knowledge through sympathy was of greatest importance to Senghor, for as he pointed out, this was exactly the way in which the Negro-African had traditionally known the world around him. We all know that the Negro is a man of nature, Senghor has said. He lives off the land and with the land. He is a sensualist who permits nothing between subject and object. He is sound, odour, rhythm, form and colour; he feels rather than sees, senses within his flesh, projects his own being into another and thus knows it. The Negro reason is not discursive but synthetic, not antagonistic but sympathetic. Negro reason never kills what it is trying to understand by categorizing it and squeezing it of its sap. The white man's reason is analytical through use but the Negro approaches the world intuitively through participation. Hence, 'the black man's sensitivity, his emotional power. . . . [What] strikes the Negro is less the appearance of an object than its profound reality, its surreality; less its sign than its meaning. Water enchants him because it flows, fluid and blue, particularly because it washes, and even more because it purifies.'[2]

Here, then, was Europe moving towards a position which had always been occupied by Africa, and the significance of this philosophic rapprochement could scarcely be overstated for it involved nothing less

---

[1] Senghor, *On African Socialism*, vii–viii, 46, 68–71.
[2] Senghor, 'African-Negro Aesthetics', *Diogenes*, no. 16, winter, 1956, 23–4.

his African-oriented slogans, he claimed no uniqueness for an African way of life—his programme was essentially the economics of modernization applied to Africa. His professed African solution was no more than an African response to the exigencies of the African environment, and his African personality was only the African dealing with the problems of a developing economy. Africans studied African history or African geography because Africa was where they lived. They busied themselves with tropical medicine because this was the kind of medicine they needed in their daily lives. There was, in fact, no African mystique. Little concerned with humanistic questions, Nkrumah referred only occasionally to the need for the arts and letters in Africa in counterpoint to his constant emphasis on rural electrification, better urban water supplies, or the manufacture of fertilizers.[1]

Senghor's image of Africa was far more embracing, though no less theoretical. He has been described as an eclectic—borrowing trade union organization from French socialism, dialectics from Marx, or modern technology from the West, and applying these to traditional African values in order to build a new African civilization. Certainly as a practical politician he has been faced with down-to-earth problems of government and economic planning which call for utilization of solutions where they can be found. Nevertheless, Senghor has been no pragmatist, but a builder of philosophical systems in the best continental European style. His expressed objectives convey the scent of the scholar's closet; his picture of Africa's new civilization is cast in terms that strongly suggest European idealist thought, and more particularly, French existentialism.

Senghor's conception of what he calls African socialism begins with an exhaustive and erudite analysis of Marxism which he rejects in its Leninist-Stalinist mutation because of its atheism and materialism, but also more generally for two additional reasons. First, Marxism purports to be universal in its application but turns out to be of especial value only to the European proletariat which has profited along with the European bourgeoisie in the exploitation of colonial peoples. Second, Marx's philosophy was based on a view of the world limited by the scientific knowledge of Marx's own day which posited a universe of concrete substance and measurable dimension functioning according to fixed laws and knowable through observation and discursive reasoning. With the twentieth century came new theories of knowledge in the West born of the scientific revolutions which presented a universe far less tangible and palpable, indeterminate in its actions, and at once finite and

[1] *I Speak of Freedom*, 121.

be blown off the earth at this moment of rising expectations, and saw better uses for the vast sums spent on armaments, in the form of underwriting the needs of the developing countries of the world. Unable to deal with the great powers in their individual weakness, African states, said Nkrumah, must band together and through their positive neutrality exert pressure on the giants to divert attention and resources from a nuclear arms race to massive technical assistance for the new and needy nations of the world.[1]

Such a positive and articulate programme enunciated by an attractive, energetic leader, the first to engineer political independence in West Africa's post-war world, had strong appeal to Africans and captured the imagination of European observers as well. Unhappily, Nkrumah emerged in time, not as an architect of African modernization, but as an idealist corrupted by delusions of infallibility, not as a cool head capable of giving stability to new independence but as a romantic who confused his personal judgment with absolute truth and his self-esteem with universal public approval. The result was a steady deterioration of Ghana's political and economic affairs and a growing isolation of Africa's first pan-Africanist by Africa's own leaders. The national economy of Ghana was brought to a point of bankruptcy by a combination of maladroit policy and excessive zeal for industrialization. Preoccupation with the dangers of political opposition resulted in a one-party state with Nkrumah leading a government increasingly isolated from the country it governed, increasingly corrupt and increasingly inefficient. Many of Nkrumah's views on international affairs were unexceptionable, but his brand of pan-Africanism was so extreme as to leave him virtually alone among African leaders who might concur in his general objectives but who rarely acquiesced in the means for achieving them. When Nkrumah fell from power early in 1966, his passing delineated with awful clarity the gap that had developed between the ideals he had expressed so winningly and the reality of his failure.[2]

Like Kwame Nkrumah, Léopold Senghor regarded the new Africa as a unity; like Nkrumah he thought consciously of Africa's posture in the modern world and offered an articulated system through which that posture might be achieved. Yet the two men were worlds apart, not so much in their objectives as in their techniques, their style. Nkrumah's universe was defined by political methods and economic goals. Despite

---

[1] *I Speak of Freedom*, 117–18; *Africa Must Unite*, 199–200.
[2] Dennis Austin, *Politics in Ghana, 1946–1960*, 363–421; *West Africa*, no. 2543, Feb. 26, 1966, 231, no. 2544, Mar. 5, 1966, 262–3.

Some West African leaders like Sékou Touré shared Nkrumah's enthusiasm for African economic unity and condemned African participation in the European Economic Community as a step towards the creation of an African proletariat vis-à-vis a European bourgeoisie. Others, while agreeing with the overall objective of economic development, were less sure about methods. Senghor spoke for most of French-speaking West Africa when he described his objective of a state socialism which provided development planning and government operation of certain sectors of the economy but which allowed ample latitude for the encouragement of private capital from abroad. Further, Senghor reached exactly opposite conclusions from Nkrumah concerning the Common Market, insisting that co-ordination within the Market area would prevent the balkanization of African states and enable them to gain much needed credits in trade with Europe. Among leaders of independent Nigeria, there was initially the feeling that Africa could gain little from joining a European union but that cautious attempts should be made for economic co-operation among African nations. National development plans were an essential part of Nigeria's efforts to modernize, but considerable encouragement was given to foreign aid and investment and less fear was expressed than in the case of Nkrumah over the danger that foreign assistance would necessarily lead to a new economic domination of Africa by the more developed nations of the world.[1]

For Kwame Nkrumah, the search for modernization was the starting point, not only for domestic policy, but for much of his strategy in foreign affairs. If his slogan, 'Neo-colonialism', reflected fear that there were newer and more insidious forms of colonial domination, his 'African Personality' meant that the African valued his freedom to work out his destiny in his own way, not in ways imposed upon him by either malign or well-meaning outsiders. If 'pan-Africanism' expressed a reasonable desire to develop political and economic strength through unity, 'Positive Neutrality' and 'Non-alignment' were doctrines which sought to utilize that unity to preserve past, present and future gains for an independent Africa. Modern warfare and arms races were obviously expensive and highly dangerous phenomena, Nkrumah insisted. African nations, valuing their newborn independence and looking forward with hope to a brighter future through economic revolution, did not want to

[1] Ali A. Mazrui, 'African Attitudes to the European Economic Community', *International Affairs*, Jan., 1963, vol. 39, no. 1, 30; L. S. Senghor, *On African Socialism*, 16–17, 57–9, 155; Sir Abubakar Tafawa Balewa, *Nigeria Speaks*, 57, 137–42, 147; Balewa, 'Nigeria Looks Ahead', *Foreign Affairs*, Oct., 1962, vol. 41, no. 1, 135.

stamped out and replaced by an integrity in public life equal to the task of national development.[1]

Such an analysis was close to the classic formula for modernization. One of the basic purposes of the attack on traditionalism, Nkrumah explained, was the necessity for effecting a revolution in agricultural production. Productivity had to be raised significantly and changed from subsistence farming to a commodity cultivation carefully designed to provide adequate food for a steadily rising population while supplying local industry with raw materials and producing cash crops which could pay for necessary imports. In this respect, cocoa was a particularly vital West African crop for earning international exchange, but under the British it had been encouraged to the dangerous exclusion of diversification. Hence, said Nkrumah, greater attention had to be given to other agricultural products—fruit, palm products, rubber, coffee, spices and tobacco—in order to free the country from the risks of price fluctuations on the international markets. Beyond this, agreements with other major producers like Nigeria or Brazil could be effected further to control and stabilize the market situation.[2]

Nevertheless agricultural reform was insufficient without complementary industrialization. In Ghana this meant major developments like the Volta River project designed to provide national power coverage along with the manufacture of aluminium for an expanding world market. It also meant new industries to supplement the old economy as with the modern fishing and canning establishment at Tema, or improved commercial facilities in the form of Ghana's new merchant fleet and modernized ports. To finance these developments, foreign investment would be needed, but Nkrumah argued that the state should assume as great a share of the investment burden as possible in order to forestall attempts by former colonial powers or other nations striving to gain control of Africa's actual and potential riches. In this connection, Nkrumah warned that association in the European Common Market would surely thrust back the new African nation to its subservient colonial position as provider of raw materials for Europe. Much more sensible, he urged, was an African common market which would pool and co-ordinate resources and develop large-scale unified buying and selling policies with which to confront the economically sophisticated and powerful West.[3]

[1] Kwame Nkrumah, *I Speak of Freedom*, 30, 37, 47, 53, 104; Nkrumah, *Africa Must Unite*, 64–5, 100, 104–5.
[2] *Ibid.*, 108–10, 121.
[3] *I Speak of Freedom*, 86–7; *Africa Must Unite*, 160, 168–9.

first step to economic advance, partly because it eliminated once and for all the exploitation of colonialism, and partly because it freed African leadership to effect fundamental changes in African society prerequisite to economic development. Among English-speaking West Africans there were further divisions between those who hoped to force the pace of modernization through rigorous state authority, and those who took a more relaxed view of government planning, and laid proportionately greater emphasis on the preservation of democratic political institutions.

Two West African leaders in particular—Kwame Nkrumah and Léopold Senghor—were successful in constructing forceful and articulate philosophies describing the aspirations of the independent West African. Nkrumah was the first, and perhaps the more successful, of the two in giving currency throughout Africa to his ideas. Stressing the close relationship between political action and economic objectives, he pointed out how political independence presented the opportunity to alter the pattern of traditional agriculture, to create a corps of technicians capable of operating the mechanics of a complex society, and to develop new social values consonant with the new economic system. This would require, he continued, a high degree of state control; hence there had to be an effectively centralized government and an end to such divisive institutions as tribalism, regionalism and federalism. The central authority would organize the countryside, not through the chiefly institution or some form of federalism, but through a network of local political councils and officials responsible to the centre. Democratic processes would be honoured, but if a traditionalist or separatist opposition developed, the luxury of democracy would have to give way to authoritarianism in order to ensure the continued effectiveness of the state.

Outdated social and economic custom would have to go, Nkrumah went on. The extended family encouraged nepotism and a system of gifts and bribes which rewarded indolence, retarded productivity, opposed savings and discriminated against the energetic and resourceful. Polygamy was a further impediment as were laws of succession and inheritance designed to stifle the creative urge. Customs governing landholding would have to be revised to strengthen title and enable owners to raise capital and to finance commerce and light industry in the rural areas. A desire for systematic saving, long discouraged under traditional patterns of family responsibility, would have to be instilled in the interests of capital accumulation. Corruption and bribery were to be

to the idea of independence with his provocative emphasis on the inequities of colonial rule and his drive towards a political organization of national dimension.[1]

The dramatic breakthrough which this new leadership effected during the post-war years brought not only political freedom to Africa. It appeared as well to sound the arrival of a more thoroughgoing emancipation involving the reassertion of ancient African cultural and philosophical truths, and a determination to proclaim newly-won national independence by assuming a posture of unmistakable equality with the world's established nations. Gone, it would seem, was the partial or total deference to western standards which had characterized the attitudes of the older generation of pre-war leaders. The change was apparent in many ways–in the shift from Victorian morning coat to Nigerian agbada or Ghanaian kente cloth; in the outburst on behalf of the concept of negritude, already developed before the war but now given much greater prominence through the writing and thought of Aimé Césaire, Léopold Senghor and their followers; in the renascence of interest in Africa's past on the part of a rising group of university-trained historians; in the post-war efforts to develop a new African art and literature which enunciated cultural independence from former colonial masters and gave meaning to the image of the new nations; in the manifold movements towards pan-African co-operation; in the spate of slogans that emerged proclaiming the non-alignment of the African personality in a neo-colonial world, or pan-Africanism as a solution to the balkanization threatening African socialism.

These various manifestations of a new independence were related to one overriding objective–the establishment of modern nation-states in Africa. Since the early nineteenth century, the people of West Africa had aspired to the material advantages which western science and technology had achieved in Europe. Now, at last, the opportunity presented itself for a major African advance towards modernization. Opinions differed somewhat as to the preferred route, but there was general concurrence that political freedom, government planning and modernization of the economy were closely interrelated. Within most of the French territories there was a leaning towards gradualism in which a high degree of co-operation between the African states and France could continue. In the British areas, independence was regarded more as a necessary

[1] James S. Coleman, *Nigeria, Background to Nationalism*, 134, 220–4, 230–55, 260–7; Ruth S. Morgenthau, *Political Parties in French-Speaking West Africa*, 10–16, 138–53; Thomas Hodgkin, *African Political Parties*, 23–5, 32, 38–44; George Padmore, *Pan-Africanism or Communism*, 152–3, 175–85.

differed in detail but ultimately arrived at the same end of national independence.

Not only did the Second World War inaugurate an abrupt change in the fortunes of West African nationalism, it witnessed as well a new style in African leadership. The old élites had established their ascendancy through a thoroughgoing western education open to a small number of urban-based professional people. Leaders like Casely Hayford, Herbert Macaulay or Blaise Diagne needed only to appeal to this restricted class of which they were representatives and which constituted their political support. In the years leading up to the war, however, changes began to take place which were to affect post-war political leadership. First of all, a greater number of West Africans were becoming educated, not to the degree of the former élite, but enough to form a substantial body of literate clerks, entrepreneurs, schoolteachers, trade unionists and government workers to whom nationalist appeals against colonial rule could be made. Secondly, the systems of transportation and communication within West Africa were being expanded and refined to the point that this new educated class could be approached and organized politically in ways that would have been impossible at an earlier time. During the 1930s a new brand of popular journalism was successfully introduced which demonstrated that fresh ideas, audacity and energy might be made to rally a large political following, far greater in extent and numbers than anything previously attempted.

The war accelerated the whole process of change. Soldiers returned from abroad with a new sophistication concerning the world they lived in; state-controlled economic readjustment accentuated grievances over wages, prices and jobs; a sharply rising school enrolment further increased the size of the educated class; university students studying in France, Britain and the United States began to return home with egalitarian, radical or anti-colonial attitudes and a knowledge of the techniques of political manipulation. When the colonial governments expanded the suffrage, first in French Africa in 1946 and subsequently in the British areas, there was for the first time the opportunity for effective nationwide political organization and activity. A popular leadership emerged to take command—Léopold Senghor in Senegal, replacing Lamine Guèye with the help of rural votes; Kwame Nkrumah in the Gold Coast, easily sweeping aside the old-fashioned conservatism of J. B. Danquah; Sékou Touré in Guinea relying on a combination of trade union organization and the appeal of the magic name of his illustrious ancestor, Samori; Nnamdi Azikiwe in Nigeria rallying the country

objective, in style rather than substance. The term, assimilation, has come to identify the process by which native Africans of the French colonies have been absorbed by French culture. If Senegalese leaders from Gabriel Pellegrin and Abbé Boilat to Blaise Diagne and Lamine Guèye were thoroughly assimilated into French ways, British Africans were no less assimilated into the British version of European culture. Carr with his London tailor and his hankering for European holidays appears essentially no different from Macaulay whose cultivated flamboyance was more Edwardian than Yoruban. These surface manifestations were not superficial. They represented a deep intellectual and psychological commitment, and Macaulay's protest was just as much a part of the pattern as Carr's acquiescence. French Africans learned from France the doctrine of the unity of French culture and only slowly and reluctantly accepted the idea of independence from France. Englishmen, reserving the right of political separatism as part of their way of life, instilled this principle in the minds of their colonial people. Thus assimilated, the British Africans thought not only of modernization but of political autonomy as well.

This formative period of a century and a half was a seedbed where human aspirations to a better existence were first brought to life, where the shattering impact of western science and technology was absorbed, where Africa's posture in relation to a modern world was painfully conceived. The opportunities presented through political independence in the middle of the twentieth century did not always find West Africans prepared for the trials which confronted them. Nevertheless, the fact that they were strangers neither to Europe nor to the revolution of modernization may be traced to the exertions of those who had preceded them; that they were powerfully attracted to modernization reflected the experiences and wisdom passed down to them by their pioneer forebears.

3 *The Search for Identity in Modern Africa*

In West Africa the vision of democratic self-determination, stimulated during the First World War, soon faded before the chill of the European post-war reaction. Far different was the situation which developed at the conclusion of hostilities in 1945. The Atlantic Charter reaffirming the concept of self-government was predictably hailed in British West Africa, but, more important, it was followed by constitutional concessions to a rising popular demand which led to internal self-government and eventually to political freedom. The pattern in the French territories

they proclaimed was a European invention, and all of them were so thoroughly accustomed to the European style of living that they found difficult any personal concessions to the doctrines of Africanization they were propounding.

Thus among West African leadership the problem of racial identity became intensified. African self-assertion taught by Europe through European ideas of progress and human perfectibility, the European cult of nationalism, and European condescension towards Africa, was obliged to express itself primarily through European media. African aspiration towards self-improvement could be realized only through adoption of western standards of technology, economic development and education. The more the African struggled to improve his lot, the more he was engulfed; the more he turned from the old Africa, the more he was obliged to protect his African identity. The response of Blyden and his followers was therefore forced and understandable. Henry Carr may have been more logically correct in his acceptance of western standards, but psychologically he was out of tune with his people and his times.

Henry Carr was a realist; he saw things as they were and suited his actions and words to what he saw. Clearly, western civilization had a great deal to offer. Why deny it? Why try to forestall the inevitable? Why impede the good? More could be gained through co-operation than through opposition. The essential job was to improve the lot of the West African, and it was only a waste of time trying to score debating points in the legislative council or indulging in gaudy but ineffectual public displays. There were many who shared Carr's views. Samuel Lewis had been such a person, and so in their way were the nationalist historians Samuel Johnson and C. C. Reindorf. They longed to see their people united in fruitful accord, but a major goal was the introduction and mastery of the Christian civilization of Europe. Henry Carr was a realist, but he was no politician and no psychologist. The point was that the advantages of the West had to be introduced without admitting their superiority. Herbert Macaulay, like Blyden, saw this. With Macaulay the reaction was instinctive rather than rational; illogical, it was more profound than Carr's rationalism. In recognizing the need for both acceptance and rejection, Macaulay probed deep into the human heart to satisfy the psychological requirements of the people of West Africa.

Viewed from another perspective, both Carr and Macaulay were working towards the same goal. Both were patriots concerned with the welfare of their country–their differences lay in method rather than

essential and honoured position for the African among the world's races not only enunciated Negro equality with the white man, but demonstrated past African cultural achievements and predicted future African accomplishments.

Though some of Blyden's doctrines deeply shocked the traditionalist James Quaker and raised reservations in the mind of Samuel Lewis, his views had great appeal among the younger generation of African clergy as well as among African nationalists who made their appearance towards the end of the century. Gold Coast patriots like Mensah Sarbah, Attoh-Ahuma, James H. Brew, and Casely Hayford drew heavily on Blyden in pressing their views of the vitality of traditional institutions. In Lagos, John Payne Jackson used Blyden to chastise the British administration in Yorubaland, while those dissatisfied with the way of things within the Anglican church took the occasion of Blyden's call for independence to form their own congregation. In Senegal where the name of Blyden was probably little known the response to European expansionism by assimilated creoles like Gaspard Devès and J. J. Crespin was somewhat different, expressing itself in a struggle for political and economic control of the colony between the provincial and metropolitan mercantile interests. Unlike the British territories, there was little evidence of fundamental dissatisfaction among the mulatto population with European colonial rule.

What seems to be of greatest significance in Africa's vacillating reaction to Europe is the fact that all educated Africans, whatever their intramural differences, were increasingly dominated by European philosophies. Men like Kitoyi Ajasa, Henry Carr or Blaise Diagne who argued for greater reliance on Europe reflected a straightforward belief in the need for European economic, political, educational and intellectual standards. For their part, the nationalists of the Blyden school preached a cultural separatism for Africa but made good use of European ideas and institutions in presenting their arguments. Mensah Sarbah and Casely Hayford fell back on their British legal training and western scholarship to make their points concerning traditional Gold Coast customs. Western-style newspapers printed in European languages were the vehicles of Attoh-Ahuma, the Jacksons of Lagos, Blyden himself, Herbert Macaulay or the Young Senegalese. Education and economic development based essentially on western standards were constant demands of the nationalists; literacy was their vehicle of communication, and the economic rehabilitation they sought was only what had been proposed by English philanthropists many years earlier. The nationalism

English missionaries imbued with a sense of Anglo-Saxon superiority, unconvinced as to African capabilities and reluctant to serve under a black bishop.

Though sorely tried, Crowther bore these rebuffs with characteristic resignation and humility. His African pupils and successors were not so philosophical. They did not take easily to the concept that they were second-class human beings unable to rise above the limitations of their colour. Such notions were contrary to the Christian principles they had been taught and were refuted by their own missionary accomplishments in West Africa. Proud, aggressive individuals like James Johnson, Attoh-Ahuma and Majola Agbebi rebelled in a movement that led to the eventual establishment of independent churches in West Africa.

Moreover, it was at this moment that Europe adopted a radically new political relationship towards Africa. Within a few short decades leading up to the First World War, the continent was swallowed up and divided into colonies, and the educated, westernized African found himself thoroughly suspended between two worlds. Trained to an uncritical acceptance of the West, he was now rejected as an equal by Europe, and his country and people were made to subserve European interests. Unwilling and unable to return to a traditional Africa he no longer respected, he rose to its defence in part through loyalty and in part as an expression of national sentiments learned from the West. In the Gold Coast, for example, the educated community supported the traditional authorities as the locus of legitimate power wherein effective opposition to outside pressures could be concentrated. Men like John Mensah Sarbah and J. E. Casely Hayford were not in essential sympathy with chiefly rule—they were Europeanized Africans who wanted to be sure that their countries would emerge as modern self-directing communities; yet they were forced by Europe to resist the very civilization that was pressing in upon them. The result was an ambivalence towards the West, an acceptance-rejection which in varying forms has characterized African thinking to the present day.

During the nineteenth century the most subtle and far-reaching expression of this ambivalence emerged in the philosophy of Edward W. Blyden. Blyden would not permit the possibility of African acquiescence in Europe's double standard. To do so would risk a basic loss of self-respect, an admission of the alleged inferiority. His ingenious counter was a theory of racial equality which granted Europe all her accomplishments but which reserved large areas of achievement—particularly in moral and spiritual matters—to the Negro. Blyden's insistence on an

Quaker and A. B. C. Sibthorpe in education, William Grant and John Ezzidio in the business community.

By mid-century it was accepted that European culture was the medium needed to introduce West Africa into the modern world, and that the westernized African would himself be the essential agent in this development. Samuel Crowther and his fellow missionaries moved forward with the business of converting the indigenous people, Sierra Leone merchants began to open up the Yoruba country to the prospects of legitimate trade, Boilat and his colleagues instituted their abortive effort to establish French secondary education in St. Louis, and black men were attempting the experiment of self-government in the republic of Liberia.

Thereafter the crest of an unqualified African acceptance of Europe began to fall. It had reached its height with Africanus Horton, Paul Holle and the merchants of Freetown, all calling for increased European political and military involvement in West Africa. Horton was thoroughly committed to the idea of the westernization of African society; as a trained physician he could have done no less than demand the application of western science to age-old African medical problems, and as a sometime businessman, he had a lively interest in the economic dvelopment of his country. But Horton's plea for greater Europeanization was accompanied by his revolutionary suggestion of eventual African independence, and other voices of change soon joined his. Crowther, the apostle of Anglican orthodoxy, urged his clergy to learn local languages and argued that certain indigenous customs properly integrated into Christian religious instruction would help deepen the understanding of the people in the message of the Gospel. In Senegal a faint murmur of dissatisfaction with French administration was discernible. At Abeokuta the unique career of Reversible Johnson protested the British presence in Yorubaland. In Freetown the strident iconoclasm of William Rainy irritated the administration even as it entertained the populace.

Nevertheless, the first full measure of disillusionment came only with the demise of Bishop Crowther. Crowther had been one of the earliest and most successful African apostles of the European revolution. His quick mastery of the western, Christian way of life had led to his selection by the C.M.S. as the African on whom prime responsibility had been placed for spreading the message of the Bible and the Plough throughout West Africa. He had laboured hard at establishing missions on the Niger, and was first in the eyes of the educated African as the best example of the benefits of the policy for which he stood. Gradually his image began to tarnish, his authority to erode before the attacks of

based on a healthy exchange of West African agricultural produce for Europe's manufactured goods. Initially, it was admitted, these activities would have to be primed by European enterprise, but soon Africans trained to carry on the good work would emerge to form the leadership of self-sufficient states, black replicas of the sober, God-fearing mercantile community that constituted the essence of British society during the Victorian era.

The second movement emerged from the great Revolution of 1789 in France. The inequities of Bourbon oppression were to be swept away both in the homeland and in the overseas territories. Here, humanitarianism erupted in a more violent but a more complete fashion. There was to be no period of tutelage and transition. All men were at once free, all were brothers, all were privileged to partake of the responsibilities of self-government. The revolution undertook to guarantee not only national and individual freedom, but offered to all the prospect of immediate absorption into the French way of life. There would no longer be the division between the people of France and those of the Empire. There was only the idea of a greater France where men enjoyed the fruits of their culture, as fully in Senegal or the Antilles as in the Île de France or the Touraine.

At the points of European contact, the African response reflected a desire to absorb the standards, the values, and the institutions of the West. Reservations there were, as evidenced by the Nova Scotian uprising, the criticisms of slavery by men like Gustavus Vassa and Ottobah Cugoano, or the resistance to change among the *signares* of Senegal and the Maroons in Sierra Leone. Nevertheless the prevailing tone in the new settlements was that of assimilation of European culture–the close attachment of the mulattoes in Senegal to France, the American orientation of the Negro settlers in Liberia, the westernized flavour of the European enclaves on the Gold Coast, and particularly the emergence of the recaptives of Sierra Leone as African prototypes of British mid-nineteenth-century bourgeois respectability. Men like Hilary Teague in Liberia and Abbé Boilat in Senegal were fully representative of their communities. On the Gold Coast African leadership gravitated towards westernized merchants and clergymen–James Bannerman for example, who served as lieutenant-governor of the British territories in the early 1850s, or William De Graft, the Fanti assistant to the celebrated British Negro missionary, Thomas Birch Freeman. At Freetown the pattern was exemplified by such figures as William Fergusson in government service, George Nicol and G. J. Macaulay among the clergy, James

sensitivity which manifests itself in nagging doubts over the completeness of African independence from the West, in easily ruffled sensibilities concerning national integrity, or in a chronic desire to play a role on the international stage quite as important as the world's older, more established nations.

Between these two eras lies the second stage—the period during which Europe first introduced to Africa in a serious, systematic fashion the concept of the scientific-technological revolution, demonstrated the effect of that revolution in the development of modern European societies, and suggested the possibility that Africa might share in its advantages. It was in this period, beginning with Sierra Leone and Senegal in the late eighteenth century and continuing into the twentieth century, that West Africans first confronted this new world of the West and made their first efforts to understand it and to come to terms with it. It was to prove a difficult process for many reasons, not the least of which was Europe's colonial control over Africa. Nevertheless, it was during this period that the long metamorphosis towards modern Africa was begun, when pioneer West African leaders, grasping the significance of the revolution that confronted them, tried to bring their people into the brighter new world they saw before them.

2 *The Dilemma of Acceptance and Rejection*

The initial impulse came from Europe in two ways. First, the humanitarianism of eighteenth-century Britain led to the abolition of slavery at home, then to a growing interest in the worldwide problem of slavery which culminated in the founding of the Sierra Leone refuge in 1787, the abolition of the slave trade in 1807, the persistent efforts to sweep the slavers from the seas and the termination of slavery within the Empire in 1834. Most important of all was the concurrent conviction among British philanthropists that abolition in itself was not enough, that a programme of positive rehabilitation would be necessary to bring Africa out of her barbarism and ignorance in order that she might join Europe in the fruits of modern western civilization. Thus it was that men like Granville Sharp, Thomas Clarkson, Henry Thornton and Zachary Macaulay in the first instance, and Thomas Fowell Buxton and Henry Venn at a later period evolved their theories of African regeneration through Christianity and commerce. First abolish the slave trade, they argued, then through missionary enterprise introduce the religious and ethical blessings of a higher religious order along with an economy

THE MODERN WEST AFRICAN [459]

European contact with West Africa goes back five centuries, but the influence of Europe over this period has varied enormously. From the perspective of the twentieth-century African nation, there were three stages in Europe's relations with West Africa. The first covered the longest span of time, and bore few equals in the human misery it generated. Yet this early stage, dominated by the slave trade, was the least consequential measured by its effect on modern West Africa. Beginning in the fifteenth century, the Europeans came to trade–for gold, ivory, gum and other goods, and then for slaves. The traders were content to remain in their ships or at scattered coastal stations where they exchanged their goods for cargoes of slaves and then departed. Though students of the slave trade differ as to its impact on life in West Africa, such effect as European contact had on African society clearly was at best negative and depressive, both through the extraction of millions of men, women, and children, and the disruptive effect which slaving had on the development of stable, peaceful, progressive communities among the West African people. Nothing of consequence from Europe's vast store of scientific and humanistic knowledge seems to have been brought by the slavers, little was left but some acquaintance with guns and other war-making implements and an appetite for European products. West African society remained as it had been found, evolving primarily through internal forces and exigencies, largely unaffected by European contact.[1]

The third stage has just begun–the era of the developing nation-state. Its characteristics are familiar. West African countries have achieved political independence and are attempting with varying success to create nations with the degree of effective political control at the centre needed to organize a concerted march towards industrialization and the mechanization of agriculture. The people are poised between a traditional social order rooted in an outmoded past and a new dynamism related to the newer national economic aspirations. There is a great emphasis on planning and on education designed to provide the new nations with the trained scientists and professional cadres necessary to bring about and operate the new order. Like all periods of flux, it is an untidy time marked by political instability, clumsy economic policy, difficult social and individual adjustment. It is a period of optimism and high expectation, of youthful energy and impatience. It is also a period of great emotional

---

[1] Henri Brunschwig, *L'Avènement de l'Afrique Noire*, 16; R. Coupland, *The British Anti-Slavery Movement*, 21; J. D. Fage, *Introduction to the History of West Africa*, 86–7.

22 Epilogue: The Emergence of the Modern West African

1 *Africa and Europe – The Three Stages*

It requires no great prodigy of vision to note that the nations of West Africa in the mid-twentieth century have been and are being profoundly shaped by western ideas and institutions. The influences are most apparent in their physical aspect – the networks of highways, railroads and air lines, the burgeoning cities, the developing systems of education, or more trivial but no less significant indications such as television sets, gasoline stations, or Coca-Cola. Everywhere the move towards modernization is apparent. In the cities there is the evidence of western engineering and architecture, of industrial and commercial development, of banking establishments, of labour organizations, of western-style governments complete with civil service, and of slums and juvenile delinquency as well. On the land the change is less far-reaching and less evident, but it is there too – in the cash-crop agriculture, the experimental farms, the rural health centres, or in the power lines marching across country on their spidery supports. Least measurable is the influence which the West has exerted in the world of ideas. Some factors seem more pervasive than others; for example, the concept of nationalism. In other aspects westernization appears less pronounced. Tribal affiliations and traditional family institutions, for instance, have proved surprisingly resistant to the westernizing forces of science and the urban-industrial society; yet this is difficult ground to assess, for similar manifestations of parochialism have long been common in the West, and in Africa there are signs that these traditional social patterns are changing. Perhaps the most revealing indication of the degree to which the western way of life has installed itself in the African psyche is the thorough commitment which the African appears to have made to acquiring the advantages of this new way of life.

during his 1920–1 debate with Ofori Atta over representation. High-minded principles aside, he wanted it understood that representation went with taxation. 'After all who buys the motor-cars, the patent boots, the high collars, the fine shirts, builds the fine houses?' Those who paid for the government should be the ones who directed it.[1]

Such views were not uncommon at the time. European ideas continued to impress themselves on the educated Africans who quite naturally took on some of the middle-class mercantile thinking which their colonial masters exhibited during the post-war years. In Senegal, French assimilation had absorbed and neutralized the nationalism of Blaise Diagne and his followers. Even in Nigeria the activities of Herbert Macaulay could be regarded essentially as an effort to gain what advantage there was for a small group of educated Africans while happily indulging in a favourite role of gadfly to the British administration. To a considerable extent, Casely Hayford reflected the thinking of his times.

[1] Gold Coast, *Legislative Council Debates*, Apr. 25, 1921, 208; George Padmore, *The Gold Coast Revolution*, 52–3.

edge off such views, mellowing the uncompromising stand into something more accommodating and perhaps recognizing at last the extravagance of some of his more extreme pronouncements.

In part the stand which Casely Hayford took in his last years was circumstantial. In the surging enthusiasm which engulfed the world at the end of the First World War, all things seemed possible, the idea of human goodness and brotherhood was in the air, and self-determination was to be the hallmark of the future. The 1920s, however, came to be the period of gradual disillusion for the brave new world, in Europe as well as in Africa, and indeed for idealists the world over. African leaders saw their dreams of self-government go a-glimmering as they lost the initiative to colonial administrations unpersuaded by African arguments of self-competence and unwilling to yield the direction of growing colonial economies. For African nationalists, it was a bad period in which to live.

One further observation need be made concerning Casely Hayford and the educated African class from which he came. Their essential patriotism need not be questioned when it is remarked that they were a distinct social and economic group which tended to equate progress with the requirements of their class and leadership with the views they expressed. This was apparent in several respects. In the first place, many of their political demands were most likely to benefit the educated members of the community—a university for those who already had advanced schooling, an official policy of economic development which would open up the country and diminish exploitation by European commercial enterprise in favour of the indigenous entrepreneur, the end of discrimination in government positions so that the educated élite might replace British personnel. Even their position on land policy was not entirely disinterested; the demand for freedom from official interference was of direct assistance to the slowly emerging middle class in its efforts to gain a firmer hold on the local economy.

Beyond this, the educated community showed little fundamental belief in democratic institutions or willingness to recognize any leadership but its own. Despite the endless talk about traditional democracy, the elite were not prepared to co-operate with the chiefs except on terms which gave them undisputed leadership. Moreover, whenever they proposed schemes of representative government these invariably contained property and other qualifications on the franchise which would have placed the power squarely in the hands of the educated leaders themselves. Casely Hayford stated the case most eloquently, if ingenuously,

and more settled', he announced to the legislative council. His personal experience had shown that the advice of the educated African was being encouraged and utilized in the deliberations of the head chiefs, to the extent that his old reservations on this count had completely vanished. It was time to banish differences and join hands – the people among themselves, and all with the government – in the great work of building a new nation.[1]

4 Casely Hayford as Popular Representative

Casely Hayford's change of heart was criticized by those who felt there could be no concession either to the chiefs or to the government on the matter of representation. To some extent the criticism was justified, for he had accepted a situation he had initially opposed and agreed to work within its confines. This was in part a reflection of the man's character. By nature a compromiser rather than a fighter, he was a political realist who understood the futility of a stand on principle without power. To Casely Hayford the objective throughout the 1920s had been self-determination through a representative legislature and equality of opportunity in employment for Africans. His major effort to achieve these ends had been the National Congress, but the times were not ready for such pan-African ventures, and it failed. Within the Gold Coast he thought he could obtain increased popular representation through the educated leadership, but here again accomplishment fell short of expectations. In the end the practical politician was forced to recognize the limitations within which he worked, and he closed his career on a note of anti-climax, urging co-operation with the authorities and moderation on the part of a people who he felt could look for true political self-expression only in the distant future after a long period of tutelage.[2]

In addition to his willingness to come to terms with the inevitable, Casely Hayford in his later years may have been exhibiting some of the conservatism of age. His early career had been marked by a hot Gold Coast nationalism which struck out at the apparent inequities of alien rule and proudly defended the cultural and political traditions of a proud people. It was but natural that the passage of time would take the

---

[1] Kimble, *op. cit.*, 451–3, 494, 497; Gold Coast, *Legislative Council Debates*, Feb. 25, 1929, 155.
[2] Sampson, *Gold Coast Men of Affairs*, 29–33, 164–5; Sampson, *West African Leadership*, 24–6; Gold Coast, *Legislative Council Debates*, Feb. 25, 1929, 154, Feb. 26, 1930, 240.

the representation of the indigenous authorities to six members chosen by the head chiefs from among their number. The Native Administration Ordinance strengthened and extended the administrative and judicial functions of the head chiefs.[1]

The educated reaction to these developments was one of shocked horror. Not only was it contrary to traditional practice for chiefs to elect themselves to represent the people; far worse, the native authorities had doubled their strength in the central legislature while the educated élites were weakened, comparatively speaking. Casely Hayford represented the attitude of the educated community in his sharp criticism. The advanced coastal cities were grossly under-represented, he insisted, while the system of provincial representation was a total negation of traditional democracy, permitting head chiefs to choose legislative councillors from among their own ranks without any reference to their people. It was inevitable that the chiefs, lacking education, would be unequal to the complexities of parliamentary procedure, while the practice of having the government ratify those chiefs nominated merely ensured official control of the whole process. An artificial barrier had been raised between the towns and the country, he continued, dividing the people and depriving the mass of the population of its educated leadership. It was a patent attempt to divide and rule. 'Now that is no franchise at all', he cried. 'It is a mockery. It is a sham, a humbug. In every part of the world those who lead public opinion are qualified to do so, men of training, men of experience, men of sound education.'[2]

At first the educated leadership proposed to boycott the electoral arrangements but the practical politician in Casely Hayford soon counselled that the new constitution was a reality, the better to be endured from a position inside than outside the legislative council. When the government announced it would permit a broader number of advisers to assist the head chiefs with their many duties, Casely Hayford interpreted this as a concession to the educated community. Breaking with the more militant wing of his party, he successfully stood for election to the council and effected a reconciliation with Ofori Atta. Thereafter until his death three years later, he was an undeviating supporter of the *status quo*. 'There never was a time in my view in the history of this country when the basis of co-operation between the Government and the governed and between all classes of the community was more secure

---

[1] Kimble, *op. cit.*, 441-2, 492-3.
[2] Gold Coast, *Legislative Council Debates*, Mar. 18, 1926, 316-27; *The Gold Coast Leader*, July 3, 1926.

Having called into question the right of the chiefs to speak for the people, Casely Hayford turned next to an examination of the position of leadership of the educated elite. In the past he had maintained that the educated African was a natural leader, for it was he who had been able from earliest times to communicate with the European. More recently, with an increasing emphasis on education and literacy in everyday life, the more highly educated members of the community naturally assumed positions of leadership and were chosen by the authorities to assist in the process of government. Now, speaking in his usual succinct but fluent manner, he unfolded his argument still further before the closely attentive councillors. There was, he insisted, the question of taxation. Those who paid the taxes were the ones who had the greatest right of a voice in public disbursements.

Still, it was the broader principle of public service which the speaker chose as his ultimate argument:

The educated class represents substantially the intelligentsia and the advanced thought of British West Africa, and the principles it stands for are some of those fundamental ones that have always actuated communities that have arrived at the stage of National consciousness. It also represents the bulk of the inhabitants of the various indigenous communities and with them claims, as sons of the soil, the inherent right to make representations as to extinguishing disabilities, and to submit recommendations for the necessary reforms. It falls to me to make it quite clear that the idea that when a man is educated and has adopted European ways he loses his identity with his people is a wrong notion.... Therefore I should like that this idea that there is a distinction between the educated and other classes be removed ... We simply ask for a certain amount of interest and control in the conduct of our own affairs.[1]

The issue thus was fairly joined between the traditional authorities and the elite as to which group was best qualified to provide their people with leadership. Though the case was being argued largely on the merits, it contained an element of a power struggle reflecting the dominating personalities of the two protagonists. Involved as well was the attitude of the British administration concerned with developing a larger share of African participation in government in such a way as would utilize and reconcile both the traditional and educated forces in the Gold Coast community. The solution of the authorities tended to stress the role of the chiefs who were accorded wider legislative and judicial powers under the Constitution of 1925 and the Native Administration Ordinance of 1927. The former provided that the three representatives from the towns be directly elected by the people but doubled

[1] *Ibid.*, Apr. 25, 1921, 195, 208, 218, 220; Sampson, *West African Leadership*, 62.

élite as advisers. This was no innovation, he pointed out, for the Fanti Confederation had been just such a coalition of traditional authorities and the educated African; nevertheless, changing times also called for changing circumstances and in the modern world the educated élite could no longer sit silent in total filial piety.[1]

It was just such an arrogation of authority which lay at the basis of the attack which Nana Ofori Atta levelled at the National Congress. In an able speech before the legislative council in 1920 he challenged the right of the educated African to speak for anyone but himself. The people at large were being guided quite adequately by the traditional rulers who were at once their servants and their leaders. As long as the chiefs remained on their stools, he pointed out, it was to be assumed that the people were satisfied with their stewardship. Matters affecting their territories could only be dealt with through the chiefs themselves, and no other African could assume such authority without specific chiefly authorization. It was the native authorities, Ofori Atta concluded, who were the only natural, rightful, and legitimate embodiment of the popular will.[2]

Casely Hayford's rebuttal was just as sharp. Replying to Ofori Atta before the legislative council, he challenged the chiefs' position as popular spokesmen. Nana Ofori Atta himself as an unofficial member of the legislative council could only represent the people in that forum if they had so elected and instructed him, and as a government nominee he obviously had no such sanction. Further, it was customary for the people to make known their views through a special spokesman or linguist. The chief was not the people's spokesman, he was simply their head. How then could Ofori Atta presume to speak for the people or for the other chiefs, when none had chosen him to do so?

Beyond that, continued Casely Hayford, Nana Ofori Atta had raised a very serious principle in constitutional law. He had suggested that no one in his district could express an opinion on any question common to the whole of the Gold Coast without his chiefly consent. This was a curious and dangerous doctrine, for while there seemed to be nothing in traditional practice to prevent private individuals from commenting on matters of common interest, it was precisely the chiefs themselves who were expressly denied such a right. They were not autocrats and they certainly were not spokesmen for the people. Ofori Atta's position on this matter therefore appeared highly irregular.

[1] Casely Hayford, *Gold Coast Native Institutions*, 250–4; *The Gold Coast Leader*, Mar. 28, 1903, Sept. 7–14, 1918, Oct. 24, 1925; Gold Coast, *Legislative Council Debates*, Nov. 2, 1918, 223.
[2] Gold Coast, *Legislative Council Debates*, Dec. 30, 1920, 345–64.

also had other bases. In the first place, the Congress movement was not supported in the Gold Coast by the old Aborigines' Rights Protection Society. Secondly, it was attacked as unrepresentative of the chiefly authority by Nana Ofori Atta, Paramount Chief of Akim Abuakwa, an important representative of the traditional powers on the legislative council. The position of the Aborigines' Rights Protection Society was primarily one of pique over Casely Hayford's failure to grant what its leaders felt was an adequate voice in the affairs of the Congress. The attack of Ofori Atta was another matter, however, and Casely Hayford moved with a dispatch and thoroughness demanded by the circumstances to meet this criticism. He was able to weaken Ofori Atta's position in part by demonstrating a considerable chiefly support within the Gold Coast for the Congress; for the rest, he and his colleagues continued to claim pre-eminence as community leaders, primarily because of their western education.[1]

The question had more general application, however. Who indeed were the people's representatives? Was it the chiefs whose rule was sanctioned by tradition but whose ability to rule was increasingly called into question by the exigencies of a modern world? Was it self-appointed parvenus who had no authority in the community based on custom, but whose knowledge of the West and of contemporary legal or technical questions qualified them to advise their people? The issue was whether the old Africa or the new was going to act as the liaison between the administration and the people, and in the long view, whether the traditional authorities or the new leadership would eventually become the government of emergent Africa.

Casely Hayford had over the years given considerable support to the chiefly power. He and others continually emphasized the importance of traditional procedures in the interests of good government, and it was precisely the representatives of the educated community who successfully defended such institutions as customary land law, who fought the erosion of the chiefly authority by British action, and who recommended participation by the chiefs at both the local and central governmental level. There was, however, one qualification to this support, at least in so far as Casely Hayford was concerned. He was more than happy to assist the chiefs as long as it was understood that they would share their authority with the educated African, or at any rate use members of the

---

[1] *The Gold Coast Independent*, Dec. 18–25, 1920, Jan. 29, May 28, 1921; *Journal of the African Society*, vol. XX, 1920–21, 145; H. E. G. Bartlett to Acting Colonial Secretary, Aug. 22, 1921, Adm. 11-1/1921, Ghana National Archives; *The Gold Coast Leader*, Mar. 29–Apr. 5, Apr. 12, 1919.

those who came would understand how to conduct themselves in a constitutional manner.[1]

Such ambivalence produced conflicting views of pan-Negro leadership inside and outside West Africa. Casely Hayford always acknowledged Marcus Garvey as a powerful force in bringing the grievances of the black race before the world and proposing a remedy, and did Garvey the honour of imitation by suggesting that Britain and the United States organize a free mandated territory in West Africa under League of Nations auspices for the repatriation of native Africans and exiles from America. Still, he regretted Garvey's advocacy of force as a solution to the Negro problem which he felt greatly reduced Garvey's moral effectiveness. In this respect Casely Hayford found the constitutional approach of W. E. B. Du Bois to be superior. Du Bois, however, and Booker T. Washington as well, struck Casely Hayford as provincial in approach to the Negro question, each limiting himself to racial problems in the United States alone. By contrast, the objectives and accomplishments of Marcus Garvey or of a man like Edward W. Blyden far transcended these more limited efforts, for they were designed, not for special factions, but for the black race as a whole. Still, philosophizing in the manner of Blyden could have its limitations in the face of practical needs. The saintly J. E. K. Aggrey, for example, was far too impracticable in his theorizing about co-operation between the races. Africa could no longer be soothed by such soporifics. The African would tolerate no more buffets and curses, insults and lynchings, said Casely Hayford. 'Until white world opinion becomes radically and basically changed in the direction of respecting the common civic rights of Africans generally,' he concluded, 'it is but waste breath to preach saintliness and self-mastery to Africans.'[2]

3 *Who were the People's Leaders?*

One of the criticisms which was early levelled at the National Congress of British West Africa was that it was largely the creature of certain members of the educated community who did not represent the people of West Africa. This may in part have been a carry-over of long-standing official prejudices concerning the role of the educated African, but it

[1] *The Gold Coast Leader*, Sept. 6-13, 1919, June 19, 1920, Jan. 7, 1922; *West African Leadership*, 65.
[2] *The Gold Coast Leader*, Oct. 8, 1921, Aug. 18, 1923, May 29, 1926; Casely Hayford, *The Disabilities of the Black Folk and Their Treatment, With an Appeal to the Labour Party; Ethiopia Unbound*, 163-5.

African, while the use of Europeans as teachers inevitably promoted false standards and confused educational objectives. Casely Hayford wanted a university to serve West Africa, but significantly he recommended that it be placed inland away from the corrupting foreign influences found along the coast. He wanted academic standards of the highest attainment, but he insisted on the study of Africa as a primary responsibility, and an approach to pedagogy from an African point of view. History, therefore, would be worldwide in its context but would deal centrally with Africa's role in the world's affairs. Stress would be laid on Africa as the cradle of philosophy and religion, science studied with an emphasis on examples drawn from Africa's storehouse. Professorships of African language would be needed, for character was formed in considerable measure through environment and language was one of the most subtly influential of environmental factors. Let such a university be a centre to attract students from the world over, let the study of African institutions spread to the Negro universities of America. Clearly the products of this university would be men–'no effete, mongrel, product of foreign systems'.[1]

West African leadership of pan-Africanism, as expressed by Casely Hayford, was a curious blend of law-abiding constitutionalism and racial belligerence–possibly a measure of personal ambivalence, possibly a reflection of the strain of reconciling a clear statement of racial emancipation with the need to avoid pronouncements which might appear seditious to the colonial authorities. On the one hand, Casely Hayford's paper the *Gold Coast Leader* gave repeated attention during the post-war years to evidences of Negro world solidarity–here commenting favourably on the 1919 Pan-African Congress in Paris or the Coloured Commonwealth of Britain, there lamenting racial problems in the United States or South Africa, and the absence of coloured colonial troops at a London post-war procession, and always urging the idea for unity of the people of West Africa. It was obvious that if the black man was to command his own soul, he needed to master his destiny through political freedom. But softly, 'the force thus engendered requires guiding and needs to be controlled'. Negroes in America would naturally turn to Africa, their homeland, for guidance and refreshment, but one advantage of such rapprochement would be the opportunity given the African of teaching the proper relation between government and governed, so that

[1] Sampson, *West African Leadership*, 73, 81–2; Casely Hayford, *United West Africa*, 10–15; *Ethiopia Unbound*, 17, 161, 171, 192–7; Edward W. Blyden, *African Life and Customs*, 77–88; *The Gold Coast Leader*, May 27, 1922, Sept. 22, 1923, June 7, 1924.

substantially to the new civilisation that is about dawning.... Africa can cure materialistic Europe of the war craze, that is, Africa intelligently combined and co-operative.... Dame Africa may yet be able presently to say to materialistic Europe: if you want any of the good things of my storehouse, you must really learn to behave yourselves and not go on like a set of bandits! If that happy hour should strike in world affairs, mankind will perforce adopt a new moral perspective.... Economically Africa can starve Europe in no time.... Henceforth the slayer and the disturber of the world's peace must... keep on his best behaviour.... We desire now to found for ourselves a place in the history of mankind more abiding than any that has gone before.... It is easy to see that by promoting the unity of the Ethiopian race we shall be indirectly promoting the unity of the entire human race.[1]

West African leadership for a pan-African movement implied an intellectual and cultural sophistication which rested upon principles of education always central to Casely Hayford's philosophy of African development. The problem was both quantitative and qualitative. Quantitatively, West Africa lacked adequate numbers of institutions – primary, secondary, university and technical – to deal with the expanding needs of a growing society, and the demands of the National Congress of British West Africa to this end were simply a straightforward reflection of this need. The qualitative question was more difficult, however. Since the days of Edward W. Blyden it had been argued by many Africans that a slavish adherence to European curricula and standards would lead to slavery indeed – a slavery of the mind more insidious and overpowering than the physical slavery with which Africa had had so long to contend. What was needed, therefore, was education for the highest professional and technical proficiency which yet would not lose sight of African national and racial heritage, African social instincts and patterns of thought.

Through the Congress Casely Hayford demanded such innovations as compulsory education in the larger communities, pensions for teachers, africanization of staff, better pay and training for teachers, expansion of vocational education and the establishment of a West African university. Nevertheless, he insisted, none of these recommendations could have much impact unless the ultimate objective be kept in view of developing the unique traits of the African character. On educational questions Casely Hayford was a wholehearted disciple of Blyden.

Africa could not realize her full potential by studying an alien culture, he contended. Western education denationalized and emasculated the

[1] *The Gold Coast Leader*, July 24–31, 1920.

the Congress could not survive the loss of its founder and protagonist, and it gradually dwindled away in the years that followed.

This pan-African idea of Casely Hayford was therefore premature, to say the least, although it certainly rested on strong logic. In part it was a means to the several ends which the Congress had promoted over the years and which its author hoped might result in self-determination for West Africa as a dominion within the British Empire. In part, it was also an element in a wider search for unity among the members of the black race which manifested itself during the early years of the twentieth century. Casely Hayford himself was certainly fully aware of the psychological potentialities of his Congress and repeatedly stressed its role, not only in unifying the black race, but in establishing leadership for the world Negro cause at its source—that is, in Africa itself:

As a Congress, we must be in advance of the current racial thought of the day. We must, to a certain extent, be able to guide and control it. There is intense activity in racial progress both in the United States and in the Islands of the Sea. But, admittedly, in the last analysis, the right inspiration must come from the mother continent; and in no part of Africa can such inspiration be so well supplied as in the West.

Under West African leadership, therefore, the Negro race would come together to harness the discoveries of science and make them work for the emancipation and prosperity of those who had too long been the burden-bearers for others. Co-operation was the key to the future—co-operation, to be sure, between white and black in a genuine effort to achieve racial equality, but also co-operation among members of the black race, just as the competitive white managed to co-operate with his own in the establishment of a progressive society:

If the black man hopes to survive, he must assimilate and adopt this sort of intensive co-operation. . . . Therefore there must come a point when we must make up our minds to shoulder our own industrial, educational, political, and religious burdens . . . Hitherto the practice has been for the European to make use of the African to get there. We must change that. The African must in future make it a point to get there himself.[1]

In the end, such co-operation among Africans would lead, not only to progress for the black race, but to a favourite objective of Casely Hayford and other African nationalists—world moral leadership:

Instinctively it is being felt that in race solidarity is the coming strength of a people who have once again in the cycle of the ages to contribute

[1] *The Gold Coast Independent*, Mar. 28, 1925; *The Gold Coast Leader*, June 9, Sept. 22, Nov. 24, 1923; Sampson, *West African Leadership*, 75–6, 78–80.

African economic expansion, greater local autonomy ensuring that both capital and labour would be adequately represented in the orderly development of the land. In this connection an interesting element of African economic discrimination also showed itself in the resolution calling for restrictions on Syrians settling in West Africa.

There were other recommendations which related to the major theme of self-determination. Legal reform was said to be long overdue, both in the court structure which delegated judicial functions to inexperienced executive officers, and in the double standard which applied one law to whites and another to blacks and discriminated against Africans becoming part of the legal apparatus in their own countries. The old question of land tenure also received a full airing, the argument of the conference claiming African competence to manage his own land, and suggesting complicity between European economic interests and the colonial government in trying by deceit and force to deprive the local landholder of his property. Further, it was suggested that greater competence in local self-government could be encouraged through a strengthened press, and particularly through an expanded and improved system of education with especial emphasis on a university for West Africa. Finally, the Congress put the seal on its theme of self-determination by protesting unilateral European disposition of former German colonies in Africa when the principles of Versailles cried out for utilization of some form of local referendum in countries like Togo and the Cameroons.[1]

The idea of united action was excellent in theory, and it received a good deal of popular support throughout West Africa; yet it had a number of practical limitations. First, there was division among the African leadership especially in Nigeria and the Gold Coast which robbed the Congress movement of much strength. Next, the authorities were suspicious of the Congress as a potential source of trouble and did nothing to encourage its activities. Further, the colonies were separated and isolated so that effective co-operation was difficult. Finally, the accomplishments of the Congress over the years were doubtful, though Casely Hayford claimed to have influenced legislative council reforms and induced the founding of Achimota College. When he died in 1930,

---

[1] National Congress of British West Africa, *Resolutions of the Conference of Africans of British West Africa*; Petition of the National Congress of British West Africa to King George V, Oct. 19, 1920, Correspondence Relating to the National Congress of British West Africa, *Gold Coast Sessional Papers, no. VII, 1919–1920*, C.O. 98/33; Patriarch J. G. Campbell, *The First Conference of Africans of British West Africa*.

and a correspondence took place on the subject between them and members of the educated communities in Nigeria, Sierra Leone and the Gambia. During the war years the idea remained largely dormant, but with the end of hostilities it was revived and emerged finally in the form of the first conference of the National Congress of British West Africa, held in Accra in March 1920.[1]

The Congress launched itself with a great show of energy and high expectations, and in its major addresses and resolutions the outline of its objectives became apparent. Leading all the rest was the demand for basic reform in constitutional government which would give Africans effective parity in the legislative council, create new houses of assembly with elected majorities and power over taxation and the colonial budgets, and establish self-government at the municipal level. The tone of the conference was clear–it was high time that some such reform were effected. West Africans had long-lived traditions of self-government and they now had a growing number of educated leaders, so that Wilsonian self-determination had relevance for West Africa at least as much as for other parts of the world. The appeal to Wilsonian democracy was somewhat ambiguous, however, as the conference suggested that suffrage be limited by property and educational qualifications, should appropriate indigenous voting procedures prove inadequate.

These proposed reforms were based upon ideas of human equality–especially between the black and white races–and the conference continued in this vein by insisting on equality of job opportunity for Africans in the civil service, in appointments to the medical service and in the nomination of judges. Beyond this, equality was demanded in economic opportunity, where many elements of favouritism were said to reside. In the past, it was maintained, the natural resources of West Africa had been exploited on behalf of British economic interests. Casely Hayford himself particularly stressed the unfortunate character of duties on exports which tended to depress prices in such a way as to favour British purchasers while the taxes were borne by the local producers. Now, at the war's end, there was the movement of the Empire Resources Development Committee which was no more than an attempt to take over African resources, to make the West African a serf on his own land, and to use Africa as a device for liquidating Britain's economic losses sustained in the war. Casely Hayford urged a different approach which would make foreign capital and indigenous labour partners in West

---

[1] Sampson, *West African Leadership*, 59; *The Lagos Weekly Record*, June 26, 1920; *The Gold Coast Leader*, Aug. 10–17, 1918.

others gave instinctive assent. Leadership, as always, consisted of anticipating the common will, not of providing great originality in thought and action. Interestingly, it was when Casely Hayford introduced his one major innovation in the pattern of African nationalism that he experienced his one conspicuous failure.

There was nothing wrong with his logic or imagination. To Casely Hayford there was but one way to the achievement of the many goals of the West African, and that was the way of unity. Unity in thought, unity in aspiration, unity in objective could be effected through unity of action, united political action. Here was the key to the new and better world in men's minds. True patriotism, he wrote at the time, is love of mankind. 'I venture to commend... the coming together of entire West Africa as one man to think together, and to act together in matters of common need.' It was a proposal exciting in its prospects, but for Casely Hayford it was no new idea. In 1892 he had stood before the people of Accra and urged them to unite in harmony that their country might prosper. Four years later he had extended the idea to include all of West Africa:

Has the reader ever tried to picture to himself a united West Africa, and what it would mean—with all its hinterland opened to commerce and civilization—with the whole sphere of influence intersected by railways, telephones, and the electric telegraph—with a central national assembly—with a common literature, the product, in a sense, of native intellect—with common religion? It is a grand idea. The present age is too feeble to take it in. But it looms large in the future nevertheless. It may not be in our time. But that it is realisable is within the region of practical politics. Of one thing . . . we may be absolutely certain, namely, that it is quite possible with the spread of education to live down all intertribal jealousies; and when that has taken place, you have nearly realised the dream. Therefore it is that no opportunity should be lost of sowing the spirit of unity among the different communities of West Africa.[1]

The idea for some practical form of united action among the people of British West Africa was first mooted in the period just prior to the outbreak of the First World War. It was discussed between Casely Hayford and Dr. R. A. Savage, at that time editor of the *Gold Coast Leader*,

---

[1] Magnus J. Sampson, *West African Leadership*, 153–7; *The Gold Coast Chronicle*, Nov. 14, 1892; *The Sierra Leone Weekly News*, Feb. 8, 1896.
The idea of community among West Africans had been implicit in the thinking of Edward W. Blyden who made a number of efforts to encourage larger political units in West Africa, but nothing came of these attempts. See Hollis R. Lynch, 'Edward W. Blyden: Pioneer West African Nationalist', *The Journal of African History*, vol. VI, no. 3, 1965, 373–88.

he founded his National Congress of British West Africa in 1920, a major platform plank was the franchise, not just for the Gold Coast but for all the British West African territories. When a limited right of election came, first in parts of Nigeria and then in Sierra Leone, Casely Hayford applauded the success but redoubled his demand both for advance in the other areas and for a more thoroughgoing reform in all. When qualified elected representation came to the Gold Coast under the new Constitution of 1925, it was rejected as insufficient. Five years later at its last meeting in Lagos, Casely Hayford's National Congress recorded the continuing disappointment of its membership with the rate of progress of constitutional reform in the countries of British West Africa where 'in none have the people been accorded the right of an effective voice in their affairs'.[1]

The campaign for legislative council representation, however, was only one part of a larger concept of African progress released through the aspirations generated at the close of the First World War. The idea of national self-determination took the imagination of West Africans, not the least in the Gold Coast with its long history of agitation for a greater share in local government. With self-determination would come other benefits – better administration of government, an improved economy, more effective public health facilities, an expanded system of public education. Representative government responsible to the people whose taxes supported it was one necessary step; so too was the end of the crown colony system with its arbitrary administration responsive to pressures in Britain and aloof from the desires and needs of Africa. Not that there was any expressed aspiration to total independence. Gold Coast leaders during the 1920s, like those in Nigeria, consistently protested their devotion to the British connection. Reform there would have to be, but it would always be reform within the British Empire.[2]

The significance of Casely Hayford's role during these years was not so much in the uniqueness as in the commonplaceness of his ideas. He became the most effective leader of West Africa in his generation precisely because his views were widely shared throughout British West Africa. It was he who, more than any other, was able to formulate, articulate and promote with tireless persistence the policies to which

[1] National Congress of British West Africa, *Resolutions of the Conference of Africans of British West Africa*, 1; *The Gold Coast Independent*, Mar. 24, 1923; Resolutions of the Fourth Session of the National Congress of British West Africa, Lagos, Jan., 1930, Macaulay Papers, IV-14.
[2] *The Gold Coast Leader*, July 19, Oct. 11, 1919; *The Gold Coast Independent*, Feb. 3, 1923.

The mighty upsurge released during the First World War on behalf of democracy and national self-determination greatly accelerated demands for enlarged participation in government on the part of the people of West Africa. To be sure such demands had been voiced intermittently over the years in the Gold Coast, but the note of urgency was sharply amplified as the Great War ended. The war's influence quite aside, moreover, conditions were changing rapidly as the economy expanded, and it appeared reasonable to the administration that a more representative forum than the old legislative council would henceforth be needed to give adequate representation to local African interests. In 1916, therefore, Governor Clifford reconstituted the council, enlarging its membership from nine to twenty-one and expanding the number of unofficial delegates to nine – three Europeans representing the business community, three paramount chiefs on behalf of the regions, and three educated Africans from the coastal cities. The official membership still constituted a majority, however, and all councillors were nominated, not elected.[1]

It was not surprising that Casely Hayford took a leading part in the African response to these reforms. He had long been an outspoken critic of the legislative council, commenting as early as 1888 that a council of appointed members dominated by an official majority made a farce of representative government. Ten years later he was petitioning the government on behalf of the people of the western province of the Gold Coast for greater and popularly chosen representation on the council, and after 1916 he and others continued to press these demands. There was every precedent for a representative legislature in the traditional councils of the people, he insisted; moreover, the alleged reform of 1916 in reality advanced the situation not one whit beyond the old position, for the change was quantitative, not substantive. Even more important, expanding economic opportunity in the Gold Coast strongly suggested that both foreign capital and domestic labour would prosper with more freedom from administrative restraint. Those who sought to open up the country were bound to seek a bigger voice in its government, while the people whose toil made such development possible were similarly and appropriately concerned with a greater direction in their own affairs.[2]

Over the years, therefore, Casely Hayford and a majority of the educated community continued to agitate for legislative reform. When

[1] David Kimble, *A Political History of Ghana, 1850–1928*, 433–5.
[2] *The Gold Coast Echo*, Aug. 10, 1888; Gold Coast, *Legislative Council Debates*, Nov. 2, 1918, 219, Nov. 26, 1919, 92–9, Apr. 25, 1921, 209–13; J. E. Casely Hayford, *United West Africa*, 27–9; *The Gold Coast Leader*, Sept. 30, 1916, June 5–12, 1920.

ment control once again faced the people. The administration, concerned over the problem of deforestation, had introduced a Forest Bill designed to establish forest reserves over what it called unoccupied, uncultivated lands. The responding popular protest was characteristic, and Casely Hayford took a leading role therewith.

He drew sinister comparisons between the Forest Bill and the earlier legislation, indicating that the government was prepared to convert forest reserves into public lands, thus compromising the freedom of indigenous ownership. Furthermore, he pointed out, the government could under the proposed law acquire through the agency of the governor-in-council any land it desired for forest reserves even if such land were clearly occupied. Finally, the cost of management of the forest reserves was to be met by attaching 60 per cent of the receipts of the reserves, only the remaining 40 per cent going to the owners. Thus it appeared that the owners of the soil were, through no action of their own, to be reduced to squatters on their own land, dependent upon foreign capitalists for daily wages, and at the mercy of a government which had the authority to limit cultivation to given areas, and in the final analysis to alienate without limit such lands as it desired. Small wonder, Casely Hayford concluded, that the people opposed this legislation; and indeed, the popular opposition generated was so great that the government was eventually forced to abandon its proposals.[1]

2 Self-determination, Pan-Africanism, and the National Congress of British West Africa

The principles set forth by Casely Hayford during these years leading up to the First World War reflected in large measure the views of the community of educated Africans in the Gold Coast, a community which presumed – probably correctly – to act as well on behalf of the indigenous authorities in the land. With the war's end, however, new conditions and new issues tended to force a split between the educated African and the traditional ruler so that a more complex division emerged poising government, educated African and chiefly authority each against the others. Within this changing context Casely Hayford continued to strive for greater autonomy, though always within the confines of the British Empire, for thoughts of absolute independence had long expired since the days of Africanus Horton.

[1] Casely Hayford, *Gold Coast Land Tenure and the Forest Bill*, 19, 25–7; *Gold Coast Land Tenure and the Forest Bill, 1911* (Second Notice), 6.

and reached decisions which were reported to the district councils through specially appointed representatives. From that stage the matter was referred to the great state council composed of district representatives and their advisers, and here the king in solemn conclave finally disposed of the problem. It was a beautiful system of finely meshed machinery, said Casely Hayford, perfectly designed to satisfy all segments of the population.

As a substitute for this, Britain could offer only the legislative council with its European official members pledged to vote with the government and its unofficial African minority which understood the wishes of the people but was never able to represent those wishes in any effective manner. Under this arrangement, Casely Hayford pointed out, the governor was more powerful than the English king himself, the administration was directed by individuals not responsible to the taxpayers whose revenue sustained the government, and the only way the people could secure redress was via the unsatisfactory process of petition. Plainly, said Casely Hayford, the solution was a representative assembly in which the chiefs took full part and all sections of the community were represented.[1]

Beyond this, the critic continued, it was necessary to emphasize the further consideration of Africa's communal method of property holding, so uniquely effective among the cultures of the world. Here again, it appeared that, by ignorance or design, the government was prepared to disregard traditional proficiency. There was some evidence, Casely Hayford warned, to show that official land legislation was no more than a technique for moving the people off their land in order to create a cheap labour supply, but whatever the motive, it was essential that government should not become overlord or owner of the land. Only the cultivator could be the owner; the creation of landlords could only mean serfdom for the African on his own land, and the consequences of this were incalculable.[2]

Still the government persisted in its foolish course, said Casely Hayford. In 1898, through the agency of the Aborigines' Rights Protection Society, the people had persuaded the Colonial Office to withdraw legislation designed to govern so-called public lands in ways contrary to native law. Thus the Concession Ordinance of 1900, while providing for the leasing of land, protected against alienation and clarified the status of individual ownership. Now in 1911 the old threat of govern-

[1] *Gold Coast Native Institutions*, 7, 120–1, 124–9, 164–5, 253–4.
[2] *The Truth About the West African Land Question*, 4, 7, 38–9.

alien administrator on the whole had abetted their disintegration by assuming that he was dealing with a savage people. Human sacrifice such as was practised in Ashanti was commonly cited by Britishers who conveniently forgot Britain's own history of witch hunts and hangings for sheep stealing. Local chiefs were held to be unable to govern their people by those who systematically weakened the authority of the chiefs by unseating them arbitrarily and packing them off to prison like common criminals.

With sensitive administrators like George Maclean, said Casely Hayford, these difficulties rarely arose, but many officials exceeded their authority as defined in the Bond of 1844, often with results as disastrous to British interests as to local institutions. It was evident, he continued, that England was in the Gold Coast primarily for trade; yet the actions of her agents often depressed normal commercial intercourse. Between Ashanti and the coast, for instance, there had long existed a profitable exchange conducted by Ashanti merchants coming to the coast to exchange gold, ivory and other products for the manufactured goods of Europe. This prosperous commerce was shattered by the English position on slavery after 1874. The Ashanti middlemen had many slaves among the retainers in their caravans. When they reached the coast these slaves were induced to run away with the result that the merchants often were obliged to abandon their goods for lack of manpower to transport them back to Ashanti. Long-standing goodwill and mutual confidence had thus been destroyed by British bungling, and it was unlikely that the once thriving exchange could be restored by the authorities through railroad communication and the miserable counterfeit of government stores in the hinterland.[1]

Similarly, British intransigence complicated the political life of the country. The Colonial Office in London failed to recognize that representative government was the very essence of the indigenous state system, that self-government in which all adults had a voice was as perfect and efficient as any such system extant. Furthermore, the nature of the British relationship on the Gold Coast had rested initially upon divided responsibilities—England being charged only with external affairs while internal government remained with the local authorities. Nonetheless, these factors had been studiously ignored. Under the indigenous system major issues were thoroughly studied and debated at various governmental levels. First, the village and town councils met

[1] *The Gold Coast Echo*, Oct. 9, 1888; *Gold Coast Native Institutions*, 30, 95–9, 161–2, 243, 260; *The Truth About the West African Land Question*, 91.

African habits of living be encouraged. With no image of servile imitation constantly before him, the European would soon come to regard the African far more seriously than was the usual case. For the African it would nourish the roots of his self-respect, and the process had no need to stop with the continental shores. Beginning in Africa itself the movement could become worldwide, securing the idea that Africa had her own history, customs and institutions which could be neglected in the present no more than in the past, and which could help sustain and strengthen the Negro who dwelt abroad in the lands of his oppression equally with his brother who remained at home in Africa.[1]

Essentially, however, Casely Hayford's posture was one of attack, not defence. His indictment of European colonial rule implied a moral superiority on the part of the black man which in turn suggested that in the final reckoning before God or the judgment of history, Africa and not Europe would prove to have been the greater force for human progress. Europe's weakness was her preoccupation with the material. Her love of strife and her courage seemed always to lead to bloodshed, while her misguided search for wealth eventually turned up naught but dross. For his part, the black man was physically and intellectually the equal of any on earth; sociologically he had made a unique contribution to the idea of family life; while spiritually he occupied a sphere peculiar to himself. When the West had exhausted its energies in the futile effort to achieve those things which satisfy not, the world would turn to Africa for inspiration, for only in Africa was to be found the spirit of pure altruism, the leaven of all human experience. 'The nation that can, in the next century show the greatest output of spiritual strength,' Casely Hayford concluded, 'that is the nation that shall lead the world.'[2]

Such pronouncements of a higher morality on the part of the materially depressed have crowded the pages of history and formed the basis for much religious activity. No doubt Casely Hayford took them not at their literal value but as a rallying cry to accompany the specifics of his more practical, historical criticism of British administration on the Gold Coast. For him, the crux of Britain's failure to institute effective equitable government rested on her unwillingness or inability to understand and utilize ancient and honourable local traditions and institutions of statecraft. The initial entry of the British had tended to upset local institutions, and instead of attempting to rebuild and preserve these institutions, the

[1] *Ibid.*, 168–9, 173–5, 185–6; Casely Hayford, *Gold Coast Native Institutions*, 234; *The Lagos Standard*, Oct. 7, 1903; Casely Hayford, *The Truth About the West African Land Question*, 101.
[2] *Ethiopia Unbound*, 1–2, 9, 62–3.

must remain a hewer of wood and drawer of water in his own country.[1]

For a time, continued Casely Hayford, the African too was naïve. He had accepted the white man at his word, and had put his faith in Christianity and the West, only to be cheated and deceived. All appeared lost for the European was strong and relentless before Africa's weakness and ignorance. Yet all was not lost. There was a gentler persuasion, Casely Hayford suggested, that might succeed where direct force could not. Many peoples had been compelled through history to bow to superior power, but no nation had ever succumbed which had refused to yield up its soul. It was still possible for the African to work out his own salvation, and once he had clearly delineated the image of his own standards and the logic of his own thoughts, he would sooner or later prevail. After the occupation of Kumasi, for example, newer coastal-type houses had been erected alongside the more frail impermanent traditional compounds, but in the long run was it not the intangible that mattered most? Would not the symbols of European authority ultimately fade while the Ashanti people still maintained their gods, their treasures, their golden stool, and their way of life safe from the contamination of alien contact?

Freedom, therefore, meant that each people was obliged to follow its own genius, not the alien standards of another race. For Africa this meant the heartbeat of the traditional village where the people had worked their fields in peace and harmony time out of mind. Behind the steady activity of the village stood the moral strength of the community with its ancestor worship, its contemplative existence and its spiritual simplicity. This was the backbone of Africa, said Casely Hayford, the village hinterland untouched by Europe with its frantic bustle, its ethical disorientation and its adherence to a misleading materialism:

You cannot think great thoughts in Africa by adopting wholesale the hurry and the bustle and the way of life of the European. Nature did not intend it. Those who attempt it end in trouble. Nay, worse. It means death. For even the dual man cannot serve both God and Mammon. And no worse burden could be imposed by civilisation on African nationality than the burden of a double life, the arch-enemy of Truth.

These idealized professions of faith were not enough in themselves, Casely Hayford continued. If the idea of an intrinsic African culture was to take root it would need visible, tangible symbols for the benefit both of the African and the European. It was essential that national dress and

[1] *Ethiopia Unbound*, 68–9, 81–4, 98–9.

self-government, defrauded of their economic resources and stripped even of the very essentials of their culture and way of life. Through some deception they had been lulled into accepting the blandishments of Europe, waking too late to evade the trap which closed on them. Forced to accept European political control, recognizing even the value of certain aspects of western civilization, they moved to protect those material and spiritual qualities of their society which could still be salvaged and which symbolized their search for independence and self-assertion.

In the Gold Coast it was Casely Hayford who was becoming by the turn of the century the most articulate and influential advocate of African national consciousness. Matching Mensah Sarbah's expertness on indigenous law and institutions, and succeeding Attoh-Ahuma as the leading editorial critic of the colonial régime, he added his own measure of protest over the years in the form of lofty but withering analyses of the effects of British rule in West Africa.

His attack was twofold. On the one hand he undertook to point out the moral and ethical shortcomings of colonial occupation while at the same time he criticized practical blunders caused by European administrators badly grounded in West African history and the workings of indigenous institutions. The ethical argument in turn pursued an essential duality which stressed the hypocrisy of materialistic Europe compared with the simple idealism of unspoiled, persecuted Africa. The European had professed Christian love and the desire to assist long-suffering Africa through abolition of the slave trade and the introduction of the more progressive aspects of western civilization. In fact, however, said Casely Hayford, they came to deprive the country of its riches, gutting the soil of its precious metals and enlisting the Africans as soldiers to fight imperialist wars, spilling African blood that now the Dutch, now the English, might profit. Not content with this quick havoc, they introduced alcoholic spirits along with the Gospel, cynically urging moral excellence on a people they were leading down the road to physical decay. The European Christian chaplains, far from teaching the message of peace and brotherhood, joined in the debauch, accepting colonial appointments as sinecures that they might help perpetuate notions of racial superiority and patterns of racial segregation. Only a few misguided government officers deviated from the standard—too honest to understand that indigenous chiefs were not to be encouraged to govern their people or children to attend schools, too naïve to distinguish between the professed policy of human brotherhood and the practical circumstances that the African

a natural flair for compromise to bring to life the master politician. A follower of the ideas of Edward Blyden, he lacked the old reformer's didactic persuasiveness, relying on indirection to achieve his objectives. *Ethiopia Unbound* was characteristic. A declaration on behalf of negritude as powerful as Blyden's best, it generated its argument through its subtleties and its sophisticated idealism, not through the purity and power of its logic.

Casely Hayford was typical of his generation. Born into a prominent Gold Coast family in 1866, he was educated at the Wesleyan Boys' High School in Cape Coast and at Fourah Bay College. For a while he served as a high-school principal in Accra until he lost the position through political activity, then found an abiding interest in newspaper work as a young editor on several local journals. For a time he worked as a law clerk in Cape Coast, and finding the law to his taste, he proceeded to Cambridge and London to complete his education and professional training. In 1896 he was back in the Gold Coast, a practising barrister and at once a leader in the controversy which was then reaching a climax between the authorities and the people over the government's attempt to regulate the administration and alienation of land in the Gold Coast. Asked by the Aborigines' Rights Protective Society to prepare a brief contesting the proposed legislation, Casely Hayford accumulated such copious material on indigenous Gold Coast institutions as to place himself alongside Mensah Sarbah as an accomplished student of traditional society as well as one of the most energetic informed advocates of African rights in the face of British colonial administration.[1]

This was a period of lively African reaction to colonial rule. In Lagos Herbert Macaulay was contributing his essays in the local press stressing the arrogance of the government's officers, and John Payne Jackson was beginning to recoil from his earlier generous views of colonial administration in Yorubaland. In Sierra Leone, Samuel Lewis was moving towards his falling out with Governor Cardew while Ernest Parkes could already see the end of his brief period of official influence. Still farther up the coast in Senegal, the creole interests were contesting the colony's trade with the French merchants of Bordeaux as forces slowly took shape which were to erupt in 1914 with the election of Blaise Diagne. Everywhere the bloom of the early missionary and philanthropic effort had faded. West Africans felt cheated of their land, deprived of their right of

---

[1] Magnus J. Sampson, *Gold Coast Men of Affairs*, 161-2; Sampson, *West African Leadership*, 12-13, 15, 24-7; Brandforth Griffith to Lord Knutsford, June 28, 1889, C.O. 96/202; Gold Coast, *Legislative Council Debates*, Dec. 4, 1930, 392-3; J. E. Casely Hayford, *Gold Coast Native Institutions*, xi-xiii.

his homeland only to discover heartache and ambiguity in what he saw there. One of his first visits was to the simple church of his boyhood, and when he arrived it was the hour of prayer. As he renewed acquaintance with the familiar but ageing faces, he was saddened by the inappropriateness of the scene. A Sankey hymn was being sung by the children in their Manchester homespun to the laboured accompaniment of a wheezy old harmonium. At the head of the choir stood the schoolmaster elegant in his cutaway coat, glazed cuffs, high collar and patent-leather shoes, but a bit of a fool in this costume so inappropriate to the people and the land. The minister was a white man preaching to a black congregation while outside the church a notice announced another service to be held later for Europeans only. The stranger returned home turned away in sadness and in anger. All at once he saw with a burst of insight what the mission of his life would have to be. He would dedicate himself to saving his people from the national and racial death which awaited them, practising these emasculated sentimentalities and shameless slanders proclaimed in the name of Christ. His people would have to be taught to recapture the virile religion of their past, to turn aside from a civilization which came with the Bible in one hand and the gin bottle in the other, which dismembered their tribes, alienated their lands, appropriated their goods, and drained the strength away from their time-tested authorities and institutions.[1]

The book was to a considerable extent an exercise in autobiographical reminiscence as the vehicle for a personal profession of faith in the black race. Its author was a Cape Coast barrister and political figure, Joseph E. Casely Hayford who, like the protagonist in his story, had prepared himself in England for a legal career and returned to his home in the Gold Coast to lend his voice to the African protest against the inequities of British rule. His was to be a persistent voice over the years – intelligent and incisive in its criticism, resourceful and energetic in its proposals, sincere and courageous in its profession of patriotic faith; yet Casely Hayford, for all his insight and sensitivity, for all his liberalism and humanity, was no crusader and certainly no revolutionary. Poised against his contemporary, Attoh-Ahuma, who thundered forth his condemnation of the vagaries of British rule with bluff forthrightness, Casely Hayford was subtle, ironic, oblique. An accomplished legal practitioner and scholar like his colleague Mensah Sarbah, yet he was more at home in the political arena where his talents as writer and speaker joined with

---

[1] J. E. Casely Hayford, *Ethiopia Unbound*, 65–75; *The African Times and Oriental Review*, Nov., 1912, vol. I, no. 5, lit. suppl., 7–8.

21 The Metamorphosis of Casely Hayford

1 *Casely Hayford Defends Africa's Traditional Institutions*

In 1911 there appeared in London an unusual literary work entitled *Ethiopia Unbound*. The book was unusual primarily in its form and tone — a loosely constructed piece which appeared to be a novel but which included large portions of intellectual autobiography, of historical, philosophic and literary references, and which was spun out in such a shifting evanescent fashion as to create a dreamlike illusion of unreality. Characters drifted in and out of the loose and insubstantial narrative which was frequently interrupted by long treatises in which the author was able to set forth his ideas on matters which interested him or by dialogues conducted between idealized characters in a stilted language appropriate to their artificial aspect.

Cast as fiction, the work was in fact an attempt to rally the black people of the world in defence of their own culture, their own accomplishments, their own racial integrity. The African, it seemed to say, had to learn to be himself, not to be content with a role as counterfeit white. It was permissible for him to pursue his university study and professional training in Europe, but it was not satisfactory for him to turn into a black European. Aware of his own identity, he could take from Europe that which was useful and reject that which was inappropriate, employing the essential African soul as touchstone. Looking beyond the crudities of traditional African life he might probe the inner meaning and deeper purpose of the ancient social systems of Africa, clothing them with modern techniques and directing them towards newer contemporary objectives. In such a way could he best serve the cause of Negro independence and manhood.

The protagonist in *Ethiopia Unbound* was a Gold Coast man who had gone to London for a time to read law, and who had finally returned to

as to details. In one particular, however, Ajasa felt strong personal convictions. Why, he demanded, must so much attention be lavished on instruction in the vernacular, when it was clear that a knowledge of English was essential both for commercial and social reasons? 'The languages and traditions of the natives of this country are not worthy of preservation', he observed, adding, 'A language without a literature is only of interest to the philologist. The traditions for the most part consist of faint records of comparatively recent tribal wars. They do not possess the slightest historical or literary value.'[1]

Ajasa's long tenure in the legislative council may be taken as a measure of the appreciation of the authorities for his support. Active in debate, he occasionally registered a mild demurrer over a particular piece of legislation, or defended the practice of the elected Lagos members of putting questions to administrative officers, 'not with the intention of embarrassing the Government', for, 'our duty here is to assist the Government in every possible way by bringing matters to their notice'. In the main, however, he gave full and loyal backing to official policy in a way which suggested some lack of independent judgment or will. Perhaps typical of the man was his reaction to the reorganization of the legislative council in 1922. Having first gone on record as opposing the move, Ajasa then quickly shifted to conform with the official line:

We have the eyes of many fixed on us ... They are watching us to see whether the negro has any capacity for self-government on modern lines ... Self-government must in any case be a matter of the distant future, but we can begin to afford evidence ... whether or not we have that capacity ... Let us give proof of our ability to attain the high ideals which have been placed before us ... Failure will bring down upon us the curse of generations to come, because the hands of the clock will be set back for us as a race, we do not know for how many countless years.[2]

Herein lay the essential difference between Kitoyi Ajasa and Henry Carr. The former lacked confidence in his people for he lacked confidence in his own independence of judgment. Carr, on the other hand, reached conclusions regarding colonial rule which, though not always popular, were based on his best estimate of the value of European civilization to African society. His faith in his own people did not falter because he never lost faith in himself.

[1] *Ibid.*, Aug. 19, 1920, Mar. 20, 1925, Feb. 5, 1926; Nigeria, *Legislative Council Debates*, May 5, 1926, 38.
[2] *Ibid.*, Oct. 31, 1923, 27–8, Feb. 19, 1926, 98.

to a fine art-the art of finding clever and cunning ways to [pander] to the wishes of the mob.[1]

If most Nigerians, either the people or their leaders, were incapable of mastering the intricacies of representative government, Ajasa had no doubts as to where to turn for respite. British rule in West Africa had been long and satisfactory, and Nigerians looked forward to many years of continued enlightened rule. When difficulties arose, they did not come from governmental disinterest in the needs of the people, but from popular ignorance of official objectives. Educated natives had a responsibility in this situation to help broaden the base of popular understanding of government policy. The government was unqualifiedly for the people, but if the system was going to work smoothly, the people would have to learn reciprocally to be for the government. The burden of proof it seems, was Nigerian, not British.[2]

Ajasa began publication of his *Nigerian Pioneer* in 1914, at Lugard's behest so it was said, and the paper quickly gained a reputation for cleaving to the administration line. Thomas Jackson accused it of practising a 'cult of flunkeyism and toadyism... which considers servility and hypocrisy as the *ultima thule* of imperial loyalty', and there was evidence to back these charges, in substance if not in severity. During that busy year, the *Pioneer* stoutly defended the work of the governor-general, especially in his amalgamation of greater Nigeria, criticized the people of Abeokuta for causing the Ijemo rioting, and congratulated the administration for its foresight in bringing a modern water supply to Lagos. On the controversial issue of the Provincial Courts Ordinance, Ajasa admitted that there might be evidence of some judicial irregularities but these were being rectified. Furthermore, a system of jurisprudence appropriate for advanced societies could scarcely be considered appropriate for the Nigerian people, 'just emerging from barbarism'.[3]

As with most of his compatriots, Ajasa saw education as the means for achieving the long struggle away from African primitivism. There were many aspects of education which needed attention-the proper training of craftsmen and enlightened farmers in order that the wealth of the country might be intelligently exploited, the careful education of the talented minority which would constitute responsible leadership, and the inculcation of standards of character. Since the European was a specialist in educational techniques, it were wise to follow his suggestions

[1] *The Nigerian Pioneer*, Feb. 13, 1925.
[2] *Ibid.*, May 5, 1922, Oct. 17, 1930.
[3] *The Lagos Weekly Record*, Dec. 5 & 12, 1914; *The Nigerian Pioneer*, Mar. 24, 1914, Jan. 8, 1915.

by all means make use of it. If traditional African social institutions remained virile and efficient, leave them alone. There was nothing doctrinaire in this point of view; it was purely pragmatic.

Ajasa appears to have been something else again. Whether because of his long period of residence and training in England, whether in response to a basic personal conviction, or whether the result of a somewhat less reflective approach to the world around him, Ajasa was a much more thoroughgoing, uncritical proponent of British colonialism, and a much less enthusiastic adherent of native African ways. To begin with, he shared little of Carr's belief in the perfectibility of the African and the future promise of his world. Sometimes commenting in the columns of his newspaper, sometimes debating in the legislative council, he played down African readiness for the proper exercise of representative government. He was lukewarm towards the constitutional reforms in 1922, pointing out that there was no tradition of elected representatives in Nigeria; moreover, the people were largely uneducated and incapable of understanding either the evils of ignorance or the need for a popularly elected government. Democracy was a delicate mechanism which worked, Ajasa assured his audience, only in the hands of experts. When mishandled, the administration became saddled with men elected not for patriotism and probity but for their ability to harass the government and cajole the people. What resulted was a raising of the vulgar to the top and a flinging of the worthy into the dust heap. Better to keep the old system of executive appointment of the people's representatives, until they became qualified to choose their own. Apparently qualification would be long coming, in Ajasa's judgment, for five years later, in 1927, he still argued that representative government was something for the distant future.[1]

Part of the African problem related to the primitive uneducated masses, but part was the responsibility of faulty leadership. What was the trouble?

The tendency of man, especially of the primitive man, is towards and for things bad, and human beings had in the past preferred and in some parts of the world, do still, prefer to worship bad malignant gods rather than those that are good. It is this instinct of the primitive mind ... that is still responsible for the unfortunate position of Lagos today. Leadership connotes the possession, in the leader, of superior ideas, of balanced judgment and the ability to 'lead'. Among those who profess and call themselves leaders of the mass of Lagos, leadership has been reduced ...

[1] *The Nigerian Pioneer*, Feb. 24, Mar. 3, 10, 1922; Nigeria, *Legislative Council Debates*, Aug. 23, 1927, 54.

2 An African Reactionary–Kitoyi Ajasa

The public career of Henry Carr, his ideas and attitudes on the range of problems which dominated Nigerian affairs during his day, and particularly his identification with the pro-western approach to African civilization, suggest another Nigerian public figure who was a contemporary of Carr and who has often been coupled with Carr as a reactionary opponent of African nationalist aspirations. This was Sir Kitoyi Ajasa, the founder and editor of *The Nigerian Pioneer*, barrister and long-time unofficial member of the Nigerian legislative council, friend and adviser of Sir Frederick Lugard during the latter's years as governor-general of Nigeria. Ajasa was born in Lagos in 1866, of probable Egba parentage. Much of his schooling was completed during a long residence in England which was concluded in 1893 when he was admitted to the bar. Returning to Lagos at that time, he began what developed into an extensive legal practice over the years, and gradually came to be associated with the government, first as an unofficial member of the legislative council starting in 1906 and later through membership in Lugard's Nigerian council. When the legislative council was reconstituted in 1922, he was appointed as the unofficial member for Lagos, a seat which he occupied until 1933, at which time he was replaced by Carr. At various times he held other public positions including the chancellorship of the Anglican diocese of the Niger, and membership on the committee appointed in 1930 to investigate the Aba riots. In 1928, Ajasa was knighted in recognition of his many public services.[1]

The parallel between the two men is tempting–their similar admiration of European culture and British colonial administration, their close association with the government, their successive holding of the same seat as unofficial member for the colony in the legislative council, even the similarity of honours bestowed upon them by the crown–but the similarity is superficial and there was, in fact, an important difference between the two. Carr's respect for European civilization was earned; that is, he compared what Europe had to offer with what was available in Africa, and concluded that Africa had much to gain through adoption of certain European institutions and ideas. Basically, he was interested in the improvement of African society, and he cared little from whence came the means. If Africa could learn something from western education,

---

[1] Allister Macmillan, *The Red Book of West Africa*, 128; Adeoye Deniga, *The Nigerian Who's Who for 1934*; *The Lagos Daily News*, Sept. 28, 1931.

different races, the deeply scored characters and heredity marks, to allow such easy effacement. The African remains at heart an African in spite of his Europeanization, for the highest ideals of humanity are the common heritage of a common humanity in all its diversity.[1]

Henry Carr, therefore, like so many of his fellow Africans, was searching for the means of reconciling western and African civilization. During his years, his views had none of the popular support that came to Herbert Macaulay, for the tide of African nationalism was running strongly and Carr seemed to represent a rigid and unreconstructed version of an earlier, more trusting, less sophisticated attitude towards Europe. To be sure, Carr's philosophy of African progress was conservative in the sense that he sought the best for his people and he saw this partly in terms of what Europe had to offer. But his ideas were not backward-looking. They were based on his best estimate of the circumstances in which he lived and his best projection of the future of the Nigeria in which he believed.

The importance of Carr's contribution to African thought and African development must not be measured by the degree to which he differed from the views of Herbert Macaulay. Carr was a reflective man whose thoughtfulness led to an articulated philosophy for the progress of Africa and whose courage enabled him to stand firm for his views in the face of long public attack. An admirer of Europe he undoubtedly was, but this did not mean uncritical acceptance; rather it reflected the experimental mind ready to try the new, unmindful of the criticism of those who could not move without the backing of precedent. Moreover, Carr's sense of innovation was always positive and constructive—witness his recommendations for the rehabilitation of the House of Docemo which, far from weakening and humiliating that institution, would have enabled it to resume its ancient and honourable position of leadership within the Lagos community. Further, Carr never lost sight of the image of an African society developing within the range of its own needs. His recommendations for curricular changes in the schools stemmed from a conviction that if Africans were to be trained to live effectively in an African society, they would need to know their own world first—its history, its geography, the shape of its social structure and the texture of its ideas. Finally, Carr was yet able to look beyond the parochialism of an African community to broader perspectives. All his educational or religious thinking ended with the view of a higher morality which owed no allegiance to any one nation or people.

[1] *Ibid.*, Mar. 9, 1938, 159–63.

Carr's European orientation did not mean that he ceased to regard himself as an African, or that he failed to look forward to the day of Nigerian self-government. Neither did it mean, moreover, that Carr was an uncritical admirer of the English. He knew of far too many examples of unscrupulous and dishonest Englishmen in Nigeria exploiting the African for their personal profit. As society progressed from a reliance on status to a reliance on contract, the possibility arose of the native African being subjected to price fixing and marketing combines, to depressed wages and working conditions, by European firms co-operating with each other for these purposes. At this point, said Carr, it behoved the government to assume its rightful role of regulator, not for the purpose of further suppression, but 'to strengthen the weak, to rescue the fallen and reclaim the straggler'.[1]

In the face of the evident advantages which he saw in European civilization, Carr could find little sympathy for the African point of view which categorically turned its back on external influences as foreign and corrupting. 'Custom is but the collective experience of the individuals who belong to the race in the past,' he pointed out, 'and if in changed and changing conditions, a community is altogether to be ruled by its custom, such a community is to be ruled by the dead ... to be forever fettered to the corpse of a dead system'. At the same time, he was not surprised by the emergence of such a narrow attitude. It arose initially as a reaction to the shallow and ungenerous prejudice of those who first introduced foreign customs, proclaiming their superiority, and then criticized their use by native Africans as clumsy, ridiculous and inappropriate. In just such a way had the English of the Renaissance been treated with contempt by the Italians they sought to imitate, even as they were condemned by some of their own thoughtless and less imaginative countrymen as corrupters of national customs and traditions. This type of cultural fertilization was a natural and highly useful process, leading to the adoption of better methods of social organization, scientific processes, or artistic achievement, quickening the imagination and enabling the shuffling off of outdated values or inefficient techniques. Yet with all the benefits of cultural borrowing, Carr realized that the African would never lose sight of his essential self. He would always be an African:

It should not for a moment be supposed that an African ceases to be an African because he acquires European culture or grafts it upon his own. Nature is too jealous of the bounds which she has set between the

[1] Diocesan Synod of Western Equatorial Africa, *op. cit.*, 12–13; Nigeria, *Legislative Council Debates*, Mar. 7, 1940, 190–2, Jan. 15, 1941, 144.

the country, but times changed and customs that could not be altered merely imposed the dead hand of tradition on the people. As for illegitimacy, this was just as great an offence against native custom as it was against Christian law. Adultery and polygamy might have sufficed in societies where propagation of the species and gratification of the passions were the chief ends in view. But there was another view:

the view of marriage which regards it chiefly in the light of its action on the two persons primarily associated, having its motive in their mutual attachment and respect, as a union which is the most effective agency for the spiritual and moral improvement of both persons by the daily practice of self-denial, self-forgetfulness, and living for others . . . the Christian view of marriage is like law or government, one of those great conquests over nature, one of those eternal moral landmarks, which man should on no account let go again, and at no price efface.[1]

Carr's abiding belief in the fundamental rightness of Christian civilization quite naturally led him to an appreciation of what he regarded as the enlightened colonial administration of Nigeria by Great Britain. This appreciation stemmed from two basic qualities in Carr's make-up. First, he was a pragmatist undisturbed by romantic illusions or partisan preconceptions. Second, he was no respecter of tradition. If innovation was good and useful, it should be adopted for the social good. Novelty held no terrors for Carr, only ignorance and superstition. He was quite prepared, therefore, to recognize the good that Europe had brought to Africa, and to make the most of it. British administration was responsible for the physical development of the country, just as British philanthropy had contributed so fully to its moral regeneration. All over the world, the English rule had gone beyond the exercise of authority and the collection of revenue 'to seek the redemption and elevation of the people'. This had been done always with a full regard for the traditional usages and authorities, so that changes such as the introduction of western education were instituted without unnecessary interference with local custom, ancestral rights or chiefly prerogatives. Nevertheless, British presence in Nigeria fundamentally meant change, and change for the better. 'There can be no doubt about it,' insisted Carr, 'the further progress of our race depends upon our ability to adopt the law of reason rather than of conscience, upon our courage to discard the terrors and bogeys of taboo and make the fullest use of modern invention for the happiness and development of mankind.'[2]

[1] *Ibid.*, 5–13, esp. 10–11.
[2] *The Nigerian Pioneer*, Aug. 28, 1925; *Special Report on the Schools of Southern Nigeria*, 6–7; Miscellaneous Notebook, Carr Papers.

out self-restraint, he went on, there was only licence and this way led straight to anarchy. Hence at the bottom of all education was the proper training of character. Intelligence was a great gift, but without character, intelligence lacked direction, like science without the ethical guidance that comes from the humanities. In 1902, Carr addressed a group of schoolchildren on the subject of academic prizes:

Prizes are always very few. . . . But the habits of industry and steady application which you cultivate in order to qualify for a prize are in themselves abiding possessions. . . . remember you are sent to school, not to win prizes, but to be trained for life. Mere cleverness will not win real success in life; for this end good character counts . . . far more than mere cleverness. . . . There is nothing more despicable than characterless cleverness.[1]

Henry Carr was a religious man, and his ethical and moral beliefs were rooted in a profound faith in a godhead from whence came these standards of human behaviour. To the same schoolchildren he had addressed on the subject of prizes, he was able to add his conviction that a good character was a Christian character, and that each student and each teacher would be able best to perform his function of learning and teaching in a spirit of Christian obedience. From religious experience and practice, moreover, flowed other virtues. More particularly, Carr saw in church organization and government the training ground for political self-government. When in 1907 the Anglican church in West Africa addressed itself to plans for the establishment of a province of West Africa, Carr expressed the hope that consequent questions of administration and discipline would bring ecclesiastical and secular affairs together and unite first the people of Nigeria and then those of Nigeria with the people of the neighbouring Gold Coast. 'Out of the business of this assembly', he asserted, 'there will . . . grow the sense of a unity which would not only be ecclesiastical but also political.' It was a utopian dream, but it did look forward to later supranational movements like the National Congress of British West Africa.[2]

Carr's religious beliefs brought from him forthright, if not exceedingly popular, declarations on two social issues which had been troubling the people of West Africa during the years before and after the turn of the century—illegitimacy and polygamy. In no way was plural marriage defensible, declared Carr. Polygamy had, it was true, been the custom of

[1] Carr, *General Report for the Year 1898 on the Schools of the Colony of Lagos*, 11–12; Diocesan Synod of Western Equatorial Africa, *Report of Speech Delivered in Synod, May, 1907, by Mr. Chancellor Carr*, 13–15; *The Lagos Standard*, July 2, 1902.
[2] Diocesan Synod of Western Equatorial Africa, op. cit., 3–4.

As always these specific recommendations were rooted in sound educational objectives. Elementary education, said Carr, kept idle children off the streets and converted them into useful, productive citizens. Technical education was essential for an expanding industrial society. Adult education introduced literacy and brought the main body of the population into closer touch with the changing world. Finally, secondary and higher education provided schoolteachers, and more particularly, trained leadership for a modern Nigerian state.[1]

In an ultimate sense, said Carr, the function of education was to clarify the national purpose and provide the means for its achievement. This might be done in many different ways and certainly not to be neglected was an appreciation of the traditional art and culture of a society. Among the Yoruba, for example, were the celebrated proverbs containing the distillation of 'the didactic poetry and the social and political philosophy of the Yoruba people', which had exerted such a beneficent influence on the Yoruba man. More generally, said Carr, in Nigeria, 'we require a system of education under which our boys and girls . . . will be trained to take an interest and a pride in their work . . . through which they will get their livelihood. We want young people . . . to be trained with a view to their own contribution to the prosperity and happiness of the community.'[2]

In 1941 when Carr was making these remarks, he was thinking in terms of reducing unemployment and developing local industries in Nigeria. For Carr, however, the final reckoning of any educational system was its success in producing adults who might live productive lives in an adult world. In terms of patriotism this meant 'neither a vindictive passion nor an aggressive impulse; on the contrary the aspiration of a true patriot is that his country should be looked upon as the founder or sustainer of a virtuous civilization not inferior to that of the leading nations of the world'. More generally, it meant the inculcation of moral strength, a sense of good taste, a devotion to truth, personal kindness, thrift, courage, prudence and perseverance. Freedom of the individual had been one of the great achievements of civilization, said Carr, but it had been gained only through the understanding of self-restraint. With-

of Surprise Visits to the Schools in the Colony of Lagos', July 31, 1893, Africana Collection, University of Ibadan Library; *Special Report on the Schools of Southern Nigeria*, 6, 7; Carr, *General Report for the Year 1897 on the Schools of the Colony of Lagos*, 4.

[1] Nigeria, *Legislative Council Debates*, Mar. 6, 1935, 116–18, Mar. 25, 1937, 132–3, Nov. 30, 1937, 139, Mar. 7, 1940, 195–7.
[2] Introduction by Carr to Julius Ojo Cole, *A Collection of Yoruba Thoughts*; Nigeria, *Legislative Council Debates*, Jan. 15, 1941, 143–4.

The question of practicality obviously related to choice of subject-matter and teaching techniques. Here Carr was the consistent pragmatist. In Old Calabar when he made a special report on the schools of southern Nigeria, he expressed reservations concerning the curriculum:

I listened to a lesson in English History given by the principal teacher ... It seemed to me that too much time was wasted on such abstract ideas as 'civilization', 'education', 'art', and 'industry', and too little attention given to concrete facts and positive information ... it did not seem to me that the children took any intelligent interest in the history of the early British Kingdoms. If history should be taught at all, it should begin with the history of Old Calabar, the Protectorate and West Africa. ... The same lines should be followed in geography. The pupils should first be taught to observe what is round about them ... the aim being to bring them into contact with nature and the life they have to live.

'We should ... guard against over-ambitious schemes of study,' he concluded, 'and ... instruct the children in such subjects as are likely to come before them in their ordinary life.'[1]

Translated into specifics, this meant not only a concentration on African over English history but a preference for utilitarian courses in commercial arithmetic, bookkeeping, drafting, shorthand and French, rather than the vast array of subjects then being offered, including English literature, classics, algebra, and geometry, most of which were badly taught and of little relevance to the immediate needs of the students. In this connection, Carr urged much more attention to English usage by means of comparative linguistic training between English and native languages. The expression in a native language of ideas originally formulated in English was not enough. It was important that translation back and forth be perfected in order both to widen the circle of ideas and to strengthen a student's proficiency in English. Carr offered many other practical suggestions over the years – for example, the use of local currencies for the better teaching of arithmetic, the encouragement of western secular education for Muslims, the maintenance of at least nominal school fees in order to strengthen a sense of civic responsibility and self-reliance, a liberal government loan policy to enable the schools to plan ahead and grow in anticipation of community growth and needs, government demonstration schools where fruitful experimentation might take place and the founding of an institution for the training of teachers.[2]

[1] Ibid., 4.
[2] The Lagos Weekly Record, Jan. 29, 1898; Carr, 'Amendments desirable to make in the Education Rules, 1891', Dec. 20, 1897, and 'Extracts from a Report

characteristic victimization of the weak, the ignorant and the superstitious. And there was no doubt in Carr's mind but that there were thoroughgoing scoundrels in Lagos who made a business of feeding on ignorance and fanning the flames of superstition for their own personal advantage.

Whatever the rightness of Carr's position, however, it was a difficult one to argue effectively in a public forum, particularly against the popular position of Macaulay who succeeded in seriously embarrassing the government over the eleko question in 1920 while assisting at the same time in the Apapa land case which was such an important step in establishing the rights of indigenous land ownership. Despite his efforts, therefore, Carr's tenure as Resident was not a conspicuous success, although there were some who felt that he could have been much more effective in that post had the government been willing to use him in a decision-making capacity rather than merely as a go-between for the administration with the traditional authorities.[1]

Throughout his life, however, Henry Carr's major preoccupation and professional activity was in the field of education and it was there that he evolved his most complete system of ideas concerning African life and development. Characteristically his philosophy of education was a declaration of high-minded and clear-sighted principle on which were based specific educational techniques designed to respond to particular practical objectives. Carr began with a frank analysis of the goals and consequent advantages and limitations of missionary education. It had to be remembered, he pointed out, that the missionaries had used education for the primary objective of gaining converts to Christianity. In terms of its utility in the world of affairs, the mission curriculum had its necessary limitations—it offered little that was of practical day-to-day value, but it did instil certain social and moral standards which were prerequisite to the establishment of a new and improved order. With changing conditions, however, would have to come changing educational tactics. 'With the extension of Government occupation and of commercial enterprise,' observed Carr in 1900, 'the Missions ... will not forget that the children whom they are training to live in heaven have first to get through [this] world. They will teach them in a practical manner to be industrious, truthful, obedient, respectful, honourable, clean, tidy.'[2]

---

[1] Macaulay, *Henry Carr Must Go*, 18; *The Nigerian Pioneer*, July 28, 1922. Though he named no names, Carr's remarks about scoundrels seem clearly to refer to Macaulay. See also Nigeria, *Legislative Council Debates*, Dec. 3, 1935, 92–3.

[2] Carr, *Special Report on the Schools of Southern Nigeria*, 5, 7.

embarrass the government. His palace had become a centre of intrigue against the administration, and he had taken as his guides certain educated Africans who also entertained views critical of the government. It was Carr's emphatic view that the whole city would have been far better off if the eleko had been replaced by someone of character, and this opinion he placed unequivocally before his superiors.

For such an attitude he was roundly attacked, and though he maintained a public silence, he defended himself vigorously within the privacy of the government. Pointing to his long service in various departments dealing with native affairs, he strenuously denied the allegation that he did not associate with 'natives' and particularly avoided illiterates. His association with people of all stations was widespread, but he made a distinction between association and exploitation:

I number many illiterate men amongst my friends, but in associating with them I have steadily aimed at assisting them gradually to raise their standard of life and action. I have not associated with them in order to confirm them in habits and practices of which they might have been ashamed if they had known better. I have not cultivated their friendship in order to have irregular relations with their daughters under the cloak of 'native customs and practice' . . . I have not been amongst them for their charms and amulets, not to flatter them or to exploit them or to live upon them, nor yet to encourage them and aid them in their ignorant opposition to constituted authority or to feed them with lies and falsehoods in order to gain their applause or a cheap popularity. I have on the contrary earnestly striven to get them to eschew intrigue, bribery and corruption, dissimulation and concealment.[1]

Herbert Macaulay later insisted that Carr had been responsible for the official government position regarding the eleko affair and that Carr's attitudes had been conditioned by an overweening pride and vanity in his office and its power. This shot was far off the mark, but Carr's observations at the time were revealing in other ways. First of all, he clearly showed a respect for authority as such, and particularly he respected the British régime for the improvements it had introduced in Nigeria. Further, he revealed a strong sense of human perfectibility which was happily combined with a down-to-earth realism. Hence he entertained no romantic illusions about the limitations of the illiterate native population of Lagos, but, Macaulay to the contrary notwithstanding, did have a firm belief in their capacity for self-improvement. Finally, he harboured only the most profound contempt for charlatanism with its

[1] Resident to Lt. Governor, Sept. 19, 1919, Macaulay Papers, IV-30; 'Notes and Comments on Petition dated 17th October, 1919 . . .', *Ibid.*, V-13.

force in the life of the people. The controversy over the eleko question carried on from Lugard's time down to the mid-thirties, long after Carr had retired from his position as Resident, but he continued to maintain that the House of Docemo should not be destroyed, neither should it be turned into a subsidized curiosity. It should instead be led back to a productive participation in the affairs of its people. In 1935, Carr maintained publicly that the stipend for the eleko ought to be substantially raised over the official rate then allowed so that the king might live in a manner appropriate to his position. But this should be done with an important proviso:

The House of Docemo ... is in a very backward position, and something should be done ... to bring them to the front and teach them to take an intelligent interest in the affairs of the country. It is an old family: sentiments of respect and honour for them exist in the community and whatever is respected and honoured is worthy of encouragement. It should be of such a character as to foster respect and honour, to develop a higher level of appreciation of and also guidance in the affairs of the country. ... we should not only think of a grant to the head of the House of Docemo, but we should think of establishing an institution in which the sons of the House could be educated: where they could be given an intelligent education which would lead them to take their proper place in the community and continue the traditions of the old Ruling House.

And Carr went on to express the hope that members of the family would be able to fill positions in the legislative council, combining service for their own generation with the respect for the traditions of their forefathers.[1]

Carr's views, though eminently sensible, were probably politically impracticable at the time the eleko controversy broke out during the years of the First World War. There had been protracted trouble over the administration's decision to finance the new Lagos water supply through a ratepayer tax, and the city had finally divided over the issue with the party of Herbert Macaulay continuing to oppose payment and enlisting the eleko's support of this view. Carr had little respect for the reigning eleko of that time, Prince Eshugbayi, whom he considered weak and inept, vain and open to bribery. As far as Carr was concerned, Eshugbayi had allowed himself to be bought by cheap flattery and cash, and so had come first to oppose the water rate and later to be drawn into an intramural dispute among the Muslims of the city in such a way as to

---

[1] Miscellaneous Notebook, Carr Papers; Nigeria, *Legislative Council Debates*, Mar. 6, 1935, 115.

dent, Carr was dropped squarely in the middle of the eleko question. The position of the Macaulay party was unequivocal. Docemo, the original eleko, they said, had been, practically speaking, fleeced of his kingdom, and his descendants were yet without redress. It was high time the British administration did something to re-establish equity by at least providing the office of king with an appropriate pension which would enable him to live in dignified retirement. For their part, the authorities resented the dubious role which the eleko had been playing for some years in the local political manœuvring, and in his tactics of obstruction towards much-needed public improvements such as a modern water supply. To the administration, the eleko was a relic of a dead past, and the best thing that could happen was for him to fade away as a public figure.

Henry Carr had studied the eleko problem with his usual care. He fully recognized its complications, and characteristically he had arrived at conclusions which were thoughtful and thoroughgoing, and possibly more constructive than those of either Macaulay or the administration. He held the view that the popular image of the House of Docemo was badly distorted by romantic nonsense. The traditional allegiance to the dynasty had been turned by sentimentalists into a kind of religious cult which concentrated on idealized visions of past glories. Actually, times had long since changed, said Carr. Lagos was now living under foreign domination, to be sure, but of a government which had effected vast improvements which the people, whatever the degree of their nationalism, accepted with genuine appreciation. Psychologically, however, they had received a shock which tended to make them live in two dissociated worlds—the real workaday world in which material betterment and more effective government were gratefully accepted, and the fantasy world involving their traditional social, religious and political affiliations and loyalties.

It was no solution, Carr contended, to perpetuate this dead and decaying relic of the royal house, by subsidizing it, placing it on the dole so that it might deteriorate in splendour. Whatever the original meaning and function of the House of Docemo, the true test of its royal leadership henceforward would be how effectively it could change in tune with the times. To put the king, his family and entourage on pension would further erode self-respect and lead to a wasting idleness. Much better that the royal family be given the opportunity to improve its grasp of modern affairs through education, so that it could exercise a constructive leadership in the community it served, and once again become an active

reasons of health, but more particularly, contending that the government should be careful to avoid 'all invidious distinctions which may humiliate an African in his own eyes and those of others'. There is no evidence that Carr carried this particular issue, but in a larger sense he succeeded when Lugard, convinced of Carr's abilities, appointed him in 1918 as Provincial Commissioner of the colony, a move which was viewed with doubt both in Britain because it placed an African over Europeans, and in Lagos where among certain elements of the population Carr was regarded as too pro-British to be able effectively to understand and deal with the African point of view.[1]

Either Lugard did not fully understand the local political situation in Lagos, or he entertained an excessive confidence in Carr, for by naming Carr as Resident – the title which was later given the position – he placed his African deputy in a position of extreme delicacy, a position which the incorruptible and apolitical Carr may not have been best qualified to occupy at that precise moment. For Lagos during the period of the First World War was a honeycomb of division within the native African community – between conflicting groups of Muslims, between warring Christian church factions, between nationalists of different degrees of intensity, between tribal groups and rival economic interests, between the educated and the uneducated, and between factions within the body of westernized Africans. In addition, there was a mounting discontent with British rule which added its complication to the divisiveness within the city. During his administration, Lugard had managed to alienate substantial portions of the Lagos population, and antipathy towards him and his programme tended to become mingled with the factionalism already plaguing the community. With his long years of service in the colonial government, Carr would have already been suspect in some quarters, and the ultimate endorsement by the governor-general was promptly regarded as the final straw.

Much of the internal tension within the city showed itself in the long-drawn-out controversy with the British administration over the activities and function of the traditional authority of Lagos, the House of Docemo. Since 1913 when the question of an annual allowance for the king had first been raised by Herbert Macaulay and others, the role of the eleko in the community had posed a chronic problem for Lugard, and he had made little progress towards its solution. With his appointment as Resi-

---

[1] Notebook no. 3, S. W. Grier to Miss Douglas, Sept. 30, 1943 in Notebook no. 6, *Ibid.*; Letter, Lagos chiefs to the Secretary, Southern Provinces, Aug. 16, 1917, Macaulay Papers, IV-30.

Inspector of schools in 1915. Already this was much more than had ever been achieved by a Nigerian in the civil service. The government was glad to be able to advance an African of evident ability who could serve as an excellent liaison with the local people. The African community was gratified to have one of its own members as part of the administration—it was not only an honour but, from the African point of view, it increased efficiency in government and facilitated the placing of local grievances before the authorities.[1]

Others may have been pleased, but not Henry Carr. By 1903, after fourteen years of faithful and skilful service, Carr had come to the conclusion that he was being unjustly passed over while younger, less qualified British officers were placed in superior positions. He was with difficulty dissuaded from resigning at the time, and later he did abandon the service to study law when he discovered that no effective attention had been paid to his complaints. The issue was a private one in part, for Carr had great personal pride and a sense of dignity which was too easily bruised. There were Europeans, he pointed out, who resented the idea of an African occupying a position with authority over European personnel. Their reaction was understandable, if mean-spirited, as was the natural inclination of each new official to deprecate the accomplishments of his predecessor, merely in order to exalt his own status. Normally there was little harm done, for the predecessor was far off in another position in another part of the world. With Carr, however, it was different. 'I am as it were a permanent understudy and have the mortification of seeing younger men with defective knowledge of local conditions constantly placed over me to disparage me and depreciate my labours ... I stand damned because the policy seems to be that I am not to go further than I am. This places me at a great disadvantage ... wounding ... my own self-respect.'[2]

A sense of personal discrimination, no doubt, played a large part, but Carr's misgivings went beyond the individual. When in 1915 he became Chief Inspector of schools, Carr objected that he was not given the same leave allowances being granted to Europeans in the same grade of appointment. The governor-general, Sir Frederick Lugard, pointed out that these allowances were established solely on the basis of hardship in climatic adjustment, which in Carr's case was non-existent. Carr, however, persisted in his demand for special consideration, explaining first of all that many West Africans were in the habit of visiting Europe for

[1] Gwam, *op. cit.*, 5; *The Lagos Standard*, Apr. 1, 1903.
[2] Gwam, *op. cit.*, 5, 6; Notebook no. 5, Henry Carr Papers.

positions in the colony which would therefore have to be staffed by ex-patriots.

At a later time, Macaulay went on, Carr as protégé of the governor-general, Sir Frederick Lugard, had been promoted to the position of Resident of the colony, a superfluous office in Macaulay's opinion, in which Carr performed no service but to acquiesce in the slander of the people of Nigeria, particularly in connection with the affair of the eleko's staff of office, the facts of which Carr had used his position as Resident to misrepresent. It was Carr, concluded Macaulay, who had urged the official persecution of the eleko until his enforced retirement to the deserved impotence of private life. What credibility can be given to this sweeping indictment? How can these two views of Henry Carr be reconciled?[1]

Henry Carr's ancestry was typical of the Lagos society into which he was born in 1863. As with so many contemporaries, his family had returned in the mid-century waves of émigrés from Sierra Leone and resettled in Yorubaland. His father was a native of Abeokuta but family fortune dictated that the boy be reared from his earliest days in Lagos by a mother prematurely widowed. Education, which was to play a major theme throughout his many years, quickly placed its hallmark on young Carr. He took to schooling eagerly and easily, making such quick progress as early to be singled out for distinction. He was sent to Sierra Leone for secondary training on the strength of outstanding work in the lower forms, and carried on brilliantly in Freetown until he finally emerged from Fourah Bay College in 1882 with an honours degree from Durham University in mathematics and physical sciences. After a few years' experience teaching, Carr was appointed chief clerk in the colonial service and sub-Inspector of schools in the Lagos colony. That was in 1889, the first year of a term of government service which lasted until his retirement thirty-five years later in 1924.[2]

No doubt Carr's government career began, in so far as the colonial administration was concerned, as no more than that of an able young African filling a minor post in the civil service. He was too capable, however, for matters to rest there, and advancement followed—up to a point. He became successively Deputy Inspector and Inspector of schools, then after temporary service in the colonial administration, he returned to the department of education, eventually to become Chief

---

[1] Herbert Macaulay, *Henry Carr Must Go*.
[2] Adeoye Deniga, *Nigerian Who's Who for 1922*; *West African Pilot*, May 9, 1944. The fullest information regarding Carr's life is found in L. C. Gwam, 'Dr. Henry Rawlinson Carr', *Ibadan*, no. 17, Nov., 1963, 3-8.

20 The Conservative Nationalists: Henry Carr

1 *The Rationalism of Henry Carr*

Henry Rawlinson Carr—the name rolls off the tongue with a substantial quality which appeared to befit its owner: Henry Carr, broad-faced and square-jawed, a stocky figure carefully groomed in well-tailored clothes of conservative cut, austere in manner and forbidding in appearance; Carr, schoolteacher and educator, government officer trained in the law, precise and careful in movement and speech, slow to express a public opinion but lucid and thoughtful in those so expressed; Carr, the bibliophile; Carr the omnivorous and catholic reader; Carr the man of monumental moral strength screened behind a formidable exterior and protected by an excessive shyness.

This was one view of Henry Carr, but there was another, more widely held by the Lagos community in which he lived—a portrait conceived in the mind of his long-time enemy, Herbert Macaulay, and broadcast incessantly throughout Lagos by Macaulay in a relentless, untiring effort to discredit the reputation of Henry Carr. This other Carr was pictured as a man whose unusual intellectual talents, encouraged by special educational opportunities, had been perverted by a failure of character. Carr's training had qualified him for service in the colonial educational establishment, but, said Macaulay, while the quality of schooling under his direction showed no apparent improvement, Carr was unflagging in his demands for promotion and salary increases. There was a growing suspicion in Lagos, continued Macaulay, that Carr's total attachment to foreign western standards of thought and action had effectively divorced him from any sympathetic contact with his people. After years of labour in the school system, his best estimate of the students under his supervision was that on the whole they were inadequate in intelligence and reliability, and unqualified to fill clerical and teaching

Viewed from the perspective of subsequent events, the career of Blaise Diagne becomes clearer. If he achieved his finest moment during the years of the First World War in defence of African nationalism in Senegal, it was racial pride as much as personal esteem that gave him the motive force. In his later career, his spirited support of French colonialism appeared to be an abdication of the hero's role in return for the mere emoluments of his official position. Yet when he had left the scene, those who had criticized him most sharply were content to carry on much as he had before. Doubtless, in light of the realities of French colonial policy, there was nothing else to be done. Or almost nothing. Before he died Diagne told a close friend how he had suffered for years from a growing sense of divorce and solitude in his role as deputy, how the flatteries heaped upon him had led to a kind of corruption almost as degrading to the spirit as slavery, how pride had yielded to the honours lavished on the public official leaving the inner man bereft and deserted.[1]

3 A Political Postscript

To a certain extent the activities of Blaise Diagne were ultimately resolved in the early career of Lamine Guèye. It was Guèye, born in the protectorate the son of a citizen of the Four Communes, who benefited directly from Diagne's exertions in 1915 and 1916. It was Guèye who earned his doctorate of law from the University of Paris with a study of the changing constitutional status of the Senegalese of the Four Communes resulting from the citizenship laws sponsored by Blaise Diagne. It was Guèye who came to form a nucleus of political opposition to Diagne during the 1920s, but it was Guèye who like Diagne believed in the essential rightness of assimilation. In his time at the conclusion of another World War, Lamine Guèye placed his name on another law which revolutionized the constitutional standing of the people of French Africa—the *loi Lamine Guèye* which extended the citizenship of France to all inhabitants of the French overseas community. This legislation both vindicated and repudiated the work of Blaise Diagne. More than that it pointed the way to a new age, for out of the expanded political rights which France granted her colonials after the Second World War, came the changes which looked past Lamine Guèye to the era of Léopold Senghor.

[1] R. Delavignette, *Les Vrais Chefs de l'Empire*, 254–5.

car where the people might not yet be ready for citizenship but where they were entitled to a more direct voice in their affairs. Somehow these fine sentiments never materialized in the form of concrete legislation. Much the same was true for economic affairs. As far back as 1919 Diagne had glibly announced the need for legislation guaranteeing improved working conditions, arbitration, leisure time and other labour reforms, but years passed and no action was taken. Instead Diagne busied himself with protecting the franchise of the powerful Bank of West Africa which provided him with a fine house in Dakar for his trouble.[1]

The political opposition to Blaise Diagne was never able to overthrow him and he retained his parliamentary seat and his control over the patronage in Senegal until his death in the spring of 1934. In part the failure of his opponents came from the fact that they shared with Diagne the very weaknesses of which they complained. Politics in Senegal between the two World Wars came less from strongly held principles or well-defined economic and social groups as from a jockeying for power among factions within the Four Communes. Galandou Diouf was for years the enthusiastic lieutenant to Diagne but broke with him in 1928 primarily because he thought he could beat Diagne for the office of deputy from Senegal. After Diagne's death, Diouf succeeded as deputy but there was no essential change in policy. The break between the two had been accompanied by charges that Diagne was an agent of imperialism while his former aide had been captured by the communists. There was little conviction in these charges which were mainly a local reflection of party alignments in France. Lamine Guèye, now the ally, now the opponent of Diagne, himself fell out with Diouf once the latter became deputy. The label of communist was thenceforward reversed, with Diouf in the role of colonialist and Guèye struggling to fight off the stigma of communism. Again these labels meant little. Diouf was simply the chief of the party in power and Guèye became the opposition. When the Popular Front arrived in France in 1936, Guèye bid for its support to assist him locally, but for all the talk of socialist principles, the Guèye party remained essentially a faction within the Four Communes concerned primarily with gaining control over local politics.[2]

[1] *L'Ouest Africain Français*, Jan. 14, 21, Feb. 25, Mar. 10, 24, 1928, Nov. 23, 1929, Apr. 5, 1930; *Journal Officiel*, Chamber of Deputies, July 11, 1927, 2525–7. Such criticism failed to give credit to Diagne for obtaining substantial subsidies for ground-nut culture during the early 1930s. See A. Villard, *Histoire du Sénégal*, 179.

[2] Guyonnet, op. cit., 8–10; *La France Coloniale*, Apr. 12, 1928; Diouf, op. cit.; Buell, op. cit., I, 956–7; J. Suret-Canale, *Afrique Noire, Occidentale et Centrale, L'Ere Coloniale, 1900–1945*, 565–6; Morgenthau, op. cit., 131–4.

over the Communes like a medieval prince, rewarding his friends, punishing his enemies, gerrymandering electoral districts to ensure voting majorities, bringing official pressure to bear on voters, and even falsifying the balloting when such a measure seemed necessary. The result of this activity had been a series of victories for Diagne who was regularly returned as deputy from Senegal, but little concrete political advance for the people he purported to represent.

Many of Diagne's critics were former lieutenants and colleagues like Galandou Diouf who went back to the old days of the Young Senegalese party before the First World War, and Jean D'Oxoby, a French journalist who had founded the Diagnist paper, *La Démocratie du Sénégal* in 1914 but who had finally broken with his old chief during the mid-twenties. With Diagne's concurrence, they alleged, the general council had been replaced in 1920 by the colonial council in a move supposedly designed to effect administrative economies while broadening local representation to include French subjects in the protectorate. Actually this development merely gave the administration a tighter control over the affairs of Senegal by packing the colonial council with chiefs responsive to official direction. Thus constituted, the council had quickly degenerated into a body without authority or prestige.[1]

In part these protests reflected a struggle for political power, but there was also a measure of genuine dissatisfaction over what seemed to be political representation of increasing conservatism which failed to take account of the aspirations of a younger generation of educated Africans reaching out in their turn for political and economic advantage. Prominent in this new generation was Lamine Guèye who had been educated in Paris and who was the first West African to hold a French doctorate of law. Guèye accused Diagne of a do-nothing policy which allowed the administration steadily to erode African authority in the municipalities by restrictions on the activities of the mayors while native lands were appropriated for official use on the flimsiest of pretexts.

Diagne spoke in noble and fluent accents, his critics insisted, concerning the political rights of Africans but when it came to achievement, his record was dismal indeed. From time to time he proposed limited extension of the suffrage which would permit greater representation in the French parliament–colonial senators, more deputies for Algeria, and parliamentary delegates for evolving areas such as Dahomey or Madagas-

---

[1] *Conseil Colonial*, Nov., 1922, 55–60; *La France Coloniale*, Aug. 30, 1928; M. Guyonnet, 'La Presse au Sénégal jusqu'en 1939, Bibliographie', 7–8, G. Diouf, 'Discours Prononcé ... la 8 Septembre 1934', Univ. of Dakar library.

which were teaching the native to understand that these advantages were part of the path of progress along which he was being led. (Applause.)

The speaker asked to be excused but to cries of 'No, no! Speak, speak!' he continued. Diagne leaned forward, his features working with the emotion that welled within him, transferring to his audience the patriotic fervour he felt. He waited, then began his final measured remarks. 'It is indispensable that we deputies from the colonies raise our voices in protest every time the idea of patriotic unity is in danger of eclipse, especially when we perceive the insufficiency and uncertainty of the arguments which thus give us the right to intervene!' The applause rang out through the chamber as Diagne descended from the rostrum and returned to his place where his colleagues greeted him with their warmest congratulations.

Later, Diagne recalled the circumstances of his speech. His remarks, he said, were based on forty years' experience, twenty-four as a civil servant and sixteen as deputy from Senegal. He was convinced that there was no more selfless, friendly colonial power than France, that wherever she planted a colony, a new bit of France was created. It was absurd, he said, to think of separate countries based on some arbitrary distinction like skin colour. There could only be unity of nationality even to the extent – he smiled mischievously – of teaching to little Africans the much maligned phrase, 'our ancestors the Gauls'. People who live in the same house, he concluded, have the same material and moral interests. To be sure the policy of assimilation could not always be applied at once. First there had to be association so that the resources of the new countries could be properly developed. But after association with its material progress would surely come the final assimilation of the spirit.[1]

Such elevated notions were perhaps sincere, and certainly Diagne strongly believed in the efficacy of French colonialism. There were others, however, who took a more jaundiced view of Diagne's activities, seeing in them not high-mindedness but self-seeking, regarding him as a leader who let slip the opportunity for service in the search for power, whose pride corrupted his will, who sold his responsibilities to the people of Africa for a comfortable life as the vassal of the colonial administration and the big merchant establishments of Bordeaux.

In the first place, it was alleged that Diagne had never attempted to represent the people of Senegal but had contented himself with the affairs of his constituents in the Four Communes. Worse still, he ruled

---

[1] *Journal Officiel*, Chamber of Deputies, Jan. 30, 1930, 276–7; *La Dépêche Coloniale*, Feb. 13, 1930; *La France Coloniale*, Feb. 19, Nov. 12, 1931.

with a deceptive nonchalance, though as he began to speak, his essential sophistication soon became apparent in the vigour, the elevated concepts, the persuasiveness, the logic and the colour of his remarks. 'I belong to those', he began, 'who believe that France's traditional posture . . . can only find its resolution in unity both of conception and doctrine, a unity of the spirit between France and the peoples or races scattered across her overseas territories. (Applause.) . . . I remember from my youth the basis for my belief that a greater France constitutes a complete unity.'

The speaker now told his listeners, amidst repeated bursts of applause, how he as a boy in Goree had acted as amanuensis for illiterate Breton sailors who wished to write to their families at home. Here indeed was an example of how colonization had brought benefits which eventually had been returned to their source. 'Does this not demonstrate that to the extent we develop a policy of justice, a policy of equality, a policy of goodwill which progressively leads the native to the level of his tutor, we will be repaid in proportion?' (Hear! Hear!). 'Now we hear that in Indo-China it is a mistake to teach the history of France to children who can never really understand the essence of France.' The speaker paused and surveyed the rows of delegates before him. Then, in measured tones, 'I say that this theory is false.'

It was true, Diagne continued, that the customs and traditions of all peoples were to be respected, but unity was still the key to colonization, and 'education . . . would constitute the cement, the indissoluble bond between us'. (Hear! Hear!) Thus France would have to proclaim loudly, loyally and courageously her devotion to the students of Indo-China who in their inexperience and isolation might be subjected to the temptation of communists or others. 'Let us say to these young people that between them and us there is not and can never be a breach. . . . There are not two countries. There is only one nation, the one which we love. Thus it is that we all arrive at the idea of nationhood.' (Applause.)

Look at these other systems of colonial rule. Diagne's voice was heavy with scorn. See how imperfect they are. Why? Because they are based on material considerations. 'We need not go to them for instruction.' (Hear! Hear!) But French colonial philosophy was superior precisely because it rested, not on tangible interests alone, but on a conception of humanity composed both in the heart and the mind. The image of French colonial practice was not to be found in the occasional atrocity, in the crimes and shortcomings which are the weaknesses of all mankind. It was to be found in the education, the benevolence and the firm justice

country has made enormous progress ... Let us be guided by our hearts but also let us not lose sight of the material needs of these peoples that we may recognize not only the interests of France but also of those under her tutelage. My argument is humanitarian, and is buttressed by my personal experience as representative of the very races you are pretending to defend at this moment.[1]

During and after the conference, Diagne defended his stand. He could not vote for many sections of the final text, because he feared they jeopardized France's military security by placing excessive restrictions on the activities of her colonial military establishment. Furthermore, he saw great good in the educational and social side of military conscription. In many parts of Africa famine forced the people into the forest in search of roots, while resultant malnutrition led to epidemics and a high infant mortality. Modern civilization would change all that, but civilization could be introduced only through improved transportation and communication which in turn meant the mustering of a local labour supply for such activities as road building and railroad construction. As they contributed to national development, moreover, indigenous labourers learned the utility of good work habits and mastered a trade which enhanced their subsequent productivity. His were the observations, he continued, of one who not only came from a colonial area but who had spent many years living in various parts of the French colonies. He was not likely to be deceived either by the misguided zeal of those who knew nothing of local conditions or those, like the British, who hid their own policies of forced labour behind the sophistries of indirect rule.[2]

Six months earlier, in January 1930, Blaise Diagne had arisen before another assembly to define his image of an ideal colonial system. The occasion was a debate before the French Chamber of Deputies over the colonial budget. Diagne had not intended to speak until one of the deputies remarked that Indo-China might eventually become an Asiatic state only loosely connected with France by economic and political ties. Shocked by such heresy, Diagne scribbled on the back of an envelope the words, 'Extremely dangerous thesis', and passed the message on to the Secretary for Colonies. That night he became so agitated he could not sleep, and resolved to address his fellow delegates as soon as possible.

Mounting the rostrum a few days later and turning to face his colleagues, Diagne presented a different, more polished figure from the stump speaker of 1914. Still slender, greying slightly, he carried himself

[1] League of Nations, *International Labour Conference*, 1930, I, 282–3, 290–1.
[2] *Ibid.*, I, 301, 328, 340; *L'Ouest Africain Français*, June 28, Aug. 9, Sept. 6, 1930; *La France Coloniale*, July 3, 1930.

military conscriptees engaged in such activities as road and bridge building, sometimes as labourers requisitioned for private concerns. Abuse was even more acute in Equatorial Africa. During his Congo travels in 1925, André Gide encountered incidents where workers were deprived of their pay and brutally treated when they failed to produce their prescribed production quotas, and he reported women forced to execute heavy road repairs under appallingly difficult conditions. The railroad between Point Noir and Brazzaville was constructed by huge gangs of conscriptee labour which were fed by means of massive food requisitions forced on the people of the area. Sanitary and working conditions on the railroad became so bad as to raise questions in the Chamber of Deputies. It was suggested that the mortality rate was as high as 60 per cent and that many thousands had perished in constructing the line.[1]

Under these circumstances the French colonial record came under sharp attack at the conference, and the worker delegates tried to secure the passage of resolutions closely defining and limiting the quality and applicability of forced labour in the colonies. The final texts called for the end of forced labour, but contained so many qualifications and promised such policing difficulties as to represent no significant improvement of the general situation. Diagne consistently opposed the suggested reforms and proved to be an eloquent defender of the *status quo*.

Speaking before the assembled delegates, Diagne argued that France was second to none in her desire to put an end to what was called forced labour, that his own presence at Geneva was the symbol of France's wish for the good of her colonial people. Nevertheless humanitarian motives had always to be tempered with realism in the interests of the people on whose behalf they were invoked. Of what good were finesounding liberal decrees for people who could not understand their meaning, whose society would literally be annihilated under such legislation? We must not fashion a double-edged weapon, Diagne insisted, which freed the colonial peoples from the bonds of servitude only to plunge them into an inferiority which colonial policies were specifically designed to eradicate. The world was making vast material strides. Was it right that the less fortunate people of the world should be denied their share of this advance?

For these reasons we must voice our reservations in the interest of the people whom you wish to protect. Remember that over forty years my

[1] Charles Cros, *La Parole Est à M. Blaise Diagne*, 117; Buell, *op. cit.*, I, 1042–3, II, 27–8, 262–3; André Gide, *Travels in the Congo*, 66–73; *L'Ouest Africain Français*, Mar. 28, 1931. See also Ruth S. Morgenthau, *Political Parties in French-Speaking West Africa*, 1–6.

the American Negro laboured under many indignities and inequalities, and the French African would always seek to advance the condition of his less fortunate brother, but this could never be effected by preaching revolution in Africa. Progress could come only through peace and order whereby French African leadership would bring about the development of the mass of its people. 'We Frenchmen of Africa wish to remain French,' said Diagne, 'for France has given us every liberty and accepted us without reservation along with her European children.'[1]

Clearly this was not the same Diagne who had fought the European power in 1914 to preserve the privilege of citizenship for the people of the Four Communes, and by implication, to press for the political and civil rights of all Africans living under French colonial rule. Perhaps the political realist had become reconciled to a colonial régime he was powerless to resist. Perhaps he was already moving towards the accommodation with Bordeaux which was to take place in 1923 whereby Diagne's political ascendancy in Senegal was recognized in exchange for commercial freedom in West Africa for the mercantile houses of the Gironde. Perhaps he simply began to identify himself increasingly with France and her polished European culture rather than with Africa and her unreconstructed millions. At any rate, during the 1920s his posture on colonial affairs was difficult to distinguish from that of the French political Right; hence when French colonialism needed a defender, what more logical choice was there than Blaise Diagne, the African product of that colonial system?

Diagne's most notable service to the French colonial system came in 1930 on the occasion of the International Labour Organization conference on forced labour. France was represented by a number of delegates, but the Tardieu government especially selected Diagne as an official representative to speak on behalf of France's colonial record which was far from being above criticism. Officially, France opposed the use of forced labour by private concessionaires, and approved limited forced labour on public works only in areas where the local population had not sufficiently evolved to permit the development of a free labour supply. In practice, however, there was evidence of chronic abuse involving government acquiescence and participation. In French West Africa, workers were regularly recruited for both private and public purposes, sometimes in the form of draft labour for public works, sometimes as

---

[1] *Ibid.*, 139; Henri Charpin, 'La question noire', *La Revue Indigène*, no. 167-8, Nov.-Dec., 1922, 280-1.

prepared to support a position which implied criticism of French colonial administration. As presiding officer he quashed a resolution criticizing Belgian colonial policy and substituted an innocuous statement in the face of what Du Bois regarded as a clear majority in opposition. When the final resolutions were passed he secured the inclusion of a passage to the effect that of all the colonial powers only France provided constitutional and social equality for her African citizens, a proposition which though literally true was most eloquent in what it neglected to say concerning France's colonial peoples.[1]

Despite Du Bois's essential advocacy of White-Negro equality within a national context, Diagne had come to regard him as a dangerous internationalist of Bolshevist leanings. The first congress, Diagne argued, had offered 'us French' the opportunity to effect a moral union with their brothers from other parts of the world, but always within the bounds of their respective nationalities. French Africans already possessed freedom and equality and hoped by associating themselves with the Americans to point up the discrepancies between the liberal policy of France and the restrictive régime to be found in America. Such a rapprochement became impossible during the second congress, Diagne continued, because of the radicalism of Du Bois and his American contingent. However, before the meeting ended, Diagne claimed to have subdued Du Bois and to have established an atmosphere of greater reasonableness. The congress concluded as the French group succeeded in placing on the record a vote congratulating France on her colonial policies.

Diagne's position was based on his expressed conviction that the development of the African could only come through peaceful co-operation between the white and black races. 'To isolate the black race,' he wrote, 'and to let it work out its own evolution is ridiculous. . . . The evolution of our race is essential because mankind, at the end of the war, needs the betterment of all the people of the world, but to do this requires the co-operation of everybody.' What this meant specifically became clearer in Diagne's reaction to Marcus Garvey at the time that Garvey was inviting support for his African colonization project. Diagne's rebuff was complete. French Africans, he said, wanted nothing to do with a movement which might divorce them from a France who had taken them in as her own and who alone was capable of effecting the progress of the black race. The Negro in French Africa recognized that

[1] W. E. B. Du Bois, *The World and Africa*, 7–12, 236–40; Joseph Péyrat, 'Un Congrès pan-noir', *La Revue Indigène*, no. 151–3, July-Aug.–Sept., 1921, 143.

THE ASSIMILATION OF BLAISE DIAGNE

deputy's enthusiastic support, the Colonial Ministry in Paris began to explore means for extending the quality of full municipal incorporation to a range of towns in the colony and protectorate, presumably in recognition of the sacrifices which Africa had rendered France during the late conflict. It was not long, however, before there were second thoughts. How would the new system be administered? Who would have the right to vote and in what elections? Were the Africans really ready for greater self-government? Would the Europeans be dominated by the African vote? Could this or that town sustain financial viability as an incorporated commune? Gradually the fine picture of democracy in action faded, to be replaced by a colonial régime of increasing severity and arbitrary authority. Even the old general council was abolished and replaced by a colonial council, ostensibly more liberal in membership but actually much more responsive than its predecessor to domination by the administration.[1]

Subtle changes were beginning to show themselves in the attitudes and manner of the deputy from Senegal, as well. He had easily defeated Carpot for re-election in 1919, but more interesting at this time were his activities in connection with the pan-African congresses which the American Negro leader, W. E. B. Du Bois, organized in the years immediately following the war. The first of these was timed to coincide with the Versailles peace conference. Du Bois hoped to unite world Negro opinion in an effort to gain some voice in the disposition of the former African colonies of Germany, and proposed the formation of an internationalized refuge for Negroes in Africa to which Portuguese Africa and the Belgian Congo might eventually be added. It was a utopian dream but so indeed had been the idea of a congress in the first place, until Du Bois sought the help of Diagne. Diagne obtained the agreement of Clemenceau and the congress was duly held in Paris. Few practical results came of it although Du Bois felt that his assembly had been instrumental in putting forward the idea which grew into the Mandates Commission of the League of Nations directing the affairs of the former German colonies.

At Du Bois's instigation another pan-African congress followed in 1921, meeting successively in London, Brussels and Paris. Diagne once again participated but this time his role was more equivocal. This second congress stressed the idea of racial equality as a foundation on which national self-determination might be erected, but Diagne was not

[1] See correspondence of Gov. Gen. Angoulvant, etc., 1918, 1919, N.A.P.O.S. Senegal VII, 7 bis.

soldiers to become voters with us even as we become soldiers with them.'[1]

The governor-general would not yield and returned to France where he was shortly thereafter killed in action. The deputy, who had once cited the Dutch Van Vollenhoven as an example of successful assimilation, carried out his assignment with characteristic vigour, recruiting the necessary contingents and creating a series of incidents which served to demonstrate his determination that the dignity of Blaise Diagne and the African people be preserved. Arriving at Dakar at the beginning of his tour, he insisted on the most meticulous attention to protocol and censured those who failed to honour his presence properly. At Conakry, when the president of the chamber of commerce, a prominent businessman, failed to greet the official party, Diagne had him dismissed from his position on the administrative council. At another stop he publicly humiliated a number of European merchants who had not presented themselves at the station when his train arrived.

Such Draconian measures were as deeply resented by the Europeans as they were cheered by Diagne's followers. His opponents put out that his mission was so unpopular that he was in danger of assassination in Dakar. After the armistice his recruitment role was sharply attacked in the general council as superfluous to the war effort. Finally, he was alleged to have been paid a bounty for each soldier recruited, a libel for which Diagne subsequently won a suit for damages. Yet through it all Blaise Diagne had won much more than personal damages. As he later put it, he had won, or thought he had, political, cultural and social equality for his people. 'France is today a country of 100,000,000 people, and all Frenchmen, whatever the colour of their skin, understand now and forever what it means to fight and to die together in defence of their fatherland.'[2]

2 *The Decline of an African Liberal*

In the blush of enthusiasm which followed the war's end, it appeared as though Diagne's vision of a greater France might be realized. With the

---

[1] Diagne to Minister for Colonies, July 26, 1916, N.A.S. 17G15; *L'A.O.F.* Mar. 6, 1915; Buell, *op. cit.*, II, 9n; R. Delavignette and Ch.-A. Julien, *Les Constructeurs de la France d'Outre-Mer*, 424–6; *La Démocratie du Sénégal*, June 6, 1914, May 16, 1915; *La France Coloniale*, Apr. 3, 1930.
[2] *L'A.O.F.*, Apr. 21, 1914; J. Carde to Minister, Feb. 15, 1918, Gov. Gen. G. Angoulvant to Minister (?), June 29, 1918, Report of special police inspector, Jan. 31, 1918, N.A.S. 17G15; *Conseil Général*, Senegal, Dec., 1918, 147–8; *Le Temps*, Nov. 27, 1924; *La Revue Indigène*, no. 165–6, Sept.–Oct., 1922.

hours the crowd dispersed without further incident. The authorities were shocked over a race riot barely averted and what they regarded as irresponsible conduct on the part of a government official. Diagne was totally unrepentent, however, and explained to the mayor of Dakar the next day that he was determined to have universal respect for the person and office of deputy even at the risk of breaking the peace.[1]

Such an aggressive atittude was reflected in the chronic skirmishing Diagne carried on against his political enemies, attacking them in his party newspaper and trying to use his influence with the local authorities to have the opposition press silenced and its directors sent off for army service in France. In itself such politicking would have meant little had it not been underlain by a deep-seated resentment on the part of both African and European—the former bitter over his shabby treatment, and the latter indignant at having been forced by circumstances to grant privileges he did not consider appropriate. In 1918 the matter came to a head when France in desperate need of soldiers turned once again to Africa for help. The government of Georges Clemenceau, seeking 75,000 riflemen from West Africa, planned a vast recruitment campaign and placed Diagne in charge as a Commissioner of the Republic with a rank equal to that of Governor-General Van Vollenhoven.

Van Vollenhoven was opposed to the recruitment plan, partly because he felt other Allied European colonies in Africa should have been required to contribute their fair share of soldiers, partly because he felt that French West Africa with over 100,000 troops already in the field would be badly crippled and an easy prey in the economic struggle that was sure to follow the war's end. Moreover, he resented Diagne's appointment which created a confusion of power within the area of his authority. Diagne's support for the plan was equally uncompromising. In the first place, it gave a tremendous psychological lift to the people of West Africa to have one of their own in such an exalted position. Secondly, it placed them as full-fledged Frenchmen squarely in the fight to save the mother country and western civilization from ruin. Thirdly, it opened up the possibility for extending French citizenship beyond the limits of the Four Communes to include all West Africans fighting for the mother country. As Diagne had already stated concerning the military contingents from West Africa, 'We want all those who are not voters but only

[1] Report of the Police Commissioner of Dakar, Mar. 4, 1915, Diagne to Mayor of Dakar, Mar. 2, 1915, Lt. Gov. to Gov. Gen., Mar. 6, 1915, N.A.S. 17G15.

The issue might have remained at that point but for the mounting manpower needs at the front as the nations of Europe set about the business of slaughter on a massive scale. In 1915 Diagne successfully introduced a bill providing for mandatory military service for the people of the Four Communes on the basis of full French citizenship. When certain questions were raised over the status of children of African citizens born outside the Communes, a second law was enacted the following year which eliminated all doubt: 'The natives of the incorporated communities of Senegal and their descendants are and remain French citizens.' There would no longer be any effective administrative or judicial interference with the citizenship of the people of the Four Communes. Not only were they entitled to all rights and privileges pertaining thereto but, unlike other French citizens, they retained their special civil rights conferred in 1857. Thus they and their descendants became French citizens in perpetuity regardless of where they were born, and they were free to follow Muslim law on domestic matters including polygamy anywhere in the world that French law obtained. In danger of losing normal civil and political rights, they had finally secured privileges unique within the French empire.[1]

There was a sequel to the legislative successes of Blaise Diagne in 1915 and 1916, a sequel which emerged from France's continuing need for military manpower and which was expressed in terms of human pride – pride of the French in their civilization, pride of the Africans in their new status, and pride of the deputy from Senegal in his position. The sequel began with an incident which occurred in the central square at Dakar on another spring evening, in March 1915. Diagne was reading a notice on the post office bulletin board when two dogs began quarrelling nearby. The European owner of one called off his dog, using the name 'Blaise'. Flaring at once, Diagne confronted him, stating that he would permit no one to name a dog after the deputy from Senegal to the French parliament. Hot words followed; Diagne called the other a fool and a military slacker and tried to hit him. The two were separated by the police but soon another scuffle developed during which Diagne was called a 'dirty nigger'. Again the police intervened, whereupon the thoroughly aroused Diagne went off seeking help, returning later with over one hundred Lebou 'to teach a lesson to those who lack respect'. Fortunately the dog owner and his party had retired and after several

---

[1] Guèye, *op. cit.*, 35–47; *La Démocratie du Sénégal*, Sept. 12, 1914, Dec. 11, 1915; *L'A.O.F.*, Feb. 14, 26, 1915; *Journal Officiel*, Chamber of Deputies Oct. 21, 1915, Oct. 1, 1916.

wish to have an opinion! Since when? And besides, they aren't French because though they may elect, they are not to be elected. To hell with that.

Then, social exploitation:

Everyone knows what this is—to maintain the native in a state of inferiority which leaves him the slave of a few big merchant houses not much different from the old slavers . . . look at the agents of these houses, arriving in the Colony down and out, unable to read and write and who, having bought land for a few pennies, sell it back to the government for ten, fifteen, or twenty times the purchase price. These wretches, now grown fat, become insolent . . . while the plundered native dances attendance. Let's give the gate to that sort of exploitation.

Finally, economic exploitation:

The natives . . . have lived largely by trade. They have enriched our commerce through their initiative and hard work. Our schools used to train native students in all subjects. Since the Colony has become the haven of all the freebooters and undesirables from the metropole, the native has been denied schooling by the hateful exclusiveness of this whole pack of brigands. . . . Enough of that.

There must be a new way of doing things:

Between them and us the difference is clear. All natives must understand that they can no longer allow themselves to be made fools of by those who want them to believe they must turn their backs on all progress for the African personality. . . . The truth, the truth of France, is with us.[1]

The essential issue remained, however. Diagne had campaigned with a pledge that if elected he would put an end to the regulations excluding the people of the Four Communes from the mandatory military service required of all Frenchmen. Honouring this commitment proved difficult. When a general mobilization was called in the summer of 1914, the Diagne party moved to have the Senegalese of the Four Communes included on the same basis as Frenchmen of the metropole. There was immediate and effective local opposition. The authorities expressed pleasure over the desire of the people to serve the mother country but found that any change in the regulations governing conscription would require legislative action which could not be taken until after the war; meanwhile now in the moment of crisis it was unseemly of the Senegalese to haggle over legal fine points when France needed all her sons, at once and without condition.

[1] *Journal Officiel*, Chamber of Deputies, July 7, 1914; *La Démocratie du Sénégal*, May 23, July 8, 1914, May 16, 23, 1915.

solid bloc of protest, the French and creole strength was seriously divided.[1]

When Blaise Diagne returned home early in 1914, therefore, he found a situation already congenial to the exercise of his unusual political talents. Facile in the give and take of political debate, he was able to move a crowd to emotional heights, not so much with a precision of logic as with an incomparable control of expression and timing, playing on his listeners, stirring their sympathies, their prejudices, their hopes, their fears. To this he added a sure political touch, a long experience in dealing with the French colonial system, and an ability to focus the campaign on the issue of racial discrimination which was troubling the African electorate and which constituted his best chance of success. Add to this the appeal of a humble background, an unusual intelligence and the courage to stand up to the Europeans and creoles, and there emerged a figure towards whom the African voter was easily drawn as the embodiment of his own frustrations and his own aspirations. Diagne captured a large share of the Lebou vote of Dakar, scored heavily in Rufisque and Goree, and made enough inroads into the mulatto stronghold of St. Louis to carry the day. At that, had the creoles not indulged in a suicidal last-minute split, Diagne would have been beaten.[2]

The election concluded, Diagne moved rapidly to meet the difficulties which lay ahead. The colonial administration was suspicious, the political opposition resourceful and dangerous, and the anti-assimilationists were more implacable than ever. Leaving for Paris, he headed off a move by his opponents to have his candidacy invalidated, and successfully defended his right to be seated in the Chamber of Deputies. In Senegal he kept his name before the people, writing belligerent newspaper articles which accused the mulattoes and Europeans of continued racial discrimination and a calculated campaign to prostrate the Africans—limiting their educational opportunity, bankrupting them with excessive taxation and usurious interest rates on loans, and expropriating the lands of the Lebou.

First, there was political exploitation:

So long as the natives pledge their votes naively to individuals whose principles are unclear and who use their position for self-enrichment, all goes well . . . But if the natives step out of line to the point of expressing a political opinion, oh well . . . the cry is anarchy! . . . So! the negroes

---

[1] *La Démocratie du Sénégal*, Nov. 20, 27, Dec. 25, 1913; W. Ponty to Minister for Colonies, June 24, 1914, N.A.P.O.S. Senegal VII, 34d.

[2] *L'A.O.F.*, Apr. 19, 1913, Apr. 27, May 5, 6, 1914; *Paris-Dakar*, May 16, 1934; Telegram, W. Ponty to Minister, June 15, 1914, N.A.P.O.S. Senegal VII, 81.

In light of these developments the election for deputy in 1914 would surely have developed into an unusually sharp contest even without the novelty of Blaise Diagne as the first pure-blooded African to contest the parliamentary seat. Already there had come into being a small but well-organized political movement, the Young Senegalese, consisting of the most educated and advanced elements among the African population—teachers, legal aides, minor officials, clerks and petty traders—but indirectly representing the larger body of Africans in the Four Communes affected by the government's restrictive measures. The philosophy of these Young Senegalese was simple. They believed completely in the French idea of assimilation and looked forward to the day when Senegal would be no more than another French province along with Brittany, Burgundy or the Gironde. They had succeeded in electing a few members to the local municipal councils as well as to the general council of the colony and were already vocal in their criticism of official policy which they claimed to be the product of anti-African discrimination practised by the Europeans and creoles.

Another source of potential opposition to the political power of the creole oligarchy were the Lebou of Dakar. These fishing people, despite long contact with France, were scarcely more assimilated than they had been in the eighteenth century when their favourite avocation had been the plundering of French shipwrecks on the Cape Verde shore. Their religion was Muslim, their language Wolof, and their attitude towards French culture one of indifference. In 1914, moreover, they were particularly resentful towards the administration. Part of the difficulty lay in disputes with the French over land titles in Dakar, and part was the result of ill-understood public health measures following several severe yellow-fever epidemics during the preceding summers. Normally, the Lebou spread their votes among the European and creole office seekers, but united behind a single candidate of their own, their numbers could prove decisive.

As the forces of disaffection grew in strength, the essential weakness of the mulatto and European position became more apparent. The creoles traditionally were spilt into two or more groups reflecting personal, family or commercial competition, and the Europeans rarely were able to agree on any single leader. In 1914 the creoles and Europeans presented between them no fewer than eight candidates including François Carpot, so that while the African vote was potentially a

of the Four Communes, Ministry for Colonies, May 31, 1915, N.A.P.O.S. Senegal VII, 7 bis.

decree only after each application had followed a tortuous course through the administrative machinery, thus effectively limiting the number who might qualify for citizenship by this route.

The second step was the odious decree of August 16, 1912, which placed under the jurisdiction of native courts directed by French administrators all the indigenous people of French West Africa 'who did not have in their country of origin the status of European nationals'. This ambiguous language was interpreted by the Senegalese at the very least as denying the availability of French courts to all black Africans who by chance or necessity resided outside the jurisdiction of these courts; worse still, the decree might be interpreted as placing the original population of the Four Communes totally under the rigorous and arbitrary *indigénat*, the native law which obtained in the interior. The opposition within the Four Communes was immediate and intense, and indeed the authorities seemed to have overstepped themselves in this instance, for within a year, they felt obliged to withdraw the decree.[1]

While these restrictions were being imposed on the civil and political rights of the Senegalese in the Four Communes, additional limitations had been introduced from another quarter. To Frenchmen the privilege of citizenship had come to involve the duty of military service, and under a conscription law of 1905, all French citizens were obliged to perform two years of service in the armed forces. For a time this regulation appeared to apply to the people of the Four Communes, but in 1910 only naturalized Senegalese were permitted to perform army service, all others being invited to serve in a special African contingent made up of volunteers and conscriptees taken on four-year enlistments, these enlistments implying no rights and privileges of citizenship and granting inferior claims to civil sevice positions than those accorded full French citizens. Thus by the eve of the First World War the question of citizenship in the Four Communes had become linked with the duty of military service–if all citizens of France were obliged to render this service, it was argued, then those who performed this military duty must be regarded as French citizens. It therefore became the object of the Senegalese in the Four Communes to be included within the definition of military conscription.[2]

[1] *Cour de Cassation*, Apr. 26, 1909; Lamine Guèye, *De la Situation Politique des Sénégalais Originaires des Communes de Plein Exercice*, 27–31; Decree regulating the conditions of accession to French citizenship by natives of A.O.F., May 25, 1912, N.A.P.O.S. Senegal VII, 7 bis; Runner, *op. cit.*, 29–31; *L'A.O.F.*, Oct. 18, 1913.

[2] Guèye, *op. cit.*, 33–9; R. L. Buell, *The Native Problem in Africa*, II, 5–7; *La Démocratie du Sénégal*, Sept. 12, 1914; Note on the status of the Senegalese

the decree of 1857 could not by that fact be citizens and could not therefore be voters.

This judgment appeared to apply only to those born outside the Four Communes. Natives of the Communes presumably still maintained their citizenship with all its rights and privileges. In 1908, however, the *Cour de Cassation* handed down its historic decision of July 22 which defined the citizenship and voting rights of the people of the Four Communes. In this case the lieutenant-governor of Senegal had removed approximately 1,500 names from the voting rolls of Dakar on the grounds that their personal status as Muslims deprived them of their citizenship and, consequently, of their political rights, including the right to vote. When it reviewed this case, the high court took a different view. It ruled that political rights and civil rights were distinct—possession or lack of the one did not necessarily govern the status of the other. In the case of the people of the Four Communes, their political rights had been clearly established by the French electoral law of 1884, and they therefore could not be deprived of the vote. At the same time, the court continued, the civil status of those originating in the Four Communes was governed by the decree of 1857 which guaranteed the special rights of Muslims. Since these special rights were not consonant with the French civil code, the Muslims of the Four Communes were not French citizens. Thus it appeared that while French citizenship was not a prerequisite to political rights, the quality of citizenship could be maintained only by those individuals whose personal status was governed by the French civil code.[1]

Further limitations followed in quick succession. In 1909 the high court ruled that only individuals actually born in the Four Communes were eligible to vote, and the following year an important administrative decision established a double standard for voting throughout Senegal. It was decreed that while Europeans and creoles could participate in all elections in Senegal regardless of where they lived, non-naturalized Africans could not vote unless they were physically resident in the Four Communes. Thus it was possible for the authorities to disenfranchise anyone simply by sending him to another part of the colony.

In 1912 two further steps were taken. First, a rigorous decree was put into effect which required difficult and lengthy qualifications for Africans seeking French citizenship through naturalization. Not only did each applicant have to show proof of his devotion to France but he had to be able to read and write French and be willing to give up his personal status if he were a Muslim. Final citizenship was granted by presidential

---

[1] *Cour de Cassation*, July 24, 1907, July 22, 1908; Moreau, *op. cit.*, 178–85.

could hardly be expected to take their places alongside Frenchmen from the metropole. The genius of French culture was a subtle thing not accessible to everyone and perhaps totally beyond the reach of people of such completely different background and customs. As for civil and political privileges which had long been practised in Senegal, these were not intrinsic or based on constitutional prerogatives and could be perfectly simply removed by decree whenever the occasion demanded.[1]

This dramatic shift in French colonial philosophy was soon reflected in a series of decrees, administrative orders and court decisions taken between 1907 and the outbreak of war in 1914 by which the civil and political rights of the people of the colony of Senegal were steadily eroded. Originally the privileges of French citizenship for Senegalese had rested in the law of 1833 granting full civil and political rights, as supplemented by that of 1848 freeing all slaves. To this was later added a special civil status decreed by Governor Faidherbe in 1857 which allowed Senegalese Muslims to resort to their own courts in such matters as marriage or inheritance, where they preferred to be governed by Islamic law. The right to vote in the Four Communes had arisen more informally, for the custom had developed after 1848 that all those who could give evidence of five years' residence in the Communes were considered eligible for the franchise.

Philosophies of colonialism quite aside, the Gallic mind was troubled by the dual status which allowed Senegalese to define their civil condition both by the French code and Faidherbe's 1857 decree. How could one man be monogamous, another polygamous; one governed by European ethical principles, the other by exotic and possibly salacious doctrines drawn from the Koran—and both be Frenchmen? It was an impossibility. Essentially the question was not one of ethics, but one of logic. In 1907 the *Cour de Cassation*, the supreme court of appeal in Paris, moved to clarify the situation. In that year it sustained a ruling by the electoral board of St. Louis disqualifying a voter on the grounds that he had been born not in the Four Communes, but in the Protectorate of Senegal. The court declared that under French electoral law only French citizens had the right to vote and it then went on to assert that individuals who maintained their special civil status as Muslims under

---

[1] *L'A.O.F.*, Nov. 22, Dec. 14, 1913, Mar. 21, 1914; Inspector-General Verrier to Minister for Colonies, July 21, 1905, Ministry for Colonies Note on Political Rights of Natives in Annexed Territories, June 17, 1907, N.A.P.O.S. Senegal VII, 7 bis; Paul Moreau, *Les Indigènes d'A.O.F.: Leur Condition Politique et Economique*, 192–3; Jean Runner, *Les Droits Politiques des Indigènes des Colonies*, 151–2.

teenth century at which time the cry of discrimination in job placement and advancement had first been raised. It was alleged that both in the commercial firms and in the government, the local African population was being shunted aside in favour of newly-arrived immigrants from France who were receiving choice assignments and better pay despite the claim that in many cases they were no more than opportunists come to the colony to extract what personal advantage they could from its bounty. The authorities and the Bordeaux firms were accused of colour prejudice, until then mercifully lacking in Senegal, but the government, while admitting that racial prejudice was in evidence, blamed West Indians come to Senegal who had brought their hatred of white men with them.[1]

Whether racial prejudice was real or imaginary, whether it was caused by the blacks or the whites, there was no mistaking another concurrent development aimed at limiting the political and civil rights of the Africans of the Four Communes. Since the days of 1789, Frenchmen had paid at least lip service to the ideas of liberty, equality and fraternity as applied to France's colonial empire. There could be no distinction between Frenchmen living in France and those living overseas, it was argued. All joined together in a mystical union to enjoy the fruits of political equality and freedom, and the community of spirit established by French language and culture. Such assimilationist notions may have seemed plausible during the quiet days when the French empire contained only a few scattered islands and one or two African footholds, but now that France possessed a huge empire sprawling across Africa and south-east Asia, to many Frenchmen these doctrines seemed sadly out of tune with reality.

It was now argued that many of the peoples recently come under French control were still in a barbarous state which clearly precluded their being treated on equal terms with citizens of France. But did this not raise questions concerning others in Algeria, Senegal and elsewhere who had been undergoing assimilation for generations with little evidence of progress? Critics cited the great majority of those living in the Four Communes who were said to be crude, arrogant, lazy fellows scarcely worthy of the political and civil rights they claimed; yet were sentimental Frenchmen prepared to place this fertile colony in the inexperienced hands of the very people from whom they had originally taken it? Even those rare Africans who had shown some mastery of French civilization

[1] See above, 371. Gov. H. Lamothe to Minister, Nov. 17, 1894, N.A.P.O.S. Senegal VII, 7 bis.

candidate of the people. I am not ashamed to be a black man.' Diagne concluded his appeals on a note of triumphant defiance. They would not be treated like slaves. They were Frenchmen and they would carry the day.

It was a moment of supercharged emotion. On this first night as with all the others, the audience burst into prolonged and enthusiastic applause and while the candidate was accepting the congratulations of those clustering about him, a thrill of pride ran through the crowd. For the first time in their lives many of his listeners felt that they could hold up their heads as men, that in the slight figure standing before them they perceived a new hope for a better future. Years later the event was still remembered in all its detail, the moment when a man of courage, self-respect and dignity had instilled the sense of these same qualities in his listeners and destroyed their long-lived feelings of inferiority.[1]

To be sure, Blaise Diagne had introduced a novel personal note into the politics of Senegal, but his appeal was circumstantial as well as individual, for events had been leading over many years to the issue he defined on that spring evening in St. Louis. Discrimination there had been against the pure-blooded Africans of the Four Communes, and it was steadily increasing in its severity. In the first place, Senegal had long been operated on the mercantilist principle that a colony be subordinated to the economic interests of the mother country. Whenever this principle was challenged, it was invariably to the exclusive advantage of the local creoles who maintained no especial sense of identity with the blacks. To most creoles the Africans were but the descendants of former slaves, slow to adapt themselves to the civilizing influence of French culture, and burdened with the superstitions of their Muslim faith. Their labour as well as their vote was something to be converted into creole or French profit. Since the early days of the Third Republic, therefore, while the representatives of the merchant houses of Bordeaux fought with the St. Louis trading firms for economic and political ascendancy, both found it useful to exploit the African population as fully as the traffic would bear.

A second source of friction had been developing since the late nine-

[1] *Paris-Dakar*, Apr. 30, May 7, 1955; Lt. Gov. Cor to Gov. Gen. W. Ponty, Jan. 14, 1914, W. Ponty to Minister, Jan. 31, 1914, Reports of the Police Commissioner of St. Louis, Mar. 20, Apr. 29, 1914, N.A.P.O.S. Senegal VII, 81; Lt. Gov. to Gov. Gen., Oct. 8, 1907, Feb. 10, 1909, Minutes of Police Commissariat of Kaolack, Apr. 10, 1913, N.A.S. 13G77. In his detailed analysis of the election, G. Wesley Johnson concludes that Diagne's appeal was based primarily on his fight for the basic rights of French citizenship for the Africans of the Four Communes. See G. W. Johnson, 'The Ascendancy of Blaise Diagne, and the Beginnings of African Politics in Senegal', *Africa*, vol. XXXVI, no. 3, July, 1966, 235-53.

THE ASSIMILATION OF BLAISE DIAGNE

There was a bustle on the platform as the introductions began. Perhaps it was Mody M'Baye who spoke first—a minor political figure who never let slip an opportunity to assure an audience that the time was drawing nigh when the Africans would assert themselves, claim their rights as French citizens, and establish their ascendancy over the creoles and the whites. This would have brought smiles, for M'Baye was chronically in a state of protest and not infrequently in difficulties with the authorities, but was hardly a person to be taken seriously. Now, however, the main speaker rose and faced the audience. Few had ever laid eyes on him before, and what they saw did not impress them greatly—a tall, slender, frail-looking man already well past the prime of youth, unprepossessing in a worn khaki suit.

Blaise Diagne began to speak. He started quietly, citing the long history of loyalty which the people of Senegal had shown to the principles of the great Revolution of 1789, and reviewing in vivid detail the familiar story of how the Senegalese had contributed to the birth of the French Republic. Suddenly the lights went out and all was darkness, noise and confusion. The meeting appeared to be over before it had fairly begun. Then, one by one, storm lamps came on and gradually the crowd settled down. Finally the speaker resumed, noting the now-empty seats vacated by the creole nabobs who had satisfied their curiosity and turned off the city lights to ensure that the rally would go no further. But Diagne had anticipated such a move and had brought along the auxiliary lamps which now illuminated the proceedings.

With a totally African audience before him, Diagne spoke in a different vein—on this night and thereafter through this surprising campaign giving effective voice to the matters that were troubling the people. The Africans were being discriminated against, he would assure his listeners, and murmurs of assent would come back from the crowds. The big mercantile firms had the colony in a stranglehold, reaping huge profits and forcing up the cost of living for the jobholder and small farmer. Now, he would warn, the authorities were moving to take away the civil and political rights of the people. Their citizenship and legal privileges were being called into question; if they did not fight this development then and there, in a few short years all would be lost. However, there was no need for despair. The people remained united, and united they would prevail. Repeatedly he gave the warning. 'The majority of the voters are black,' he shouted, 'and it is their interests which must be represented.' The audiences were rapt. 'Yes, my father was a cook and my mother a kitchen helper, and I am proud of it. Your candidate is the

19   The Assimilation of Blaise Diagne

1 *Blaise Diagne Secures French Citizenship in the Four Communes*

It was a pleasant evening in the spring of 1914, but the usual quiet in the centre of St. Louis was disturbed by the murmur of the crowd gathering in the twilight. In a few weeks an election was to be held to determine who would represent Senegal in the Chamber of Deputies in Paris over the ensuing four years. This was reason enough for the people to come out to see the candidates, to hear what they had to say. On this particular evening, however, there was much greater novelty to draw the crowd. The candidate who would address the people was a black—not a mulatto from the reigning creole oligarchy or even a representative of metropolitan France. This was unprecedented. Never had an African attempted to reach such high office. Occasionally a Frenchman captured the prize, but usually the deputy was a creole, like the incumbent, François Carpot, lawyer and member of a distinguished St. Louis family. Worse still, this challenger was said to be a nobody, a minor official in the colonial customs service, a Serer of humble parentage who had years before left his home for the obscurity of his unremarkable career. Scarcely anybody had ever heard of him.

The square was filling fast and, as the darkness deepened, the lights were turned on. At the front of the audience were the leading creole citizens of St. Louis, comfortably installed in the choice seats, chatting quietly, enjoying their after-dinner cigars, mildly curious to examine the upstart challenger. To be sure, the Africans of the four incorporated cities of Senegal—St. Louis, Dakar, Goree and Rufisque—had long possessed the vote, but they were for the most part an ignorant unlettered folk who had been easily persuaded by their betters to vote as they were told. There was no danger that it would be any different this time. Indeed, of the cluster of candidates, this African had about the poorest chance, and with so many in the field it appeared likely that Carpot would win again without difficulty.

In searching Macaulay's recurrent fulminations for a reasonable motive, the suspicion grows that he could not bear to admit that Carr might have had qualities of mind and character to which he aspired in vain. During one of his assaults on Carr, Macaulay sneeringly remarked, 'His political character has derived a positively carmine tinge... from that supercilious air of self-conceit, the offspring of an irresistible fascination engendered in his ill-cultured mind by the nauseous and revolting phantoms of his own supreme superiority.' In fact, it was Macaulay whose self-conceit was the more inflated, whose sense of superiority needed constant nourishment. Macaulay was the supremely popular figure, the darling of the people of Lagos; by comparison Carr was remote–respected but not loved. Still Macaulay showed all the signs of psychological insecurity which required ever larger doses of popular acclaim. Clever, articulate, celebrated and on the side of the angels in his espousal of the causes of the day, he may have lacked Carr's simple integrity and he may have realized instinctively that his emotional response to the world around him was unequal to Carr's quiet thoughtfulness. Carr was the one person he could not surpass. Deep down there was an admiration which unhappily mutated into jealousy, and out of jealousy finally arose hatred.[1]

[1] *The Lagos Weekly Record*, May 24–31, 1924; H. Macaulay, *Henry Carr Must Go*, 27.

3 'Henry Carr Must Go!'

During Macaulay's years of ascendancy, both his influence and following outside Lagos were small, and even in that city he had his opponents. Although late in his career he was shunted aside by the younger elements of Lagos grown dissatisfied with his political monopoly, at the height of his powers it was a group of conservative Africans who opposed him – uneasy over his inflexible anti-government posture, and uncomfortable in the presence of his flamboyant public manner. Men like Dr. John Randle, Sapara Williams, Kitoye Ajasa and Henry Carr were prominent, influential members of the Lagos community whose aspirations for the development of Africa involved close association with European ideas and institutions. In the circumstances they viewed the baiting of the British administration as thoughtless and unconstructive. If future African civilization was to require the assistance of Europe, why waste time and energy in hindering British efforts and heckling British officials? For his part, Macaulay with his limitless energy, his thoroughgoing self-confidence and his unswerving fixity of purpose, had more than enough ammunition remaining from his assaults on the government to indulge a concurrent vendetta against the conservatives, and his attacks on the one were paralleled over the years by assaults of similar violence on the other.

Chief among his targets was Henry Carr. The origins of Macaulay's antipathy towards Carr are obscure. Partly it could have arisen out of differences in viewpoints as to Africa's needs and objectives; yet the opinions of the two men were not so very far apart in terms of ultimate goals. Both were thoroughly assimilated into European culture which both agreed would play an important part in Africa's future. Both were devotedly loyal to the British crown and saw Nigeria as a permanent part of the British commonwealth of nations. The differences were therefore of degree rather than kind, of methods and not of objectives, rooted as much in personal antipathy as in differences over principle. In its early stages, Macaulay's hostility centred on Carr's role as Resident of the colony in resisting Macaulay's efforts on behalf of the House of Docemo. Later it became a recurrent complaint – a peevish, tiresome attack through newspaper and pamphlet which picked up issues twenty years old as though they had occurred the day before and generated violent outbursts over matters seemingly long since dead and forgotten. Carr, who made few public appearances and statements and who never commented publicly on Macaulay, was known to have dismissed these performances as 'the ravings of a lunatic' but they could not have failed to trouble him.

Macaulay was disqualified from holding public office because of conviction for fraud in 1913, but even out of office he was able to use his control over the Democratic Party to keep himself in the popular eye and to give full voice to his opinions on state matters. What other utility of a more general public nature the party may have had was much more open to question. The elected members of the council were a tiny minority of that body and could entertain no hope, either through eloquence or political influence, of swaying issues or affecting legislation. Through the years they kept up a show of effectiveness by assuming watchdog functions which they periodically announced. 'Under our constitution, it is not possible . . . to offer such an opposition which . . . might lead to the overthrow of your Excellency's administration', remarked E. O. Moore, the second Lagos member and Democratic Party regular, in 1926. 'But I do think it is the duty of the Unofficial Members of this council to offer strenuous opposition to any Government measure or policy which, in their opinion, is not conducive to the best interest of the country.' And so issues continued to be debated and the departmental officers continued to be questioned, but to very little ultimate effect. The official majority, complained another party candidate and council member, Dr. C. C. Adeniyi-Jones, 'has not only nullified the principle of the franchise but has practically reduced the unofficial members, especially the elected members, to the role of mere recording instruments of official sweet will'.[1]

Over the years, therefore, the Democratic Party continued to elect its candidates, and the sound and fury of debate persisted without cease, accompanied by the strident complaints of Macaulay in the public press. Gradually the routine became academic and popular interest in the elections declined. Not until 1938, when the Democratic Party was unseated and a new group of younger leaders appeared on behalf of new issues, did political interest revive. By that time, Macaulay's best years as an effective political leader were behind him. Briefly he re-emerged during the period of the Second World War as co-sponsor with Nnamdi Azikiwe of the National Council of Nigeria, but the fires had burned down, and the new effort was too much. In 1946 he died while campaigning over issues which looked forward to a new era of Nigerian political ideas which went well beyond Macaulay's nineteenth-century liberalism and parochialism.

[1] *The African Mail*, Oct. 3, 1915; Nigeria, *Legislative Council Debates*, Feb. 19–20, 1926, 99; Adeniyi-Jones, *op. cit.*, 11.

elementary morality and the principle of elementary common-sense strongly forbid.[1]

Next to the land issue, the question of taxes in southern Nigeria preoccupied Macaulay. In the early years of the twentieth century he had participated in the agitation against the collection of a water rate to pay for the installation of a modern water supply in Lagos. In the twenties, he was still arguing, petitioning, and editorializing against local taxation, and using essentially the same arguments as had been employed before. In 1927 he directed the opposition of the Democratic Party to a tax bill involving a direct head tax on individuals. This was contrary to the traditions of indirect taxation in southern Nigeria, said Macaulay; furthermore, as a tax form typical in the administration of primitive societies, it was *infra dig.* for the advanced community of Lagos. Finally, it violated the essential principle of 'the great constitutional rule that taxation ought to be coincident with representation; that only those who shared in the power should be called upon to bear the burden of Government'.[2]

The constitutional changes of 1922 which permitted the election to the legislative council of three unofficial members from Lagos and one from Calabar had led at once to the development of political organization. It was Macaulay along with Thomas Jackson of the *Weekly Record* who founded the original Nigerian National Democratic Party in 1923, primarily for the purpose of contesting the three Lagos seats. The party's constitution spoke of the usual devotion to principles of democratic representative government, and advocated reforms which might have been expected – among other things, the abolition of the provincial court system, improved public health facilities, economy in government and the end of discrimination in the civil service. It also urged the principle of local self-government within a commonwealth of nations 'linked by a common sentiment of loyalty to the King-Emperor'. Despite the party's patrician leadership and the voting requirements which limited the franchise to no more than three or four per cent of the city's 100,000 population, the party claimed and commanded a large local following.[3]

[1] Buell, *op. cit.*, I, 756–7; C. C. Adeniyi-Jones, *Political and Administrative Problems of Nigeria*, 14–18; Nigeria, *Legislative Council Debates*, May 3, 1926, 18–20; H. Macaulay, *An Antithesis . . . on the Public Lands Acquisition (Amendment) Ordinance, 1945*, esp. 13.
[2] Nigerian National Democratic Party, *Petition Against the General Tax (Colony) Bill, 1927*, 2, 'Memorandum of Objections Against . . . The General Tax Ordinance', Macaulay Papers, IV-16; Adeniyi-Jones, *op. cit.*, 22–30.
[3] *Constitution, Rules and Regulations of the Nigerian National Democratic Party*; *The Lagos Weekly Record*, June 9, 1923; *The African Messenger*, May 8, 1926.

fied. In order to protect land in southern Nigeria from acquisition by foreigners, land legislation had required that all land sales be approved by the governor. Nevertheless, said Macaulay, in a 1926 petition to the Undersecretary of State for the Colonies, this did not prevent alienation by the state for which compensation usually could not be obtained without recourse to the courts, while the fear remained that appropriation might be a first step towards the establishment of a plantation system and introduction of forced labour:

Let the people be secure in the possession of their lands ... we are concerned about our countrymen whom some people are wont to call 'savages' ... If these people ... are deprived of their communal rights ... they are sure to become labourers and be made to work by compulsion.

This view might be difficult to understand in light of the firm policy which had been announced by Governor Clifford against any attempted exploitation by British commercial interests through the imposition of a plantation system. Nevertheless the question had been mooted frequently in high British business circles, while plantations and compulsory labour were enough of a commonalty in other African colonies to raise genuine fears in Nigeria at the time.[1]

The other major complaint voiced by Macaulay and other nationalist leaders over the years was that land appropriated by the government was frequently taken merely to lease back to private interests for private gain or for the convenience of the European community. When in 1945 an ordinance was passed converting all government-acquired land into crown land even where the original public purpose had been fulfilled, Macaulay thought he saw a conspiracy to deprive the people of their land and to reduce them to wage slaves:

To vest our Communal Lands in the Crown after they shall have been acquired piece by piece ... when the purpose for which such communal lands were acquired shall have been fulfilled ... is, to say the least, a deliberate plan, by legal ramifications, to deprive the native inhabitants ... of a great portion of the communal lands ... upon the possession, occupation, and use of the soil of which the prosperity of the African communities ... wholly depends. This would be a most inconsiderate act which will reduce the ... native communities from their inherent position of producers in their own right of the fruits of the soil, and of free traders in that produce, whereby they shall become slaves on their own soil; an undesirable policy which the precepts of

[1] E. M. Hunt to Macaulay, Aug. 8, 1921, *Ibid.*, IV-10; 'Memorandum Submitted to the Ormsby-Gore Hearing, 1926 ... on Behalf of the Nigerian National Democratic Party', 9–15, *Ibid.*

mattered little that the king was to have no administrative functions or political importance, nor did it even matter in the end that Cameron was obliged to settle the matter himself, making a choice which was satisfactory to everyone, after the chiefs were unable to agree. The principle had been achieved that the traditional ruler was important to the people of Lagos even though his functions had become largely ceremonial, and it was finally established that his election could only be performed in accordance with proper traditional procedure. More important still, it was conceded by the administration that African leadership could not be coerced or cajoled by a high-handed government; rather their loyalty to England and their reliance on the workings of British justice entitled them to the fullest protection of British constitutional safeguards. Having laboured so long and so hard to obtain these sanctions, Macaulay was justifiably exultant at the outcome.[1]

The eleko question had been only one of several matters which Macaulay had raised with Governor Lugard in 1913; chief among the others was the related issue of land ownership and the right of a government to expropriate private land for public purposes. The problem arose out of conflicting views of land ownership. As in the Gold Coast, the British administration tended to regard land as belonging to the crown whereas African tradition placed ownership, not with the king, but with the people. Under this latter view, the government in acquiring political control by treaty or annexation could not at the same time assume residual land ownership which continued to rest with the community or the individual. Macaulay did not contest the ultimate right of government to expropriate private land for public purpose, provided appropriate compensation were made; he did, however, suggest that the administration did not always adhere to its original declared purpose, so that on occasion lands acquired by government were put to private use and profit quite outside the limits of the original public function.[2]

Part of the problem of crown ownership was clarified in the Apapa land case which was successfully argued before the English privy council in 1921 by Chief Oluwa with the assistance of Herbert Macaulay. The decision, which was hailed by the Lagos community, fixed ultimate ownership of the lands ceded by Docemo in 1861 with the chiefs and not with the British government, which meant that land could not be expropriated without proper compensation. Yet Macaulay was not satis-

[1] *The Lagos Weekly Record*, Jan. 20, 1923; I. B. Thomas, ed., *The House of Docemo*, 86–102, 121–6; *Nigerian Gazette Extraordinary*, Aug. 29, 1933; *West Africa*, July 11, 1931, 844; *The Lagos Daily News*, Sept. 1, 1933.
[2] *The Lagos Weekly Record*, Mar. 8, 1913; Macaulay Papers, IV-1.

and responsibility. Although the original treaty did not call for a pension to be paid to Docemo's heirs, it had computed his stipend on the basis of income from export duties. Now in 1920, said Macaulay, the government's annual revenue amounted to almost £5,000,000, yet the king was brushed aside with a pittance, his stipend suspended at the pleasure of the colonial administration, and he himself hectored without reason and deprived of his office. 'Is this', he wanted to know, 'a wise manifestation of consistent and broadminded colonial statesmanship, or is it the ominous vibration of an oscillating administrative pendulum?'

More than that, Macaulay continued, the government since 1901 had declared the eleko to be a private person, but it actually treated him as a public figure. He had been made a member of the Central Native Council formed in 1901 to advise the governor on native affairs, and he continued to serve on that council. Furthermore, Macaulay asked, if the king were a private citizen, how could he be suspended from office, and later reinstated to a presumably non-existent position? Why was so much fuss being made about the eleko's staff which could only have been under the circumstances an article of private property and a family heirloom? 'It is a notable fact', said Macaulay, 'that while other lands under British dominion are pursuing political agitation by recourse to riot and insurrection, British West Africa is pursuing a modified form of home rule by the most constitutional methods.' The implication was clear – let not the administration push the people beyond the limits of endurance.[1]

Macaulay's case placed the government in a foolish position which was further complicated by a petition of 17,000 signatures gathered in 1922 requesting that the eleko be reinstated. The petition was ignored and there followed several years of skirmishing between the administration, which established and seated a rival claimant to the throne, and the legitimist party led by Macaulay who continued to agitate for the return of the true eleko to his proper place. Finally persistence, as well as the correctness of Macaulay's position, carried the day. In the 1930s the moderate administration of Sir Donald Cameron sought a way out of the impasse. A commission was formed to determine the proper method for choosing the eleko, and its recommendation, relying in considerable measure on the detailed testimony of Macaulay, was that the choice be made in strict accordance with the ancient traditions, including use of the appropriate oracle if necessary. The governor accepted this recommendation and charged the chiefs with the full responsibility for settling their intramural disputes and electing their own prince. It

[1] *Justitia Fiat*, 3–6, 45–6.

publicly the eleko's staff of office and in a newspaper interview explained that this staff belonged to the king of Lagos, recognized as such by the 16,000,000 people of Nigeria. Through clumsiness, the administration in Lagos misinterpreted the statement as an assertion that the eleko was king of all Nigeria, then foolishly and myopically persisted in this faulty interpretation, finally deposing the eleko when he refused to repudiate an incident for which he was not responsible and which in any event contained an inaccurate version of what had taken place. From this point onward, the African case was irresistible and Macaulay proceeded to exploit it with masterful thoroughness.

In 1921 he published *Justitia Fiat*, a long and detailed defence of the eleko's position, a defence which he based chiefly on moral grounds, the subtitle reading, 'The moral obligation of the British Government to the House of Docemo'. Docemo, the reigning eleko in 1861, Macaulay explained, had ceded his territory to Britain in order to secure protection for his people and to end the infamous slave trade in the coastal area. There were, however, a number of inequities involved in the transaction. First, the king had had no authority to cede ownership of the land of his domain, since he exercised only sovereignty thereupon and not ownership. Secondly, because of the disagreement over the status of land ownership, the treaty was never properly ratified by the eleko's White Cap chiefs, the residual owners of the land of Lagos. Thirdly, there was evidence that the king had been under considerable pressure from the English to sign a treaty for which he had little enthusiasm, and on signing, he had been advised only by individuals who were clearly sympathetic to the British position. The validity of the treaty was therefore open to question on technical as well as moral grounds.[1]

There were, however, other complications. Initially Docemo had been asked to cede his territory in perpetuity to the British crown in return for protection, and it was only after the protest of his chiefs over the land ownership issue that it was stipulated he would receive an annual grant equal to his income from customs duties prior to the treaty, a sum estimated at approximately £2,000. No provision was made for his heirs despite the perpetual cession of sovereignty, and in practice he actually received only half the estimated pension during the remaining twenty-four years of his life. Eventually, out of dire need, his successors were granted a modest stipend of a few hundred pounds but it was clearly stated that this was a 'compassionate allowance' and not a right, and that the eleko was to be considered a private citizen devoid of public function

---

[1] H. Macaulay, *Justitia Fiat*, 3, 37–42; *The African Messenger*, Mar. 23, 1922.

contribution to the world of ideas in West Africa was consequently minimal, although his importance as a nationalist leader was undeniable. His credo consisted of embarrassing the British administration wherever possible and of sustaining the effort as long as necessary. In the end, the agitation consumed a lifetime.

Macaulay became an outspoken critic of the British during the administration of Sir Walter Egerton who directly preceded Lugard as governor. Along with his continuing objections over the cavalier treatment of traditional African rulers by British administrative officers, Macaulay began to complain of official policy on matters of public improvements, land legislation and taxation. Early in Lugard's administration, Macaulay headed a committee of the Lagos Auxiliary of the Antislavery and Aborigines Protection Society which pressed the new governor for redress concerning several matters. Chief among these was the question of the king or eleko of Lagos, and this issue was to occupy Macaulay almost to the point of obsession for the following twenty years. The basic issue was simple. In 1861, the eleko had ceded the territory of Lagos to England by treaty and had been given an annual pension as part of the settlement. This allowance had been drastically reduced for his successors with the result that the state of the royal house had deteriorated over the years. In raising the matter with Lugard, Macaulay had several motives in mind. First, he realized the value of the traditional ruler of Lagos as a rallying point of local cohesiveness. Moreover, there was a plausible case that the eleko was at least morally entitled to more than the nominal allowance he was then receiving. Finally, the eleko issue provided a splendid opportunity to publicize the high-handed methods of a colonial government in action.[1]

The interview with the governor was unsuccessful and further events so hardened Lugard's unfavourable judgment that he ultimately suspended the eleko's stipend temporarily on the grounds that he had exceeded the authority of his office in making some local appointments among the Muslims of Lagos. Clearly the administration was embarrassed by a traditional ruler whose position had meaning for the people but who possessed no actual power. It was a situation made to order for the guerilla political tactics which were all that were permitted the African leadership of the day. In 1920, while Macaulay was in England in connection with a land case being argued before the privy council, he displayed

[1] *The Nigerian Chronicle*, Mar. 18, 1910; *The African Mail*, May 13, 1910; *The Lagos Weekly Record*, Mar. 8, 1913. The full history of the Eleko affair from its inception is set forth in R. L. Buell, *The Native Problem in Africa*, I, 662–7, and Perham, *op. cit.*, 264–71.

slightest criticism were characteristics peculiarly attuned to the emotional needs of an evolving West African society in Macaulay's day. When after the constitutional changes of 1922 a small number of unofficial members were elected to the Nigerian legislative council, they at once proved active in debate, and specialized in directing numerous questions to governmental departments dealing with details of administration. More particularly, these questions were often aimed at real or imaginary inequalities in the relative official treatment of Europeans and Africans, and it was apparent that the African representatives greatly resented any legislation which appeared to reflect any doubts over African capabilities and loyalties. Macaulay's personal idiosyncrasies to a considerable extent reflected a community sense of long-standing outrage at having to bow and scrape, to smile and endure, in face of the interminable condescension and hostility of the official and unofficial resident Europeans. Witness, for example, the humiliation visited on Macaulay when he was apprehended in the midst of a surveying commission in the Ibadan area in 1923. Whatever the merits of the suspicion that he was engaging in political activities, one can readily imagine his feelings at being hauled peremptorily before the District Officer, told he was an unsavoury character, and packed off without ceremony on an uncomfortable night train back to Lagos. It is easy to picture the scene—the British resident maintaining his cold, precise, but condescending and contemptuous manner, and Macaulay bland, polite, reasonable, with only a hint of mockery to betray the hot fury that boiled beneath the surface.[1]

Despite Macaulay's reputation for erudition and literary prowess, he was more a man of action than a man of thought. Despite his position as a leader of the West African community, his career of leadership boiled down to an unceasing campaign of pressure on the British administration based on the single and single-minded idea that Africans should have a greater role in self-government to offset official arbitrariness, mismanagement and favouritism towards the European community. He appears to have reflected less upon ultimate goals for West Africa than his contemporary, Henry Carr. Despite his own personification of the westernized African, he does not seem to have been concerned with the difficulties of reconciling the two worlds of Europe and Africa as was James Johnson. Least of all did he attempt in the manner of Blyden to fashion a philosophy of Africanness for the society he lived in. His

---

[1] Margery Perham, *Native Administration in Nigeria*, 260–1; James S. Coleman, *Nigeria: Background to Nationalism*, 145–52; *The Lagos Weekly Record*, May 12, 1923.

prolixity, and in its way it was an impressive *tour de force*. Today, however, his essays seem strained, self-conscious, illogical and redundant. Surely their argument could have had but little influence on the average citizen of Lagos in his day whose literary equipment was hardly equal to the rigours of this typical harangue:

How can it ever be argued with any modicum of reason and commonsense that because the three elected African Members of the Legislative Council of Nigeria who represent the Municipal Area of Lagos press persistently for the replacement of Europeans by competent Africans who by merit are suitable to be so transposed, therefore pointing out to Government of the fact that one African holding a somewhat high and yet anomalous office in the Service with a high salary is overdue, and long overdue for pension according to Law, and that that African official was only pitchforked into that anomalous office in order ostensibly to get rid of him from an equally important public office in which he was considered an eyesore at least, if not an undesirable unit on account of his colour, tantamounts to a contradictory policy pursued by the very leaders of the party responsible for the election of the three African members who so press for the advancement of Africans, and at once becomes a manifest conspiracy to 'drive from office' that same redundant African officer who happens to be the one African Resident in Nigeria![1]

What becomes increasingly apparent in an analysis of Macaulay's activities is that self-regard was a constant factor guiding his judgments and actions in public affairs. His appearance and dress were unforgettable and they were meant to be. Self-centred, he enjoyed the centre of the stage, and self-centred, he like to be on stage alone, to accept the full applause of the groundlings. There were some who found him incapable of accepting criticism or advice, and savagely vindictive towards those who did not do him the homage he demanded and needed. If it is true that he was unusually generous and open-handed in time and money, who but Herbert Macaulay would have used the columns of his own newspaper to publicize the fact? And when he was released from prison in February 1929 after serving a six-month term for criminal libel, who but he would have devoted his paper for days to descriptions of the people of Lagos 'mad with joy' over this event of unparalleled consequence?[2]

Still, an overdose of personal ego and a thin skin sensitive to the

[1] Thomas, *op. cit.*, 7–9, 15, 22, 39, 53, 97; *West Africa*, July 11, 1931, 844, 846; May 25, 1946, 469, June 8 1946, 517, June 29, 1946, 582; Owen Johnson, 'People I Have Met', Macaulay Papers, IV–8; Increase Coker, *Seventy Years of the Nigerian Press*, 16–17; *The Lagos Weekly Record*, May 3, 1924.

[2] Thomas, *op. cit.*, 95–7; *The Lagos Daily News*, Feb. 25, 26, 27, 28, Mar. 1, 5, Apr. 18, 1929.

considered outstanding both for their style and content; *Justitia Fiat*, his defence of the House of Docemo, for example, was celebrated not only in Nigeria but in England where it was much admired for cogency and thoroughness. Macaulay's reputation as a pamphleteer, moreover, was matched by an undoubted personal magnetism. Tall and dignified in bearing, his great black bow tie paralleling the flamboyant wings of his enormous white moustache, he was a familiar sight on the streets of Lagos as he hurried along in conversation with a companion, but always ready with a wave of a hand for a passer-by or a coin for a street-corner beggar. Patrician though he was, he was readily accessible to all people of all stations; westernized though he was, he possessed genuine sympathy and understanding for the customs and institutions of traditional African life; Christian though he was, he maintained an easy and close rapport with the Muslim community of Lagos throughout his long public career.

As an individual, Herbert Macaulay possessed a highly developed artistic sense. An accomplished violinist, he enjoyed giving public concerts as well as informal musicales at his home, Kirsten Hall, which was significantly named after a musician friend. Long before the advent of high-fidelity phonographs Macaulay was advertising the value of symphonic recordings through gramophone concerts at his home, and he was a great patron of locally staged operetta and drama. Witty and charming in conversation, he relied on wide reading in a well-stocked library to provide him with the wealth of anecdote which sprinkled his conversation, and his collections of paintings, ceramics and silver were a well-known adjunct to his cultivated household.

It was, however, his public image which gave him the popular following on which he built his political power. In addition to his great personal charm, he was unsurpassed as a public speaker. His rich voice commanded immediate attention, yet soothed with its resonance. His vivid anecdotes, heavy irony, quick humour and powerful invective were ready ingredients for a successful speaker. Being able to speak in Yoruba as well as English he had access to wider and more appreciative audiences, and his uncanny sense for the popular side of contemporary issues no doubt rallied a large following behind him. It must have been manner more than matter which gave contemporary success to his speeches, for his writing does not stand critical analysis or measure up to its initial reputation. Macaulay was one of those individuals who never used one word where two would do just as well, and it was not uncommon for him to spin out sentences of two hundred words or more of complex syntax. To be sure this was the relic of a baroque Victorian

the subjugation of a Native Ruler who, standing upon his ancient rights, refuses to give up those rights and yield placid obedience to the wishes of an Official Magnate.

Macaulay never lacked for irony to sauce the rolling periods of his Victorian prose. Now we are expected to believe, he concluded with heavy indignation, that it is, of all things in this newborn twentieth century, the ancient practices of slaving and human sacrifice which necessitate the subjection of native towns and the destruction of native kings along with 'quiet tradesmen and beggars, blacklegs and idlers, women and children, guilty or not guilty, regardless of the value of lives'.[1]

This deep sense of outrage never seemed to leave Macaulay throughout his long life and it constantly characterized his tireless efforts to check, to circumscribe, to erode and to replace the power of the British colonial administration in Lagos. Yet he was in no sense a revolutionary. He has been described as a typical nineteenth-century liberal of moderate old-fashioned views, and not once did the slightest hint of Nigerian separatism from Britain ever intrude itself in his writing. If his creed was liberalism, however, it included as well the idea of democratic local self-government, a concept which fitted not at all with contemporary European doctrines of colonial government and white supremacy.

Even more pronounced than his liberalism was Macaulay's sense of history. Most of his writing in pamphlets and newpapers was in the form of political or legalistic tracts disputing this or that issue over which the Nigerians and their government were momentarily at odds. Macaulay's arguments were invariably and exhaustively historical. His grasp of local history was legendary and he was widely read in western history so that his presentations were frequently garnished with long asides which perhaps began by examining the activities of Martin Luther, switched to the campaigns of George Washington, moved on to the career of Charles I and ended with a bit of Biblical commentary. His historical knowledge made him quite aware that England's nineteenth-century hegemony had been preceded by centuries of much more modest achievement. At the same time he was familiar with the ancient powers and accomplishments which the local African kingdoms had enjoyed in better days. Thus he was not to be confounded by arguments claiming European ascendancy over an innately inferior Africa.

By all accounts Macaulay was a man of unusual intellectual and social gifts. His vast energy thrust him fully into the great controversies of his day; indeed he was often their instigator. His journalistic tracts were

[1] *The Lagos Standard*, June 7, July 12, 1905, May 16, 1906.

revolutionize traditional patterns of trade even as the British administration radically altered the traditional political configuration. During the incumbency of Governor Egerton, the colony of Lagos was amalgamated with the protectorate of southern Nigeria, the harbour of Lagos was improved, railways, highways and telegraph lines were constructed, and a consequent expansion of internal and external trade effected. In the process, traditional rulers may not always have been treated with outstanding tact, and it was this arrogant and heavy-handed exercise of power that irked the African leadership in Lagos and led to protests by individuals like Macaulay.

In 1905 Macaulay published a sharp criticism of the deportation and imprisonment of two leading chiefs of Ilesha. Taking initial exception to a report in the British press which spoke of inferior 'nigger chiefs' encouraged to consider themselves on a par with Europeans by unscrupulous 'nigger barristers', he began by pointing to the numbers of Africans who had obtained major scholarships at the Inns of Court, who had repeatedly done valuable and successful legal work for the British government, and who in the case of Samuel Lewis had won a knighthood as the capstone to a long and distinguished career.

More serious than these gratuitous, though minor, insults, however, were the 'arbitrary use of power . . . ruthless disregard of the most commonplace courtesy . . . [and] arrogant indifference to pledges and assurances', which had led to the banishment and detainment of the chiefs. With the exception of the Ijebu, said Macaulay, the Yoruba city states had all come under British suzerainty by treaty which guaranteed local self-government while delegating authority over external affairs to the British administration centred at Lagos. Macaulay kept up the complaint of British violations off and on throughout a twelve-month period – instead of building up the strength and authority of the native rulers, the British were illegally assuming powers they did not possess and allowing inexperienced young district officers to make decisions for which they lacked all authority. Summing up Egerton's administration, he complained:

> We have invariably been told that Punitive Expeditions were employed for the opening up of Trade:– for the punishment of natives who perhaps massacred one or two European Commissioners who may have insisted upon entering a native town on a Fetish Day against all appeals from the king and his Chiefs: – for the terrorisation of a Negro king who should find it inconvenient to supply at a moment's notice, sufficient Provisions and Provender for a mighty official and his retinue while passing through that native province:– and not infrequently for

stitutional safeguards to hold off and weaken colonial policy and administration.

2 Herbert Macaulay Criticizes Britain's Colonial Adminstration

Herbert Macaulay, as assimilated and europeanized an African as the continent ever produced, was one of the leading nationalists of his era. He was, moreover, superbly endowed by both heredity and environment to assume the position of leadership which he occupied in Lagos during the forty years before his death in 1946. First of all, he was a member of the West African élite, the repatriated Aku from Sierra Leone, who formed an important section of the aristocracy during Macaulay's lifetime. More than that, he was born into the topmost stratum of that society. His maternal grandfather was none less than the revered Bishop Crowther, and his father, Thomas Babington Macaulay, an early product of the C.M.S. mission training programme, was the founder and distinguished director of the C.M.S. grammar school in Lagos, as well as friend and confidant of Sir John Glover during the latter's residence in Lagos as administrator of the colony. Young Herbert, born in 1864 one of seven children, was brought up in a manner proper among Victorian mission circles. In his later years he recalled how he had been dressed in purple velvet breeches and matching coat twice each day for prayers, and how, after years of kneeling, the nap of the fabric had worn so that he had two white patches at the knees. With religious instruction went a full measure of secular schooling as well, and the boy attended primary and secondary schools in Lagos until he took employment as a clerk in the public works department of Lagos in 1881. On the strength of his work in this position, he was sent to England in 1890 on scholarship to study engineering, returning three years later with a degree in civil engineering. After a few years' service as a government surveyor, he established himself independently in 1898 as a practising engineer, architect and surveyor.[1]

Macaulay's career as the gadfly of the British administration in Nigeria began not long thereafter, and characteristically he found his most effective medium for criticism in the public press. It was during the early years of the twentieth century that the British administration consolidated its hold over its Nigerian territories. The country was pacified and a transportation and communication system introduced which was to

[1] Macaulay Papers, V-9; Isaac B. Thomas, *Life History of Herbert Macaulay, C.E.*, 1-6.

more inclined than their Gallicized counterparts to think of local self-government rather than political liberty, of African nationalism rather than equality before the law, and of an African cultural integrity rather than the fraternity of all men. The differences between the two groups should not be pressed too far, however, for there were substantial numbers of Africans in the coastal towns of British West Africa as thoroughly assimilated into western culture as were the Franco-Africans of Senegal; indeed, it was because, rather than in spite, of their English training that they were able to think in terms of African cultural nationalism. Those who assumed leadership at this time all showed the indelible mark of Europe—James Brew or Casely Hayford on the Gold Coast, Samuel Lewis of Sierra Leone, Sapara Williams, Henry Carr, and Herbert Macaulay in Nigeria, or the ubiquitous West African, Edward Blyden.

Within this group of English-trained African leaders there was a further distinction. One line of thought ran close to the French philosophy of assimilation, and sought as great accommodation as possible between Europe and Africa. If African institutions were sufficient, well and good. When, however, it appeared that European institutions were superior to those of native Africa, then it was necessary to clear away the debris of the old order and bring in the new as quickly as possible. Henry Carr was probably the leading exponent of this group which included an important membership—Samuel Lewis, Sapara Williams, John Randle of Nigeria, J. E. K. Aggrey, and during his last years, Casely Hayford. These men were genuine patriots, as greatly interested as were their nationalistically-minded contemporaries in the welfare of their people. Perhaps they excelled the nationalists in their concern for modernization; in any event, since they often saw Europe as the prototype, they argued that African progress was to be achieved through mastery of western science, not through emotional appeals to African nationalism, through western education and literacy, not through indigenous cultural institutions.

The other point of view took its lead from the cultural nationalism of Blyden, and employed its European background to stand off the European intrusion as much as possible. European-educated ministers like Majola Agbebi turned their training to the propagation of a native African Christianity. European-educated newsmen like the Jacksons used their skills to call into question the efficacy of western colonial government. European-educated political figures like Herbert Macaulay and John Mensah Sarbah called on their ability to manipulate British con-

Europe. There were the growing number of Africans who had studied Europe long and hard, who therefore understood the strengths and weaknesses of the West, and who could utilize European knowledge and skills in addition to those of Africa to prepare an effective African response to Europe's intrusion. These Africans, educated, sophisticated and informed, were able to lay a groundwork of ideas and institutions which led ultimately to political independence in mid-twentieth century. In so doing they of course traded away forever the standards, the beliefs, the way of life, the world view, indeed the very essence of traditional Africa, and substituted something still African-rooted to be sure, but far more western in its aspirations and motivations.

Though this second group of Africans looked to Europe for much of its inspiration and philosophy of action, it was by no means a homogeneous body, either of persons or of opinion. There were, for example, the differences which existed between Africans trained in the British and those trained in the French traditions of European culture. French-influenced Africans were more completely persuaded that the only course for Africa was total adherence to European standards; to become completely French was the goal. They were less likely, therefore, to assert their rights as Africans or to proclaim the cultural integrity of the Negro then they were to insist on full equality as Frenchmen within the worldwide French community. The mulattoes of the Four Communes of Senegal, for instance, consistently thought of themselves as French. When they quarrelled with the administration, it was a family affair among Frenchmen, not an expression of African nationalism. When at last the pure-bred Africans of Senegal ousted the creoles and established their own political ascendancy, it was not to reassert African political or cultural independence; it was to assure that they too, like the creoles, would be accorded full recognition as Frenchmen.

The situation in the English territories was somewhat different. First of all, the British held no particular brief for a policy of assimilation. English missionaries, moreover, were much more active than their French counterparts in developing primary schools, and consequently a far larger proportion of less thoroughly educated—hence, less assimilated—Africans resulted. Finally, British ideas of democratic government and colonial administration, hammered out in the years after the breakdown of the imperial system in colonial America, had resulted in a policy of eventual autonomy within the framework of a world commonwealth of British nations. Thus Africans in the British territories were somewhat

18 The Liberal Nationalists: Herbert Macaulay

1 *Africa's Accommodation of Europe*

During the years that closed the nineteenth and opened the twentieth century, European dominance over West Africa steadily increased, and the African reaction to Europe rose proportionately. Broadly speaking, the reaction came in two quite different ways from two totally different segments of the African population. On the one hand there was the reaction of traditional African society fighting to maintain its timehonoured ways, unprepared to deal with the forces closing in on it, only dimly aware of the new possibilities for advancement, yet unable to master the techniques which might be made to alter a world without destroying it. Whether it was a tough Lat Dior or an effete head of the House of Docemo, a religiously inspired Mamadu Lamine or a commercially shrewd Jaja of Opobo, a military prodigy like Samori or a confused minor chief in a Niger River village, all were incapable in the final analysis of coping with Europe. Europe could not be ignored, neither could it be absorbed. It could not be repelled nor could it be changed. Those, like the Oil Rivers chiefs, who were quickest at adapting themselves to the exigencies of the European presence were best able to survive for a time. Those, like the Eleko of Lagos, who succumbed to pressure were quickly shunted aside, to become minor curiosities or, in this particular case, a pawn in another and different type of African-European struggle. Those who chose military resistance were the ultimate inevitable victims of superior fire power. Courage and tenacity as with Lat Dior or military skill as with Samori could not in the long run match the rocket and the Gatling gun. In the end all that traditional Africa could muster was the dead weight of its inert populations, and this proved more to Africa's disadvantage than to Europe's.

There was, however, another and more effective African reaction to

to have but one party, the party of union. . . . before they consider themselves from Senegal or from the Metropole, the people of Senegal are, above all, Frenchmen, and most of all Frenchmen in the depths of their hearts.[1]

Unlike most creoles of his day, Louis Huchard harboured a genuine affection for the African, both in the colony and in the protectorate of Senegal. In place of discrimination and exploitation, he wanted to see education and economic development, for the people of Senegal were not only entitled to this sort of help in return for what they had contributed to France, but they were obviously well qualified, with proper assistance, to make the most of the advantages of French civilization. In these views, Huchard reflected attitudes which were increasingly in the minds of the Senegalese Africans themselves, so long excluded by choice and circumstances from the benefits of the French occupation. Slowly they were developing a self-awareness and a desire for some share of the fruits of their own land and the benefits of western technical efficiency. Thus Huchard anticipated views which were to come to full flower within two decades with the rise of the Young Senegalese and the appearance of Blaise Diagne.

[1] *Ibid.*, Sept. 19, Oct. 2, 1897, Dec. 31, 1897–Jan. 8, 1898.

which by Huchard's definition was a form of indirect rule of the most corrupt sort. To begin with, the colonial service seemed to consist largely of inexperienced adventurers, where people of intelligence and tact were needed. These were easily bribed, he asserted, by corrupt, venal chiefs who were thus able to maintain a feudal tyranny over their people. In France there were regular elections to forestall usurpation of power, but in Senegal, where French blood had flowed that liberty might flourish, there remained only oppressive despotism. The administration permitted local chiefs to remain in power, to collect taxes as they pleased, to practise household slavery, and to carry on brigandage without interference. To Huchard, what was needed was a system of elected chiefs, representative of their people, literate, educated and enlightened. They in turn could be responsible to district officers who might appropriately be drawn from among the mulattoes and educated Africans who knew the people and how best to help them. Then at last might end the degrading spectacle of 'weariness, suffering, despair . . . everywhere the unhappy people plundered at the least pretext, everywhere the most shocking extortions practised with impunity under the protection of the Native Affairs Department.'[1]

Thus Huchard and his editorial colleagues had much fault to find with French administration in Senegal. To them, the metropolitan commercial interests were extracting huge profits from the country and yet were unwilling either privately or through government to reinvest a reasonable share of these profits. As for the government in Paris, it clearly served the pleasure of French economic interests, refusing to develop the country, to educate the native and to reform the administration in conformity with the great principles of 1789.

But criticism of the French colonial administration and condemnation of the merchants of Bordeaux did not mean disenchantment with France herself and a desire for political independence. The people of Senegal might be crippled by ignorance and confused by superstition, but they aspired to a better life through France—for them France would always be the mother country, and to France they would always turn:

It is evident that a country does not achieve satisfactory development if cordiality and a perfect union does not bind together its people. It is time to make peace, realizing that all of us in Senegal are Frenchmen and brothers. We do not say, Senegal for the Senegalese. We think that Senegal should be for all Frenchmen, for those born on Senegal soil as well as for those born on the soil of France. It is the height of happiness

[1] *Ibid.*, Nov. 15, 30, 1896, Apr. 8, 1897.

French, so little Senegalese, that they would vote for anyone for the smallest leaf of tobacco.[1]

Despite the fears implicit in this little piece of apocrypha, the Devès party scored an impressive win in 1897, but the basic conditions against which Huchard was struggling did not greatly change. Ultimate power in the colony had always been with the governor-general and his aides, and for all the talk of assimilation and the rights of man, official policy continued to treat the colonies as existing basically for the benefit of the mother country. One charge to which Huchard returned again and again was that of favouritism in job placement and advancement for individuals emigrating from France, and correspondingly rising colour prejudice against the African. The commercial houses consistently discriminated in favour of Europeans, excusing themselves by pointing out that Africans preferred to work for the government. This was true, admitted Huchard, in so far as government jobs offered better pay and working conditions, but this was only a natural choice for personal betterment. Within the government, moreover, there was a vicious discrimination, particularly odious in the communications and native affairs offices. It was hinted that General A.-A. Dodds, a mulatto from St. Louis and the conqueror of Dahomey, was the victim of prejudice in the Ministry of Navy and Colonies, and there were many other suspected victims of discrimination–for example, Charles Molinat retired too early as director of the bank in St. Louis, two young well-qualified Senegalese recently discharged by the public works department, and another refused a scholarship to study in France for no apparent reason. It was the French who had come to Senegal who were the villains:

You . . . grandsons of those who forged the first chains for Senegal, you have deceived us as your grandfathers deceived ours . . . History has carefully recorded the time when your ancestors . . . led [ours], living corpses, from Africa to America, and you reaped the benefits . . . Gigantic fortunes which permit you to corrupt the ignorant masses . . . date from that time of misery and social injustice. With superb talent for profit, you knew how to identify among the Senegalese, the women who could advance you . . . In the commercial houses built with the money from these marriages . . . It is Senegalese money which enriches you . . . You have destroyed everything . . . every day you wound us in all our ideas, our fibres, our feelings, our desires, our hopes.[2]

One form of French discrimination over which Huchard was particularly exercised was the system of government in the protectorate,

[1] *Ibid.*, July 31, 1896, Feb. 15, May 15, 1897; Governor-General to Minister for Colonies, Jan. 16, 1897, N.A.P.O.S., Senegal VII, 68.
[2] *L'Afrique Occidentale*, Oct. 31, Nov. 30, Dec. 15, 1896, May 1, June 26, 1897.

If economic exploitation was the end, the means to the end were various, and the chief of these was political. The old battle which had been waged through the 1880s by Devès, Crespin, and others for control of the general council and the office of deputy continued into the nineties without let up. On the one hand there were the representatives of the metropolitan commercial houses who in alliance with certain creole interests had managed to keep a controlling hand on most of the colony's political affairs. Opposed were a group of mulattoes from St. Louis and Dakar who rallied around the local merchant empire, the house of Devès, and who made a show of representing the African vote. In the heyday of Gaspard Devès and J. J. Crespin, this devotion to native rights had been somewhat hypocritical, but with Huchard, the fight for native rights was real enough. As the general council elections in the autumn of 1897 approached, Huchard mounted an increasingly active attack against the entrenched interests from Bordeaux. He accused them of making common cause with the colonial administration to restrict public works where these were most needed and to initiate them where they were largely useless, to refuse a reapportionment of council seats which would reflect the growing importance of Dakar and Rufisque, and to permit the worst sort of election frauds designed to place on the rolls ignorant, illiterate Africans whose vote might easily be bought. In his indignation Huchard was capable of occasional heavy irony. At the court of the justice of the peace in St. Louis, he tells us, it was a common scene to find a questionable voter trying to establish his eligibility. Asked for witnesses, the applicant would produce two who, needless to say, spoke no French and probably did not even know Wolof:

[They] have come to swear by the name of Christ, which means nothing to them, that the future elector is twenty-two years old, born in a village on the railroad line. Now, these villages have only existed since the construction of the road, that is between ten and twelve years at most.
 Then ... the witnesses add that the future elector has lived in St. Louis for a long time, the son of Amadou and Coumba ...
 If you insist on knowing what they mean by a long time, they will answer twenty-five or thirty years. Thus we find that the future voter has lived in the city not only since his birth, but several years before that. If you examine more precisely his antecedents, you will be surprised to learn ... that Amadou and Coumba are not his father and mother ... but the owners of this future French voter, a slave bought in the protectorate for twenty pieces of guinea cloth or three cows under the paternal eye of one of our highly decorated administrators.
 After that, you will not be surprised to find on the rolls, children ten years old, English or Portuguese subjects, and individuals so little

classic manner. Huchard did more than merely talk about this injustice. He established an independent company for marketing the ground-nuts of the Cayor farmers, and almost immediately found himself in court on a charge of defrauding the natives. The case was decided just as *L'Afrique Occidentale* brought forth its first issue, and it was a complete vindication and acquittal for Huchard. Those whom he had allegedly swindled testified that no such fraud had taken place but rather that they had obtained much better prices dealing with Huchard's organization.[1]

Instead of economic exploitation, Huchard counselled economic development, with France taking the lead in planning and investment. What the country needed most of all was diversification. Her economy was stunted by its reliance on ground-nut culture. Actually there were many other agricultural products which should be explored, particularly those which had application to industry. Huchard suggested the introduction of rubber in the Casamance, cocoa in Guinea, cotton, tobacco and indigo. The government could do a great deal to help, not through direct action since private investment should always be encouraged, but indirectly through low interest-bearing loans, and through a massive programme of public works to open up the country. As early as 1885, he was urging cheap credit for farmers, and in issue after issue of *L'Afrique Occidentale*, he called for more railroads, lower shipping rates, better harbour facilities and improved systems of irrigation.[2]

Huchard urged industrial development as well, with emphasis on mining. The complaint in France had always been that colonial industry ought not to be encouraged for fear that it might compete with home industry, but this, said Huchard, was a short-sighted view. Clearly a more productive colonial population increased the overall economic health of the whole empire. The real reason for reluctance lay elsewhere—in the selfish attitude of those already making profits from the colonies as they stood, who wanted no development of the land and its people which might upset the system:

> We who live in close touch with the powers that be here, know that they are opposed in principle to any change. They did not want the Dakar-St. Louis railroad any more than they want better schooling: ignorant people being easier to exploit than individuals capable of reasoning... the syndicate dislikes big changes which open new horizons to those it is accustomed to exploiting to the hilt.[3]

[1] *Ibid.*, July 14, Aug. 31, Sept. 30, 1896, Aug. 8, Oct. 2, 1897.
[2] *Le Réveil du Sénégal*, July 19, 26, 1885; *L'Afrique Occidentale*, Aug. 31, Oct. 15, 31, 1896, Oct. 24–30, 1897.
[3] *Ibid.*, Sept. 15, 1896, Apr. 8, May 1, 1897.

The first issue of *L'Afrique Occidentale* appeared symbolically on Bastille Day 1896 to proclaim Senegal's loyalty to the mother country. Huchard took the occasion, however, to enunciate his principles which made a careful and effective distinction between France and the beauties of her colonial policy on the one hand, and the selfish machinations of metropolitan commercial interests on the other. These latter, he said, had for years pursued a calculated exploitation of the country, carrying off the riches of the land and treating the colony as their private preserve to be used for their own selfish ends. 'France established herself in this country several hundred years ago but the development of the land and its people has not kept pace with the brilliant march of progress noted elsewhere. This is particularly unfortunate when we see what other European nations have accomplished in nearby territories.' France herself, continued Huchard, was not to be blamed for she had bestowed upon Senegal the full benefit of her noble principles of human rights, but these had been accompanied by economic interests which blurred the distinction between justice and privilege, and placed the people at the mercy of a rapacious commercial combine. As for our paper, said Huchard,

We think that the prosperity of a country is illusory when a few capitalists alone pursue their activities while the natives have not sufficient means to improve their land and assure their independence... Furthermore, we feel that concern for the future, and for the welfare of the people... can come only from those who live and die in their country, attached to it by bonds of blood and the cult of ancestors. It is imperative that the riches produced from the land remain with the land... So long as this country is exploited by a political-financial system of exportation, confusing the local interests with those of overseas, we who believe that our fatherland was not given us by God to make us unhappy, or the rights of citizens bestowed by the Republic to make us outcasts, we see our duty to oppose the transformation of our land into a farm and our people into its livestock.[1]

At the root of the problem was a syndicate of large commercial houses from Bordeaux. These were able to control the ground-nut market, setting an arbitrary purchase price for the raw nuts from the farmers, regulating the processing plants, permitting no independent local merchants to deal in the ground-nut trade, and selling the finished product in France at a handsome profit. Thus, said Huchard, Senegal had become not a part of France to be developed in brotherly affection, but a conquered territory to be exploited, a colony to be milked dry in the

[1] *L'Afrique Occidentale*, July 14, 1896.

sented the new spirit of commercial enterprise which had taken hold in the land.[1]

The demise of *Le Réveil* and *Le Petit Sénégalais* in 1886 and 1887 left Senegal without a local press once again, just at a time when political developments and economic activities within the colony required the encouragement of an expanding journalistic enterprise. Yet the reasons were not obscure. Readership in St. Louis was numbered only in the hundreds despite her thousands of population, and the other centres, still much smaller, showed a similar proportion of literacy. Those who were literate, moreover, were French or thoroughly assimilated creoles who thought of themselves as French. News for them was news of the metropole, and this they could obtain from the metropolitan newspapers regularly brought in by ship. Nevertheless, there was too much happening within the colony for this situation to continue unchanged, and in 1896 three papers were founded. From that time forward, first Senegal and then the other territories of French West Africa began to be served with increasing regularity by local journals.

Of the three papers which appeared in 1896, *L'Afrique Occidentale* is of particular interest. Its editor, chief writer and moving spirit was Louis Huchard, a creole from Dakar who had contributed several pieces to *Le Réveil* dealing with the economic development of Senegal, who was a minor political figure in Dakar during the late decades of the nineteenth century, and who, like J. J. Crespin, was a sometime legal counsel who had turned the major share of his attention to other matters. He had early associated himself with the Devès-Crespin party which meant that he was infrequently in a position of political power, but it may also have accounted for the brand of liberal nationalism he brought to his editorial columns. Huchard seems to have been one of those persons who by constitution had always to defend the underdog. As early as 1885 he was arguing forcefully for the economic prospects and potentialities of the African population and twenty-eight years later we find him still defending African rights and initiative as a matter of principle. His editorial policy for *L'Afrique Occidentale* consistently reflected this same preoccupation with the injustices visited by the strong upon the weak, combined with the notion that France should and could do much more than she was to help her offspring Senegal realize its economic potential.[2]

[1] A. Villard, *Histoire du Sénégal*, 162–4; Roger Pasquier, 'Villes du Sénégal au XIX Siècle, *Revue Française d'Histoire d'Outre-Mer*, vol. 47, 1960, 3e et 4e trimestre, 412–25.
[2] *Le Réveil du Sénégal*, July 19, 26, 1885; Minute of Police Commissariat of Kaolack, Apr. 10, 1913, N.A.S. 13G77.

the immense task of bringing the interior under more direct French influence. He broke the power of El Hadj Omar along the Senegal River, tamed the Moors on its north bank, began the subjugation of the Cayor and opened up the regions to the south of Cape Verde. Nevertheless, the process of pacification was only begun with Faidherbe, and had to be supplemented later by major campaigns deep into the interior and by a variety of local police actions. By 1895, however, the territory defined as Senegal had been almost totally pacified, a fact which brought fundamental economic changes in its wake.

With the necessity for conquest and consolidation at an end, the port cities of Senegal, sustained in the past by their modest and intermittent trade with the interior, took on added importance. St. Louis, to be sure, by the end of the nineteenth century was expanding but slowly if at all, and there was fear in the old capital that other centres might eventually replace her as the prime metropolis of Senegal. By far the largest port on the coast north of the English colony at Freetown, St. Louis had a population of about 20,000 and she was moreover the administrative, commercial, and social centre of the colony. For her part, the island post of Goree had long since seen her best days and was quietly fading away in a genteel obscurity to become eventually a suburb of Dakar.

Dakar herself, located on the tip of Cape Verde, had been founded as an administrative centre by Pinet-Laprade in 1857. During its first twenty years the city managed to attract only 1,500 inhabitants but thereafter the figure rose rapidly. In 1895 the population was up to 8,000, and by the eve of the First World War Dakar replaced St. Louis as the seat of government and commercial centre for French West Africa, with a population of 25,000 and a thriving commerce to match. The fourth seaport was Rufisque, located about a dozen miles down the bay from Dakar. A small town of 1,200 in 1878, Rufisque had risen to over 8,000 by 1895 and almost doubled itself again by 1914. Rufisque was the commercial city *par excellence*. She had come into existence as a port for the shipping of ground-nuts and ground-nut products which were much in demand on the French market. Her quick expansion during the late decades of the century was a direct reflection of the final pacification of the Cayor which had somewhat reluctantly turned from herding and feudal warfare to ground-nut farming. In 1885 Rufisque was already exporting approximately forty per cent of Senegal's ground-nut tonnage. By 1910 she controlled four-fifths of the total ground-nut exports for the colony which had then risen to almost three times the 1885 figure. If St. Louis was a decaying relic of a former time, Dakar and Rufisque repre-

members of the town council. Why not give the community representation to balance the taxation to which it was forced to submit? The present arrangement, Jackson declared in 1917, 'is practically reducing the council proceedings to a mere farce and converting the Council itself to a recording machine of the Governor's sweet will'.

Jackson, along with others – E. O. Moore, in particular – kept up a steady demand for council representation and after the war a new ordinance finally granted election of three members on a franchise limited by property qualifications. By that time – the year was 1920 – Jackson was not to be satisfied with an arrangement which restricted the popular representatives to a powerless minority, and obscured the proceedings of the council by failing to publish its debates. Furthermore, he had become concerned with a larger issue – direct representation of the African on the much more influential legislative council. In 1922 a new constitution called for the popular election of three representatives from Lagos and one from Calabar to sit in the legislative council. Once again Jackson expressed his disappointment, pointing out that this small concession made only the barest show of responsible government, burying the people's representatives under the overwhelming majority of the official legislative council members. Nevertheless he and Herbert Macaulay moved to form a political party which successfully contested the first Lagos elections held in 1923, and continued to dominate Lagos politics for the ensuing fifteen years. The main figure of these years, however, was Macaulay himself, and analysis of this later period may therefore most appropriately be deferred until the ideas and activities of the great Nigerian nationalist are studied.[1]

5 Nationalist Journalism in a French-African Setting

The establishment in 1895 of a federated government for all the French possessions in West Africa anticipated a pacification of the interior which had not yet been fully achieved. In the days before Faidherbe, France had occupied but a modest empire in West Africa – a small number of trading posts and two relatively minor coastal ports serving as outlets for a trade which depended in large measure on the political temper of the independent tribes inhabiting the inland country. Faidherbe, like Captain John Glover or Ernest Parkes, realized that economic development rested squarely on peaceful commerce, and instituted a policy of pacification which by negotiated treaty and military persuasion began

[1] *Ibid.*, July 29, 1911, Feb. 3, 1917, June 28, 1919, May 12, July 14, 1923.

sympathetic policy that the Educated Native will cease to be the bug bear that haunts its political dreams.[1]

By the time Lugard's term had come to its end, the break was complete. Jackson welcomed his successor, Sir Hugh Clifford, with unrestrained joy, comparing his reputation for clear vision and enlightened administration with the oriental despotism of his predecessor:

> The news . . . has been received with great joy and gladness by the loyal natives of Nigeria. So overwhelming is the people's emotion that . . . in the inmost recesses of their hearts they have offered . . . some silent prayer to the God of the Negro for his tender mercies in delivering his dusky children from the baneful effects of an inglorious administration . . . Sir Frederick has earned the notorious distinction of being the originator of a system of government . . . the most infernal system that has ever been devised since the days of the Spanish Inquisition for the express purpose of humiliating and depressing the units of any loyal and progressive community. . . . Its 25 lashes, its public floggings . . . its maintenance of so called 'white prestige' at all costs, its subjection of the Judiciary to the Executive, and its obnoxious Criminal Code bespeak an administrative system which is the exact prototype of German Kultur in Africa.

Jackson's send-off to Lugard was unequivocal. 'For six long years', he complained, 'we have lived under the cramped condition of a military dictatorship when the law from being a means of protection had become an instrument of crime and oppression in the hands of unscrupulous officials. . . . The last administration had made the very name of the white man stink in the nostrils of the native.'[2]

War's end and Lugard's departure brought eventual reassessment of British colonial policy, quite possibly in response to the reform agitation of Lagos newsmen like Jackson and of other leaders among the African community-Herbert Macaulay in particular. In his own day, J. P. Jackson had criticized the British crown colony system as a benevolent despotism which made an empty show of responding to popular feeling through the appointment of a few unofficial legislative council members, but which in fact ruled arbitrarily through the governor and his overwhelming official majority in the council. Thomas Jackson had begun to pick up the complaint of a community taxed but unrepresented during the war years, particularly in connection with the Lagos town council. The people of Lagos had no say in matters of municipal development and taxation, he complained, for the governor appointed all twelve

---

[1] Perham, *op. cit.*, 600; *The Lagos Weekly Record*, Apr. 29 & May 4, 1916, July 21 & 28, 1917.
[2] *Ibid.*, Feb. 1-22, 1919, Jan. 10, 1920.

same reasons. No more than the Nigerians were the Senegalese willing to lose their standing and give up their constitutional gains, to be pushed back to a tribal status and made to submit to arbitrary government. No amount of argument in favour of efficiency would be likely to sway them from this view.[1]

Under different circumstances there might have been the possibility of accommodation between the governor and his journalistic tormentors. Lugard made occasional efforts to explain his position to the Lagos community, and sometimes these interviews eased the strained atmosphere. In 1916, Jackson requested and received an interview with Lugard which continued unbroken for three hours during which a wide range of matters was discussed. Lugard, who had never met Jackson prior to that moment, found him intelligent and felt he had made good progress with the editor in explaining official policies. Evidently Jackson agreed for he reported to his readers a worthwhile discussion covering numerous sore points over which the governor was 'the very incarnation of patient and sympathetic hearing [displaying] a versatility of knowledge which was equally surprising and impressive'. But fundamental positions and attitudes remained unchanged so that the old mistrust soon returned to plague both governor and governed. On one occasion Jackson attempted to analyse the impasse from his point of view. Who was the educated native, he asked.

Invariably he is a son of the soil and a member of a subject race who ... happens to be blessed (cursed from the official point of view) with the indispensable adjunct of a liberal education. He also wields ... a surprising command of the English language by which he has been able to express himself most clearly and intelligently; criticise with logical precision the political measures of the Government; advance unanswerable arguments against untoward administrative policies; and give articulate expression to the thoughts, the feelings and the wishes of his less enlightened brethren. ... the Nigerian Government has always viewed the educated native with a considerable amount of suspicion and distrust, presumably because he has proved such a faithful guardian of the people's rights and liberties and also a veritable stumbling block to the realisation of some of the nefarious schemes of the Administration ... the attitude of the educated native is founded upon a sociological law ... that the function of society is the evolution of personality ... The advanced or progressive units of the race will be those who through the process of natural selection can boast of elasticity or adaptation or who have the greatest power of making conscious adjustments to ever changing conditions. It is only when the Nigerian Administration recognises this truism by adopting a more liberal and

[1] See below, 398. See also *L'Afrique Occidentale*, Apr. 8–16, 1898.

disaffection among a liberty-loving people whose loyalty is proverbial and utilising that very spirit of disaffection as a means for their further humiliation. Never was imperial infatuation fraught with graver dangers.[1]

The worst feature of this whole dismal policy to a man of Thomas Jackson's thinking was Lugard's pet reform of the southern courts. For Lugard it was a plain step forward from an inefficient court system which encouraged unethical legal activity, which did not provide adequate judicial coverage of large areas, and which put many of the lower courts in the hands of semi-educated native clerks. As reformed, the system brought justice within the reach of all by establishing provincial courts to be directed by the local British political officers. It effected economies by using executive officials for judicial functions, and it improved the administration of justice by giving the power of decision to officials familiar with the people, their language and customs.[2]

This was hardly likely to impress the Lagos intelligentsia. Jackson saw tyranny and mismanagement in the hands of inexperienced young political officers. He forecast the disappearance of British justice before a policy of political favouritism. He deplored the banning of counsel to the accused, the limitations of the right of appeal and the use of corporal punishment. He argued that the system put the judiciary at the mercy of the executive, introducing some of the worst features of oppressive German colonial rule:

> Graver and wiser heads stand aghast at this apparent passing away of the true ideals of British Justice and the supersession thereof by a spirit of Militarism . . . With gloomy foreboding they murmur at the sworn determination of the Administration to ride rough-shod over the feelings of the people and with bated breath the rumour is spread that an evil star has arisen over Nigeria and its peoples cast upon anxious times.[3]

The essential reason for this attitude was not difficult to understand. The African leadership in Lagos, aware of the opportunities which western education and western political and economic developments held out for Nigeria, was flatly unwilling to see this phase of Africa's development rolled back and lost. Precisely the same reaction was forthcoming at exactly the same moment when the people of the Four Communes of Senegal resisted French efforts to reorganize the courts in the same name of efficiency. And the reaction was identical for precisely the

---

[1] *Ibid.*, May 23, 1914, Mar. 6, 1915, Oct. 14, 1916.
[2] Perham, *op. cit.*, 424–30.
[3] *The Lagos Weekly Record*, Oct. 17, 1914, Dec. 5 & 12, 1914, Jan. 2, 1915, Oct. 14, 1916.

rapprochement between the governing body and the governed may be established which is the keynote of a sympathetic and an enlightened form of government.' The governor could not have disagreed more. In his eyes, the educated native of Lagos was the worst possible agent to express the 'aspirations of the public', and western democracy was hardly the appropriate form of rule for the Africa he felt he knew.

But Jackson pressed on. He attacked the water rate scheme repeatedly, insisting that it ran counter to traditional views regarding taxation. He made pointed references to the Boston Tea Party and the loss of the American colonies by another British government too narrow and inflexible to take account of local opinion and too arbitrary to give much attention to democratic processes. When the massacre at Ijemo gave Lugard his excuse for bringing Egba independence to an end, Jackson suggested that the new treaty had been signed under duress and without popular approval. The administration's intention to inspect and register private as well as government schools was regarded by Jackson as a blow at political freedom, since in West Africa whenever educational opportunities were limited, some form of domination, physical or mental, inevitably followed with a consequent wholesale confiscation of property.[1]

The main fire, however, was directed against the amalgamation of northern and southern Nigeria, and the reflection that this reform gave of an official determination to rule arbitrarily. The so-called indirect rule in the north had always been a farce, said Jackson. The emirs had been stripped of their power, put on a salary – which incidentally was paid for through southern taxes – and the region was run like a military satrapy by Lugard's commissioners. The south, accustomed to a different régime based on constitutional government, found itself subjected to the same sort of arbitrary administrative rule, while the legislative council was reduced to the impotence of a municipal assembly. 'Need there be any wonder that [this] policy ... should have failed to commend itself to a people whose main characteristics are an intense patriotism, a fervid devotion to the cult of freedom and an irresistible capacity for expansion?' There was no rhyme or reason to it all, just a burning desire to curtail individual rights and to extend despotism:

The attempt to set back the hands of the clock of progress by foisting upon the more favoured states the despotic rule of the Northern Provinces thereby giving them a foretaste of militarism can only be construed as a set purpose to wound the susceptibilities of and create a spirit of

[1] *The Lagos Weekly Record*, June 6, 13, July 11, Sept. 19, Oct. 10, 1914.

the city whom he thought arrogant, loud, conceited and quite unrepresentative of the overwhelming proportion of the country's population. Unable to fit Lagos in his system of colonial administration, Lugard set about to change it—to neutralize and restrict it. Herein lay the crux of the dispute between the administration and the city's leadership in which Jackson was to take a conspicuous part.[1]

Lugard's policy involved a number of related moves designed to tighten up and make more efficient the government of the country by extending to the southern provinces the administration which had been worked out in the north. He in effect reduced the legislative council to the status of a municipal council for Lagos; he tried, though unsuccessfully, to transfer the capital to Kaduna; he instituted a more rigorous control over school inspection; he took advantage of unrest in Abeokuta to bring that quasi-independent city under full British protection; he tried repeatedly to limit the freedom of expression of the Lagos journals; he concluded arrangements for a public water supply in Lagos, instituting a rate which was regarded as unrepresented taxation by the people of the city. Most resented of all was his reform of the court system of the southern provinces for it appeared in African circles as an attempt to substitute arbitrary administrative justice for traditional British jurisprudence guided by professional judges.

It was not long before the local Lagos papers had opened a full-scale attack against the governor. The 'scurrilous local yellow press', he called them, pouring out their 'columns of venomous abuse often bordering on sedition or libel', but it was not as simple as all that. To be sure they had little access to government sources of information and often had to make do with their imaginations; further, an anti-government posture was a popular posture, and newspapers were thus tempted to push to extremes in their search for a wider circulation. Nonetheless, there was a good deal of moment to their arguments, and, though they tended to be long-winded and heavily baroque in style, they were well written. Indeed it was their very effectiveness which added to official irritation at their activities.[2]

Jackson was indefatigable in his pursuit of the governor and his administration. When he first assumed direction of the *Record*, he enunciated his editorial policy: 'Politically . . . it will be our duty to educate or enlighten public opinion . . . whilst a corresponding obligation is entailed to place continually before the eyes of the Government the legitimate desires and aspirations of the public . . . so that mutual

[1] Margery Perham, *Lugard, The Years of Authority*, 581–6.
[2] *Ibid.*, 597, 598; Ikoli, *op. cit.*

and by 1905 was working regularly for his father. By the time he assumed the editorship, therefore, he was well experienced and ready to exercise full control over the paper's policies.[1]

A change in editorial emphasis was soon apparent. John Payne Jackson's style had been reasonably genial and muted, and his criticism of the English administration was tempered and balanced, much in the fashion of Blyden. More than that, J. P. Jackson frequently spoke in generalities rather than in specifics. He talked of such things as the nature of the African character, the superiority of African marriage customs, family solidarity and its relation to traditional government, the relative merits of Christianity and Islam, or the applicability of European individualism to Africa. Thomas H. Jackson, on the contrary, was not content with generalities. He was interested in specific issues requiring specific solutions. To be sure they involved principles, but the time for mere talk had passed, and it was necessary to see principles translated into action. Actually, the times were changing. African leaders were no longer content to theorize and ruminate over their situation. Like it or not, their countries had become colonies during the generation before the First World War, and the general question of the relations between Europe and Africa had been crystallized in particular issues involving colonial administrations, or European control of African churches. The change had been signalled by Blyden's call for an independent church in 1891. By 1914, it was manifest in Nigeria in a whole series of conflicts which set the paternal rigidity of a colonial administration against the stiffening resistance of a people who yearned for a voice in their own affairs.

Thomas Jackson was one of a small group of younger journalists recently come on the scene and they all were in varying degrees set upon establishing a new pattern. The *Lagos Standard* like the *Weekly Record* had been a product of the nineties, but in 1908 Chris Johnson founded the *Nigerian Chronicle*, and in 1914 the *Times of Nigeria* was reorganized under the direction of James Bright Davies. All were quick to take aim at the government and the governor-general presented them with an admirable target. Lugard appeared as the embodiment of all their frustrations, the realization of their worst fears. His administrative experience in Nigeria had been in the north, and the patterns of government he had worked out there did not readily accommodate Lagos. The city was atypical, westernized, accustomed to European cultural and political institutions. Lugard was especially put off by the educated leadership of

[1] Allister Macmillan, *The Red Book of West Africa*, 109.

to him and to them; and . . . that religion which separates a man from his people and makes him stand off from them in contemptuous scorn, is a religion not from God but from the devil.[1]

Whatever the merits of these charges, they reflected sincere beliefs on Jackson's part and a sense of his people having been wronged. It is not surprising that some of this hostility to Europe appeared in Jackson's ideas on education as well. Africans did not want to be turned into black Englishmen, he explained. They desired an education which made use of Europe's assets but did not destroy the essential African. More and better teachers were needed to produce a practical training that would suit the everyday needs of the people. An education that was too bookish and too rooted in European materials merely encouraged indolence and produced a youth with an inadequate, irrelevant training. Native languages should be employed to encourage independent thought and imagination; the discipline of manual training should be introduced to instil habits of regularity and industry; and every effort should be bent on making the African known to himself and to his countrymen. Clearly, the influence of Blyden was strong right up to the final thought. We know the Africans can learn to make money, and become successful in commerce, said Jackson, but what of their influence in the world of ideas? 'Can they produce any effect upon the *thought* of the world? Can they say anything to shape the ideas of humanity in the direction of progress and thus do something to lift the human race?' The implication was that, with proper education, they could. 'Ideas, not money, rule the world', he concluded. As with Blyden, he saw Africa's contribution to the world in terms of its spiritual rather than material needs.[2]

4 *The Militant Newspaperman—Thomas Horatio Jackson*

John Payne Jackson remained as editor of the *Weekly Record* until the spring of 1914 when he was replaced by his son, Thomas Horatio Jackson. J. P. Jackson had come originally from Liberia and his parents were American Negroes, but a long residence in Lagos had made him at least a naturalized Nigerian. It was in Lagos that his son was born in 1879, and it was there, as well as in Liberia and Sierra Leone, that Thomas Jackson was educated. Although he worked briefly as a clerk in a commercial house, he showed an early interest and capacity for journalism

[1] *Ibid.*, Nov. 28, 1891, July 2, 1892, May 2, June 6, 1896, Oct. 23, 1897.
[2] *Ibid.*, Mar. 7, July 4, 1896, June 5, 1897, Apr. 22, 1899, July 21, 1900.

Lagos during the nineties, rested not only on the encouragement of African institutions but on the corresponding depreciation of European culture. Yet Jackson, like so many of his contemporaries, could not escape the western standards which surrounded him in all aspects of the colony's life. He was clearly proud in 1893 over the appointment of Dr. J. F. Easmon as chief medical officer in the Gold Coast, and took the opportunity to note the existence in the British colonial administration of two African school inspectors, an assistant colonial secretary and a Queen's advocate. An even greater honour was the knighting of Samuel Lewis of Freetown and on this occasion Jackson expressed the hope that many others might have the ability and opportunity to follow in his footsteps.[1]

Of those European influences corrupting the African and diverting him from his true objectives, Jackson was most critical of the Christian mission churches. When Blyden first mooted the possibility of an independent African church, Jackson was cool towards the idea, but he soon changed his view after the death of Bishop Crowther and the establishment of the Delta Pastorate as independent of C.M.S. authority. What angered Jackson particularly was the unwillingness of the Society to appoint an African successor to Crowther. What had happened to all the fine talk of a native clergy distinguished for its piety and scholarship? Why, if an African bishop was a natural development a generation earlier, was a similar appointment not even more appropriate thirty years later? 'Have the native divines ... so suddenly lost the respect and esteem in which they were held? Or is all this balderdash about non-fitness but another name for prejudice?'

To Jackson these were but rhetorical questions. The missionary record in West Africa had not been impressive. Missionaries had managed to proselytize freed slaves living outside British coastal forts, but they had made few converts within the great tribes and not a single important chief from the interior had ever been persuaded to join a Christian church. The recent C.M.S. policy of replacing native clergy with English missionaries, said Jackson, was a clearly retrogressive step after years of faithful service by African divines. Europeans did not seem to understand that Africa was not convinced by the record of Europe—that the African regarded European militarism with suspicion, and more and more favoured Islam over European Christianity:

The culture ... which hinders a man from honouring his father and his mother and places him out of sympathy with his people is a curse

[1] *Ibid.*, June 3, 10, 1893.

and morally depressed. The mixed population of Lagos was a good example of this racial degeneracy and so too were the creoles of Freetown and the Americanized Negroes of Liberia.

The trouble lay not so much in making use of European ideas and institutions as in making them an absolute end in themselves. When the African lost sight of the fact that he had his own peculiar racial character with its own assets and liabilities, he stood in danger of losing his way and perishing in pursuit of unnatural foreign standards:

Everything is conspiring to force upon the Anglicised African the necessity of re-allying himself with his people from whom his training has divorced him. The past . . . has abundantly shown that when he is dissociated from his people his position is one of disqualification and ineptitude. . . . The African with all his defects possesses a mind which is clear and unobstructed by visions of varying and conflicting interests by reason of the simple life he lives . . . It is lack of confidence in his own things which is the great trouble with the Anglicised African. . . . He . . . must know that no man has said the last word for the world and it may be that the despised life customs of the African will after all prove to be the most potential for good for men. We see the European customs which are so much admired producing results which we cannot say are either beneficial or advantageous to man. . . . we know that human life means more than rushing after money, and that the Golden Rule is more potent for good for man than the golden calf, and there can be no doubt that there is more happiness to be found for man in the simple and contented life of the African than in all the inventions and contrivances of Europe. As for ourselves we feel that the inventions of Europe have not only perverted God but nearly effaced Him with its people; and that the lot will fall to Africa ultimately to teach Europe God in the sense of establishing a primary admonition of loving one's neighbour as oneself.

'It is now seen', insisted Jackson, 'that the only useful course is to stimulate the people to civilize themselves. And the native of West Africa should employ the stimulus of European civilization . . . to civilize himself by ameliorating and advancing his own methods and institutions, remembering always that artificial life however brilliant or promising perishes with its possessor.' It was important that the so-called civilized African maintain contact with his racially pure brothers of the continental tribes. There he would find preserved African ways which had been long tested and which would sustain him. 'Put the aborigines well in front,' warned Jackson, 'go back to the simplicity of your fathers—go back to health and life and continuity.'[1]

This brand of cultural nationalism, so much in the atmosphere of

[1] *Ibid.*, Dec. 17, 1892, Aug. 3, 1895, July 11, 1896, June 5, 1897, Oct. 19, 1912.

munal, Jackson continued, land ownership was individual, not only in Lagos but throughout southern Nigeria. The land was divided among members of the family and passed on to family descendants upon death, for this was the only basis on which economic security in Africa rested. In northern Nigeria the British claimed native land tenure to be based on occupancy rather than ownership, with occupancy ensured by a system of rents. The rental was a European, not an African, institution, Jackson insisted; moreover, the assertion that through conquest ultimate ownership had devolved on Britain through the Fulani emirates did not square with the fundamental pattern of ownership which was much older than these latter-day conquests. In the south, furthermore, no such pattern and no such conquest had ever been established. Consequently application of the northern system in the south would constitute a revolutionary departure from traditional land-holding patterns. Through misguided philanthropy, therefore, the British authorities were very foolishly attempting a complete change of fundamental land law which could lead only to the conversion of the native into a squatter on his own land, and which would alienate private holdings to the state on the mistaken assumption that they were unoccupied public lands:

> It can hardly be said to be reasonable . . . to take the laws of one set of people to define the laws of another set of people whose customs and usages are quite different; nor is it rational to set up the law and its interpretation of one community as a standard by which the law of another community is to be governed. The life of the native of West Africa is of a communal order. The life of the European in Europe and elsewhere is individualistic. The law of the African must naturally conform to the communistic principle . . . To contend that ownership does not exist in the one case because it does not take the form it assumes in the other, is equivalent to divesting the word ownership of all meaning.[1]

Judging both from the flavour of his editorial comment and the frequency with which he reproduced the articles and correspondence of Edward W. Blyden, Jackson must have come increasingly under the influence of Blyden's thinking. He was one of the early advocates of the use of African dress as functionally appropriate to African climate, but his resistance to European culture was deeply embedded in principles of racial exclusiveness closely resembling the ideas of Blyden. The Negro was well known for his ability to adapt to foreign cultures, said Jackson, but the results were not always felicitous. Contact with Europe tended to produce Africans who were physically weak, materially impoverished

[1] *Ibid.*, Aug. 24, Sept. 7, 1912, July 20, 1913.

and trouble at present engendered and lead to that profitable development which it is the aim and interest of British rule to promote.[1]

As the years went on, the situation causing Jackson's complaint became worse rather than better. British control over the interior slowly tightened until by 1914, when the northern and southern provinces and Lagos were amalgamated as the Colony and Protectorate of Nigeria, all pretence of independent native authority was dropped. Under Sir Frederick Lugard, the governor-general, the administration was greatly strengthened and standardized, and Abeokuta, that last vestige of African independence, was finally integrated into the colonial government of Nigeria. At about the same time, the British administration was engaged in a re-examination of land tenure law with a view to protecting ownership of land from alienation to foreign interests. This development, however, rather than pleasing the African population, greatly upset a people whose customs, traditions, and economy were rooted in long-standing patterns of land ownership and occupation, and who felt that this ownership was being challenged and replaced by sinister alien controls.

No one felt or expressed these African misgivings more eloquently than John Payne Jackson. The basic difficulty, said Jackson, was that Europeans were applying their own standards of social order and land tenure to a totally different African situation. In Lagos, for example, the land-holding pattern had been based on original ownership by fishermen from the neighbouring island of Iddo. They had established a system of individual ownership as a usufruct held collectively, and this arrangement had not been altered by the subsequent Benin conquest which introduced the Docemo line of kingship. Hence land which appeared to be public was in fact still privately held, and the treaty between Docemo and the British in 1861 could not involve the cession of residual land rights which Docemo had never possessed. The English erroneously thought that land in Africa ultimately belonged to the community as represented by the king who allotted parcels to individuals or families as needed. When the British administration tried to protect native land from alienation to foreign speculators, therefore, it tried to assume residual rights it in fact did not possess and claimed ownership of public lands which were actually privately held.[2]

Though African social structure and land management were com-

[1] *Ibid.*, Jan. 2, Feb. 27, 1897, Mar. 19, 1898, Aug. 12, 1911, Jan 20, 1912, esp. Jan. 16, 1897.
[2] *Ibid.*, July 10, 1897, Apr. 16, 1898, Sept. 30, 1911.

British rule can be rendered effective for improving the native. But wherever ... the imposition of rule is attended with the endeavour to impose upon the natives ideals foreign to them the result can and must be only obstructive and calamitous.[1]

Though in part this attitude reflected Jackson's genuine belief in the efficacy of African customs and institutions in an African setting, there was another factor at work. Once peace had settled over the land, Jackson began to detect signs that the reality of British protection in the interior did not measure up to his expectations. There was a marked tendency on the part of the British officials to ignore the fact that the native rulers were the actual law in the land. British officers tended to humiliate and depreciate chiefs and princes publicly before the eyes of their subjects. Hausa troops in the interior were permitted to conduct themselves without adequate restraint, and military force was utilized far too frequently with nothing more highminded in view than British commercial advantage. As in the Gold Coast of Mensah Sarbah, European administrators, ignorant of African customs and traditions, imposed alien standards on the land, and made no effort to consult Africans familiar with local needs and the time-tested means used to fulfil those needs. Any African would know that native authority rested not on police force but on the seclusion, form and ceremony surrounding the king. When a chief was chastised in any way before his people, he naturally lost face in their eyes and was unable thereafter to enforce his rule. This situation, brought about by indiscreet and arrogant officers, was then cited by those same officials as an example of the ineffectiveness of local authorities in keeping a firm hand on local law and order. In reality the ineffectiveness was not African but British:

The tendency of British rule as initiated in the hinterlands of Lagos, the Gold Coast and Sierra Leone has been too much in the line of martial or military force and hence is not indicative of that progressive development and general welfare which it ought to produce. There has been too much forcible and unwarranted interference ... with native rule and institutions ... The distrust and dread inspired by the military regime in the hinterland of this Colony would seem to tend to completely demoralize and paralyse all commercial enterprise ... The British officer stationed in the country cannot be too strongly impressed with the fact that British law as such only extends to the zone marking the actual limits of the Colony proper, and that beyond that zone Native authority predominates. If this fact is well impressed upon the Native ruler and the British officer, it will at once put an end to the disquietude

[1] *Ibid.*, May 16, 1896.

the sooner will it have performed an act of the most prodigious and urgent necessity in the cause of humanity and philanthropy.

Annexation, said Jackson, was the only effective answer.[1]

When the actual military expedition was sent against the Ijebu, Jackson never wavered. Deploring the necessity for force, he continued to exonerate the English, placing the responsibility on native intransigence and explaining to his readers that savagery and ignorance must inevitably and properly fall before the pressure of civilization. Later he took some exception to what he felt was an unduly harsh post-war policy involving banishment of one of the Ijebu chiefs, but he does not seem to have shared James Johnson's sense of outrage over the Ijebu occupation, and when Governor Carter followed in 1893 with his peace-making mission throughout Yorubaland, Jackson was full of congratulations and encouragement:

> Destined as it is to endeavour to put an end to the intertribal warfare which for scores of years has disturbed and disrupted the entire hinterland; and to restore the country to tranquillity and enable the people to follow pursuits of peace and industry; as also to establish good and permanent understanding between the various interior tribes and Her Majesty's Government; the Expedition may be regarded as prolific with issues for the future of this Colony, and should have the sympathy and well wishes of all.[2]

Peace in the land once achieved, Jackson relaxed his unbending attitude towards the people of the interior. He was in fact far from being a black Englishman, and consistently urged the importance of African culture and customs. This was at once reflected in his view of how the interior protectorates ought to be administered. By all means the British should govern as much as possible through the traditional authorities of the people, supplementing rather than supplanting their rule. Native law might appear severe and oppressive on occasion but it often was the best response to the circumstances and requirements of local conditions. In co-operation with the benign influence of British administration it could be employed to encourage moral and social advancement without the necessity of the disruption and disorganization which new customs and laws often entailed:

> It is only by recognizing and building up the elements of good existing in a people that any real and permanent result can be attained ... and

[1] *Ibid.*, Nov. 7, Dec. 5, 19, 1891, Jan. 23, Mar. 5, Apr. 9, 1892.
[2] *Ibid.*, May 7, 28, Oct. 15, 22, 1892, Jan. 14, 1893.

of the Egba and Ijebu who distrusted the British while remaining hostile towards Ibadan and other inland towns whose trade they wished to cut off. Blockading the roads, they soon reduced the Lagos markets to inactivity, leaving the streets deserted and mournful, the trading canoes idle and shopkeepers fretting in front of their displays to which no one came to buy. The Ijebu soon added to this injury the insult of a calculated snub to the acting British governor who had travelled to Ijebu Ode in a fruitless effort to reach some sort of accommodation. When the new governor, Gilbert Carter, arrived on the scene towards the close of 1891, he tried once more to reach agreement and once again the British were rebuffed. In 1892, the last resort of military action was decided upon.

Jackson attacked the Yorubas of the interior, accusing them of selfish motives and corrupt conduct in keeping the civil wars alive. How could one determine who was most at fault in comparing 'the ambitious intrigues of the Ilorins; the insidious suspicions of the Ibadans; the pusillanimous apprehensions of the Okitis; the wily duplicity of the king of Oyo; the diplomatic subtlety of the Egbas; the mercenary astuteness of the Ijebus; and the unscrupulous cupidity engendered by a long and continued state of rapine'? Still, the immediate problem involved the reopening of the roads that trade might flow again. The Lagos government had been reasonable and moderate, but it had to be firm in seeking an equitable solution even to the extent of using force. 'We are as much opposed as any one to the employment of violent measures,' Jackson announced in the spring of 1892, 'and should only advocate their being resorted to as a last and extreme necessity . . . we feel confident that in this determination we have the endorsement and sympathy of all right-minded intelligent natives.' Ultimately it was a question of the end justifying the means:

No matter how loth Her Majesty's Government may be to acquire additional territory, and extend the sphere and assume the responsibility of settled government in the interior; the obstructive policy of the adjacent tribes and the uncompromising and insulting attitude assumed by them . . . has left it no choice . . .

It is utterly impossible in the interest of the commercial progress and prosperity of the Colony, and the welfare of humanity generally, that the vast interior Yoruba country should be permitted to be longer restricted and hampered by the cupidinous whims and extortionate caprice of the tribes contiguous to this Colony; or that the extreme lawlessness and outrageous banditism which for scores of years has been the blight and curse of the country should continue to obstruct the progress of legitimate commerce and healthy development. The sooner therefore that the Government remove the one and obliterate the other,

and practice were leading some to consider the necessity of forming African churches independent of control by the European parent societies. It was at this same time, moreover, that Africans, rebuffed by the patronizing attitude of Europeans, were turning to a re-examination of previously discounted African culture–resuming African names, wearing African traditional dress and giving sympathetic study to African history and customs.

This was the time when the agonizing and frustrating years of warfare among the Yoruba were approaching the climax which would lead to the solution of peace but at the price of loss of independence to British power, when the commercial promise of the British occupation of Lagos would be realized, but African self-respect would be further eroded in the process. These issues were clearly of great importance to the people of Lagos who were often sorely divided over them, and whose differences of opinion found outlet not only in face-to-face discussion but through the columns of the local press.

Though an African nationalist, Jackson in his early editorials was consistently generous both towards British policy and British officials. Plainly worried over the possibility of French and German expansion in West Africa, he considered their colonial régimes harsh and absolutist and urged vigorous action on the British authorities so that British commerce might be saved and the native population given continued protection under the benevolent regard of the British colonial administration. It was true that the English had at one time led all others in pursuing the slave trade in West Africa, but Jackson felt they had long since atoned for this sin through the vigorous way in which they had subsequently moved to extinguish the traffic. Now, in a later era, said Jackson, they were proving themselves by far the best colonizers by extending to their subjects the full liberties and privileges of English democracy. The British government and its people had inspired the love and affection of the Negro everywhere through a uniformly kind and humane treatment and through the efforts of that great nation to eliminate injustices imposed upon Negroes by other countries.[1]

This cordial view of the British influence in Africa reflected in part Jackson's belief, shared by many Lagosians, that only strong action by the administration at Lagos could bring about the peace in the land necessary for the commercial health of the country. Relations with the interior after 1890 were deteriorating to the point that trade out of Lagos had been virtually halted, largely as a result of the xenophobic policies

[1] *The Lagos Weekly Record*, Sept. 12, 1891, Jan. 30, Sept. 10, 1892.

linked by a series of highways, but the constant Yoruba civil wars had imposed a serious restriction on traffic with the interior; hence Lagos merchants and officials were constantly seeking ways of bringing the wars to a conclusion. It is in the light of the city's commercial interests that the extension along the coast to include Badagry and Lekki must be understood. In the same way, the pressure of Glover and his successors on the inland nations—notably the Egba and Ijebu—was part of an effort to stabilize and pacify Yorubaland in order that the roads might again be opened to regular traffic. By 1891 after a generation of diplomacy, a final peace was about to be negotiated, but not without a last spasm of violence and not without the suspicions and misunderstandings born of decades of warfare.[1]

3 John Payne Jackson and the Assertion of African Culture

John Payne Jackson, the founder and editor of the *Lagos Weekly Record*, was an impecunious man whose erratic personal life was conditioned by a weakness for strong drink which resulted in occasional suspension of his journal's activities. In 1890 he had persuaded the Lagos merchant, R. B. Blaize, to turn over to him the publication of Blaize's *Lagos Times*. Renamed *The Lagos Weekly Times* the paper carried on under Jackson's direction until late in the year when Blaize, discovering to his horror that his journal and its funds were being mismanaged by an alcoholic editor, dismissed Jackson and assumed personal direction of the paper under its old name of *Lagos Times*. Jackson somehow managed to find other support, possibly from the wealthy Lagos physician, Dr. John Randle, for by midsummer of 1891 he was back in business with the *Lagos Weekly Record*. From that time forward the paper continued to thrive at least from a journalistic point of view. For all his personal shortcomings, Jackson was a thoughtful student of current events and an exhaustive commentator on their significance. For almost a quarter of a century his columns proved influential and instructive to his contemporaries, even as they do to the modern observer.[2]

The *Lagos Weekly Record* made its appearance at a time when many interesting developments were occupying the thoughts of the people of Lagos. It was during this period that doubts over missionary policy

---

[1] *Nigeria Magazine*, no. 69, Aug., 1961, 107–21, 131–55; A. L. Mabogunje, 'Lagos, A Study in Urban Geography', 48–78; *C.M. Intelligencer*, 1877, 245–7, 1881, 683–91; *The Lagos Weekly Record*, Dec. 2, 1911.

[2] *The Lagos Times*, Dec. 20, 1890; Ernest Ikoli, 'The Nigerian Press', *West African Review*, June, 1950, 626.

the Marina, the broad waterfront avenue, where they were able both to supervise their mercantile activities and enjoy the refreshment of the onshore breezes from the sea.

During the thirty-year period leading up to 1891, the city had seen many physical changes. The Old Town was not greatly altered; the mud-wall thatched-roof compounds covered a somewhat larger area and the density of population was higher than formerly, but these characteristics were not readily apparent to the casual observer. Crowded conditions and lack of sanitary facilities seemed to invite epidemics but actually there was even greater danger from fire, for the people were greatly attracted to public festivities, and at little provocation would issue from their compounds firing guns and Chinese crackers which often ignited nearby thatched roofs. It was just such a celebration which had led to the destruction of Breadfruit Church in 1877 in a great fire which devastated large sections of the city.

It was in other areas of the city that the changes were much more marked. Along the waterfront, the Marina had been extended the length of the island, and numerous wharfs pushed out into the lagoon where those ships able to breach the bar were moored. During the administration of Captain Glover an attempt at town planning had resulted in the laying out of a number of streets which imposed a gridiron pattern on the newer parts of town but left unaffected the crowded narrow alleys of Old Town. Wells were also constructed and a system of kerosene street lights offered a minimum of illumination on the main thoroughfares at night. More striking still was the imposing baroque of the Brazilian houses which dominated the area between Old Town and the Marina. Their coloured façades were rich with the ornamentation of balustrade, pilaster and cement sculpture, embellishing the gables, dormers and turrets of these multi-storeyed dwellings designed in the grand manner. At Ebute Metta on the mainland, a suburb had come into existence after the anti-Christian disturbances in Abeokuta in 1867 and here were housed the Christian Egba refugees. This population did not make up more than a fraction of the Lagos total, however, and the community was still too far removed from the main centre of Lagos activity to be more than a relatively unimportant adjunct.

For African, European and repatriate alike, trade was the near-universal occupation of Lagos, and it was the city's success at commercial enterprise which accounted both for its healthy growth and for its insistent interest in the affairs of the interior. Commerce meant trade specifically with the towns of Yorubaland with which Lagos was naturally

in the contribution they were able to make to the growing body of ideas taking form in the West Africa of their day.

2 End-of-century Lagos – A setting for African Journalistic Enterprise

The Lagos which greeted John Payne Jackson's *Weekly Record* in 1891 was still a small town of some 35,000 population, but it already was giving clear indication of developing into the major West African commercial, cosmopolitan centre it was later to become. In the thirty years which had followed the British occupation of 1861, great changes had indeed taken place which were amply to justify Blyden's exclamation of surprise and admiration over the material progress of the city. The slave trade had long since departed taking with it the lurking fear and sense of doom which had characterized the old Lagos. Commerce had not suffered as a result; in fact, trade had expanded approximately tenfold over the years as the products of the interior, led by palm oil, converged on the lively port over an ever-expanding number of trade routes.

If Lagos was still a small city, it made up for its lack of size in the cosmopolitan quality of its population and atmosphere. Its crowded streets and noisy markets contained not only the crews of visiting merchantmen but a variety of individuals from the peoples of West Africa, the Americas and Europe. The blue-clad Yoruba women predominated in the markets of the Old Town, but there were also to be seen many others – the stately Hausa in their long white robes, Krumen and Fanti who still worked the surf boats unloading vessels unable to cross the treacherous harbour bar, refugees from the interior towns of Abeokuta, Oyo, Ibadan and Ijebu Ode come to Lagos to escape persecution, war and slavery, and tribesmen from the far interior including Nupe, Fulani and Kanuri. Numerically small but economically and socially important were the repatriates from Brazil and Sierra Leone – Yoruba whose forebears had been enslaved generations earlier and who had later returned to their homeland, settling not in original villages which they had never known, but preferring to remain in the big city on the coast. Among the Europeans, Englishmen predominated but there were Americans, French and a smattering of others. The European colony was small, however, never exceeding a scant two hundred and fifty. Apart from government officials, the Europeans divided into merchants and missionaries. The latter had been forced to congregate in Lagos as a result of the Yoruba wars and the Christian persecutions at Abeokuta, but for the merchants Lagos was a natural habitat. They lived typically along

with a verve which often lacked journalistic dispassion and needlessly aroused local animosities.

Another group became editors only for brief periods or for special purposes in careers that centred on other activities. Hilary Teague divided his energies between careers devoted to journalism and public service. Blyden in his long and active life was the originator or occasional editor of several journals in Freetown and Monrovia, and a continually prolific contributor to a wide range of English-language newspapers in West Africa. Similarly, William Rainy, while primarily a barrister, also directed a number of Freetown papers during his residence in that city. In Lagos, Majola Agbebi at various times served as an editor, as did Attoh-Ahuma in the Gold Coast. Another clergyman, James Johnson, though only briefly serving as a newspaper editor, was constantly appearing before the West African public through the columns of the local papers. Merchant families like the Devès in St. Louis and the Bannermans and Brews in the Gold Coast were publishers as was the Lagos entrepreneur, R. B. Blaize. At a later time public figures like Casely Hayford in Cape Coast and Herbert Macaulay in Lagos gained much of their popular influence through their editorial activities. Much the same could be said for Kitoyi Ajasa who, important though he was as director and owner of *The Nigerian Pioneer*, is more appropriately cast in the role of legal counsel and public official.[1]

African newspapermen, therefore, in the sense of full-time professional journalists, were comparatively rare before the period of the First World War. The point need not be laboured, however, since the distinction between professional and avocational newsmen appears to have had no particular significance either with respect to the community influence of individual points of view or the importance of their contribution to a peculiarly African philosophy. The figures discussed in this chapter – Louis Huchard of Senegal, and the Jacksons, John Payne and Thomas Horatio, of Nigeria – happen to have been full-time journalists, but their interest lies not so much in their professional identification as in the shape of their thought, less perhaps in the popular extent of their influence than

[1] See above, 93–100, C. H. Fyfe, 'The Sierra Leone Press in the Nineteenth Century', *Sierra Leone Studies*, n.s., no. 8, June, 1957, 226–36; K. A. B. Jones-Quartey, 'Sierra Leone and Ghana: Nineteenth Century Pioneers in West African Journalism', *Ibid.*, n.s., no. 12, Dec., 1959, 230–44; Roger Pasquier, 'Les Débuts de la Presse au Sénégal', *Cahiers d'Etudes Africaines*, 1962, 477–90; David Kimble, *A Political History of Ghana*, 182 n., 409, 517–18. There were government gazettes in Sierra Leone and the Gold Coast early in the nineteenth century, but unofficial, privately owned newspapers began in Freetown in 1855 and in Accra in 1857. An early paper, the *Anglo-African*, appeared in Lagos during the mid-'sixties.

17 The Journalist in West African Thought

1 *The Newspaper as an Agent of West African Nationalism*

West African intellectual activity in the nineteenth century tended to originate and develop where the opportunity for expression existed. At first such possibilities were limited largely to the missions. Early Africans literate and articulate enough to formulate and to express thoughts on African affairs were usually clergymen with mission-school education and views conditioned by that education. In addition there was a mercantile and professional leadership, for the most part mission-educated and, with some exceptions, sturdy lay supporters of the various mission churches in West Africa. In some instances, these were less inclined to assume a self-conscious, vocal, intellectual leadership, being content to build up their businesses and serve their communities quietly in public positions such as justices, municipal officials, jurymen, or legislative councillors.

In time another group of men came to have a growing voice in the West African world of ideas, men whose activities gave them unusual opportunity for influence within their communities. These were the newspapermen – editors and publishers – who made their first appearance in Liberia late in the 1820s and subsequently in Sierra Leone and the Gold Coast during the 1850s and 1860s. In Lagos, the first regular newspapers appeared during the 1880s, while Senegal, old in years and in sophistication, was a surprising last in the field, not producing a local paper until 1885. Many of the early editors were as much printers as true journalists for they often established newspapers as business ventures to supplement their income from job-lot printing. This did not mean, however, that they were indifferent to the political or social questions of their day; on the contrary, they tended to adopt as their own many of the grievances of their readers, and plunged into political and religious issues

of the Gold Coast were bound to be attracted to the English nation with its noble constitution which protected the liberty of the individual, but 'it is almost easier for a camel to go through the eye of a needle than for any man of average intelligence to be constitutional out here ... The local government is at bottom an absolute monarchy.' Later he remarked that it was of the greatest good fortune that Mensah Sarbah's *Fanti Customary Laws* had been published at a time when the Gold Coast government was adopting Star Chamber tactics. The appearance of this volume helped re-establish a sense of legislative responsibility in the face of an arbitrary executive, and thus preserved the peace and justice which all people sought through their governments.[1]

Resistance to despotism was not enough, however. It was also essential that the African actively cultivate his own institutions, to return to the simple life, to re-establish contact with nature and mother earth in the manner of the ancestors. This did not mean primitivism but rather a refreshment of the spirit, weary with the conceits of an effete European civilization. Back to the land, urged Attoh-Ahuma. Let the noble ploughman be preferred to the counterfeit European pushing his pen in a counting house. 'Free men ... eke out miserable lives as clerks ... they could sit *every man under his vine and under his fig tree, none making him afraid.*' Beyond this, there had to be a conscious search for national unity, for nationhood in race, in political objectives and in a concentric system of government. Some of these views might appear at first to be retrogressive, but in fact they pointed the way forward to a new and more vital nationhood by means of the traditional African technique of drawing on the accumulated vitality of those who had come before.[2]

Finally, there was the necessity to make use of what European civilization had to offer, not slavishly but creatively, not in blind imitation of externals but with a sensitivity to inner qualities, and a discrimination that distinguished what was irrelevant and what was of value to the African experience. Then would the African of the Gold Coast bring together in his own society the most potent elements of both his and Europe's way of life, then might he view at last 'his ultimate reversion to the simplicity of his forebears, sobered and matured with all that is excellent in Western civilisation and religion'.[3]

[1] *The Gold Coast Methodist Times*, Sept. 15, 1897; Attoh-Ahuma, *West African Celebrities*, 249, 251.
[2] *The Gold Coast Leader*, Jan. 28, 1922; Attoh-Ahuma, *The Gold Coast Nation and National Consciousness*, vii–viii, 6–11, 46–7.
[3] *Ibid.*, 37–42; Attoh-Ahuma, *West African Celebrities*, 253–4, 257.

driving, somewhat exaggerated, literary style rarely failed to appeal to his readers.[1]

It was therefore in manner rather than matter that he most differed from Mensah Sarbah. Both men were equally tenacious in their opposition to the government's attempt to gain tighter control over the disposition of apparently unoccupied lands. Where Mensah Sarbah fought the measure with constitutional weapons in the council chamber, however, Attoh-Ahuma tilted with the enemy publicly before the fascinated gaze of his readers:

> No legislation about imaginary Public Lands can be applicable in the Gold Coast. The idea is preposterous, outlandish, unthinkable and ... not to be ... foisted upon us without revolutionizing the fundamental distinctions of *Mine* and *Thine*. Another white elephant that is still at large is ... *Settler's Rights*. Before Europe ever dreamed of coming into contact with our Ancestors we were the absolute possessors of the field ... It is an inversion of thought for any one to label us as Settlers. We submit most respectfully that those Administering the Government ... are the Settlers. We are natives of the Soil ... there is everything to make us justly proud of our branch of the comparative history of nations. Here we have lived for centuries.[2]

This truculence delivered *con brio* lifted Attoh-Ahuma's pronouncements above the level of ill-temper, and characterized his style on most matters. His exhortations to his countrymen to protect the integrity of their traditional institutions bypassed the intellect and drove straight to the heart:

> We need to think for ourselves, to find out the eternal principles that underlie every thought and idea indigenous to the nation ... We have fought valiantly for what we deemed were our Ancestral Rights in the past, and would fight again, if those rights were menaced tomorrow—but the greatest calamity of West Africa that must be combated tooth and nail ... is the imminent Loss of Ourselves.... Rather let men rob our lands ... but let us see that they do not rob us of ourselves. They do so when we are taught to despise our own Names, Institutions, Customs and Laws ... The days are coming, however, when not to stand by the nation and its true life shall mean the eternal forfeiture of all claim to respect and reverence.[3]

For Attoh-Ahuma the task of preserving national integrity involved a series of related processes. In the first place, there was the necessity for vigilance against governmental tyranny. As rational beings the people

---

[1] *The Gold Coast Leader*, Jan. 28, 1922; Sampson, *op. cit.*, 77–80.
[2] *The Gold Coast Methodist Times*, Sept. 30, 1897.
[3] Attoh-Ahuma, *West African Celebrities*, 2–3.

National Prosperity', yet who urged his people to 'go Fantee' with all the advantages of 'western education and civilisation . . . that will enable us to realise our individuality'.[1]

Born in 1863, a year before Mensah Sarbah, he was soon marked for religious training leading to a career in the Wesleyan church. After receiving his secondary education at Cape Coast, he went to England to prepare for the ministry, then returned to Africa in 1888 where he worked for some years as a minister and school administrator under Methodist auspices in the Gold Coast. For a time he directed the Accra Grammar School and then founded successively the Accra Collegiate School and the African Methodist Episcopal Zion College, but none of these institutions prospered under his direction for he was apparently an indifferent administrator. In 1903 he became associated with Mensah Sarbah in the foundation of the Fanti Public Schools Limited, an effort to provide secondary education in the larger towns. Later, during the period of the First World War, he returned to active work in the ministry, retiring in 1919, two years before his death.

If Attoh-Ahuma's professional accomplishments were not especially noteworthy, he more than made up for their shortcomings through his achievements as a publicist and practitioner of African nationalism. During the 1890s he took over the editorship of the *Gold Coast Methodist Times*, commenting freely and forcefully on political matters, especially during the controversy over the government lands bill which reached its climax in 1897. When he was forced from the *Methodist Times* because of his outspoken, extra-religious editorializing, he moved his activities to the editorial office of the *Gold Coast Aborigines*, an organ of the Aborigines' Rights Protection Society. Still later he joined forces with the *Gold Coast Leader*, for many years the journalistic vehicle for J. E. Casely Hayford. In 1911 he published *The Gold Coast Nation and National Consciousness*, a strong statement on behalf of African nationalism which was apparently based upon his newspaper writings. In these various journalistic activities and as a leader and sometimes secretary of the Aborigines' Rights Protection Society, Attoh-Ahuma was able to realize his undoubted gifts of expression both in the spoken and written word. His stately graceful carriage and great organ-like voice, his humorous agreeable manner and serenity of disposition made him formidable either in conversation or public pronouncement, while his

---

[1] *The Gold Coast Leader*, Jan. 28, 1922; S. R. B. Attoh-Ahuma, *The Gold Coast Nation and National Consciousness*, vii-viii, 40; Attoh-Ahuma, *Memoirs of West African Celebrities*, x, 254, 257.

member of the legislative council he deplored both the tendency of the authorities to treat the unofficial representative as a destructive opposition and the reciprocal inclination of the unofficial member to become no more than an agent of obstruction and criticism. Like Samuel Lewis in Sierra Leone, he regarded himself as an integral part of the government whose role it was to advise the executive in the interests of more efficient equitable government, and he was disappointed when this ideal failed to materialize. Perhaps, as has been suggested, Mensah Sarbah lived in an age when moderation was ill appreciated, and constructive constitutional reform in government and society could not be achieved in the face of the forces which were driving the government and the governed apart.[1]

4 *The Baroque Nationalism of Attoh-Ahuma*

If the sweet reasonableness and scholarship of Mensah Sarbah were one man's approach to the problem of preserving an African identity under alien rule, the career of the Reverend Samuel Richard Brew Attoh-Ahuma indicated that there were other roads to the same objective. Attoh-Ahuma was in many ways the antithesis of his studious contemporary. Where Mensah Sarbah was withdrawn and introspective, a man of few words, artistic, sensitive and subtle, Attoh-Ahuma was an extrovert whose dominating rococo personality was appropriately fitted in a massive frame and whose convictions were sustained by a dynamic prose style and commanding public presence. Poised against Mensah Sarbah's precise but colourless manner, Attoh-Ahuma performed in the grand fashion. He was one of those who changed his westernized name to an African form–from S. R. B. Solomon to Attoh-Ahuma–as befitted the grandson of a former king of James Town, Accra. It was he who criticized the black whiteman as 'a creature, a freak, and a monstrosity', who wrote a book celebrating the exploits of the great men of Africa's past, lamenting only that he had missed many others 'owing . . . to the arbitrary and gratuitous custom of foisting foreign and fanciful names upon our people', who demanded of his countrymen that they adopt what he termed a 'Backward Movement' to the simple life of earlier times which was in reality a step away from 'foreign accretions and excrescences', and a step forward towards 'National Resurrection and

[1] Gold Coast Legislative Council, Oct. 16, 1905, C.O. 98/15; Sampson, *op. cit.*, 21.

for protracted periods which made it difficult to conform to this stipulation.[1]

Mensah Sarbah's exertions were part of a concerted community opposition, the more impressive since the intention of the proposed legislation had been to protect African land-holders from the dangers of alienation of their holdings. The result was that the British government yielded and ultimately proposed legislation governing concessions which no longer contained the offensive sections concerning the validity of African land titles, especially in connection with the so-called public lands. These recommendations proving satisfactory, the new legislation was approved in the legislative council where Mensah Sarbah gave it his support, thus symbolizing the concurrence of the African community.[2]

The philosophy and career of John Mensah Sarbah were devoted to bringing together the best of the sometimes conflicting worlds of Africa and Europe on behalf of an evolving African society. He recognized clearly that the traditional way of life would have to change, but he was a moderate and an evolutionist and stressed the continuity of institutions, not just for their own sake, not even as a necessary manifestation of cultural integrity, but because he knew things would work better if these institutions were properly utilized.

Under these circumstances he urged the importance of strengthening the traditional authorities so that they might evolve with the times, bringing with them the best of the values of the traditional world—respect for age and authority and the strong sense of community solidarity. He quite agreed that the individual initiative encouraged by the West was a valuable concept which could lead to much social progress, but excessive individualism sometimes engendered selfishness, class antagonism and poverty. The best of both worlds was Mensah Sarbah's objective—not the dead hand of traditionalism but the strength of the ancient community virtues; not the mischievous influence of unchecked individualism but the valuable thrust of constructive activity.[3]

This desire for a balance between the old and the new led to his plea that the educated African be given a wider role to play, and his own career was a demonstration of how a member of the educated community could serve both the administration and his own people. As an unofficial

---

[1] Kimble, *op. cit.*, 330–57; *The Gold Coast Chronicle*, July 27, Aug. 14, Sept. 2, 30, Nov. 5, Dec. 12, 1897.
[2] F. M. Hodgson to J. Chamberlain, Mar. 5, 1900, enclosure, C.O. 96/358.
[3] Redwar, *op. cit.*, v–vi.

alienation by European concessionaires seeking mineral, timber or other rights. It was felt that European speculators often took advantage of unlettered chiefs to gain control of land without adequate compensation, and that such sharp practice could only be effectively blocked if the government established itself as the owner or trustee of the land. In the Gold Coast bills were introduced in 1894 and 1897 designed to check the traffic in land concessions, initially by declaring waste and forest lands to be crown lands, but later, in the face of African opposition, by vesting in the government the right of administration, but not of ownership, of these lands. Specifically it was proposed that African land titles no longer be taken for granted, that outright African ownership be obtainable only by application to the governor, that certain lands be declared vacant unless demonstrably in use, that inheritance of land be henceforth governed by English law, and that concessions to Europeans for practical purposes be available only by government action.

The African community was totally and unalterably opposed to the proposed legislation as a violation of traditional practices and a move to confiscate the property of the people. The local newspapers were outspoken in their criticism, public demonstrations were mounted and petitions circulated, and an organization was formed, the Aborigines' Rights Protection Society, to direct the popular protest. Mensah Sarbah, who had been instrumental in the founding of the society, soon took a direct hand in the attack, appearing before the legislative council to plead against the government proposals.

His arguments were thoroughgoing and lengthy, but reduced themselves to three essential points all rooted in the traditional custom of the country. In the first place, he said, there was no such thing in the Gold Coast as land without an owner. The mere fact that land was not being cultivated did not prove it was not owned; indeed, under African custom, all land, whether waste land, forest land or otherwise, was always under ownership. Secondly, the government proposed henceforward to make those who had been land-owners mere settlers on their own land. Such an action was entirely illegal, under British as well as native jurisprudence, for the crown could only appropriate land by conquest, cession or treaty—not by legislative action. Thirdly, settlers on the land were liable to lose even their settler rights if they did not demonstrate their frequent utilization of the land; yet the pattern of crop rotation in the country called for long stretches in which fields lay fallow and hence technically unused, whereas many land-holders were out of the country

basis... the towns of this Colony will become the centres of renewed activity, a public judiciary will restore public order, trust and confidence, public... sanitary work shall then be more satisfactorily, successfully, expeditiously and economically undertaken, commercial prospects brightened and civil disputes being adjudicated by natives conversant with their peculiar native laws, customs and usages, peace, prosperity and harmony shall dwell in our midst. Then will be dispelled forever the cloud, the weighty cloud of despair that has rested on us for a long while.

The pressures for and against this and subsequent municipal ordinances resulted in a standstill. The laws went on the books despite the protests, but the towns remained unincorporated for many years for want of popular support. The more spirited elements in the African opposition spoke of the tyranny of unchecked despotism which consistently reneged on its promises of municipal improvements. Mensah Sarbah, equally determined in opposition, continued, however, in his more measured criticism, suggesting that the ideal solution lay in forming a municipal government which utilized the best available in both the African and the British experience.[1]

A desire to preserve what was valuable in traditional institutions and to utilize the training of educated Africans motivated Mensah Sarbah in his recommendations concerning the functions of the chiefly courts. The relation of British to indigenous government had long been a difficult question for the administration which had veered now towards utilization of the traditional chiefs as a means for indirect rule, now towards subordination of the chiefs to European officials. In 1878 and 1883 the jurisdiction and powers of native authorities had been defined, but by the very process of definition their authority was circumscribed and identified in the public mind with the British administration, particularly since these acts gave the colonial governor the power to suspend or dismiss chiefs on cause. Gradually, therefore, the chiefs became enmeshed in the web of British administration, their independence and prestige steadily declining and their function slowly altering from that of heads of government to that of minor administrative officials. The community of educated Africans in the Gold Coast tended to resist this erosion of the power of traditional authorities, and rose to defend the chiefs.

Mensah Sarbah was one of their leading spokesmen, arguing that the

[1] David Kimble, *A Political History of Ghana, 1850–1928*, 418–21; W. Brandford Griffith to Lord Knutsford, June 18, 1889, and enclosure, June 28, 1889 and enclosure, C.O. 96/202; *The Gold Coast Chronicle*, May 23, 1892, July 6, 1897; *The West African Mail*, Oct. 13, 1905.

African had always regarded administration of justice as a fundamental index of leadership, that the right of chiefly dismissal lay with the people and not with the British crown, and that the best way of preserving the strength and effectiveness of indigenous rulers was to give them a responsible measure of direct control over the government of their people. His appeal was in vain and had little effect in checking the movement towards centralization. During a legislative council debate in 1910 over the amendment of the Native Jurisdiction Ordinance of 1883, Mensah Sarbah urged increased responsibility for the indigenous courts and a curtailment of official interference in the judicial process. Specifically he called for greater authority in the native courts in keeping the peace, for the use of chiefs as advisers to the Supreme Court in cases involving customary law, and for a reduction of types of cases which could be appealed from head-chief courts to district commissioners. Although some of these suggestions were subsequently adopted, both he and T. Hutton Mills, his unofficial colleague on the legislative council, failed to carry their major recommendation that chiefs be suspended or dismissed, not through arbitrary action by the governor, but by resolution of the council itself, taken after full public debate.[1]

Characteristically, some of the deepest misunderstandings between the government and the people of the Gold Coast came over the question of land ownership. It was the common problem encountered in all colonial territories. European practice was conceived in terms of private ownership, or public ownership with private leasing. Individuals could purchase title to land or in the case of public lands these rights could be negotiated through long-term rents. In the British colonies there was a tendency to regard land as belonging to the crown, a direct reflection of British practice based on ancient feudal rights and privileges. The African position was that all land, whether or not in cultivation, was owned by someone–a head of household, a family, a community or a tribe. It could not be alienated outside the community, it could not be used as a basis for taxation, and rents were normally not charged for its use. Most certainly, land did not fall to colonial governments, especially if their rule was not based on conquest, for clearly a foreign régime could not be supposed to represent the interests of the local people.

The essential difference between these divergent views was heightened when colonial governments felt compelled to protect African land from

---

[1] Kimble, *op. cit.*, 458–69; Sampson, *op. cit.*, 19–20; *Fanti National Constitution*, 134–5; Gold Coast Legislative Council, July 2, 4, 1910, C.O. 98/19.

Tema, 470
The Ten Lost Tribes, 263, 265
Third Republic, France, 235, 238, 242, 394
Thornton, Henry, 58, 460
Tirailleurs sénégalais, 77, 234
Torrane, G., 259
Touré, Sékou, 467, 471, 478, 479
Townsend, Henry, 199
Trade, African-European, 44-5
Trade, legitimate, 179
  in Senegal, 70-1, 164, 165, 169, 171, 173, 365
  in Liberia, 89-90, 95
  in Sierra Leone, 119, 136, 298, 312, 319-20, 325
  in Yorubaland, 198, 200-1
Trarza Moors, 170, 242
Tucolor, 163, 168, 223
Turner, Nat, 87
Twi, 258

United Native African Church, 231, 292
United States Civil War, 85

Vai, people, 215
Valentin, Durand, 238
Vallon, Admiral, 244
Van Vollenhoven, J., 403, 404
Vassa, Gustavus, 35-6
  criticizes slavery, 35, 40-2, 44, 45, 461
  and Sierra Leone, 36, 46
Venn, Henry, 146, 187, 193, 194, 280, 282, 460
  and African 'rehabilitation', 180-1
  on African leadership, 182, 186, 187, 291
Volta River project, 470
Voting rights,
  in Senegal, 251, 396, 403-4

Walo, 75, 79, 83, 164-5, 167, 170, 173, 174

War of American Independence, 48, 53, 65
Washington, Booker T., 450
Wealth of Nations, 44
West Africa, 446
  response to Europe, 18, 109, 112, 374-7, 460
  nationalism in, 18
West African Countries and People, 114, 126
West African Reporter, The, 138, 142, 300
West African university, 446
  proposed by Africanus Horton, 121-2, 129
  and W. Grant, 139
  Blyden's ideas on, 228
  and Casely Hayford, 449
Western Echo, The, 329
West Indies, 33, 37, 42, 72, 82, 135, 166, 174, 179, 210, 235
Wheatley, Phillis, 33, 34
White Cap chiefs, Lagos, 384
White Plains, 101
Wilberforce, William, 40
Wolof, 68, 82, 84, 159, 163, 234, 267, 269

York, store ship, 60
Yoruba, language and people, 110, 131, 177, 182, 184, 187, 189, 208, 271, 277, 306, 347, 424
  Oyo Yoruba characterized by Samuel Johnson, 270
  and *History of the Yorubas*, 272, 273
  discussed by James Johnson, 284
Yorubaland, 123-4, 135, 177, 197, 198, 208, 348, 352, 416, 435
  civil wars, 131, 197, 271, 272, 273, 349, 350, 351
Young Senegalese, 209, 373, 398, 464

Zong, slaver, 43

INDEX [511]

surveys life in Sierra Leone, 266–8
criticizes Nova Scotians, 268
extols liberated Africans, 268–9
Sierra Leone nationalist, 269–70, 277–8
as Europeanized African, 270, 276, 462
Sierra Leone, 27, 28, 46, 47, 68, 85, 90, 95, 110, 111, 113, 117, 119, 130, 131, 135, 140, 149, 178, 212, 345, 435, 445, 460
founding of, 48–9, 50–1
under Sierra Leone Co., 51–2, 55, 56, 58, 59, 60–4
trial by jury, 52, 151, 152–3, 312–13, 316
land policy, 52, 55–6, 62, 63, 64
legislative council, 65, 133, 150, 298, 307–9
British government begins, 66
compared with Liberia, 85–6, 88
influence in West Africa, 85–6, 314
and Africanus Horton, 122–3
'creoles', 136, 208, 298–302, 303, 305, 311, 312, 315, 316, 318, 320, 324, 325, 356
concept of effete 'creoles', 136, 138, 297–302, 316, 324–5
native African church, 142–5, 148–9
life described by A. B. C. Sibthorpe, 266–8
protectorate established, 298, 312, 315, 318, 324
hut tax, 318
and Syrians, 325
Sierra Leone Company, 51, 52, 54, 130, 131, 269, 311
administration in Sierra Leone, 51–2, 58, 60–5
and quitrents, 56, 62, 63, 64, 65
end of rule, 66
Sierra Leone Weekly News, The, 316
Signares, 70, 71, 82, 162, 461
character, 69
Slavery, 52, 53, 72, 179

European attitude towards, 25, 34
abolition of by Britain, 25, 28, 48, 105, 179, 460
abolition of by France, 25, 71, 84, 238, 396
and manumission, 33, 238
Cugoano's criticism of, 35–40, 44–6
Vassa's criticism of, 35, 40–2, 44, 45
in United States, 86
domestic, 261, 286, 295, 315, 322
Slave trade, 18, 25, 27–8, 31, 72, 73, 328, 459
abolition of, 31, 40, 48, 66, 71, 76, 95, 97, 98, 106, 110, 130, 142, 177, 460
and occupation of Lagos, 198
and C. C. Reindorf, 259
and Sierra Leone interior, 315
The Slave Trade and Its Remedy, 280
Sleight, John, 238
Smith, Adam,
ideas of, 26–7, 44
Sofa, warriors, 319, 323, 324
Solomon, S. R. B., see Attoh-Ahuma, S. R. B.
Somerset, James, 21, 48
Sor Island, 236
Soyinka, Wole, 477
Sudan, western, 234, 319, 322, 324
Sundiata, 478

Taylor, Moses, 143
Teague, Hilary, 93, 102, 108, 109, 288, 346, 461
editor of *Liberia Herald*, 93
on agriculture, 96
on manufacturing, 96
on Liberian state, 97, 98
on indigenous peoples, 98, 99–100
and Liberian Declaration of Independence, 98–99
and Liberian Constitution of 1847, 99–100
Teilhard de Chardin, Pierre, 475